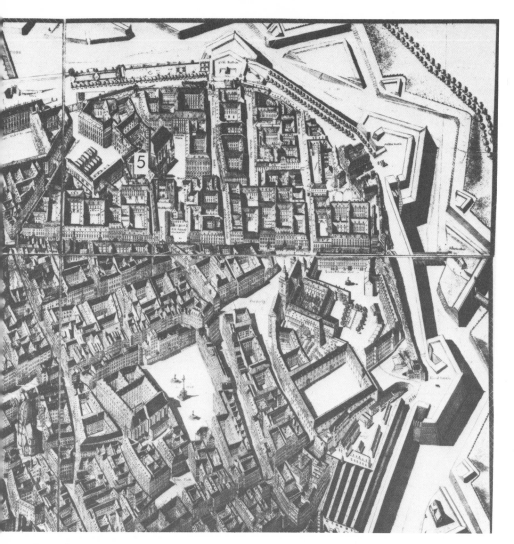

Legend
1. Schwarzenberg Palais
2. Kärntnerthor-Theater
3. Redoutensaal
4. Burgtheater
5. Hofburgkapelle

A History of the Oratorio

A History of the Oratorio

VOLUME 3

THE ORATORIO IN THE CLASSICAL ERA

By Howard E. Smither

THE UNIVERSITY OF NORTH CAROLINA PRESS

CHAPEL HILL AND LONDON

© 1987 The University of North Carolina Press

All rights reserved

Manufactured in the United States of America

Library of Congress Cataloging-in-Publication Data
(Revised for volume 3)

Smither, Howard E.
A history of the oratorio.

Includes bibliographies and indexes.
Contents: v. 1. The oratorio in the baroque era:
Italy, Vienna, Paris.—v. 2. The oratorio in the baroque
era: Protestant Germany and England.—v. 3. The
oratorio in the classical era.
1. Oratorio. I. Title.
ML3201.S6   782.8'2'09   76-43980
ISBN 0-8078-1274-9 (v. 1)

The publication of this work was made possible in part through
grants from the National Endowment for the Humanities, a federal
agency whose mission is to award grants to support education,
scholarship, media programming, libraries, and museums, in order to
bring the results of cultural activities to a broad, general public.

To Ann

℘ Contents

ᔧ *Illustrations*

Music Examples

℘ *Preface*

The present volume continues *A History of the Oratorio*, two volumes of which were published in Chapel Hill in 1977: volume 1, *The Oratorio in the Baroque Era: Italy, Vienna, Paris*; and 2, *The Oratorio in the Baroque Era: Protestant Germany and England*. This volume starts where the previous two stopped and, like them, its purpose is to report on the present state of knowledge in the field of oratorio history. It is intended for the student of music, but the student of cultural history, with little musical background, may find at least parts of the work useful.

In the prefaces to both of the previous volumes I wrote that the third volume would treat the history of oratorio since the Baroque era, and, indeed, I originally intended this one to extend into the twentieth century. Nevertheless, the enormous amount of important source material available for the oratorio since the Baroque era has necessitated an expansion of the project. In the interest of treating the history of the oratorio with sufficient detail to represent responsibly the genre and the research done on it to date, I have limited this volume mainly to the eighteenth-century oratorio in early Classical and Classical styles. A fourth volume, on the oratorio in the nineteenth and twentieth centuries, is in progress.

The term "Classical era" used in the title of the present volume requires some explanation, for it has a broader meaning here than in some musicological literature. Rather than adopting a restrictive interpretation of the term, in which it refers only to the time of late Haydn and Mozart and of Beethoven,[1] I have preferred Friedrich Blume's view that "The beginnings of what music historiography designates as the Classic period reach back to before the middle of the 18th century, into the generation of Johann Sebastian Bach."[2] Thus I include some oratorios from as early as the third decade of the eighteenth century—works which exhibit characteristics of melody, texture, and harmonic rhythm that are closer to what is generally described as Classical style than to Baroque. In musi-

1. As in Engel, "Quellen," p. 285; Feder, "Bemerkungen," p. 305; and Rosen, *Classical Style*, p. 7. For a survey of meanings of "Classical," see Daniel Heartz, "Classical," *New Grove*, 4:449–54.
2. Blume, *Classic and Romantic*, p. 18.

cological literature the new style before the mid-century has been called *galant*, "pre-Classical," and "early Classical"; the last-named term is favored here, because *galant* (although used in the time) is vague, and "pre-Classical" describes the music as an antecedent to a style rather than as a style in its own right. Although Blume's argument for a "Classic-Romantic" period seems convincing for the history of music in general,[3] I find so many changes in the libretto, music, and social function of oratorio in the early nineteenth century that I prefer to divide the history of this genre shortly after 1800. For the most part *The Oratorio in the Classical Era* ends around 1800, but the coverage must occasionally be extended to about 1820 in order to trace the Italian oratorio through the decline of the Metastasian type and to include exceptional cases, such as the oratorios of Jean-François Le Sueur and Stepan Anikievich Degtiarev.

Continuing the approach begun in the previous volumes, this one is organized first by language of oratorio text and by geographical area: the oratorio in Italian, within Italy and abroad; the oratorio in English, in England and the New World; the oratorio in German, in the Catholic South and the Protestant North; the French oratorio in Paris; and the oratorio in other languages—Spanish, Portuguese, Danish, and Russian. The least amount of previous research has been done on works in "other languages"; it may well be that oratorios in Spanish and Portuguese (on the Iberian Peninsula and in the New World) and oratorios in Scandinavian and Slavic languages were more numerous and important than the brief summary in chapter 10 makes them out to be, but that we cannot know until further specialized studies in those areas are undertaken. In an introductory section before the discussion of oratorio in a given language I raise the question of terminology and genre, whose definitions I continue to view as relative to the language and culture in a given time and place. (See the discussion of terminology and genre in volume 1 of this study, pp. 3–9.)

The oratorio in each language is treated under three headings: first, the social context of the oratorio, primarily the occasions, sponsors, and locations of performances, and at times the performing forces as well; second, the libretto; and third, the musical characteristics, first generally and then specifically, through commentary on individual oratorios. The specific oratorios treated have been selected to show a variety of styles and approaches. Not all the oratorios selected are "great" works, yet I hope that each will contribute to the understanding of the genre's characteristics in a given musical, linguistic, cultural, and geographical context. To facilitate comparison of works I have treated the musical aspects of the individual oratorios in approximately the same order: vocal forces, solo roles, overall form (including a structural outline of each oratorio), instrumentation, instrumental numbers, arias, ensembles, and choruses.

3. Ibid.

In most cases the music examples have been reduced from orchestral scores. Transposing instruments have been notated at sounding pitch. The examples are as faithful to their sources as possible within the limits of the reductions necessary to save space. In every instance the main source of a music example is given in its heading. Any editorial changes of musical substance are indicated in square brackets. If significant changes were made on the basis of another source, they are placed within curved brackets and a note to that effect follows the example. Texts have been edited (usually by punctuation marks, capitalization, and spelling) without comment. Texts for which authoritative editions are available, such as those in the critical edition of Metastasio's works, conform to those editions. In all tables and diagrams which include indications of keys or tonal areas, upper case indicates major and lower case, minor. In the text, however, only upper case is used, which means "major" unless the word "minor" follows. The system of pitch notation used in the text is the Helmholtz system, according to which octaves are designated as follows, beginning with three octaves below middle C: CC, C, c, c′, c″, c‴, etc.[4]

Footnote references to works listed in the bibliography are given in short form. An asterisk following a reference means that the work is entirely or substantially music. The date of this preface is also that of the bibliography. Works that appeared after that date were not consulted, unless (as in a few instances mentioned in footnotes) they were sent to me in manuscript or proof copy.

Unless otherwise indicated, composers' names are standardized according to the version used in *New Grove*; for composers who are not in *New Grove* but are in *MGG*, the *MGG* spelling is used. Some musical terms in the volume change according to the general practice of the language and region of the oratorio being discussed: for instance, in treating the Italian and German oratorio I use the Italian *aria*, but for the English and French works, *air*; likewise, *recitativo obbligato* and *accompanied recitative* are synonyms.

Any scholarly work of broad scope represents but a stage in a continuous process of ongoing research. Yet I would hope that a work which attempts to synthesize the thought represented in specialized studies and to integrate that thought with first-hand investigation of primary sources might reflect our understanding of a subject at a given historical moment and provide a springboard for future investigation. The stimulus for further research is one of this volume's important goals.

My work on this project has required the assistance and cooperation of a large number of people to whom I should like to express my appre-

4. For details, see Llewelyn S. Lloyd, "Pitch Notation," *New Grove*, 14:787, Example 1, number (1).

ciation. At my own institution, the University of North Carolina at Chapel Hill, I am grateful for the help of the Music Library staff; that staff has changed during the period in which the volume was in progress, but all members have been extremely helpful, especially James Pruett (formerly Music Librarian, currently Chairman of the Department of Music), Margaret Lospinuso, Kathryn Logan, and Ida Reed. I especially wish to thank the staffs of the Division of Performing Arts at the Library of Congress, and the Music Divisions of the New York Public Library at Lincoln Center and the British Library at the British Museum. Most of the libraries found in the list of library abbreviations provided me with materials, and I am thankful to them for their help. Some staff members of European libraries extended themselves considerably to make rare materials available to me, and to them I offer a special note of thanks: in West Berlin, Dr. Rudolf Elvers, of the Musikabteilung, Staatsbibliothek der Stiftung Preussischer Kulturbesitz; in Dresden, Dr. Ortrun Landmann, of the Musikabteilung, Sächsische Landesbibliothek; in Leipzig, Frau Ellen Roeser, of the Musikbibliothek der Stadt Leipzig; and in Lübeck, Frau Renate Schleth, of the Musikabteilung, Bibliothek der Hansestadt Lübeck.

The University of North Carolina at Chapel Hill has generously supported this project. I much appreciate the research funds of the James Gordon Hanes Professorship, which I used for travel, the purchase of research materials, and the payment of research assistants. Research assistants were also made available to me through the Department of Music and the University Research Council, and I should like to thank not only the Department and Council, but the assistants themselves: for bibliographical work, Sara Ruhle, Leanne Langley, Paul Cauthen, Leslie McCall, and Scott Warfield; for the first drafts of musical examples, proofreading the entire volume, and making many useful suggestions, Christine de Catanzaro. I am also grateful to numerous other students, who were not my assistants but who helped me more than they knew, simply by participating in seminars, writing papers, theses, and dissertations (noted within the body of the volume), and by reacting to ideas. Especially helpful was the group of twelve participants in my 1978 seminar on oratorio history, sponsored by the Summer Seminar Program of the National Endowment for the Humanities.

I wish to thank Joyce L. Johnson and Carol Bailey Hughes, who read the manuscript with special attention to their expertise in oratorio—the former in Italian oratorio and the latter in Russian oratorio—and Henry L. Woodward, who offered valuable suggestions for the entire work. I thank the staff of the University of North Carolina Press, particularly C. David Perry for his help with editorial and computer problems and Elisabeth P. Smith, whose editing of the manuscript resulted in many improvements. Whatever infelicities may remain are clearly my responsibility.

I gratefully acknowledge major grants for work on this project: in

1979–80, a Kenan Leave from the University of North Carolina at Chapel Hill and a fellowship from the National Endowment for the Humanities; and in 1984–85, a Departmental Leave from the University of North Carolina and a fellowship from the John Simon Guggenheim Foundation, which were used for work on this volume as well as on the fourth one, still in preparation.

To my wife, Ann Woodward, I owe a special debt of gratitude for interest in the project, for countless hours of listening to me as I worked out problems relative to the book, for reading and reacting to the manuscript, and for constant, loving support.

Chapel Hill, N.C.   HOWARD E. SMITHER
December 1985

❧ Abbreviations

Libraries

With few exceptions, the library sigla are those used in *New Grove*, which in turn are based on those in the publications (series A) of the Répertoire Internationale des Sources Musicales (RISM; Kassel). The exceptions are new sigla for a few libraries not listed in *New Grove* or RISM. Throughout the volume, within a series of library sigla, a national sigillum applies without repetition until it is contradicted.

A	Austria	
	GÖ	Furth bei Göttweig, Benediktinerstift
	Wgm	Vienna, Gesellschaft der Musikfreunde
	Wn	_____, Österreichische Nationalbibliothek, Musiksammlung
B	Belgium	
	Bc	Brussels, Conservatoire Royal de Musique
	Br	_____, Bibliothèque Royale Albert Ier
BR	Brazil	
	Rn	Rio de Janeiro, Biblioteca Nacional
C	Canada	
	Tu	Toronto, University of Toronto, Faculty of Music
CS	Czechoslovakia	
	Pu	Prague, Státní Knihovna ČSSR, Universitní Knihovna
D	Germany	
	As	Augsburg (BRD), Staats- und Stadtbibliothek
	Au	_____, Universitätsbibliothek
	B	Berlin (W), Staatsbibliothek Preussischer Kulturbesitz
	Bds	Berlin (E), Deutsche Staatsbibliothek, Musikabteilung
	Dl	Dresden (DDR), Bibliothek und Museum Lobau
	Dlb	_____, Sächsische Landesbibliothek
	DT	Detmold (BRD), Lippische Landesbibliothek
	FUl	Fulda (BRD), Hessische Landesbibliothek

	Hs	Hamburg (BRD), Staats- und Universitätsbibliothek
	HEu	Heidelberg (BRD), Universitätsbibliothek
	HR	Harburg über Donauwörth (BRD), Fürstlich Oettingen-Wallerstein'sche Bibliothek
	KNth	Cologne (BRD), Theaterwissenschaftliches Institut der Universität
	LEm	Leipzig (DDR), Musikbibliothek der Stadt
	LÜh	Lübeck (BRD), Bibliothek der Hansestadt
	Mbs	Munich (BRD), Bayerische Staatsbibliothek
	MZp	Mainz (BRD), Bischöffliches Priesterseminar
	W	Wolfenbüttel (BRD), Herzog August Bibliothek
	WÜu	Würzburg (BRD), Universitätsbibliothek
E	Spain	
	Bc	Barcelona, Biblioteca de Cataluña
	Bf	_____, San Felipe Neri
	Mn	Madrid, Biblioteca Nacional
F	France	
	Pn	Paris, Bibliothèque Nationale
	Pc	_____, Conservatoire National de Musique (in Pn)
	Po	_____, Bibliothèque-Musée de l'Opéra
GB	Great Britain	
	Cu	Cambridge, University Library
	Ge	Glascow, Euing Music Library
	Lbl	London, British Library
	Lcm	_____, Royal College of Music
	Ob	Oxford, Bodleian Library
	T	Tenbury, St. Michael's College
I	Italy	
	Ac	Assisi, Biblioteca Comunale
	Bam	Bologna, Biblioteca della Casa di Risparmio (Biblioteca Ambrosini)
	Bas	_____, Archivio di Stato
	Bc	_____, Civico Museo Bibliografico Musicale
	Bca	_____, Biblioteca Comunale dell'Arciginnasio
	Bsf	_____, Convento di S. Francesco
	Bu	_____, Biblioteca Universitaria
	Fas	Florence, Archivio di Stato
	Fc	_____, Conservatorio di Musica Luigi Cherubini
	Fm	_____, Biblioteca Marucelliana
	Fs	_____, Seminario Arcivescovile Maggiore
	Fsf	_____, Archivio della Congregazione dell'Oratorio in San Firenze

FOLc	Foligno, Biblioteca Comunale	
Li	Istituto Musicale Luigi Boccherini	
Ma	Milan, Biblioteca Ambrosiana	
Mb	_____, Biblioteca Nazionale Braidense	
Mcom	_____, Biblioteca Comunale	
Ms	_____, Biblioteca Teatrale Livia Simoni	
Msartori	_____, Claudio Sartori, private collection	
MAC	Macerata, Biblioteca Comunale Mozzi-Borgetti	
MOe	Modena, Biblioteca Estense	
Nc	Naples, Conservatorio di Musica S. Pietro a Majella	
Nf	_____, Biblioteca Oratoriana dei Filippine	
Nlp	_____, Biblioteca Lucchesi-Palli (in Nn)	
Nn	_____, Biblioteca Nazionale Vittorio Emanuele III	
Pu	Padua, Biblioteca Universitaria	
PAc	Parma, Conservatorio di Musica Arrigo Boito	
PESo	Pesaro, Biblioteca Oliveriana	
PLcom	Palermo, Biblioteca Comunale	
PLn	_____, Biblioteca Nazionale	
Ras	Rome, Archivio di Stato	
Rc	_____, Biblioteca Casanatense	
Rf	_____, Archivio dei Filippini	
Rli	_____, Accademia Nazionale dei Lincei e Corsiniana	
Rn	_____, Biblioteca Nazionale Centrale Vittorio Emanuele III	
Rsc	_____, Conservatorio di Musica S. Cecilia	
Rv	_____, Biblioteca Vallicelliana	
Rvat	_____, Biblioteca Apostolica Vaticana	
Vgc	Venice, Biblioteca della Fondazione Giorgio Cini	
Vcg	_____, Biblioteca Casa di Goldoni	
Vmc	_____, Museo Civico Correr	
Vnm	_____, Biblioteca Nazionale Marciana	
Vsmc	_____, S. Maria della Consolazione detta Della Fava	
P	**Portugal**	
C	Coimbra, Biblioteca Geral da Universidade	
La	Lisbon, Palácio Nacional da Ajuda	
Lcg	_____, Fundação Calouste Gulbenkian	
Ln	_____, Biblioteca National	
Lt	_____, Teatro Nacional de S. Carlos	
Pm	Oporto, Biblioteca Pública Municipal	
PL	**Poland**	
GD	Gdánsk, Biblioteka Polskiej Akademii Nauk	
Wu	Warsaw, Biblioteka Uniwersytecka	
WRol	Wrocław, Biblioteka Ossolineum Leopoldiensis	

US   United States of America
    NYp   New York, Public Library at Lincoln Center and
            Museum of the Performing Arts
    Pu   Pittsburgh, Carnegie Library
    Wc   Washington, D.C., Library of Congress, Music Division

USSR Union of Soviet Socialist Republics
    Lsc   Leningrad, Gosudarstvennaya Ordena Trudovovo
            Krasnovo Znameni Publichnaya Biblioteka imeni
            M. E. Saltïkova-Shchedrina

Other Abbreviations

For bibliographical abbreviations, see the Bibliography. Other abbreviations are either standard in scholarly writing about music or are explained at first occurrence. Note that if abbreviations of vocal parts (S,
soprano; A, alto; T, tenor; B, bass) are not separated by spaces or punctuation, those parts sing together. (For example, SS might indicate a duet
for two sopranos or a chorus for two soprano parts, depending on context; and SATB could indicate either a quartet or a four-part chorus.)

PART I
The Italian Oratorio

CHAPTER I

Social Contexts of the Italian Oratorio

Introduction: Terminology and Genre Definition

Characteristic primarily of areas with Roman Catholic traditions, oratorios in Italian and Latin were performed in a wide variety of social contexts, not only in Italy but also in Northern and Eastern Europe and in the Iberian Peninsula. The present chapter focuses upon the sponsors and social contexts of oratorios with librettos in the Italian language but also includes those in Latin. The latter, less widely cultivated, were usually like the former in virtually every respect but language. Therefore what is said below of oratorios in Italian may be understood as applying also to those in Latin unless a distinction is explicitly made. Wherever the Italian oratorio was cultivated, it retained essentially the same features and was described in approximately the same terms. Although the Italian oratorio's libretto and music are treated mainly in chapters 2 and 3, a few words of introduction to terminology and genre definition are useful here.

In the context of the period and areas treated in the present chapter, what meaning or meanings of the word *oratorio* can be extracted from designations in printed librettos and musical sources and from writings about oratorio? Eighteenth-century Italian writings about oratorio are few, and all were written by poets and literary theorists and critics.[1] Among the earliest of the writings is Arcangelo Spagna's "Discorso dogmatico," printed in his *Oratorii overo melodrammi sacri* (Rome, 1706), which is discussed in volume 1 of the present study.[2] A contemporary of Spagna, the important Arcadian theorist Giovanni Mario Crescimbeni

---

1. On early eighteenth-century literary criticism of the Italian oratorio, see Baker, "Marcello," pp. 122–32. Reimer, "Oratorium," pp. 1–7, treats oratorio terminology from the seventeenth to the early nineteenth centuries but relies primarily on non-Italian sources.

2. Smither, *Oratorio*, 1:294–99. Spagna's "Discorso" is reprinted, together with a German translation, in Schering, "Beiträge."

treats the oratorio briefly in his *L'istoria della volgar poesia* (Rome, 1698; 2d ed., Rome, 1714; 3d ed., Venice, 1730–31).[3] Apostolo Zeno's dedication to his collected oratorio librettos, *Poesie sacre drammatiche* (Venice, 1735), deals with his approach to the libretto.[4] Francesco Saverio Quadrio's *Della storia e della ragione d'ogni poesia* (5 vols; Bologna and Milan, 1739–52) includes a section on oratorio in volume 3 (1744), which depends heavily upon Spagna.[5] Outside of Italy, among the dictionaries that define *oratorio* with specific mention of the Italian use of the term are Sébastien de Brossard's *Dictionaire de musique* (Paris, 1703), Johann Gottfried Walther's *Musikalisches Lexikon* (Leipzig, 1732), James Grassinau's *A Musical Dictionary* (London, 1740), and Jean Jacques Rousseau's article "Oratoire" in the *Encyclopédie* (vol. 9; Neuchâtel, 1765) and in his own *Dictionnaire de musique* (Paris, 1768).[6]

A unifying thread that runs through all of these writings is the concept of oratorio as a dramatic work, much like an opera, but with a religious text; Spagna, Crescimbeni, and Quadrio state explicitly that the oratorio is not staged—with scenery, costumes, and acting—in the manner of opera.[7] The following brief description of the Italian oratorio in the eighteenth and early nineteenth centuries is derived primarily from the present author's study of a large sample of printed librettos and musical sources called oratorios in the period, but the description also conforms to the definitions of the term and descriptions of the genre found in the above-listed sources.

The term *oratorio*, when applied to a work with an Italian or Latin text in the period 1720–1820, usually refers to the genre identified by the same term in the first two decades of the eighteenth century.[8] Until late in the eighteenth century, the characteristic libretto of an oratorio continues to reveal a two-part general structure, alternations of poetic meters intended for recitative and aria (as in *opera seria*), few choruses and ensembles, and biblical or hagiographical subject matter. The librettos of Metastasio were particularly favored and became models for other poets. Late in the eighteenth century, changes made in the oratorio libretto more or less parallel those made in serious opera, e.g., more

3. See Schering, "Beiträge," pp. 67–70, for a reprint from the 3d ed. of the comments on oratorio.

4. The dedication and statements about oratorio in some of Zeno's letters are discussed and quoted in Smither, *Oratorio*, 1:384–90.

5. See Quadrio, *Della storia*, 3/2:494–500.

6. For quotations from and discussions of the definitions of *oratorio* in these dictionaries, see Reimer, "Oratorium," pp. 2–3.

7. For Spagna's and Crescimbeni's statements, see Schering, "Beiträge," pp. 52 and 68, respectively; both statements are quoted in Smither, "Sacred Opera," p. 89. For Quadrio's statement, see Quadrio, *Della storia*, 3/2:497.

8. For descriptions of the Italian oratorio of the early eighteenth century, see Smither, *Oratorio*, vol. 1, chaps. 7 and 8.

choruses and ensembles and fewer simple recitatives. The music of an oratorio was much like that of an *opera seria*. During the course of the eighteenth and early nineteenth centuries, the musical changes in oratorio were mostly in the details of style and structure and were similar to changes in serious opera. Indeed, the major oratorio librettists and composers worked mainly in opera, and the sponsors and audiences for oratorio were often the same as for opera.

The type of composition commonly called *oratorio*, and so designated in all the writings from Spagna through Rousseau mentioned above, was also called by a variety of other terms. These terms usually relate to the poetic composition, for the prevailing concept of a vocal genre was that of a literary work intended to be set to music (just as an opera was a drama intended for music—*dramma per musica*). Zeno used three synonyms for the same works in this genre: *oratorio* in personal correspondence, *azione sacra* in librettos printed for individual performances, and *poesie sacre drammatiche* on the title page of his collected edition (but each work within that edition is called an *azione sacra*).[9] A glance through the present volume's appendix A, which includes title-page quotations of representative Italian and Latin oratorios, will reveal other synonyms for *oratorio* in addition to those used by Zeno, among which are *cantata, carmina, componimento da cantarsi, componimento per musica, componimento poetico da cantarsi nell'oratorio, componimento sacro, dialogo, dramma armonico, drama sacrum,* and *sacro componimento drammatico*. The three most common terms for the genre are *oratorio, azione sacra,* and *componimento sacro*. Thus far no genre distinctions have been discovered among the works identified by these various terms, except for *cantata*: this term usually labels works that are shorter than those called *oratorio*, but exceptionally *cantata* is used for a longer piece that could equally have been labeled *oratorio*.

Most patrons and institutional sponsors of oratorio performances tended to foster traditions established in the Baroque period: oratorios continued to be performed in oratories, churches (but not during Mass), private palaces, and theaters. At times the performers' platforms or theatrical stages were elaborately decorated. Yet the normal manner of performance continued to be that described by Spagna, Crescimbeni, and Quadrio, that which we might call a concert performance. Oratorios were characteristically presented with the orchestra on the platform together with the singers, who, music in hand, performed their parts with neither costumes nor acting in the operatic sense.

From the mid-eighteenth century on, however, works identified by the term *oratorio* or one of its synonyms—works like traditional oratorios in libretto and music—were increasingly staged in the manner of operas.[10]

9. See the discussion in ibid., 1:385–86.
10. On this practice, see Smither, "Sacred Opera," pp. 95–96.

More prominent in Italy than elsewhere, this practice was particularly important from the 1780s to the 1820s in Naples, where staged oratorios were given in the theaters during Lent. (See the section "Theaters," later in this chapter.) The staging of works called *oratorio* brought about a semantic change. In Italy of the late eighteenth and early nineteenth centuries, *oratorio* is used in two senses: the traditional sense, that of a sacred drama in concert performance; and a new one, that of an *opera sacra*. The new sense found its way into a music dictionary in the early nineteenth century: Pietro Lichtenthal's *Dizionario e bibliografia della musica* (Milan, 1826) defines *oratorio* as either a staged or an unstaged work, and in his article on *opera*, he includes *oratorio* as a species of opera. The sacred opera, or staged oratorio, remained exceptional, both as opera and as oratorio, and may be seen as a symptom of the social changes that, in the late eighteenth and early nineteenth centuries, initiated the decline of the Italian oratorio.

Italian and Latin Oratorio in Italy

The number of oratorio performances that must have been given in Italy during the eighteenth century is staggering to contemplate. In Rome, for example, each of two oratories—at the Chiesa Nuova and the church of San Girolamo della Carità—appears to have sponsored about twenty to twenty-five performances per year (the majority in the second half of the century) as is shown later in this chapter; private patrons, colleges, confraternities, and other institutions also sponsored oratorios—perhaps five to ten per year—which would bring the annual Roman average to between forty-five and sixty performances. Venice, Bologna, and Florence might have been as active as Rome; perhaps next were Naples, Milan, Palermo, Perugia, and Genoa; and these followed by Macerata, Padua, Foligno, Faenza, Lucca, Pesaro, Modena, Siena, Catania, Chieti, Pistoia, and a host of smaller cities and towns.[11] For Italian society,

11. The order of cities in this list follows the number of extant oratorio librettos printed in the eighteenth century for performances in each city as recorded in Claudio Sartori's tentative catalogue (Sartori, "Catalogo"), which would appear to represent only the proverbial tip of the iceberg. According to my count, Sartori includes the following number of oratorio librettos for these cities: Rome 385, Venice 312, Bologna 295, Florence 184, Naples 120, Milan 83, Palermo 74, Perugia 51, Genoa 44, and Macerata through Pistoia 41 down to 14.

Evidence derived from printed librettos, of course, must be considered incomplete and provisional—librettos were probably not printed for all performances, not all printed librettos survive, and surely not all surviving librettos have been located and catalogued. Although the numbers suggest that the first four cities listed were the most active in the performance of oratorios, more studies of local oratorio history would produce a more accurate estimate. For the oratorio in

oratorio was clearly an important genre, cultivated in small towns and large cities and available to all strata of society.

The Congregation of the Oratory

For nearly two hundred years, from the early seventeenth to the early nineteenth centuries, the Congregation of the Oratory—the members of which were known variously as the Fathers of the Oratory, the Oratorians, or the Philipine Fathers—was among the most active and consistent sponsors of oratorio performance throughout Italy. This community of secular priests together with its adjunct association of laymen was formed in Rome during the 1550s around St. Philip Neri (1515–95) and began its activities at the church of San Girolamo della Carità. The oratory of that church served for the informal religious services, or "spiritual exercises" (with music, mostly *laude*) led by Neri. In 1575 Neri's community was formally designated the Congregation of the Oratory; in the following year he and his disciples moved to a new church, popularly called the Chiesa Nuova—officially, Santa Maria in Vallicella —and they used a nearby oratory for their spiritual exercises. The priests at San Girolamo maintained a close relationship with the Oratorians and continued Neri's traditions in their own oratory. In the first half of the seventeenth century, when dialogues and oratorios began to be performed in such spiritual exercises, these two locations became the principal Roman centers of oratorio performance—a position that they retained until the early nineteenth century. A close relationship between the activities of the Oratorians at the Chiesa Nuova and the priests at San Girolamo appears to have continued throughout the eighteenth century and beyond, but those at the Chiesa Nuova seem to have been the more active oratorio sponsors. The oratory designed by Francesco Borromini and completed in 1640, which stands next to the Chiesa Nuova today, was the main Roman location of oratorio performances for nearly two-hundred years.[12]

Beginning in the late sixteenth century—at first in Italy but then in northern Europe, the New World, and the Far East—Oratorians established new communities modeled on the Congregation in Rome.[13] By the

Perugia, a study based mostly on librettos but partially on archival materials is Brumana, "Perugia."

12. In this chapter, oratorios said to have been performed "at the Chiesa Nuova" and "at San Girolamo" will refer to those performed in the oratories at those churches. For background on these and other Roman oratories and on their music in the sixteenth and seventeenth centuries, see Smither, *Oratorio*, 1:39–57, 121–24, 159–67, 207–15, 259–60.

13. For a list of nearly 200 oratories and the dates of their establishment, see Gasbarri, *Spirito*, pp. 184–87.

mid-eighteenth century, more than one hundred such communities existed in Italy, and many of them—possibly all in varying degrees—followed the Roman practice described below of performing an oratorio during a spiritual exercise. The Italian cities in addition to Rome where Oratorians were probably the most active as sponsors of such performances are Bologna, Florence, and Venice—possibly less active in this respect were the Oratorians in Genoa, Naples, and Perugia.[14]

The following description of the Oratorians as sponsors of oratorio performances focuses primarily on Rome, which served as the model for other cities, and draws upon what is known of the closely related activities of the priests at San Girolamo.[15] To illustrate Oratorian sponsorship outside Rome, Florence is important in the following discussion, both because the Florentine Oratorians were so active and because their activity has been carefully documented by archival research.[16]

The Oratorio Season. In seventeenth-century Rome, the Oratorians at the Chiesa Nuova and the priests at San Girolamo della Carità established a tradition of performing oratorios within a spiritual exercise conducted in the evening every Sunday and other feast day during the winter months, from All Saints (1 November) to Palm Sunday. This tradition was still flourishing at the turn of the century. A document of the Roman Oratorians dated 1696 refers to payment "for the music of the oratorio for the evenings of feastdays in winter";[17] the traveler François Raguenet wrote that in 1697 at San Girolamo oratorios were performed "every Holy Day night from All Saints to Easter";[18] and a Roman Oratorian document of 1701 mentions payment "to provide for the evening Oratorios on feastdays."[19] The Oratorians in Florence at the church of San Firenze and those in Bologna at Santa Maria di Galliera followed the same tradition, as probably did those in other cities.[20]

The annual number of performances around the turn of the century at the Chiesa Nuova and San Girolamo is not known, but it may have been more than thirty in each location. Lists of performances sponsored by the Florentine Oratorians indicate that thirty-two to thirty-seven orato-

14. This conclusion is based on my survey of printed librettos (much aided by Sartori, "Catalogo") and on the results of: Johnson, "Oratorio"; Hill, "Florence II"; and Brumana, "Perugia."

15. Little research has been done on oratorio cultivation at San Girolamo. Whatever differences may have distinguished the patterns of oratorio performance there from those at the Chiesa Nuova must await further investigation.

16. Hill, "Florence II."

17. The document in I-Ras, Registro 170, 12 April 1696, is quoted in Johnson, "Oratorio," p. 49.

18. Raguenet, *Comparison*, p. 22, n. 16.

19. Johnson, "Oratorio," p. 49.

20. On Florence and Bologna respectively, see Hill, "Florence II," p. 249, and Vitali, "Colonna," pp. 133–34.

rios were given in each of the three seasons of 1668–70 and 1693–94.[21] Outside the traditional season, Oratorians occasionally sponsored performances on special days, such as the feasts of SS. Nereus and Achilleus (12 May), St. Philip Neri (26 May), and the Nativity and Assumption of the Virgin Mary (8 September and 15 August, respectively).[22]

The performances, which took place within a religious service (described in the next section), were free to the public and financially supported by the Oratorians or private patrons. The number of performances and musicians hired fluctuated according to the available financial support. Early in eighteenth-century Rome, performances at the Chiesa Nuova were at times supported by such patrons as Cardinals Pietro Ottoboni (1667–1740) and Benedetto Pamphili (1653–1730) and Prince Francesco Maria Ruspoli (1672–1731).[23] Beyond that period, however, little is known of such private patronage at the Chiesa Nuova. The practice there would seem to have paralleled the Florentine one of paying for performances by funds from the Oratorians' dues, the direct support of specific Oratorians and their families, endowments from legacies, and income from real estate.[24] Rarely is a specific patron mentioned on the title page or in the dedication of a libretto printed for an Oratorian performance, whether in Rome, Florence, or elsewhere. At San Girolamo in Rome, on the other hand, librettos printed throughout the century frequently bear dedications,[25] probably indicating financial support by the dedicatee.

The number of oratorio performances at the Chiesa Nuova may have diminished during the early eighteenth century,[26] and the normal number of performances by the Florentine Oratorians appears to have been somewhat smaller in that century than in the late seventeenth.[27] By mid-

21. Hill, "Florence II," p. 249.

22. Johnson, "Oratorio," p. 47.

23. Gasbarri, *Oratorio fil.*, p. 65; Johnson, "Oratorio," p. 50.

24. For eighteenth-century documents referring to payments for performances at the Chiesa Nuova in Rome, see Johnson, "Oratorio," pp. 47–66, passim. and her Appendix A. For details of financing oratorio performances by the Florentine Oratorians in the seventeenth and eighteenth centuries, see Hill, "Florence II," pp. 254–55.

25. This conclusion is based on my survey of oratorio librettos and of the librettos listed in Sartori, "Catalogo."

26. Cf. Johnson, "Oratorio," p. 48: "Oratorios were only occasionally presented earlier in the eighteenth century. . . ." On pp. 45–52, Johnson sees the performance activities of the Oratorians increasing steadily throughout the eighteenth century. The focus of her work is on the oratorio at the Chiesa Nuova from 1770 to 1800; it remains to be seen whether further research on the earlier decades of the century would reveal more performance activity there than is currently known.

27. According to Hill, "Florence II," p. 249, "The eighteenth-century lists [of oratorios] show a slight reduction in the number of performances; normally

century at the Chiesa Nuova in Rome, however, a full season of oratorios had been resumed. In 1747 oratorios were being performed with some regularity during the winter months, but with basso continuo only, rather than orchestra—this in contrast to the practice of the Florentine Oratorians who used small string ensembles for virtually all the performances for which records exist.[28] To make their performances more attractive, the Roman Oratorians approved in 1747 the proposal "that violins be introduced in the oratorios in music during winter, in hopes of greater attendance."[29] A report of expenses for music in the season 1767–68 (among the few such reports that survive) attests to performances with orchestra at the Chiesa Nuova every Sunday evening and on special feast days between All Saints and Palm Sunday and every evening during the week following Christmas.[30] This level of sponsorship continued until near the end of the century. During the 1780s, active and prosperous years for the Oratorians, a special platform for the orchestra and singers was constructed in the oratory; about thirty oratorios, a different one each week, were performed during the season; and many new oratorios were added to the repertoire.[31] According to Johnson, "by the late eighteenth century, the oratorios at Vallicella [the Chiesa Nuova] had eclipsed the popularity of those at San Girolamo della Carità, the only other oratory with a season equivalent to Vallicella's. . . ."[32] Not only were the seasons equivalent, but these oratories appear to have presented oratorios on the same evenings, according to Charles Burney, who says that on Friday, 16 November 1770, he heard the first half of an oratorio at the Chiesa Nuova and then went to San Girolamo to hear another oratorio.[33]

By the mid-1790s Rome had entered a period of political and social unrest and the Oratorians had fallen on hard times. They had to cut expenses: in 1794 the number of oratorios performed was reduced by one half; in 1795–96 the maestro di cappella, Pasquale Anfossi, was not paid extra, as he had previously been, for accompanying the oratorios, although he continued to do so. Notice survives of only four oratorio performances in 1795, nine in each of the years 1796 and 1797, two in

between twenty-two and twenty-nine oratorios were heard during each of those later seasons [for which lists of oratorios survive]." Lists survive for the seasons 1668–1670, 1729–30, 1738–42, 1751–55, 1758–64 (p. 248).

28. Ibid., pp. 257–58.

29. Document in I-Rf, C I 10, 11 September 1747, quoted in Johnson, "Oratorio," p. 54.

30. I-Ras: Fondo Congregazione dell'oratorio, Busta 112, No. 7: "Giornale per le spese della Prefettura della Musica di Chiesa Nuova." For a brief discussion of the document, see Johnson, "Oratorio," pp. 55–57; and for excerpts, see ibid., pp. 657–66.

31. Ibid., pp. 59–60.

32. Ibid., pp. 58–59.

33. Burney, *France and Italy*, p. 378.

1798 (the year the French troops occupied Rome and Pope Pius VI fled to Siena), and none in 1799 and 1800.[34] The oratorios began again at least by 1802, for two librettos printed in that year attest to performances at the Chiesa Nuova,[35] and a list of expenses from 1804 shows that ten oratorios were performed there in November and December.[36] Printed librettos suggest that the Oratorians in Rome continued occasional sponsorship of oratorio performances until well past the middle of the nineteenth century.[37] The extent to which the Oratorians in Florence and other cities continued to sponsor oratorio performances in the early nineteenth century is not known, but one might reasonably assume that their sponsorship also diminished.

The Spiritual Exercise. The context for oratorio performances at the Chiesa Nuova, and possibly at San Girolamo,[38] continued to be the spiritual exercise that had originated with Philip Neri in the late sixteenth century. The service consisted of one or more opening prayers (in the eighteenth century a litany, the Salve Regina, and the Pater Noster), a sermon recited from memory by a small boy, music, a sermon by a priest, and more music.[39] Neri wrote of the boy's sermon and the music, "Practice has shown that by inserting the pleasure of spiritual music and the simplicity and purity of boys into the serious exercises done by serious persons one draws many more people of every sort."[40] In the sixteenth and early seventeenth centuries the music included *laude*, spiritual madrigals, and dialogues. After the mid-seventeenth century, when the two-

34. Johnson, "Oratorio," pp. 61–66.

35. See appendix A: *Il paradiso perduto* (1802) and *La virtù in gara* (1802).

36. The list is quoted in Johnson, "Oratorio," pp. 733–34.

37. In my survey of extant oratorio librettos, I have seen thirty-two printed in Rome between 1802 and 1830 with title pages indicating Oratorian sponsorship; four indicating sponsorship by the priests at San Girolamo; and forty-one without indication but with composers and librettists named who were active at either the Chiesa Nuova or San Girolamo. Thus, at least seventy-seven oratorios were performed in Rome, probably at these oratories, in this twenty-eight year period.

38. The close relationship between these two oratories (cf. Alaleona, *Oratorio*, pp. 155–62) makes reasonable the assumption of similar services, despite inadequate research thus far on activities at San Girolamo.

39. For references to these elements in the Oratorians' services in the sixteenth century, see Smither, *Oratorio*, 1:52–53; and in the seventeenth century, pp. 56–57, 123–24, and 167.

40. Translated from Marciano, *Oratorio*, 1:37. For the full context of this quotation, see Smither, *Oratorio*, 1:52. Neri probably derived the idea of sermonizing by a boy from similar practices in sixteenth-century Florentine confraternities, with which he was familiar from his own boyhood. Cf. Hill, "Florence I," p. 132; Cistellini, "Neri," pp. 64–66; and *Processo*, vol. 2, pp. 324–25, n. 1645. On sermons by adolescent boys in the Florentine confraternities, see Trexler, "Ritual in Florence," p. 220.

part oratorio became the norm in this service, the oratorio's first part was performed before the sermon and the second part after it.[41] A document of the Bolognese Oratorians at Santa Maria di Galliera shows that they adopted the same service shortly after the founding of their Oratory, in 1616;[42] and the Florentine Oratorians at San Firenze introduced the service in 1652, "in order to conform as nearly as possible to the institution of Rome."[43] Like the Oratorians in Bologna and Florence, those in other cities would probably have followed the model of Rome in this regard.

This type of service continued throughout the period under discussion, as is clear from archival documents and comments by travelers who heard performances sponsored by Oratorians. In the first issue (July 1766) of Johann Adam Hiller's weekly music journal published in Leipzig, a report on music in Italy includes the following:

> In Bologna one meets the best musicians in all Italy. Next to the beautiful church *the Madonna di Galliera* there is a splendid chapel [i.e., oratory], where they perform oratorios or spiritual concerts [Oratoria oder geistliche Concerte *(Concerts spirituels)*], which last at least three hours, every Sunday in winter, from All Saints Day to Easter. Although these oratorios are given at night, nevertheless full outward decency and the greatest silence prevails there. It is generally a drama of two acts, in which the content is taken from Holy Scripture or church history. Before the piece there is Mass, and a short discourse by a young boy, which serves as an introduction to the oratorio. Between the two parts or acts likewise a Philippine [Father] gives a discourse, so that meanwhile the musicians can rest.[44]

Visitors to the services of the Oratorians seldom fail to mention the role of the young boy. In his account of a visit to Rome, the French traveler Coyer emphasized the boy's performance, which he found particularly impressive. On 26 March 1764 he wrote, "In another church, before an *Oratorio*, performed with all the apparatus of a delicious music, a child of eight to nine years, in cassock and surplice, climbed

41. See Archangelo Spagna's comments, published in 1706, but describing seventeenth-century practice, paraphrased and quoted in Smither, *Oratorio*, 1:167.

42. I-Bas: Fondo demaniale, *Padri Filippini di Santa Maria di Galliera*, 112/5995, mazzo 6. The document is quoted in full in Vitali, "Colonna," pp. 133–35.

43. I-Fs: *Libro di ricordi ordinari* A, p. 22. A longer passage of the document from which this quotation is taken is quoted and translated in part in Hill, "Florence II," p. 251.

44. Translated from "Einige Anmerkungen über Italien, aus des *Abbé Richard description historique et critique de l'Italie etc. à Paris 1766*," *Wöchentliche Nachrichten und Anmerkungen die Musik betreffend*, 1 (1766): 47.

onto a chair to preach to the faithful; that ecclesiastical marionette would have astonished you with his air of assurance, with his tone of pathos, and his gestures."[45] Burney, who is less complimentary about the boy's sermon, provides a rather full description of the service and its music on Sunday, 11 November 1770:

> In the afternoon I went to the Chiesa Nuova, to hear an oratorio in that church, where the sacred drama took its rise. There are two galleries; in one there is an organ, and in the other a harpsichord; in the former the service was begun by the matins in four parts, *alla Palestrina*; then the *Salve Regina* was sung *a voce sola*, after which there were prayers; and then a little boy, not above six years old, mounted the pulpit, and delivered a discourse by way of sermon, which he had got by heart, and which was rendered truly ridiculous by the vehicle through which it passed. The oratorio of Abigail, set to music by Signor Casali, was then performed. This drama consisted of four characters, and was divided into two parts. . . .
>   Between the two parts of this oratorio, there was a sermon by a Jesuit, delivered from the same pulpit from whence the child had descended. I waited to hear the last chorus, which, though it was sung by book, was as light and unmeaning as an opera chorus, which must be got by heart. . . .[46]

Most of Burney's comments about the order of this service are verified by an Oratorian document of about the same time, which gives minute details.[47] There are, however, some discrepancies: Burney surely did not hear an oratorio "in that church," strictly speaking, for such performances invariably took place in the oratory attached to the church; and what Burney calls "matins" was probably a litany, traditional in this period for the oratory service, as mentioned above. Burney's comment about the last chorus's being "sung by book" could as well pertain to the entire work and to the tradition at this and other oratories. The music was characteristically read—neither memorized nor acted—and it was virtually sight-read. In both Rome and Florence new oratorios appear to have been rehearsed only once, and repeat performances, even in subsequent seasons and with different singers, were not rehearsed.[48] The performers were all male, and castrati sang the upper parts.[49]

Burney does not mention the audience, but it would probably have

45. Translated from Coyer, *Voyages*, 1:279.
46. Burney, *France and Italy*, pp. 363–65.
47. The document is in I-Rf: C III 15, and is quoted in full in Johnson, "Oratorio," pp. 31–35 (in English), and pp. 719–21 (in the original Italian).
48. Ibid., p. 60; Hill, "Florence II," p. 257.
49. This point is mentioned in a letter of 1783 by a visitor to Rome, published in *Magazin der Musik* 2/1 (1783): 990.

consisted of 150 to 200 men of various social positions.[50] The audience probably thought of the event more as a concert than a religious service, for in public announcements in Rome the oratorios were so regarded.[51] Oratorio, after all, was the only operatic type of music available to Romans except during Carnival time, when opera was permitted.[52] Only exceptionally were women admitted to the oratory at the Chiesa Nuova, to that at San Firenze in Florence, and probably to oratories in other cities as well.[53] An exception in Florence was the performance for the inauguration of the new oratory on 3 December 1775. Exceptions in Rome included the celebration of female saints—the feasts of the Assumption (15 August) and St. Cecilia (22 November), among others— and certain special events, such as the 1772 performance of the oratorio *Daniello*, composed by the thirteen-year-old Maria Rosa Coccia and dedicated to Maria Sforza-Cesarini. When women were admitted, they were seated separately from men, "for the uprightness of the persons, and the decorum of the place," according to a Roman Oratorian document.[54]

How long the Oratorians continued the traditional service that Burney describes is not known, but in 1824 it was still used. Georg Ludwig Peter Sievers, who published a report in the periodical *Cäcilia* on the musical life of Rome in that year, says that the oratorians were performing oratorios every Sunday and feast day from 1 December to Easter—a shorter season than in the eighteenth century—and he describes the service:

Before the beginning of [the service] a litany is sung with organ accompaniment. The first sermon, remarkably enough, is given every time by a young boy. . . . After the ending of the [sermon] begins the oratorio. Then the members of the audience (which means men, for women are not admitted, for this service takes place in the evening and the oratory is only sparsely lighted) pull out of their pockets a libretto together with a small piece of candle; they light the latter at the holy lamp, and with the help of [the

50. The estimate of the number in the audience is based on the the number of librettos normally printed (cf. Johnson, "Oratorio," p. 56) and the approximate seating capacity of the oratory at the Chiesa Nuova.

51. Ibid., pp. 36–37.

52. For information on eighteenth-century musical life in Rome, including both opera and oratorio, see ibid., pp. 20–44.

53. On the exceptional admission of women to the oratory at the Chiesa Nuova in Rome, see ibid., pp. 30, 35; on the same subject at San Firenze in Florence, see Hill, "Florence II," pp. 249–50.

54. I-Rf: C III 15, translated in Johnson, "Oratorio," p. 35; original Italian, p. 721. A Florentine Oratorian document testifying to the separation of men and women at the performance of 1775, mentioned above, is I-Fsf: *Ricordi* B, p. 108 (3 December 1775), quoted in Hill, "Florence II," p. 249, n. 12.

candle] they follow the text. After the first part of the oratorio begins the second sermon; the candles are extinguished and the audience either listens or (what happens more often) leaves the church until the second [part] begins, when the wax candles are lighted anew. The oratorio begins a half-hour after sundown (*a mezz'ora di notte*) and often lasts three hours.[55]

Sievers says that the composers represented that year were Giovanni Paisiello, Pasquale Anfossi, [Pietro Alessandro] Guglielmi, Ferdinando Paer, Girolamo Mango, and Paolo Bonfichi, and that the performances tended to be musically poor and poorly attended.[56] By the 1820s, the long tradition of the Italian oratorio and the oratory service would seem to have lost its vitality.

Although the preceding account of the sponsorship of oratorio performances by the Congregation of the Oratory has focused on Rome and Florence, where most of the archival research has been done, printed librettos suggest that the Oratorians in both Bologna and Venice might have been as active as those in Rome and Florence. In Venice virtually every extant libretto of an Italian-language oratorio performed in the eighteenth century names the Congregation of the Oratory as its sponsor.[57] (The conservatories, considered below, performed oratorios in Latin.) Archival studies of the Oratorians' activities in these cities—and in Genoa, Naples, Perugia, and others—are needed before we can accurately estimate the extent and patterns of oratorio sponsorship by the Congregation of the Oratory throughout Italy.[58] But the Oratorians were by no means the only sponsors of oratorio performances in Italy. Probably the second most active sponsors were the confraternities of laymen found in virtually every Italian city.

Lay Confraternities

Variously called *confraternita, arciconfraternita, compagnia,* or *congregazione,* the lay confraternities of the seicento and settecento mostly continued or imitated institutions founded in the late Middle Ages and Renaissance.[59] A confraternity was a club—a voluntary association of

55. Sievers, "Rom," pp. 208–9.

56. Ibid., pp. 209–10.

57. More information on Venice will be offered in the forthcoming book, Arnold, *Oratorio in Venice,* not yet available as of this writing.

58. For the city of Perugia, a good beginning has been made by Brumana, "Perugia."

59. The *arciconfraternita* differed from the *confraternita* not in kind but in higher rank: only the former was permitted to establish affiliated institutions of the same type. (Cf. Pio Ciprotti and Vittorio Bartoccetti, "Confraternita," *Enciclopedia cattolica,* 4:col. 261.)

laymen—established by ecclesiastical decree for the promotion of pious and charitable practices, increased public worship, and religious education.[60] The brothers of a confraternity met regularly in a church, oratory, or chapel to participate in ritual, educational, and organizational meetings; they wore distinctive clothing for ritual and public processional purposes. Confraternities exerted a powerful influence on religious, festive, and social life throughout Italy and Mediterranean Europe, as Ronald Weisman indicates:

> Apart from the parish mass, confraternal ritual was one of the most common forms of religious experience for southern Europeans in the early modern period. Throughout Mediterranean Europe, confraternities planned and directed much of the festive life and public charitable activities of their communities. The confraternities provided their members with certain vital forms of social insurance in life and in death. Confraternities were also commissioners of works of art, and were thereby major sources of patronage for the Renaissance artist. Confraternal activity clearly contributed in many ways to the spiritual and material needs of townsmen in the late medieval and early modern world.
>
> But beyond being a place to pray, and an institution providing charitable distributions and other services to the community, the confraternity, like the family and guild, was one of the principal forms of sociability available to males in premodern European society. . . .[61]

In Italian cities, towns, and villages, the confraternity's role in planning and directing ritual and festive life, not only for the brothers but also for the community at large, included the sponsorship of musical performances. In the seicento and settecento, the works performed by confraternity sponsorship were often oratorios.

The musical aspects of Florentine confraternal ritual and festivity have been more fully documented by archival research than those in other cities.[62] The extent to which the Florentine confraternities may be taken to represent those of Italy at large is still unknown. So far as oratorio sponsorship is concerned, however, the available evidence of non-Florentine activity—largely derived from printed oratorio librettos—would im-

60. Lumbroso and Martini, *Confraternite romane,* p. 13.

61. Weissman, *Ritual Brotherhood,* p. ix.

62. For the history of such activities of the Florentine Compagnia dell'Arcangelo Raffaello in the period 1583–1655, see Hill, "Florence I." For the same confraternity's oratorio sponsorship, together with that of several other confraternities in Florence, from 1655 to 1785, see Hill, "Florence III." I wish to thank Professor John Walter Hill for making that article available to me in typescript prior to its publication.

ply some similarity between the Florentine confraternities and those in other cities.

Florentine life depended heavily on confraternities. In 1785, when Grand Duke Peter Leopold suppressed them for reasons of his Enlightenment view of religion—he also saw them as a political and economic threat—247 confraternities existed in Florence.[63] At least one included about 500 members so that virtually every man in the city may well have belonged to a confraternity. In Rome, by comparison, Lumbroso and Martini list only 164 confraternities established between 1264 and 1776;[64] available data does not reveal how many were still functioning in the settecento. The Florentine confraternities were legalized again in 1790 but never regained their former significance.

Although the Congregation of the Oratory, as indicated above, sponsored most of the oratorios heard in certain cities, in Florence oratorios were heard in at least thirty-one locations outside the Oratorians' premises. The vast majority of such performances took place in the oratories of about fourteen confraternities, five of which stand out as the most active: the Compagnia dell'Arcangelo Raffaello; the Compagnia di S. Giovanni Evangelista; the Compagnia della Purificazione della Gloriosa Vergine Maria, et di San Zanobi, detta di San Marco; the Congregazione ed Ospizio di Giesù, Maria, e Giuseppe e della SS. Trinità detta del Melani posta nella Compagnia di San Marco; and the Compagnia di S. Jacopo. Except for the Congregazione ed Ospizio, these confraternities originated in the Renaissance for the religious education of adolescent boys not destined for the clergy. By the seventeenth century, however, all but the Compagnia di S. Giovanni Evangelista had become clubs for middle-class adults.[65] Possibly sparked by a relatively short-lived spirit of competition, these five groups sponsored oratorios most actively between 1690 and 1710. In that period they performed from two to twelve oratorios per year, with an average of seven or eight.[66] Confraternal sponsorship in Florence tapered off after 1710, diminished drastically after 1725, and continued sporadically until 1785.

If the confraternities never equaled the Oratorians in the number of

63. Unless otherwise indicated, all the following information on the Florentine confraternities and their oratorio sponsorship derives from Hill, "Florence III."

64. Lumbroso and Martini, *Confraternite romane*, pp. 441–45.

65. For details of the history of the Compagnia dell'Arcangelo Raffaello, which performed *sacre rappresentazioni* in the sixteenth century, spiritual dialogues with and without scenery and costumes in the early seventeenth century, and then oratorios in the later seventeenth century, see Hill, "Florence I." According to Hill, "Florence III," the other four confraternities mentioned here had similar traditions. For further details on the adolescent confraternities in Renaissance Florence, see Trexler, "Ritual in Florence."

66. The numbers derive from Hill, "Florence III," Appendix, "Oratorios Produced by Lay Confraternities in Florence After 1650."

works sponsored, they clearly exceeded them in the sumptuousness of performances. The performances, normally given between Christmas and Easter, were free and open to the public and usually financed on an ad hoc basis by the brothers of a confraternity. Such performances also included larger and more varied orchestras than those of the Oratorians as well as better personnel, often including singers from the opera rather than the church musicians who performed in the Oratory. At times the confraternity brothers lavishly decorated their oratories to approximate a theater and constructed special galleries to accommodate the large crowds they anticipated. A description by the diarist of the Compagnia di S. Jacopo of the elaborate and elegantly decorated structures erected in that confraternity's oratory for the performance of Benedetto Marcello's *Joaz* on Easter, 17 April 1729, shows the lengths to which the brothers went to create a theatrical environment for the performance:

A stage having been erected, it seemed well to make it go all the way, that is, taking the entire front of the altar platform. The altar was moved forward, so that the first stairs of the platform served as the stairs of a false altar. The said stage was made with the most beautiful architecture, since with several levels of seats for the performers, it was in such a form that each one of the performers who participated was clearly distinguishable even from the street. Here and there on the sides of the said stage there were doors through which to enter from below, made from gilded wood and with door curtains of damask trimmed with gold. And over the middle of each one of these doors there was a wooden candelabrum carrying 15 candles and two other candelabra of pure crystal, each one carrying five candles. The front of the stage and the performers' seats were decked with yellow and red silk with azure flounces on top. The whole facade of the altar was covered with crimson taffeta with gilded flounces. The first and second rows were decorated, for their entire length, with brass tendrils and candles, so that it looked like a real theatre for its magnificence. . . . At 4 p.m. the company was opened and at 5:30 it was so full that even with the 30 extra benches that were put up, there were people even in the centre aisle, the sacristy and right up to the stage, so that no more could get in. . . . At 6:15 the said oratorio began. . . . In the second aria of the first part Sig. Franc[es]co Veracini, celebrated violinist, played a most beautiful *sinfonia a solo* which caused great applause, and at 9:15 the aforesaid oratorio finished, everything having taken place with good order and to the glory of the Lord God.[67]

67. I-Fas: Compagnie religiose soppresse 1246, no. 10, p. 405. Quoted from Hill, "Veracini," pp. 264–65. The entire document, which includes the number of singers and instrumentalists, is transcribed in Hill, "Life and Works," pp. 969–76, and is translated in part and discussed in ibid., pp. 109–13. For another

Not only did the confraternities outdo the Oratorians in sumptuousness of decor and music, but also in the makeup and size of the audience, which regularly included both men and women and could number as many as 600 persons—if the number of librettos printed provides an indication of audience size.[68] In the early settecento, the intermission activities between an oratorio's two parts included both a sonata played by a virtuoso and a sermon, but after the mid-century the sermon was dropped.

Evidence from printed librettos suggests that confraternities in Florence were more active as sponsors of oratorio performances than those in other cities. Nevertheless, in virtually every large city of Italy, and many smaller ones as well, confraternities sponsored oratorios from time to time. Virtually any major feast day of the church year might be an occasion for a confraternity's performance of an oratorio, but the season of Lent, and particularly Holy Week, were favored. In Bologna, for example, oratorios were sponsored on Good Friday by the Arciconfraternita di Santa Maria della Morte,[69] and during Lent by the Arciconfraternita di Santa Maria della Vita;[70] in Milan, in early January by the Congregazione dell'Immacolata Concezione,[71] and every Friday in Lent by the Congregazione del Santissimo Entierro in San Fedele;[72] in Rome, on the Fridays of Lent by the Arciconfraternita del Santissimo Croci-

---

description of a confraternity oratorio, dating from 1712, see Smither, *Oratorio*, 1:286–88.

68. According to Hill, "Florence III," in 1748, 600 copies of the libretto were printed for an oratorio performance at the Compagnia della Purificazione.

69. App. A: *L'Abele* (1739), *Adamo ed Eva* (1775), *L'angelica costanza* (1720), *I conforti di Maria* (1723, 1734, 1745), *Debora e Sisara* (1795), *La deposizione dalla croce* (1787), *Gesù Cristo deposto dalla croce* (1794). (In this and following footnotes, "app. A" [appendix A] refers to the location of information taken from the title pages of librettos sponsored by the organization under consideration. Such title pages are provided in appendix A because they offer more details about the oratorio and its context than are included in the text.)

70. App. A: *L'appostolo dell'Etiopia: S. Matteo* (1726), *Il beato Riniero* (1742), *La caduta di Gerusalemme* (1727), *La decollazione di S. Gio. Battista* (1721), *L'esiglio di S. Silverio papa e martire* (1720).

71. App. A: *L'adorazione delli tre re magi* (1722), *La colpa originale piangente alle culle* (1723), *Dialogo pastorale a gloria del nato Redentore* (1720), *Gesù bambino adorato* (1726).

72. Giovanni Battista Sammartini was the maestro di cappella for this confraternity. Most of his works composed for the confraternity's Lenten services were cycles of brief, dramatic cantatas, usually with three personages. For what appears to be a typical Sammartini cycle, see app. A: *La passione di Gesù Cristo, e i dolori della Vergine Madre in cinque cantate* (1743). Sartori, "Catalogo," lists librettos for twenty-seven performances of such cantatas sponsored by this confraternity between 1725 and 1773.

fisso,[73] and on Good Friday by the Congregazione della Santissima Nascita di Maria Vergine.[74]

Although most confraternities established in the late Middle Ages and early Renaissance drew members from throughout a city, from the sixteenth century on new confraternities were often parish oriented.[75] Among these were the confraternities of Christian Doctrine, established for the sole purpose of providing boys (sometimes girls too) with a basic religious education.[76] In the seicento and settecento some such confraternities would hold an annual *disputa della Dottrina Christiana*, a kind of contest, in which two teams of boys—as many as one hundred each in a large parish—would face each other on platforms at the front of a church. The first in line on one side would pose a doctrinal question to the first on the other. A boy who hesitated or could not answer had to leave the platform. The last boy remaining was proclaimed and crowned Emperor, the *Imperatore della Dottrina Cristiana*, and presented with honors and gifts.[77] From time to time an oratorio would enliven such festivities. In Bologna in 1763, for instance, an oratorio formed part of the ritual of the "solemn coronation of the Emperor of the Christian Doctrine";[78] also in Bologna, in 1752, at the church of San Sigismondo, an oratorio marked "the occasion of solemnly giving the Cross to the boys of the Christian Doctrine";[79] and in Rome, on 4 January 1735, at the church of San Marco, a Christmas oratorio brightened "the occasion of the solemn dispute on the Christian Doctrine to be done by the parish girls [zitelle parrocchiane],"[80] in a rare instance of female participation. Oratorios sponsored by confraternities of the Christian Doctrine were characteristic in the settecento but were also found in the the late sei-

73. This confraternity was more active in the seventeenth century than the eighteenth. It continued its tradition of performing oratorios every Friday in Lent until 1710 and revived the performances again in 1725 for only one year. For more information, see Smither, *Oratorio*, 1:207–15.

74. App. A: *Oratorio per la santissima Vergine addolorata* (1738 and 1739), *La passione di Gesù Cristo nostro signore* (1755), *La SS. Vergine addolorata* (1729, 1733, 1736, 1737, and 1745).

75. On the Florentine parish confraternity, see Weissman, *Ritual Brotherhood*, pp. 206–8.

76. For descriptions of confraternities of Christian Doctrine, see ibid., p. 213, and Lumbroso and Martini, *Confraternite romane*, pp. 132–34. According to Hill, "Florence II," p. 109, n. 5, some of the Florentine city-wide confraternities mentioned above were also confraternities of Christian Doctrine, but they appear to have had more varied activities than the parish confraternities established strictly for doctrinal instruction.

77. Lumbroso and Martini, *Confraternite romane*, p. 134.

78. App. A: *Il paradiso terrestre* (1763).

79. App. A: *Il trionfo della croce* (1752).

80. App. A: *Componimento sagro per musica sopra la nascita de Redentore* (1735).

cento.[81] If young boys occasionally heard oratorios during their early years in this context, some of those who attended colleges a bit later would have renewed their familiarity with the genre.

Educational Institutions

Colleges. In eighteenth-century Rome—unlike Florence—the *collegi,* or boarding schools for young men, seem to have been far more active sponsors of oratorios than the confraternities. Most active were the Collegio Nazareno, operated by the Congregazione delle Scuole Pie (or the "Scolopi"); the Collegio Germanico-Ungarico, by the Jesuits; and the Collegio Clementino, by the Somaschi. No archival studies exist of the music in these colleges during the eighteenth century, but extant librettos suggest that each may have sponsored at least one oratorio annually. The title pages of librettos for performances at the Collegio Nazareno usually identify the works as cantatas, but many would seem to approach the oratorio in their two-part structure, dramatic text, and duration. The performances were virtually always given "on the occasion of the public academy" in the college, and the subject usually related to the Nativity of the Blessed Virgin (feast day, 8 September).[82] The works performed at the Collegio Clementino, usually called oratorios, virtually always celebrate the feast of the Assumption (15 August).[83] At the Collegio Germanico, the title-page wording of most oratorio librettos does not include an occasion but simply states the performance location.[84] A few Roman librettos attest to performances, on rare occasions, at the Collegio Capranica and the Seminario Romano.

Probably less frequently than in Rome, oratorios were given at colleges in cities elsewhere in Italy, as shown by the following sample of places

81. For one dating from 1683 in Bologna, see Smither, *Oratorio,* 1:280.

82. App. A: *Cantata per la Natività della Beatissima Vergine* (1739). At times a more specific title precedes the indication of the feast day, as in app. A: *Elia al Carmelo. Cantata per la Natività della Beatissima Vergine* (1761).

83. App. A: *Oratorio per l'Assunzione della B.ma Vergine* (1730).

84. App. A: *Il martirio di S. Ferma* (1733). I am grateful to Dr. Joyce L. Johnson for giving me information from her unpublished research about performances at the Collegio Germanico-Ungarico that are not represented by librettos in Sartori, "Catalogo."

In some years the Collegio Germanico-Ungarico seems to have borrowed repertory from the oratories at the Chiesa Nuova and San Girolamo della Carità: *Il trionfo di Mardocheo* by Giovanni Batista Borghi, was performed in 1774 and 1785 at the Chiesa Nuova and in 1778 at this college; *S. Elena al Calvario* by Nicola Luciani, was performed in 1779 at San Girolamo and 1780 at the college; and *Il popolo di Giuda,* by Antonio Sacchini, was performed in 1768 and 1777 at the Chiesa Nuova and 1769 at the college. (See app. A for these libretto title pages in full.)

and occasions of performances. In Bologna an oratorio was given on 6 February 1725 by Dominican students for their annual celebration of the feast of St. Thomas Aquinas and also to acknowledge the recent election of Pope Benedict XIII (1724–30)—Bologna, of course, was in the papal state. About six weeks later (20 March), apparently the same oratorio was given in Milan, again by Dominican students and for St. Thomas Aquinas, but the pope's name was omitted from the libretto's title page.[85] Colleges operated by the Scolopi in various Italian cities and even in small towns sometimes performed the same kinds of works (perhaps some of the same works) as were given at the Collegio Nazareno in Rome and for the same kinds of occasions. For instance, at Urbino in 1760 the Collegio de' Nobili delle Scuole Pie performed for a public academy a work called a cantata, on the subject of the Nativity of the Blessed Virgin, which may be one of the works of the same title that were performed at the Nazareno in Rome in the years 1753–57, 1760, and 1780 (perhaps in other years as well).[86] In 1752 in Murano, near Venice, a work called a cantata, on the subject of the Assumption of the Virgin, was performed in a public academy at the Collegio di San Lorenzo Giustiniani, also operated by the Scolopi.[87] In Florence in 1759 an oratorio formed part of a public ceremony in which the rhetoric students at the Scuole Pie celebrated the opening of a new oratory at the school.[88] In Perugia until about 1770 oratorios were occasionally performed in three colleges: the Collegio della Compagnia di Gesù, the Collegio del Seminario, and the Collegio della Sapienza.[89]

Conservatories. In Venice, aside from the Congregation of the Oratory, the most active sponsors of oratorios were the four hospitals or conservatories: the Ospedale della Pietà, the Ospedale degl'Incurabili, the Ospedale dei Mendicanti, and the Ospedale dei Derelitti ai Santi Giovanni e Paolo (called the Ospedaletto). The performances were given by the girls who studied there, who, after the completion of their studies, usually either married or entered convents.[90] The oratorios that they performed were always in Latin, a rare language for oratorio outside Venice.[91]

85. Both the Bologna and Milan title pages, app. A: *L'umiltà coronata.*
86. App. A: *Cantata per la Natività della Beata Vergine* and *Cantata per la Natività della Beatissima Vergine.*
87. App. A: *Cantata per l'assunzione della Beatissima Vergine.*
88. App. A: *L'innocenza vendicata.*
89. For details, see Brumana, "Perugia," p. 119, and Brumana's chronological list of librettos, with full title-page citations, on pp. 125–58.
90. On the Venetian conservatories, see Arnold, "Conservatories"; Meyer-Baer, "Conservatories"; and Smither, *Oratorio,* 1:290–91.
91. Latin oratorios were performed in Rome by the Arciconfraternita del SS. Crocifisso until 1725; in Naples at times for All Souls Day (for examples, see the works by Francesco Feo mentioned in chap. 3; also app. A: *Rubri maris trajectus*

Extant printed librettos suggest that each conservatory may have given one to five oratorios per year throughout most of the settecento and that all the conservatories increased the number of such performances around the mid-century.[92] For the Incurabili more librettos are extant from the 1760s than from any other decade; for the other three, more from the 1780s, possibly the peak decade of oratorio performance in Venetian conservatories.[93] About twice as many librettos are extant from the Mendicanti as from any other conservatory.[94]

The title pages of about half of the extant librettos printed for the conservatories cite performance occasions. At the Incurabili, the Mendicanti, and the Ospedaletto, a typical annual occasion is *dum recolitur solemne triduum hebdomadae majoris* ("to contemplate the solemn *triduum* of Holy Week"—i.e., the three-day period of Maundy Thursday, Good Friday, and Holy Saturday).[95] Some librettos are more specific about the context of oratorios in this *triduum*. For instance, the title page of a libretto for a performance in 1758 at the Incurabili refers to the oratorio as a *sacra isagoge ad psalmum Miserere* ("a sacred introduction to the Psalm 'Miserere' "—i.e., Psalm 50 in the Vulgate,"Miserere mei, Deus");[96] a libretto for an oratorio given there in 1764 terms the work an *introductio ad psalmum Miserere*;[97] and librettos printed for the Mendicanti in 1750 and 1767 call the oratorios *carmina praecinenda psalmo Miserere*.[98] In a libretto of 1760 for the Mendicanti an additional detail is mentioned: Vespers on Good Friday is the service in which the oratorio introduced Psalm 50.[99] Although most librettos do not mention Vespers, comments of visitors to Venice, some of which are cited below, stress Vespers as a characteristic oratorio occasion.

Other than Holy Week, feast days of special importance to a given conservatory afforded occasions for oratorio performance. Numerous

---

[1773]); and occasionally in Palermo (see app. A: *Aemulatio inter divinum amorem*).

92. For more information, see the forthcoming work, Arnold, *Oratorio in Venice*.

93. According to my analysis of Sartori, "Catalogo," the most active decade at the Incurabili was the 1760s: 11 extant librettos; at the other three, the 1780s was the peak decade: Mendicanti, 29 librettos; Ospedaletto, 17; Pietà, 16; Incurabili, only 4; total extant from the 1780s, 66 librettos.

94. Mendicanti, 104 librettos; Pietà, 50; Incurabili, 45; Ospedaletto, 44. Further research is needed to determine whether these numbers reflect the relative number of oratorio performances in the conservatories.

95. App. A: *Jonathas. Actio sacra* (1771, Mendicanti), *Pharisaei conversio ad sepulchrum* (1782, Ospedaletto), and *Vexillum fidei* (1761, Incurabili).

96. App. A: *S. Petrus et S. Maria Magdalena*.

97. App. A: *Sacrificium Abraham*.

98. App. A: *Aqua e rupe Horeb* and *Tertia dies, sive Pium ascetarum colloquium*.

99. App. A: *Sermo discipulorum Christi*.

librettos attest to oratorios at the Mendicanti on the feast of St. Mary Magdalene (22 July),[100] at the Incurabili on the feast of the Transfiguration (6 August),[101] at the Ospedaletto on the Assumption (15 August),[102] and at the Pietà on the Nativity of the Blessed Virgin Mary (8 September).[103] A few librettos were printed for performances on Christmas, Easter, and Pentecost.

Further evidence of the social context of oratorio in the Venetian conservatories is offered by the comments of foreign visitors. Lalande, for instance, who visited Venice in 1765, says that in the four conservatories on "each feast and Sunday they do Vespers with music, and often an *oratorio*. . . . The Pietà is the one of the four that has the best reputation, with regard to the good music and the power of the instruments; the Mendicanti for the excellence of the voices: the music is executed behind a slightly closed grille [*grillage peu serré*] and one has the pleasure of seeing there the excellent musicians playing their instruments with delicacy, with grace, and with the power and science of the best masters."[104] Visiting Venice in 1769, Grosley also commented on the Vespers with oratorios and motets in the conservatories:

[When] the *oratorio* [is] performed by the *conservatories*, every body makes the afternoon service. . . . These conservatories have alternately vespers in music, very finely performed, and concluding with a grand motet, [the libretto of] which is sold by women who let chairs to sit on; the words are nothing but a most wretched uncouth jumble of Latin phrases in rhyme, and stuffed rather with barbarisms and solecisms, than any thing of sense and propriety; indeed, the author is generally the sexton. On this paltry ground, however, is wrought the most delicate music, of which both the vocal and instrumental parts are performed only by the girls of the house (whom you see through the grate, which is hung with a very slight crepe) fluttering about and throwing themselves into all the attitudes required in the execution of the most spirited music.[105]

Burney, who visited Venice in August of 1770, says that at each of the four conservatories "there is a performance every Saturday and Sunday evening, as well as on great festivals. I went to the *Pietà* the evening after my arrival, Saturday, August 4. . . . The composition I heard tonight did not exceed mediocrity."[106] On 14 August, however, Burney lavished high

100. App. A: *Sancta Maria Magdalena* (1740).

101. App. A: *Coronatio Salomonis* (1780).

102. App. A: *Triumphus Judith* (1757). On p. 17 of the libretto is added the text of a *Carmina sacra in vesperis solemnibus*; on p. 20, that of a *Carmina sacra recinenda in aliis vesperis*.

103. App. A: *Moyses in Nilo* (1771).

104. Lalande, *Voyage*, 8:204.

105. Grosley, *Italy*, p. 264.

106. Burney, *France and Italy*, p. 139.

praise on Sacchini's oratorio *Machabaeorum mater* and on the performance of it that he heard at the Ospedaletto.[107] In 1775 Coyer visited Venice and commented on the "beautiful Vespers and oratorios" that he heard the girls perform at the conservatories.[108]

The conservatories of Naples, unlike those of Venice, trained only boys, some of whom became leading composers of opera and oratorio. In the seventeenth and eighteenth centuries there were four such institutions: the Conservatorio di Santa Maria di Loreto (after 1807, Real Collegio di Musica), Conservatorio della Pietà dei Turchini (merged with Santa Maria di Loreto in 1807), Conservatorio di Sant'Onofrio a Capuana (merged with Santa Maria di Loreto in 1797), and Conservatorio dei Poveri di Gesù Cristo (closed by 1743).[109] During the late seventeenth and early eighteenth centuries these conservatories performed sacred operas, usually composed by students as valedictory exercises. Closely related to oratorio by subject matter and operatic style, the works differ from oratorios of their time in their characteristic three-act structure, inclusion of comic characters, and performance with operatic staging, costumes, and acting.[110] The practice of performing such operas in the conservatories had ceased by 1730.[111]

Visitors to Naples do not mention oratorio performances in the conservatories, but a few librettos show that some were performed there. For instance, in 1765 the student Vincenzo Bellini (probably the grandfather of the nineteenth-century opera composer of the same name) composed an oratorio performed at Sant'Onofrio;[112] and in 1780 an oratoriolike work was given at the Pietà for the feast of Santa Maria del Carmine.[113] More research is needed on eighteenth-century music in the Neapolitan conservatories before further assessment of their oratorio activities is possible.

Other Social Contexts, Public and Private

The sponsors and occasions of oratorio performances treated thus far account for the majority of oratorios performed in the settecento, but a great many other contexts are also found.

Feasts of Patron Saints. In the smaller towns of Italy, more often than the larger ones, the feast day of the town's patron saint seems to have been an occasion for an oratorio performance. Together with special religious

107. Ibid., p. 171.
108. Coyer, *Voyages*, p. 210.
109. Renato di Benedetto, "Naples," *New Grove*, 13:25, 29.
110. App. A: *Il trionfo della castità di Santo Alessio* (1713), *La divina providenza* (1720), and *Il martirio di S. Eugenia* (1722).
111. Renato di Benedetto, "Naples," *New Grove*, 13:28.
112. App. A: *Isacco figura del Redentore*.
113. App. A: *Pel le nozze di Salomone*.

services, processions, and secular events, the oratorio formed part of the town's annual rite of protection as is often clear from the libretto's title page. In the Abruzzi mountain town of L'Aquila, for instance, an oratorio was performed on 6 October 1789 "to solemnize the festival of the glorious protector Sant'Emidio,"[114] and in 1801 an oratorio was sung "in the cathedral church to celebrate the anniversary of the prodigious liberation from the earthquake on the day 6 October 1762, in thanks to the most beloved tutelary Sant'Emidio, bishop and martyr."[115] Whether in smaller or larger communities, oratorios performed on such occasions had patriotic, civic, and political significance as well as religious. If the patron saint protected the city, so did the public officials, and their names, too, were sometimes listed on a libretto's title page. On that of the libretto of 1789 for L'Aquila, for instance, one finds the names of the city's administrators (*procuratori*). At Civitavecchia, near Rome, from the 1720s to the 1770s, oratorios were occasionally performed to celebrate the feast day of the city's protectress, Santa Ferma (or Fermina).[116] Late in the century the title pages of librettos for this occasion list the members of the town's administrative body (*magistrato*), who dedicate the oratorio to the patron saint.[117]

The scope of the social events surrounding performances for patron saints is usually difficult to reconstruct, but for the feast of Santa Rosalia (4 September) in Palermo of the 1720s and 1730s some detailed accounts survive. According to pamphlets printed in 1721 and 1728 that describe the festivities and include librettos of the vocal works performed,[118] the feast was celebrated by a four-day festival of religious services and processions, parades with elaborate floats, fireworks, and special music, including oratoriolike works. In both of these years two such works were performed: a dramatic dialogue of sacred-patriotic content, with four personages, sung from a triumphal float ("carro trionfale") at the end of the first day's activities; and a Latin sacred dialogue, "Music within Vespers" ("Melos inter Vespras"), on the third day. The title page of each pamphlet provides a long list of Palermo's senators, each amply identified by his full title.

114. App. A: *Il sacrifizio di Gefte.*
115. App. A: *Il vota di Jefte.*
116. The printed librettos use one or the other of these spellings; Enrico Josi's article "Civitavecchia," *Enciclopedia cattolica*, 3:col. 1767, uses "Firmina."
117. App. A: *Gioas. Componimento sagro da cantarsi nella sera della festività di Santa Fermina protettrice della città di Civita Vecchia* (1774).
118. App. A: *L'armeria e la galleria dell'augustissima casa d'Austria aperte ed esposte* (1721) and *L'Ester palermitana S. Rosalia applaudita con giubilio universale della Sicilia* (1728). These are the only two such documents I have seen, but those of 1725 (*Corteggio degli angeli*), 1730 (*Simulacro della gloriosa*), and 1731 (*Santita coronata della vergine*), listed in Sartori, "Catalogo," are probably similar. These would provide useful material for a study of these fascinating occasions.

Another description of the broad social context for an oratorio in honor of a patron saint is Burney's account of the events he witnessed in 1770 at Figline, a small town about thirty miles from Florence:

> At four o'clock in the evening, the games began in the great square, which is a large piece of ground of an oblong form. There were 1500 peasants of the neighborhood employed upon this occasion, who had been three months in training: they had the story of David and Goliath to represent, which was done with most minute attention to the sacred story, and the *costume* of the ancients. . . .
>
> At Vespers I heard the same story *sung* in an oratorio, set by the Abate Feroce, in which Signor Fibbietti, the tenor, had a capital part, to which he did great justice: during this performance, the whole town was illuminated in an elegant manner, and there were very ingenious fireworks played off in the great square; and, in justice to the pacific disposition of the Tuscans, I must observe, that though there were at least 20,000 people assembled together on this occasion without guards, yet not the least accident or disturbance happened. . . .[119]

According to the title page of its printed libretto,[120] the oratorio that Burney heard was performed as part of a "solemn three-day celebration [*nel solenne triduo*] . . . in honor of Santa Massimina, virgin and martyr . . . beneficient protectress" of Figline.

Forty Hours Devotion. The *Quarant'ore*, or Forty Hours devotion, was practiced in Italy from the sixteenth century to commemorate the period of Christ's entombment.[121] During the three-day observance a consecrated Communion Host was exhibited continuously for forty hours in an ornate monstrance on an altar in a church or oratory. In the seventeenth century the decorations surrounding the monstrance became extremely elaborate, establishing a tradition that continued until well into the nineteenth century. At times the entire chapel of a high altar would be transformed into a large, illusionistic theatrical scene (called a *teatro*, *apparato*, or *macchina*) with deep perspective.[122] Intended to interpret and glorify the Eucharist, which was prominently displayed, the scene often represented a biblical story treated allegorically. Scenes for the Forty Hours devotion resembled theatrical scenery in construction but apparently not in function—they seem not to have been used as back-

119. Burney, *France and Italy*, pp. 237–38.
120. App. A: *Il trionfo di David nella disfatta di Golia.*
121. For a study of music in the Forty Hours devotion of the seventeenth and eighteenth centuries, see Smither, "Forty Hours," which includes bibliography and a list of forty-one oratorios and cantatas performed in the Devotion. See also Smither, *Oratorio*, pp. 41–44 and 377–78, and Ozolins, "Pasquini," pp. 168–78.
122. For the development of decorations for the Forty Hours devotion, with illustrations, see Weil, "Forty Hours."

ground for acting. An *apparato* would be brilliantly illuminated for a special service, including prayers, a sermon, and music, held on each day. Although the Forty Hours devotion might be held during any time of the year—in some cities it was held by churches in rotation as a perpetual prayer—the last three days of carnival were favored. Thus, as carnival reached its peak, this visually sumptuous ceremony would function as a spiritual counterbalance to the season's worldly spectacles and excesses and a preparation for Lent. The service occasionally went beyond the visual emulation of the theater by introducing non-liturgical, operatic music—a spiritual cantata or an oratorio in Italian.

The tradition of performing such music in the Forty Hours devotion dates from the early period of oratorio history: in Palermo, an oratorio-like work was performed on this occasion in the Jesuit church during carnival as early as 1650.[123] Printed librettos show that oratorios were given, perhaps sporadically, in Palermo's churches for Forty Hours devotions until at least 1754, when a truncated version of Metastasio's *La morte d'Abel*, set by Girolamo Abbos, was sung "in the *quarantore* of carnival at the church of the Gesù."[124] In Milan at the church of Santa Maria presso San Celso, from the late seicento through much of the settecento, cantatas and occasionally oratorios were sung "to the glory of the Most Holy Sacrament exposed . . . on the occasion of the spiritual exercises" held on the final Saturday through Monday of carnival.[125]

Rarely do the printed librettos of such works provide information about the visual decorations of the Forty Hours devotions, but some of the librettos for performances in Foligno are fascinating exceptions. The oratorio *Giuditta*, set by Giuseppe Carcani, according to the libretto's title page, was to be sung in "in the venerable oratory of the Good Jesus of Foligno, for the occasion on which, in the last three days of carnival of the year 1745, is exposed there, solemnly, for the public adoration of the faithful, the Most Holy Sacrament, in a *macchina*, representing the triumph of the same Judith."[126] Printed at the end of the libretto is a full-page, detailed description of the *macchina*. This scenery represents the same story as the oratorio and places the Eucharist in the center in the midst of clouds.[127] In the service for which the oratorio was sung, the visual, literary, and musical elements—and no doubt the sermon—com-

---

123. *L'Abramo* (Palermo: Pietro Coppola, 1650), in I-PLcom. For full title-page citation, see Ozolins, "Pasquini," p. 169, n. 72.

124. App. A: *La morte d'Abel* (1754).

125. App. A: *Cantate a gloria del santissimo Sacramento* (1729). Sartori, "Catalogo," lists comparable titles for similar cantatas performed in 1689, 1710, 1718, 1725, 1736, 1741, 1742, and 1744. For the title page of an oratorio intended for the same place and occasion, see app. A: *L'Abramo. Sacra azione a lode del Santissimo Sacramento* (1755).

126. App. A: *Giuditta figura di Cristo, di Maria, e della Chiesa* (1745).

127. The full text of the scenery description is given in Italian and English translation in Smither, "Forty Hours."

bined to communicate the allegorical theme and glorify the Eucharist. Librettos of 1749 and 1751 for similar services at Foligno indicate that scenes and oratorios were based on the themes of Daniel in the lions' den and the sacrifice of Abraham.[128]

Court and Private Occasions. In Rome at the Vatican Apostolic Palace, from the 1670s until at least 1740, cantatas and oratorios were heard by visiting cardinals on Christmas Eve after the pontifical vespers.[129] Whether such works were given at the Vatican on other occasions is not known. Elsewhere in Rome, oratorios and dramatic cantatas were performed in large halls, theaters, and chapels of a number of private palaces on a variety of religious and political occasions—among others, in the theater of the Cancelleria Apostolica for Christmas Eve meetings of the Accademia dell'Arcadia (1727, 1730);[130] in the garden (made into an amphitheater) of the palace of San Marco, by command of Pietro Capello, Venetian ambassador to the Holy See (1727);[131] in the palace of Cardinal De Acquaviva, minister from Aragon to the Vatican, on the occasion of the promotion to cardinalate of the royal infante of Spain, Don Luis (1735);[132] in the private chapel of the duchess of Giovenazzo during the Christmas season (1757);[133] and in the Campidoglio apartment of Prince Rezzonico, a Roman senator, during Holy Week (1790).[134] In virtually any Italian city an oratorio might occasionally be sung in a context similar to those mentioned for Rome. In Palermo there seems to have been a tradition throughout much of the settecento of performing oratorios on the Saturdays of Lent in the Royal Chapel Palatine, often called on libretto title pages "the venerable royal chapel, Nostra Signora della Soledad, of the noble Spanish and military officials." (The title pages are sometimes in Spanish, but the oratorio texts are in Italian.)[135]

The entrance into a convent of a woman from a noble or at least a wealthy family was another private occasion for the performance of an

128. App. A: *Per la solenne esposizione del SS. Sagramento in una machina rappresentante Daniele nel Lago de' Leoni* and *Per la solenne esposizione del SS. Sagramento in una machina rappresentante il sagrificio d'Abramo.*

129. Cf. Smither, *Oratorio*, 1:275–76. This tradition has not been fully investigated. For a late example of a libretto title page for an oratorio performed on this occasion, see app. A: *Componimento sagro per musica da cantarsi nel Palazzo Apostolico* (1740).

130. For a discussion of the 1727 performance, see Smither, *Oratorio*, 1:269–74. The libretto for the 1730 performance is virtually identical to that for 1727.

131. App. A: *L'umiltà coronata.*

132. App. A: *Per la promozione al cardinalato.*

133. App. A: *Gioas re di Giuda* (1757).

134. App. A: *La passione di Gesù Cristo nostro signore* (1790).

135. App. A: *El materno amor di Maria SS. del la Soledad* (1739), *Maria vergine confortata* (1753), and *Giocabbe* (1799).

oratorio or a dramatic cantata. In Florence, for instance, in 1752 an oratoriolike work was sung "in the church of the noble religious [nuns] of San Pier Maggiore, on the occasion of the entrance into the convent of the illustrious Signora Contessa Maria Cammilla Pierucci"; in 1742 a similar piece marked "the solemn entrance into the venerable convent of the Most Holy Conception, called the New Convent in Via della Scala, of the most illustrious Signora Margherita Ginori, with the name of Donna Caterina Teresa Maria Margherita"; and another, in 1747, solemnized the entrance into the convent of San Martino in Via della Scala of "the most illustrious Signora Contessa Maria Elisabetta Barbolini."[136] Title pages of librettos attest to performances of oratoriolike works for this type of occasion in Bologna, Naples, and Palermo,[137] among other cities and even smaller communities. A similar type of occasion, but by no means as frequently solemnized by an oratorio, was the ordination of a priest or the celebration of his first Mass. Two Neapolitan examples are an oratorio of 1771 "for the first Mass celebrated by the Reverend Signor D. Giuseppe Cerlone" and an oratorio of 1775 sung "in the house of Signor D. Angelo Perrotti on the occasion of the first Holy Mass that the new priest D. Pietro Perrotti, his most worthy son, celebrates."[138]

Theaters. Beginning in at least the early eighteenth century oratorios were occasionally given concert performances on elaborately decorated stages in halls and theaters within private palaces. In Francesco Maria Ruspoli's palace in Rome, for instance, Handel's *La Resurrezione* (1708) was performed with the orchestra and singers seated on an ornate stage with a proscenium, erected in a large hall. According to extant sketches (possibly from 1708) of decorations intended for Holy Week performances in a hall and a theater in Cardinal Pietro Ottoboni's Roman palace, the Cancelleria, the orchestra and singers were apparently to be grouped together on a stage; and an engraving that records the actual decorations for a performance in Ottoboni's theater on Christmas Eve 1727 shows a stage-set representing a long hall inside a palace, with the instrumentalists arranged on semicircular risers and the singers seated, while singing, with books in their hands, in the center of the stage.[139]

136. App. A: *Il trionfo della vocazione religiosa* (1752), *La sposa de' sacri cantici* (1742), *Il trionfo della religione* (1747).

137. App. A: *Il sacrifizio d'Abramo* (Bologna, 1732), *Invito alle spirituali nozze con Gesù* (Bologna, 1779), *Rut nel campo di Booz* (Naples, 1759), *Lo sposalizio di Abigaille con Davide* (Naples, 1767), *Li sacri sponsali dell'anima religiosa col verbo incarnato* (Palermo, 1739), *Il trionfo della casta Susanna*, (Palermo, 1742).

138. App. A: *Componimento per musica* (1771) and *I portenti del Divino Amore* (1775).

139. For discussions of and bibliography on the Ruspoli and Ottoboni decorations, with illustrations of the latter, see: Smither, *Oratorio*, 1:264–74; Smither,

The occasional use of private or public theaters as concert halls for oratorio performances continued throughout the century. A case in point dating from 1776 is François-Hippolyte Barthélémon's *Jefte in Masfa*, commissioned by the grand duke of Tuscany, Leopold I, and performed at the Florentine Teatro di Via del Cocomero. According to the composer's daughter,

> The Duke's wish was to have [the oratorio] performed in *action* at the theatre, the story being calculated for the display of fine dresses and striking scenery; but the bishop would not allow it. It was therefore performed as an Oratorio, the orchestra being arranged as in London, on the stage, with the addition of plate glass to hide the scenes; the partition that is placed before the principal singers, being tastefully covered with yellow satin and trimmed with silver fringe; so that, with a profusion of wax-lights and elegantly-cut chandeliers, the effect was both novel and striking, and created repeated bursts of applause.[140]

The bishop's decision to prohibit an operatically staged performance must have come late. The scenery had already been constructed by the time of the performance, for there was "plate glass to hide the scenes"; and the librettos had probably been printed, for the title page includes the words *da rappresentarsi*, more common in this period for operatic than concert performances. That the duke would have preferred to see the work "performed in *action*" rather than "performed as an Oratorio" is a symptom of changing tastes. The operatic presentation of oratorios was becoming increasingly common.

The staging of oratorios with operatic scenery, costumes, acting, and memorized roles appears to have been highly exceptional before the mid-eighteenth century.[141] An unusual and instructive example of such a performance of a sacred work sponsored in 1736 by the Oratorians in Naples is *Giuseppe riconosciuto*, composed by Giuseppe Terradellas, identified in the printed libretto as a student at the Conservatorio dei Poveri di Gesù Cristo.[142] The libretto differs considerably from the sa-

---

"Sacred Opera," pp. 91–94 and 101 (items 1–4); and Smither, "Oratorio," *New Grove*, 13:670, ill. 5.

140. [Henslowe], "Barthélémon," p. 7. For the title page of the libretto printed for this performance, see app. A: *Jefte in Masfa*.

141. For two exceptions previously noted, see Smither, *Oratorio*, 1:276; and Schering, *Oratorium*, p. 116, n. 1. A possible third exception is cited by Victor Crowther in a letter to *The Musical Times*, 119 (1978): 838, but I have yet to find clear evidence that this example was operatically staged. For a discussion of the relationship to oratorio history of some early seventeenth-century sacred dialogues and "incunabula of the oratorio" that were staged in a Florentine confraternity, see Hill, "Florence I," pp. 127–33.

142. App. A: *Giuseppe riconosciuto* (1736).

cred operas performed at the Neapolitan conservatories in the early decades of the century: it is based on an Old Testament text rather than the life of a saint, it uses an oratorio text by Metastasio as a point of departure (but that text is heavily revised), and it does not include comic personages. The new version is longer and divided into three acts rather than the two parts of Metastasio's original. In a preface to the libretto, the anonymous poet who revised it wrote:

> To show for the first time in a theatre Joseph Recognized by His Brothers in Egypt is indeed not to wish to degrade the most honorable idea of the Abate Pietro Metastasio, which formerly was presented in another manner, but rather to make the sublime sentiments that fill the *melodramma* of that author more suitable for instructing the people by adding the liveliness of scenic representation. . . . With great hesitation was the task [undertaken] of arriving at such variation, addition, and reshaping of it that it could be done with the art of acting. It remains that the reader, in separating the good things from the bad, neither deprive the first [author] of his due honor, nor the second author of his merited sympathy.[143]

Although this preface refers to the presentation as being "in a theater," according to the libretto's title page the work was given within the vesper exercises (*nell'Essercizi Vespertini*) of the Oratorians. Thus for this performance (and perhaps for others) the Oratorians of Naples would appear to have erected a theatrical stage in their oratory. The tone of the preface is defensive on behalf of what the author apparently considers an innovation: he seeks to justify his revision of Metastasio and the departure from the usual way of performing that poet's oratorio.

This revised work presents an ambiguous combination of two genres, opera and oratorio. To date, the work appears to be an isolated example of such ambiguity in eighteenth-century Italy up to its time, but later in the century such ambiguity may well have led to the change in the application of the word *oratorio* and the practice of performing oratorios. From the mid-century on, librettos printed for performances with stage action indicate a growing interest in the operatic performance of works that are essentially traditional oratorios.[144] In an essay on theater reform, published in 1779, the Neapolitan Saverio Mattei advocates the establishment of a sacred tragic theater in Naples that, he says, could open "with the inimitable sacred tragedies of Metastasio, that is, with his almost divine oratorios, which are truly accomplished *tragedies*."[145]

143. Preface to app. A: *Giuseppe riconosciuto* (1736).
144. For title pages of fourteen librettos printed for staged performances of oratorios between 1744 and 1818 in Corato, Ferrara, Florence, Lucca, Mantua, Modugno, Naples, Palermo, and Pistoia, see Smither, "Sacred Opera," pp. 102–3, items 15–28.
145. Mattei, "Filosofia-Salmi," 6:215. For more on Mattei's proposed re-

Perhaps Mattei's essay contributed to an increased interest in staged oratorios. At the very least, it reflects the thought of his time.

By the 1780s the word *oratorio* or one of its traditional synonyms (most frequently *azione sacra*) was often applied to sacred works with stage action.[146] In Naples—at the Teatro del Fondo, the Teatro Nuovo sopra Toledo, and the Teatro San Carlo—staged oratorios were presented in about half of the Lenten seasons between 1786 and 1810, after which fewer such works were performed.[147] In 1786, for instance, the Lenten work at the Teatro Nuovo sopra Toledo was a pasticcio, *Il convito di Baldassarre: oratorio*, performed with operatic staging—the names of the costume and stage designers are listed in the printed libretto.[148] When Goethe visited Naples he attended a performance of Giuseppe Giordano's *La distruzione di Gerusalemme: azione sacra* at the Teatro San Carlo on 9 March 1787, and he saw little difference between this Lenten offering and secular opera: "Here, during Lent, they perform sacred operas [*geistliche Opern*]. The only difference between them and profane operas is that they have no ballets between the acts; otherwise, they are as gay [*bunt*] as possible."[149] The practice of presenting oratorios in the manner of operas became widespread in the late eighteenth and early nineteenth centuries. In Florence, for instance, at the Teatro di Via della Pergola, the staging of oratorios as operas during Lent appears to have begun in 1791 when the grand duke Ferdinand III allowed the theater to remain open during that season provided that a "dramma sacro" would be performed and that the proceeds would benefit the poor of the Congregazione di San Giovanni Battista.[150] The work staged was Pietro Alessandro Guglielmi's *Debora e Sisara: azione sacra*, first performed two years earlier in Naples during Lent.[151] Similar works were staged in Florence during most Lenten seasons for the next two decades.[152]

The frequency in the use of the word *oratorio* and its synonyms in a

---

forms, see Smither, "Sacred Opera," pp. 89–90. Mattei's essay on theater reform is printed both in Mattei, "Filosofia-Salmi" and Mattei "Filosofia-Riforma."

146. On the Italian oratorio with stage action in the late eighteenth and early nineteenth centuries, see Pasquetti, *Oratorio*, pp. 465–98, passim; Schering, *Oratorium*, pp. 241–45, and Smither, "Sacred Opera," pp. 89–90, 95–96.

147. This conclusion is based on a survey of printed librettos and on the list (incomplete) of works performed at Neapolitan theaters in Florimo, *Napoli*, 4:250–406.

148. App. A: *Il convito di Baldassarre* (1786).

149. Goethe, *Italian Journey*, p. 187; Goethe, *Die italienische Reise*, p. 215.

150. Morini, *La Pergola*, p. 83.

151. App. A: *Debora e Sisara* (Florence, 1791). See the discussion of this work in chap. 3.

152. Morini, *La Pergola*, pp. 83–174.

new context reflects a semantic change. *Oratorio* came to be used in two senses: for a sacred dramatic work that was not acted, as well as for one that was acted. In the new sense, the word *oratorio* is synonymous with *sacred opera* (*opera sacra*). As defined in Pietro Lichtenthal's *Dizionario e bibliografia della musica* (Milan, 1826), an oratorio is: "A species of drama, the subject of which is a theme selected from sacred history, performed by singers with the accompaniment of an orchestra, either in a church, or in a hall, or indeed on a theatrical stage—in this last case one means *Opera sacra*, and it bears the mark of the usual *Opere in musica*, having the same form and conduct."[153] In the same dictionary, under the heading "Opera," Lichtenthal says, "The Italians distinguish four kinds of operas: *Opera sacra*, *Opera seria*, *Opera semiseria*, and *Opera buffa*."[154] He describes all these except *opera sacra*, for which he refers the reader to the article "Oratorio." Thus by Lichtenthal's time the terms *oratorio* and *opera sacra* had become synonyms, but the old synonyms for *oratorio*, those dating back to the beginning of the eighteenth century or earlier, are still in use. Gioacchino Rossini's *Il Mosè in Egitto*, first staged at the Neapolitan Teatro San Carlo in 1818, illustrates the synonymous use of the terms *oratorio*, *azione*, and *opera* in Italy: in its printed libretto the work was called an *azione tragico-sacra*;[155] in the autograph manuscript, the original title page in a copyist's hand calls the work, "Oratorio/Mosè in Egitto";[156] the Neapolitan newspaper *Giornale delle Due Sicilie* reported on 27 February 1818, "Rossini is finishing the writing of the music of an *oratorio* for the Royal Theater of San Carlo";[157] but late in his life Rossini added a new cover to the autograph manuscript and wrote, "Il Primo/Mosè Opera/Mio Autografo/G. Rossini."[158]

Italian Oratorio Abroad

Outside of Italy, Italian oratorio was cultivated most consistently at Roman Catholic courts and in cities where Italian opera was important. Oratorios were usually heard during Lent—when theaters were closed to secular works and opera singers were available—but rarely in other seasons. The limited number of occasions for the performance of Italian

153. Lichtenthal, *Dizionario*, 2:78.
154. Ibid., 2:77.
155. See Radiciotti, *Rossini*, 1:317, n. 1, for quotation of libretto title page.
156. Rossini, *Mosè**, vol. 1, f. 1.
157. Quoted in Radiciotti, *Rossini*, 1:319, n. 3.
158. Rossini, *Mosè**, vol. 1, recto of unnumbered folio preceding first numbered folio. In Isotta, "Mosè," p. 569, the work's revision for the Paris stage in 1827 is considered to be its transformation from an oratorio to an opera.

oratorios explains the relatively small production in this genre beyond the Italian peninsula.

Court and Private Patronage

In German Lands. From at least the 1640s to 1740, the Viennese Habsburg court—a stronghold of Italian opera—consistently sponsored Lenten performances, in the court chapels, of sacred dramatic music in Italian.[159] Emperors Ferdinand III (1637–57) and Leopold I (1658–1705) sponsored both oratorios and *sepolcri*. The Viennese oratorios were comparable to those of Italy, but the *sepolcri* were shorter than oratorios, in one structural part, limited to the theme of the Passion and Crucifixion, and intended to be performed with costumes, acting, and scenery—which always included a model of the sepulchre of Christ. During the reigns of Joseph I (1705–11) and Charles VI (1711–40) the *sepolcro* was abandoned.[160] The Holy Week tradition of erecting, in the Hofburgkapelle (see endpapers, no. 5), a scene representing the holy sepulchre continued, but the musical works—typical two-part oratorios—sung in the presence of this scene are not known to have been acted. The title pages of the librettos printed for the performances of such works characteristically include the formula "applied to His [Christ's] most holy sepulchre and sung [*cantato*—not *rappresentato*, as with the *sepolcro* title pages] in the most august chapel" of the emperor.[161]

The reign of Charles VI's daughter, the musically talented and educated Maria Teresa (1740–80), brought a change in Viennese patronage.[162] An opera enthusiast, she reorganized and supported the Viennese theaters, yet her rationalistic outlook and political and economic difficulties—particularly early in her reign—were apparently not conducive to maintaining the same type and degree of musical activity at court as her forebears had done. Oratorios were no longer heard in the court chapel. The Viennese aristocracy now assumed a more active role in musical patronage, and especially important was Field Marshal Joseph Friedrich, Prince of Saxen-Hildburghausen, in whose palace (the Palais Rofrano, now the Palais Auersperg; see Figure I-1) concerts were pre-

159. For a discussion of this sponsorship, see Smither, *Oratorio*, 1:366–80.

160. The list of performances at court provided in Weilen, *Theatergeschichte*, shows that the *sepolcro* virtually disappears after 1705.

161. For characteristic title pages of such librettos, see app. A: *La cena del Signore* (1720), *La passione di Gesù Cristo signor nostro* (1730), and *Isacco figura del Redentore* (1740).

162. For musical patronage in Vienna during the time of Maria Teresa's reign, see: Richard Schaal, "Habsburg," *MGG* 5:cols. 1207–8; Theophil Antonicek, "Vienna," *New Grove* 19:719–23; Hadamowsky, "Barocktheater," pp. 65–67.

sented on Friday evenings during the winter months. Giuseppe Bonno (1711–88) directed these concerts from about 1749 to 1761, and his oratorio *Isacco figura del Redentore* (see Figure I-2) was staged as an opera there in 1759.[163] The extent of Italian oratorio performances at this and other private palaces in Vienna from the 1740s on has not been investigated. The relatively few extant printed librettos from the 1740s through the 1760s—by Bonno, Georg Cristoph Wagenseil (1715–77), Johann Adolf Hasse (1699–1783), and Ignaz Holzbauer (1711–83), among others—shed little light on the social contexts of performances, but some of these works were possibly performed at Lenten concerts in the Burgtheater. With the establishment in 1771 of the Tonkünstler-Societät, oratorios were regularly given in public concerts; during Advent and Lent—in the Kärntnerthor-Theater until 1783 and thereafter in the Burgtheater (the court theater, also called the Nationaltheater).[164]

If the Viennese imperial court ceased to sponsor oratorios from the 1740s on, other Roman Catholic courts in German-speaking lands continued to do so—particularly the electoral courts, of which the one at Dresden may be singled out for the length and consistency of its oratorio tradition. Lutherans since the Reformation, the electors of Saxony became Roman Catholics beginning in 1697, when Friedrich August I (r. 1694–1733) converted to Catholicism to strengthen his claim to the Polish crown. He ruled as King August II, "the Strong," of Poland from 1697 until his death in 1733. Upon his religious conversion he established the Roman Catholic "Royal Polish and Electoral Saxon Chapel" but also retained the Lutheran chapel.[165] As at the Viennese Habsburg court of the same period, so also in Dresden Italian opera became an important ingredient of social life except during Lent, when Italian oratorio served to highlight the season. Beginning at least in 1730, oratorios were heard annually in Dresden on Good Friday, Holy Saturday, or both.[166] During the reign of Elector Friedrich August II (King August III of Poland, 1733–63), the splendor of court life increased, as did that of Italian opera and oratorio performance. The defeat of Saxony in the Seven Years War (1756–63) and subsequent economic difficulties restricted the court's musical life, particularly opera production. But Italian oratorios, economically more modest than operas, were still heard annu-

163. Angermüller, "Bonno," *New Grove* 3:27–28.
164. On oratorio performances in these theaters, see Hanslick, *Concertwesen*, pp. 5, 18, 30–35.
165. Fürstenau, *Dresden*, 2:13.
166. Ibid., 2:44, gives 1730 as the earliest documented Holy-Week performance of an Italian oratorio in Dresden but speculates that the tradition began earlier. According to Seibel, *Heinichen*, p. 44, Heinichen composed an Italian oratorio, *La pace di Kamberga*, dedicated to Elector Friedrich August I, but this would probably not have been a Holy-Week oratorio. Regarding Heinichen's Holy-Week cantata (or oratorio), dated 1728, see below, n. 173.

FIGURE I-I. The Palais Rofrano (now the Palais Auersperg), in Vienna. This palace was the residence of Field Marshal Joseph Friedrich, Prince of Saxen-Hildburghausen, who sponsored oratorio performances directed by Giuseppe Bonno between 1749 and 1761. (Eighteenth-century drawing by Salomon Kleiner; from Eisler, *Das barocke Wien*, pl. 189.)

ally at the climax of Holy Week. The Italian-oratorio tradition continued in Dresden through the first quarter of the nineteenth century.[167]

The composers active for at least a part of their careers in the sumptuous environment of the Dresden court during the eighteenth and early nineteenth centuries and who wrote Italian oratorios for performance there include: Johann David Heinichen (1683–1729), Jan Dismas Zelenka (1679–1745), Giovanni Alberto Ristori (1692–1753), Johann Adolf Hasse (1699–1783), Johann Georg Schürer (1720–86), Domenico Fischietti (ca. 1725–after 1810), Johann Gottlieb Naumann (1741–1801), Joseph Schuster (1748–1812), Franz Seydelmann (1748–1806), Ferdinando Paer (1771–1839), and Francesco Morlacchi (1784–1841). The oratorios of Hasse—by far the most famous of these figures—were the ones most often repeated in Dresden and most widely performed throughout Europe.

In Dresden oratorios were normally given in the Catholic court chapel, as the librettos printed for these occasions virtually always indicate.[168] In 1708 Elector August I remodeled a 1664 opera house as the Catholic

167. Engländer, *Naumann*, p. 51, n. 7.

168. For a characteristic title page of an oratorio performed in Dresden, see app. A: *La deposizione dalla croce di Gesù Cristo* (1748).

ISACCO.
FIGURA
DEL
REDENTORE.
AZIONE SACRA
DA RAPRESENTARSI
IN
MUSICA.

VIENNA,
Nella Stamparia Arci-Teſcovile appreſſo G, L, N, de Ghelen,
L'Anno M. DCC LIX.

FIGURE I-2. Title pages of the libretto to Metastasio's *Isacco*. Although the composer's name is lacking, this is probably the libretto printed for Giuseppe Bonno's setting of 1759, staged in the Viennese palace of Field Marshal Joseph Friedrich, Prince of Saxen-Hildburghausen. As with most Italian oratorio librettos printed for Viennese performances, this one includes Italian and German on facing pages. (Courtesy of A-Wn.)

Isaac.

Ein
Vorbild
Des
Erlösers.
Vorgestellet
In einer
Geistlich-Musicalischen
Aufführung.

V. Engelshofen.

3147:

WIEN,
Gedruckt mit von Ghelischen Schriften, 1759.

FIGURE I-3. The Viennese Burgtheater (center; see endpapers, no. 4), where oratorios were performed in Lenten concerts beginning in the mid-eighteenth century. (Engraving by C. Postl; from Eisler, *Das bürgerliche Wien*, pl. 88.)

chapel,[169] and in 1739 August II began construction of a splendid new Catholic court church. Dedicated in 1751, the new church served as the main location for oratorio performances,[170] but at times the oratorios on Good Friday or Holy Saturday were also heard earlier in Holy Week at open rehearsals, which took the form of court concerts.[171] Few specifics are known about the religious services that would probably have formed a context for these performances, but oratorios were sometimes sung before a model of the holy sepulchre, after the manner of the Viennese court prior to 1740 and of other centers, particularly in Austria and Bohemia. The title pages of at least two librettos for oratorios by Johann Georg Schürer include the same formulation, "applied to the Most Holy Sepulchre," as do Viennese title pages of the early eighteenth century.[172] Heinichen's *Oratorio Tedesco al Sepolcro Santo* (1724)—a German-language work, as explained in its Italian title—was surely intended to be sung before a model of the holy sepulchre, as probably were

169. Fürstenau, *Dresden*, 2:34.
170. Ibid., 2:270.
171. Engländer, *Naumann*, p. 103 and n. 7.
172. See app. A: *Il figliuol prodigo* (1747) and *Isacco figura del Redentore* (1753).

FIGURE I-4. The Kärntnerthor-Theater (see endpapers, no. 2), the location of oratorio performances sponsored by the Viennese Tonkünstler-Societät between 1772 and 1783. (Anonymous colored engraving; from Eisler, *Das bürgerliche Wien*, p. 99.)

his two Italian cantatas that are designated *Cantato al sepolcro di nostro Signore.*[173]

Although at the Dresden court the Italian oratorio tradition was particularly long and consistent, Italian oratorios were performed at least sporadically at the court chapels of electors and prince-bishops located in a number of other German-speaking cities, including Bonn, Mainz, Mannheim, Munich, Salzburg, and Würzburg.[174] The details of oratorio

173. Seibel, *Heinichen*, pp. 44 (oratorio) and 46 (cantatas). The first of these cantatas, "Come? S'imbruna il Ciel!"—an autograph manuscript in D-Dl—bears the information "1728. 42 Minuten." With this length and its four personages (Maria Vergine, Maria Magdalena, S. Giovanni, and Centurione), the work might well be classified as an oratorio.

174. For characteristic title pages of oratorio librettos printed for performances in these cities, see app. A: *Sant'Elena al Calvario* (Bonn, 1740); *Gioas re di Giuda* (Mainz, ?1772–74); *La conversione di S. Ignazio* (Mannheim, 1740), *La Passione di Gesù Cristo* (Mannheim, 1754), *I pellegrini al Sepolcro* (Mannheim, 1768); *Abramo* (Munich, 1731); *Per la morte del Redentore* (Würzburg, ?1730).

The following are among the few writings that shed light on the cultivation of oratorio in these cities. Bonn and Munich: Brandenburg, "Bonn"; Mainz: Gottron, *Mainz*, pp. 122–23 and 137–40; Mannheim: Walter, *Geschichte*, pp. 181–88, 362–68; Munich: Münster, "München" and Münster, "Torri." On the per-production at such centers remain largely uninvestigated. The evidence of printed librettos, however, suggests that in consistency and length of tradition, Mannheim was second only to Dresden. As in Dresden, so also in the other German cities listed above, the libretto title pages most frequently name Good Friday and Holy Saturday as performance occasions—some librettos are less specific, giving the occasion as Lent or Holy Week, but a few name a feast day outside of Lent.

In Other Areas. Aside from courts in German lands, the one outside Italy that most actively cultivated Italian oratorio was in Portugal. The enthusiasm of the royal court in Lisbon for Italian opera—and particularly Neapolitan opera—began during the prosperous reign of John V (r. 1706–50),[175] but court performances of Italian oratorios appear to have begun only with the reign of José I (r. 1750–77) and to have extended through that of Maria I (r. 1777–1816). Printed librettos suggest that at least one Italian oratorio may have been performed every year in Lisbon—either at court or elsewhere—from the late 1760s (perhaps earlier) to at least the first decade of the nineteenth century.[176] During Lent oratorios were heard at court, in the Ajuda palace;[177] but some works fulfilled the double function of solemnizing Lent and celebrating a royal birthday or nameday. Examples of such double-function performances are those of *Il Gioas re di Giuda* by António da Silva, sung "in chamber, in the presence of the royal most faithful majesty, the most august Lady Maria I, Queen of Portugal, of the Algarvi etc., on 31 March 1778, the most felicitous birthday of her royal faithful majesty, the most august Lady Maria Vittoria, Queen Mother"; *La passione di Gesù Cristo signor nostro* by Luciano Xavier dos Santos, sung "in the Royal Palace of the Ajuda, to celebrate the august name of the most serene Lord Don Giuseppe, Prince of Brazil, 19 March 1783"; and Joseph Haydn's *Il ritorno di Tobia,* sung at the Ajuda for the same prince's name day on the same date in 1784.[178]

Among the oratorio composers active in Lisbon were Pedro Antonio Avondano (1714–82), Giuseppe Scolari (?1720–after 1774), Luciano

---

formance of Caldara's oratorios in Salzburg, see Schneider, *Salzburg,* pp. 96–99, and the additions and corrections to Schneider in Kirkendale, U., *Caldara,* pp. 89–91.

175. Robert Stevenson, "Lisbon: 1," *New Grove,* 11:25.

176. Isolated performances of oratorios modeled on the Italian genre but in the Portuguese language may be documented as early as 1719, but not at court. These are considered in chap. 10.

177. The palace library (P-La) still houses printed librettos and manuscript scores of Italian oratorios.

178. For these title pages quoted in full, see app. A: *Il Gioas re di Giuda* (Lisbon, 1778), *La passione di Gesù Cristo signor nostro* (Lisbon, 1783), and *Il ritorno di Tobia* (Lisbon, 1784).

Xavier dos Santos (1734–1803), João Cordiero da Silva (ca. 1735–1808 or later), António da Silva, João Pedro de Almeida Motta, Braz Francisco de Lima (1752–1813), and António Moreira (1758–1819). Some of the more important composers not active in Lisbon but whose oratorios were performed there are Nicolò Jommelli (1714–74), Antonio Sacchini (1730–86), Joseph Haydn (1732–1809), and Giovanni Paisiello (1740–1816).

In Slavic lands, court patronage of Italian oratorio was less important than sponsorship by religious orders or—late in the century—performances in public concerts.[179] Exceptional as a patron, Cardinal Wolfgang von Schrattenbach, Bishop of Olomouc (1711–38), sponsored one or two Italian oratorio performances each year during Lent in Brno from the late 1720s through the 1730s. According to printed librettos, the works were composed largely by Italians and some had been written originally for the Habsburg court in Vienna. Among the Italian composers of oratorios performed in Brno are Antonio Caldara (1670–1736), Leonardo Leo (1694–1744), Nicola Bonifacio Logroscino (1698–1765 or 67), Girolamo Pera, Francesco Polli, Nicola Porpora (1686–1768), and Pietro Giuseppe Sandoni (1685–1748). Thus far the only known native composer of Italian oratorios for Schrattenbach was Václav Matyáš Gurecký (1705–1743), who was employed by the bishop and had studied with Caldara in Vienna.[180]

In Poland most Italian oratorios were performed in Warsaw, according to information given in printed librettos. Although the locations of such performances are largely unknown, the repertoire during the "Saxon" period of King Augustus III tends to be that of the Dresden court, and one might reasonably assume that the performances were court sponsored. Italian oratorios were at least occasionally performed during the reign of King Stanislaw II (r. 1764–95). On 2 April 1784 La passione, by Giovanni Paisiello (1740–1816), was heard in Warsaw, "in the presence of his majesty the king of Poland in the oratory of the court," and in 1791 Debora e Sisara, by Pietro Alessandro Guglielmi, was given during Lent in the oratory of the same court.[181]

The Russian court was a stronghold of Italian opera during the reign of Empress Catherine the Great (r. 1729–96); late in her reign Italian oratorio appears to have occasionally substituted for opera during Lent. Although most such performances were given in subscription concerts

179. Current knowledge about oratorio in Slavic lands is regrettably limited, and the information given here on this subject is provisional. Further research is much needed.

180. Jirí Sehnal, "Václav Matyáš Gurecký," New Grove, 7:850–51. For the title-page wording of an oratorio by Gurecký, see app. A: Giacobbe (Brno, 1731).

181. See app. A: La passione di nostro signore Gesù Cristo (Warsaw, 1784) and Debora e Sisara (Warsaw, 1791).

either in St. Petersburg or Moscow, a libretto for Paisiello's *La passione* dated 1782 suggests that the work was first performed late in that year at Catherine's court, in St. Petersburg; in March, 1783, a subsequent performance took place in St. Petersburg's Catholic church.[182]

On the few performances of Italian oratorios in Denmark and Sweden, see chapter 10.

Religious Orders

In predominantly Roman Catholic areas of German and Slavic lands, religious orders sponsored oratorio performances, usually during Lent but occasionally for special feasts or celebrations. In German-speaking areas, the majority of these works were in the native language, but a few were in Italian or Latin. The Jesuits—who continued to cultivate the Latin school drama in their educational institutions—were among the more active sponsors of Italian and Latin oratorios, until the suppression of the order in 1773. Characteristic are their performances of: Metastasio's *La passione di Giesù Cristo nostro signore*, in a setting by Pietro Carlo Grua (ca. 1700–1773), at their church in Bamberg on Maundy Thursday and Good Friday, 1754; Pallavicino's *I pellegrini al sepolcro di nostro salvatore*, set by Hasse, at Innsbruck on Good Friday and Holy Saturday, 1769; and the same work in a Latin translation, as *Peregrini ad sepulcrum servatoris nostri*, in Fulda on Good Friday, 1768.[183] But the Jesuits were by no means alone in this activity. For example, in 1725 the Benedictines at the monastery of Our Lady of Monferrato, in Vienna, celebrated their patron saint's feast day with a performance, in the presence of Emperor Charles VI, of Caldara's *Il trionfo della religione e dell'amore*;[184] in 1726 the Servites, in their Viennese church, celebrated the feast of St. Thomas Aquinas by performing an oratorio (anonymous in its printed libretto), *La religione trionfante in S. Tomaso d'Acquino*.[185] At the musically active Benedictine abby of Kremsmünster, in Austria, oratorio formed an integral part of musical life.[186] Franz Sparry (1715–67, director of music from 1747) composed Latin and German oratorios for Kremsmünster;[187] and Georg Pasterwiz (1730–1803, direc-

182. Mooser, *Annales*, 2:347; Mooser, *Opéras*, p. 105.

183. See app. A: *La passione di Gesù Cristo nostro signore* (Bamberg, 1754), *I pellegrini al sepolcro* (Innsbruch, 1769), and *Peregrini ad sepulcrum servatoris nostri* (Fulda, 1768).

184. See app. A: *Il trionfo della religione e dell'amore* (Vienna, 1725).

185. See app. A: *La religione trionfante in S. Tomaso d'Acquino* (Vienna, 1726).

186. Kellner, *Kremsmünster*, is a useful reference work for oratorio at this abbey, despite the absence of the words *oratorio* and *Oratorium* from the book's index.

187. Ibid., pp. 375–77, 408–9.

tor of music from 1767–83) performed his own oratorios and those of many others, including a remarkably early one, Leonardo Leo's *Sant' Elena al Calvario* (1732 or 1734), given in 1773 for the abbot's name-day.[188]

The librettos known to date suggest that religious orders in Bohemia and Moravia were more active sponsors of Latin and Italian oratorios than those in Germany or Austria.[189] In Prague and its environs from the 1720s to the 1770s, the Premonstratensiens, Jesuits, and Benedictines (in that order of frequency) appear to have sponsored performances of oratorios in Latin, to the virtual exclusion other languages, whereas the Crucifers of the Red Star (an order active mainly in Bohemia) sponsored mostly Italian oratorios, with an occasional Latin or German one.[190] The same orders and others (including the Franciscan Capuchins) are known to have sponsored a few Latin and Italian oratorios elsewhere in Bohemia, Moravia, Silesia, Poland, and Slovenia.[191] By far the most characteristic occasion for all such performances in these areas was Good Friday, and some of the librettos reveal that the works were sung before a model of the holy sepulchre—particularly the Jesuit performances in the 1720s and those of the Crucifers of the Red Star in the 1750s.

Public Concerts, Performances in Theaters

Although Italian oratorios were performed mainly in a religious context—in court chapels and in monastery and parish churches—they were occasionally heard in public concerts, which became increasingly prominent throughout the century. Supported and attended primarily by the middle classes, such concerts developed first in England and then on the

188. On Pasterwiz's performances of oratorios, see ibid., pp. 450–53, 458, 469–71; and on his performance of Leo's oratorio, see ibid., pp. 364 and 455.

189. The following conclusions are based largely on my analysis of the Bohemian and Moravian oratorio libretto collections as listed and described in Poštolka, "Strahow" and Bužga, "Osteroratorien" and on Kamper, *Hudební Praha*, chapter 3 (on oratorio), pp. 153–78, and the lists in the Kamper's appendix, pp. 243–53. See also Lauschmann, "Pražské oratorium." More specialized studies on the oratorio in Slavic lands are required to determine whether these studies fully represent oratorio there. As more evidence comes to light, I suspect that other Eastern European and predominantly Roman Catholic areas—those of present-day Yugoslavia and Hungary, for instance—will emerge as important for the cultivation of Italian and Latin oratorios by religious orders.

190. Cf. Poštolka, "Strahow," p. 92, where the librettos listed on pp. 99–144 are classified according to sponsoring religious order and locale.

191. For references to a few oratorio performances in Ljubljana, Slovenia (Yugoslavia), see Cvetko, *Musique slovène*, pp. 128–33.

FIGURE I-5. Title page of Metastasio's *Isacco*, set by Josef Mysliveček and printed for a performance sponsored by the Sacred Military Order of the Crucifers of the Red Star in the church of San Francesco on Good Friday, 1778, in Prague. (Courtesy of CS-Pu.)

Continent. In English, German, and Slavic areas, and in Lisbon, public concerts in Lent tended to include at least an occasional Italian oratorio.

During Handel's time in London, oratorio became a standard feature of the Lenten concerts held in the major theaters—a feature that continued until well into the nineteenth century. Although these concerts were dominated by English oratorios (see Table IV-1 and the discussion of it), Italian oratorios were occasionally heard from the 1730s through the 1770s—thereafter, even more rarely. To mention a few of the Italian works among London's Lenten offerings: in 1734 at Lincoln's Inn Fields, *David e Bersabea*, by Nicola Porpora (1686–1768);[192] in 1757 at the Theater Royal in Drury Lane and in 1764 at an unnamed theater, Hasse's *I pellegrini*, with additions by Felice Giardini (1716–96);[193] in 1765 and 1770 at the King's Theater in the Haymarket, Jommelli's *La passione*;[194] in 1770 at the same theater, *Gioas re di Giuda*, by Johann Christian Bach (1735–82), with Metastasio's text "much altered and encreased" by Giovanni Gualberto Bottarelli;[195] and in 1795, *Debora e Sisara* by Pietro Alessandro Guglielmi.[196]

In German cities where public concerts were becoming important,[197] Italian oratorios began to appear on programs in the second third of the century. They were performed in Frankfurt as early as 1738;[198] throughout the century, however, most oratorios heard in that city were in German. During the winter of 1754–55 in Hamburg, Giovanni Battista Locatelli's opera troupe performed in concert the oratorio *Il sacrificio d'Abramo* by Francesco Zoppis (ca. 1715–81);[199] and in Hamburg concerts from 1762 to 1765, one to five Italian oratorios (by Avondano, Galuppi, Hasse, Lorenz Kühl, and Zoppis) were heard each year.[200]

Leipzig is of special interest for its cultivation of the Italian oratorio beginning in the mid century. The Leipzig concert series directed by Johann Friedrich Doles (1715–97) began in 1743 as a private, middle-class society called the Großes Konzert, and sometimes the Kaufmannskonzert. The performances, which took place at the Inn Zu den drei

192. Michael Robinson, "Porpora," *New Grove*, 15:126–27. See app. A: *David e Bersabea* (London, 1734).

193. 1757 performance: *London Stage*, 2/4:558; 1764 performance: libretto *The Pilgrims*, in F-Pn.

194. 1765 performance: libretto *La passione*, in F-Pn and US-Wc, according to Sartori, "Catalogo"; 1770 performance: libretto *La passione*, in GB-Cu: S 721.d.70.4/5.

195. Libretto: *Gioas rè di Giuda*, in GB-Cu: S 721.d.70.4/4.

196. See below, Tables IV-1 and III-7.

197. On the emergence of public concerts in Germany, see Preußner, *Bürgerliche Musikkultur*.

198. Israël, *Frankfurt*, p. 28.

199. According to Sittard, *Hamburg*, p. 80. (Sittard spells the composer's name "Zappi.")

200. See the newspaper notices quoted in Menke, *Telemann*, pp. 47–63.

Schwanen, were attended by subscribers and guests—occasionally noblemen. In Holy Week of 1749 the Großes Konzert initiated a special series called the Concerts spirituels. (That name, well known since the founding of the Parisian series called "Concert spirituel" in 1725—which, however, did not perform Italian oratorios—would also be adopted during the eighteenth century in other cities, including Berlin, Hannover, and Schwerin.) The Leipzig Concerts spirituels presented an Italian oratorio every year from 1750 through 1756. Most of the works were by Hasse, the famous Kapellmeister of nearby Dresden whose Roman Catholic works could not be heard in Leipzig's churches.[201] The Großes Konzert and Concerts spirituels were suspended during the Seven Years War, but when they were reestablished in 1763 by Johann Adam Hiller (1728–1804), the repertoire for Lent—and sometimes for Advent as well—again consisted largely of Italian oratorios, and again Hasse dominated the programs.[202] The construction of the new Gewandhaus in 1781 finally gave the Leipzig public a much-needed concert hall, and at the founding of the Gewandhaus concert series, the directors stipulated: "In Advent and Lent, instead of the usual concerts, Concerts spirituels will be given, in which oratorios, serious operas, and other vocal works will be performed."[203] Although the repertoire of the Concerts spirituels in the Gewandhaus included oratorios in Italian, the majority were now in German.[204] The change of taste reflected in this repertoire—from Italian- to German-language works—is by no means unique to Leipzig, but represents the ever growing desire of European audiences for oratorio—indeed for vocal works in general—in their own languages.

In Vienna, the founding of the Tonkünstler-Societät, in 1771, was important both for that city's concert life and for the cultivation of Italian oratorio.[205] An association of musicians established by Florian Leopold Gassmann (1729–74) for the purpose of providing pensions for the widows and orphans of its members, the Societät gave concerts each Advent and Lent for its own benefit. This was Vienna's earliest regular, public-concert series, and it began by focusing on Italian oratorio. The

201. For descriptions of the Concerts spirituels and lists of the works performed, see Schering, *Leipzig*, 3:268–69, and Dörffel, *Festschrift*, 1:4–7.

202. For a list of the works performed during Advent and Lent from 1763 through 1778, see Schering, *Leipzig*, 3:403.

203. Document quoted in Schering, *Leipzig*, 3:483, and in Dörffel, *Festschrift*, 1:16.

204. For a list of oratorios performed at the Gewandhaus from 1782 through 1802, see Schering, *Leipzig*, 3:492; and for a list of oratorios and other religious works performed from 1782 to the late nineteenth century, see Dörffel, *Festschrift*, 1:184–87.

205. For details of the Tonkünstler-Societät's organization, history, and repertoire, see Hanslick, *Concertwesen*, pp. 18–35, and Pohl, *Tonkünstler Societät*, pp. 43–68.

main work on the inaugural concert, in Lent of 1772, was Gassmann's oratorio *La Betulia liberata*. As was characteristic of the subsequent programs of the Societät, that oratorio was not the only work performed. It was preceded and followed by symphonies—by Joseph Starzer (1726 or 1727–1787) and Franz Aspelmayer (1728–86) respectively—and between the two parts of the oratorio a violin concerto was performed by Franz Lamotte (?1751–?1781). Every concert from 1772 until 1777 featured an Italian oratorio—by Hasse, in concerts of 1772 through 1774; Carl Ditters von Dittersdorf (1739–99), 1773, and 1776; Giuseppe Bonno, 1774; Haydn, 1775; Bertoni, 1775; Gassmann, 1776; and Salieri, 1777. From 1778 to the end of the century, the programs show clear evidence of the same change of taste as evidenced in Leipzig of the 1780s.[206] The trend favored works in German, rather than Italian—the last performance of a complete Italian oratorio in a Societät concert was given in 1788.

Leipzig stressed Italian oratorio presumably because of its proximity to Dresden, and Vienna did so because of its tradititonal cultivation of the genre in that language; but other cities were more like London in rarely including Italian oratorios in their concert offerings. Scattered concert performances may be documented by printed librettos and other sources beginning in the 1750s in Prague, the late 1760s in Berlin, the 1780s in Moscow and St. Petersburg, and the 1790s in Lisbon. Virtually all such performances were given in Lent.[207] Of special interest is the first performance in Berlin of Handel's *Messiah*: it was sung in Italian, in a concert organized by Johann Adam Hiller in the cathedral on 19 May 1786, by a massive performing force in imitation of the Handel Com-

206. For details of the change of taste within the concerts of the Tonkünstler-Societät, see Edelmann, "Haydns *Il ritorno di Tobia*."

207. Among the sources for concert performances in these cities are:

Prague. Librettos printed for performances mostly at the Royal Theater: Zoppis, *Sacrificio d'Abramo*, 1756, in CS-Pu and I-Mb (the same work as performed in Hamburg, 1745–55); Hasse, *Cantico de' tre fanciulli*, 1763, in CS-Pu: 65 D 1232; Antonio Ferradini, *Giuseppe riconosciuto*, 1763, in CS-Pu: 65 E 3944; Domenico Fischietti, *La morte d'Abel*, 1763, in CS-Pu; anon., *Isacco figura del Redentore*, 1765, in CS-Pu: 65 E 3170; Jommelli, *La passione*, 1765, CS-Pu.

Berlin. Librettos printed for performances at the Liebhaberkonzerte: Hasse, *La caduta di Gerico*, n.d. (?1770s or ?1780s), in D-KNth:OT Inv. 9866; Dittersdorf, *La liberatrice . . . Ester*, 1775, D-B: Mus. Ms. 5010 (libretto bound with score); libretto for the Concerts spirituels: Johann Friedrich Reichardt, *La Passione*, 1784, D-Mbs: P.o.it. 655.

Moscow and St. Petersburg. See Mooser, *Opéras*, pp. 22, 64, 92, 105.

Lisbon. Librettos printed for oratorios sung in the "Nuova Sala della Assemblea di San Carlo": Giuseppe Giordani, *La distruzione di Gerusalemme*, 1796, in I-Rc, Carvalhaes 4513; Paisiello, *La passione*, 1797, in P-Lt, Lcg. See also Fonseca Benevides, *Theatro de S. Carlos*, p. 23 and the list on his pp. 419–30.

memoration of 1784 in Westminster Abbey (for details, see chapter 4).[208]

As we have seen, the theatrical performance of oratorios—with scenery, costumes, acting, and memorized roles—was highly exceptional in Italy before the mid-eighteenth century; such performance of Italian oratorios appears slightly less exceptional outside Italy. Prior to the mid-eighteenth century, six Italian oratorios are thus far known to have been performed as operas—all six are by Pietro Torri (1650–1737) and were written for the elector of Bavaria, Maximiliam II Emmanuel (r. 1679–1726), between 1692 and 1737.[209] From the mid-century on the number of oratorio performances that are in every sense operatic increases but does not rival the number found in Italy. In Munich, other such performances date from 1749 and the 1750s; in Bonn at the court of the elector of Cologne (the elector of Bavaria's brother), from 1746, 1758, and 1774; at Kremsmünster, Georg Pasterwiz's setting of Metastasio's *Il Giuseppe riconosciuto* was staged in 1777; and in Vienna, staged performances date from 1759, 1788, and 1791.[210] In Prague, the earliest known operatic performance of an Italian oratorio dates from Lent, 1749, when an anonymous *Isacco figura del Redentore* was produced in Prague's theater by the opera company of Giovanni Battista Locatelli (1713–90).[211] Such performances may be documented in Lisbon beginning with Lent of 1773,[212] and in Moscow with Lent of 1783.[213]

208. This was not the first performance of *Messiah* in Germany; it was performed in Hamburg in 1772 (language uncertain) and 1775 (in German). See below, chap. 6.

209. For documentation, see Smither, "Sacred Opera," pp. 96 and 103. For the title page of a libretto printed for one of these works, see below, app. A: *Giacob* (Valenciennes, 1709).

210. For citation of libretto title pages for all but the Pasterwiz work, see Smither, "Sacred Opera," pp. 103–4. On the Pasterwiz oratorio, see Kellner, *Kremsmünster*, pp. 469–71.

211. For a discussion of the work and a quotation from the printed libretto's title page, see Teuber, *Theater*, pt. 1, pp. 203–4. Later librettos show an occasional staged oratorio in Prague during Lent throughout the second half of the century.

212. See app. A: *La Betulia liberata* (Lisbon, 1773); see also the discussions and lists of staged and unstaged works in Fonseca Benevides, *Theatro de S. Carlos*, pp. 49, 97, 108–9, 117–18, 140, 144–45, and 419–30.

213. See Mooser, *Opéras*, p. 22.

CHAPTER II
The Libretto and Music of the Italian Oratorio

The Libretto

The Metastasian Libretto

The type of oratorio libretto commonly called "Metastasian" received an important impulse from the contributions of Apostolo Zeno (1668–1750) and Pietro Metastasio (1698–1782), the two most significant librettists of their time; yet it was the sole creation of neither librettist, for in its essentials it appeared early in the eighteenth century and antedates their works.[1] Zeno did, however, introduce important changes in the oratorio libretto, and Metastasio retained those changes in his.[2] Their librettos are classic (or even "classical") for their clear, simple structure and elegant language—reflections of the classicizing influence of the Arcadian Academy. Zeno and Metastasio were members of the Academy and were dedicated to its ideal of improving Italian literature by returning to ancient principles.[3] Metastasio's librettos are classic in another sense, for they held the position of classics—models of excellence in Italian oratorio—throughout much of the eighteenth century; the Metastasian libretto became archetypal for the age.[4]

Metastasio's oratorio librettos were set by an astonishing number of composers, far more than those of any other poet of his time, and were frequently imitated by other poets.[5] One of the reasons for his immense

1. For a summary of Archangelo Spagna's "Discorso" of 1705, which anticipates some of Zeno's changes in the oratorio libretto, see Smither, *Oratorio*, 1:294–305; and on Spagna in relation to Zeno, see ibid., p. 388.

2. On these changes, see ibid., pp. 386–93.

3. For an extended treatment of the Arcadian Academy and its relationship to Italian dramatic art in general and oratorio in particular, see Baker, "Marcello," pp. 69–132.

4. Cf. the definitions of "classical" and the discussion of Metastasio in this regard in Daniel Heartz, "Classical," *New Grove*, 4:450–52.

5. To the extent that Sartori, "Catalogo," may be assumed to include a reason-

popularity is surely his carefully polished and mellifluous verse, which was eminently suited to the musical styles of his time. As his librettos represent the main stream in Italian oratorio, the following treatment of the libretto will focus on them. Yet many of the traits found in his librettos and described below also appear in those of certain contemporaries, both older and younger than he and similarly influenced by the Arcadian Academy. Among his best and best-known contemporaries, in addition to Zeno, are Pietro Pariati (1665–1733), Stefano Benedetto Pallavicino (1672–1742), Domenico Lalli (pseudonym of Nicolò Bastiano Biancardi, 1679–1741), and Giovanni Claudio Pasquini (1695–1763). A multitude of lesser poets wrote oratorio librettos representing the general principles (but rarely the elegance of language) found in Metastasio's works.[6]

In 1729 Metsastasio was invited to Vienna by Emperor Charles VI to replace Zeno as the Habsburg court poet.[7] Between 1730 and 1740, for Holy Week performances in the court chapel, Metastasio wrote his seven Viennese oratorio librettos: *La passione di Gesù Cristo* (1730, first set by Antonio Caldara), *Sant'Elena al Calvario* (1731, Caldara), *La morte d'Abel* (1732, Georg Reutter), *Giuseppe riconosciuto* (1733, Giuseppe Porsile), *Betulia liberata* (1734, Reutter), *Gioas re di Giuda* (1735, Reutter), and *Isacco figura del Redentore* (1740, Luca Antonio Predieri).[8] His Viennese period, 1729–82, is as appropriately called the "Metastasian era" in Italian oratorio as it is in Italian *opera seria*.[9] Metastasio's oratorio librettos were at times modified by other librettists from the 1730s on,[10] but only near the end of the century did a general

---

able sample of the Italian oratorio libretto before 1800, it is noteworthy that Sartori lists at least 366 librettos printed for different performances of Metastasio's seven Viennese oratorios and only 25 of Zeno's 17 oratorios. Also according to Sartori, most librettists' oratorios, like most of Zeno's, appear to have been set only once or twice. In Metastasio, *Opere*, 2:1322–25, Brunelli lists the following numbers of composers in the eighteenth and nineteenth centuries who set Metastasio's oratorios: *Betulia*, 33; *Isacco*, 27; *Giuseppe*, 25; *Gioas*, 24; *Abel*, 22; *La passione*, 19; *Sant'Elena*, 14.

6. Sartori, "Catalogo," lists over 400 eighteenth-century librettists of Italian oratorios, most of whose works remain to be studied. For comments on some librettists whose works were performed at the Congregation of the Oratory in Rome, see Johnson, "Oratorio," 1:146–68.

7. For general information on Metastasio and his oratorio librettos, and for bibliography, see Smither, *Oratorio*, 1:390–95.

8. Metastasio's first libretto, *Componimento sacro per la festività del SS. Natale* (Rome, 1727), less representative of the Metastasian oratorio than those listed, will not be treated here. For a discussion of it, see Smither, *Oratorio*, 2:269–74.

9. Cf. Pasquetti, *Oratorio*, p. 400; and Daniel Heartz, "Metastasian Serious Opera," in *New Grove*, 13:555–58.

10. On *Giuseppe riconosciuto* modified for operatic staging as early as 1736 in Naples, see the reference in chap. 1, n. 142.

movement away from the Metastasian model begin. Even then, however, some elements of the model remained.

The relationship between Metastasio's librettos for opera and those for oratorio is close, yet important differences distinguish the genres. Among the similarities are the approximate number of characters (usually six or seven in the operas, four to six in the oratorios); the consistent alternation between recitatives in *versi sciolti* (a free mixture of seven- and eleven-syllable lines, with irregular rhyme) and closed pieces, usually arias in two rhymed stanzas written to accomodate the prevailing da capo musical setting; the few choruses and even fewer ensembles (mostly duets, or *arie a due*); and the usual *lieto fine*, or happy ending. An obvious difference is the oratorio's sacred and devotional subject matter, with dramatic conflicts based on moral issues derived from religious history and doctrine, versus opera's secular and usually historical subject matter, with conflicts based on the opposing claims of love and duty, passion and reason.[11] Other differences are the oratorio's two-part division, absence of scene numbers and variety of "scene" structure, relative brevity, and greater reflective, narrative, and descriptive emphasis, versus the operas' three-act division, scene numbers and relative consistency of scene structure, greater length, and greater dramatic emphasis. Throughout the Metastasian period, the general characteristics of the Italian oratorio predominate, but there are exceptions—some oratorios, for instance, that are Metastasian in other respects have one or three parts, rather than the usual two.

Subject Matter and Treatment. As may be seen from his oratorio titles, Metastasio selected five of his subjects from the Old Testament, the most important source for Zeno and many of his predecessors.[12] *La passione* is Metastasio's only New Testament text and *Sant'Elena* his only hagiographical one. Available evidence suggests that performances of oratorios with Old Testament texts were far more numerous throughout the Metastasian period than were those with New Testament, hagiographical, or other religious texts such as allegories of faith and morals and texts derived from church history.[13]

All of Metastasio's librettos respect the three dramatic unities: time (the drama unfolds within a twenty-four hour period), place (the drama

11. For a brief characterization of Metastasio's opera librettos, see Michael F. Robinson, "Metastasio," *New Grove*, 12:216.

12. Cf. Smither, *Oratorio*, 1:299, 388.

13. This conclusion is based on my survey of the librettos in Sartori, "Catalogo," in which there would seem to be about three times as many titles based on the Old Testament as on the New, and about twice as many on the Old Testament as on hagiography. The list of oratorios sponsored by the Congregation of the Oratory in Rome between 1770 and 1800 given in Johnson, "Oratorio," 1:71–74, includes four times as many Old Testament oratorios as New Testament or hagiographical ones.

does not change locale), and action (only one dramatic action takes place). For this reason much action is narrated in the past tense rather than conveyed through dialogue in the present. The result is a libretto of considerable dramatic restraint. In *Isacco*, for instance, the place is the home of Abraham, Sara, and Isaac, and therefore only after Abraham and Isaac return home from Mount Moria and tell Sara about the nature of the sacrifice does the audience learn of it; there is no dialogue on Mount Moria, where the dramatic events of Abraham's preparation to sacrifice his son and the divine intervention take place. In *Betulia*, because the place is the city of Bethulia, the audience learns of Judith's experiences in the Assyrian camp (including her beheading of the enemy commander, Holofernes) only after she has completed the deed and returned to the city. Holofernes is not even a personage in that work, and thus Metastasio, with customary restraint, rejects the dramatic potential of dialogue between him and Judith.

The most dramatically active librettos are the five based on the Old Testament, for Metastasio capitalizes on the dramatic conflicts of the biblical stories whenever he can do so without violating his classic principles. The other two librettos are more reflective than dramatic, yet not lacking in dramatic tension. In *La passione*, which takes place after the Crucifixion, Peter, who was not present, asks John, Mary Magdalene, and Joseph of Arimathea to tell him about it. The drama of the Crucifixion unfolds as they answer his questions by relating the brutal, gory, and intensely emotional details, and all four comment and reflect on the drama and its religious meaning. The place of *Sant'Elena* is Calvary, where the third-century St. Helen and the other personages are in search of the tomb and cross of Jesus. The libretto emphasizes religious reflection rather than dramatic conflict. Tension is created by doubt: the uncertainty of whether the cross that has been found is truly the cross of Jesus. The doubt is dispelled by a miracle, which is explained in past tense to St. Helen.

Throughout Metastasio's librettos, copious footnotes document the biblical and other writings (mainly by the early church fathers) on which he bases specific lines of poetry. Despite the scholarly appearance, however, poetic and dramatic license abounds. To serve his poetic-dramatic conception, Metastasio freely invented personages and episodes not found in the sources. In *Isacco*, for instance, he added (without documentation or explanation) the character Gamari, a companion of Isaac; Gamari's presence facilitates dialogue and dramatic action. In the same work he introduced Sara, Abraham's wife, who is not in the biblical story, but in this case he gives reasons in the *Avertimento* at the beginning of the libretto: "The silence of the sacred Text has left in doubt whether Abraham communicated to Sara the divine command to sacrifice his own son; whence we—among the opinions in which the Expositors are divided—have embraced that which asserts [that he did], as more useful for the conduct of the action, for the movement of the affections, and for the resemblance of the figure [of Christ], which we have proposed to express."[14] The combination of careful documentation and poetic-dramatic license found in Metastasio's oratorios is also characteristic of Zeno's and of those by some other earlier librettists, particularly in librettos for Vienna; and the same combination is found in the oratorios of some later poets as well. Zeno and subsequent librettists continued to avoid the role of God. In *Abel* and *Isacco*, which are based on stories in which God speaks to Cain and Abraham respectively, Metastasio introduces an angel, as an emissary of God, who conveys God's message.

In most of his Old Testament librettos Metastasio follows traditional Christian exegesis by interpreting events and personages of the Old Testament as prefiguring those of the New. This is by no means new to the oratorio libretto, for both in Italy and Vienna librettists had occasionally followed the same tradition in the seventeenth and early eighteenth centuries.[15] Not only in *Isacco figura del Redentore*, but in *Abel* as well, the title role is conceived as a figure of Christ.[16] Frequently in both works the allusions to Christ are clear in the poetry and sometimes supported by footnotes to relevant passages in the New Testament. Early in part I of *Isacco*, for instance, in a recitative interpreting Isaac's birth by the elderly Sara as prefiguring the virgin birth of Jesus, Abraham tells Isaac:

Abramo:	Abraham:
Sì, figlio: il tuo natale	Yes, son, your birth
Costò un prodigio alla natura. I suoi	cost nature a miracle. It violated
Ordini violò. D'arida pianta	its order. You are the miraculous
Tu sei mirabil frutto.[17]	fruit of a barren plant.

14. Translated from Metastasio, *Opere*, 2:679. In a footnote at the word "Expositors," Metastasio lists several authorities, beginning with St. Augustine.

15. Among the examples of such librettos are two anonymous ones on the Cain and Abel story, one set by Francesco Scarlatti, *Agnus occisus ab origine mundi in Abele* (Rome, 1699; I-Rvat: R.G. Miscell. G 75, int. 16), and the other by Alessandro Scarlatti, *Il primo omicidio* (Venice, 1707), printed in Scarlatti, *Oratorii*, vol. 4, and discussed in Smither, *Oratorio*, 1:338–42; and two Viennese *sepolcri* set by Antonio Draghi: Nicolò Minato's libretto on the sacrifice of Isaac as a figure of the Passion of Jesus, *Il sacrificio non impedito* (Vienna, 1692), mentioned in Smither, *Oratorio*, 1:378–80, with Figure VIII-4, and the anonymous *Il secondo Adamo* (Vienna, 1699). For more on the two Draghi works, see Schnitzler, "Draghi," pp. 154–55, 387, and 397.

16. For a discussion of *Abel*, see below in chap. 3, where it is treated in relation to the setting by Leonardo Leo.

17. Metastasio, *Opere*, 2:681. Metastasio does not include a New Testament footnote for this passage.

Later in part I, Isaac is about to leave his mother, who is weeping for she knows he must be sacrificed, to go with his father; and in prefiguring the words of Jesus on the Cross as He asks John to care for His mother, Isaac makes the same request of Gamari:

Isacco:	Isaac:
Ah sì, Gamari amato,	Ah, yes, dear Gamari,
Tu, che fosti fin ora il mio diletto,	you who have been my beloved,
Tu, che su questo petto	who on this breast
Giungesti a riposar, prendine cura	have rested your head, take care of her
in vece mia. Mentre sarò lontano,	in my place. While I am far away,
Con l'opra tu l'assisti e col consiglio.	assist her with work and counsel.
Madre, fin ch'io ritorni, ecco il tuo figlio.[18]	Mother, until I return, behold your son.

After numerous other references to the New Testament, near the end of the oratorio Abraham has a vision of the future in which he fully clarifies the role of Isaac as a figure of Christ.[19] New Testament references are relatively few in *Giuseppe* and *Betulia*, but only in *Gioas* are they totally absent.

Recitatives. In Metastasio's oratorios, recitative and aria function much as they do in opera, but with certain exceptions. Although in both genres the recitatives convey the dramatic action and the arias reflect on the situation or a personage's feelings, in oratorios the recitatives tend to include more descriptive and narrative qualities. A reflective recitative, whether solo or dialogue, often treats a theological point or reveals a personage's religious experience or emotional state, sometimes quite impassioned; and such a passage is often followed by an aria that brings the episode to a climax. This procedure is well illustrated in *La passione* by the opening recitative and aria, sung by Peter, who expresses his utter bewilderment and remorse after his denial of Jesus:

RECITATIVE

Pietro:	Peter:
Dove son: Dove corro?	Where am I? Where do I hasten?
Chi regge i passi miei? Dopo il mio fallo	Who controls my footsteps? Since my failure

18. Ibid., 2:689. Metastasio's footnotes: for line 3, John 13:23, 22:20; line 7, John 19:26.

19. Ibid., 2:699–70.

Non ritrovo più pace:	I find peace no more;
Fuggo gli sguardi altrui: vorrei celarmi	I flee the glances of others, I would hide
Fino a me stesso. In mille affetti ondeggia	even from myself. Among a thousand affects wavers
La confusa alma mia. Sento i rimorsi,	my confused soul. I feel remorse,
Ascolto la pietade; a' miei desiri	I harken to pity; to my desires
Sprone è la speme, è la dubbiezza inciampo:	hope is a spur, doubt it is an obstacle;
Di tema agghiaccio, e di vergogna avvampo.	I freeze with fear, and blaze with shame.
Ogni augello che ascolto,	Every bird that I hear
Accusator dell'incostanza mia	seems to me the accusor of my inconstancy,
	the bird heralding the day.
L'augel nunzio del dì parmi che sia.	
Ingratissimo Piero!	Ungrateful Peter!
Chi sa se vive il tuo Signore? A caso	Who knows if your Lord lives? Not by chance
Gli ordini suoi non sovvertì natura.	does nature alter her order.
Perché langue e si oscura	Why does the sun languish and grow dark
Fra le tenebre il sole? A che la terra,	among the shadows? Why does the earth,
Infida ai passi altrui, trema e vien meno,	unfaithful to its usual course, tremble and fail,
E le rupi insensate aprono il seno?	and the mindless rocks open their breasts?
Ah che gelar mi sento!	Ah how cold I feel!
Nulla so, bramo assai, tutto pavento.	Nothing do I know, much I desire, everything I fear.

ARIA

Giacché mi tremi in seno,	Since you tremble in my breast,
Esci dagli occhi almeno	pour forth at least from my eyes
Tutto disciolto in lagrime,	all dissolved in tears,
Debole, ingrato cor:	oh weak, ungrateful heart;
Piangi, ma piangi tanto	Weep, but weep so much
Che faccia fede il pianto	that the tears may bear witness
Del vero tuo dolor.[20]	to the truth of your grief.

20. Ibid., 2:551–52.

The state of confusion to the point of being lost, which is expressed in Peter's recitative, occurs in other oratorios by Metastasio and those by other poets and is also found in opera of the time.[21]

Metastasio had to emphasize the narrative and descriptive elements of recitative more in oratorio than in opera, for his oratorios, following the norm in his time, were written for concert performance in the imperial chapel, and the context was at least nominally devotional. The poet needed to convey verbally the kinds of visual appearances and actions that would have been conveyed in an opera by the costumes, scenery, and acting. The narrative and descriptive passages are woven into the dialogue, for a separate narrator's role, or *testo*—important in seventeenth-century Italian oratorios—had been abandoned around the turn of the century.[22] The oratorios are filled with examples of comments in recitative that would have been superfluous in opera. In *Betulia*, for instance, each time Judith enters one of the characters either comments that she is approaching or names her immediately upon her entrance, and twice her dress and behavior are fully described.[23]

Metastasio's recitatives, although written in *versi sciolti* and thus without consistent rhyme, are skillfully unified by a variety of techniques, including rhetorical repetition, alliteration, assonance, and rhymed couplets. Unusually rich in such techniques is the opening recitative of *La passione*, quoted above, with its striking repetition of "Dove," which immediately and forcefully establishes Peter's utter confusion. This is a typical recitative for its free mixture of seven- and eleven-syllable lines and concluding rhymed couplet, but it includes more rhymed couplets and assonance than most.[24] Less ornate and thus more characteristic are the two fragments quoted above from *Isacco*, "Sì, figlio: il tuo natale" and "Ah sì, Gamari amato."

Arias and Duets. All of the arias in Metastasio's oratorios have two rhymed stanzas, usually of four lines each.[25] Most of the oratorios include twelve arias, six in each part. The principal characters usually sing three, one aria in one part of the oratorio and two arias in the other part, whereas the least important characters sing one per part or only one in the oratorio. An aria usually follows a passage of recitative, either dia-

21. For comments on scenes of confusion in the oratorios, see Johnson, "Oratorio," 1:107–8.

22. For Arcangelo Spagna's early eighteenth-century views of the *testo*, see Smither, *Oratorio*, 1:296–97.

23. Metastasio, *Opere*, 2:633–34, 638–39, 645.

24. Note the rhymed couplets at the line endings "inciampo"/"avvampo," "mia"/"sia," "natura"/"oscura," "meno"/"seno," and "sento"/"pavento"; and the line endings with assonance at "corro"/"fallo," "Piero"/"caso," and "terra" following the preceding couplet "natura"/"oscura."

25. Less frequently the arias include the following numbers of lines: $4 + 3$ (cf. Peter's aria, quoted above), $3 + 4$, $3 + 3$, $4 + 6$, $6 + 4$, $6 + 6$, and $5 + 4$ (once).

logue or solo, and serves as a culminating point, as does Peter's aria quoted above, following his solo recitative. In Metastasio's operas an aria usually concludes a scene—a numbered division of an act consisting of a single unit of dialogue or monologue—and the character who sings it usually leaves the stage when finished (the "exit-aria" convention). In his oratorios the "scenes" are not so designated, and the units that one might call scenes have greater variety of structure. Occasionally in the oratorios an aria precedes a character's "exit";[26] usually, however, the character who sings an aria takes part in the dialogue that follows it, after at least a brief rest, but sometimes that character must continue immediately with recitative. For instance, after Peter's aria quoted above, "Giacché mi tremi in seno," he remains "on stage" and, in recitative, immediately introduces a Chorus of the Followers of Jesus with the words, "Ma qual dolente stuolo / S'appressa a me? . . ." ("But what sorrowing multitude approaches me?").

Most of the arias in Metastasio's oratorios may be classified by content according to four broad types: dramatic, religious, comparison (simile or metaphor), and sententious.[27] The majority of the arias are of the dramatic type, that is, they derive directly from the dramatic situation and are responses to it.[28] Among the examples are "Giacché mi tremi in seno." The religious arias might praise God, express a belief in God, or preach a sermon.[29] An excellent example is the following aria sung by John in *La passione*:

Giovanni:	John:
Dovunque il guardo giro,	Wherever I turn my glance,
Immenso Dio, ti vedo:	Immense God, I see Thee:
Nell'opre tue t'ammiro,	In Thy works I marvel at Thee,
Ti riconosco in me.	I recognize Thee in me.
La terra, il mar, le sfere	The earth, the sea, the spheres
Parlan del tuo potere:	Speak of Thy power:

26. No "exits" are marked in Metastasio's oratorio librettos, but one may assume a hypothetical exit if the character does not participate in the following unit of text, which happens seven times each in *Abel* and *Gioas*, six times in *Isacco*, once in *Giuseppe*, and not at all in the other three. Some librettists who followed Metastasio's principles marked the "exits," along with other "stage" indications in their librettos for unstaged oratorios, to help the reader-listener imagine the implied action.

27. Some of the arias do not fit into these four types and are best understood in terms of their specific texts and contexts. For more detail about aria types in the oratorios than can be presented here, see Johnson, "Oratorio," 1:112–22, and Arcari, *Metastasio*, pp. 139–87. The present section on arias depends heavily on Johnson's valuable treatment.

28. Johnson, "Oratorio," 1:121, Table 10, lists twenty-eight arias of this type from Metastasio's oratorios.

29. See ibid., Table 9, p. 119, for a list of fourteen such arias.

Tu sei per tutto; e noi   Thou art everywhere; and we
Tutti viviamo in te.[30]   All live in Thee.

In the comparison arias—common also in *opera seria*—a personage compares his condition or dramatic situation to an image in nature: the sea, a storm, a bird, an animal, a tree, a plant, etc.[31] Usually the aria's first stanza presents the image of nature, and its second stanza relates the image to the personage or situation. In *Betulia* Judith's first aria is a characteristic example. In her preceding recitative she has warned that if the city of Bethulia is to be saved, the rulers and the people must avoid both the extremes of despair and false hope. Thus the following comparison:

Giuditta:	Judith:
Del pari infeconda	Equally barren
D'un fiume è la sponda	is the bank of a river
Se torbido eccede,	whether it overflows in turbulence
Se manca d'umor.	or lacks moisture.
Si acquista baldanza	One acquires presumption
Per troppa speranza,	through too much hope,
Si perde la fede	one loses faith
Per troppo timor.[32]	through too much fear.

The arias of the sententious type, of which there are only a few in the oratorios, focus on a maxim or a proverb.[33] In *Giuseppe*, Joseph's first aria is a clear example.

Giuseppe:	Joseph:
E legge di natura,	It is a law of nature
Che a compatir ci mova	that one moves us to pity
Chi prova una sventura	who experiences a misfortune
Che noi provammo ancor:	which we also experienced.
O sia che amore in noi	Either love kindles in us
La somiglianza accenda,	a likeness,
o sia che più s'intenda	or one understands more,
Nel suo l'altrui dolor.[34]	in his own sorrow, that of another.

Arias may also be classified according to their essential affect, whether it be one of joy, peace, anger, lamentation, remorse (as in Peter's "Giacché

30. Metastasio, *Opere*, 2:561.
31. See Johnson, "Oratorio," Table 7, p. 115, for ten such arias in the oratorios.
32. Metastasio, *Opere*, 2:635.
33. For a list of four such arias in the oratorios, see Johnson, "Oratorio," 1:116, Table 8.
34. Metastasio, *Opere*, 2:607.

mi tremi in seno," quoted above), or any other. The affect, of course, is of primary importance to an understanding of the composer's setting of the text.

The only ensembles in Metastasio's oratorios are duets: one each in *La passione* and *Sant'Elena*, none in the other oratorios. In these duets the personages are never in conflict, but in agreement, as is characteristic of ensembles in the oratorio libretto in general. In *Sant'Elena* the duet "Dal tuo soglio luminoso," sung by St. Helen and Eudossa, is written as if it were an aria, with two stanzas of three lines each and religious in content. In *La passione* the duet "Vi sento, oh Dio, vi sento," between Peter and Mary Magdalene, is dramatic, in that it responds to the preceding recitative, and consists of one stanza each for the two to sing separately, followed by two more stanzas that they are to sing partially together and partially in alternation.

The varied meters of Metastasio's arias and duets may be related generally to the emotional quality of the texts, as was acknowledged by various writers of his time and indeed in Metastasio's own writing.[35] In general the shorter meters, such as the *quinario* and *senario* (lines of five and six syllables) were considered appropriate for agitated emotion; the longer meters, such as the *settenario* and *ottonario*, for neutral expression; and the *decasillabo*, for serious, philosophical, or sorrowful expression. According to Johnson, Metastasio "used a variety of meters in his oratorio texts, with *settenario* and *ottenario* the most frequent, due to the flexibility of their accent patterns. Within the scheme of the oratorios there appears no strict arrangement of the meters for the arias; but a pattern of sorts does emerge, in which there was one short line (*senario*) aria and one very long line (*decasillabo*) aria per oratorio. The shorter verse never opened either part of the oratorio, but seems to have occurred at a dramatic high point, near the end of a part."[36]

Choruses. Metastasio's oratorios include few choruses. Following the tradition he inherited from his predecessors, he placed a chorus at the end of each part of every oratorio. *Abel*, *Giuseppe*, and *Isacco* have these final choruses only, whereas *La passione*, *Sant'Elena*, and *Gioas* each has an additional chorus within one of its parts. Only *Betulia* includes more than three choruses: in part I, two internal choruses (both in alternation or combination with a solo personage, Ozia) plus a one-line exclamation "Al campo, al campo!" and a final chorus; and in part II, a final chorus in alternation with Judith plus another one-line entrance, "All'armi, all'armi!" The final choruses of the oratorios tend to summarize and moralize and are written in *versi sciolti*, the style used for recitatives.

35. For a study of the literature on meters in relation to emotional quality and of the meters in Metastasio's oratorios, see Johnson, "Oratorio," 1:122–39 (Table 11 on pp. 136–39 lists Metastasio's oratorio arias and their meters).

36. Johnson, "Oratorio," 1:135.

Such verses were also traditional for madrigals of the sixteenth and seventeenth centuries, as well as for the final chorus, called *madrigale ultimo*, in an oratorio of the seventeenth and early eighteenth centuries.[37] Metastasio would seem to have continued the tradition of the *madrigale ultimo*, without using that label. The few internal choruses, which are more closely related to the dramatic action than are the final ones, are written in regular meter with rhyme. In all the oratorios but one the choruses are named as groups of personages in the drama; only in *Abel* is the word *coro* used without further designation.

Modifications of the Metastasian Libretto

Until at least the 1780s Metastasio's oratorios were often set to music virtually intact,[38] and most librettos by other poets followed the principles of his librettos.[39] When modifications were made in Metastasio's oratorios, such as substitutions, deletions, or additions of arias or recitatives, they usually did not significantly change the general character of the libretto. For instance, in Nicolò Jommelli's setting of Metastasio's *Isacco* (Venice, 1742), the libretto retains its essential character despite the insertion of two new arias and a brief recitative that were clearly intended to heighten the dramatic effect and sharpen the characterization.[40] More drastic are the modifications of Metastasio's text of *Betulia* in Jommelli's setting (Venice, 1743). The composer deletes the roles of two minor characters, Cabri and Amital, who are of minimal importance to the dramatic development (other characters sing their essential lines of recitative, but not their arias); and in part II he makes several large cuts in the recitatives (especially in theological discussions), probably for reasons of economy and dramatic continuity, and adds an aria for Judith.[41]

37. Cf. Smither, *Oratorio*, 1:197, 306, 311–12, 332. As late as 1715 in Vienna, Johann Joseph Fux's oratorio *La fede sacrilega* labels the final chorus *madrigale*; see ibid., p. 114.

38. For a few of the numerous examples, see the printed librettos of Johann Adolf Hasse's *Giuseppe* (Dresden, 1741; D-B: Mus. Th 257); Giuseppe Maria Orlandini's *Gioas* (Florence, 1744, performed in Pistoia; I-Rc: Z.III.1.CCC); Andrea Bernasconi's *Betulia* (Munich, 1755; I-Mb); Giuseppe Bonno's *Isacco* (Vienna, 1759; A-Wn: 759,242-B, TB) and his *Giuseppe* (Vienna, 1774; CS-Pu: 9 H 4971); and Florian Leopold Gassmann's *Betulia* (Vienna, 1776; CS-Pu: 9 J 3548).

39. All the librettos set by Johann Adolf Hasse that are not by Metastasio, for instance, follow the principles of the Metastasian libretto, except that three are short, one-part works.

40. The inserted arias are Abramo's "Col tuo braccio" and Sara's "Sollecito, dubbioso"; the inserted recitative precedes the latter aria. For a discussion of these additions and their effect, see Cauthen, "Jommelli," pp. 114–20.

41. The deletion of the two characters was evidently a practical matter, accord-

These changes in *Betulia*, which tend to reduce the reflective and religious content and hasten the dramatic action, are closer to the type that became increasingly prominent in the ensuing decades and led to the decline of the Metastasian libretto.

In the late eighteenth century two broad, interrelated categories of change appear in the oratorio libretto, one offering more possibilities for musical variety than the Metastasian libretto, and another creating greater dramatic action and interest. In both categories Italian oratorio followed the lead of opera, as it had done since the seventeenth century.

Greater musical variety resulted from a change in the libretto's usual pattern of alternation between recitative and aria. Although alternation is retained, recitatives are shorter and arias fewer, and other closed pieces take the place of arias.[42] A genre new to oratorio, the cavatina (in a single stanza), sometimes appears instead of an aria (still normally in two stanzas), and ensembles are more numerous—not only duets, the most common ensembles of the Metastasian libretto, but also trios, quartets, and even quintets. Internal choruses become more numerous, and oratorios increasingly begin with choruses. The two parts of oratorios still commonly end with choruses, but some end with ensembles and others with choral-ensemble or choral-solo complexes. A number of these departures from the Metastasian libretto are found, for instance, in three of the texts set by Pasquale Anfossi (1727–97): *Il sagrifizio di Noè uscito dall'arca* (Rome, 1783, librettist unknown) includes four arias, three cavatinas, one duet, one trio, and four choruses; *Il figliuol prodigo* (Rome, 1792, libretto by Carl'Antonio Femi), opens with a trio-chorus complex and includes nine arias, one arioso, two cavatinas, two duets, another trio, and a chorus at the end of each part; and *La morte di San Filippo Neri* (Rome, 1796, libretto by Femi), begins with a chorus and in part I includes eight arias, two duets, a trio, an internal chorus, a closing rondo for a solo personage and chorus, and in part II a closing chorus.[43] The work by Domenico Cimarosa (1749–1801) that is known both as *Assa-*

---

ing to the printed librettos (which are quoted in Cauthen, "Jommelli," p. 9 and n. 16). The largest cuts for the remaining characters are those in which Ozia tries to convince the pagan Achior that there is one God. (For a description of all the modifications, see ibid., pp. 120–22.)

42. For a detailed treatment of the changes in the oratorio libretto of the late eighteenth century, see Johnson, "Oratorio," 1:143–68 and the catalogue of oratorios performed at the oratory of the Chiesa Nuova from 1770 through 1800 in ibid., 2:388–633. A perusal of the outlines of the fifty-three oratorios in the catalogue provides an excellent indication of the changes in the oratorio libretto late in the century. The present discussion relies on Johnson's catalogue and discussions of individual works, together with the present author's survey of librettos in the period under discussion.

43. For outlines and discussions of all three works and for lists of sources, see Johnson, "Oratorio," 2:429–34, 398–407, and 418–24, respectively.

lonne (written for Florence, 1779) and *Absalom* (revised for Venice, in Latin, 1782) illustrates well the late-century interest in ensembles, for it includes (in its Italian version) one duet and four trios (two of which are ensemble finales), as well as five arias, one arioso, and one internal chorus.[44]

The desire to increase the dramatic interest of Italian oratorio—to make it more like opera—was expressed in writings about oratorio and revealed in librettos from time to time throughout the century but became particularly prominent beginning in the mid-century. An early writing that reflects this desire is Arcangelo Spagna's treatise of 1706, in which he advocates changes, including the abandonment of the *testo*, to make the oratorio "un perfetto melodramma spirituale," despite its performance without staging, costumes, and action.[45] Zeno, too, wished to place greater emphasis on drama in oratorio, which is no doubt why he increased the proportion of recitative to aria. He preferred such designations as *dramma sacro* and *azione sacra* to *oratorio* and published the collected edition of his oratorio librettos under the title *Poesie sacre drammatiche* (Venice, 1735).[46] The performing circumstances for which Spagna, Zeno, Metastasio, and most other Italian librettists wrote their oratorios dictated that the works would not be acted but given concert performance, usually in a devotional context; yet oratorios were acted on rare occasions early in the century and more frequently beginning in the mid-century, as pointed out in chapter 1. Some acted performances retained the traditional characteristics: for instance, Giuseppe Bonno's *Isacco* (Vienna, 1759) used Metastasio's libretto unchanged.[47] For most such performances, however, either a Metastasian libretto was modified to make it more suitable for a staged production or a new libretto was written for the occasion. The libretto of the staged oratorio influenced the oratorio as a traditional concert piece. Indeed, some oratorios originally staged in theaters were subsequently performed as concert works in oratories and concert halls (e.g., P. A. Guglielmi's *Debora e Sisara*, discussed in chapter 3).

The increase of dramatic action and interest—whether for the purpose of staging or not—is revealed in several aspects of the new oratorio libretto. Unity of place is less strictly observed than in the Metastasian works. The greater freedom allows more dramatic action during recitatives and requires less past-tense narration of action that had taken place in another locale. Reflective and narrative recitatives are fewer. More

44. This description is based on the manuscript in I-Rf, as reported in Johnson, "Oratorio," 2:467–68.

45. For a discussion of Spagna's treatise and for further bibliography, see Smither, *Oratorio*, 1:294–99, and Smither, "Sacred Opera," p. 89.

46. For further information on Zeno's librettos and for bibliography, see Smither, *Oratorio*, 1:384–90.

47. The printed libretto is in A-Wn: 759,242-B,TB.

numbers are dramatic, that is, the arias, cavatinas, ensembles, and choruses tend to be linked directly to their dramatic context, and fewer are of the religious, sententious, and comparison types. Personages in ensembles are not necessarily in agreement as they are in the Metastasian libretto, but dramatic conflict and plot development can take place during an ensemble; and ensemble finales at times replace final choruses. Some of these characteristics are seen in a revision of Metastasio's *Isacco* for a staged performance at Bonn in the theater of the elector of Cologne, Clement Augustus, in 1746 (see Figure II-1). Although in Metastasio's libretto the action presumably takes place entirely at the home of Abraham and Sara, in this version that locale is only one of five, which include a grotto surrounded by a forest, a road that leads to the summit of Mount Moriah, a forest near Abraham's home, and a meadow. In part I much of the libretto is by Metastasio, but some of his recitatives and arias are deleted and new ones added; part II, however, has been largely rewritten for theatrical purposes.

More striking for their dramatic qualities than such revisions of Metastasio's oratorios, however, are librettos written for works originally intended to be staged, particularly the Neapolitan oratorios, or sacred operas, staged during Lent in the late eighteenth and early nineteenth centuries.[48] In addition to the dramatic characteristics mentioned above, such works feature several changes of locale and scenery, visually splendid ceremonial and military scenes with solo-choral or ensemble-choral complexes, and battles raging on stage. Among the most popular of these was *Debora e Sisara* with a libretto by Carlo Sernicola, set by Pietro Alessandro Guglielmi (1728–1804) for performance at the Teatro San Carlo in Naples during Lent of 1788. Particularly striking in this libretto is the finale of part I, in which four personages represent two sides of a conflict that concludes with the inevitability of war between the Israelites and the Canaanites. In part II the war takes place (on stage), the Israelites are victorious, and Sisara (the Cananite general), is executed by a woman, Giaele. The solo-choral finale is a massive Israelite prayer. This work and others equally dramatic and equally unlike the Metastasian oratorio was performed frequently—both staged in theaters and in concert versions in oratories—throughout Italy and north of the Alps until the 1820s.[49] With the growing popularity of this type of libretto, which served both as a sacred opera or staged oratorio and a traditional oratorio for concert performance, the Metastasian libretto

48. For lists of such works, see the reference in chapter 1, n. 144.
49. The work exists in several versions. Printed librettos for performances (in various versions) known to me are: Bologna, 1789; Florence, 1789; Naples, 1789; Livorno, 1790; Warsaw, 1791; Palermo, 1792; Bologna, 1795; Longiano, 1795; Naples, 1795; Lisbon, 1796; Livorno, 1798; Florence, 1803; Lisbon, 1806; Venice, 1806; Rimini, 1808; Ferrara, 1808; Milan, 1810; Palermo, 1815; Palermo, 1818; Rome, 1821; Chieti, 1827.

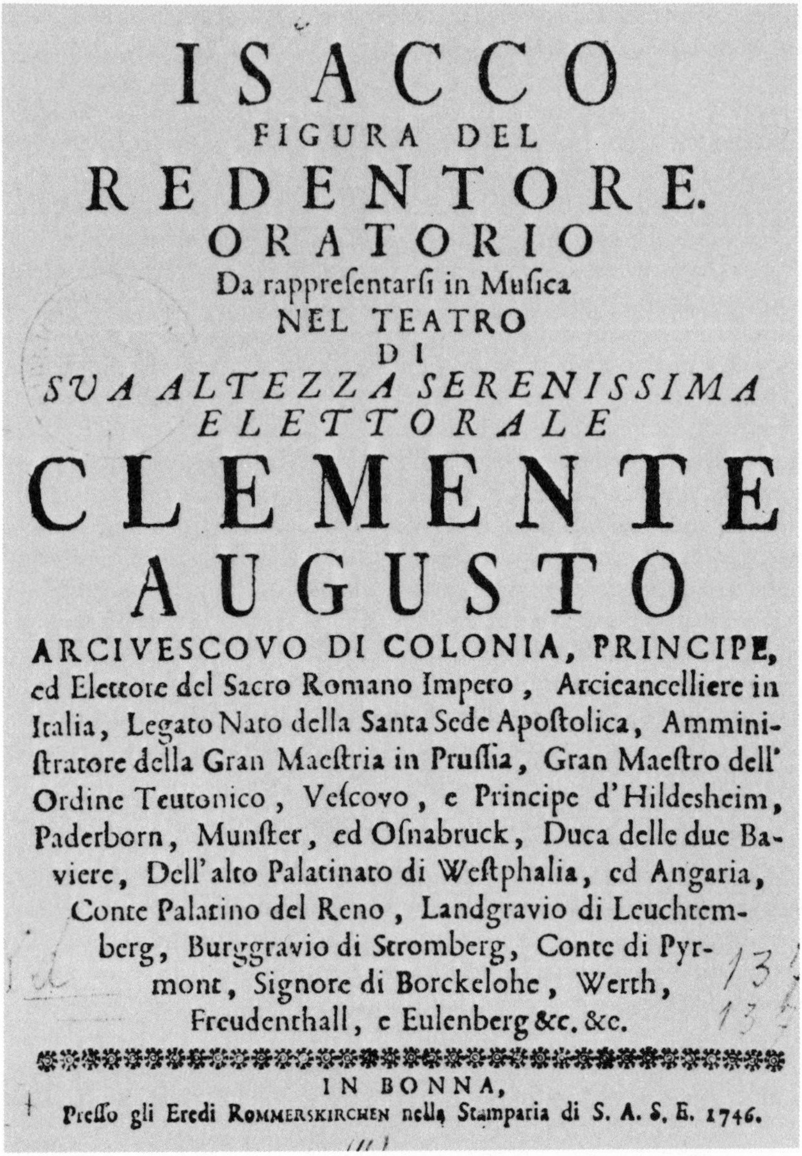

ISACCO
FIGURA DEL
REDENTORE.
ORATORIO
Da rapprefentarfi in Mufica
NEL TEATRO
DI
SUA ALTEZZA SERENISSIMA ELETTORALE
CLEMENTE
AUGUSTO
ARCIVESCOVO DI COLONIA, PRINCIPE,
ed Elettore del Sacro Romano Impero , Arcicancelliere in
Italia, Legato Nato della Santa Sede Apoftolica, Ammini-
ftratore della Gran Maeftria in Pruffia, Gran Maeftro dell'
Ordine Teutonico , Vefcovo , e Principe d'Hildesheim,
Paderborn, Munfter, ed Ofnabruck, Duca delle due Ba-
viere, Dell' alto Palatinato di Weftphalia, ed Angaria,
Conte Palatino del Reno , Landgravio di Leuchtem-
berg, Burggravio di Stromberg, Conte di Pyr-
mont, Signore di Borckelohe , Werth,
Freudenthall, e Eulenberg &c. &c.

IN BONNA,
Preffo gli Eredi ROMMERSKIRCHEN nella Stamparia di S. A. S. E. 1746.

FIGURE II-I. Title page of Metastasio's *Isacco* revised for a staged
performance at the electoral palace in Bonn, 1746. The poet who revised the
libretto and the composer are anonymous. (Courtesy of F-Pn.)

became obsolete. Although Metastasio's oratorios were still set by some composers, they were rarely used in their original form.[50]

The Music: General Characteristics

The broad outlines of the Italian oratorio and certain aspects of text setting remained relatively stable throughout the century under consideration, despite striking changes in stylistic and structural detail. Stability marks two aspects conditioned by the libretto: the two-part division of the work as a whole and the pattern of alternation between recitative on the one hand and aria, ensemble, or chorus on the other.[51] Also stable is the musical interpretation of the affects and imagery of texts. In the early nineteenth century, composers continue to follow many old traditions of rhetorical text treatment, such as long coloratura passages and large skips in an aria of anger, sighs in an aria of plaintive affect, chromatic inflections for tearful texts, and both obvious word painting and more subtle interpretations of words and ideas. Another aspect of stability is the tradition, basic in dramatic music, of relating an aria's musical style and at times its structure to the dramatic importance, social station, or religious significance of the personage who sings it. For instance, in such widely separated works as Leo's La morte d'Abel of the 1730s and Haydn's Il ritorno di Tobia of 1775—or Bertoni's David poenitens of the same year—an angel, as an emissary of God, is given special treatment that will distinguish him from lesser personages; likewise a saint, a prophet, or any heroic figure will be distinguished by musical means. Also reasonably consistent from the beginning to the end of the period is evidence in many works of tonal planning for an oratorio as a whole. A work usually begins and ends in the same key, and the arias, ensembles, and choruses are often in keys that contribute to tonal unity and symmetry; but the keys of some numbers in most works appear to have been selected for other reasons, such as appropriateness to the affect of a text.[52]

50. For examples of Metastasio's oratorios set with changes to suit the taste of the late eighteenth century, see: Gioas . . . The poetry by Metastasio, much altered and encreased by G. G. Bottarelli, set by Johann Christian Bach for London in 1770 (lib. in GB-Cu: S721.d.70.4/4); Gioas, set by Antonio Cartellieri for Vienna in 1795 (lib. in CS-Pu: 9J3549); and Betulia, set by Joseph Schuster for Dresden, 1796 (lib. in D-B: Mus. T 92/3).

51. Although changes in the libretto late in the century reflect an interest in greater musical variety, as indicated above, such changes do not modify the principle of alternation.

52. See chapter 3, Tables III-1 through III-6 and III-8, for the tonal centers in the Italian oratorios treated in that chapter. Throughout this volume I suggest relationships between keys and affects of texts in specific oratorios. The principle that certain keys are appropriate for certain affects was important to many

The focal point of the present discussion is change in musical style and structure. The changes are not, of course, peculiar to the Italian oratorio but are found in opera and other vocal genres, and to some extent in instrumental music as well. When closely examined, changes in musical style and structure throughout the eighteenth century seem to be continuous, complex, and multidirectional, not necessarily away from a certain style of the past nor toward a certain style of the future. Some contemporaneous composers write in what seem to be quite different styles, and a single composer will make subtle or bold changes from one work to another; even within one work, a composer will combine elements from apparently different styles. Seen at close range, the music exhibits more variety than homogeneity, despite some widely accepted conventions. Nevertheless, within the complex and initially bewildering multiplicity of change through the eighteenth century, one inevitably discerns patterns, and for the sake of discussion the perceived phases of change must be given labels, however inadequate some of them may seem. The present author uses terms that have become traditional in treatments of eighteenth-century styles: Baroque, early Classical (sometimes called *galant* or pre-Classical), Classical, and late Classical. (There is little in the Italian oratorio until around 1820 that one could identify with Romantic style.)

For the purpose of understanding the patterns of change in the music of the Italian oratorio, works treated below are grouped into three large, overlapping periods: from the 1720s to the 1760s, which includes oratorios in the older, late-Baroque and the newer, early Classical styles and those in mixtures of the older and newer styles; from the 1760s to the 1780s, early Classical and Classical styles; and from the 1780s to about 1820, Classical and late Classical styles (with suggestions of Romantic). In the first two of these periods, oratorios in Italian were produced in far greater number than those in any other language; Italian oratorios were composed by virtually all the major and minor composers of Italian opera, in Italy and abroad, and also by composers active in churches and monasteries throughout Italy and known only in their locales. In the third period came the waning of the traditions—especially the religious traditions—which had provided occasions for the performance of Italian oratorios for more than a century and a half. Appendix B is a provisional list of over 200 composers who wrote Italian oratorios between 1720 and 1820; the list includes the number of oratorios (many of which are lost) that each composer is thought to have written and the cities in which the works were first performed, according to current information. The conclusions of the present discussion are based on a sample of the extant oratorios by composers in that list.

(perhaps most) eighteenth-century theorists and composers, but they often disagree on the details of that principle. For a study of this subject, see Steblin, *Key Characteristics*, chapters 3–7.

From the 1720s to the 1760s

Because the oratorio in late Baroque style was treated in volume 1 of this study, little is said of it here, and no specific works representing that style are discussed in chapter 3. Good representatives of the late Baroque style in this period are the works of Johann Joseph Fux (1660–1741), Antonio Caldara (1670–1736), Giuseppe Porsile (1680–1750), and Georg von Reutter (1708–72), all active at the relatively conservative Habsburg court in Vienna;[53] Jan Dismas Zelenka (1679–1745) and Nicola Porpora (1686–1768) in Dresden;[54] and Benedetto Marcello (1686–1739) in Venice.[55] In their oratorios the arias, ensembles, and choruses characteristically have a linear bass line and thus an essentially contrapuntal texture, relatively quick harmonic rhythm, a rich harmonic vocabulary, and melodic lines that tend to be spun out by sequential treatment of motives. Yet some of their oratorios suggest the early Classical style, as do Caldara's oratorios of 1712–15 (but he returned to a contrapuntal style at Vienna beginning in 1716) and Porpora's *Nascita di Gesù* (1748).[56]

Among the characteristics of the early Classical style are a simple, tuneful melodic line organized by measures clearly grouped into balanced phrases and decorated by triplet figures and Lombardic rhythms (i.e., "inverted" dotted patterns, also called the "Scotch snap"); a simple, thin, homophonic texture, often of only two or three real parts (with violins in unison, violas doubling basses, and winds doubling strings); an essentially nonlinear bass line, at times using the *Trommelbass* (long series of repeated notes in the bass, forming a pedal point) and occasionally such chordal figures as the Alberti bass; a restricted harmonic vocabulary with slow harmonic rhythm; and the occasional use (beginning in the mid-century) of an orchestral effect often called the "Mannheim crescendo."[57] In its general effect, this music is lighter and more immedi-

53. For comments and bibliography on the oratorios of Caldara, see Smither, *Oratorio*, 1:355–61, 397–98; on those of Fux, see ibid., 1:407–15. Forthcoming facsimiles are Caldara, *Joaz**, and Reutter, *Betulia**.

54. On the oratorios of Zelenka, see Oschmann, "Zelenka." Modern editions of Zelenka's *Sub olea pacis et palma virtutis* (1723; made by Susanne Oschmann from the manuscript in D-Dlb: Mus. 2358-D-2) and *I penitenti al sepolchro del Redentore* (1736; made by Reinhold Kubik from the manuscript in D-Dlb: Mus. 2358-D-9) are available from the Deutsches Musikgeschichtliches Archiv Kassel. For information, see "Mitteilungen," *Die Musikforschung* 34 (1981): 520, and 36 (1983): 64. A forthcoming facsimile is Porpora, *Nascita di Gesù**, a work composed for Dresden.

55. On the oratorios of Marcello, see Baker, "Marcello." A forthcoming facsimile is Marcello, *Joaz**.

56. On Caldara's style changes, see Smither, *Oratorio*, 1:358–61, 397–98.

57. For detailed descriptions of early Classical style that are broadly applicable to the period but specifically focus on the symphonies of Johann Stamitz, see Wolf, *Stamitz*, pp. 96–110 (on phrase structure in Baroque and early Classical styles), 165–77, 226–42, 293–305 (on the general characteristics of the Stamitz

ately accessible—in its time, regarded by its proponents as more "natural"—than music in the older, Baroque style.

Oratorio composers who represent the newer, early Classical direction, but who sometimes mixed the newer and older styles, include Francesco Feo (1691–1761), Leonardo Leo (1694–1744), Johann Adolf Hasse (1699–1783), Baldassare Galuppi (1706–85), Giuseppe Bonno (1711–88), Ignaz Holzbauer (1711–83), and Nicolò Jommelli (1714–74). The first three and Jommelli were trained in Naples, an important center for the newer style in both opera and oratorio, and they composed all their oratorios before 1750. As may be seen from the cities listed in appendix B, Feo, Leo, Galuppi, and Jommelli wrote their oratorios for first performances in Italy, whereas the others wrote principally for courts in German-speaking lands: Hasse mainly for Dresden, Bonno for Vienna, and Holzbauer for Mannheim. Galuppi's twenty-seven oratorios (of which only two survive in musical sources) distinguish him as among the most prolific oratorio composers of his time.

Although Feo and Leo were born only three years apart, were fellow students in Naples, and were then active as composers in that city, they adopted remarkably different approaches to the new style. In his oratorios composed between 1723 and 1734, Feo incorporates most of the early Classical characteristics mentioned above, but occasionally uses Baroque phrase structure.[58] In Leo's oratorios, on the other hand, the new tendencies are more obviously mixed with Baroque traditions.[59] This mixture is seen at times in the combination of clearly balanced phrases together with a relatively complex texture and rich harmonic vocabulary, and at other times in simple texture and harmony but melodic lines developed through a sequential, spinning-out procedure.

Hasse also mixes the old and new styles, particularly in his earlier oratorios. For instance, his *Daniello* (for Vienna, 1731), *Serpentes ignei in deserto* (Venice, ca. 1730–33), *Il cantico de' tre fanciulli* (Dresden, 1734), and *I pellegrini al sepolcro di Nostro Signore* (Dresden, 1742) all include fugal texture in their opening *sinfonie*; in the last three of these works, the fugal sections use two fugue subjects (or a subject and countersubject) and are found within movements suggesting the French overture, a Baroque form. Some arias in Hasse's *Serpentes ignei in deserto* mix Baroque texture and the new melodic style: in the arias "Incerta vivendo" and "Spera o cor," for instance, the basso continuo parts often

---

early, middle, and late symphonies, respectively). On the "Mannheim crescendo," see Wolf's pp. 298–302, and see below, chap. 3, n. 36.

58. See Feo's three works called *Oratorium pro defunctis* (1723, 1725, and 1728) and *Tobias* (1731), in F-Pc: Ms. 1955–59; and *San Francesco di Sales* (1734), in I-Vsmc. A forthcoming volume of facsimiles, Feo, *Oratorium pro defunctis**, includes two of the oratorios by that name from F-Pc.

59. See his *La morte d'Abel*, treated in chapter 3.

move in stepwise motion and in counterpoint with the voice, yet the vocal melody, especially in the former, has simple, clearly balanced phrases; in the same work, the arias "Coeli audite" and "Dolore pleni humiacentes" more consistently reveal early Classical features.[60] Perhaps the best example of early Classical style in Hasse's oratorios is his last one, *La conversione di Sant'Agostino* (Dresden, 1750).[61]

Clearly representing the early Classical style are the two surviving oratorios of Galuppi (*Adamo caduto* of 1747 and *Il sacrifizio di Jephtha* of 1749),[62] Holzbauer's single surviving oratorio (*La Betulia liberata* of 1760, revised 1774),[63] and Jommelli's four surviving oratorios all from the 1740s.[64] Rarely does one find in these works a trace of Baroque texture or phrase structure in arias, unless used for a consciously "learned" purpose.[65] In the oratorios of virtually any composer of the period, regardless of his characteristic orientation, learned style—even an extended fugue—might appear in the final choruses of parts I and II; yet operatic choruses, in simple chordal style, are also found. In the work of some composers, Jommelli for instance, a higher incidence of contrapuntal choruses in oratorio than in opera distinguishes oratorio style.

Musical sources are extant for all of Bonno's oratorios—*Eleazaro* (1739), *San Paolo in Athene* (1740), *Isacco figura del Redentore* (1759), and *Il Giuseppe riconosciuto* (1774)—and these works provide an excellent means of tracing style change within one composer and one genre.[66] The first two are clearly in the contrapuntal, late-Baroque style of Fux; the third is early Classical, and the fourth Classical. Although *Isacco* and *Giuseppe* are much alike in some respects, they differ significantly in texture and harmony, instrumentation and orchestration, and aria structures; these aspects of *Giuseppe* are more like those of composers in the next period (discussed below) than the ones treated in this section.

Despite differences in details of musical style, both late-Baroque and early Classical oratorios share the da capo form, or a slight modification

60. For sources, see the manuscripts in A-Wn: Supp. Mus. No. 2110 and a better copy in D-Mbs: Mus. Mss. 1169. For brief quotations from these arias, see Kamieński, *Hasse*, "Notenbeilagen," pp. 1–2.

61. See the treatment of this work in chapter 3.

62. The present author used copies of *Adamo* in I-Vnm: Mss. Cod. It. IV-1021 = 10794, and in I-Vsmc (no number); and of *Il sacrifizio di Jephtha* in I-Vsmc (no number). A forthcoming facsimile is Galuppi, *Adamo**.

63. I am grateful to Professor Eugene K. Wolf for having sent me a microfilm of the manuscript of this work in D-Mbs: Mus. Mss. 2288 I-II.

64. They are listed in chapter 3, together with the discussion of Jommelli's *La passione*.

65. As in Jommelli's *La passione*; see the reference in chap. 3, n. 38.

66. The music manuscripts of the first three are in A-Wn: 17054, 17060, 17088, respectively; and a manuscript of the fourth is in A-Wgm: III 7943/ Q747. A forthcoming facsimile is Bonno, *Isacco**.

of it, in arias and most ensembles. Standard in both oratorio and opera by the beginning of the century, the da capo form continued to be characteristic through the 1750s, began to wane in the 1760s, and virtually disappeared by the 1780s. The structure as commonly found in oratorios from the 1720s on is illustrated in Table II-1, where "R1," "R2," and "R3" represent orchestral ritornellos, any of which might be omitted but all are usually present; "S1," "S2," and "S3" stand for solo vocal passages; "D.C." abbreviates "da capo" (indicating a repetition of the entire A section); and "D.S." abbreviates "dal segno" (a return not to the beginning but to a sign, "§," marked at some point after the beginning).[67] The first stanza of a typical two-stanza aria text is usually sung twice (in S1 and S2) in the A section. In some arias, however, there are text repetitions within S1 and S2, and in others the first stanza is sung once only. The second stanza is usually sung once (S3) in the B section (but here, too, text repetions may occur). The A section is a binary form, with tonal motion during S1 either to the dominant (for an aria in major) or the relative major (aria in minor); S2 begins either in the tonic or in the new key but quickly returning to the tonic, and the A section closes in the tonic with a strong cadence that will eventually be the aria's final cadence. The B section tends to be shorter than A and tonally unstable, but one or two keys (often the relative minor for an aria in major) will usually be established within it. The B section usually contrasts with A; the type of contrast depends on the second stanza's affect and the composer's interpretation of it. In addition to a contrast of tonal area, the B section might contrast in orchestral scoring, meter, tempo, and melody, but at times B borrows melodic material from A. The only difference between the da capo aria and the type of dal segno shown in Table II-1 is the return to the sign, rather than to the beginning. In this case a return to the sign will effect a deletion of the opening ritornello and allow the singer to begin S1 without delay. The composer might, however, insert a few measures of preparatory ritornello (sometimes functioning as a retransition to the A section), as indicated in Table II-1 by "(R)" before the D.S.

Both of these forms, and many variants of them as well, are found in the oratorios of virtually all the composers mentioned above as representatives of late-Baroque and early Classical styles. Near the end of the period from the 1720s to the 1760s, however, composers increasingly

---

67. For more details on the forms illustrated in Tables II-1, II-2, and II-3, see Ratner, *Classic Music*, pp. 272–79 and Rosen, *Sonata Forms*, chapter 4, "Aria," pp. 27–68. For contributions relative to my discussions of those three tables, and especially Table II-3, I am grateful to the members of my graduate seminar on aria structures, given at the University of North Carolina in the fall of 1985; the students' wide-ranging exploration of and reports on the varied aria forms in early Classical and Classical works were extremely helpful.

TABLE II-I
Typical Structures of Da Capo and Dal Segno Arias

	Da Capo Aria								
Sections:	A					||	B	||	D.C.
Rit. & Solo:	R1	S1	R2	S2	R3	||	S3	||	
Major key:	I	I-V	V	*I ---------		||	new key(s)	||	
Minor key:	i	i-III	III	*i ---------		||	new key(s)	||	
Text stanzas:		1		1		||	2	||	

	Dal Segno Aria with R1 Deleted from Repeat								
Sections:	A	§				||	B	||	D.S. (§)
Rit. & Solo:	R1	S1	R2	S2	R3	||	S3	||	(R)
Major key:	I	I-V	V	*I ---------		||	new key(s)	||	(I)
Minor key:	i	i-III	III	*i---------		||	new key(s)	||	(i)
Text stanzas:		1		1		||	2	||	

*S2 often begins in V (major key) or III (minor key) and quickly returns to the tonic.

abbreviated the da capo form by using the dal segno indication in various other ways, which affect the lengths of the vocal passages. Three characteristic dal segno structures of this type have been termed "half da capo," "condensed da capo," and "quarter da capo" forms.[68] These are illustrated in Table II-2. To produce a half da capo aria, the composer writes the dal segno abbreviation after the B section and places the sign in approximately the middle of the A section, at the beginning of S2 (see the sign's location in the diagram of the half da capo aria in Table II-2); he might include a few measures of ritornello or retransition (marked "(R)" in Table II-2) after the B section to prepare the return to S2. For a condensed da capo aria the brief ritornello following B is again an option, but in this case the composer writes out S1 up to the beginning of its modulation (see S1 after section B in Table II-2), then uses the dal segno to begin at the corresponding point of S2. Thus he condenses the A section by deleting R1, the second part of S1, and all of R2, and he substitutes the beginning of S1 (written out) for the beginning of S2. The condensed da capo results in approximately the same degree of abbreviation as the half da capo but is used when the S2 section begins in the "wrong" key (V instead of I, or III instead of i) or begins with melodic

68. This terminology is used in Downes, "Johann Christian Bach," pp. 390–412.

TABLE II-2
Half, Condensed, and Quarter Da Capo Arias

Half Da Capo Aria

	A			$\S$		B		D.S. ($\S$)
Sections:	A			$\S$		B		D.S. ($\S$)
Rit. & Solo:	R1	S1	R2	S2	R3	S3	(R)	
Major key:	I	I-V	V	*I - - -		new key(s)	(I)	
Minor key:	i	i-III	III	*i - - -		new key(s)	(i)	
Text stanzas:	1			1		2		

Condensed Da Capo Aria

	A			$\S$		B		D.S. ($\S$)
Sections:	A			$\S$		B		D.S. ($\S$)
Rit. & Solo:	R1	S1	R2	S2	R3	S3	(R) S1	
Major key:	I	I-V	V	V - - I - -		new key(s)	(I) I	
Minor key:	i	i-III	III	III - I - -		new key(s)	(i) i	
Text stanzas:	1			1		2		1

Quarter Da Capo Aria

	A			$\S$		B		D.S. ($\S$)
Sections:	A			$\S$		B		D.S. ($\S$)
Rit. & Solo:	R1	S1	R2	S2	R3	S3	(R) S4	
Major key:	I	I-V	V	V - - I - -		new key(s)	(I) I	
Minor key:	i	i-III	III	III - I - -		new key(s)	(i) i	
Text stanzas:	1			1		2		1

*S2 often begins in V (major key) or III (minor key) and quickly returns to the tonic.

material other than that of S1. In the quarter da capo aria, again a brief ritornello might be used after the B section, but this time the composer will write a new vocal setting (marked "S4" in Table II-2) of the beginning of the first stanza, in the tonic key, and then use the dal segno for a return to the point at which S2 reaches the tonic key; this procedure is similar to that for the condensed da capo, except for the new music, S4, which substitutes for the beginning of S1 and precedes the dal segno. The structures presented in Tables II-1 and II-2 are those most frequently encountered in this period, but they are often modified. Detailed analysis of individual arias from this period reveals myriad adaptations of these forms to a multitude of text types and dramatic purposes; and other forms, including binary and through-composed, are occasionally found.

Holzbauer's *La Betulia liberata* (performed in Mannheim, 1760 and 1774, and in Vienna, 1761) provides examples of all three of the dal segno forms listed in Table II-2.[69] None of the twelve arias in this work is of the full da capo type, but five are half da capo arias and five condensed, and two have quarter da capo form. The only extant source of this work appears to date from 1774.[70] It is not known whether Holzbauer used the dal segno indications to modernize his work for the late performance or whether the forms as we see them were in the original version; if they were, the work would be exceptional for the total absence of the full da capo form. Such abbreviations of da capo form, rare in oratorios of the mid-century, become increasingly prominent in the 1760s and 1770s. In her study of oratorios performed at the Chiesa Nuova in Rome, Johnson found only occasional abbreviations of the da capo form among oratorios between 1740 and 1765, but in those between 1765 and 1790, the da capo is totally replaced, at first by abbreviations using the dal segno indication, and then by other forms.[71]

Most recitative in oratorios from the 1720s to the 1760s is in simple style accompanied by the continuo alone. Early in the period, recitative accompanied by the orchestra, and in Italy usually called "obbligato" recitative, appears only once or twice per oratorio, at particularly important points in the libretto.[72] By the end of the period, however, oratorios tend to include as many as four or five obbligato recitatives;[73] and these become even more important after the 1760s.

A significant aspect of change in oratorios during the course of the century is the structure of the introductory instrumental number (sinfonia or overture) at the beginning of part I—the only instrumental number in most oratorios. Introductory pieces are usually motivically independent of the work as a whole. Oratorios largely in Baroque style will often begin with either a French overture or an Italian three-movement sinfonia with the tempo sequence fast-slow-fast and with binary forms in all three movements. Early Classical oratorios usually begin with an Italian sinfonia, but exceptionally an opening piece is in two movements or only one.[74] A one-movement introductory piece in binary or sonata

69. I am grateful to Mr. Steven M. Shearon for having made available to me his unpublished study of the work's aria forms.

70. See above, n. 63, for location of the source. Professor Eugene K. Wolf has kindly written to me his conclusion, on the basis of staving and watermarks, that the score, mostly autograph, represents the revised (new) version of 1774.

71. Johnson, "Oratorio," pp. 287–90, 345–46.

72. As in Leo's *La morte d'Abel*, with one obbligato recitative; see the discussion of that work in chap. 3.

73. The works by Hasse and Jommelli, treated in chapter 3, have five such recitatives each.

74. Both the Hasse and Jommelli works treated in chapter 3 have one-movement opening pieces.

form becomes increasingly prominent late in this period and in the following one.

The main changes in instrumentation and orchestration between the 1720s and 1760s are in the varieties and uses of wind instruments. In works essentially in Baroque style, the winds, usually grouped in pairs, play a strictly subsidiary role, doubling strings or playing harmonic support, except on the rare occasions when they are used in a concertato capacity; the same applies to the earliest works in the new style. The winds (still used in pairs) are treated with greater independence as separate sections, or families, in the orchestra late in this period and more frequently in the next.

From the 1760s to the 1780s

Oratorios produced in this period represent early Classical and Classical styles, which differ primarily in texture and harmony, instrumentation and orchestration, and aria structures. In the Classical style homophonic textures are activated by accompanying lines of greater melodic and contrapuntal interest; the *Trommelbass* is less prominent; the number of real parts increases; the orchestra is larger, the viola part is more frequently independent of the bass line, and the wind instruments are often independent of the strings; the harmonic vocabulary is richer, with more frequent, complex modulatory excursions away from a prevailing tonal area; da capo arias are rare, but dal segno arias comparable to those illustrated in Table II-2 are frequently used, as are "transformed" da capo arias (discussed below); and the brief cavatina occasionally replaces the aria as a solo number.

Most of the composers who represent this style were born between the 1720s and the 1750s. Among the more important figures who wrote oratorios for Italy, some of which survive in musical sources, are: Ferdinando Bertoni (1725–1813), whose nearly fifty oratorios, mostly for the Mendicanti in Venice, make him probably the most prolific oratorio composer of the eighteenth century and whose *David poenitens* is treated in chapter 3; Pasquale Anfossi (1727–97), most of whose twenty-two oratorios were composed for the Congregation of the Oratory in Rome and whose works reflect the changes in style from the 1760s to the 1790s;[75] Antonio Sacchini (1730–86), whose eight Italian and Latin oratorios were composed for Bologna, Venice, and Rome;[76] Wolfgang Amadeus Mozart (1756–91), whose only traditional Italian oratorio,

75. For comments on Anfossi and his oratorios, see Johnson, "Oratorio," pp. 174–89, 287–387 passim, and 392–434. Forthcoming facsimiles are Anfossi, *Giuseppe** and Anfossi, *Betulia**.
76. A forthcoming facsimile is Sacchini, *Esther**.

La Betulia liberata, was commissioned for performance in Padua, completed in 1771, but apparently never performed;[77] and Josef Mysliveček (1737–81), a Bohemian active mainly in Italy (known there as "il divino boemo") who wrote four oratorios, including *Isacco figura del Redentore* (for Florence, 1776, performed in Munich, 1777, as *Abramo ed Isacco*) of which Mozart wrote in that year, "all Munich is talking about his oratorio *Abramo ed Isacco*, which he produced here."[78] The works from the 1760s and some from the 1770s (such as that just mentioned, composed by the fifteen-year-old Mozart) reveal a blend of early Classical and Classical style traits, whereas most works from the 1770s and 1780s are more clearly Classical in style. Less important than the abovementioned composers but one who has attracted some scholarly attention is Luigi Gatti (1740–1817), who wrote four oratorios dating from the 1770s to the 1790s, two of which were for Mantua and Brescia.[79]

Outside of Italy, Vienna and Dresden were of special importance for the Italian oratorio. In Vienna, the concert series established by the Tonkünstler-Societät (discussed in chapter 1), significant for the cultivation of Italian oratorio especially in its first decade, included oratorios by some of the best composers of this period, most of whom were active in Vienna. A few of the Italian oratorios included in the first decade of Societät concerts were: *La Betulia liberata* (performed in 1772 for the inaugural concert of the series), the only oratorio by Florian Gassmann (1729–74), who founded the Society;[80] *La liberatrice del popolo giudaico, ossia l'Ester* (hereafter called *Ester*, performed in 1773), by Carl Ditters von Dittersdorf (1739–99), the composer of three oratorios in Italian and one in Latin;[81] *Il Giuseppe riconosciuto* (1774), by Giuseppe Bonno; *Il ritorno di Tobia* (1775, treated in chapter 3), the only Italian oratorio by Joseph Haydn (1732–1809); *La passione di Gesù Cristo* (1777), one of at least four Italian oratorios by Antonio Salieri (1750–1825); *La passione di Gesù Cristo* (1778), the only Italian oratorio by Joseph Starzer (1726 or 1727–87). All of these and most of the other Italian oratorios performed on this series use librettos essentially of the Metastasian type and are in Classical style.[82] A notable exception to the Metastasian oratorio is Mozart's *Il Davidde penitente* (K. 469, per-

77. Cf. the "Vorwort," by Luigi Ferdinando Tagliavini, to Mozart, *Betulia liberata**, p. VII.

78. Translated from letter of W. A. Mozart to L. Mozart, 11 October 1777, in *Mozart Briefe*, 2:46, letter 347. A forthcoming facsimile is Mysliveček, *Passione**.

79. Gehmacher, "Gatti."

80. A forthcoming facsimile is Gassmann, *Betulia**.

81. A forthcoming facsimile is Dittersdorf, *Ester**.

82. For complete lists of works performed at concerts of the Tonkünstler-Societät, see Hanslick, *Concertwesen*, pp. 30–35; and Pohl, *Tonkünstler-Societät*, pp. 43–68.

formed by the Societät in 1785), a one-part work with a reflective text, no personages, and music largely adapted from his mass K. 427/417a.[83]

Johann Gottlieb Naumann (1741–1801) was the principal composer of Italian oratorios in Dresden after Hasse's departure. Of his eleven works in this genre between 1767 and 1801, all but one were for the Dresden court. Of special interest for understanding the changes in oratorio style and form from the early Classical 1760s to the Classical 1780s are Naumann's two completely different settings of Metastasio's *La passione*, the first written for Padua in 1767 and the second for Dresden in 1787.[84] Among Naumann's younger Dresden contemporaries who composed Italian oratorios in Classical style are Joseph Schuster (1748–1812, four oratorios) and Franz Seydelmann (1748–1806, three oratorios).

In works of this period arias are still composed in various abbreviations of the da capo form, chiefly those shown above in Table II-2, but they tend to be longer. Often the first stanza of the text is sung twice in S1 and twice in S2, rather than once each (as in Table II-2), and a brief ritornello might follow each repetition of that stanza.

In addition to the modifications of da capo form previously treated, a new approach to the aria results in a structure that is hereafter called the "transformed da capo aria." As illustrated in the first two schemes of Table II-3, in writing a transformed da capo aria of the A1-B-A2 type, the composer uses neither da capo nor dal segno signs; instead, he rewrites the first A section, A1 in Table II-3; the rewritten version is labeled A2 in the table.[85] The first A1 section no longer has a "closed" tonal scheme (as in the da capo and dal segno forms) but remains "open," for it ends in the dominant (in major) or the mediant (in minor). Sometimes A1 has a tonal plateau in the new key (as shown in the table) and is thus tonally comparable to the exposition in a sonata form; at other times A1 is tonally more like the first section in a binary form that does not firmly establish the new key until the end of its A section. As with the traditional da capo form, the first stanza of the text might be sung twice, once each in S1 and S2 (see the first scheme in Table II-3), or only once in the A1 section; following the new tendency to expand, however, the first stanza might be sung twice each in S1 and S2. Another possibility for A1, but one less frequently used, is illustrated in the second and third schemes of the same table: both stanzas of the aria text are sung in A1, the first in S1 and the second in S2. Some of the ritornellos indicated in the Table II-3 might be omitted (as they might be in da capo

83. For a modern edition, see Mozart, *Davidde penitente** (an edition has not yet appeared in the Mozart *Neue Ausgabe sämtlicher Werke*).

84. The sources for both works are in D-Dl: Mus. 3480/D/7 (1767 setting) and Mus. 3480/D/6 (1787 setting). A forthcoming facsimile of both is Naumann, *Passione**. For a comparison of these settings, see Troutman, "Naumann."

85. For arias that use the schemes shown in Table II-3, or modifications of them, see the works discussed in chapter 3 by Bertoni, Haydn, and Guglielmi.

TABLE II-3
Some Schemes of Transformed Da Capo Arias

A1-B-A2 Form: Stanza 1 in A1, Stanza 2 in B

Sections:	A1					B	A2				
Rit. & Solo:	R1	S1	R2	S2	R3	S3	R1	S1	R2	S2	R3
Major key:	I	I-V	V	V - - - - -		new key(s)	*I ----------------------				
Minor key:	i	i-III	III	III - - - -		new key(s)	*i ----------------------				
Text stanzas:		1		1		2	1				

A1-B-A2 Form: Stanzas 1 and 2 in All Sections

Sections:	A1					B	A2				
Rit. & Solo:	R1	S1	R2	S2	R3	S3	R1	S1	R2	S2	R3
Major key:	I	I–V	V	V - - - - -		new key(s)	*I ----------------------				
Minor key:	i	i-III	III	III - - - -		new key(s)	*i ----------------------				
Text stanzas:		1		2		1 and 2	1		2		

A1-A2 Form: Stanzas 1 and 2 in Both Sections

Sections:	A1					A2				
Rit. & Solo:	R1	S1	R2	S2	R3	S1	R2	S2		R3
Major key:	I	I-V	V	V - - - - -		*I --------------------				
Minor key:	i	i-III	III	III - - - -		*i ----------------------				
Text stanzas:		1		2		1		2		

*Occasionally A2 begins in another key and quickly returns to the tonic.

and dal segno arias), and R1 in A2 is usually omitted. The A1 section could, however, have as many as five ritornellos (some quite brief), if they are used between stanza repetitions within S1 and S2.

The B section of the transformed da capo aria is often fully comparable to that of the traditional da capo or dal segno aria, with the same elements of contrast, and with the usual statement of the second stanza in S3. Yet the B section at times suggests the greater tonal instability of the development section in a sonata form;[86] and when the B section

---

86. Cf. Charles Rosen's discussion of "the partial transformation" of what he calls the "trio section" (his questionable designation for the B section of a da capo aria) "into a more dynamic relation to the whole form" in Rosen, *Sonata Forms*, p. 67. In Hunter, "Haydn's Aria Forms," p. 54, the B section is called the "development section," a term Hunter uses (recognizing its frequent need for

derives some of its melodic material from A1, the comparison with a development section becomes even closer. The second formal scheme shown in Table II-3—which, however, is infrequently found—uses both the first and second stanzas, with some of their original motives, in the B section; this procedure makes a comparison between the B section and a development section even more apt. Nevertheless, one rarely finds in B sections the kinds of motivic manipulation and the textural devices that characterize most development sections in instrumental works.[87]

The A2 section is entirely in the tonic, except for a possible brief beginning in another key (as shown in Table II-3) and for local excursions to other keys; thus A2 suggests a sonata-form recapitulation. In a remarkable number of instances, however, A2 begins as quite a free recapitulation, with a text setting that bears only a vague resemblance to that at the beginning of A1; but, in accord with what Edward Cone has called "sonata principle," the second half of A2 tends to be a more faithful recapitulation (in the tonic) of the last part of A1 (originally in the new key).[88]

The third formal scheme illustrated in Table II-3 is one that omits the B section. Its A1 and A2 sections have the characteristics of the second formal scheme in the same table. In the transformed da capo aria of the A1-A2 type, R3 will sometimes function as a retransition to A2; at other times a brief vocal retransition, with words selected from either the first or the second stanza, or with appropriate, newly invented exclamations, will precede and prepare for A2. The A1-A2 form is roughly comparable to the instrumental form variously termed "sonata form without development," "abridged sonata form," "sonatina form," "slow-movement form," or "exposition-recap form."[89]

The structural type illustrated in the first two schemes of Table II-3 has been called a "sonata-form," "modified da capo," or "compressed da capo" aria, but it is better described as a "transformed da capo" aria.[90] The dal segno arias illustrated in Tables II-1 and II-2 are all modifica-

---

qualification) for "non-specific reference to the longer central sections of most arias" in Haydn's operas.

87. For B sections of Haydn's arias that are said to be much like instrumental development sections, see Hunter, "Haydn's Aria Forms," p. 195, Table 6:1, and pp. 203–4.

88. According to Cone, *Musical Form*, pp. 76–77, "the sonata principle . . . requires that important statements made in a key other than the tonic must either be re-stated in the tonic, or brought into a closer relation with the tonic, before the movement ends."

89. On these terms, see Hunter, "Haydn's Aria Forms," pp. 53, 55; Rosen, *Sonata Forms*, p. 28; LaRue, Review of Rosen, *Sonata Forms*, p. 563, n. 5.

90. Before arriving at this conclusion, I used the term "sonata-form aria," but with qualification, in Smither, "Haydns *Il ritorno di Tobia*," p. 173 and n. 26. The term "sonata form" is used throughout Hunter, "Haydn's Aria Forms"; "sonata form with central trio section," in Rosen, *Sonata Forms*, p. 56; "modi-

tions and compressions of the da capo aria, and all retain the essential ternary features of that form: the A section closing in the tonic, B contrasting with A, and the exact repetition of all or part of A (via the da capo or dal segno indication). The first two schemes in Table II-3, on the other hand, represent a transformation of da capo form—a transformation, indeed, for its character has been radically changed. Tonally it is no longer a ternary form. The tonality arches from the tonic at the beginning, through the new key at the end of A1 and one or more new keys in B, to the return to the tonic in A2. This tonal arch integrates the previously separate sections of the da capo aria into a tonal whole; in respect to tonal integration, the transformed da capo aria is similar to sonata form, as suggested above, and clearly resulted from the application of the same principles of tonal organization that led to sonata form. Whether those principles developed first in instrumental or in vocal music would be virtually impossible to establish; they may have been applied to both at about the same time.

Despite the similarity of organizing principles, however, the sonata form and the transformed da capo aria have different antecedents and sometimes different emphases; they are best distinguished today by different terms. The transformed da capo takes its point of departure from a convention of vocal music: the setting of a two-stanza text intended for da capo form. Many of the same Metastasio aria texts—and Metastasian texts by other poets—that had often been set in da capo or dal segno forms came to be set as transformed da capo arias. Within the context of both oratorios and operas, the transformed da capo aria functioned exactly as the da capo aria had done—and, indeed, as the dal segno aria continued to do. Sonata form has been described as a "synthesis of a three-part design and a two-part tonal structure";[91] although the same may be said of some transformed da capo arias, often their three-part design is much more prominent than is that of sonata form. This prominence is especially striking when B contrasts with A1 and A2 in affect of text and in musical style (at times written in a new tempo and meter) and stands in bold relief against A1 and A2.[92] In such cases, the character of the B section asserts the traditional tripartite aspect of the structure more than do most development sections in sonata forms;[93] such arias may be

fied da capo," in Downes, "Johann Christian Bach," pp. 413–14; and "compressed da capo," in Ratner, *Classic Music*, pp. 276–79.

91. James Webster, "Sonata Form," *New Grove*, 17:489.

92. See the example in Rosen, *Sonata Forms*, pp. 57–66, from Mozart's *Zaide*, "Tiger, wetze nur die Klauen," in which the B section changes to Larghetto and 3/8 time and strongly contrasts with the Allegro and C of A and A'.

93. In Ratner, *Classic Music*, p. 279, the relationship of an aria with this type of B section to the older, tripartite, da capo aria is recognized: "When the middle section of a compressed [i. e., transformed] *da capo* aria is set in a different style and tempo than that of part I, the traditional effect is retained—the contrast of two sentiments."

called tonally binary only with the proviso that an important "parenthesis," the B section, intervenes between the tonally open A1 and the closed A2.

The A1-A2 aria scheme, shown third in Table II-3, is reasonably interpreted as yet another transformation of the da capo form. This transformation is effected by both tonal integration and the removal of the B section.

Although the aria forms already mentioned are those most prominent in this period, numbers called "cavatina" sometimes take the place of arias. Various structures are labeled "cavatina," but that word seems most often used for a number with a short, one-stanza text, set in simple style and binary form, roughly approximating the A section of a da capo form or the A1-A2 form.[94] Occasionally numbers called arias are in simple binary, rondo, or through-composed forms. Ensembles, duets in particular, tend to be set in modifications of the various forms used for arias.

The proportion of obbligato recitative to simple style tends to increase in oratorios during the course of the eighteenth century.[95] As mentioned above in reference to the previous period, an oratorio from the 1720s or 1730s might include one or two obbligato recitatives, whereas one from the mid-century might have as many as four or five. From the 1760s to the 1780s the tendency to increase further the number and length of such recitatives is notable. Haydn's *Tobia*, for instance, includes eight long obbligato recitatives. Yet considerable variation persists among oratorios in the number and length of such recitatives: Mozart's *Betulia* includes only two, and the works by Anfossi sung at the oratory in Rome include between one and five.[96]

The increase in the number of ensembles and choruses in this period has already been treated in the discussion of the oratorio libretto, and the structures of ensembles, as mentioned above, are similar to those of arias. The general trend to increase the number of choruses departs from the Metastasian libretto and was favored by some composers who wrote works for the concerts of the Tonkünstler-Societät, where the performing forces were large. One such work is Dittersdorf's *Ester*, which includes seven choruses; Haydn's *Tobia* included only three in its original version, but the composer added two more for the 1784 revival (see Table III-5). The original three included choral alternations with an ensemble of soloists (personages in the drama), a combination that becomes increasingly prominent in the period. Choruses tend to include both chordal homophony and imitative counterpoint, and at times have extended fugues, as do the final choruses for parts I and II of Haydn's *Tobia* and the

94. For two examples, see nos. 4 and 10 in Bertoni's *David*, discussed in chap. 3.

95. Cf. Johnson, "Oratorio," pp. 329–36.

96. Cf. the descriptions of Anfossi's oratorios in ibid., pp. 392–434.

central chorus in part I of Dittersdorf's *Ester* ("Fra le sventure estreme"); yet the choruses in some oratorios of the time are in simple, chordal, operatic style throughout, as are those in Bertoni's *David poenitens*.

The sinfonia of an oratorio in the Classical style tends to be either a three-movement piece as are those for early Classical oratorios or a one-movement sonata form, sometimes with a slow introduction. The three-movement sinfonia may have been more prevalent in Italy in this period.[97] In Vienna, however, the one-movement sinfonia (often called an overture) seems to have been favored: every oratorio mentioned above as having been performed in concerts of the Tonkünstler-Societät during the 1770s (as well as Bertoni's *David*) has this type of sinfonia. Yet in 1772 when Hasse revised his *Sant'Elena al Calvario* (originally composed for Dresden in 1746) for a concert in this series, he retained a three-movement sinfonia. An interesting feature of Haydn's *ouverture* (his term) for *Tobia* is the motivic relationship between the slow introduction and the first chorus, a relationship seldom found in introductory pieces for oratorios in this period. Somewhat more frequent, and found in the Haydn work, is a direct connection, without pause, between the end of the one-movement sinfonia and the beginning of the oratorio's part I.

From the 1780s to ca. 1820

After a history of more than a century and a half as an important Italian vocal genre, the oratorio enters a period of decline in frequency of performance and in social and musical significance. The growing importance of the *opera sacra* as a Lenten theatrical work—considered a type of oratorio in this late period—is symptomatic of the musical, social, and religious changes that render the traditional, unstaged, Italian oratorio obsolete. Nevertheless, some of the best composers of Italian opera still wrote traditional oratorios, as well as staged ones, in which they introduced some of the musical styles and structures of contemporary serious opera.

Among the most notable changes in the musical structure and style of oratorio are those that reflect the concomitant modifications of the Metastasian libretto (discussed above): ensembles and choruses become more numerous, important, and dramatically conceived; solo-choral and ensemble-choral numbers become more frequent and longer, particularly at the beginnings and endings of the two parts; the final number of an oratorio occasionally reveals the influence of the comic-opera finale.[98] Recitatives tend to be shorter and more often set in obbligato style. On the whole, the pattern of alternation between recitative and aria is retained, but passages of simple and obbligato recitative are increasingly

97. Cf. ibid., pp. 302–9.

98. For a discussion of the choruses and ensembles (including the ensemble finale) in this period, see ibid., pp. 377–87.

mixed with other solo styles (arioso, cavatina, aria) and with ensembles or choruses to form larger and more varied musical units. The da capo aria is totally abandoned, and the dal segno is rare. Continuing to appear in this period are the transformed da capo aria (but sometimes drastically modified) and the cavatina, but other forms are used with increasing frequency: the rondo, the "two-tempo" aria (slow-fast, comparable to the cantabile-cabaletta of nineteenth-century opera), and the short, through-composed aria. With some composers the melodic style of arias tends to be simpler, with fewer elaborate coloratura passages; recitative style is sometimes introduced into arias. Changes in instrumentation and orchestration are particularly striking, and orchestral color is more fully exploited to reinforce the dramatic effect: the brass and woodwind sections are larger and more prominent (clarinets become standard and trombones begin to appear), and the harp is occasionally introduced. As in both opera and instrumental music of the time, so also in oratorio the range of dynamic level is increased, and dynamics are combined with orchestral scoring to create more striking dramatic effects than are characteristic of the previous period.

Some of the composers mentioned above in relation to the previous period lived on into this one and continued to write traditional oratorios in essentially Classical style but introduced some of the new structural and stylistic features. Among them are Anfossi in Rome (in the 1790s), and Naumann, Schuster, and Seydelmann in Dresden. Anfossi's *Il figliuol prodigo* (1792) and *La morte di San Filippo Neri* (1796) were mentioned in the section on the libretto for their emphasis on ensembles and choruses.[99] *Il figliuol prodigo* also includes several two-tempo arias, a through-composed aria, and a long solo complex (beginning at "Che pena inaspettato"), which moves through obbligato, simple, and obbligato recitatives, then to a cavatina, another obbligato recitative, and an aria. In the same work the trio "Mille larve" represents the new dramatic trend by including contrasting sentiments for the three singers, whose melodic lines contrast as well. Of the three Dresden composers mentioned above who continue to compose in an essentially Classical style but whose works also suggest nineteenth-century technique, Seydelmann is especially noteworthy for his setting of Metastasio's *La morte d'Abel* (for Dresden, 1801). Highly effective for its powerful, dramatic approach to both the orchestral and vocal writing, this oratorio has been called "not only the most significant work that Seydelmann ever wrote, but also one of the most significant works that were produced by the entire Hasse school after Hasse's death."[100]

99. The information on the Anfossi works is based on ibid., pp. 398–406.

100. Cahn-Speyer, *Seydelmann*, p. 99: " . . . ist nicht nur das bedeutendste Werk, das Seydelmann überhaupt geschrieben hat, sondern auch eines der bedeutendsten Werke, die von der ganzen Hasseschen Schule nach Hasses Tod

Among the composers who more fully represent the newer, late-Classical (and even early Romantic) styles and forms are Pietro Alessandro Guglielmi (1728–1804), Giovanni Paisiello (1740–1816), Domenico Cimarosa (1749–1801), Niccolò Antonio Zingarelli (1752–1837), Simon Mayr (1763–1845), Ferdinando Paer (1771–1839), Francesco Morlacchi (1784–1841), and Gioacchino Rossini (1792–1868).[101] Although Guglielmi was of the same generation as many composers who worked mainly in early Classical and Classical styles, his *Debora e Sisara* (libretto by Carlo Sernicola), first performed as a staged work in Naples at the Teatro San Carlo during Lent of 1789, became one of the most famous works of its kind, performed in both staged and unstaged versions throughout the late-eighteenth and early nineteenth centuries. Although the aria forms of this work are conservative, the dramatic approach of its libretto and musical style are characteristic of the time. Most of Paisiello's five or six oratorios were written for Naples after 1787, but the one which was best known, and was widely performed throughout Europe, is a setting of Metastasio's *La passione* (1783), written for St. Petersburg. Paisiello set Metastasio's text with few changes, yet the setting reflects new approaches to oratorio composition: the arias show relatively little relationship to the old da capo, dal segno, or A1-B-A2 forms described above; the vocal style tends to be simple, yet includes an occasional coloratura passage; and the numerous obbligato recitatives, often with elaborate orchestration, help to negate an impression of old-style alternation between recitatives and arias. Similar tendencies are found in Cimarosa's *Il sacrifizio di Abramo* (first staged, Naples, Teatro San Carlo, 1786) in the version used at the Roman Oratory in 1795. In varying degrees and ways the new styles described above are to be found in Zingarelli's *Gerusalemme distrutta* (Naples, 1794), which was widely performed throughout Europe in both staged and unstaged versions (as at the Roman Oratory, 1796). Morlacchi's two oratorios, both composed for Dresden, are settings of Metastasio's *La passione di Gesù Cristo* (1812) and *Isacco figura del Redentore* (1817); the second of these was said to have been one of his best works.[102] Rossini's only oratorio is *Mosè in Egitto: azione tragico-sacra*, first staged at the Teatro San Carlo

---

hervorgebracht worden sind." Cahn-Speyer discusses the work at some length on pp. 99–102 and provides some long and convincing musical examples on pp. 260–301.

101. Johnson, "Oratorio," comments on oratorios by Guglielmi (p. 539), Paisiello (pp. 588–97), Cimarosa (pp. 466–93), and Zingarelli (pp. 623–33). The only detailed studies that exist of oratorios by the composers in this list, however, are those of Rossini's *Il Mosè*. A forthcoming facsimile is Paisiello, *Passione**.

102. For historical but not analytical information on this work see Ricci des Ferres-Cancani, *Morlacchi*, pp. 59–61 and 110–11.

during Lent of 1818, revised for a performance in the same theater in 1819, used as the basis of his *Moïse et Pharaon* (first performed at the Paris Opéra in 1827), and widely performed throughout Europe as a sacred opera, but rarely as a traditional unstaged oratorio.[103] This work, which well represents the end of the Classic style and turn to the early Romantic, also represents the high point and virtually the end of the Neapolitan staged oratorio, or sacred opera.

103. For a facsimile of the autograph manuscript, see Rossini, *Mosè**; for a list of librettos attesting to the widespread performances of this work and the French version between 1818 and 1835, see the text-critical study, Gossett, "Operas of Rossini," pp. 421–29; Gossett treats the other sources of the work on pp. 394–420. Among the historical and critical writings on this work are the following: Conati, "Rossini," 394–429 (a text-critical study of *Il Mosè*); Isotta, "*Mosè*"; and Isotta, *Rossini*.

Selected Italian Oratorios

The six works treated in this chapter represent the Italian oratorio from the early to the late-Classical styles, both in Italy and north of the Alps. Leo's oratorio, originating in Italy, reveals a mixture of Baroque and new, early Classical styles; Hasse's, composed in Dresden, is early Classical but not quite up to date for a mid-century work; but Jommelli's, written for Rome, reveals traits that more fully represent the mid-century. Bertoni's oratorio, composed for a Venetian conservatory, shows a mixture of early Classical and Classical styles; Haydn's, composed for the Tonkünstler-Societät in Vienna, is Classical and one of the best oratorios of its time; and Guglielmi's, probably the most popular work of its kind in the late eighteenth and early nineteenth centuries, reveals the direction that Neapolitan oratorio and sacred opera were taking in the late-Classical period just before the Italian oratorio's demise.

Leonardo Leo: La morte d'Abel

One of the leading Neapolitan composers of opera and sacred music in his day, Leonardo Leo (1694–1744) studied in Naples with Nicola Fago (1677–1745) at the Conservatorio della Pietà dei Turchini.[1] As a student he composed two sacred operas in 1712 and 1713,[2] and he began his professional career as an opera composer in 1714. From 1720 on, he

1. For biographical surveys and brief discussions of Leo's music, see: Helmut Hucke, "Leo," *MGG*, 8:cols 622–30; Hucke, "Leo," *New Grove*, 10:666–69; and Pastore, *Leo*. A critical survey of writings about Leo is found in Hardie, "Leo," pp. 3–43.

2. *S. Chiara, o L'infedeltà abbattuta* (1712), *Il trionfo della castità di S. Alessio* (1713). In Pastore, *Leo*, pp. 15 and 95, the second of these works is called an oratorio. Yet according to the printed libretto (in I-Nn: 73.A.28 [3]) the work neither functioned as nor had the structure of an oratorio. It was in the usual three acts of the Neapolitan sacred dramas performed in the conservatories and was done as an opera, with five stage sets.

LEONARDO LEO MRO DI CAPPELLA NAPOLITANO

FIGURE III-I. Leonardo Leo (1694–1745).
(Anonymous oil painting in I-Bc.)

composed at least one serious opera virtually every year, and in many years one or more comic operas as well.

In addition to his reputation for opera, Leo was highly regarded as a composer of church music and oratorios. Skilled in contrapuntal techniques, he wrote several didactic works, and late in life became interested in the reform of church music. He is known to have composed at least six oratorios, but the musical sources of only three fully authenticated works are extant: *Oratorio per la SS. Vergine del Rosario* (1724?; Naples, 1730), and two settings of Metastasio texts, *Sant'Elena al Calvario* (Naples 1732 or Bologna 1734) and *La morte d'Abel* (Naples, ca. 1732–

34, or Bologna, 1738).[3] That the two works with Metastasio texts exist in numerous manuscript copies throughout Europe (unlike most of Leo's operas) attests to their considerable popularity.[4] Leo's music is conservative in comparison with that of his Neapolitan contemporary Leonardo Vinci.[5] His *Abel* well illustrates a blend of the old and new styles found in many Italian oratorios of the 1720s and 1730s.

Leo sets Metastasio's *Abel* in complete and virtually unmodified form.[6] The cast of characters consists of Abel (S), Cain (T), Eve (A), Adam (B), an Angel (S) and a Chorus (SATB). As mentioned in chapter 2, in this libretto as in *Isacco* the title role is portrayed as a figure of Christ. In part I Abel is presented as the good shepherd, who knows and values his flock and whose flock knows him. Because Abel's sacrifice of a lamb was so pleasing to God, Cain becomes insanely jealous of his brother. An Angel (as an emissary of God) urges Cain to realize his faults and confess his sins, and Abel tries to make peace with Cain. By the end of part I, however, Cain sees himself as surrounded by those who have turned against him—his brother, mother, and father—but at Eve's insistence upon a reconciliation with Abel, he feigns a change of attitude. Eve

3. Conflicting and questionable dates are found in the literature for these three oratorios: cf. Hell, *Opernsinfonie*, pp. 554, 560, and 564; Hucke, "Leo," *New Grove*, 10:688; and Pastore, *Leo*, pp. 96, 100. For title pages of librettos printed for performances of *La morte d'Abel*, see app. A: *L'Abele* (Bologna, 1739) and *La morte d'Abelle* (Florence, 1738). The other three oratorios, surviving only in printed librettos, are *Dalla morte alla vita di S. Maria Maddalena* (Atrani, near Amalfi, 1722), *S. Francesco di Paola nel deserto* (Lece, 1738), *Il verbo eterno e la religione* (Florence, 1741, lib. by C. F. Taviani). On another oratorio, *Saul e Gionata*, attributed to Leo in a manuscript in D-LEm, see Wolff, "Leo"; Hucke, in "Leo," *New Grove*, 10:688, considers the work of doubtful authenticity.

4. As late as 1783 in Berlin Johann Freidrich Reichardt performed in a Concert spirituel a large portion of Leo's *La morte d'Abel* and wrote glowingly of the work. See his remarks quoted in Carl Friedrich Cramer's *Magazin der Musik*, 1 (Hamburg, 1783): 568–73; for more on the same work, see ibid., 2/1 (1784–85): 135–42.

5. On the conservatism of Leo's operas, see Hardie, "Leo," p. 76; Hucke, "Leo," *MGG*, 8:626; and Hucke, "Leo," *New Grove*, 10:667.

6. The source used for this study is the manuscript in I-Nf: MS 420.4, in which only an occasional word deviates from Metastasio's text. For a modern arrangement (called an *elaborazione*) by Giuseppe Piccioli, see Leo, *Abel**-P1, and Leo, *Abel**-P2. The arrangement (in which no sources or editorial changes are indicated) differs in numerous respects from the manuscript used by the present writer: notes are different, slurs and dynamics are added, instrumentation is changed, tempo marks are modified, for some da capo arias only the first A section is supplied, large cuts (of recitatives and arias) are made, and some sections are recomposed—all of which drastically alter the work's structure and style. The recording conducted by Carlo Felice Cillario (issued by Musica Sacra, AMS 21 STE; and The Musical Heritage Society, MHS 1743–44) is based on Piccioli's arrangement. A forthcoming facsimile is Leo, *Abel**-F.

rejoices, but Adam is uneasy, for he sees the calm in Cain's face belying a tempest in his breast. The final chorus of part I is a peroration on envy and a prayer for defense against it.

In a brief soliloquy at the beginning of part II, Cain decides that his brother must die, for the false peace with him is unbearable. When Abel enters, Cain addresses him as "dear brother." He says he is about to go to the field to offer a sacrifice to God, and asks Abel to accompany him. Before the brothers leave, Eve appears, and they tell her where they are going. As the Christ figure, yet unaware that he is the victim, Abel tenderly takes leave of his mother. After their departure Eve weeps for joy at Abel's tender words, but Adam is worried that the two brothers have gone into the field together. Eve sees Cain in the distance, and wonders why he is returning so soon and alone. Then she is shocked to see him covered with blood. The Angel asks Cain where his brother is. After Cain's reply ("Am I my brother's keeper?") the Angel furiously decrees his punishment. Cain laments, as does Eve, for she has lost both her sons. Cain sees no hope for pity, but Eve counters that divine pity is greater than any fault of ours. When Adam approaches, bearing the body of Abel, Eve's impassioned description of the scene suggests portrayals of Jesus' descent from the Cross. In the oratorio's final recitative Adam has a vision of the future in which he sees a new Abel whose bloodshed will save humanity. Like the final choruses of most Metastasian librettos, this one has a moralizing text but is more strongly penitential and self accusing than most. Each of us has a part in the crime: we detest the ways of the impious, yet we tread that path; we abhor Cain, yet we do not see him in us.

The outline of the work in Table III-1 shows its tonal structure as reflected in its sinfonia, arias, and choruses. Both final choruses are in D, although the opening sinfonia is in G. In part I, all arias but that of Cain (which reveals his tormented state) are in major keys, but in part II, in which the tragedy occurs, the only aria in major is that of the Angel whom Metastasio has placed significantly in the center of each part. In part I, nos. 5–7 are related as V-I-I in the main key of the oratorio. On the whole, however, affect may have been a more important criterion than tonal symmetry for Leo's selection of keys in this work.

The instruments (as designated in the manuscript source examined for these comments) consist of strings, oboes, and horns—the winds never play concertato parts.[7] The opening sinfonia, the only instrumental number in the oratorio, is in three movements, the first of which uses some traditional Baroque conventions but combines them in an unusual manner. The movement unfolds through the alternation of two textural and thematic units, shown in Examples III-1a and III-1b, in which A ap-

7. In Leo, *Abel**-P1, pp. 43–50, Cain's aria "Alimento il mio proprio tormento," the obbligato solo part for oboe is not in the source, which states, for that aria, "oboè di ripieno," indicating that the oboes double the violins.

TABLE III-I
Leo, *Abel*: Structural Outline

Numbers	Keys
[Sinfonia]	G
PART I	
1. Aria. Abel, "Quel buon pastor son io"	B♭
2. Aria. Eva, "Qual diverrà quel fiume"	G
3. Aria. Caino, "Alimento il mio proprio tormento"	c
4. Aria. Angelo, "Con gli astri innocenti"	F
5. Aria. Abel, "L'ape e la serpe spesso"	A
6. Aria. Adamo, "Con miglior duce"	D
7. Coro, "O di superbia figlia"	D
PART II	
8. Aria. Abel, "Questi al cor fin ora ignoti"	f
9. Aria. Adamo, "Dunque si sfoga in pianto"	g
10. Aria. Eva, "Dall'istante del fallo primiero"	d
11. Aria. Angelo, "Vivrai, ma sempre in guerra"	C
12. Aria. Caino, "Del fallo m'avvedo"	f
13. Aria. Eva, "Non sa che sia pietà"	e
14. Coro, "Parla l'estinto Abelle"	d-D

proximates the opening of a French overture, and B (in the same tempo) begins as a two-part canon and continues in a light, contrapuntal texture. The formal structure of the movement, with tonal centers indicated, is approximately:

$$\begin{array}{ccccc} A & B & A' & B' & A'' \\ \text{G: I - V/V} & \text{v - II} & V & i & I \end{array}$$

The second movement, in 6/8 time and E minor (without tempo mark but probably slow), features a simple texture with the melody in the first violins accompanied by the other strings playing pizzicato. The sinfonia closes with a dancelike allegro in G major and 3/8 time.[8] The second and third movements, less Baroque in style than the first, exhibit early Classical texture, simple harmony, and periodic melody especially at their beginnings, as does Example III-2, the beginning of the third movement.

All the arias have da capo form, the same tempo in both sections, and orchestral accompaniment (as opposed to continuo only). All but two (nos. 9 and 11) begin with instrumental ritornellos, and in both exceptions the personage who finishes the preceding recitative also sings the aria—unlike Hasse's normal practice when the ritornello is omitted (see

8. The last movement is marked 3/8 but barred in 6/8.

EXAMPLE III-1. *La morte d'Abel*—Leo (I-Nf: MS 420.4, ff. 1v, 2v–3).

Example a:

Example b:

below, n. 24). Four of the six arias in major keys move to the relative minor in the B section (nos. 1 and 4–6), which is a frequent practice in the time;[9] three of the six in minor move to the relative major (nos. 9, 10, and 13) and two to the dominant minor (nos. 8 and 12). In most of the arias the character, if not always the melodic material, of the B section is similar to that of the A; in the few exceptions the musical contrast in B is related to the contrasting affect in the text. One such exception, number 2, is a comparison aria in which the first stanza (A section, see Example 3a) speaks of a river with turbulence at its source; Leo paints the wave images in both the orchestral and vocal lines. In the second stanza (B section, Example III-3b), which dwells on the misery of

9. Cf. Strohm, *Opernarien*, p. 220.

EXAMPLE III-2. *La morte d'Abel*—Leo (I-Nf: MS 420.4, f. 9).

(In the source, beginning at measure 3, bar lines are written as in 6/8 time.)

Eve's sons, the turbulent wave motion in G major gives way to a lyrical, pathetic expression in G minor.

Like the sinfonia, the arias show a mixture of old and new styles. Usually beginning with a clear, periodic structure, the arias often continue, particularly in melismatic sections, with lines "spun out" in Baroque fashion. As in the new style, the vocal line dominates and is frequently doubled—exactly or in modified form—by the first violin or another orchestral part; but the active continuo and rich harmonic vocabulary reflect older practice. Examples III-3 through III-5 are characteristic. Example III-3a shows a grouping of short, balanced phrases, but an active accompaniment, which, in this instance, paints the text. Closer to traditional Baroque practice is Example III-3b with its sequential treatment and syncopation for rhetorical effect in the vocal line and its chromatic inflections in the bass. The torment of Cain is reflected in Example III-4 (from no. 3 in Table III-1) by a restless rhythmic style and active continuo, which show little relationship to the early Classical style.[10] In Example III-5 (from no. 6) the periodic structure and simple accompaniment suggest the new style, yet the descending bass line is

10. The word *arioso* in that example is found in the source at the beginning of the continuo line, where all tempo marks are placed. The word designates the character of performance, and has nothing to do with the structure of the number, which is a da capo aria.

EXAMPLE III-3. *La morte d'Abel*—Leo (I-Nf: MS 420.4, ff. 25–25v, 30v).

Example a:

What will become of that river, in its long course, . . .

EXAMPLE III-3. continued

Example b:

My miserable sons! Ah, one sees expressed . . .

EXAMPLE III-4. *La morte d'Abel*—Leo (I-Nf: MS 420.4, ff. 33–33v).

EXAMPLE III-4. continued

I feed my own torment . . .
(In the source, 3/8 time signature but bar lines as in 6/8.)

contrapuntal in conception. Perhaps it is also extramusical, symbolizing the idea of "miglior duce" ("better leader") or the "primo sentier'" ("the first path" of righteousness, which Adam says Cain has lost). The aria closest to early Classical style is illustrated in Example III-6 (from no. 8), Abel's final aria, before he and Cain depart. The simplicity of texture continues throughout, but the periodicity at times dissolves into a "spinning out" procedure.

The arias are all preceded by recitatives, which with only one exception are in simple style, without vocal melismas or strongly marked rhythmic patterns. The single obbligato recitative highlights the dramatic point, near the end of part II, at which Eve angrily dismisses Cain in utter frustration and then sees Adam approach, carrying the body of Abel; this recitative begins in simple style, but instruments are added as the dramatic tension increases.

Both choruses begin with a powerful statement in unison and octaves and then alternate chordal and imitative styles; and both close with fugal sections. Whereas the final fugue of the first chorus is brief, that of the last chorus is unusually extended for an Italian oratorio. It is in the style of the choruses that this oratorio is least like an opera.

EXAMPLE III-5. *La morte d'Abel*—Leo (I-Nf: MS 420.4, ff. 55–55v).

With the better leader in the long journey, so that a ray of light remain with you, [return to the first path, now lost].

(In the source, bar lines as in 4/2 time.)

EXAMPLE III-6. *La morte d'Abel*—Leo (I-Nf: MS 420.4, ff. 74v–75).

EXAMPLE III-6. continued

mo- ti   non in- ten-   do, e non sa-   pre-   i

Violone

These internal motions of my blood, hitherto unknown to my heart, I do not understand, and I would not know...

Johann Adolf Hasse: La conversione di Sant'Agostino

Among the most significant opera composers of his time, Johann Adolf Hasse (1699–1783) was born in northern Germany where he also received his first training and began his professional career.[11] He spent most of the 1720s in Italy, primarily in Naples where he studied with Alessandro Scarlatti and became highly successful as a composer for the Neapolitan stage. From the 1730s he traveled frequently and widely but lived mostly in Dresden, Venice, and Vienna. His principal position, held from 1730 to 1763, was that of Kapellmeister at the musically celebrated electoral court in Dresden. He composed more than sixty operas during the half-century 1721–71, at least eleven oratorios between 1730 and 1750, and many sacred and instrumental works, intermezzos, and cantatas.

The first three of Hasse's oratorios were composed in the early 1730s for performances in Vienna at the imperial court chapel and in Venice at the Ospedale degl'Incurabili; his subsequent oratorios were written for the Dresden court.[12] The two works for Venice have texts in Latin (nor-

11. On Hasse and his oratorios and operas, see: Sven Hansell, "Johann Adolf Hasse," *New Grove*, 8:279–93; Kamieński, *Hasse*; Millner, *Hasse*; and the foreword by Arnold Schering to Hasse, *Sant'Agostino**, pp. III–XII.

12. *Daniello* (Vienna, 1731; lib. Zeno; 2 pts.); *Serpentes ignei in deserto* (Venice, ca. 1730–33; lib. B. Bonomo; 1 pt.); *S. Petrus et S. Maria Magdalena* (Venice, ca. 1730; 1 pt.); *Il cantico de' tre fanciulli* (Dresden, 1734; lib. S. B. Pallavicino; 2 pts.); *Le virtù appiè della croce* (Dresden, 1737; lib. Pallavicino; 1 pt.); *Giuseppe riconosciuto* (Dresden, 1741; lib. Metastasio; 2 pts.); *I pellegrini al sepolcro di Nostro Signore* (Dresden, 1742; lib. Pallavicino; 2 pts.); *La caduta di Gerico* (Dresden, 1743; lib. G. C. Pasquini; 2 pts.); *La deposizione dalla croce*

mal for oratorios in Venetian conservatories), and these plus one oratorio for Dresden are exceptionally brief and in one part. Otherwise Hasse set texts of the Metastasian type. The music of his oratorios is much like that of his operas and represents the main stream of Italian music in those genres from the 1730s to at least the early 1760s. Of the same generation as Leo, Hasse better typifies the early Classical style in his oratorios than does Leo, although Hasse's early oratorios show some evidences of the continuing Baroque tradition, as mentioned above in chapter 2. Hasse's oratorios were performed throughout Europe, in both Roman Catholic and Protestant centers. The most widely disseminated of his oratorios appear to have been *I pellegrini al sepolcro di Nostro Signore*,[13] *Sant'Elena al Calvario*,[14] and the work selected for special consideration below, his last oratorio, *La conversione di Sant'Agostino*.[15]

Maria Antonia Walpurgis (1724–1780), the librettist of *Sant'Agostino*, was the daughter of Elector Karl Albert of Baveria.[16] Just three years before writing the libretto she had married Friedrich Christian, later the elector of Saxony, and had moved to Dresden. Important in Dresden as a patroness of artists and musicians, she was also a singer, keyboard player, and poet, and in 1747 she became a member of the Arcadian Academy. She based *Sant'Agostino*, her first major work, on a five-act Latin Jesuit play, *Idea perfectae conversionis sive Augustinus*, by Franz Neumayr (1697–1765), a work first performed in Munich in 1739.[17] The theme of her libretto, the conversion of a sinner to sainthood, had been common for oratorios since the seventeenth century,[18]

---

di Gesù Cristo salvatore nostro (Dresden, 1744; lib. Pasquini; 2 pts.); *S. Elena al Calvario* (Dresden, 1746; lib. Metastasio; 2 pts.); *La conversione di S. Agostino* (Dresden, 1750; lib. M. A. Walpurgis; 2 pts). The above list is based on that of Hansell, "Hasse," *New Grove*, 8:289. Locations are given for first performances of first versions only. For information on revisions, see Hansell's list. Five additional oratorios attributed to Hasse are of doubtful authenticity.

13. Available in modern edition (made from manuscript in D-Dlb: Mus. 2477-D-14) by Michael Koch from Deutsches Musikgeschichtliches Archiv Kassel. For information see "Mitteilungen," *Die Musikforschung* 36 (1983): 64.

14. A forthcoming facsimile is Hasse, *Sant'Elena**.

15. The following comments are based on the edition by Arnold Schering: Hasse, *Sant'Agostino**, which takes into consideration the principal manuscript sources.

16. For biographical information on her, with bibliography and comments on this oratorio, see Yorke-Long, "Maria Antonia" and Arnold Schering's foreword to Hasse, *Sant'Agostino**, pp. VI–VIII.

17. Printed in Neumayr's *Theatrum asceticum, sive meditationes sacrae in theatro Congregationis Latinae B. V. Mariae . . . Exhibitae Monachii, Verni Jejunii Tempore ab Anno 1739. usque ad Annum 1747 . . .* (Ingolstadt: August Vindel, 1747), pp. 1–172. For a detailed comparison of Neumayr's play and this oratorio, see Kamieński, *Hasse*, pp. 195–98.

18. Cf. Smither, *Oratorio*, 1:300.

but the style and structure of her work were modeled largely on Metastasio's oratorios. In fact, Metastasio played an editorial role in the libretto, which Maria Antonia had sent him. He returned it with praise and did not change the general structure but only details: he modified some of the grammar and word order, changed some verses, and revised for clarity and concision.[19] Surely because the librettist was a royal princess, special pains were taken in printing the libretto. For the oratorio's first performance—on Holy Saturday, 28 March 1750, at four o'clock in the afternoon in the Dresden court chapel—copies of the libretto were printed in Italian only, Italian and German on facing pages, and Italian and Polish (unusual even in Dresden, the residence of the Polish king).[20] Her libretto also had the distinction of being translated into German by Johann Christoph Gottsched.[21]

The libretto's personages are St. Augustine (A); Simpliciano (T), a priest; Monica (S), Augustine's mother; Alipio (A), a friend of Augustine; Navigio (B), Augustine's brother; a Voice (S); and a Chorus. As the oratorio begins, Simpliciano is trying to console Monica who despairs that Augustine will ever change his wicked ways and who weeps and prays for her son. In the course of part I, Simpliciano, Monica, Alipio, and Navigio describe by intense, colorful, and at times metaphorical rhetoric Augustine's inner conflict between good and evil and try to persuade him to reform. He would like to change and knows he should, yet he finds worldly pleasures so enticing that he cannot. He sees no hope. The final number of part I, a chorus in alternation with Monica and Alipio together, draws on the Crucifixion theme—for in Dresden oratorios were Holy-Week pieces—by praying that the Divine Blood not be shed in vain for Augustine. At the beginning of part II, Monica is in agony over the turmoil of her son, but Simpliciano and Alipio are sure that Augustine will win his struggle against evil. The dramatic climax (unlike anything in an oratorio by Metastasio) is achieved through a convention of the stage—indeed, a *deus ex machina*: at the mid-point of part II, Simpliciano, Monica, and Navigio withdraw to observe Augustine during a recitative soliloquy.[22] As her son struggles, Monica grows fearful and does not want him to be left alone, but suddenly he cries out to God for help. A Voice responds: "Take, take and read." He finds in his hands "the book of the apostle to the gentiles" (in the Neumayr play, the

19. See the letter, Metastasio to Baron Wetzel, 17 January 1750, quoted in Kamieński, *Hasse,* pp. 193–94.

20. A contemporary announcement of the first performance is cited in Kamieński, *Hasse,* p. 191. A libretto of 1750 entirely in Italian is in D-B: Mus. Th 247; librettos with Italian and German, and with Italian and Polish on facing pages are in D-KNth: OT Dresden.

21. Kamieński, *Hasse,* p. 193.

22. The "stage" action for the withdrawal is printed in the libretto: "Si ritriano tutti in disparte." Similarly, the exits are marked, "parte," following exit arias throughout the libretto.

book is explicitly Paul's Epistle to the Romans, chapter 13); he reads, achieves a sudden revelation, is overwhelmed with joy, and sings an aria of repentance, "Or mi pento, oh Dio." Apparently out of hiding now, Simpliciano warns Augustine that he may be deceiving himself, but Augustine is certain of his conversion. Monica and others rejoice for him. Simpliciano sings a recitative and final aria, exhorting all unhappy souls to follow Augustine's example and drawing on the theme of the Crucifixion. The oratorio closes with a chorus of praise that urges every timid heart to value the example of Augustine's conversion.

The oratorio's structure is shown in Table III-2. Tonal planning in this work seems to have been carefully done for a combination of structural and affective reasons. The main tonal center is B-flat, the key of the *Introduzione* and final chorus. The first and last numbers of part I are in the dominant (nos. 5–6 relate as I-V), and part II opens in the subdominant and closes in the tonic (nos. 10–11 relate as V-I). Most other keys are closely related to B-flat. The two arias in more distantly related sharp keys, numbers 3 and 9, may be in those keys for reasons of affect, for both have optimistic texts: number 3 speaks of the hope one may have in God and number 9 of Augustine's newly discovered love of God. Affects of pathos—weeping, anguish, emotional turmoil—characterize virtually all the other arias, the single exception being the priest's exhortation, number 10, which, as the penultimate number, is logically in a key close to the work's tonal center. The only aria in minor—again surely for affective reasons—is number 4, Augustine's expression of remorse, doubt, and suffering.

The instrumentation consists of strings, pairs of flutes, oboes, horns, and bassoons, plus continuo.[23] The woodwinds usually double the strings; the horns, in the few numbers that include them, fill in the harmony. In two arias (nos. 1 and 8), however, the flutes have concertato parts, possibly for affective purposes, as both arias have tearful texts. The *Introduzione* is in one movement marked "Allegro non troppo però, ma con molto spirito" and is written in an active, energetic rhythmic style suggestive of the concerto. Much of the time the *Introduzione* proceeds with simple, relatively slow harmonic rhythm and sparse, two-part texture (with much doubling of upper and lower voices). The final cadence is immediately followed by a four-note transition in the continuo, which connects the *Introduzione* to the opening simple recitative.

Only three of the arias (nos. 1, 7, and 10) have the full da capo form, and all three are sung at important structural positions: Monica's arias begin parts I and II, and Simpliciano's is the last aria of the oratorio, his priestly exhortation. For all others Hasse uses the dal segno sign and always for the same purpose: to delete the opening ritornello by placing the sign just after it. In each dal segno aria the B section is followed by a

23. For the number of manuscript orchestral parts that Schering saw in the Königliche Bibliothek in Dresden, see Hasse, *Sant'Agostino*, p. XIII.

TABLE III-2
Hasse, *Sant'Agostino*: Structural Outline

Numbers	Keys
Introduzione	B♭
PART I	
1. Aria. Monica, "Piangerò, ma figlio amato"	F
2. Aria. Alipio, "Sento orror del tuo delitto"	E♭
3. Aria. Simpliciano, "Non abbandona mai Iddio"	A
4. Aria. Agostino, "Il rimorso opprime il seno"	c
5. Aria. Navigio, "Come fra venti insani"	B♭
6. Coro, Monica, Alipio, "Inspira o Dio"	F
PART II	
7. Aria. Monica, "Ah, veder gia parmi il figlio"	E♭
8. Aria. Alipio, "Piange, e quel pianto avviva"	C
9. Aria. Agostino, "Or mi pento, oh Dio"	D
10. Aria. Simpliciano, "A Dio ritornate"	F
11. Coro, "Si lodi il Ciel pietoso"	B♭

brief orchestral retransition to the key of the A section. This retransition incorporates material from the opening ritornello and thus substitutes for it. In four arias (nos. 3, 7, 8, and 10) Hasse begins the B section in the same key as the A, and introduces the contrasting key only after one or more phrases of B. Only three of the arias in major keys move to the relative minor for the B section (nos. 2, 5, and 10); the aria in minor (no. 4) moves to the relative major. In four arias (nos. 1, 3, 7, and 9) the B section contrasts with A in both tempo and meter. In most of the arias Hasse uses for the B section melodic material that is related to or virtually the same as that of A, and he does so in two of the arias that have contrasting meters and tempos (nos. 3 and 9). For instance, in Example III-7 (from no. 9, Augustine's aria of penitence), the vocal line at the beginning of the B section (Example III-7b) is a variant of that at the beginning of S1 in the A section (Example III-7a). The only aria that begins without an opening ritornello is number 1, in which Monica responds to Augustine, who concludes the preceding recitative.[24]

The balanced phrase structure and gentle melodic curves in the vocal lines of Example III-7 are characteristic of this oratorio as a whole and of Hasse's later style in general. Although his phrase and period structures are frequently not simple groupings of 2 + 2 or 4 + 4 measures, he is careful to relate phrases in such a way as to convey a feeling of balance.

24. According to Millner, *Hasse*, p. 41, in Hasse's operas this is the usual context of an aria without a ritornello.

EXAMPLE III-7. *Sant'Agostino*—Hasse (Hasse, *Sant'Agostino**, pp. 96–97).

Example a:

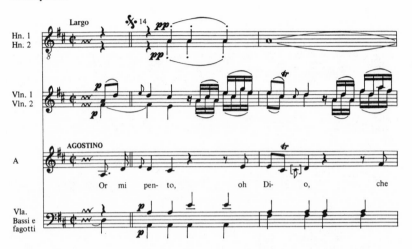

Now I repent, oh God, that [I began] so late to love Thee . . .

EXAMPLE III-7. continued

Example b:

Ah piteously consent [to give] me one of Thy tender glances . . .

For instance, in Example III-8, the beginning of the oratorio's first aria, the melodic contours and rhythmic patterns in the first nine measures of the vocal line suggest the groupings: 3, 1 + 1, and 2 + 2 (elided with next group); and measures nine through fifteen: 4 + 3. Example III-9, the beginning of the first vocal section in Simpliciano's final aria, is typical of early Classical style for its triplets and Lombardic rhythms, in addition to its balanced phrasing and repetition of one-measure motives.[25] Even in setting the text of a stormy comparison aria with an image of "insane winds," Hasse maintains his structural balance, as may be seen in Example III-10. Throughout the oratorio Hasse's word painting is secondary to phrase balance and smooth vocality of line: he avoids extremes of contrast. Examples III-7 through III-10 well illustrate the textures of the

25. Hasse's phrases of three two-measure groups (as suggested at the beginning of this example) in his operas is noted in ibid., p. 211.

EXAMPLE III-8. *Sant'Agostino*—Hasse (Hasse, *Sant'Agostino**, pp. 12–13).

EXAMPLE III-8. continued

EXAMPLE III-8. continued

I shall weep, but beloved son, how much more, because of your fate, will you make me weep thus?

EXAMPLE III-9. *Sant'Agostino*—Hasse (Hasse, *Sant'Agostino**, pp. 109–10).

EXAMPLE III-9. continued

Return to God, forsake error: love merits being demonstrated to you; . . .

EXAMPLE III-10. *Sant'Agostino*—Hasse (Hasse, *Sant'Agostino**, p. 51).

EXAMPLE III-10. continued

As in insane wind the sea moans in agitation: . . .

oratorio's arias: the vocal line reigns supreme and the orchestra, with its delicate and simple accompanying material, rarely intrudes. One of the orchestral parts usually doubles the vocal line, as in all the examples but III-8, where the voice is not doubled at the beginning but briefly exchanges motives with the flute in measures 9–12. The harmonic rhythm of the arias is slow and the bass lines are simple, often with repeated notes, as seen particularly in Example III-8, but the *Trommelbass* (long series of repeated notes, usually eighth notes, in the bass), so popular in the mid-century, is scarcely suggested in this work.

The simple recitatives tend to be traditional with syllabic text setting and long notes in the continuo, but occasionally the continuo punctuates with sudden bursts of quick notes for text emphasis and painting. At the ends of several simple recitatives a tempo mark (adagio or largo) is indicated to provide a metrical close, but melismas are rare. *Sant'Agostino* reflects a growing interest in obbligato recitative: five sections of recitative are in this style, and four of them begin as simple recitatives to which instruments are added as the dramatic tension increases. Among these four is the climactic conversion scene, a complex of simple and obbligato recitative that illustrates several of Hasse's procedures. In Example III-11a (the beginning of Augustine's soliloquy), the continuo provides rhythmic punctuation in the first three measures, simple harmonic support in the next four, and text painting (for the word "onde," waves) in the last two. In Example b, the Voice (of God) is introduced by strings in unison and octaves, and, in the return to simple style that follows, the continuo puncutates with an ascending run. In

EXAMPLE III-11. *Sant'Agostino*—Hasse (Hasse, *Sant'Agostino**, pp. 86–87, 89, 90–91, 93–94).

Example a:

Oh violent remorse! Everything accuses me. In every flower so vile in the evening, and in the morning so beautiful, I find the image of my vain pleasure. From every sublime wave . . .

EXAMPLE III-11. continued

Example b:

Take, take and read, Augustine! I am to take and read!

Example c:

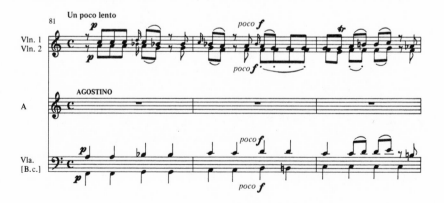

EXAMPLE III-II. continued

Oh infinite goodness. Clearly now I know, only your mercy . . .

Example d:

EXAMPLE III-11. continued

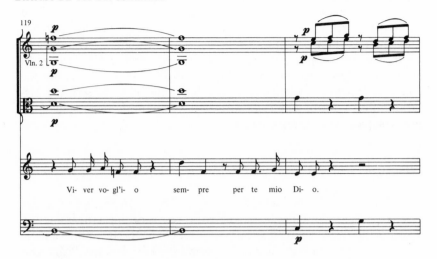

My promises let earth and Heaven hear: I want to live always for Thee, my
God. From this instant . . .

Example c, Augustine reads silently during sigh motives in the strings,
and then he proclaims his newly found faith to a background of sustained strings. And in Example d, he begins to make promises to God,
with accompaniments first of short chords, then of an ascending run in
the violins to paint "Ciel" (Heaven), then of sustained chords, and finally of strings punctuating with repetitions of an ascending motive.

The first of the two choruses includes the soloists Monica and Alipio.
The chorus has a binary structure comparable to the A section of a da

capo aria. The soloists begin each main section, and their material is then repeated and extended by the chorus in a combination of imitative and chordal texture. The final chorus is longer and more complex, and has four sections corresponding to four segments of the text. The sections are in different tempos and alternate between duple and triple meter. As in the first chorus this one mixes chordal and imitative texture, but the final section, allegro, is a short fugue (clearly the most conservative element of the oratorio) with *colla parte* orchestration; the beginning of the fugue is quoted in Example III-12.

Nicolò Jommelli: La passione di Gesù Cristo

Born in Aversa, a few miles north of Naples, Nicolò Jommelli (1714–74) received his early training there with the director of the cathedral choir, Canon Muzzillo.[26] From 1725 he was a student in Naples at the Conservatorio di Sant'Onofrio, where his teachers were Ignazio Prota and Francesco Feo, and from 1728 he studied at the Conservatorio della Pietà dei Turchini with Nicola Fago, Giovanni Sarcuni, and Andrea Basso. Leo, Hasse, and Vinci, active composers in Naples during Jommelli's student years, probably influenced his musical style. From 1737 when he began his professional career until 1754 he was active mainly in Italy as a composer of opera but also of sacred music, oratorio, and works in other genres. His positions included that of maestro di cappella at the Ospedale degl'Incurabili in Venice (from 1742 or 1743 to 1747)[27] and maestro coadiutore of the papal chapel in Rome. In 1749 he composed and produced two operas in Vienna that were successful and were highly praised by Metastasio. From 1754 to 1769 he served as the Oberkapellmeister at the court of Karl Eugen, the duke of Württemberg, in Stuttgart, where he increasingly departed from traditional *opera seria* practices. Among the traits of his Stuttgart operas are a more flexible format than the Metastasian one of alternating recitatives and arias, and an increase in the number of ensembles, choruses, obbligato recitatives, and programmatic orchestral pieces. Jommelli spent his late years in Naples, where his new style was little appreciated. From 1769 he also consistently supplied music to the Lisbon court, which was enthusiastic about his late operas.

The most authoritative list of Jommelli's oratorios and sacred cantatas

26. For a detailed but out-of-date biography, see Abert, *Jommelli*; more up to date but brief treatments are McClymonds, *Jommelli*, pp. 1–17, and idem, "Jommelli," *New Grove* 9:689–95.

27. The date 1743 is given in most sources for the beginning of his tenure at the Incurabili, but a libretto of his oratorio *Isacco* (Venice, 1742; copies in I-Mb and Vcg) first noted in Cauthen, "Jommelli," p. 3, n. 6, identifies him as the *maestro di cappella* of that Ospedale.

EXAMPLE III-12. *Sant'Agostino*—Hasse (Hasse, *Sant'Agostino*, pp. 121–22).

And if you wish to be strong, everyone is strong . . .

includes sixteen such works.[28] According to the earliest extant printed
librettos, their dates lie between 1740 and 1755, and all were first performed in Naples, Palermo, Pistoia, Rome, or Venice. Of the approximately nine pieces that seem best classified as oratorios rather than cantatas, musical sources of only four, settings of Metastasio texts, are
extant: *Isacco figura del Redentore* (Venice, 1742), *La Betulia liberata*
(Venice, 1743), *Gioas* (Venice, 1745, Latin translation as *Joas* by G. B.
Visino), and *La passione di Gesù Cristo* (Rome, 1749).[29] The premieres

28. McClymonds, "Jommelli," *New Grove*, 9:694. For a study of Jommelli's
oratorios, see Cauthen, "Jommelli."

29. On the classification of Jommelli's works as either oratorios or cantatas,
see Cauthen, "Jommelli," pp. 5–7. The manuscript source in I-Ac of *Gioas*,
attributed to Jommelli, is of doubtful authenticity, according to ibid., pp. 126–
31. If the manuscript is not *Gioas* by Jommelli but by another composer, the
number of musical sources of Jommelli's oratorios is reduced to three. A volume
of facsimiles including Jommelli's *Betulia* and *Passione* is Jommelli, *Betulia**.

FIGURE III-2. Nicolò Jommelli (1714–74). (Anonymous oil painting in I-Bc.)

of the first two of these took place at the Venetian oratory (of the Congregation of the Oratory), attached to the church of Santa Maria della Consolazione, called "Santa Maria della Fava"; *Gioas* [*Joas*], at the Ospedale degl'Incurabili while Jommelli was the maestro di cappella there; and *La passione*, in Rome.[30]

30. For more information on the first performances of these four works and on subsequent performances, see Cauthen, "Jommelli," pp. 8–15. See app. A for the

Jommelli's *La passione* was commissioned by Cardinal Henry Benedict, Duke of York, who was a grandson of King James II, the last Stuart king of England. During the cardinal's exile in Rome he became one of the city's important patrons of the arts. The printed libretto for the first performance is lost, and the place and occasion of the premiere are unknown; the oratorio may have been performed in the cardinal's residence or his church, Santa Maria in Campitelli.[31] *La passione* is extant in more manuscript sources than any of Jommelli's other oratorios and appears to have been more widely performed than the others. Surviving printed librettos testify to numerous performances in Italy from its origin until 1780, as well as performances in London (1770), Prague (1765, 1767), Copenhagen (1775), and Lisbon (1786); the work was among the few eighteenth-century oratorios in any language to be printed in score, and it is the only complete vocal work listed in the Breitkopf manuscript catalogue.[32]

Metastasio's first libretto for Vienna, *La passione*, dates from 1730 and was first set to music by Caldara. Jommelli set the libretto without change. The personages are Peter, (T), John (A), Magdalene (S), Joseph of Arimathea (B), and a Chorus of Followers of Jesus (SATB).[33] Part I begins with a recitative and aria by Peter (text quoted in full in chapter 2), which expresses his anguished confusion and remorse after his denial of Jesus. Peter then sees a group of Jesus' followers approaching; the chorus addresses disconsolate humanity: "How great the price of your sins." Magdalene, John, and Joseph were apparently a part of the group that approached, for Peter, who was absent from the Crucifixion, now begins to ask them about it. The remainder of part I consists of reflections—recitatives, arias, and a duet—on the Passion story as Peter's questions are answered. The language is intense, at times harsh and gory. By the end of part I the Passion story has been told; the final chorus interprets the Crucifixion, and closes with the thought, "The slaughter of the Redeemer brings salvation to the just and death to the wicked." Part II begins with another question by Peter: "And is the deceased Lord still unburied?" Joseph explains that Jesus was buried in a sepulchre of stone. Peter wishes to visit it, but Magdalene stops him, for the sun is setting, the seventh day is for rest, and John adds that the sepulchre will be guarded. The personages reflect on the wickedness of those who tortured

---

title page of a libretto for a performance in Rome, 1755, of *La passione di Gesù Cristo signor nostro*.

31. For more details and bibliography, see ibid., pp. 12–13.

32. For a list of performances, see ibid., p. 14; the score was printed in London by Robert Bremner, ca. 1765–70, the years of the London performances (cf. bibliography, Jommelli, *Passione**); for locations of manuscript sources, see McClymonds, "Jommelli," *New Grove* 9:694; and for the Breitkopf catalogue listing, see Brook, *Breitkopf*, cols. 298–99.

33. In the published version, Jommelli, *Passione**, the part of Joseph is transposed up an octave and notated in the treble clef.

and crucified Jesus, and on the terrible vengeance that hangs over "un-faithful Jerusalem." There follow several detailed prophesies of and re-flections on the destruction of Jerusalem, after which John turns to thoughts of the many figures of Christ throughout the Old Testament and reflects that God is found everywhere. Magdalene feels lost without Jesus, abandoned without a guide, but Peter counters that they are not abandoned, for Jesus left them with thousands of examples to imitate. After the soloists express their certainty that Jesus will arise and triumph over death, the final chorus confirms their hope, which "blossoms amidst our tears and teaches us, on the uncertain paths of human life, to trust in Heaven's help."

The structural outline of the oratorio is shown in Table III-3.[34] The main tonal center is E-flat, the key of the overture and of the endings of parts I and II.[35] The tonal centers in the last two numbers of part I relate as V-I. (The final chorus of part I ends on the dominant, for rhetorical effect; see below.) Flat keys predominate: of the sixteen vocal numbers plus the overture, ten are in flat keys, six in sharp keys, and one in C major. The two arias in D major (nos. 4 and 10) both have texts of rage. The aria with possibly the most exalted verses in the entire libretto—verses quoted in chapter 2, referring to an omnipresent and omnipotent God—is the only aria in E major (no. 13).

The oratorio is scored for strings, flutes, oboes, horns, and continuo; the winds are never used as solo instruments, but in pairs they at times take part in dialogues with the strings or voice. The overture is unusual for its first movement, which is influenced by French-overture style but has neither the structure nor tonal arrangement of the French overture:

	A	B	A′	B′	A″
No. of meas.:	4	17	3	21	3
Key, E♭:	I	I-V	V	V-I	I

The brief A sections, marked adagio e staccato, have dotted rhythms as at the beginning of a French overture; the B sections, allegro moderato, begin imitatively but continue in homophonic texture. Of special interest in the B section is an early instance of the so-called "Mannheim cre-

34. The main source used for for the following discussion of the music is the print, Jommelli, *Passione**, which has been verified by reference to the manu-script, GB-Lbl: Add. 14136. A modern piano-vocal version that includes most of the arias but not the overture, duet, or choruses, is Jommelli, *Passione**(pv).

35. For a discussion of the tonal centers in Jommelli's oratorios in relation to those of his operas and to theoretical comments of the time, see Cauthen, "Jommelli," pp. 16–26; see Cauthen's pp. 22 and 26 for an argument that the key of E-flat is of special significance in Jommelli's works and may have been chosen because of its appropriateness for a Passion. According to Hell, *Opern-sinfonie*, p. 378, n. 111: "Die Tonart *Es-Dur* ist innerhalb der in der vorlie-genden Arbeit behandelten Sinfonien ein Einzelfall."

TABLE III-3
Jommelli, *La passione*: Structural Outline

Numbers	Keys
Overture	E♭
PART I	
1. Aria. Pietro, "Giacchè mi tremi in seno"	F
2. Coro, "Quanto costa il tuo delitto"	g
3. Aria. Maddalena, "Vorrei dirti il mio dolore"	E♭
4. Aria. Giuseppe, "Torbido mar, che freme"	D
5. Aria. Giovanni, "Come a vista di pene"	c
6. Aria. Maddalena, "Potea quel pianto"	G
7. Aria. Pietro, "Tu nel duol felice sei"	C
8. Duetto. Pietro, Maddalena, "Vi sento, oh Dio"	B♭
9. Coro, "Di qual sangue"	E♭ (closes on V)
PART II	
10. Aria. Giovanni, "Ritornerà fra voi"	D
11. Aria. Giuseppe, "All'idea dei tuoi perigli"	E♭
12. Aria. Pietro, "Se la pupilla inferma"	A
13. Aria. Giovanni, "Dovunque il guardo giro"	E
14. Aria. Maddalena, "Ai passi erranti"	F
15. Aria. Pietro, "Se a liberarsi"	G
16. Coro, "Santa speme, tu sei ministra"	E♭

scendo" (see Example III-13), which appeared earlier in some of Jommelli's works than in the symphonies of Mannheim composers.[36] In Example III-13 the crescendo is indicated (in mm. 16–18) by abbreviations for *piano* (P), *rinforzando* (rinf), and *forte* (f, or fe). With its *Trommelbass*, sustained horns, and rising violin line with repeated figures, this passage is characteristic of the context in which Jommelli and others soon after him used the orchestral crescendo. This example reflects one facet of the newest instrumental style in the mid-century, a style absent from Hasse's oratorio examined above. The second movement of the overture is a simple allegro in 3/8 time and early Classical style, with a binary form.

Of the twelve arias all but three have da capo form, which makes the work structurally (but not stylistically) more conservative than Hasse's *Sant'Agostino*. In the three arias for which Jommelli used the dal segno

36. For full discussions and bibliography of the orchestral crescendo, see Wolf, *Stamitz*, pp. 231–39 and 298–302, and Hell, *Opernsinfonie*, pp. 354–67. Hell (p. 364) and Wolf (p. 235) give the Italians, and especially Jommelli, credit for priority in using the orchestral crescendo, as found in Jommelli's sinfonia to *Artaserse* (1749); the passage quoted in Example III-13, contemporaneous with *Artaserse*, was first noted in Cauthen, "Jommelli," pp. 78–80.

EXAMPLE III-13. *La passione*—Jommelli (Jommelli, *Passione**, pp. 1–2).

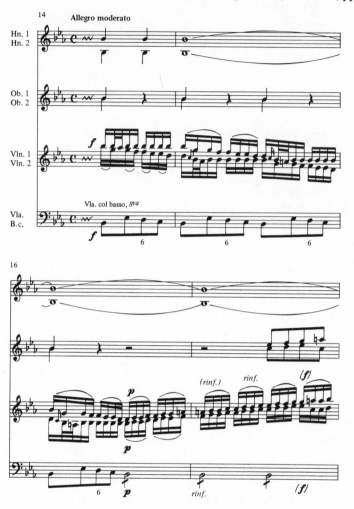

EXAMPLE III-13. continued

(Note: The dynamic markings in curved brackets show their placement in the manuscript GB-Lbl: Add. 14136, ff. 2v–3.)

(nos. 5, 13, and 14), he used it as Hasse did—which followed the trend of the time—to delete the opening ritornello.[37] A majority of the arias in major keys and the duet are conventional in moving to the relative minor for the B section (nos. 1, 3, 4, 8, 10, 11, 13, 14, and 15—but 13 and 14 do so only after moving to the subdominant), and the only aria in minor moves to the relative major. Changes of tempo and/or time-signature for the B section are found in nos. 1, 5 (see below, Example III-15a-b, the beginnings of S1 and the B section respectively), and 8. In all but two of the arias Jommelli uses totally new melodic material in the B section. The exceptions are nos. 3 (see below, Example III-14a-b) and 10; but even in these arias, the material in B that is derived from A is considerably modified.

With few exceptions the numbers of this oratorio well represent the up-to-date, mid-century, early Classical style: balanced and relatively short phrases, simple, homophonic texture, and slow harmonic rhythm; in some numbers the *Trommelbass* functions as a pedal point beneath changing chords but at times it serves to activate several measures of static harmony. The only numbers in which "learned," contrapuntal style is characteristic are the three choruses and one of the arias, number 11,

37. This is essentially his use of the dal segno even in no. 14, where the sign falls within the S1 of section A; at the end of section B in that aria Jommelli adds a reworked setting of the first three poetic lines of A as a transition to the original setting of the fourth line of A within S1.

in which the initial melody of A sounds like a fugue subject (with an alla breve time signature), at times treated in stretto.[38]

The most distinctive aspect of this oratorio—in fact, of all Jommelli's oratorios—is the composer's preoccupation with the musical interpretation of his text's dramatic, affective, and pictorial features. Examples III-14 through III-16 illustrate this and other aspects of his style. Example III-14a shows the beginning of number 3 (the only aria without a ritornello), in which Magdalene responds to Peter's first question—rather, she says she would like to respond but is overwhelmed with emotion. The vocal line's opening two-measure phrases, articulated by sigh motives followed by rests and accompanied by off-the-beat chords, immediately reveal the intensity of her emotion, her gasping for breath; in measures 9–10 the line returns to the E-flat on which the melody began, to paint the words "mi ritornano sul core"; and in measures 11–17 the melisma on the word "risonar," broken with rests, expresses the resounding of her "mournful accents" on her heart. The B section (Example III-14b) begins with melodic material derived from A and retains the same style of accompaniment, for Magdalene's emotional state has not changed. A clear, traditional example of the rhetorical figure *suspiratio* (from which the style of the entire aria is derived) is found on the words "l'interrotto sospirar" (mm. 98–103).

Example III-15a-b, from number 5 (S1 in section A and the beginning of section B) illustrates the aria with two affects. John, who has been describing the Passion, asks at the beginning of the aria why Jesus did not arm himself with thunderbolts or heavenly spheres to destroy his enemies. Jommelli set this section with jagged melodic lines, strong dynamic contrasts in the orchestra, and word painting (of the thunderbolts, mm. 43–46, in the violins). The B section (Example b) begins with a striking change: in the adagio, almost an obbligato recitative, John suddenly and dramatically realizes ("Ah, I understand") why the suffering was allowed; and in the larghetto his explanation begins with a leap of an octave to a long note (to paint "infinite Mind") accompanied by violins in imitative, "learned" style.

Example III-16a-b illustrates Jommelli's setting of one of the comparison arias. This text describes the way in which an experienced swimmer supports a boy who is learning to swim. At first (the aria's A section) the experienced swimmer places his hand under the boy's chest for support; then (B section) he removes his hand, stands aside, watches attentively, and if he sees the boy become afraid, supports him again. (The comparison with God's help when man's hope falters is not explicit in the aria verses but is implied in the preceding recitative.) As usual, Jommelli takes full advantage of the images Metastasio has provided. In Example a, the voice rises to a high g″ on "librarsi" (in this context, "to float" or perhaps "to swim") and holds it for four and one-half measures, while

38. Part of the aria is quoted in Cauthen, "Jommelli," pp. 94–96.

EXAMPLE III-14. *La passione*—Jommelli (Jommelli, *Passione**, pp. 25, 28).

Example a:

EXAMPLE III-14. continued

EXAMPLE III-14. continued

-len- ti a ri- so- nar.

I would like to tell you my sorrow but from my lips my mournful accents return to resound more painfully on my heart.

Example b:

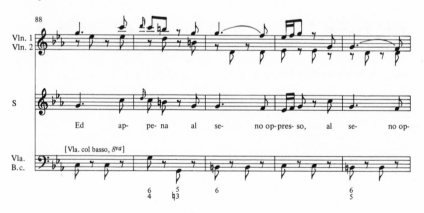

Ed ap- pe- na al se- no op-pres- so, al se- no op-

EXAMPLE III-14. continued

And my overwhelmed breast is scarcely permitted an interrupted sigh.

Example a:

EXAMPLE III-15. continued

Why, at the sight of such fierce pain, did you not arm yourself with thunderbolts or [heavenly] spheres . . .

Example b:

EXAMPLE III-15. continued

Ah, I understand: the infinite Mind did not wish to impede the great work . . .

EXAMPLE III-16. *La passione*—Jommelli (Jommelli, *Passione**, pp. 114–15).

Example a:

EXAMPLE III-16. continued

If in the midst of waves [a boy wishes to float] . . .

EXAMPLE III-16. continued

Example b:

Then he moves away and watches attentively, but if he perceives fear in [the boy] he supports him . . .

the strings and continuo depict waves; the text is repeated (mm. 33–38), and this time, as the phrase "in mezzo all'onde" is repeated, the voice, too, paints the waves. The harmony of the excerpt is almost entirely static, changing only in measures 30–32. The beginning of the B section (Example b) relates melodically to the beginning of A by reversal: down an octave and up a fifth, rather than down a fifth and up an octave. Now the experienced swimmer steps aside: chords on weak beats, rests at ends of phrases, and fermatas combine to interpret the suspense expressed in the text, and the virtual shout on the second syllable of "attento" gives it a second meaning ("watch out" or "be careful"). In measure 152 the waves begin again in the strings, the text speaks of fear ("tema") and the long notes in measures 156–58 (on "lo sostiene") paint the support by the experienced swimmer.

The simple recitatives of *La passione* are all without melismas, metrical sections, or quick-note punctuations found in the Hasse work. Like Hasse's oratorio, however, this one has five obbligato recitatives, which reflect the growing interest in such recitative—this is a larger number than is found in Jommelli's other oratorios.[39] Three of these five are preceded by passages in simple style. The obbligato recitatives interpret the text in much greater detail than do Hasse's. Jommelli was known, even in his earlier operas, for the dramatic power of his obbligato recitatives, and they became an important feature of his Stuttgart operas, as mentioned above. The first vocal utterance of this oratorio is set in obbligato style; the text, revealing Peter's confusion and remorse (Example III-17; see the full text quoted in chapter 2), is accompanied by dotted patterns in the strings to reflect an agitated emotional state. At the words "Among a thousand affects wavers my confused soul" (m. 12), Jommelli paints the word "ondeggia" (translated in the example as "wavers" but alternates might be "rolls, waves, tosses, undulates") with an arpeggio effect in the strings. Another case in point is the final obbligato recitative of the oratorio (Example III-18). Previously Magdalene's aria (no. 14) has expressed a feeling of loss without Jesus; and Peter, in a brief simple recitative, has told her that He left us many examples and symbols. Jommelli begins the obbligato recitative at the point where Peter interprets the Crucifixion: the crown of thorns teaches us to flee evil thoughts, the pierced hands teach us to abhor greed, etc. The entire first half of the recitative is unified by the solemn march figures (perhaps to represent Jesus as king, crowned) shown in the example, in which the two flutes play brief solo passages.

As is characteristic of oratorios in the period, the choruses are the least operatic numbers of the oratorio. Jommelli uses learned style in all three. The first chorus, number 2, is in ABA form, in which the A section is imitative and the B section, for soprano and alto, is mostly in parallel thirds. The concluding chorus of part I is in two sections, the first in

39. See ibid., pp. 53–55.

EXAMPLE III-17. *La passione*—Jommelli (Jommelli, *Passione**, p. 7).

EXAMPLE III-17. continued

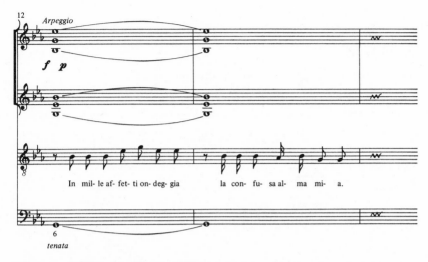

Where am I? Where do I hasten? Who controls my footsteps? . . . Among a thousand affects wavers my confused soul . . .

EXAMPLE III-18. *La passione*—Jommelli (Jommelli, *Passione**, pp. 110–11).

EXAMPLE III-18. continued

EXAMPLE III-18. continued

Dal-le sue ma-ni cru-del-men-te tra- fit-te

The sacred temples crowned with thorns teach us to flee evil thoughts. From his hands, cruelly pierced, . . .
(Additions made on the basis of the manuscript GB-Lbl: Add. 14136, ff. 155–56, are placed within curved brackets.)

duple meter and mostly chordal style and the final in triple meter and fugal style. The last few measures move from the tonic to the dominant of E-flat major, to express the word selected from earlier in the chorus for its ending, "pensaci, pensaci" ("let us reflect"). In certain contexts, of course, part I would be followed by a sermon, which would explain the selection of "pensaci" for the ending. In any event, the dominant closing on that word makes a striking rhetorical effect. The final chorus is in two sections, the first in alternating chordal and imitative style, and the second fugal, with separate subject for each of two segments of text.

Ferdinando Bertoni: David poenitens

Ferdinando Bertoni (1725–1813) was born in Salò, near Brescia.[40] Little is known of his earliest training, but in 1743 he studied with Padre Martini in Bologna and then went to Venice, which was to become his permanent home. In 1745 he composed his first opera, a genre for which he was to become well known. He was also active as a composer of sacred music and oratorios, as well as various other vocal and instrumental works. In 1752 he became first organist at St. Mark's basilica, and in 1785, maestro di cappella (succeeding Galuppi); from at least 1757 he served as maestro di cappella at the Ospedale dei Mendicanti. Though not a native of Venice, the city honored him as one of its great composers. He was elected to the Accademia filarmonica in Bologna (1773), and his works were admired throughout Europe. He made two trips to London to direct performances at the King's Theatre during four seasons, 1778–80 and 1781–83.

As an oratorio composer, Bertoni was astonishingly prolific. With nearly fifty oratorios to his credit—composed between 1746 and 1785, a particularly active period for oratorios in the conservatories—he probably wrote more than any other composer of the eighteenth century.[41] His five oratorios in Italian were first performed in the oratory of St. Philip Neri, and the remainder, in Latin, were virtually all written for the Mendicanti. The musical sources of all but nine are lost. The work with the largest number of surviving sources and thus probably the best known is *David poenitens*.[42]

First performed at the Mendicanti in 1775, *David poenitens*, like many oratorios written for the Venetian conservatories, was intended to be sung during the *triduum* of Holy Week as an introduction to the *Miserere* (Psalm 50). Despite this intention, indicated in its printed libretto, the work actually received its premiere "on Palm Sunday, when, unannounced, the Emperor Joseph II attended a performance."[43] Later the same year, the oratorio was performed in Vienna on an Advent concert of the Tonkünstler-Societät in the Kärntnerthor-Theater.

40. For information on Bertoni's life and works, see Sven Hansell, "Ferdinando Bertoni, *New Grove*, 2:645–48.

41. Next most prolific, according to my count, would seem to have been Bertoni's older contemporary Galuppi, who composed twenty-seven oratorios. Alessandro Scarlatti composed over thirty, some of which date from before the turn of the century.

42. The sources used for the following comments on *David poenitens* are the manuscript in A-Wn: 19115; the printed libretto for the Venetian performance of 1775 in I-Bc: Lib. 7418; and that for the Viennese performance of 1775 in D-DT: Mus. t-8. See app. A for the title pages for both librettos. A forthcoming facsimile is Bertoni, *David**.

43. Sven Hansell, "Ferdinando Bertoni," *New Grove*, 2:646.

The anonymous librettist of Bertoni's *David poenitens* derived his story from 2 Kings (or 2 Samuel), chapter 24, in which King David, to determine the extent of his power, orders a census of his people and is punished by God for his pride. Because the oratorio was sung by the young women of the Mendicanti, it is written for sopranos and altos only.[44] There are seven personages and a chorus: King David (S); Bethsabaea (S), David's wife; Joab (A), the general of the army; Gad (S), a prophet; Sadoc (S), a priest; Areuna the Jebusite (A); an Angel of the Lord (S); and a Chorus of the People of Israel (SSAA). The librettist followed the main events of the biblical story, but for dramatic and musical interest he embellished it and added the personages Bethsabaea and Sadoc.

Part I opens with an episode of praise for the king and expressions of the beauties and joys of the kingdom. The mood of rejoicing is broken when Bethsabaea tells David she is troubled at hearing of his command that a census be taken, and she fears he will be punished. David tries to defend himself, but he becomes worried about the consequences of his act. Joab had been charged with taking the census, for which he sent the army into all the regions of the kingdom. Having completed his enormous task, Joab makes his report to David, who is filled with remorse for his sin of pride. The prophet Gad tells David that God will give him a choice of three punishments for his sin: seven years of famine, pursuit by his enemies for three months, or a pestilence for three days. David chooses the pestilence, and part I ends with a prayer for the suffering Israelites. Part II opens with David's long penitential soliloquy in an obbligato recitative and an aria: he expresses his anguish at seeing others suffer for his sin and asks God to turn against him but spare his people. After an angry aria by Bethsabaea about David's pride and shame, Gad enters with a command from God: David is to go with Gad to the region of the Jebusites. David agrees, and when they arrive at the threshing floor of Areuna the Jebusite (the place where God halted the Angel of death, according to the biblical account), Gad tells David that God wishes him to build an altar there. David does so and offers a sacrifice on the altar; he and the chorus praise God. An Angel appears to tell David, in an obbligato recitative and an aria, that God has heard his prayers and forgiven him, and that peace and joy will now reign. The score ends at this point, but the printed libretto for the Venice performance includes two lines of recitative in which David introduces the *Miserere*. The Viennese performance evidently was not followed by the *Miserere*, for the Viennese libretto omits the brief recitative introduction to the psalm and instead repeats the chorus sung prior to the Angel's appearance (no. 13 in Table III-4) as the closing number. (With this repetition the work

44. The names of the seven soloists are included at the beginning of the Venetian libretto and of the manuscript score used for these comments.

TABLE III-4
Bertoni, *David poenitens*: Structural Outline

Numbers	Keys
Sinfonia	D
PART I	
1. Aria. Areuna, "Mecum date signa amoris"	D
2. Coro. "Cantate sodales"	C
3. Aria. Sadoc, "Anima excelsa vive?"	A
4. Cavatina. Bethsabaea, "Pacis dilectae"	F
5. Aria. Joab, "O quam dulce in praelio mori"	C
6. Aria. Gad, "Plange, suspira, et geme"	D
7. Quartetto. "Exaudi deprecantes!"	B♭
PART II	
8. Aria. David, "Dextra aeterna!"	E♭
9. Aria. Bethsabaea, "Oves duxisti errantes"	A
10. Cavatina. Gad, "Tremebundi suspirantes"	D
11. Duetto. David, Bethsabaea, "Celer ut agna"	G
12. David, Coro. "Fronte pronta mente pura"	E♭
13. Coro. "Concentu harmonico laetae"	F
14. Aria. Angelus, "Dum serena dies beata"	D

would conform to the long tradition of ending an oratorio with a chorus but would end in the wrong key (F rather than D) unless the chorus were transposed.)[45]

The libretto for Bertoni's *David poenitens* differs in several respects from the Metastasian type: the unities of time and place are ignored; neither part I nor II closes with a chorus;[46] three internal choruses (nos. 2, 12, and 13) are more than the usual number; and three of the solo numbers (1, 4, and 10) have texts of only one stanza—in the sources, two of these (4 and 10) are called *cavatina* rather than *aria*. The libretto does, however, retain the Metastasian feature of regular alternation between verses for recitative and those for closed numbers. As the title of the oratorio indicates, the work focuses on David's penitence, which he expresses most eloquently in part II. In contrast to part I, in which he sings only simple recitatives, in part II he is featured: first in his obbligato recitative followed by an aria (no. 8), then in his prayerful duet with

45. I have not, so far, located the score or parts used for the Viennese performance.

46. The quartet at the close of part I is an ensemble of personages, not marked *coro* in the score nor in the Venetian libretto, although the Viennese libretto calls it *Quartetto coro*; the *Miserere*, probably sung by a chorus at the Mendicanti, was not a part of the oratorio, but the librettist clearly assumed its presence.

Bethsabaea (no. 11), and finally in another prayer in which the chorus joins him (no. 12).

The tonal center of the work as a whole is D major, as Table III-4 indicates: the sinfonia, beginning of part I, and end of part II are in that key, as is one internal number in each part (nos. 6 and 10). The flat keys furthest from D major were possibly chosen for reasons of affect: in part I, the closing quartet in B-flat major, a prayer for mercy; and in part II, numbers 8 and 12 in E-flat major, which reveal David's penitence. (David's obbligato recitative at the beginning of part II, not listed in the table, begins in C minor and prepares for number 8.)

The instruments required for the work are strings, continuo, and pairs of oboes, flutes, horns, and trumpets. The wind instruments usually fill in harmony, punctuate, or double the stringed instruments. At times, however, the pairs of winds have solo passages: the trumpets play fanfares in the martial aria of Joab (no. 5), and the flutes accompany and play interludes in Bethsabaea's cavatina (no. 4; see below, Example III-20) and the coloratura aria of the Angel at the end of the oratorio (no. 14; see Example III-22).

The only instrumental number is the sinfonia, a one-movement work in sonata form with a brief development section and without repeat signs for either the exposition or the development-recapitulation. Example III-19a illustrates the beginning of the sinfonia, which is typical of the early Classical style found not only in this number but often throughout the work: homophonic texture, slow harmonic rhythm, *Trommelbass*, and simple, balanced phrases. Not all phrases are as simple as these, but Bertoni's mode of musical thought is usually symmetrical; where asymmetries occur they clearly result from expansions or contractions of basically symmetrical structures. The second section of the exposition, in the dominant, has the contrasting theme shown in Example III-19b, which again illustrates the simple phrasing, harmony, and texture (with parallel thirds in the violins doubled at the lower octave in the violas) so characteristic of the work.

In the arias, cavatinas, and duet, Bertoni uses neither da capo nor dal segno forms, but the transformed da capo instead: the A1-B-A2 form in numbers 3, 5, 6, 8, 9, 11, and 12; the A1-A2 form in numbers 1, 4, and 10.[47] In the A1-B-A2 arias, the B sections, always settings of the second stanza of text, are written approximately as B sections of da capo or dal segno arias had been: shorter than A1 and A2, and predominantly modulatory but momentarily establishing one or two keys; the B section of the duet remains in the dominant. Of the six arias with B sections, four move to the relative minor (but in most cases not immediately). In the two cavatinas, the A1 section closes on the dominant without having modulated to that key.

47. On the transformed da capo, see Table II-3 and the accompanying discussion.

EXAMPLE III-19. *David poenitens*—Bertoni (A-Wn: 19115, [ff. 2–2v, 3v–4]).

Example a:

EXAMPLE III-19. continued

Example b:

EXAMPLE III-19. continued

Throughout the oratorio Bertoni emphasizes both simple, attractive tunes and coloratura passages, the latter more for vocal display than for dramatic interpretation of the text. Example III-20, from the beginning of the first vocal section of Bethsabaea's cavatina (no. 4), illustrates well the pleasant simplicity of the vocal style. In the recitative preceding this number David has told Areuna and Bethsabaea of his growing anxiety about the decision to have a census taken, and he and Areuna have departed. Alone, Bethsabaea sings this brief number, one stanza of three lines, expressing her desire for peace. As is often the case, the singer's line is doubled, exactly or slightly ornamented, by an instrument, in this case, the first violin. The phrases are clear and balanced: the first phrase of five measures is a four-measure phrase extended by one measure to repeat the word "amatae." The parallel thirds in the violins and the accompaniment of arpeggiated triads in the viola are characteristic of this work, but the predominant role of the flutes beginning in measure 23 is unusual. Whereas most of the arias include coloratura passages, the cavatinas do not.

Probably the most dramatic aria text of the libretto is the penitential one that David sings (Example III-21), following his obbligato recitative at the opening of part II. Bertoni does not ignore the drama of the text, which he expresses by dotted accompanying figures (mm. 11–12), an agitated violin part and dynamic contrasts (mm. 15–19), affective rests in the vocal line after "Dextra aeterna" and "in te peccavi," and a coloratura passage (mm. 21–23). Yet the aria retains the work's usual simple style of harmony, texture, and phrasing, and the pleasant accompaniment of parallel thirds and sixths in the violins (mm. 11–15, 24).

Clearly the most virtuosic aria of the oratorio is that of the Angel, the

EXAMPLE III-20. *David poenitens*—Bertoni (A-Wn: 19115, [ff. 49v–51]).

EXAMPLE III-20. continued

Blessed image of beloved peace, sweetly come to me.

EXAMPLE III-21. *David poenitens*—Bertoni (A-Wn: 19115, [ff. 100–101v]).

EXAMPLE III-21. continued

Eternal arm [of God]! before Thee I have sinned, spare the people of Sion! Spare the innocent people! Turn thy hand against me.

closing number, which testifies to the remarkable skill of Laura Risegari, the student at the Mendicanti who performed it. Example III-22 shows the end of the A1 section. The long coloratura on the word "fortunata" ("happy") extends for nine measures and reaches a high C-sharp in measure 105—for safety's sake, the first flute supports the soloist by playing in unison with her, and the second flute plays parallel thirds below. The flutes are more important in this number than in any other.

As usual with eighteenth-century Italian oratorios, the forms and styles of ensembles are similar to those of arias. The duet between David and Bethsabaea (no. 11) is a transformed da capo of the A1-A2 type; in this instance, however, the first part of A1 is greatly abbreviated in A2. The quartet (no. 7) uses a similar A1-A2 scheme. The text, a prayer for those suffering in the plague, consists of four stanzas of four lines each. The tempos, groupings of personages, verse-lines of text, and tonal centers of the quartet may be diagrammed as follows (abbreviations: B, Bethsabaea; A, Areuna; J, Joab; S, Sadoc):

	Section A1 Allegro				
Personages:	a4	B	A	J	S
Verse-lines of text:	1–4	5–6	7–8	9–10	11–12
Tonal centers in B♭:	I	V	v	V	ii

	Section A2				*Coda* Allegro assai
	a4	BS	AJ	BS	a4
	1–2	5–6	9–10	11–12	13–16
	I	I	I	I	IV-I

Thus the first twelve lines of text are sung in the A1 section, which moves from tonic to dominant, with a turn to the supertonic at the end; the A2 section remains in the tonic and is an abbreviation of A1, in which duos replace solos; the final section is shorter than the other two, functions as a coda in quicker tempo, and moves from IV to I. The style of the quartet is light, operatic, virtually devoid of counterpoint, and thus strikingly different from the traditional finale (usually a chorus) for part I or II of an oratorio. Example III-23a shows the first entrance of the voices, in homorhythmic style, characteristic of most of the number. Example III-23b is taken from the end of the first *a* 4 section. The texture is essentially homophonic, and the manner of repeating text (in mm. 52–58) is clearly what one might expect from an opera—even a comic opera, despite the text—of the same period.

Most of the recitatives are in simple style and quite plain. Of the five obbligato recitatives, the first two emphasize the oratorio's joyful beginning and are sung by Areuna at the beginning of the oratorio, in prepara-

EXAMPLE III-22. *David poenitens*—Bertoni (A-Wn: 19115, [ff. 66v–69]).

EXAMPLE III-22. continued

EXAMPLE III-22. continued

EXAMPLE III-22. continued

EXAMPLE III-22. continued

Live, exult, and be happy, may beloved peace reign with you.

EXAMPLE III-23. *David poenitens*—Bertoni (A-Wn: 19115, [ff. 77v–78, 79v–80v]).

Example a:

EXAMPLE III-23. continued

Graciously hear our prayers! Be mindful of the wretched people!

Example b:

EXAMPLE III-23. continued

[We are wandering lambs] without a leader and without hope . . .

tion for his aria (no. 1) and then in preparation for the first chorus (no. 2). The remaining three obbligato recitatives prepare for other important numbers: the ensemble that closes part I (the recitative is a dialogue among the four personages who sing the ensemble), David's penitential aria (no. 8), and the Angel's aria (no. 14). The most dramatic obbligato recitative is David's, at the beginning of part II, which opens with a majestic orchestral tutti of fourteen measures in C minor. Bertoni pays more attention to interpreting the dramatic aspects of his text in this recitative than in any other, yet even here such interpretation is minimal. In Example III-24a, for instance, from the point at which David com-

EXAMPLE III-24. *David poenitens*—Bertoni (A-Wn: 19115, [ff. 93v–94v, 98–98v]).

Example a:

Ec- ce! au- dio gen- tes se-mi a- ni- mes mo- rien- tes . . .

EXAMPLE III-24. continued

Behold! I hear the people half dead, dying . . . Cruel, inhuman, barbaric, insane king!

Example b:

Divine, angered right hand, armed with just fury . . .

ments on the suffering and dying of his people, the orchestra appropriately and effectively plays sigh motives under the sustained B-flat of the oboes (mm. 21–24, 27–28); yet, when David accuses himself as a "cruel, inhuman, barbaric, insane king," the orchestra enters with some relatively ineffectual chords. Near the end of the recitative, where David speaks of God's just fury (Example III-24b), Bertoni increases the tempo to allegro and the rhythmic activity to sixteenth notes in the strings. Again, however, the orchestral expression seems to fall short of the text's meaning.

Whereas the styles of the oratorios discussed above—by Leo, Hasse, and Jommelli—are distinguished from operas by the serious and at times learned style of their choruses, in this work by Bertoni the choral style seems to differ little from that of opera. Like the passages of the ensemble illustrated above, the choruses are simple, essentially homophonic, often homorhythmic, and rarely contrapuntal. The chorus in which David participates is a kind of rondo structure, ABAB'AA', in which the A sections are David's solos (in the tonic), the B sections are for chorus (in closely related keys), and the final A' is for chorus (in the tonic).

Joseph Haydn: Il ritorno di Tobia

A composer of central importance to the establishment and mature development of the Classical style, Joseph Haydn (1732–1809) was born in Rohrau, Austria, about twenty-five miles east of Vienna.[48] In 1740 he was accepted as a choirboy under Georg Reutter the younger, Kapellmeister of St. Stephen's Cathedral in Vienna. The extent of Haydn's education at the choirschool is not clear, but he did receive instruction in singing and evidently in keyboard instruments as well. Having left the choirschool in 1749 or 1750, he worked as a freelance teacher and performer until he received his first regular appointment, probably in 1759, as Count Morzin's music director. The most important position of his career was that of Kapellmeister to the Esterházy family beginning in 1761 and continuing, at least nominally, for the rest of his life. From 1761 until 1790 Haydn's work was largely at one of two Esterházy residences: first at the palace in Eisenstadt (about twenty-five miles south of Vienna); and beginning in 1766–67, mainly at the more elaborate palace called Esterháza (on the south side of the Neusiedler See, in western Hungary). Except for occasional visits to Vienna, Haydn lived for nearly thirty years in the relative isolation of the Esterházy establishments. Yet music was important at the Esterházy court, and Haydn's life of composition and performance was intense; he became a brilliant com-

48. For a brief summary of Haydn's life and works and for bibliography, see Jens Peter Larsen and Georg Feder, "Joseph Haydn," *New Grove* 8:328–407. The most detailed work, in five-volumes, is Landon, *Haydn*.

poser of works in virtually all the genres of his time. Upon the death in 1790 of Haydn's patron Prince Nikolaus, his successor Prince Anton dismissed most of the musical establishment at Esterháza, retained Haydn as Kapellmeister in name only, and kept him on full salary but gave him no duties. Haydn moved to Vienna, and in this new period of freedom he visited London twice, in 1791–92 and 1794–95, to be featured as composer and musical director of the famous Salomon concerts. In his later years he again became active as the Esterházy Kapellmeister, but his duties were light, and he continued to live in Vienna as one of Europe's most celebrated composers.

Well known for his great importance in the development of Classical instrumental styles and genres, particularly the symphony and the string quartet, Haydn also composed in a variety of vocal genres, but more in Italian opera and in church music than any other. That the composition of oratorios was not one of his duties at either Eisenstadt or Esterháza accounts for his having composed only one work in this genre during his long period of active service for the Esterházy family.[49] Yet that work, *Il ritorno di Tobia*, is an outstanding example of the late-eighteenth-century Italian oratorio.[50] His better-known late oratorios, *The Creation* and *The Seasons*, were first performed with German texts and are discussed in chapter 8, on oratorio in the German language.

Tobia was composed in Esterháza for performance in Vienna at the Lenten concerts of the Tonkünstler-Societät in the Kärntnerthor-Theater on 2 and 4 April 1775.[51] This was Haydn's first major commission for Vienna since entering the Esterházy service. Characteristic of the large forces used for the Tonkünstler-Societät concerts, the orchestra, chorus, and soloists for the premiere of *Tobia* possibly numbered more than 180 performers.[52] The oratorio was enormously successful and called the attention of the Viennese to Haydn's extraordinary ability; the major composers of the city could now see in him a powerful rival.[53] *Tobia* was performed again at concerts of the Tonkünstler-Societät in 1784 (with two added choruses and numerous cuts, mostly to shorten the arias) and

49. The tradition in Eisenstadt of performing an annual oratorio in the German language on Good Friday was evidently discontinued in 1762. Cf. Landon, *Haydn*, 1:313, 369.

50. For a general discussion of the relationship of this work to the tradition of Italian oratorio, see Smither, "Haydns *Il ritorno di Tobia*."

51. See Fig. III-3 and app. A for the title page of the 1775 libretto, in CS-Pu: GY 3500. For more on the Tonkünstler-Societät, see chap. 2.

52. Schmid, "*Tobia*," p. 297; Schmid in "Vorwort" to Haydn, *Tobia**, p. VII; and Landon, *Haydn*, 2:214. According to Holschneider, "Die *Judas-Maccabäus* Bearbeitung," p. 179, n. 11, the records (in A-Wsa) of performers participating in the concerts before 1780 do not survive.

53. It was evidently this rivalry that delayed Haydn's entrance into the Tonkünstler-Societät until he was received as an honorary member in 1797. For details, see Landon, *Haydn*, 2:215, 418–20, 4:246.

IL RITORNO
DI
TOBIA,
AZIONE SACRA
PER MUSICA
DI

Gio. Gaſtone Boccherini Luccheſe,
Poeta de' Ceſarei Teatri di Vienna,
e frà gli Arcadi Argindo Bolimeo.

DA CANTARSI
NE' TEATRI PRIVILEGIATI
DI VIENNA
L' ANNO 1775.

PRESSO GIUSEPPE KURZBOECK,
STAMPATORE ORIENT. DI S. MAJ.
IMP. R. A.

FIGURE III-3. Title page and folio 2r of the libretto printed for the first performance of Haydn's *Il ritorno di Tobia*. The title page bears the name of the librettist, Giovanni Gastone Boccherini, but not of the composer, whose name is given beneath the list of interlocutors on folio 2r (Courtesy of CS-Pu.)

INTERLOCUTORI.

TOBIT Ceco, Conforte di

ANNA, Madre di

TOBIA, Spofo di

SARA.

L'ANGIOLO RAFFAELLO, in figura
d'Azaria.

CORO D'Ebrei Servi di Tobit.

L'Azione fi rapprefenta ne' fubborghi
di Ninive;

Il luogo è un Atrio terreno nell' Abita-
colo di Tobit, con diverfe porte;
alcune introducenti à più alti ap-
partamenti; ed altre contigue alla via di Campagna.

*La Mufica è tutta nuova del Sig. Giufep-
pe Haydn, Maeftro di Capella di
fua Altezza il Principe Nicolò Efter-
bazy di Galantha.*

A 2   PAR-in 1808 (in a new version by Haydn's former student, Sigismund Neu-komm).[54] Performances during Haydn's lifetime outside Vienna include those of 1777 in Berlin, at a Konzert der Musikliebhaber; 1783 in Rome, at the Oratory of St. Philip Neri; 1784 in Lisbon, at the Ajuda Palace for the nameday of the prince of Brazil; and 1802 in Leipzig, at a Gewandhauskonzert.[55]

The libretto of Haydn's *Tobia* was written by Giovanni Gastone Boccherini (1742–ca. 1800), an older brother of the more famous Luigi. Giovanni Gastone was a dancer, poet, and member of the Arcadian Academy; in 1772 he wrote opera librettos for Florian Gassmann and Antonio Salieri. Sometime after 1781 he went to Madrid but details of his later life are unknown.[56] Boccherini's text is based on the Book of Tobias, chapters 5–12, in the Vulgate Bible (and the Protestant Apocrypha). Frequently used as a source of oratorio librettos as well as other literary and visual art works, the Book of Tobias has traditionally served to exemplify familial devotion, the virtues of obedience to God, and God's intervention in human affairs.[57] The libretto assumes some familiarity with the biblical story, which may be summarized (and much simplified) as follows: While the Israelites are in Nineveh as the captives of the Assyrians, the blind and aged Tobit sends his son, Tobias, to the city of Rages to collect a longstanding debt of silver from Gabelus. Tobias seeks a guide and finds Azarias, who is actually the Archangel Raphael in disguise. On the journey to Rages, they camp by the Tigris river, and Tobias, while washing his feet, is attacked by a monstrous fish. Tobias accepts Raphael's advice to pull the fish out of the water, remove its entrails, and save the heart, gall, and liver as medicines. When they arrive at Rages, Raphael advises that they lodge with Tobias's kinsman, Raguel, whose daughter's name is Sara, and that Tobias ask for Sara's hand in marriage. Tobias knows that Sara has had seven husbands and all have been killed by a devil, but Raphael tells him that placing the liver of the fish on burning coals will drive away the devil. Tobias and Sara are married, Tobias is saved from the devil, the debt is collected, and the newlyweds return with Raphael to Nineveh. Meanwhile, Tobit and his wife, Anna, are worried about Tobias, who has been gone longer than expected. Eventually the three travelers arrive at Tobit's home, and Ra-

---

54. For a discussion of these performances in relation to changing taste in Vienna and within the concerts of the Tonkünstler-Societät, see Edelman, "Haydns *Il ritorno di Tobia*."

55. Extant librettos printed for the first three of these performances are found at D-B: Mus. T 91/2 (Berlin, 1777); I-Nc, Rsc, Vgc (Rome, 1783); and I-Fc Rc, PAc, Vgc (Lisbon, 1784). On the Leipzig performance of 1802, see Schmid, "*Tobia*," p. 305.

56. C. Mutini, "Giovanni Antonio Gastone Boccherini," *Dizionario biografico*, 11:59–60.

57. For a historical and literary survey of the Tobias story, see Zimmermann, *Tobit*.

phael tells Tobias to anoint Tobit's eyes with the gall of the fish to heal them. Tobias follows Raphael's instructions and restores his father's sight. Raphael identifies himself as an archangel and disappears.

The personages of the libretto are Tobit (B), Anna (A), Tobias (T), Sara (S), the Angel Raphael (S) disguised as Azarias until the end, and a Chorus (SATB) of Hebrew Servants of Tobit. The action takes place in Nineveh at the home of Tobit and Sara and is concerned mainly with the anxious waiting of the mother and father for their son, his return with Sara and Raphael, the restoration of Tobit's sight, and the revelation that Azarias is Raphael. The libretto opens with a chorus, combined with solos by Anna and Tobit, which is a prayer for mercy for the unhappy mother and father who have waited so long for their son's return. In the ensuing recitatives and arias, Anna and Tobit are characterized as opposites: Anna is of weak faith, anxious, certain that a catastrophe has befallen her son; Tobit is pious, generous, hopeful, convinced of God's mercy. Anna sees Azarias (Raphael) in the distance returning alone and is even more certain that her son has met with misfortune. When Raphael arrives, she impatiently questions him, and by answering her questions he gradually reveals the story of the journey—the fish, the marriage, the saving of Tobias from a devil—and he predicts that Tobias will restore Tobit's sight. Eventually Tobias and Sara arrive; they and Anna gather around Tobit and kneel at his feet for his blessing. Anna repents for her impatience and lack of faith and hope, and Tobias tells Tobit he will restore his sight. Part I ends with the chorus, combined with the five soloists, in prayer for the success of Tobias's attempt to heal his father's eyes. Part II is concerned with Tobias's administration of the medicine to Tobit's eyes. The dramatic tension builds through a series of unsuccessful attempts. At first the fish's gall burns unbearably in Tobit's eyes, but Raphael assists; finally all the gall enters Tobit's eyes, and the "unclean scales" fall away. But when Tobit tries to open his eyes, the light is too bright, again the pain is excruciating, and he refuses to try again. Anna and Tobias (in a duet) show the weakening of their faith. But then in the denouement, a long obbligato recitative for the full cast: Sara reveals that Tobit's sight has been restored and tells how she, on Raphael's instructions, gradually accustomed his eyes to the light; Tobit enters and rejoices at seeing his family; Azarias enters, and Tobit wishes to reward him; Azarias refuses the reward, reveals that he is Raphael, explains that he, on behalf of God, has done all in answer to the prayers of Tobit and Sara, predicts that proud Niniveh will be overthrown and Jerusalem will be rebuilt, and ascends to Heaven on a cloud. The final chorus and the remaining four personages praise God for his compassion.

This is essentially a Metastasian libretto: Boccherini observes the unities of time, place, and action; events which occurred in another time and place are narrated in past tense; the libretto proceedes mainly by alternation between recitatives and arias; the only ensemble is a duet; and each part closes with a chorus. The 1775 version includes eight numbers in part I and seven in part II (see Table III-5), which is normal for a Metastasian libretto.[58] Boccherini's arias, however, differ from those of the Metastasian libretto in their tendency to greater length and irregular lengths of lines (no. 10b, for instance, has sixteen lines of irregular lengths). The choruses added in 1784 (nos. 5c and 13c) slightly modernize the work and contribute to its symmetry, for they occur at about the same place in each part. From the dramatic standpoint the libretto is hardly compelling, but it offers opportunities for varied musical settings (including two traditional comparison arias, 2b and 12b), and Haydn responds to the text with imaginative and moving music.

As Table III-5 shows, the work begins and ends in C: the overture (Haydn's term, *ouverture*) begins with a largo introduction in C minor to an allegro di molto in C major, and the final chorus of part II is in C. The key of C is used internally only for numbers 5b and 5c. Some of the other keys may have been selected for affective reasons; for instance, E-flat is used in the opening choral-soli prayer for mercy for the sorrowing Anna and Tobit, and again for the duet (no. 15b) in which Anna and Tobias despair that Tobit will ever see again. Tonal symmetry is of special importance in this work. Table III-6 illustrates some symmetries between parts I and II: the first two arias of part I (2b and 3b) are in the same keys as the first two of part II (10b and 11b); and the keys of the last three numbers of each part are a tritone and a third apart.[59]

The availability of a large orchestra for the concerts of the Tonkünstler-Societät is reflected in the instrumentation: strings and continuo, plus pairs of flutes, oboes, bassoons, English horns, French horns, trumpets, trombones, and timpani—the largest orchestra of any Italian oratorio discussed thus far. In several of the numbers the instruments are used with particular effectiveness in the service of the text.[60] Perhaps the most subtle orchestral sonorities in the oratorio are those in Sara's aria, number 11b, in which she expresses such joy at being with Tobias's family that she seems to be among angels rather than men. The aria is scored for flutes, oboes, English horns, bassoons, and French horns, with all strings muted throughout. The English horns contribute a particularly delicate hue to the orchestral sound of this aria, and all the winds play

58. Throughout the following discussion, *Tobia* is described in its 1775 version unless otherwise specified. The discussion is based on the modern edition: Haydn, *Tobia**.

59. That part I ends in D major and the first aria of part II is in the same key might seem to contribute to the work's tonal coherence; yet the perception of that contribution is weakened by the obbligato recitative at the beginning of part II (discussed below), which strongly emphasizes B-flat major for about forty measures.

60. Note especially the trumpets in the martial aria 2b, the English horns in nos. 11b, 13b, and 15b, and the powerful sound of the combined oboes, English horns, French horns, and trombones in 13b. Muted violins are used in nos. 6b, 11b, 15b, and 16 (obbligato recitative).

TABLE III-5
Haydn, *Tobia*: Structural Outline

Numbers	Keys
Overture	c-C
PART I	
1. Coro, Anna, Tobit, "Pietà d'un'infelice"	E♭
2b. Aria. Anna, "Sudò il guerriero"	D
3b. Aria. Tobit, "Ah tu m'ascolta"	F
4b. Aria. Raffaelle, "Anna, m'ascolta!"	A
5b. Aria. Anna, "Ah gran Dio"	C
5c. Coro [1784]. "Ah gran Dio!"	C
6b. Aria. Tobia, "Quando mi dona un cenno"	E
7b. Aria. Sara, "Del caro sposo"	B♭
9. Coro with soli. "Odi le nostre voci"	D
PART II	
10b. Aria. Raffaelle, "Come se a voi parlasse"	D
11b. Aria. Sara, "Non parmi esser fra gl'uomini"	F
12b. Aria. Tobia, "Quel felice nocchier"	G
13b. Aria. Anna, "Come in sogno un stuol"	f
13c. Coro [1784]. "Svanisce in un momento"	d-D
14b. Aria. Tobit, "Invan lo chiedi, amico"	A
15b. Duetto. Anna, Tobia, "Dunque, oh Dio"	E♭
17. Coro with soli. "Io non oso alzar"	C

Note: The numbers in this table are those in the edition, Haydn, *Tobia**. Except for nos. 5c and 13c, the table is based on the 1775 version.

TABLE III-6
Haydn, *Tobia*: Comparison of Keys in Numbers of Parts I and II

		Part I								
Overture	1	2b	3b	4b	5b	[5c]	6b	7b	9
c-C	E♭	D	F	A	C	[C]	E	B♭	D
		└─── m3 ───┘				[1784]	└─ tritone ─┘└─ M3 ─┘		
		Part II								
		10b	11b	12b	13b	[13c]	14b	15b	17
		D	F	G	f	[d-D]	A	E♭	C
		└─── m3 ───┘				[1784]	└─ tritone ─┘└─ m3 ─┘		

solo at various times and thus stand in relief against the muted and often pizzicato strings.

The overture is unusual for its anticipation of the opening chorus of the oratorio. The main motive of the introductory largo section in C minor (Example III-25a, mm. 1 and 5, vln. 1, ob. 1), becomes important in the initial chorus in E-flat (Example III-26a and b). The slow introduction and chorus are separated by the light allegro in sonata form, for which the mode changes abruptly to major and the meter to triple (Example III-25b). The second section of the exposition introduces new material, and the development manipulates motives from the beginning of the exposition. The end of the allegro, marked *perdendosi*, modulates to E-flat and closes with a fermata on the dominant of that key to form a direct connection with the chorus that begins immediately. The return to the overture's largo motive at the beginning of the chorus is all the more powerful thanks to the intervening allegro.

Haydn did not use the full da capo form in *Tobia*, but two arias in succession—nos. 6b and 7b, sung by Tobias and Sara—use the dal segno indication to achieve the half da capo form: in both arias, Haydn places the sign at a point that calls for the repeat of only the second half of the A section.[61] In eight of the work's eleven arias (nos. 2b, 3b, 4b, 5b, 11b, 12b, 13b, and 14b), Haydn uses the transformed da capo (A1-B-A2) as does Bertoni in *David poenitens*. Yet the B sections in most of the arias in this scheme differ markedly from those in Bertoni's, for Haydn's B sections tend less to establish keys than to move through them; at times the tonal flux (but not the motivic technique) suggests an instrumental development section. In four of the arias (nos. 2b, 11b, 12b, 14b) Haydn sets both stanzas of the text in A1 and then repeats some or all of the lines of those stanzas in B with musical-textual "development," and repeats some or all of them again in A2 (cf. the model in Table II-2, second illustration). In aria 13b Haydn responds to the text in yet another way: in A1 he sets the first stanza of the text (expressive of darkness and fear) in minor; in B, he manipulates the same text; and in A2 he sets the second half (expressive of light and confidence) in major. (In this aria, however, A2 might almost be labeled C, for its relationship to A1 is tenuous). In the duet, with its long text of six stanzas, Haydn sets stanzas 1–2 as solos by Tobias and Anna, respectively, in A1-A1, tonally comparable to a sonata-form exposition and its repetition; stanzas 3–4 in the B section as dialogue and ensemble phrases in the dominant; and stanzas 5–6 as ensembles in the tonic to music that formed the last half of A1. Thus A2 is musically a half recapitulation.

Haydn's setting of individual poetic lines and words are traditional, but the word painting is more detailed than one usually finds in orato-

61. On the half da capo form, see Table II-2 and accompanying discussion. For the 1784 performance, Haydn made an ornamented version of the aria 6b, which is discussed in Schmid, "Zierpraxis."

EXAMPLE III-25. *Tobia*—Haydn (Haydn, *Tobia**, pp. 1, 21).

Example a:

EXAMPLE III-25. continued

Example b:

EXAMPLE III-26. *Tobia*—Haydn (Haydn, *Tobia**, pp. 28, 30–31).

Example a:

EXAMPLE III-26. continued

Have mercy on an unhappy one, have mercy on an afflicted parent . . .

EXAMPLE III-26. continued

Example b:

EXAMPLE III-26. continued

Have mercy on an afflicted one, on an unhappy parent . . .

rios of the period. The comparison arias, numbers 2b and 12b, well illustrate the tradition and detail. In 2b, an aria of four stanzas rather than the usual two, Anna angrily reproaches Tobit for wasting his time with piety (which she regards as a mark of his pride) for his only reward is suffering:

Anna:
  Sudò il guerriero,
Ma gloria ottenne;
Tremò il nocchiero,
Ma s'arrichì.
  Geme tal'ora
L'agrigoltore;
Ma lo ristora
La messe un dì.
  Tu passi gl'anni
fra pene e pianti
E sono i danni
La tua mercè.
  Chiaro si vede
Che fra tuoi vanti,
Un vero merito
Giammai non c'è.

Anna:
  The warrior sweated,
but obtained glory;
The helmsman trembled,
but he grew rich.
  At times
the farmer groans;
but one day the harvest
will repay him.
  You spend the years
in pain and weeping,
and injuries
are your reward.
  It is plain to see
that with all your pride
true merit
never do you have.

Haydn changes styles and rhythmic-melodic figures to interpret the various images in the text. Example III-27a illustrates the martial setting for the warrior in lines 1–2; lines 3–4 (not in the example) are interpreted by trembling sixteenth notes in the first violins; the farmer in the second stanza (Example b) is represented by a folklike tune, first sung by Anna, then played by the oboe; the third stanza, with references to Tobit's pain and weeping, evokes chromatic steps (Example c, mm. 41–43, voice, vlns., b.c.), which also effect the modulation to the dominant; and the word "giammai" ("never," emphasized as "not *ever*") of the last stanza (Example d) is set to one of the oratorio's longer coloratura passages.

    Number 12b is a traditional comparison aria in which Tobias sees his own nearly completed task of healing Tobit's eyes as comparable to that of a helmsman who is happy when he sights the port from afar but must not rest from his toil lest the breeze blow the ship off course. Haydn responds with the expected wave music in the strings (Example III-28) but adds another detail—a series of large skips (mm. 32–33) to paint the words "da lungi scorge il porto" ("from afar sights the port"). An aria that well repays careful examination is number 10b, in which Raphael predicts and describes the end of the world; the text is filled with images that Haydn interprets musically in detail—trembling, darkness, falling

EXAMPLE III-27. *Tobia*—Haydn (Haydn, *Tobia**, pp. 60, 62–63, 65–67).

Example a:

The warrior sweated, but obtained glory . . .

Example b:

At times the farmer groans . . .

EXAMPLE III-27. continued

Example c:

You spend years in pain and weeping . . .

Example d:

Never do you have [true merit].

EXAMPLE III-28. *Tobia*—Haydn (Haydn, *Tobia**, pp. 390–91).

The happy helmsman who from afar sights the port [he had] longed for . . .

stars, heaven, the earth disappearing from beneath the feet of men, waves disappearing from the sea, the highest God.

Haydn's *Tobia* reflects the growing tendency in oratorio to increase the proportion of obbligato recitatives to those in simple style. Eight of the fourteen recitatives are in obbligato style and use orchestral motives for interpretation of the text and for musical unification. One of the most imposing of the obbligato recitatives is that which begins part II, number 10a, "Oh della santa fé," sung by Anna, Sara, and Raphael. The text expresses hope that Tobit's eyes will soon be healed. This long (109 mm.) recitative is introduced by an orchestral passage of thirty-four measures that serves as an introduction to part II; the recitative is unusual for its triple meter throughout and its tonal stability (in B-flat) for the first forty measures, after which it modulates freely and closes on the dominant of E minor, just before Raphael's aria (no. 10b) in D major. Another imposing obbligato recitative, which is even longer (177 mm.) than number 10a, is number 16, in which all five soloists participate. This is the denouement, the text of which has been described above. The recitative uses the entire orchestra except for trombones, as does the final chorus for which it prepares, and is filled with dramatic orchestral punctuations. Particularly effective is the point at which Azarias reveals himself as Raphael, with a fanfare that includes brass and timpani; shocked at his words, the other soloists interrupt the recitative with an awe-inspired, measured ensemble of whole and half notes, with the words, "Ah perdono, pietà guerrier celeste!"

After the first performance of *Tobia*, a Viennese newspaper reported on Haydn's success and mentioned: "Especially his choruses glowed with a fire that was otherwise only in Händel."[62] The reference to Handel is appropriate, for the considerable amount of learned style in all three of the 1775 choruses (nos. 1, 9, and 17) recalls the Baroque, as does the careful attention to text painting. (The style of these choruses is diametrically opposed to the simplicity of those in Bertoni's *David poenitens*—a work that reflects Venetian practice but which, as mentioned above, was performed on the same series as Haydn's oratorio later in the same year.) In number 1, learned style is evident at the first choral entrance (Example III-26b) and frequently thereafter; the counterpoint, however, is balanced by chordal, declamatory style in this and the other choruses. The final choruses of both parts I and II close with extended fugues that are similar in several respects and contribute another element of symmetry to the work. Both fugue subjects (Example III-29a from no. 9 and 29b from no. 17), begin with an ascending fourth, return one step, ascend again, and curve back; in both fugues, the order of voice entrances is BTAS; and near the end of both fugues pedal points and chordal texture (traditional procedures in this context) are introduced. All three of the 1775 choruses include soloists: in number 1 the soloists alternate with the chorus within a free sort of exposition-recapitulation structure; number 7, prior to its closing fugue, has a choral refrain that is sung after solos by each of the five personages; and number 17 begins with the soloists, then a choral passage precedes the final fugue.

Neither of the two choruses added in 1784 (nos. 5c and 13c) includes a fugue, but both use imitative and chordal texture. In the oratorio's 1784 version, the chorus 5c continues directly from the preceding aria, the last few measures of which were deleted so that the two numbers could be joined. (The text of that chorus begins with the same words as the preceding aria, but the continuation is different.) The second of the 1784 choruses is musically related to its preceding aria: the second stanza of the chorus's text is set to the same melodic material as the second stanza of the aria's text, for the ideas of those second stanzas are related. In all the choruses of this oratorio Haydn is careful to paint and

62. K. k. priviligierte Realzeitung, no. 14 (6 April 1775), p. 219, as translated in Landon, *Haydn*, 2:215.

EXAMPLE III-29. *Tobia*—Haydn (Haydn, *Tobia**, pp. 267–68, 563–65).

Example a:

Restore the light to Tobit, oh Author of light . . .

Example b:

We shall gain greater glory and greater happiness.

express his text in detail, but number 13c is particularly rich in this regard and is among the most powerful expressions in the oratorio.

Pietro Alessandro Guglielmi: Debora e Sisara

Born in Massa, about twenty miles north-west of Lucca, Guglielmi (1728–1804) is said to have received his early training in Lucca under Giacomo Puccini (1712–81).[63] With the patronage of the duchess of Massa, Guglielmi went to Naples in 1746 to study at the Conservatorio di Santa Maria di Loreto, where his teacher was Durante and his better-known fellow students included Pasquale Anfossi, Tommaso Traetta, and Antonio Sacchini. It was probably in 1754 that Guglielmi left the conservatory; his earliest opera, the genre for which he was to become best known, dates from 1757. Between 1763 and 1776 he traveled widely for performances of his operas in Rome, in cities of northern Italy and particularly Venice, and in London where, from 1767 to 1772, he and Felice Alessandri shared the musical directorship of the King's Theatre in the Haymarket. Guglielmi continued his operatic career in Naples from 1772 to 1793, when he was called to Rome as maestro di cappella at St. Peter's; from 1797 he held the same post at the church of San Lorenzo in Lucina. In Rome he composed most of his church music but continued to write operas. He was elected to membership in the Neapolitan Nobile Accademia di Musica (1777) and Instituto Nazionale (1799), and was a member of the Roman Accademia di Santa Cecilia and Institut National des Sciences et des Arts.

Between 1764 and 1802, Guglielmi wrote at least seven oratorios, mostly for concert performances at the Congregation of the Oratory in Rome and for Lenten staged performances in Neapolitan theaters.[64] Of these works, *Debora e Sisara* was by far the best known in Guglielmi's

63. The great, great grandfather of the more famous Giacomo Puccini (1858–1924). For information on Guglielmi's life and works, see: James L. Jackman, "Pietro Alessandro Guglielmi," *New Grove*, 7:793–97.

64. The following list of first-performance places, institutions, dates, and librettists (if known), is based on Jackman, "Guglielmi," *New Grove*, 7:797, with corrections based on information from printed librettos: *La madre de' Maccabei* (Rome, Congregation of the Oratory, 1 November 1764; lib., Giuseppe Barbieri); *Debora e Sisara* (Naples, Teatro San Carlo, Lent, 1789; lib., Carlo Sernicola); *La passione di Gesù Cristo* (Madrid, Caños de Peral, Lent, 1790); *La morte d'Oloferne* (Naples, Teatro del Fondo di Separazione, Lent, 1791; after, and with quotations from, Metastasio, *Betulia liberata*), *Gionata Maccabeo* (Naples, Teatro San Carlo, Lent, 1798; lib., Onorato Balsamo?), *Il solenne trattenimento de' fratelli dell'Oratorio di S. Filippo Neri sul monte di S. Onofrio* (Rome, Congregation of the Oratory, 1 June 1800; lib., Giovanni Battista Rasi), *Il Paradiso perduto* (Rome, Congregation of the Oratory, 1 November 1802; lib., Rasi).

time and is said to have been "almost universally regarded as one of the most sublime works of the late 18th century."[65] Composed for the Lenten season of 1788 at the Neapolitan Teatro San Carlo, the work was performed frequently for about two decades in Italy and abroad (see Table III-7) and sporadically to the 1820s. Slightly more than half the performances of *Debora e Sisara* that are listed in Table III-7 were given in theaters and were certainly or probably staged (but not the London performance, no. 16); the remainder probably were not staged, for they were given in oratories and halls in which staging was not characteristic. The adaptability of this work to both staged and unstaged performance no doubt contributed to the frequency with which it was heard. *Debora e Sisara* is among the antecedents of an even more famous work of the same genre, dating from thirty years later: Gioacchino Rossini's *Mosè in Egitto* (1818), composed for Lenten performance in the same theater, and on occasion given as a traditional, unstaged oratorio in concert hall, oratory, or church.[66]

Carlo Sernicola's libretto for *Debora e Sisara* is derived from the biblical story in the Book of Judges, chapter 4, which had been an important source of oratorio librettos since at least the early eighteenth century. In the biblical account the people of Israel are suffering under the yoke of Jaban, the Canaanite king, whose general is Sisara. The Jewish prophetess Debora tells her people to rise up against Sisara and asks the captain, Barac, to assemble an army. He does so, but fears the outcome of a battle with Sisara and asks Debora to accompany him. She agrees and predicts that Sisara will fall by the hand of a woman. The Israelites win the battle, but Sisara escapes and flees to the tent of Jahel, the wife of Haber, with whom Sisara is at peace. Jahel allows Sisara to hide in her tent, but during his sleep she drives a nail "through his brain fast into the ground: and so passing from deep sleep to death, he fainted away and died" (Judges 4:21). When Barac comes in pursuit of Sisara, Jahel reveals to him the dead leader.

The librettist makes clear in the prefatory *Argomento* that he interprets the biblical story as a tribute to the courage and moral strength of women, and his drama celebrates the heroism first of Debora and then Giaele (Jahel): "The Highest God, wishing to make known that women equally as well as men are capable of that counsel, of that fortitude, which are sought to support great matters and to govern peoples, after the deaths of several leaders who with the name of judges had governed His people, made their government fall into the hands of a prophetess by the name of Debora. . . . Filled with divine spirit, Debora showed no less

---

65. Jackman, "Guglielmi," *New Grove*, 7:794. See also Florimo, *Napoli*, 2:341.

66. Including "the church of Saint Patrick in New York," according to a printed libretto with an English title, *Moses in Egypt: A Sacred Oratorio* (n.p.: J. H. Turney, for L. Da Ponte, 1832).

TABLE III-7
Guglielmi, *Debora e Sisara*: Provisional List of Performances, 1788–1827

Year	City	Place and/or sponsor	Occasion and/or date
1) 1788	Naples	Teatro S. Carlo	Lent
2) 1789	Bologna	Oratorio, S. Filippo Neri	—
3) 1789	Florence	Oratorio, S. Filippo Neri	Feast, 8 December
4) 1789	Naples	Teatro San Carlo	Lent
5) 1790	Ferrara	Sala de' sig. Intrepidi	Lent
6) 1790	Pisa	Teatro dei fratelli Prini	Lent
7) 1791	Florence	Teatro di via della Pergola	Lent
8) 1791	Genoa	Oratorio, S. Filippo Neri?	—
9) 1791	Prague	Teatro Nazionale	December [Advent]
10) 1791	Rome	Oratorio, S. Girolamo della Carità	—
11) 1791	Warsaw	Oratorio di corte	Holy Week
12) 1792	Palermo	Teatro S. Cecilia, Nobili Associati	Lent
13) 1793	Milan	Teatro alla Scala	Autumn
14) 1795	Bologna	Oratorio, S. Maria della Morte	Good Friday
15) 1795	Longiano	Church, Minori Conventuali di S. Francesco	Feast, 26 July
16) 1795	London	King's Theatre in the Haymarket	Lent
17) 1795	Naples	Teatro S. Carlo	Lent
18) 1796	Lisbon	Nuova sala della Assemblea nel Reggio Teatro di S. Carlo	Lent
19) 1798	Livorno	Teatro, Accademici Avvalorati	Lent
20) 1803	Florence	Teatro in via della Pergola	Lent
21) 1806	Lisbon	Reggio Teatro di S. Carlo	Summer
22) 1806	Venice	Teatro Venier in S. Benedetto	Lent
23) 1808	Rimini	—	Feast, S. Antonio di Padova
24) 1808	Ferrara	Teatro Comunale	Lent
25) 1810	Milan	Teatro alla Scala	Lent
26) 1815	Palermo	Teatro Carolino	Lent
27) 1818	Palermo	Teatro Carolino	Lent
28) 1821	Rome	Oratorio, S. Filippo Neri	—
29) 1827	Chieti	—	Feast of S. Giustino

The table is based primarily on evidence in printed librettos.

courage in war than she had shown prudence in time of peace. . . ." After relating Giaele's courageous act, he summarizes: "and in that manner by one woman such a signal war began and by another it was concluded."[67]

The libretto includes seven personages: Debora (S); Sisara (T); Alcimo (S), Sisara's son, not in the biblical story; Barac (B); Giaele (S); Araspe (S), another nonbiblical personage, who is a confidant of Sisara and Alcimo; and Aber (T); plus choruses of Hebrew and Canaanite soldiers. In part I Debora urges war against Sisara and agrees to accompany Barac into battle. To gain time for preparation, Barac asks Aber to approach Sisara about a peace conference. When Aber does so, Sisara at first refuses, but his son, Alcimo (portrayed as a person sensitive to human values, unlike his father), has a premonition of disaster and pleads with his father at least to discuss peace. Sisara agrees, and arrangements are made for the conference. At the end of part I the conference takes place, but anger erupts on both sides. In the recitative that precedes the quartet finale, Sisara says he will meet the Israelites on the battlefield. The quartet expresses the anger and confusion of Debora, Barac, and Sisara, while Alcimo is still trying in vain to play the role of peacemaker. Part II begins with reflections on various feelings before the battle. Then the actual conflict is described in the libretto's notes on stage action, including the darkening of the sky and the tempest on the side of the Canaanites, the death of Araspe, the fleeing of Sisara, and the victory of the Israelites. In the scene following Sisara's flight from the battlefield, he is exhausted, confused, and lost (the scene begins with "Ove son? Ove fuggo?" an expression long familiar in oratorio and opera), but he finds his way to Giaele's tent. She invites him in and goes into the tent when she knows he is asleep. The Israelites enter with choruses of thanksgiving, and during the recitatives and choral-solo complexes, Giaele appears and pulls open the door of her tent to reveal the dead Sisara (tutti: "Oh vista!"; Alcimo: "Ah padre!"). In the course of further recitative and an aria-chorus complex, Alcimo can see no further reason to live, and he kills himself (Giaele, Aber, Barac: "Oh spettacolo!"; Debora: "Oh orrore!"). The choral-solo finale reflects on the power of God, the Israelites' debt to him, and their penitence.

Although this libretto for the most part continues the traditional alternation between recitative and aria, ensemble, or chorus, it is a long way from the Metastasian libretto. Not only is unity of place ignored and unity of time questionable, but far more dramatic action takes place than was characteristic of most oratorios even at the end of the century. This is, of course, to be expected of a work originally intended for staged

67. The quotations are translated from the libretto *Debora e Sisara: Azione sacra* (Naples: Vincenzo Flauto, 1788), pp. 5–6 (copy in the Schatz Collection at US-Wc: ML48/.S4241), but virtually the same *Argomento* was reprinted in many of the later printed librettos.

presentation, yet it seems to have retained its popularity even without staging, when the audience needed to read the descriptions of action printed in the libretto in order to understand the work.

As might be expected for a work which had so many performances, *Debora e Sisara* exists in numerous sources that differ from one another. Some differences are insignificant, but others are major. Given the minimal research thus far on Guglielmi's music, the amount of contact the composer had with the various versions is not known. The source used for the present discussion is that in a manuscript at the New York Public Library.[68] Most of that version corresponds to the libretto printed in 1788 for the first performance;[69] in part I the differences are minor, but in part II they are more significant. The version of the New York manuscript might date from as early as 1791, for its part II shows many correspondences with part II of a libretto printed in 1791 for a performance at the court in Warsaw (see Table III-7, no. 11).[70]

The oratorio as represented in the source selected for these comments (see the outline in Table III-8), begins with a sinfonia in B-flat; parts I and II end in that key, which is also heard twice within each part. Both parts begin with keys closely related to B-flat, as are most keys of the oratorio. In regard to the use of sharp keys, it is of interest that numbers 2, 5, and 10, in A, D, and D, respectively, are either prayers or refer to prayers.

The instrumentation includes strings and pairs of flutes, clarinets, oboes, bassoons, horns, and trumpets; and in two numbers a harp is used, both times to accompany Debora. In number 14 the harp plays throughout Debora's aria, which reflects her serene peace and confidence as she prepares to lead the battle against Sisara; and in number 20, a prayer in which the chorus and Debora alternate, the harp accompanies her solos.

The opening sinfonia begins with an adagio introduction, followed by an allegro in sonata form, with a modified recapitulation that begins in the subdominant. The allegro makes considerable use of solo winds. Two other instrumental numbers are a march (between nos. 15 and 16), for clarinets, horns and bassons, played as Sisara marches off with his his squadron; and a sinfonia, which follows the quintet (no. 16). That sinfonia—a noisy battle symphony played during the simultaneous raging of a battle and a thunderstorm—is introduced by the following stage directions: "When the quintet is finished, the signal of the battle is given.

68. US-NYp: *MRHI+. The provenience of the manuscript is given on its title page as follows: Presso "Gio.i Ricordi Editore ed Incisore di musica tiene negozio Copisteria, e Stamperia di musica, nella Contrada di Pescheria Vecchia vicino alla Piazza de Mercanti in Milano . . ." Ricordi was located in that contrada between 1808 and 1812, according to Richard Macnutt, "Ricordi," *New Grove*, 15:851.

69. See app. A for the complete title page and library location.

70. See app. A for title-page quotation and library location.

TABLE III-8
Guglielmi, *Debora e Sisara*: Structural Outline

Numbers	Keys
[Sinfonia]	B♭
PART I	
1. Coro, Debora, Giaele, Aber, "Ah! qual viltade"	E♭
2. Aria. Giaele, "Ah l'ira tua giammai"	A
3. Aria. Debora, "Sento già qual voce"	C
[4. Aria. Aber, "Preveggo già l'ire"	B♭
5. Aria. Barac, "D'una donna per mano s'avvenga"	D
6. Duet. Sisara, Alcimo, "Al mio contento in seno"	G
7. Aria. Sisara, "Tuoni il cielo"	B♭
8. Aria. Araspe, "Quando il periglio è certo"	C
9. Aria. Alcimo, "Non merta il mio amore"	F
10. Coro d'Israeliti, "Con prieghi aspettasi"	D
11. Quartet. Deb., Bar., Sis., Alc., "Perfido!"	B♭
PART II	
12. Aria. Barac, "Fra quai dubbj in volto"	g
13. Aria. Araspe, "Giacchè scacciar non sai"	D
14. Aria. Debora, "Non ascolto in tal momento"	B♭
15. Aria. Giaele, "La speme, che in Dio"	F
16. Quint. Sis., Ara., Deb., Bar., Alc., "La mia destra"	C
17. Aria. Sisara, "Io cedo a detti tuoi"	B♭
18. Coro d'Israel., Abe., Bar., Deb., Alc., "Dagli affanni"	D
19. Aria (Alcimo, "Non ha cor") & Coro d'Israeliti	F
20. Coro ("Quanto a te dobbiam gran Dio"), Debora	B♭

Source, US-NYp: *MRHI+, except for bracketed no. 4, found in US-Wc: M2000/.G84 D3/Case.

Araspe is struck down. Sisara meanwhile, seeing his camp destroyed, jumps down from his carriage and flees precipitously, while Debora and Barac wander through various streets, following small remaining groups of the Canaanites, and gradually the storm ceases."[71]

Of the twelve arias (excluding no. 19, which includes chorus), eight (nos. 2, 3, 4, 5, 7, 8, 9, and 12) are cast in the A1-B-A2 form of the transformed da capo aria. In these eight the first stanza of the text is set in A1 and A2 and the second in B. One aria (no. 13) has the A1-A2 form, with both stanzas set in both sections. The duet and one aria (nos. 6 and 14) are ternary forms (with A closing in the tonic). Only one aria (no.

71. Translated from *Debora e Sisara: Azione sacra* (Warsaw: P. Dufour, 1791), p. 57.

15) has a dal segno form, in which the sign is used to delete the opening ritornello. The structure of number 17 is unusual: it might be heard as a free rondo, but the "refrain" is not always in the tonic; the strangeness of this structure seems to reflect the uncertainty of Sisara, who vacillates between the impulse to accept Giaele's invitation to rest in her tent and the contrary impulse to continue fleeing for his life.

The arias in the oratorio well represent the Classical style as found in Neapolitan opera of the 1780s. Although they include ample opportunity for vocal display at intense moments, their style is otherwise simple, with balanced phrases, slow harmonic rhythm, and orchestration calculated to support and add color to the vocal lines but not to compete with them. Example III-30 (from no. 2) is characteristic. The opening ritornello, of which about one-third is shown in the example, illustrates the tunefulness of the work; the burst of sixteenth notes in the flutes and strings (mm. 2 and 4) and the sudden tutti, marked *forte*, (mm. 6–8) are typical contrasts. In the recitative preceding this aria, Debora has inspired Giaele with courageous words, and the aria is her simple expression of hope that the wrath of God will never be deadly for her people.

Illustrating the type of coloratura found in the work is Example III-31 (from no. 3). Debora has just agreed to accompany Barac into battle, and in this aria she expresses her response to her inner voice, which urges immediate battle: "I feel that voice in my breast, it speaks to me and strengthens me; now the fault is to delay, ah, one [must] run to triumph." Like the previous example, this one begins in a simple style (the voice enters for the first time in measure 17), but the syncopated accompaniment in the violins (first heard at the beginning of the opening ritornello) suggest Debora's excited state. When she arrives at the words "ah, si corra a trionfar," the final syllable provides an occasion for an elaborate coloratura that continues for nine measures (and repeats later in the aria).

The oratorio includes three ensembles: a duet (no. 6), the quartet-finale to part I (no. 11), and the quintet (no. 16). The duet between the father and son, Sisara and Alcimo, written in a relatively simple and lyrical style, proceeds mostly in parallel thirds and sixths in the first and third sections (A1 and A2). More complex is the quartet, for this represents the ensemble finale much as it is found in comic opera. Here, however, the motivation for confusion is anything but comic, for the ensemble represents the breakdown of peace negotiations—a breakdown complete with shouting and name calling on both sides. Solos and various groupings of soloists into ensembles lead to a concluding, agitated, operatic *stretta* for all voices and full orchestra. The quintet, in part II, is not in the original 1788 libretto; in the version presented here it substitutes for an aria. When the substitution was added is not known (nor is it certain that it was Guglielmi's work), but it is present in the 1791 Warsaw libretto. Like the quartet just discussed, the quintet is intended to

EXAMPLE III-30. continued

EXAMPLE III-30. continued

EXAMPLE III-30. continued

Ah, let thy wrath be never deadly for us . . .

EXAMPLE III-31. *Debora e Sisara*—Guglielmi (US-NYp: *MRHI+, ff. [66–66v, 68–69v]).

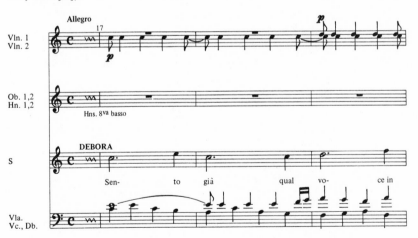

EXAMPLE III-31. continued

EXAMPLE III-31. continued

EXAMPLE III-31. continued

I feel that voice in my breast . . . ah, one [must] run to triumph.

represent conflict—here, the verbal conflict of enemies just before they clash in battle—and the procedures of this ensemble are comparable to those of the quartet.

Most of the recitative in the oratorio is in simple style, but obbligato recitative is used seven times, usually at points of extreme dramatic tension. The longest of the obbligato recitatives is the dialogue between Sisara and Giaele in part II, beginning with Sisara's "Ove son, ove fuggo?" (leading to his aria, no. 17). Here the orchestral passages between vocal sections are long and dramatic, to portray Sisara's confusion and exhaustion after the battle, Giaele's gradual manipulation of Sisara into her tent, and his hesitations and changes of mind.

The chorus is used in five numbers, and virtually all choral writing is in chordal style. Soloists are combined with the chorus in three of the five numbers (1, 19, and 20). The first of these is an opening solo-duo-choral complex: the Hebrews begin by lamenting their condition, in a largo sostentuo section, during which Giaele and Aber sing a brief duo of hopelessness; then the tempo changes to allegro spirituoso and Debora vigorously rejects their self pity, as she sings coloratura passages between and soaring above the *sotto voce* choral statements. Number 19 is the aria-choral complex in which Alcimo laments the death of his father and then kills himself, and the chorus responds with shock. The choral-solo finale of the oratorio is a prayer in which Debora and the chorus alternate. The two choruses that do not include soloists (nos. 10 and 18) are both marches; in number 10 the chorus alternates with a wind band.

* * *

Through the course of the eighteenth century, the Italian oratorio—the earliest and by far the most widely cultivated and influential type—clearly reflected the principal changes in the musical style of the period. In varying degrees the Italian oratorio was a model for the genre in other languages. Although the English oratorio was in large measure the creation of Handel and shows various influences, the basics of the genre are clearly Italian—Handel, after all, had first composed oratorios in Italy, and in England he modified what he had learned in Italy to suit English taste. Yet in his hands the English oratorio became a specific, Handelian type; and after Handel's death in 1759, the genre in England retained its essentially Handelian traits for the rest of the century and beyond.

PART II
The English Oratorio after Handel

CHAPTER IV

Social Contexts of the English Oratorio

Introduction: Terminology and Genre Definition

In 1763 a small, anonymous book appeared in London under the title, *An Examination of the Oratorios Which Have Been Performed This Season at Covent-Garden Theatre*. The author, Robert Maddison, wrote it essentially to support the views of John Brown, whose treatise on the relationship between poetry and music had recently appeared; a pasticcio setting of Brown's libretto, *The Cure of Saul*, had just been performed at Covent Garden.[1] Near the beginning of his *Examination*, Maddison raises the question of what an oratorio is, and confesses, "I never was more puzzled in my life, than to tell what it is, there are so many discordant opinions about it." He continues:

> At *one end* of the *town*, an *Oratorio* is a sort of sober, solemn entertainment; which, by way of *mortification* in *Lent*, is served up to the public on *fish* and *soup days*; and so the admirers of *Acis and Galatea*, and *Alexander's Feast*, have slyly slipped them in under the names of *Oratorios*, just as a good catholic friend of mine, who was a great lover of *Pork* and *Pease*, used to call it *Sturgeon* whenever he eat it in Lent. On the contrary, at the *other end* of the *Town*, an *Oratorio* is a bundle of diverting songs and choirs, tied together, with a little solemn nonsense, during which, you may talk, sleep, or stare, without any interruption, either to your own, or the audience's entertainment. Now, for my part, I have a very different idea of a genuine Oratorio, and here I present it to the reader, under the dry form of a definition.
>
> An *Oratorio* then is a *Poem*, accompanied with *music*, where, unincumbered with the absurdity of a *dramatic exhibition*, they jointly affect the mind, by a representation of some great and interesting subject, impressed with all the force of their combined powers. I say unincumbered with a *dramatic* exhibition, because an *Oratorio*, if *acted*, becomes immediately an *Opera*, with the addi-

1. On Brown's treatise and his libretto, *The Cure of Saul*, see chapter 5.

tional impropriety of a *continued chorus*, and an almost unavoidable want of *unity*, both in *time* and *place*. . . .[2]

There would seem to be much truth in both Maddison's caricature in the first paragraph and his definition in the second, so far as the performance and the generally accepted definition of oratorio in England are concerned. Maddison adheres to a characteristic eighteenth-century view when he speaks of oratorio as first of all a poetic genre and secondly a musical one. In London, oratorios were given largely during Lent on Wednesdays and Fridays in the theaters. Although Handel did not regard his *Acis and Galatea* and *Alexander's Feast* as oratorios, they were often included as Lenten offerings in the theaters, as if they were oratorios, simply because they were performed in the manner of an oratorio. And the manner of oratorio performance in England was unstaged—"unincumbered with a *dramatic* exhibition."

Although Maddison regards the oratorio as "a representation of some great and interesting subject," he does not specify that the subject be religious; yet he seems to imply such a subject when he says the admirers of the secular *Acis and Galatea* and *Alexander's Feast* had "slyly slipped them in under the names of *Oratorios*," and with few exceptions the works generally called oratorios in eighteenth-century England were based on religious subjects. An exception beyond the two noted by Maddison is a work by Thomas Arne. One of his most popular stage pieces of the mid-century, the masque *Alfred* (1742), was revised as *Alfred the Great* and given, presumably again as a masque, on Friday, 12 May 1753, at the King's Theatre in the Haymarket. But during the Lenten oratorio season of 1754, *Alfred the Great* was advertised as "done in the manner of an Oratorio" for its performance at the Theatre Royal in Drury Lane on Wednesday, 27 March.[3] Subsequent public references to the work sometimes referred to it as "the Oratorio of Alfred";[4] and an undated libretto printed in London for a concert performance calls the work *Alfred the Great: An Oratorio. As perform'd at the Theatre-Royal in Drury-Lane.*[5]

From Handel's death in 1759 to the early nineteenth century, the English oratorio is Handelian in several senses: the terminology and genre definition are essentially Handel's; his works remain important in the oratorio repertoire; other oratorio composers follow the Handelian model at least in certain externals if not in musical style; and the continuing tradition of giving oratorios in the London theaters during Lent was begun by Handel. The performance of Handel's music in London and at the provincial festivals acquired significant ritual and political

2. [Maddison], *Examination*, pp. 3–4.
3. *London Stage*, 4/1:417.
4. Ibid., 4/1:423, 425.
5. Copy in GB-Lbl: R. M. 5. e. 6 (5).

dimensions, as recent research has shown.[6] The Handelian oratorio is so important in the following pages that a brief review of Handel's treatment of the genre is in order.

The English oratorio was Handel's creation, that is, his highly successful modification of an essentially Italian genre to suit English taste;[7] and he dominated the genre in England from the time of his first oratorio in English, *Esther* (1718), until long after his death. The texts of his English oratorios are sacred, usually dramatic, in three acts (sometimes called "parts") as opposed to the Italian two, and his English works place far greater emphasis on the chorus than do contemporary oratorios in Italian. Exceptions to Handel's use of the term *oratorio* for a setting of a dramatic text with personages are his designations of three works with nondramatic texts as oratorios: *Israel in Egypt, Messiah*, and the *Occasional Oratorio*; and in one instance, Handel used *oratorio* for a concert of miscellaneous works.[8] (In the later eighteenth century, the use of *oratorio* for a concert of sacred music during Lent was revived; also late in the century, *oratorio* was sometimes used in the provinces as a synonym for *festival*.)[9] In Handel's early oratorios he drew the musical styles of his recitatives and airs from Italian *opera seria*; in the later oratorios, however, he increasingly departed from the da capo air and certain other *opera seria* conventions. The choruses of Handel's oratorios were modeled on English sacred choral music. With the exception of a 1732 performance of *Esther*, Handel's oratorios were given in concert, usually in London's theaters during Lent, and they continued to be heard in that context until well into the nineteenth century.

England

The sources of information on the English oratorio after Handel are numerous but have never been fully explored. The treatment of the subject in this chapter and the following one must be considered provisional, pending further specialized research in this field.

6. Weber, *Musical Classics*. I am grateful to William Weber for allowing me to see the manuscript of his book in progress, in which the performance in England of "ancient" music—by Handel and some of his contemporaries and predecessors—in the later eighteenth century is perceptively and convincingly interpreted as both ritual and political behavior. That interpretation does not form a significant part of my study, but Weber's work should be consulted for details. For a revealing account of what Handel's oratorios meant to his admirers in the second half of the eighteenth century, see Myers, *Anna Seward*, which includes numerous quotations from the letters of this ardent Handelian.

7. On the few English antecedents of the Handelian oratorio, see Smither, *Oratorio*, 2:175–78, 182–88.

8. For more details on terminology, see ibid., 2:349–50.

9. Pritchard, "Musical Festival," p. 50.

Oratorios in the Theaters. Handel's immediate successors as managers of the Lenten oratorio series in London's theaters were John Christopher Smith the younger (1712–95) and John Stanley (1712–86).[10] Smith, the son of Handel's treasurer and principal copyist, was a composer and organist who had assisted Handel in his later years; Stanley was a composer and celebrated blind organist who had directed some of Handel's oratorios in the 1750s. Beginning in 1760 Smith and Stanley jointly organized the oratorio concerts at the Theatre Royal in Covent Garden, and in 1770 they moved to the Theatre Royal in Drury Lane.[11] When Smith left the series in 1774 he was replaced by the composer-harpsichordist Thomas Linley Sr. (1733–95), and upon Stanley's resignation (1786, shortly before his death),[12] the composer-organist Samuel Arnold (1740–1802) succeeded him. Rivals to these oratorio series included the concerts, also held in theaters, directed in 1761–62 and 1773 by Thomas Augustine Arne (1710–78); in 1768–73 and 1776–77 by Arnold (sometimes together with Edward Toms); in 1770–71 and 1775 by Johann Christian Bach (1735–82); and in 1774, 1779, and 1784 by François-Hyppolyte Barthélemon (1741–1808). In the period immediately following Handel's death, the concerts in these series typically followed Handel's model: an oratorio would form the main evening's offering, and instrumental music, often concertos, would be performed between the acts; later, concerts of oratorio excerpts became more frequent than complete oratorios.

Virtually all of these series were overwhelmingly devoted to Handel's music. Table IV-1, which lists the oratorios given in London theaters during nine Lenten seasons from the year after Handel's death to the turn of the century, represents, in general, the repertoire and main locations of oratorio performances in London during this forty-year period.[13] As the lists of 1760 and 1765 show, the oratorio series at Covent Garden had no rivals. Most of the works are by Handel, and his *Messiah* (characteristically announced as *The Messiah*) closes the season, as it tends to do for most of the later eighteenth century (cf. all the lists except those of 1790–1800). The series of 1760 and 1765 are characteristic for their

10. This paragraph is based mainly on McVeigh, "Violinist," pp. 47–48; the volumes of *London Stage* that treat the theatrical seasons mentioned; and the articles in *New Grove* on the persons mentioned.

11. For details of the Lenten oratorios during Stanley's period, see Williams, "Stanley," 1:42–47.

12. Williams, "Stanley," pp. 57–58.

13. Table IV-1, for which the source is the volumes of *London Stage* for the years in question, lists the name of the composition as given in the source but omits the numerous comments and longer versions of titles, which would well repay further investigation for a more detailed understanding of the social context of oratorios in the theaters.

TABLE IV-I
Oratorios in London Theaters: Nine Lenten Seasons, 1760-1800

Dates			Theaters, Oratorio Titles, Composers, Comments

1760

February
F	22	CG	*Samson*
W	27	CG	*Samson*
F	29	CG	*Paradise Lost*, Smith

March
W	5	CG	*Paradise Lost*, Smith
F	7	CG	*The Triumph of Time and Truth*
W	12	CG	*Zimri*, Stanley
W	19	CG	*Judas Maccabaeus*
F	21	CG	*Judas Maccabaeus*
W	26	CG	*The Messiah*
F	28	CG	*The Messiah*

1765

February
| F | 22* | CG | *Judas Maccabaeus* |
| W | 27 | CG | *Alexander's Feast, Coronation Anthems* |

March
F	1	CG	*Israel in Babylon*, Handel pasticcio by Toms
W	6	CG	*Samson*
F	8	CG	*Judas Maccabaeus*
W	13	CG	*Israel in Egypt*, "With considerable alterations and Additions."
F	15	CG	*Solomon*
W	20	CG	*Samson*
F	22	CG	*Judas Maccabaeus*
W	27	CG	*The Messiah*
F	29	CG	*The Messiah*

1770

March
[Th	1	KH	*La passione*, Jommelli]
F	2	CG	*The Messiah*
F	2*	DL	*Samson*
W	7	CG	*Judas Maccabaeus*
W	7*	DL	*Judas Maccabaeus*
[Th	8	KH	*La passione*, Jommelli; *Stabat Mater*, Pergolesi; "Grand Chorus," P. C. Guglielmi]
F	9	CG	*The Resurrection*, Arnold
F	9*	DL	*Gideon*, Smith

TABLE IV-1
continued

Dates			Theaters, Oratorio Titles, Composers, Comments
W	14	CG	*Samson*
W	14*	DL	*Alexander's Feast, Coronation Anthems*
[Th	15	KH	*La passione*, Jommelli; other works as March 8]
[F	16	CG	*The Passion*, Jommelli. "Oratorio from the Italian of Metastasio. Never Performed. The Music by Sg Jomelli With additional Choruses by Leo, Graun, and others."]
F	16*	DL	*Acis and Galatea, Ode for St. Cecilia*
W	21	CG	*The Messiah*
W	21*	DL	*Judas Maccabaeus*
[Th	22	KH	*Gioas Re di Giuda*, J. C. Bach]
F	23	CG	*The Resurrection*, Arnold
F	23*	DL	*The Messiah*
W	28	CG	*Israel in Babylon*, Handel pasticcio by Toms
W	28*	DL	*Alexander's Feast, Coronation Anthems*
[Th	29	KH	*Gioas Re di Giuda*, J. C. Bach]
F	30	CG	*The Resurrection*, Arnold
F	30*	DL	*Samson*
April			
[W	4	CG	*The Death of Abel*, Piccini. "From the Italian of Metastasio. . . . with additional chorusses (sic)."]
W	4*	DL	*The Messiah*
[Th	5	KH	*Gioas Re di Giuda*, J. C. Bach]
F	6	CG	*The Resurrection*, Arnold
F	6*	DL	*The Messiah*
1775			
March			
F	3	DL	*Judas Maccabaeus*
W	8	DL	*Samson*
W	8*	KH	*Samson*
F	10*	DL	*Judas Maccabaeus*
F	10	KH	*The Messiah*
W	15	DL	*Acis and Galatea, Ode for St. Cecilia's Day.* "In the Ode will be introduced two *songs* from Handel's Oratorios."
F	17	DL	*Alexander's Feast*, two Coronation Anthems
F	17*	KH	*The Messiah*
W	22	DL	*L'Allegro, il Penseroso*, two Coronation Anthems
W	22*	KH	*Samson*
F	24	DL	*The Messiah*
F	24*	KH	*Alexander's Feast*, Coronation Anthems
W	29	DL	*The Fall of Egypt*, Stanley
W	29*	KH	*Judas Maccabaeus*

TABLE IV-1
continued

Dates			Theaters, Oratorio Titles, Composers, Comments
F	31	DL	*The Messiah*
F	31*	KH	*Alexander's Feast,* Coronation Anthems
April			
W	5	DL	*Acis and Galatea, Ode for St. Cecilia's Day* (as 15 March)
W	5*	KH	*Judas Maccabaeus*
F	7	DL	*The Messiah*
F	7*	KH	*The Messiah*
1780			
February			
F	11*	DL	*Alexander's Feast, Ode for St. Cecilia's Day*
W	16	DL	*Judas Maccabaeus*
F	18*	DL	*Acis and Galatea,* "Also the music in *Bonduca* . . . by the late Henry Purcell."
W	23	DL	*Samson*
F	25*	DL	*L'Allegro, il Penseroso ed il Moderato*
March			
W	1	DL	*Joseph*
F	3*	DL	*Acis and Galatea;* music in *Bonduca,* Purcell
W	8	DL	*Judas Maccabaeus*
F	10*	DL	*L'Allegro, il Penseroso, Ode for St. Cecilia's Day*
W	15	DL	*The Messiah*
F	17*	DL	*The Messiah*
1785			
February			
F	11*	DL	"The Music that was selected for the Commemoration of Handel, in Westminster Abbey and the Pantheon, the 26th and 27th of May, 1784."
W	16	DL	*The Messiah*
F	18*	DL	*Acis and Galatea, Ode for St. Cecilia's Day*
W	23	DL	*L'Allegro, il Penseroso, The Coronation Anthems*
W	23	LH	*Judas Maccabaeus*
F	25*	DL	*Alexander's Feast,* "Also some of the pieces that were selected and performed for the Commemoration of Handel . . ."
March			
F	4*	DL	*Judas Maccabaeus*
F	11*	DL	*Samson*
W	16	DL	*The Messiah*
W	16	LH	*Judith,* Arne
F	18*	DL	*The Messiah*

TABLE IV-I
continued

Dates			Theaters, Oratorio Titles, Composers, Comments

1790

February

F	19	CG	*The Messiah,* "preceded by *God save the King*"
F	19	DL	*The Messiah,* "preceded by *God save the King*"
W	24	CG	"A Grand Selection of Sacred Music from the performances in Westminster Abbey"
W	24	DL	"A Grand Selection from the Works of Handel that were performed at the Pantheon and Westminster–Abbey"
F	26	CG	"A Grand Selection of Sacred Music," Handel
F	26	DL	*Redemption,* Handel pasticcio by Arnold

March

W	3	CG	"A Grand Selection of Sacred Music," Handel
W	3	DL	"A Grand Selection from the Works of Handel"
F	5	CG	*Judas Maccabaeus*
F	5	DL	*Acis and Galatea,* "Also a Grand Selection"
W	10	CG	"A Grand Selection of Sacred Music," Handel
W	10	DL	"A Grand Selection from the Works of Handel"
F	12	CG	*The Messiah*
F	12	DL	"A Grand Selection from the Works of Handel"
W	17	CG	"A Grand Selection of Sacred Music," Handel
W	17	DL	"A Grand Selection from the Works of Handel"
F	19	CG	"A Grand Selection of Sacred Music," Handel
F	19	DL	*Alexander's Feast, Acis and Galatea*
W	24	CG	"A Grand Selection of Sacred Music," Handel
W	24	DL	"A Grand Selection from the Works of Handel"
F	26	CG	"A Grand Selection of Sacred Music," Handel
F	26	DL	*Redemption,* Handel pasticcio by Arnold

1795

February

F	20	CG	"A Grand Selection of Sacred Music, from the Works of Handel"
[F	20	KH	*Debora and Sisara,* P. A. Guglielmi]
F	27	CG	*Alexander's Feast*; "Part III. A Grand Miscellaneous Act," mostly Handel
F	27	KH	"A Grand Selection of Sacred Music Chiefly from Handel"
W	4	CG	*L'Allegro ed il Penseroso*; "Part III. A Grand Miscellaneous Act," all Handel
F	6	CG	"A Grand Selection of Sacred Music, from the Works of Handel"
W	11	CG	*The Messiah*
F	13	CG	"A Grand Selection of Sacred Music," mostly Handel

TABLE IV-I
continued

Dates			Theaters, Oratorio Titles, Composers, Comments
W	18	CG	*Acis and Galatea*; "Part III. A Grand Miscellaneous Act," mostly Handel
F	20	CG	*The Messiah*
W	25	CG	"A Grand Selection of Sacred Music," Handel
F	27	CG	"A Grand Selection of Sacred Music, from the Works of Handel"

1800

February

F	28	CG	"A Grand Selection of Sacred Music, from the Works of Handel"

March

W	5	CG	"A Grand Selection of Sacred Music, from the Works of Handel"
F	7	CG	*The Messiah*
F	14	CG	*Alexander's Feast*; "Part III. A Grand Miscellaneous Act," Handel
W	19	CG	"A Grand Selection of Sacred Music, from the Works of Handel"
F	21	CG	*Acis and Galatea*; "Part III. A Grand Miscellaneous Act," mostly Handel
W	26	CG	*The Messiah*
F	28	CG	*The Creation*, J. Haydn

April

W	2	CG	*The Creation*, J. Haydn
F	4	CG	*The Creation*, J. Haydn

Source: *London Stage*, vols. for the years cited.
Abbreviations
  CG   The Theatre Royal in Covent Garden
  DL   The Theatre Royal in Drury Lane
  LH   The New or Little Theatre in the Haymarket
  KH   The King's Theatre in the Haymarket
  F   Friday
  W   Wednesday
All oratorios are by Handel unless otherwise indicated.
Dates marked with an asterisk are command performances, announced:
  "By Command of Their Majesties."
Oratorios sung in Italian are given in brackets.
Titles and comments in quotation marks are taken from contemporary announcements.

inclusion of *Judas Maccabaeus* and *Samson*, which, together with *Messiah*, were the most frequently performed of Handel's oratorios in the later eighteenth century. The "Handel pasticcio" oratorio is represented in the list of 1765 by *Israel in Babylon*, arranged by Edward Toms. In addition to Handel's oratorios, which dominated the series, those by the directors of the series or by other composers were occasionally heard; for instance, oratorios by Smith and Stanley were given in 1760.

The list for 1765 in Table IV-1 shows that the oratorio on 22 February (see asterisk following date) was a command performance. Royal patronage was as important to the financial success of oratorio as to opera. A command performance—to be attended by King George III (r. 1760–1820), the queen, members of the royal family, and their retinue—would be publically announced in advance and would insure a full house, including attendance by those who were close to the court and others who might have little opportunity to see his Majesty.[14] On the night of a command performance, when the king entered his box (which he had approached through a private corridor, led by a theater proprietor, walking backward to face the king and carrying a candelabrum) the audience stood and applauded, and the king bowed. More applause greeted the other members of the family, who bowed first to the king and then to the audience. When the king was seated, the concert began. As Table IV-1 shows, in 1765 George III attended only one oratorio, but his attendance soon increased. In the lists from 1770 to 1785 his presence is noted at one or two oratorios during most weeks in Lent; in years when two or more series competed, he tended to patronize only one of the series. After 1786 the king ceased attending the Lenten oratorios; instead, he began to support the Concerts of Ancient Music.[15] In response to George III's mental illness beginning in 1788, "God Save the King" was sung in the theaters, on some evenings several times, which accounts for its presence in the list for 1790 (19 February).[16]

Nearly every Lenten oratorio season included works that are neither oratorios in the Handelian sense nor sacred, as we have seen. The examples that recur most frequently are *Alexander's Feast* (in every list of Table IV-1 beginning in 1765) and *Acis and Galatea* (in every list beginning in 1770); Arne's *Alfred the Great,* heard during Lent in 1754 (and later years), was mentioned above. If the presence of such secular works in an oratorio series seems puzzling, it appeared equally so not only to Maddison (quoted above) but also to some of his contemporaries. In a letter signed "Rectus" published in a London newspaper of 1766, the author questions the Lenten oratorio season in several respects:

14. See *London Stage*, 5/1:ccx-ccxii, for details of royal visits.

15. See Weber, *Musical Classics*, for clarification of the puzzlement expressed in *London Stage* 5/1:ccx, about the disappearance of the king from the Lenten oratorios beginning in 1786.

16. Cf. *London Stage*, 5/2:1087.

I have long endeavoured to find out the reason, why plays should not be performed on Wednesdays and Fridays in *Lent,* as well as on those days all through the rest of the season; I have never yet been able to find out that Lent makes the least difference in people's way of living, I mean in the generality of mankind . . . again, why are oratorios to be limited to this particular season? Can the time of the year render *solemnity unseasonable?* I should hope not: but am still willing to have all the respect paid to Lent, which either the laws or customs of our country seem to require; at the same time, I would have this respect paid with uniformity, and nothing introduced among the oratorios which should have the least tincture of any thing *not sacred;* where would be the difference between the performing of the oratorio of *Acis and Galatea,* or the tragedy of *Romeo and Juliet,* and let me add to the former, the oratorio of *Alexander's Feast?* How can either of these two be called sacred? one extracted from *profane history,* the other *purely fiction.*[17]

Rectus concludes with a plea that, in the interest of variety, concertos be performed during both intervals, as in the past, rather than the first only, as during the present season: "dear variety! which more than any religious motive is the reason that we so willingly give *half a guinnea* to sit at an oratorio, in the same place where at a play we can sit for *three shillings.*"

The list of 1770 in Table IV-1 shows a season of unusual competition for the Lenten audiences among three oratorio series: the Smith-Stanley series on Wednesdays and Fridays at Drury Lane, the Arnold-Toms series on the same days at Covent Garden, and the J. C. Bach series on Thursdays at the King's Theatre in the Haymarket. Bach's series was unusual, for it consisted only of Italian oratorios—Jommelli's *La passione* and Bach's own *Gioas re di Giuda.* The Drury Lane series included the usual Handel fare, plus Stanley's *The Fall of Egypt;* at Covent Garden were heard oratorios by Handel and Arnold and a Handel pasticcio by Toms. On 7 March, Drury Lane and Covent Garden rivaled each other with performances of the same work, *Judas Maccabaeus.* To compete with the King's Theatre, Covent Garden included two Italian oratorios: Jommelli's *La passione,* announced as having "additional choruses by Leo, Graun, and others"—and thus it could be billed as "never performed," that is, not the same work as at the King's Theatre; and Piccini's *La morte d'Abel,* which also included "additional chorusses," by Pergolesi, Corelli, Richter, Carissimi, "Mr. Bach," Jommelli, and Leo.[18] (To help

17. *The Gazetteer and New Daily Advertiser,* 25 February 1766, p. 1, col. 4.

18. The composers of the additional choruses are listed in the printed libretto, *The Death of Abel, an Oratorio, from the Italian of Metastasio, as it is performed at the Theatre-Royal in Covent-Garden. The Music by Signor Nicolo Piccini. With Additional Choruses by Other Eminent Masters.* Sold at the the-

draw an audience, the announcement identified Piccini as "the composer of *La buona figliuola*," which was playing at the King's Theatre that season.) The year 1775 saw the rivalry of only two series, that of Stanley and Linley in Drury Lane and of Bach in the King's Theatre in the Haymarket. Both series offered the usual Handel works—they competed with the same oratorios on 8 March (*Samson*) and 7 April (*Messiah*)—and Stanley revived his oratorio, *The Fall of Egypt*.

In the late 1770s and early 1780s oratorios became increasingly unfashionable, in part, no doubt, because the Concerts of Ancient Music had begun.[19] Rivalry among theaters during Lent began to wane, as the lists of 1780 and 1785 in Table IV-1 indicate. The repertoire in those lists is traditional (nearly all Handel, with *Messiah* at the end), but the series from 1785 through 1800 reveal the influence of the monumental Commemoration of Handel, which took place at Westminster Abbey and the Pantheon in 1784 (discussed below). Rivalry between theaters returned, and, like the Commemoration programs, those of the Lenten concerts included "grand selections" from Handel's music. In the announcements of 1785 the selections are listed only twice—on 11 and 25 February—but in 1790 no less than fourteen performances were billed as "A Grand Selection" from Handel's music; the trend of performing selections continued into the early nineteenth century. Even the performance on 26 February 1790 of Arnold's Handel pasticcio, *Redemption*, was announced as "A Sacred Oratorio selected from the Great and Favourite Works of Handel that were performed at his Commemoration in Westminster-Abbey and at the Pantheon."[20] In this later period, few oratorios were given in their entirety. In 1795 Pietro Guglielmi's *Debora and Sisara*, sung in Italian, was an exception to the usual English and Handelian offerings. Also exceptional was the performance of an oratorio by another foreigner—but by no means a stranger to London—Joseph Haydn. (See chapter 8 on Haydn's London visits.) The London performances of *The Creation* in 1800 were bound to claim considerable attention, and the work would inevitably be compared with Handel's oratorios. After the first performance on 28 Feburary a critic wrote, "Although not equal in grandeur to the divine compositions of the immortal Handel, [*The Creation*] is, nevertheless, on the whole, a very charming production."[21]

The size of the forces for the Lenten oratorios is difficult to estimate. The number of Handel's performers in the theaters varied. Exceptionally

---

ater, (n.p., n.d.). Copy in LB-Lcm: XX. G. 20 (7). The libretto is in English; whether the work was sung in English or Italian is not certain.

19. McVeigh, "Violinists," p. 44; Weber, *Musical Classics*, chapter "Concerts of Ancient Music."

20. *London Stage*, 5/2:1230.

21. As quoted from the *Morning Herald*, 29 March 1800, in *London Stage*, 5/3:2259.

FIGURE IV-I. An oratorio performance at the Theatre Royal in Covent Garden. (Aquatint by Augustus Charles Pugin and Thomas Rowlandson, published in London by Rudolf Ackermann, ca. 1809. Reproduced by permission of the Harvard Theatre Collection.)

he used a large group: in 1733 at King's Theatre in the Haymarket, about a hundred performed *Deborah* (ca. twenty-five singers, the rest instrumentalists); in his later period, however, he appears to have used an orchestra of about thirty-five to forty pieces, a chorus of about seventeen to twenty-four voices, and four to nine soloists, who joined with the choruses.[22] According to Winton Dean, Handel's "oratorio chorus was selected from the choirs of the Chapel Royal, St Paul's Cathedral and Westminster Abbey, principally from the Chapel Royal. It was exclusively male."[23] The Handelian practice surely continued for a time, but in the 1770s, newspapers began to note larger forces and women in choruses. In 1773 the *Public Advertiser* reported: "The Oratorio of Judith, composed by Dr Arne, which was performed at the Theatre Royal in Covent Garden Yesterday Evening, was received with uncommon Applause. . . . The striking Appearance of the Band and Chorus, which were much more numerous than they have usually been, received a most pleasing Addition from the Female Singers then first introduced."[24] In 1778 an-

22. For details of some of Handel's performances, see Dean, *Oratorios*, p. 103–5.
23. Dean, *Oratorios*, p. 108.
24. *Public Advertiser*, 27 February 1773, p. 3.

other newspaper reported on women in the oratorios directed by Stanley and Linley: "The Oratorios commenced last night at Drury-Lane, by command of their Majesties, with the delightful entertainment of Acis and Galatea. . . . The chorus was full, and well supported: The addition of women in the treble part is very pleasing and judicious, as they support the high sounds so much better than the boys."[25] The 1770s appear to mark a turning point, not only in London but in the provinces as well. As we shall see, in this period women choristers from Lancashire were in great demand as leaders of soprano sections in choruses at provincial festivals.

Other Contexts. Oratorios were occasionally given for charitable purposes in the chapels of London's hospitals. Beginning in 1750, Handel's *Messiah* was heard annually until 1777 at the Foundling Hospital Chapel.[26] The composer directed the performances until 1755, after which he officially turned his duties over to J. C. Smith the younger, his former student and the Chapel's organist. Yet in 1757 Handel appears to have directed *Messiah* at the Foundling Hospital, and shortly before his death in 1759, a public announcement named him as the director of the forthcoming performance there. Between the announcement and the performance Handel died, and Smith directed *Messiah*, which he continued to do annually until 1768, when Felice Giardini succeeded him and directed most of the annual *Messiah* performances until 1777, when they ceased.[27] The forces used in the Foundling Hospital Chapel apparently fluctuated; although in 1749 Handel performed there the new Foundling Hospital Anthem and excerpts from *Solomon* with "above One Hundred Voices and Performers," the annual *Messiah* probably used much smaller forces.[28]

Two other London locations of oratorios were the chapels of Lock Hospital and Middlesex Hospital. In the former, the reverends Martin Mandan and Thomas Haweis arranged annual oratorio performances, including *Ruth*, by Charles Avison (1709–70) and Felice Giardini (1716–96), given in 1763, 1765, and 1768;[29] *Judith* by Arne, in 1764; and *Manasseh* by John Worgan (1724–90), in 1766 and 1767.[30] In 1780

25. *Morning Chronicle and London Advertiser*, 7 March 1778, p. 2, cols. 1–2.

26. For comments on these performances, see Shaw, *Handel's Messiah*, pp. 44–46, 49–54, 62.

27. The performances not directed by Giardini were directed by Thomas Linley Senior (in 1773) and Stanley (1775–77). For details, see Boyd, "Stanley," and Williams, "Stanley," 1:48–50.

28. Dean, *Oratorios*, p. 105.

29. According to Christopher Hogwood and Simon McVeigh, "Giardini," *New Grove*, 7:351, in 1763, parts I and III of *Ruth* were by Avison, part II by Giardini; in 1765, I by Avison, II-III by Giardini; in 1768, all by Giardini.

30. McVeigh, "Violinist," p. 310; Mackerness, *Social History*, p. 124; *London*

Providence, by John Abraham Fisher (1744–1806), was given for the benefit of the Middlesex Hospital.[31]

Excerpts from oratorios and occasionally a complete oratorio were heard at London's most elite concert series of the later eighteenth century, the Concert of Ancient Music. This subscription series, founded in 1776, performed only "early" music (mostly composed by the generations from Purcell to Handel); thereby the series aimed to preserve the "musical classics" as an alternative to the ever increasing encroachment of modern, *galant* style.[32] Chief among the directors of this socially exclusive and politically useful series were John Montagu, the earl of Sandwich; Brownlow Cecil, the earl of Exeter; Sir Watkin Williams Wynn, a Welsh baronet; Richard, the seventh viscount Fitzwilliam; Sir Richard Jebb, Bart.; and Francis Osborne, the duke of Leeds. The musical director was the private secretary to the earl of Sandwich, Joah Bates (1740-99), an organist. Informally called the "Ancient Concerts" or the "Tottenham Street Oratorio" (after their location in the Tottenham Street Rooms), these were glittering social affairs.[33] In 1785 the series received royal patronage, after which it was often called "the King's Concerts," and the *Morning Chronicle* reported on George III's first appearance:

> The patronage of the KING has induced the Directors of this concert [series] to enlarge the room, and fit it up with suitable decorations. A superb gallery is erected for their *Majesties* and the Royal Family, at the east end of the room. The orchestra is on the model of the one which was constructed in Westminster Abbey for *Handel's* Commemoration [described below]. . . .
>
> This *concert* [series] is the only subscription one, that his *Majesty* ever honoured with his presence, and in compliment to their illustrious visitor, Handel's music will have a preference given to it by the Directors. . . .
>
> A little past eight their Majesties, the Princess *Royal*, Princess *Augusta*, Princess *Elizabeth*, and Prince *Edward*, entered the room; then the Concert commenced.[34]

Commenting on the splendor of the concert environment, one of Bates's sisters wrote that the concerts "are conducted in a most magnificent

Stage 4/2:1167, 1246; Wesley, *Journal*, 5:47 and n. 1, 106 and n. 3. John Wesley attended the performances of the Arne and Giardini works in 1764 and 1765.

31. Owain Edwards, "John Abraham Fisher," *New Grove*, 6:617.

32. For details on this series, and especially on its social and political aspects, see Weber, *Musical Classics*, chapter "Concerts of Ancient Music."

33. For the term "Tottenham Street Oratorio" and for background on these concerts, see Scholes, *Burney*, 2:178–80.

34. Elkin, *Concert Rooms*, pp. 84–85.

stile. The band is quite perfection and the best music is performed there. The presence of the royal family, and all the state court attendants make the room look grand. The room is beautifully lighted, the subscribers number three hundred, all are people of high rank and fashion."[35]

One of the rules of the Ancient Concerts was that the music performed be at least twenty years old, but in practice it tended to be older, as pointed out above. Still some mid-century works were heard. The repertoire was primarily English and Italian and was strongly Handelian—a bust of Handel adorned the concert hall. Between 1776 and 1790, excerpts from all of Handel's oratorios were given, and some in their entirety: *Jephtha*, once; *Esther, Occasional Oratorio*, and *Samson*, twice each. Secular works, not oratorios but included within Lenten series, were also performed complete: *Acis and Galatea*, twice; and *L'Allegro, il penseroso ed il moderato*, three times.[36] According to the earliest roster of performers known to date, the 1787 wordbook, there were 8 boys from the Chapel Royal, 8 "altos" (who would be male), 9 tenors, and 8 basses; 17 violins, 4 violas, 4 cellos, 2 basses, 4 oboes (oboists doubled on flute), 2 trumpets, 4 horns, 3 trombones, and 1 timpanist.[37] According to Elkin, the available forces—probably at a later date—totaled eighty-eight: a chorus of forty-three (16 boy sopranos, 9 male altos, 9 tenors, 9 basses) and an orchestra of forty-five (16 violins, 5 violas, 4 violoncellos, 2 double basses, 4 oboes, 4 bassoons, 4 horns, 2 trumpets, 3 trombones, and timpani.[38] Scholes notes that the performers included the king's private band and choirboys from the Chapel Royal, Westminster Abbey, and St. Paul's Cathedral.[39]

The Provinces: Festivals and Other Occasions

Social Context and Repertoire. In the English provinces the most important eighteenth-century context for oratorio performance was the music festival. That occasion offered the rare opportunity to marshal large enough vocal and instrumental forces in a provincial town to perform oratorios, and oratorios could draw an audience large enough for the stated purpose of most festivals: to raise funds for religious or secular

35. Letter from Ms. Furey (Bates's sister) to her sister, n.d. [after 2 February 1785], fols. 8–9, Bates letters, as quoted in Weber, *Musical Classics*, chapter "Concerts of Ancient Music," ref. to n. 110.

36. Weber, *Musical Classics*, Table II, chapter "Concerts of Ancient Music"; Weber analyses the programs between 1776 and 1790.

37. I wish to thank Professor William Weber for sending me this information, which he cites as found on pp. xiii–xvi of the 1787 wordbook.

38. Elkin, *Concert Rooms*, p. 84. Elkin does not provide a date or period in which such forces were used, but they would probably date from later than 1787.

39. Scholes, *Burney*, 2:179.

charities. Music was at first the handmaid of charity at most festivals,[40] but by the second half of the century it had begun to forsake its secondary role and dominate the event. From the mid-century on, festivals tended to expand and to change in character; charities increasingly became excuses, rather than reasons for festivals. Other purposes for festivals were to celebrate important events or anniversaries—St. Cecilia's Day, the dedication of an organ or a building, the end of an academic year, the installation of the chancellor of a university, among others— and in the second half of the century, some festivals were organized by individuals for profit. The earliest festival development took place in the south and the midlands, beginning in the first half of the century; the festivals of the north, which emerged in the second half of the century, were to a large extent a separate development, deriving from a change in the social environment and a desire for local prestige comparable to that of the more cultured south.[41]

The Three Choirs Festival is a clear example of the festival as fund raiser for a religious charity, and it is the provincial festival with the longest history; it may have begun as early as 1713 and it survives even today.[42] The event was an annual fall festival held in the cathedral towns of Gloucester, Worcester, or Hereford in rotation. In the eighteenth century it was called a "musical assembly" or a "music meeting"; the designations "festival" and "Three Choirs" date from the mid-nineteenth century. In the first half of the eighteenth century, the festival lasted two days (although most festivals in the early period lasted only one day) and emphasized charitable and religious purposes. Each day began in the cathedral with Morning Prayer, which included large-scale settings, with orchestra, of the *Te Deum, Jubilate*, and extended anthems; and in the evenings, concerts of secular music were given in other buildings of the town. Probably imitating the annual festive services known as the Sons of the Clergy at St. Paul's Cathedral in London,[43] in 1724 the organizers of the Three Choirs Festival initiated a collection to be taken up for the widows and orphans of the choir members and diocesan clergy, and later only for the dependents of the clergy.[44] From about the mid-century the festivals began to place greater emphasis on music and entertainment, but the proceeds still went to charity. Socially important balls were held after the evening concerts, and at least by the mid-century, the Gloucester

40. For an extensive and detailed social history of English festivals, upon which the following treatment of them heavily depends, see Pritchard, "Musical Festival"; on music as a "handmaid of charity," see Pritchard's pp. 11–20.

41. On the distinct and separate development of the northern festivals, see ibid., pp. 118–47.

42. On the Three Choirs Festival, see ibid., pp. 18–20; and Watkins Shaw, "Three Choirs Festival," *New Grove*, 18:792.

43. On the festivals of the Sons of the Clergy, see Pritchard, "Musical Festival," pp. 11–16.

44. Shaw, *Three Choirs*, p. 3.

horse races took place in conjunction with the music meeting there, presumably to attract a still greater crowd.

Beginning in the mid-century, oratorios—usually the Handel works most popular in the London theaters—were increasingly heard in the evening concerts at the Three Choirs Festival.[45] In Gloucester, for instance, Handel's *Samson* was given in 1748 and 1752, and his *Judas Maccabaeus* in 1754; and in Hereford, *Samson* and *Solomon* were performed in 1756. In 1757 at Gloucester *Messiah* was heard for the first time at a Three Choirs Festival; since then it has been heard annually at these festivals.[46] In 1753 and 1756 Hereford added a third evening concert, and Gloucester and Worcester followed that practice in 1757 and 1758, respectively. The festival continued to fluctuate between two and three days until 1770, when it was firmly established as a three-day affair.[47]

The year 1759 marks a momentous step in the Three Choirs Festival and in the history of oratorio, for in that year, at the festival in Hereford, *Messiah* was transferred from an evening concert to an additional concert on the third morning in the cathedral. Worcester followed in 1761, but Gloucester admitted *Messiah* to the cathedral only in 1769.[48] The change at Hereford in 1759, probably influenced by the very first performance of *Messiah* in a cathedral (at Bristol, see below) the previous year, resulted from an attempt to reconcile religious with musical elements, the service with the oratorio.[49] The change elevated the role of what was to become the most famous English oratorio in history: a morning performance of *Messiah* in a cathedral now seemed virtually equal in status to a religious service. Thenceforth at the Three Choirs Festival, the first two days began with a festal service and the third day with *Messiah*; and in other festivals, too, the practice was adopted of performing *Messiah* in cathedrals and churches, sometimes in lieu of Morning Service.[50] From 1760 to 1800, in addition to the annual *Messiah* and frequent performances of *Judas Maccabaeus* and *Samson*, oratorios by Handel included *Athalia*, *Esther*, *Israel in Egypt*, *Jephtha*, and *Joshua*. Other works frequently performed included *Acis and Galatea*; *Alexander's Feast*; *L'Allegro, il Penseroso ed il Moderato*; and *Ode for St. Cecilia's Day*. Arnold's Handel pasticcio, *Omnipotence*, was performed at Worcester in 1776. Among the few oratorios by composers other than Handel were Arne's *Judith* (Gloucester, 1766); Giardini's *Ruth* (Gloucester, 1775);

45. This paragraph and the next are based on Lysons, *Three Choirs*, pp. 13–80; Shaw, *Three Choirs*, pp. 6–29; and Pritchard, "Musical Festival," pp. 51–54.
46. Except for the "Mock" Festival at Worcester in 1875. See Shaw, *Three Choirs*, p. 10.
47. Shaw, *Three Choirs*, p. 9.
48. Shaw, *Three Choirs*, p. 12.
49. Pritchard, "Musical Festival," pp. 51–54.
50. Ibid., p. 55.

Arnold's *Cure of Saul* (Hereford, 1771) and *The Prodigal Son* (Gloucester, 1781); and Haydn's *The Creation* (Worcester, 1800). In 1785 at
Worcester, a remarkable exception to the standard repertoire of the
Three Choirs Festival was the performance of an Italian oratorio, Johann
Friedrich Reichardt's setting of Metastasio's *La passione*. (The same
work had been performed on 24 March of that year for King George III
at Buckingham Palace.)[51]

Not associated with a charity but originally with celebrations of St.
Cecilia's Day (22 November), the Salisbury Festival is a particularly early
one whose roots go back to the seventeenth century.[52] From 1748 the
Salisbury Festival of St. Cecilia, organized by a local musical society, was
an event of two days, and from 1769 of three days; the festival usually
occurred between late August and early October (rather than the original
22 November), and was held annually until 1789, again in 1792, and
sporadically until 1828. The pattern of musical performances was approximately like that of the Three Choirs Festival: in the early period, a
festal service in the cathedral was followed by an evening concert in
another building; but eventually the festal service was supplanted by a
morning concert. Oratorios began to appear in the evening concerts in
the mid-century, and to the end of the century Handel predominated,
with *Messiah* and *Judas Maccabaeus* the most frequently performed oratorios. Relatively few oratorios were given in the mornings at the cathedral, but in 1752 selections from *Messiah* were excerpted as anthems for
Morning Prayer.[53] The complete *Messiah* was first performed in Salisbury Cathedral in 1768, and it remained the oratorio most often heard
in that location. An exceptional oratorio for its Italian language, Jommelli's *La passione*, was given in an evening concert at Salisbury in 1770,
the same year in which it was performed in London by J. C. Bach at the
King's Theatre in the Haymarket (see Table IV-1, list for 1770).

In the second half of the century, music festivals became extremely
widespread throughout England.[54] Those for religious charities would

51. According to Cramer's *Magazin der Musik*, 2/1 (1784–85): 725.

52. Betty Matthews, in a communication to *R. M. A. Research Chronicle* 8
(1970):23, (see bibliography: Pritchard and Reid, "Festival Programmes") considers the Salisbury Festival to be the earliest one in England. See also idem,
"Salisbury," *New Grove*, 16:421; Husk, *Account*, pp. 93–102; and Pritchard,
"Musical Festival," pp. 41–43. For background on and lists of programs for the
festivals of Salisbury, Winchester, Cambridge, Oxford, Liverpool, Manchester,
Birmingham, Derby, Newcastle upon Tyne, and York, see Pritchard and Reid,
"Festival Programmes." Except where otherwise indicated, the following treat-
ment of festivals relies on the background and programs given by Pritchard and
Reid.

53. Shaw, *Handel's "Messiah"*, p. 57.

54. For details on festivals from the mid-century on, see Pritchard, "Musical
Festival," pp. 40–94. On festivals for the profit of individuals, see Pritchard's pp.
62–85.

retain a festal service; the others tended not to do so, but some of their concerts were usually given in churches. Several festivals—including those in Winchester, Birmingham, Derby, and Bristol—followed patterns comparable in most respects to those of the Three Choirs and Salisbury: a fall festival of one to three days, morning concerts in a church or cathedral, evening concerts in a secular location, and oratorios at first given only in the evenings but later (especially *Messiah*) in the mornings in churches. Most northern festivals, however, were one-day events and many were for the profit of the organizer. The Bristol festival of 1758 is of particular interest, for in that year the performance of *Messiah* in the cathedral marked the first time that work had been given in a church other than the Foundling Hospital Chapel in London;[55] the Bristol performance of *Messiah* established a precedent with far-reaching consequences, as we have seen. Present at that performance was John Wesley, who was impressed at the audience behavior and surprised at the performance: "I doubt if that congregation was ever so serious at a sermon, as they were during this performance. In many parts, especially several of the choruses, it exceeded my expectation."[56] In 1775 at the Winchester Festival, morning concerts in the cathedral were initiated with a performance of *Messiah*.

Some festivals were held in churches of rural villages, among them Framlingham in East Suffolk (where as many as a thousand attended), Oakley Wood near Cirencester, and Church Langton in Leicestershire.[57] A revealing report of audience reaction at Church Langton was written by the reverend William Hanbury, who states (with some exaggeration) that prior to the performance of *Messiah* in his church there on 27 September 1759, directed by the Oxford Professor of Music William Hayes (1708–77), "an oratorio was never before heard of in the country."[58] The rural audience was overwhelmed, according to Hanbury's description, which suggests the style of English sentimental writing and of literary *Empfindsamkeit* in contemporary Germany:

> The music, on so solemn a subject by so good a band, was most affecting; and to see the effect it had on different persons was astonishingly moving and strange. An eye without tears I believe could hardly be found in the whole church, and every one endeavoured to conceal the emotions of his heart: drooping heads, to render the tears unnoticed, became for a while almost general, till by now and then looking about, and finding others affected in the like manner, no concealment in a little time was made. Tears then with unconcern were seen trickling down the faces of many: and

55. Matthews, "Bristol," *New Grove*, 3:287.
56. Wesley, *Journal*, 4:282
57. Sadie, "Concert Life," pp. 22, 24.
58. Hanbury, *Church-Langton*, pp. 45, 87.

then indeed, it was extremely moving to see the pity, compassion, and devotion, that had possessed the greatest part present.[59]

For the next four years, Hanbury continued to organize festivals in Church Langton (1760–61), Leicester (1762), and Nottingham (1763), at which *Messiah* was always performed (in the morning and in church); other works given were *Judas Maccabaeus*, *Esther*, *Samson*, and *Alexander's Feast*.[60]

Diverging from the pattern of the fall festivals are those in the university towns of Cambridge and Oxford, beginning in the 1760s. They were two-day festivals, which often accompanied the closing of the academic year in late June or early July. In Cambridge the oratorios were usually performed at Great St. Mary's Church, whereas secular works and miscellaneous concerts were given in the Senate House. In Oxford oratorios were heard in the Sheldonian Theatre or the Holywell Music Room as evening concerts, but apparently not in church. An oratorio written as a "degree exercise" for the Doctor of Music at Oxford was sometimes performed at such a festival. For instance, John Abraham Fisher's exercise, the oratorio *Providence*, was given in Oxford on 2 July 1777, when he received the Bachelor of Music and Doctor of Music degrees.

Oratorios were heard at numerous "occasional" festivals: at Bristol in 1757, when *Judas Maccabaeus* and *Messiah* were performed for the dedication of the new organ in "the great Musick Room";[61] at Oxford in 1749, when performances of *Esther*, *Samson*, and *Messiah* were directed by William Hayes in the Sheldonian Theatre to celebrate the opening of Radcliffe Camera (a building of the Bodleian Library);[62] and again at Oxford in 1754, 1756, and 1759, when Hayes directed oratorios, including *Messiah*, for the Commemoration of Founders and Benefactors. After 1754 Hayes gave annual performances of *Messiah* in either the Sheldonian Theatre or the Holywell Music Room. On 10 October 1772, when Lord North was installed as chancellor of Oxford University, Samuel Arnold's *The Prodigal Son* formed part of the festivities.[63]

During the 1750s in Bath, Thomas Chilcot (ca. 1700–66) performed Handel's oratorios in theaters; and on 16–17 May 1759, in the Bath Abbey, William Hayes conducted singers from Salisbury, Worcester,

59. Ibid., pp. 81–82.
60. On Hanbury's festivals see Pritchard, "Musical Festival," pp. 55–57; and Prophet, *Hanbury*, pp. 29–70. See also Hayes, *Anecdotes*, pp. 10–11, where the financial accounts for the use of the performing parts are given. Hayes's book provides fascinating insight into the kinds of attitudes and strife that occurred behind the scenes at these festivals.
61. Pritchard, "Musical Festival," p. 87.
62. Ibid.; on Hayes's performances of *Messiah* in Oxford, see Shaw, *Handel's "Messiah,"* p. 56.
63. Roger Fisk, "Samuel Arnold," *New Grove*, 1:616.

Gloucester, and Bristol Cathedrals in performances of *Messiah* and *Judas Maccabaeus* for the benefit of the Bath General Hospital.[64] In a provincial church or cathedral a special event or time of the year might call for an oratorio or part of one. On 22 August 1759, for instance, *Messiah* was performed at the opening of St. Peter's Church in Colchester.[65] In the church of Stratford upon Avon, Arne's *Judith* was performed "on the occasion of the jubilee held there, September 6, 1769, in honour of the memory of Shakespeare."[66] Beginning in 1777, part I of *Messiah* was performed annually at Christmas in the Salisbury Cathedral.[67] At the Handelian earl of Sandwich's estate in Hinchingbrooke, the earl began in 1767 to offer performances of Handel's oratorios by as many as seventy performers. An oratorio was performed on each of the six days of his private "festivals."[68] In 1774 he imported singers from Lancashire to participate in a performance of Handel's *Jeptha* in Leicester parish church; this performance, which attracted an audience of 800, may have suggested to him the idea of the Ancient Concerts begun in London two years later.[69]

Performing Forces. Provincial festivals before the mid-century characteristically used relatively small performing groups. In 1727 at Bristol, for instance, in announcing a festival of St. Cecilia a local newspaper wrote, "above 30 voices and instruments are to be concerned," and added that among them were "several eminent and masterly hands from Bath, Wells, London, and other places."[70] Like Bristol, most provincial festivals had to draw musicians from other cities, but the Three Choirs Festival was exceptional: its forces consisted of the combined choirs of the three cathedrals (all male singers) plus instrumentalists from local music clubs. Yet before the mid-century, the total number of musicians at the Three Choirs Festival probably did not exceed fifty and included more instrumentalists than singers.[71] Handel's performance of *Athalia* at Ox-

64. Beechey, "Chilcot," pp. 181–83.

65. Williams, "Stanley," 1:47.

66. From the title page of *Judith, A Sacred Drama* (London: W. Griffin, [1769]). Copy in GB-Lcm: XX. G. 20 (5).

67. Weber, *Musical Classics*, chapter "Handel's Oratorios in London and the Towns"; Weber's source is John Marsh's Journal (in the Cambridge University Library), vol. 7, p. 566.

68. Ibid., chapter on "Handel's Oratorios in London and the Towns"; Weber's source is Joseph Cradock, *Literary and Miscellaneous Memoirs* (London, 1828), 1:117–24.

69. Weber, *Musical Classics*, "The Spread of Handel's Music, 1759–1784."

70. As quoted in Pritchard, "Musical Festival," p. 99, from *Felix Farley's Bristol Journal*, 18 November 1727.

71. Pritchard, "Musical Festival," p. 101.

ford in 1733 was unusual for its large number of musicians, described as "about 70 Voices and Instruments of Musick."[72]

Most announcements and reports of festivals do not specify the number of performers who took part; the few that do, however, show that in the mid-century, when extended choral works—mainly oratorios—were introduced into the provincial festivals, the number notably increased. For instance, an increase has been documented between 1750 and 1753 at Salisbury: on 4 October 1750, *Messiah* was first given there at an evening concert, apparently with "a total of rather more than thirty performers, vocalists and instrumentalists together";[73] in the following year, the festival forces numbered more than forty; and in 1753, between forty and fifty—the cathedral choir and local instrumentalists were supplemented by musicians from Oxford, Bath, and London.[74] Also characteristic of the time was the increase in forces at Oxford: for the festival of 1749, William Hayes advertised, "the Vocal Parts by the Gentlemen of the several Choirs in the University, and the Instrumental by near Fifty Hands from London, and other Places";[75] five years later, the *Oxford Journal*, on 5 July 1754, wrote that Hayes used "near an Hundred" musicians, including instrumentalists and well-known soloists from London;[76] and in 1756, Hayes advertised "a great Number of Voices and Instruments of every kind requisite," and he brought Handel's soloists from London.[77] At a Winchester festival between 1770 and 1783 (exact date unknown) Handel's *Joshua* was given by sixty-five instrumentalists and fifty voices—but this group appears unusually large for southern festivals.[78] In October, 1767, a festival in Birmingham for the benefit of Capel Bond employed "a numerous Band [over forty instrumentalists] with a full Chorus of 40 Voices"—the total represents an increase of nearly 100 per cent over that of 1759 in Birmingham.[79] The forces at the Birmingham festivals for the rest of the century appear to have numbered between eighty and ninety.

A pattern of common occurrence in the second half of the century was for soloists and good chorus singers to move from one festival to another.[80] For the festivals of the south and midlands, the soloists would

72. As quoted in Dean, *Oratorios*, p. 104, from the *Norwich Gazette*, 14 July 1733.

73. Shaw, *Handel's "Messiah,"* pp. 56–57.

74. Husk, *Account*, p. 162.

75. Dean, *Oratorios*, p. 105.

76. Shaw, *Handel's "Messiah,"* p. 56.

77. Dean, *Oratorios*, p. 105.

78. Pritchard, "Musical Festival," pp. 112–13.

79. Ibid., p. 115, and n. 180, where the complete instrumentation is given; quotation from *Aris's Birmingham Gazette*, 12 October 1767.

80. On the movement of singers to various festivals in 1759–60, see Pritchard, "Musical Festival," pp. 105–10.

usually be opera and oratorio singers from London (the theaters of the metropolis were inactive during the festival season); the chorus singers were often drawn from the Three Choirs, the Oxford colleges, and other festival centers. As in London's theaters, concertos would be given between the acts of oratorios, and the soloists would often be the same ones who played at the London oratorios. The musical directors were frequently imported as well, sometimes from London. In the late 1760s, when the north first began to develop festivals that would eventually rival those of the south and midlands, the choral forces were drawn from Lancashire singers, of both sexes, who had been trained within a long indigenous tradition—dating from the seventeenth century—of sight-singing and choral performance.[81] Of special importance were the carefully trained singers from Hay, Shaw, and Oldham. The Lancashire singers were soon widely recognized for their outstanding choral abilities, and both the men and women were increasingly in demand for festivals. From about 1772, however, the term "Lancashire chorus-singers" commonly designated a group of about six to eight female sopranos who were employed as choral leaders at most of the major festivals.[82] The year 1772, in Gloucester, marks the first use at the Three Choirs Festival of the "Lancaster chorus-singers," who were engaged to strengthen the treble part, previously sung by boy sopranos.[83]

The Commemoration of Handel: London, 1784

A festival of enormous significance for the history of oratorio in England, Germany, and America was the Commemoration of Handel in London, 1784, for it became a model of monumental performance. Charles Burney's book, *An Account of the Musical Performances in Westminster-Abbey and the Pantheon, May 26th, 27th, 29th; and June the 3d, and 5th, 1784. In Commemoration of Handel* (London, 1785), commissioned by George III, provides full background and descriptive details of the event.[84] Burney reports a conversation, early in 1783, among three directors of the Ancient Concerts—the viscount Fitzwilliam, Sir Watkin Williams Wynn, and Joah Bates: "after remarking that the number of eminent musical performers of all kinds, both vocal and instrumental, with which London abounded was far greater than in any other city of Europe, it was lamented that there was no public periodical occasion for collecting and consolidating them into one band; by which means a performance might be exhibited on so grand and magnificent a

81. On the singers of the north, the tradition from which they came, and the development of northern festivals, see ibid., p. 118–47.

82. Ibid., p. 143.

83. Lysons, *Three Choirs*, p. 49.

84. Burney, *Account,* consists of two sections with separate pagination: "Sketch of the Life of Handel," and "Commemoration of Handel." The latter is referred to here as: Burney, "Commemoration."

scale as no other part of the world could equal."[85] Having conceived of founding a "periodical" festival on a "grand and magnificent scale," they reasoned that the ideal year for initiating it would be 1784: the twenty-fifth year of Handel's burial in Westminster Abbey, and, according to current information, the centenary of his birth. They and the other directors of the Ancient Concerts planned the event, with Joah Bates as musical director; they secured the patronage of George III and the use of both Westminster Abbey and the Pantheon—the architect James Wyatt's elegant neoclassical structure in Oxford Street. As in many of the provincial festivals, so also in London the proceeds from the sale of tickets were to benefit charities: the Westminster Infirmary and the Musical Fund (officially, the Society of Musicians, established in Handel's time for the assistance of aged and infirm musicians and a charity to which Handel had generously contributed).

Wyatt was engaged to design the elaborate decorations and structures needed within Westminster Abbey. "The general idea," according to Burney, "was to produce the effect of a royal musical chapel, with the orchestra terminating one end, and the accommodations for the Royal Family, the other."[86] The extent of the preparations in the Abbey is reflected in a report of *The European Magazine*:

> The present organ will be taken down, and a grand gallery erected in the room, from a design of [Mr James Wyatt], for the reception of their Majesties, and all the younger branches of the Royal Family, of an age capable of relishing the performance, together with the Royal attendants. This gallery will be hung with crimson velvet fringed with gold. Over the western door of the Abbey, will be erected a large new organ, built by Mr [Samuel] Green for Canterbury cathedral, but which is to be fixed up in the Abbey on this occasion. Mr [Joah] Bates, we are informed, means to play the organ. The base of the orchestra, which will contain a band of about five hundred vocal and instrumental performers, is to be seven feet from the ground. In short, the whole will form a *coup d'oeil*, equally novel, magnificent, and splendid.[87]

The architect's achievement may be seen in the engravings of Figures IV-2 and IV-3.

At the end of February the schedule of concerts was announced in the newspapers as 20, 22, and 23 April, to coincide with the period of Handel's funeral, but for various reasons the concerts were postponed until Wednesday, Thursday, and Saturday, 26, 27, and 29 May. At the queen's request, the Commemoration was extended, at the last minute, by two additional performances, on 3 and 5 June. The concert audiences

85. Burney, "Commemoration," p. 3.
86. Ibid., p. 5.
87. *The European Magazine and London Review*, 5 (March, 1784): 165.

FIGURE IV-2. East end of Westminster Abbey, showing the royal gallery designed by James Wyatt for the 1784 Commemoration of Handel. (Engraved by J. Spilsbury after a drawing by E. F. Burney; from Burney, "Commemoration," following p. 90.)

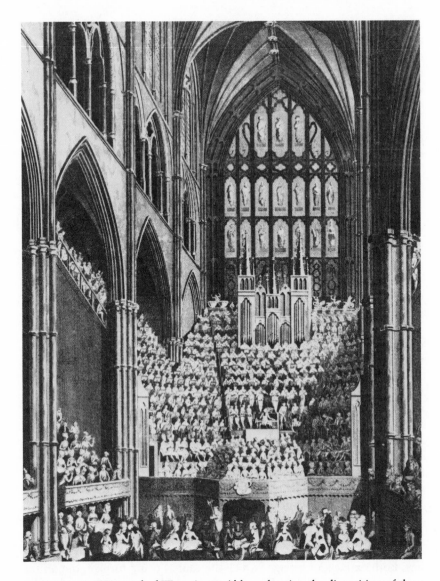

FIGURE IV-3. West end of Westminster Abbey, showing the disposition of the performers for the 1784 Commemoration of Handel. (From Burney, "Commemoration," following p. 108.)

were elegant and enormous—especially on the first and third days. Burney reports, "Many families, as well as individuals, were, however, attracted to the capital by this celebrity; and I never remember it so full, not only so late in the year, but at any time in my life, except at the coronation of his present Majesty."[88] The newspapers reported in glowing terms the grand and sublime visual and aural impressions of the concerts, and tended to manipulate the event for their various political purposes.[89]

The first concert, held in the Abbey, consisted of selections from various works by Handel—among them a Coronation Anthem, the *Dettingen Te Deum*, part of the *Funeral Anthem*, the overtures to the oratorios *Esther* and *Saul*, and the chorus "The Lord shall reign" from *Israel in Egypt*. The concert in the Pantheon, on the second night, was also one of selections, including concertos, airs, and choruses, with four numbers from the oratorios *Joshua*, *Israel in Egypt*, and *Judas Maccabaeus*. The only complete oratorio performed at the Commemoration was *Messiah*, given in the Abbey as the third concert (originally planned as the final one). The two added concerts, on 3 and 5 June, were essentially repeats of the first and third of the series.

The performing forces in Westminster Abbey, which are of special historical importance, totaled 525 persons, who were stationed as shown in Figure IV-3 and in the chart of Figure IV-4. Burney lists the name of every performer, both instrumental and vocal.[90] The orchestra members numbered 251: 48 first violins, 47 second violins, 26 violas, 21 violoncellos, 15 double basses, 6 flutes, 26 oboes, 26 bassoons, 1 double bassoon, 12 trumpets, 12 horns, 6 trombones (the trombonists played other instruments when trombones were not needed), 3 kettledrums, 1 double kettledrum (specially made for the occasion), and 1 organ. The 275 singers consisted of 60 sopranos (including 47 boys, 12 women, and 1 castrato), 48 counter tenors (no female contraltos), 83 tenors, and 84 basses. The number of singers listed includes the soloists—especially well known among them was the soprano Gertrud Elisabeth Mara (1749–1833), who had just arrived in London from the Continent. Burney comments that the "numerous band" consisted "not only of all the regulars, both native and foreign, which the capital could furnish, but all the irregulars, that is, *dilettanti*, and provincial Musicians of character, who could be mustered, many of whom had never heard or seen each other before."[91] The performances in the Abbey were not "conducted" in the modern sense but were directed from the organ by Joah Bates, with the assistance of three sub-directors who stood in the center and on each

88. Burney, "Commemoration," p. 14.

89. For some of the newspaper reports, see Myers, Handel's "Messiah," p. 192; and for the political use of the Commemoration, see Weber, *Musical Classics*, chapter "The 1784 Commemoration and its Aftermath."

90. Burney, "Commemoration," pp. 17–21.

91. Ibid., p. 13.

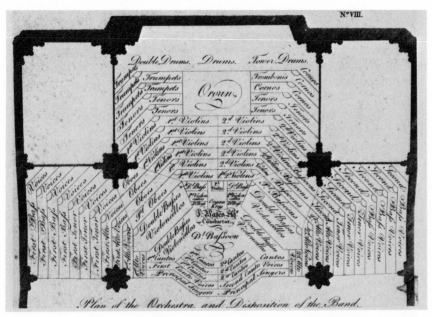

FIGURE IV-4. Seating chart for the performers at the 1784 Commemoration of Handel. (From Burney, "Commemoration," following p. 112.)

side, "for conveying signals to the several parts of that wide-extended Orchestra."[92] In a description adorned with mechanical and scientific images reflecting the emerging industrial age, Burney marvels at the precision of this massive force:

> Foreigners, particularly the French, must be astonished at so numerous a band moving in such exact measure, without the assistance of a *Coryphaeus* to beat the time, either with a roll of paper, or a noisy *baton*, or truncheon. . . .
>
> As this Commemoration is not only the first instance of a band of such magnitude being assembled together, but of *any* band, at all numerous, performing in a similar situation, without the assistance of a *Manu-ductor*, to regulate the measure, the performances in Westminster-Abbey may be safely pronounced, no less remarkable for the multiciplicity of voices and instruments employed, than for accuracy and precision. When all the wheels of that huge machine, the Orchestra, were in motion, the effect resembled clock-work in every thing, but want of feeling and expression.
>
> And, as the power of gravity and attraction in bodies is proportioned to their mass and density, so it seems as if the magnitude of this band had commanded and impelled adhesion and obedience, beyond that of any other of inferior force. The pulsations in every

92. Ibid., p. 11.

limb, and ramifications of veins and arteries in an animal, could not be more reciprocal, isochronous, and under the regulation of the heart, than the members of this body of Musicians under that of the Conductor and Leader. The totality of sound seemed to proceed from one voice, and one instrument; and its powers produced, not only new and exquisite sensations in judges and lovers of the art, but were felt by those who never received pleasure from Music before.

These effects, which will be long remembered by the present public, perhaps so to the disadvantage of all other choral performances, run the risk of being doubted by all but those who heard them, and the present description of being pronounced fabulous, if it should survive the present generation.[93]

The daily press also tended to praise the performances, which met with general approval except for those who did not like the acoustics, or would have preferred more arias sung by the Italians, or had political or religious motives for opposing such an undertaking. Some conservative evangelicals judged the veneration of Handel in the Abbey to be a profanation of a holy place.[94]

The Influence of the Commemoration: England and Abroad

Had the 1784 Commemoration been an isolated event, its influence would surely have been powerful; but it was planned to initiate a periodical festival and was repeated in subsequent years (annually from 1785 to 1791, except for 1788–89) with ever greater forces: in 1785, 616 performers are reported; in 1786, 640; in 1787, 806; and in 1791, 1068.[95] By 1791 these gigantic performances had established themselves as the epitome of festive grandiosity. Joseph Haydn attended in 1791, and the veneration of Handel that he witnessed there, and in London in general, was surely in part responsible for his two oratorios based on English sources, The Creation and The Seasons, treated in chapter 8.

In London these festivals influenced the repertoire of the Lenten oratorio series in the theaters: we have seen that their programs increasingly consisted of the "grand selections" performed at Westminster Abbey and the Pantheon, and that Messiah was one of the few oratorios performed complete. One message of the festivals seems to have been that "bigger is

93. Ibid., p. 14–15.
94. On William Cowper's strong disapproval of the performance of Messiah in the Abbey and mixed feelings by the reverend John Newton, see Myers, Handel's "Messiah," pp. 199–214; and idem, "Fifty Sermons."
95. For these figures, see Myers, Handel's "Messiah," p. 215–20; Myers doubts, however, that as many as 1068 participated at one time in 1791. For two sets of figures that differ slightly from these, see Pritchard, "Musical Festival," p. 150, n. 209.

better," a message reflected on occasion in the Lenten oratorios: for instance, in 1795 the announcement of Guglielmi's *Debora and Sisara*, together with "Grand Chorusses under the direction of Dr Arnold," at the King's Theatre in the Haymarket, carried the comment, "The Orchestra, vocal and instrumental, will consist of nearly two hundred performers."[96]

In the provinces the Handel Commemoration stimulated new festivals in smaller towns such as Wells (1787), Portsmouth (1790), Andover and Chippenham (1792), Blandford (1793), Axminster (1795), and Fareham (1796).[97] In such centers as Liverpool, Manchester, Newcastle-upon-Tyne, and Birmingham the tendency toward more expensive and elaborate festivals was intensified by the monumentality of the Commemoration.[98] The evening programs of festivals increasingly imitated the groupings of miscellaneous selections from Handel's oratorios, operas, and other works that were a feature of the Handel Commemoration,[99] and vocal and orchestral forces increased. In the fall of 1784 an avowed attempt was made in Gloucester to emulate the Handel Commemoration in London: not only were some of the same works performed, but "the trombones, the double bassoon, and double kettle-drums, which had been introduced at the Abbey, were engaged to give greater effect to the chorusses."[100] In 1788, when the royal family visited the festival at Worcester, not only were the double bassoon and double drums used, but the orchestra was "aided by the powerful support of his Majesty's private band."[101] In 1784 the Liverpool Festival used 130 performers, the largest group assembled in the area up to that time.[102]

The influence of the Handel Commemoration was felt far beyond the shores of England—in Germany and the New World.[103] Not only did German journals carry descriptions of the Commemoration,[104] but Burney's *Account* was translated almost immediately by Johann Joachim Eschenburg (1743–1820) under the title *Dr. Karl Burneys Nachricht von Georg Friedrich Händels Lebensumständen und der ihm zu London im Mai und Juni 1784 angestellten Gedächtnissfeyer* (Berlin and Stettin, 1785). In the year after the German version of Burney's *Account* appeared, Johann Adam Hiller (1728–1804) introduced *Messiah* to Berlin

96. *London Stage*, 5/3:1730.

97. Pritchard, "Musical Festival," p. 151.

98. Ibid., p. 151.

99. As may be seen from a survey of the programs given in Pritchard and Reid, "Festival Programmes."

100. Lysons, *Three Choirs*, p. 64.

101. Ibid., p. 69.

102. Pritchard, "Musical Festival," p. 163.

103. On its influence in the New World, see below, the section "Handel in America."

104. See for instance, Cramer's *Magazin der Musik* 2/1 (1784–85): 162–74 and ibid. 2/1 (1784–85), pp. 734–40.

with a monumental performance in the Berlin Cathedral.[105] Hiller's intention was to give Berliners some idea of the 1784 performance in Westminster Abbey; yet he performed the work in an Italian translation, no doubt in order to use Italian soloists, attract a large audience of opera lovers, and please his patron. Like Burney, Hiller published an account of the performance, under the title *Nachricht von der Aufführung des Händelschen "Messias," in der Domkirche zu Berlin, den 19. May 1786* (Berlin, [1786]), dedicated to Prince Frederick William, who supported the concert, and who would soon succeed Frederick the Great to the throne. Hiller begins the introduction of his report by describing the impression on German music lovers of the reports of the Handel Commemoration in London:

> The performances of various works by Handel, which were presented in London with an unusually large number of musicians and with so much solemnity at a centennial Commemoration of this famous, and, in his way, great man, have created such a sensation through reports in newspapers and journals, that the wish to have been a witness of [the Commemoration], or to hear something similar to it sometime, must necessarily have been stimulated in many places and with very many friends of music. Burney spurred on this wish even more through his enthusiastic report of the Commemoration in honor of Handel, which was undertaken at London in May and June 1784, which Professor Eschenburg translated from the English and thereby made better known in Germany.
>
> Since, however, wishes and realizations are very different from each other, one must not wonder that thus far no city in Germany has ventured to undertake something which perhaps in a hundred cities has been wished.[106]

Hiller concludes his introduction by flattering his Berlin readers and his patron: "Berlin, among all the cities of Germany, is the first that has undertaken something similar to the London Commemoration and perhaps also is the only city that could undertake it."[107]

Hiller's plan for and execution of the concert is in many respects modeled on the Handel Commemoration in London, as is his report on that by Burney. Like the proceeds for the London performance, those for this one benefited "the poor widows and orphans of deceased musicians,"[108] and like Burney's report, Hiller's provides an accounting of the

---

105. A brief report of the performance appeared in Cramer's *Magazin der Musik* 2/2 (1786): 974–76. This was not the first performance of *Messiah* in Germany, for it had been performed in Hamburg in 1772 (see chapter 6).

106. Translated from Hiller, *Messias*, p. 7.

107. Ibid., p. 8.

108. Ibid., p. 31.

income, expenses, and amount remaining for charitable purposes.[109] Like Burney, Hiller lists the instrumental and vocal forces, which total 308 (over 200 fewer than in London). The 189 instrumentalists consisted of 38 first violins, 39 second violins, 18 violas, 23 violoncellos, 15 double basses, 12 flutes, 12 oboes, 10 bassoons, 8 horns, 6 trumpets, 4 trombones, 2 timpani, 1 organ, and 1 harpsichord.[110] Of the 119 singers, including soloists, there were 38 sopranos (named are 11 women and 3 castrati; unnamed are 24 "chorus singers" [Chorsängern]), 24 altos (1 woman and 4 men named, plus 19 "chorus singers"), 26 tenors (6 named, 20 "chorus singers") and 31 basses (8 named, 23 "chorus singers").[111] Although Hiller does not provide engraved illustrations of the Berlin Cathedral, as Burney does of the Abbey, Hiller gives a seating chart for the performers (see Figure IV-5), which shows that he, unlike Bates in London, stood at the front as would a modern conductor. Again like Burney, Hiller mentions that the concert was attended by numerous persons of distinction, including the royal princes and princesses, and by many persons who came from outside Berlin.

The success of the Berlin performance of *Messiah* prompted Hiller to give the work in German at the University Church in Leipzig on 3 November 1786 with 212 musicians, and he repeated the performance there on 11 May 1787. In Breslau on 30 May 1788 Hiller gave *Messiah* again, with a force of 261: the instrumentalists numbered 151 and the singers 110.[112]

The New World

Handel in America

Eighteenth-century concert life in British colonial America and the United States followed English models. Excerpts from Handel's oratorios—*Messiah* more often than any other—were prominent in concerts of religious music. According to an unconfirmed report, in April 1769 an oratorio was presented by a Philharmonic Society augmented by army and navy officers in St. Paul's Church, Halifax, Nova Scotia, but the

109. Ibid., pp. 30–32.
110. Ibid., pp. 22–25.
111. Ibid., pp. 26–27.
112. For details of these and other German performances of *Messiah*, see Siegmund-Schultze, "*Messias*-Aufführungen"; Siegmund-Schultze prints Hiller's German translation of the *Messiah* text on pp. 73–94. On Hiller's *Messiah* in Breslau, see also Peiser, *Hiller*, p. 74; on both the Leipzig and Breslau performances, see also Myers, *Handel's "Messiah,"* pp. 271–72, where the numbers of performers differ from those given above.

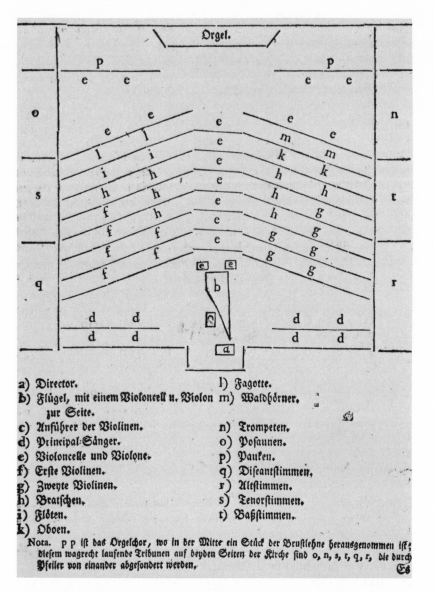

a) Director.
b) Flügel, mit einem Violoncell u. Violon zur Seite.
c) Anführer der Violinen.
d) Principal-Sänger.
e) Violoncelle und Violone.
f) Erste Violinen.
g) Zwente Violinen.
h) Bratschen.
i) Flöten.
k) Oboen.

l) Fagotte.
m) Waldhörner.
n) Trompeten.
o) Posaunen.
p) Pauken.
q) Discantstimmen.
r) Altstimmen.
s) Tenorstimmen.
t) Baßstimmen.

Nota. p p ist das Orgelchor, wo in der Mitte ein Stück der Brustlehne herausgenommen ist; diesem wagrecht laufende Tribunen auf beyden Seiten der Kirche sind o, n, s, t, q, r, die durch Pfeiler von einander abgesondert werden.

FIGURE IV-5. Seating chart for the performers at *Messiah*, directed by Johann Adam Hiller in the Berlin Cathedral, 1786. (From Hiller, "*Messias*," p. 28.)

sources of this report are unknown and thus far unsubstantiated.[113] The earliest confirmed report of a performance in America of vocal excerpts from an oratorio dates from Tuesday evening, 16 January 1770, in New York, when selections from *Messiah* were performed for the benefit of William Tuckey (1708–81); formerly a vicar-choral at Bristol Cathedral, Tuckey was the choirmaster of the Charity School of Trinity Church and an active figure in New York's musical life in the colonial period.[114] According to an advertisement in the *New York Journal* of 4 January 1770, the concert was originally scheduled to take place on Tuesday, 9 January, in "Mr. Burns's Room."[115] The first part of this "Concert of Church Music" was instrumental, but the second part consisted of "A SACRED ORATORIO, on the Prophecies concerning CHRIST, and his Coming; being an Extract from the late Mr. HANDEL'S GRAND ORA-TORIO, called the MESSIAH, consisting of the Overture, and sixteen other Pieces, viz. Airs, Recitatives, and Choruses. Never performed in America." Tuckey added a request for instrumentalists to assist in the performance: "As it is impossible that a performance of this Sort can be carried on without the kind Assistance of Gentlemen, who are Lovers of Music and Performers on Instruments; Mr. Tuckey will always gratefully acknowledge the Favour of the Gentlemen who assist him." In a subsequent notice postponing the concert until 16 January Tuckey announced that he had succeeded in engaging "a considerable number of Ladies and Gentlemen,"[116] but the size of the performing force is not known.

Tuckey repeated his performance of *Messiah* on 3 October 1770 in the Trinity Church, in conjunction with a sermon by the reverend Dr. Auchmuty, for the benefit of the Corporation for the Relief of the Widows and Children of Clergymen in the Communion of the Church of England in America. On 4 October the *New York Journal* reported, "Several pieces of Church musick, before the sermon, and after it part of the celebrated

113. The report is found in Kallmann, *Canada*, p. 56, where it is attributed to Ven. Archdeacon Armitage, "Music in By-gone Days," *Acadian Recorder* (16 January 1913), p. 7; the report is repeated in Blakeley, "Halifax," *Encyclopedia of Music in Canada*, p. 403. Yet the article McGee, "Halifax," a study of archival documents and newspaper reports in Halifax, does not verify the report. Rather, McGee states, on p. 380, that "the first record of a large musical presentation in St. Paul's is from a newspaper account in 1789 . . . on May 26, the 'Final Chorus of the Messiah and the Coronation Anthem by Handel' were performed by 'Several gentlemen and the music Bands of the Regiments who played with the organ.' " McGee cites the *Royal Gazette*, 26 May 1789.

114. On Tuckey's life and works, see Aaron, "Tuckey."

115. On this and other concerts organized by Tuckey, see Sonneck, *Concert-Life*, pp. 176–81; Aaron, "Tuckey," pp. 83–89; and Myers, *Handel's "Messiah*," pp. 249–50. Myers, on p. 249, specifies the location of this concert as "George Burns' Music Room in the New York City Tavern, situated on the west side of Broadway between the present Cedar and Thames Streets."

116. *New York Journal*, 11 January 1770.

Mr. Handel's Oratorio of the *Messiah* were performed by a considerable number of male and female voices, accompanied with the organ, very much to the general satisfaction" of "a numerous audience, consisting of most of the principal inhabitants, &c. and at which about twenty eight clergymen of the church of England of this and the neighboring colonies attended."[117] The charitable purpose of this sermon with music was similar to that of the annual Sons of the Clergy services at St. Paul's Cathedral in London and the performances of the Three Choirs Festival. Part of *Messiah* was heard again in New York at the Trinity Church in April 1772. According to an announcement, the music was to be performed as part of a service: "On Monday next will be performed at Trinity Church, part of Mr. Handle's [sic] sacred Oratorio, called the MESSIAH, on the *Passion, Crucifixion, Resurrection* and Triumphant Ascension of JESUS CHRIST: by a select Company. Divine Service will begin at half an Hour past ten."[118] Once introduced into American concerts and church services, Handel's *Messiah* became a staple, as it had long been in England; yet no complete American performance of the work is known prior to one in Boston on 25 December 1818.[119] Myers lists numerous performances of *Messiah* excerpts between 1770 and 1800 in Baltimore, Bethlehem, Boston, Charleston, New York, Norfolk, and Philadelphia.[120]

The influence of London's 1784 Commemoration of Handel may be seen in the types of programs heard in America and, on occasion, in the sizes of performing forces. On 10 January 1786 the Musical Society of Boston, directed by the composer and organist William Selby (1738?–98), presented an elaborate concert for the benefit of the prisoners in the Boston jail, in which, according to Sonneck, Selby desired "as far as possible, to unite the musical forces of Boston in a concert which would assume the proportions of a festival."[121] Like some of the morning concerts in English provincial festivals, this one was held in a church, the Stone Chapel, and mixed the liturgical elements of Morning Prayer with vocal and instrumental music.[122] The event began at eleven o'clock with the overture to Handel's *Occasional Oratorio* and included several excerpts from *Messiah* and one from *Samson*. The Music Society of Boston presented a similar and equally festive event on 16 January 1787. Again there were excerpts from Handel's *Messiah* and *Samson*, plus one from

117. Quoted in Myers, *Handel's "Messiah,"* p. 250; and Messiter, *Trinity Church*, p. 30.

118. Quoted in Messiter, *Trinity Church*, p. 30.

119. Myers, *Handel's "Messiah,"* p. 260.

120. Ibid., pp. 251–58.

121. Sonneck, *Concert-Life*, p. 275. Sonneck's assumption that this undertaking would require uniting the musical forces of Boston is reasonable, but he does not list the performing forces.

122. The order of events and a newspaper review are quoted in ibid., pp. 275–77.

Samuel Felsted's *Jonah* (see below). The *Boston Gazette* sang the praises of *"Handel! Handel! Handel!"* and particularly noted "the Hallelujah Chorus in the Messiah, in which there appears perfect illumination—the surprise and astonishment of the audience, at the performance of this divine Chorus, cannot well be described, especially at those parts where the *drums* so unexpectedly thundered in and joined in the glorious Halle- lujahs to the 'King of Kings and Lord of Lords, etc.' "[123] In New York another reflection of the Handel Commemoration was a concert orga- nized by Alexander Reinagel (1756–1809) on 20 July 1786: Maria Storer, who had performed in festivals at Bath and Salisbury, sang selec- tions from "Handel's Sacred Music, as performed in Westminster Abbey."[124]

In Philadelphia a monumental concert given on 4 May 1786 resulted from the stimulus of London's Commemoration of Handel and the im- posing concert (mentioned above) in Boston held on 10 January 1786. According to *The Pennsylvania Packet,*

> At the Reformed German Church, in Race street, was performed a GRAND CONCERT of *vocal and instrumental music*, in the pres- ence of a numerous and polite audience. The whole *Band* consisted of 230 vocal, and 50 instrumental performers; *which*, we are fully justified in pronouncing, was the most complete, both with respect to number and accuracy of execution, ever, on any occasion, com- bined in this city, and, perhaps, throughout America.
>
> The first idea of this concert was suggested to the trustees of the musical institution, by *the Commemoration of Handel*, in London, and *the Sacred Concert* in Boston. . . .
>
> The whole concluded with the exertions of the *full Band* in the performance of that most sublime of all musical compositions, the *Grand Chorus* in the *Messiah*, by the celebrated *Handel*, to these words, *"Hallelujah! for the Lord God omnipotent reigneth,"* &c. . . .
>
> Nearly one thousand tickets were sold, at two thirds of a dollar each, and the nett proceeds, after deducting for necessary expences, have been delivered to the managers of the *Pennsylvania Hospital, Philadelphia Dispensary, and Overseers of the Poor*, to be applied by them for the use of said institutions and unprovided poor.[125]

At this point in Philadelphia's history, it would seem that the vocal forces comparable to those of the London Commemoration could be mustered, but not the instrumental forces. The "musical institution" mentioned in this review was the Institute for the Encouragement of Church Music (later called the Uranian Academy), organized by Andrew Adgate, who was the director of this performance.

123. Ibid., p. 279, where the entire review is quoted.
124. Myers, Handel's "Messiah," p. 251.
125. *The Pennsylvania Packet, and Daily Advertiser*, 30 May 1786, fol. 2r.

Of special importance for the history of the oratorio in America is *Jonah* (1775), by Samuel Felsted (1743?–1802), the organist of Saint Andrew's Parish, Kingston, Jamaica.[126] *Jonah* is probably the first oratorio composed in the New World and the only one composed there in the eighteenth century; it also appears to be the the first oratorio, by any composer, to be performed in its entirety in eighteenth-century America. According to Thurston Dox, evidence in Jamaica points to a performance of *Jonah* there in 1779.[127] The earliest known performance elsewhere was on 11 June 1788 in New York.[128] According to the New York *Daily Advertiser* the work was sung in a concert "at the German Church on Nassau Street for the relief of the German Reformed Church in the city of Albany" and was flanked on the program by instrumental music and anthems.[129] Another performance was given by the Musical Society of New York on 18 June 1789, and again the oratorio was surrounded by instrumental music and anthems.[130]

In Boston on Wednesday, 14 October 1789, the *Massachusetts Centinal* announced: "On Wednesday next, will be performed at the Stone Chapel in this town, an Oratorio, or, Concert of Sacred Musick, to assist in finishing the Colonnade or Portico of said chapel, agreeably to the original design." The first part of the concert consisted of two anthems and an organ concerto by Selby, and excerpts from Handel's *Messiah* and *Samson*; the second part was devoted to

> The oratorio of *Jonah*, complete, the solos by Messrs. Rea, Ray, Brewer, and Dr. Rogerson. The chorusses by the *Independent Musical Society*; the instrumental parts by a Society of Gentlemen with the band of his Most Christian Majesty's Fleet. As the above oratorio has been highly applauded by the best judges, and has never been performed in America [but see the above-mentioned performances]; and as the first performers of this country will be joined by the excellent band of this Most Christian Majesty's squadron, the Publick will have every reason to expect a more finished and delightful Performance than ever was exhibited in the United States.[131]

Thus the singers and some of the instrumentalists scheduled to perform were evidently local, but the instrumentalists included French musicians. ("His Most Christian Majesty" was the French king's title.) It is of inter-

126. See Dox, "Felsted," based on Dox's recent research on Felsted in Kingston, Jamaica, and the United States.

127. Ibid.

128. Sonneck, *Concert-Life*, pp. 225–26.

129. Ibid.

130. Ibid., p. 202.

131. *Massachusetts Centinel*, 14 October 1789.

est that the newspaper announcement includes two uses of the word *oratorio*, which were found in England: *oratorio* designated both the concert as a whole and the genre of one work on the program. The concert thus advertised, however, was twice postponed. On Wednesday, 21 October, the *Centinel* printed on its front page the entire text of *Jonah*, but the concert had been postponed until 27 October so that it would coincide with a visit by the recently inaugurated president, George Washington, who was to visit Boston. On 28 October the *Centinel* reported, "Yesterday THE PRESIDENT honoured the Stone-Chapel with his presence to hear the Concert of Sacred Musick; but on account of the indisposition of several of the first performers, the Musick was postponed until Wednesday next. Several pieces were however given, which merited and received applause." The *Centinal* of 25 November announced a new date: "The ORATORIO, OR CONCERT OF SACRED MUSICK, Which through the indisposition of several Singers with the prevailing *Influenza*, could not be fully performed on the 27th ult. will be performed at the *Stone-Chapel*, in Boston, on Tuesday, the first day of December next, at 6 o'clock, P.M. if the weather permits, otherwise on the next day at the same hour." The weather did not permit, for on Wednesday, 2 December, the *Centinel*'s readers found that the concert was to be performed on that evening "at 6 o'clock, at the Stone-Chapel.—An original poem will be delivered by Mr. Whitewell, jun. of this town—and the Chapel will be brilliantly illuminated." Thus the vicissitudes of what is probably New World's first oratorio.

CHAPTER V

The English Oratorio: Libretto, Music, Selected Oratorios

The Libretto

In the second half of the eighteenth century the librettos of the relatively few new English oratorios are essentially Handelian: typically they are dramatic, based on the Old Testament, and divided into three acts or parts, and they include several choruses in each act. The following titles of a few Old Testament oratorios performed in London in the post-Handel period indicate some of the stories favored (in parentheses are first performance dates and places):

David and Jonathan (28 January 1761, King's Theatre in the Haymarket), music by Charles Barbandt;

Judith (27 February 1761, Drury Lane), libretto by Isaac Bickerstaffe (d. 1812?), music by Arne;

Ruth (15 April 1763, Lock Hospital Chapel), music by Avison and Giardini;

Rebecca (16 March 1764, Covent Garden), libretto possibly by Benjamin Stillingfleet, music by Smith;

Hannah (3 April 1764, King's Theatre in the Haymarket), libretto by Chrisopher Smart (1722–71), music by Worgan;

Manasseh (30 April 1766, Lock Hospital Chapel), music by Worgan;

Abimelech (16 March 1768, Little Theatre in the Haymarket), music by Arnold;

Goliath (5 May 1773, King's Theatre in the Haymarket), music by Luffmann Atterbury (ca. 1740–96);

The Fall of Egypt (23 March 1774, Drury Lane), libretto by John Hawkesworth (1715?–73), music by Stanley; and

Elijah (1785), libretto by Thomas Skelton Dupuis, music by John W. Callcott (1766–1821).

Of special interest is *Judith* by Bickerstaffe and Arne, for it clearly shows the contrast between the English and Italian approaches to oratorio. Bickerstaffe based his libretto on the same story as Metastasio's *Betulia liberata*, but his approach was quite different: *Judith* is divided into three acts rather than *Betulia*'s two parts, and in *Judith* the dramatic and choral elements assume greater proportions (see further discussion below).

Among the few oratorios composed on New Testament subjects is *The Ascension: A Sacred Oratorio* (20 March 1776, Covent Garden), with biblical words, and music by James Hook (1746–1827).[1] Texts of this type, compiled from biblical quotations, are relatively rare, despite the enormous popularity of *Messiah*, the prime example of an oratorio with such a libretto. An interesting work of this type is Arnold's *Resurrection*, which the composer, in the prefatory "Argument" in the printed libretto, describes as representing an apostolic act of worship:

> The reader of this compilation will please to consider it as a supposed act of worship of the *Apostles*, after the *ascension* of our blessed *Lord*.
>
> In order to give room for that variety so essentially necessary in an entertainment consisting entirely of *sacred* music, the piece opens with the joy of the *Disciples*, and with their gratulations to the house of *Israel*: from their own situation, exposed to the hatred and persecution of so many powerful enemies, they are led to reflect on the uncertainty of human life, and to express their entire trust and confidence in *God*, for their support under the many difficulties and distresses, with which they were sure to meet, in the course of the *ministry* they were now about to enter on.
>
> A review of the *principal* scenes of our blessed *Lord's passion*, of their own consequent despondence, and of the notice of his *resurrection* by the Angel, then follows. Order gives way to the ecstasy and transports of joy which the recollection of this great event excites: their praises to *god* on this most happy and important *occasion*, brings on a review of the promis'd blessings of the *Messiah's Kingdom*. Hence arises a natural transition of *our own* final *Resurrection*, as the consequence of *that* of *our* blessed *Lord* and *Redeemer*.[2]

Like the text of Handel's *Messiah*, those of Hook's *Ascension* and Arnold's *Resurrection* imply the narrative-dramatic action through the selection of biblical texts but do not include personages.

1. Libretto in GB-Lcm: XX.G.19d.(18).
2. *The Resurrection, a Sacred Oratorio. As it is performed at the Theatre-Royal in Covent-Garden. The music by Mr. Arnold . . . Sold at the Theater* [London: n.d.], pp. iii–iv. (copy in GB-Lcm: XX.G.19.[19]).

Of special interest for its relationship to oratorio criticism is the libretto *The Cure of Saul: A Sacred Ode*, by the clergyman, writer, and amateur musician John Brown (1715–66). The libretto is prefaced to Brown's treatise, *A Dissertation on the Rise, Union, and Power, the Progressions, Separations, and Corruptions, of Poetry and Music* (London, 1763). This *Dissertation* must have been widely read, for it was translated into German (Leipzig, 1769) by J. J. Eschenburg, and into Italian (Florence, 1772) by Oresbio Agieo (academic name of Francesco Corsetti). Brown's treatise and libretto evidently had little influence on the Italian libretto, but it may have influenced that of Germany (see chapter 6). Brown intended *The Cure of Saul* to illustrate the conclusions of his critical writing on the relationship between music and poetry in contemporary genres. In the *Dissertation* he considers oratorio as generally understood in his time to be essentially a dramatic genre, and thus he excludes *Messiah*: "Though that grand Musical Entertainment is called an *Oratorio*, yet it is not *dramatic*; but properly a Collection of *Hymns* or *Anthems* drawn from the sacred Scriptures: In strict Propriety, therefore, it falls under another Class of Composition, which we have already considered."[3] The main fault that Brown finds with contemporary oratorio lies in the unnatural and improbable qualities of recitative:

> The capital Impropriety and Defect of this Entertainment [oratorio], while it wears the *dramatic* Form, is the perpetual Recitative or musical Accompanyment in the interlocutory Parts, similar to that of *Opera*. This is a Circumstance so repugnant to modern Manners, and therefore so far out of Nature, that no Audience can be much affected by the Representation, or take Part in an Action so improbably feigned. The necessary Effect of This glaring Improbability is a general Inattention to the *Subject*, and a Regard centered chiefly on the *Music* and *Execution*.[4]

As long as oratorio "wears the dramatic form," Brown recommends that it be reformed "by destroying the *Recitative*, or perpetual *musical* Accompanyment: And in this Case, the Interlocutory Part would sink into the common Form of *Tragedy*."[5] But Brown's final recommendation to the librettist is to abandon the dramatic form and create a union of the ode and the epic:

> This Union forms what may properly be styled the *Narrative* or *Epic Ode*. . . . The intermixed Narrations must be short and animated: The Songs and Choirs various and expressive; and being frequently interrupted by the brief Recitals, may by these Means be inspirited far beyond the simple and continued Ode, which from its unbroken Length often degenerates into Languor. By this Union,

3. Brown, *Dissertation*, p. 218, footnote d.
4. Ibid., p. 216.
5. Ibid., p. 232.

all the striking Parts of the Action may be brought forth to View, while every thing that is cold, improbable, and unaffecting, may be veiled in Darkness.—The *Recitative*, or musical Accompanyment in the *narrative* Parts, will *here* lose a great Part of that Improbability which incumbers it in the *dramatic* Representation: For *here*, the *Reciter* is a professed Musician, whose Province lies in the Enthusiasm of Song; and the *Narrations* being *short* and *animated*, beyond what is possible in the continued Use of *Dialogue*, they approach nearer to the Genius of the *Ode*, and therefore may without Improbability or Impropriety receive a musical Accompanyment which approaches nearer to a full and direct Song.—And lastly, the *Songs* and *Choirs* are in their Performance so far from being unnatural, that they are no more than a powerful transcript from Nature, impelling those who hear the Recital of the Action, and are instructed in the Laws of Melody, to join in every represented Scene of Joy, Triumph, Terror, Exultation, Devotion, or Distress.[6]

Brown's *The Cure of Saul* is a "narrative or epic ode" of the type he recommends.[7] The one-part libretto, based on the story of David's soothing Saul with music, includes neither labeled personages nor passages designated for specific types of setting—recitative, air, or chorus. The style fluctuates between lines of narrative and those attributed to David, Saul, and the Chorus of Shepherds. As the text's full meaning is not always explicit, the "argument" prefixed to the libretto is essential. On the whole the poetry is better than most found in oratorio librettos of the time.

Brown's libretto was first set as a pasticcio, performed at Covent Garden on 4 March 1763, when the *Public Advertiser* called it "A *Sacred Ode* by Dr Brown. Adapted [by the author of the Ode] to select Airs, Duets and Chorusses from Handel, Marcello, Purcell and other eminent composers."[8] On 23 January 1767 at the King's Theatre in the Haymarket, *The Cure of Saul* was performed again, this time billed as "Written by Dr Brown; composed by Arnold. For the Benefit and Increase of a Fund established for the Support of Decayed Musicians and their Families."[9] The 1767 performance may have been that for which an undated libretto was printed, which includes on the title page the words, "The music composed by Mr Arnold"; that libretto shows the work divided into three parts (as opposed to the original one-part version) and includes eleven entrances of the chorus.[10]

6. Ibid., pp. 234–35.
7. For a contemporary, highly favorable piece of critical writing about this libretto, in which it is compared with several set by Handel, see [Maddison], *Examination*, quoted in chapter 4 on oratorio terminology.
8. As quoted in *London Stage*, 4/2:982.
9. As quoted in ibid., 4/2:1213.
10. Libretto in GB-Lbl: R. M. 5. e. 7 (7).

The pasticcio oratorio that used Handel's music exclusively or primarily became an important type in the second half of the eighteenth century. For such a pasticcio a new libretto and newly composed recitatives joined miscellaneous airs, ensembles, and choruses taken from Handel's works. Among the early examples are *Israel in Babylon* (12 April 1764, King's Theatre in the Haymarket), arranged by Edward Toms;[11] and both *Nabal* (16 March 1764, Covent Garden) and *Gideon* (10 February 1769, Covent Garden), with librettos by Thomas Morell (1703–84, one of Handel's oratorio librettists) and music adapted by Smith. *Nabal* was billed as drawing "music of the Songs and Chorusses entirely from works of Mr Handel."[12] Later Handel pasticcios are *Omnipotence* (25 February 1774, Little Theatre in the Haymarket), libretto by Arnold and Toms, and adapted by Arnold; *Redemption* (10 March 1786, Drury Lane), libretto possibly by W. Coxe and adapted by Arnold; and *The Triumph of Truth* (27 February 1789, Drury Lane), adapted by Arnold—about two-thirds of its numbers were by Handel, the others by Haydn, Corelli, Purcell, Arnold, Arne, Jommelli, and Sacchini.

According to the preface to the 1774 libretto of *Omnipotence*, that work, assembled from Handel's Chandos Anthems, "is divided into three parts; under the different subjects of *Creation*, *Redemption*, and *Salvation*: the endeavour, in the arrangement, hath been to retain the sublimity of the sacred texts; and the melodious illustration they have received from the genius of Mr Handel, in the full force, propriety and grandeur, they stand with in the original compositions. A few movements, for connection, are added from his other works, which are too trifling to particularise."[13] As the original texts were retained, the libretto was an exception to the usual dramatic oratorio.

The preface to the 1786 libretto of *Redemption*, quoted here in full, reveals much about the motivation for presenting this pasticcio, the enormous scope of the drama, and the method of adapting Handel's music to it:

> The judicious selection of Music, performed at the Commemoration of Handel at Westminster-Abbey, and at the Pantheon, first gave the idea of compiling and bringing into one performance, or regular drama, those great and favorite works of this justly-admired author; and I have only to regret, that the compass of time allotted for the performance of an Oratorio is so short, as to deprive me of adding many more of his capital compositions, that would have greatly enriched the performance.
>
> In the arrangement of the pieces, care has been taken not to alter the harmony, or to interfere with the melody of the voice part, excepting to divide a note, in order to accommodate particular

11. Manuscript in GB-Lbl: R. M. 19.b.6.

12. *London Stage*, 4/2:1045.

13. Printed libretto in GB-Lbl: T. 657 (7).

syllables to such words as are adapted to Italian airs.—Where-ever the text could be preserved, it has been preferred.

The drama opens with a description of the *Creation*, which being accomplished, it hastens to the grand scriptural type of *Christ*; that of Abraham's faith, in offering his son Isaac. After which, the history of Joseph being sold to the Ishmaelites, and the departure of the Children of Israel, with Moses their leader, out of the land of Egypt, conclude the first part.

The stories of Joshua, Deborah, Saul, David, and the Coronation of Solomon, slightly touched upon, compose the second part.

From the prophesies of Jeremiah and Mica, of the coming of our blessed Lord and Savior, the third part opens: his Birth, Mission, Death, and Resurrection follow; and the piece concludes with the consequences thereof—our REDEMPTION!

S[amuel] A[rnold][14]

The libretto identifies the sources of many of the texts for individual numbers: books of the Old and New Testament, John Milton's *Paradise Lost*, John Wesley's *History of the Bible*, Christopher Smart's *Psalms*, the *Te Deum*, the Communion Service, and texts of Handel's oratorios; although the accompanied recitatives are Handel's, the simple recitatives evidently have new texts and music. The music for the numbers was taken from virtually all of Handel's oratorios; from his operas *Alcina*, *Ezio*, *Rodelinda*, and *Siroe*; and from the Coronation Anthems, a *Jubilate*, and the *Funeral Anthem*. Thus Arnold's pasticcio, motivated by the Commemoration of Handel, functioned as a concert of Handel's music placed within a context created by a new libretto of monumental scope.

The Music: General Characteristics

Despite the English interest in oratorio during the second half of the eighteenth century, as evidenced in the frequent performance of some of Handel's oratorios, few new oratorios were composed. New works in this genre rarely survived beyond two or three performances. When it came to oratorio, whether in the London theaters during Lent or in the provincial festivals, the public wanted its ritualistic Handelian performance, and oratorios by other composers apparently could not satisfy that need. In a letter of 1784 John Stanley, in declining to set to music some oratorio librettos offered to him, pointed out the futility of composing oratorios: ". . . there is little reason to suppose that any other than Mr Handels musick would succeed, as people in general are so partial to that, that no other Oratorios are ever well attended."[15] Slightly

14. Printed libretto in GB-Lbl:11779.c.25.
15. Stanley to Charles Burney, 21 April 1784. The letter, in the possession of Mr. Gerald Coke, is quoted in Williams, "Stanley," 1:56.

later Burney mentioned in a letter to Sir Joseph Banks that the public was unwilling "to like any other compositions of that kind [oratorios] than those of Handel, though they have heard them so long, that they are heartily tired of them."[16] Five works from the 1760s and 1770s are treated below as examples of the newly composed English-language oratorio; the present section summarizes the musical characteristics of such works.

We have seen that the English veneration of Handel had its impact on the libretto of English oratorio. In musical style the Handelian influence is also evident, especially in choruses. In the airs one often finds an element that indigenous English Baroque and early Classical styles have in common: a simple, tuneful vocal line with balanced phrases and a relatively light texture. Unlike the early Classical style, however, is the more conservative, linear motion of the basso continuo, which tends to generate a fast harmonic rhythm; but even in the most conservative oratorios of the period, a few airs reveal an early Classical simplicity of texture and slow harmonic rhythm.

The formal structures of airs in English oratorios tend to be conservative. Da capo and dal segno airs are common, with the sign in the dal segno form frequently used to delete the opening ritornello upon the repeat to the A section. A common form is the binary air, often with a structure comparable to the A section of the da capo form. Rarely does an English oratorio include a clear example of the transformed da capo.

The conventions of word painting that derived from Baroque style and continued in early Classical and Classical styles are, of course present in the English oratorio. Handel was a consummate master of such word painting; his successors, who tried to carry on the tradition, pale in comparison—a point surely grasped by their audiences. The use of minor keys for dark affects—fear and lamentation, for instance—continued in post-Handelian England, as in oratorios in other regions and languages.

The chorus, particularly prominent in the English oratorio, reveals Handelian influence in the variety of textures; imitative, fugal, "open-work," and chordal textures are often juxtaposed in the choruses of Handel and his successors.[17] Yet the extent of that variety in the post-Handelian oratorio is tempered by the strong tendency, found also on the Continent, toward purely chordal texture.

The orchestra of the English oratorio continues to be more or less that of Handel, as do the orchestral numbers. The French overture, the most common opening instrumental number in Handel's oratorios, remains important in this period, and as with Handel the overture is often followed by a dance number such as a minuet. The Italian sinfonia, how-

16. Burney to Banks, 26 May 1784. The librettos had been offered to Stanley by Burney, on behalf of a friend of Sir Joseph Banks. The letter, in the possession of the Hyde Collection, Somerville, New Jersey, is quoted in Williams, "Stanley," 1:194 (for Williams's documentation, see 1:56, n. 55).

17. For references to examples in Handel, see Smither, *Oratorio*, 2:353.

ever, is occasionally used. The rare instrumental number within oratorios usually has a descriptive function or establishes the mood for a
change of scene.

The Music: Selected Oratorios

The following works are organized in chronological order and represent
a sample from the relatively small repertoire of new English oratorios
composed in the eighteenth century after Handel's death. The first and
third of these works, by Smith and Stanley, in a very real sense represent
Handel's followers, for, as we have seen, those composers continued his
Lenten oratorio series. The works by Arne and Worgan are closer to the
early Classical style than those by Smith and Stanley. Felsted's *Jonah* has
been chosen primarily for its historical priority as a New World oratorio;
far less imposing than the others, it is, nevertheless, an effective work by
a composer who was familiar with the English Baroque oratorio and the
early Classical style.

John Christopher Smith: Paradise Lost

The younger John Christopher Smith (1712–95), who composed *Paradise Lost,* was the son of Johann Christoph Schmidt, who anglicized his
name when he moved from Ansbach to London to become Handel's
treasurer and principal copyist.[18] The elder Smith arrived in London in
1716, and his son followed him in 1720. The younger Smith had a few
composition lessons with Handel and Johann Christoph Pepusch (1667–
1752), but most of his studies were with Thomas Roseingrave (1688–
1766). Smith occasionally composed for the theater in the 1740s and
1750s. He became the unpaid organist at the Foundling Hospital in
1754, assisted Handel in his later years, and from 1759 to 1768 conducted the annual performance of *Messiah* at the Foundling Hospital.
From 1760 to 1774 Smith collaborated with Stanley in organizing the
oratorio series in the London theaters during Lent (see chapter 4), and
from 1762 to 1772 he gave harpsichord lessons twice weekly to the
dowager princess of Wales. Upon her death George III granted Smith a
pension, and Smith bequeathed to the king the large collection of Handel
manuscripts (now in the Royal Music Library at the British Museum);
Handel had left his manuscripts to the elder Smith, who had passed them
on to his son. The younger Smith composed or arranged nine oratorios,
three of which are pasticcios of Handel's music. Of the six entirely by
Smith, only two are known to have been performed: *David's Lamentation over Saul and Jonathan* (1738; libretto by John Lockman; per-

18. On the younger Smith, see Roger Fiske, "John Christopher Smith," *New
Grove*, 17:414–16; and Mann, "Smith."

formed at Hickford's Rooms, 1740) and *Paradise Lost* (1757–58; libretto by Benjamin Stillingfleet; first performed at Covent Garden, 1760). No performances are known for *Judith* (1758, libretto by Robert Price), *The Feast of Darius* (1761, mostly from Smith's setting of Metastasio's *Dario*), *Jehosaphat* (1764), and *Redemption* (1774?, libretto by William Coxe).

His most successful oratorio, *Paradise Lost*, was performed in three Lenten seasons, 1760, 1761, and 1774.[19] The work survives in both manuscript and printed sources.[20] The manuscript source shows evidence of numerous revisions. Comparison of the printed librettos of 1760 and 1774 suggest that some of the revisions in the manuscript relate to changes made before the 1760 performance and others to changes made for the 1774 performance. On the verso of the title page of the 1760 libretto is an "Advertisement" that states, "As the oratorio was found to take up too much time at the rehearsal, the lines marked thus ' are not performed." Deleted from the 1760 performance were seven airs, seven B sections and da capos of airs and duets, and four passages of recitative. The 1774 version deleted a few more items and added a few.[21] The numbers performed in 1760, 1774, and both years are indicated in Table V-1.

The librettist of *Paradise Lost*, Benjamin Stillingfleet (1702–71), was a naturalist, amateur musician, and close associate of Smith. Stillingfleet states on the title page of the printed libretto (in both 1760 and 1774) that the work is "altered and adapted to the stage from Milton," and in the dedication to a Mrs. Montagu he clarifies the extent of his reliance on that author: "As to the piece before us, my greatest difficulty has been to bring the materials furnished by Milton into so small a compass, and at the same time to preserve some idea of the original plan. Herein all my merit, whatever it is, consists. Almost all the recitative is taken word for word from the author, and as to the songs they are in general so much

19. *London Stage*, 4/2:776, 844; 4/3:1790.

20. The main source for the following comments is the manuscript in D-Hs: MA/672, which includes the entire work. Other sources consulted are the published overture and airs, Smith, *Paradise**, copy in GB-Lbl: G. 232 (2) and GB-Lcm: XVIII.A.12.(2); the printed libretto, *Paradise Lost. An oratorio. As it is performed at the Theatre-Royal in Covent-Garden* (London: R. and J. Dodsley, 1760), copies in GB-Lbl: T.657 (5) and R.M. 5.e.6 (1), and in GB-Lcm: XX.G.20.(2); and the printed libretto *Paradise Lost. An Oratorio. Altered and adapted for the Stage from Milton . . . A New Edition, with Alterations and Additions* (London: J. Dodsley, 1774), copy in GB-Lcm: XX.G.20.(3). I have not located a printed libretto for the performance of 1761.

21. A detailed study of the manuscript of this and other Smith oratorios has yet to be undertaken. For a helpful preliminary study, see McCredie, "Smith," pp. 34–36. A dissertation in progress on the music of Smith, including the oratorios, is Small, "Smith."

his, that I have tried to compose them chiefly from the sentiments I found in him, and as often as I was able to preserve his very words."[22] Based mainly on the story of Adam and Eve as told in books 4–5, 9, and 11–12 of Milton's *Paradise Lost*, the libretto's recitatives not only quote Milton, as Stillingfleet says, but often abbreviate and paraphrase Milton's verses. The recitatives follow Milton in verse form, that is, unrhymed iambic pentameter. The airs, duets, and choruses—essentially Stillingfleet's verses but suggested by Milton—are usually in rhymed trochaic tetrameter. An interesting departure from Milton is the insertion in the 1774 version of the Anglican "Te Deum," verses 1 and 3–5, as a chorus (see Table V-1, no. 2). The personages of the libretto are Adam (S), Eve (S), and the angels Gabriel (T), Michael (B and T), and Uriel (B), who sing recitatives and airs; and the angels Ithuriel (B), Uzziel (T), and Zephon (T), who sing recitatives only.[23] The chorus (SATB) functions both as an unnamed commentator on the action and as a chorus of Angels.

Act I of the libretto begins with a scene in heaven where Gabriel, Uriel, and the other angels look down to observe with pleasure the newly created world, yet they must find Satan, the fallen angel, who lurks "in the mount that lies from Eden north."[24] The scene changes to Paradise, where Adam and Eve rejoice in the beauties and innocent pleasures of their existence. As in Milton's book 4, evening approaches, and the first parents sing the glories of the night. They prepare to repose after the labors of the day, and the angels watch over them as they sleep. Act II draws mostly on Milton's description of Adam and Eve's awakening in the morning (book 5) and of their fall from innocence (book 9). Eve tells Adam of a dream in which she tasted the forbidden fruit, but he reassures her that it was but a dream. They express their joy to the Lord for his glorious work, but the chorus and the angels sense impending doom. Eve suggests to Adam that rather than working side by side in the garden, they part, for in so doing they might accomplish more; Adam resists, for there may be dangers and temptations if they part, but eventu-

22. Printed libretto, *Paradise Lost* (1760), p. 4.

23. The vocal ranges are derived from the clefs and ranges in the manuscript score. In that source, Michael's part is written in the bass clef (range A–c') for his first recitative and air, and thereafter, in the tenor clef (range up to g'); Adam's part is in the soprano clef throughout, and the name "Master Norris" appears over Adam's part several times. This Norris has not been positively identified, but he may have been the well-known tenor, Thomas Norris (1741–90); perhaps he sang the role in 1761 or 1774. According to the published score of 1760, "Miss Young" sang the role of Adam, "Miss Brent" and "Signora Frasi" shared the role of Eve, "Mr. Beard" sang Gabriel, and "Mr. Champness" and "Mr. Beard" shared Michael.

24. This libretto summary is based on the 1760 version, which is longer than that of 1774.

ally agrees. Gabriel feels a shock—the earth is wounded, and Nature sighs: "Some evil sure betides the human pair." Eve returns to Adam, and explains that the tree of which they had been warned is not dangerous, for a wise serpent had eaten its fruit and persuaded her to do so. Exhilarated by her taste of forbidden fruit, she sings, "Yes, wisdom opens all her stores, / into my soul her treasure pours, / celestial visions strike my eyes, / I seem to mount and tread the skies." She tempts Adam, who at first refuses for fear of death, yet finally agrees out of love for Eve. Gabriel sees the "disturb'd passion" in the faces of the pair, and, in a paraphrase of Milton, he notes, "Earth trembles from her bowels, as again / in pangs, and nature gives a second groan / sky lowers, and thunder mutters, these are signs, / these can be only signs of mortal sin." The final chorus proclaims that the Lord "shall pour his vengeance" on the impious head of Satan "and give thee full due for this foul deed." In act III, mostly from Milton's book 11, Gabriel tells the angels that Michael has been sent to earth on an important errand. Meanwhile Adam blames Eve for the misery resulting from their sin and wants to banish her from his sight. She pleads that they try to go on together, and he finally agrees that they should "strive / in offices of love, how we may ease / each others burthen, in our own share of woe." Michael arrives to evict them from Paradise, to which Eve exclaims in a Miltonian paraphrase, "O unexpected stroke far worse than death! / Must I then leave thee Paradise?" As in Milton's book 12, Michael explains what the future will bring, including the coming of the Messiah to redeem mankind: "at his birth a star / unseen before in Heav'n proclaims him come. / His place of birth a solemn angel tells / to simple shepherds, keeping watch by night." The oratorio closes with the prophecy of the angelic announcement, "Glory to God on high, peace on earth, good will towards men," and a "Hallelujah" chorus.

From the structural outline, Table V-1, one may infer a tonal center of D major: in both the 1760 and 1774 versions, act II closes on the dominant and act III on the tonic of D; more numbers are in D than any other key; and more sharp than flat keys are used. (The choices of F major and minor for the two movements of the ouverture, however, do not fit the D major center.) Especially important in this work is the affective use of major and minor. The affect of the text in act I is joyous, and all keys are major. The first number in minor is 14, in which Eve is tormented about her dream of eating the fruit of the forbidden tree; and the next number in minor, 16, is a chorus of impending doom: "A voice was heard, a solemn voice, on high, / it thrice said woe, woe, woe, to those below." The texts of the other numbers in minor also relate to the catastrophe: number 20, an air of Gabriel's concern, ". . . sin, I fear, has got command"; 21, on the suffering of Nature; 29, on a violent storm that Adam sees after his fall; 31, Eve's fear of impending death; 36, Eve's anguished departure from the nuptial bower at the eviction from Paradise; and 38, Michael's comments on Satan.

TABLE V-I
Smith, *Paradise Lost*: Structural Outline

Numbers	Keys
Overture	F/f
ACT I	
1. *Chorus. "Works which he pronounced good"	G
2. +Chorus. "We praise thee o God" [Anglican "Te Deum," vs. 1, 3–5]	D
3. *Air. Adam, "Would we hold dominion given"	G
4. *+Air. Eve, "Bounteous providence divine"	B♭
5. *+Air. Adam, "Sweet partaker of my toil"	F
6. *Air. Eve, "Yes, Adam, yes the sun I see"	D
7. *+Air. Eve, "Glittering stars resplendent moon"	A
8. *+Duet. Adam, Eve, "Thou didst also make the night"	E♭
9. *+Chorus. "When chaos heard his high command"	G
10. *+Air. Gabriel, "Roses shed your rich perfume"	E
11. +Chorus. "Arise o Lord, exert thy mighty pow'r"	G
12. *Chorus. "Back, o back again to hell"	C
ACT II	
13. *+Air. Adam, "Wake my fair"	E
14. *+Air. Eve, "Cease, cease vain mimic fancy"	g
15. *+Duet. Adam, Eve, "Parent of good"	D
16. *+Chorus. "A voice was heard"	c
17. *+Chorus. "We remember when his powerful arm"	D
18. *+Air. Eve, "Time with slowest pace"	E♭
19. *Air. Adam, "Trust not over much"	G
20. *+Air. Gabriel, "Man so favour'd man so blest"	c
21. *+Chorus. "Nature now perhaps for thee"	f
22. *+Air. Eve, "Yes wisdom opens all her stores"	D
23. *+Air. Adam, "Thrilling horrors chills my veins"	E♭
24. *Air. Gabriel, "Too sure the deed is done"	D
25. *+Chorus. "But he the Lord, the judge"	A
ACT III	
26. *Air. Gabriel, "Fond man forbear"	E♭
27. +Chorus. "Sound his tremendous praise" [Music not in D-Hs MA/672.]	?
28. *Chorus. "Angels cannot higher soar"	B♭
29. *Air. Adam, "See thro' yon clouds"	c
30. *+Air. Eve, "My only strength"	G
31. *+Air. Eve, "It comes, it must be death"	f
32. *+Air. Adam, "He who rules in Heav'n"	C
33. *Air. Michael, "I come,—unpleasing errand!"	D
34. +Air. Michael, "Thou henceforth are doom'd to toil"	D
35. *+Chorus. "Righteous, Lord, are all thy ways"	A
36. *+Air. Eve, "Ah! nuptial bower"	d

TABLE V-I
continued

Numbers	Keys
37. * + Chorus. "Him these bounds cannot restrain"	G
38. * + Air. Michael, "He the gloomy prince of air"	a
39. * + Chorus. "Obedient to his mighty word"	C
40. * + Chorus. "Glory to God on high"	D
41. * + Chorus. "Hallelujah"	D

*Number included in 1760 performance.
+ Number included in 1774 performance.
* + Number included in both 1760 and 1774 performances.

The instrumentation of the work consists of strings and pairs of flutes, oboes, bassoons, horns, trumpets, and timpani. The trumpets are used in four numbers, particularly powerful choruses: the "Te Deum" (no. 2); the chorus of Angels recalling the power of God when Satan rebelled (no. 17), the only number in which the timpani have a part; and the two final choruses (nos. 40 and 41). The "ouverture" of the oratorio is a traditional French overture, with a three-measure fugue subject in the second, fast part and two measures of adagio at the end. The second movement is an andantino in minuet style and binary form, with both parts repeated.

Smith shows his conservatism in the structures of the airs. Most of the airs listed in Table V-I have a close relationship to the da capo form. According to the manuscript source, nine of those airs were originally either in da capo form (nos. 7, 19, 29) or dal segno (4, 22, 23, 32, 34, 38); in all the dal segno airs, the sign is used to delete the opening ritornello. To shorten the work, however, two da capo airs (19, 29) and four dal segno airs (22, 23, 32, 38) were truncated to the first A section of the form.[25] Eleven airs were originally written in a binary structure comparable to the A section of a da capo form. The air number 18 is cast in a ternary ABA' form, number 10 is a kind of rondo, and number 26 is through composed. Both of the duets were composed as ternary forms (no. 8, ABA'; 15, da capo) but were later shortened, in the manuscript, to the first A of the form.

As may be expected from a composer associated with Handel, Smith's style retains features of the Handelian oratorio. Yet he was, after all, a mid-century composer, and *Paradise Lost* shows him more interested in

25. On the crossed-out B sections in the manuscript, which imply deleted da capo as well, see McCredie, "Smith," pp. 35–36.

the balanced phrases and simplicity of the early Classical style than was Handel, even in his later works.[26] Among the clear examples of late-Baroque style in the airs of the oratorio is number 34 (from the 1774 version), in which Michael informs Adam and Eve that they will be driven out of Paradise. As shown in Example V-1, the first vocal entrance of the air, Smith uses a rhythmically vigorous orchestral style, comparable to an allegro of a Baroque concerto, with nearly continuous sixteenth-note motion in the orchestra. The leaping vocal line—surely to be sung in a strongly accented manner—is organized in groups of two and three measures, but balance of phrase is less important here than continuous rhythmic drive. Smith shows some interest in text painting but by no means as much as Handel, nor is Smith as imaginative. In Example V-1 the rapid sixteenth-note motion relates to the general affect of the text, Michael's fury; and the repeated ascending lines on "driven" (mm. 18–20) are probably intended to paint that word.

More characteristic of the airs in this oratorio, however, are Examples V-2 and V-3, which illustrate a blend of late-Baroque and early Classical tendencies. In Example V-2 (from no. 18), Eve, about to leave Adam to work in another part of the garden, sings of how slowly time will pass while she is away from him. Here, at the first entrance of the voice, the phrase structure of the vocal line consists of three groups of four measures, suggesting the balance of phrases found in early Classical style. Yet Baroque principles are also evident: the vocal phrases consist of a two-measure motive treated in rising melodic sequence and accompanied by motives in imitation (between the continuo and first violins). Example V-3 comes from an air sung by Eve (no. 7) as she and Adam prepare to retire; this air shows a similar mixture of Baroque and early Classical traits. Again the vocal phrases divide into three groups of four measures, but the texture is not that of a simple vocal line with unobtrusive accompaniment; rather, the accompanying instruments attract considerable attention by their rhythmic activity (probably intended to paint the "glittering" in the text) and fleeting imitations of the vocal motive at beginnings of measures.

Although Example V-4 is by no means characteristic of the oratorio, it shows that Smith on occasion composed an air in a simple, early Classical style. In this air (no. 32) Adam is not yet aware that he and Eve will be driven from Paradise, and he expresses hope that "He who rules in heav'n" will hear their prayer for help. The extreme simplicity of harmony, arpeggio figure in the second violin, total absence of counterpoint, and doubling of the vocal line by the first violin at the unison and by the viola in parallel thirds and sixths contribute to the artless sincerity of Adam's expression.

26. The "galant spirit of his vocal phrases" in Smith's Shakespeare songs is mentioned in Mann, "Smith," p. 136. For some examples of balanced phrases and simple style in Handel's Susanna (1748), see Smither, Oratorio, 2:328–29.

EXAMPLE V-1. *Paradise Lost*—Smith (D-Hs: MA/672, act 2, ff. 29v–30).

EXAMPLE V-I. continued

EXAMPLE V-2. *Paradise Lost*—Smith (D-Hs: MA/672, act 2, f. 27v).

EXAMPLE V-3. *Paradise Lost*—Smith (D-Hs: MA/672, act 1, f. 69v).

EXAMPLE V-4. *Paradise Lost*—Smith (D-Hs: MA/672, act 3, f. 26).

Most numbers are preceded by simple recitatives, but eleven recitatives are accompanied by the orchestra. Of these, only one is heard in act I, just prior to Eve's air, "Glittering stars" (no. 7). As the dramatic tension increases in acts II and III, however, accompanied recitatives become more frequent—five are found in each act. The accompanied recitatives use strings only, usually with a mixture of sustained-chord style and rhythmic figures. None of the accompanied recitatives begins as a simple recitative to which instruments are added, as often happens in the period. Occasionally tone painting is used, as in Gabriel's accompanied recitative before his air number 25; the strings punctuate, with appropriate quick-note figures, his words, "a second groan, sky lowers, and thunder mutters."

In the choruses listed in Table V-1 are found the oratorio's most obviously Handelian elements. Yet by no means all of the choral textures

Handel used are present in the work.[27] The declamatory style—incisive, strongly rhythmic, and chordal—is most frequently heard but is often relieved by passages in free imitation, unison, or "cantus firmus" style (one part in long notes and the others in shorter notes and declamatory style). Differing from Handel, however, is the infrequency of fugue; the only choral fugue in the oratorio appears at the end of the final chorus in act I in the version of 1774. Example V-5 (from no. 9) is a typical choral passage. After a nine-measure orchestral ritornello, the sopranos enter first and hold their d″, while the other voices chordally declaim the same text. After several measures of declamatory chordal style, a rising triadic figure is imitated (mm. 21–23), and all voices repeat the text in chordal texture. Throughout most of the chorus the strings have the kind of sixteenth-note activity that is seen in most of this excerpt, and the other instruments support the chorus by either doubling vocal parts or playing homorhythmically with them.

Thomas Augustine Arne: Judith

The most important composer for the London stage of the mid-century, Arne was born in London in 1710 and died there in 1778.[28] He studied violin with Michael Festing, a student of Francesco Geminiani and a member of the orchestra of the Italian opera in London. Arne began his theatrical activies in the early 1730s and within a decade established his reputation, particularly with the masques *Comus* (1738) and *Alfred* (1740). Beginning in 1742 Arne gave concerts for two seasons in Dublin. There in 1744 he introduced the first of his two oratorios, *The Death of Abel* (libretto by Arne after Metastasio's *La morte d'Abel*). From the mid-1740s he was a popular composer for London's pleasure gardens, and many of his songs for the gardens appeared in published collections over the next twenty years. Beginning in the 1750s his *Alfred,* to which he composed additional music, often called *Alfred the Great,* was at times given during Lent "in the manner of an Oratorio,"[29] as mentioned above. Arne received the degree Doctor in Music at Oxford in 1759. His oratorio *Judith* (1761; libretto by Isaac Bickerstaffe) was followed by his greatest success, an English opera in the Italian manner, *Artaxerxes* (1762; libretto by Arne after Metastasio's *Artaserse*). Also immensely popular were his nineteen songs for the pasticcio *Love in a Village* (1762).

After the Dublin performance of *Abel,* mentioned above, Arne revived the work three times in London's Lenten seasons: in 1755 and 1762 at

<hr>

27. For a summary of Handel's choral textures, see Smither, *Oratorio,* 2:353.

28. For a summary of his life and works, see Julian Herbage and John A. Parkinson, "Thomas Augustine Arne," *New Grove,* 1:605–11.

29. *London Stage,* 4/1:417.

EXAMPLE V-5. *Paradise Lost*—Smith (D-Hs: MA/672, act 1, ff. 79v–81).

EXAMPLE V-5. continued

EXAMPLE V-5. continued

EXAMPLE V-5. continued

the Theatre Royal in Drury Lane and in 1764 at the King's Theatre in the Haymarket. For the revivals of the 1760s the work was called *The Sacrifice*. Only one number from *Abel*, "The Hymn of Eve," survives in musical sources.[30]

Arne's *Judith* was first performed in public at a Lenten concert on Friday, 27 February 1761, at Drury Lane; but a private performance, or "rehearsal," had preceded the public one. On 23 February 1761 the *Public Advertiser* noted: "On Saturday last the New Oratorio called *Judith*, composed by Dr Arne, to be at Drury Lane on Friday, was rehearsed at the House of a Lady of Quality, where was present a numerous Assembly of the First Distinction, who honoured it with the highest approbation. We are assured that in the Sacred Oratorio, Sg Tenducci has obtained Permission from his Plaintiff, to sing the part which Signora Eberhardi was so obliged as to understudy for him, in Case he could not obtain such Indulgence."[31] The extravagance of the famous castrato

30. Apparently the earliest of many printed sources is *The Favourite Hymn of Eve. In the Oratorio of Abel* [London?, 1755?], a copy of which is in GB-Lbl: G 316. h. (35).

31. As quoted in *London Stage*, 4/2:846.

FIGURE V-1. Thomas Augustine Arne (1710–78). (Engraving by Richard Rhodes after a painting by Robert Dunkarton; from *Biographical Magazine* 1 [1794]: [portrait no. 5].)

Giusto Ferdinando Tenducci (1735–90) had led him to debtor's prison,[32] but he was presumably allowed to sing at the first public peformance of *Judith*. This oratorio was revived in Lenten concerts on 2 April 1762 at Drury Lane, 29 Feburary 1764 at Lock Hospital Chapel, 15 Feburary 1765 at the King's Theatre in the Haymarket, 26 February 1773 at Covent Garden, and, after Arne's death, on 3 March 1784 at the Theatre Royal in the Haymarket.[33] It was also performed in 1766 at the Three Choirs Festival in Gloucester and in 1769 at the church of Stratford-upon-Avon for a Shakespeare jubilee. The overture and airs were printed in score by John Walsh in 1764, and at least two manuscript sources survive.[34] It is of interest that a number from *Judith* was associated with the introduction of an instrument new to Covent Garden on 16 May 1767: according to a public announcement, at the end of the first act of *The Beggar's Opera*, "Miss Brickler will sing a favourite song from *Judith* accompanied by Dibdin on a new instrument called the Piano Forte."[35]

The librettist of *Judith*, Isaac Bickerstaffe, was a popular writer for the London stage and the author of the pasticcio *Love in a Village*, mentioned above. His oratorio is based on the story from the apocryphal Book of Judith, chapters 7–15, in which Judith liberates the besieged city of Bethulia from the grips of the Assyrian enemy by boldly entering the Assyrian camp and beheading the general, Holofernes. Bickerstaffe would probably have been familiar with Metastasio's well-known libretto, *Betulia liberata*, on the same story. Both librettos begin and end at the same points in the biblical narrative, but beyond this similarity they have little in common except for likenesses that derive from the common biblical source. Metastasio's work is in two parts and respects the unities of time, place, and action: his entire libretto takes place in Bethulia, Judith narrates (upon her return) the events in the enemy camp, and there is no role for Holofernes. Bickerstaffe's libretto, on the other hand, is in three acts and has Judith enter the camp and confront the enemy. In Metastasio's *Betulia liberata* the chorus is somewhat more important than in most of his librettos, as it enters four times and has

32. Roger Fisk, "Tenducci," *New Grove*, 18:687.

33. Cf. those dates in *London Stage*; the dates are for the first night in a given season, after which other performances followed.

34. The musical sources for my comments on this work are: the autograph manuscript in GB-Lbl: 3 vols., Add. 11515–11517; the manuscript copy, GB-T: 985 (now on deposit at GB-Ob, and published on microfilm, Brighton, Eng.: Harvester Press Microform Publications, n.d.); and the print, Arne, *Judith**. I consulted the following printed librettos of this work: London, 1761, in GB-Lbl: 840.k.7.(15); London, 1764, in GB-Lbl: 11777.g.39); Gloucester, 1766, in GB-Lcm: XXII.E.19.(1); Stratford-upon-Avon, 1769, in GB-Lcm: XXI.B.1.(13); London, 1773, in GB-Lbl: T.657 (2).

35. As quoted in *London Stage*, 4/2:1247.

some one-line exclamations; Bickerstaffe's libretto, however, follows English oratorio tradition by giving still greater importance to the chorus: he includes nine choruses, each of considerable length.

The libretto of *Judith* includes roles for Judith (S), the widow of Manasses; Abra (S), her handmaid; Ozias (T, S), the ruler of Bethulia; Charmis (B), an elder; Holofernes (T, S), the general of the Assyrians; an Israelite Man (T); an Israelite Woman (S); an Assyrian Woman (S); a Chorus of Israelites (SATB); and a Chorus of Assyrians (SATB).[36] At the beginning of act I the Israelites lament the siege of Bethulia, in which Holofernes has cut off their water supply; they blame their rulers for not having sought peace with the Assyrians and proclaim their readiness to submit to the enemy. Ozias promises that he will surrender within five days if God has not saved them by then. The beautiful and holy Judith, a recluse since the death of Manasses, rejects the notion that Bethulia must surrender to the enemy. She prays, is inspired to save the city, and announces to the rulers that she has a plan but will reveal it only after executing it. At the close of the act she and Abra depart from the gates of Bethulia as the Chorus of Israelites praise God for inspiring Judith. Act II takes place entirely within the Assyrian camp. Judith tells Holofernes that she and her handmaid have forsaken Bethulia because the crimes of the inhabitants are bringing the wrath of God upon them; when the time is right, she says, she will guide Holofernes's troops by secret paths into the city. Struck by her beauty and convinced of her story, Holofernes issues an order for all to allow Judith and Abra full freedom of the camp and of exit from it, so that they may respect their religious customs. Holofernes plans a banquet, invites Judith as his guest, and in the course of the evening becomes drunk with wine. At the end of act II, as Holofernes reclines his head upon Judith's breast, she sings a gentle song of sleep, as does the Chorus of Assyrians. At the beginning of act III, Judith and Abra are back in Bethulia, and Judith relates the tale of Holofernes's drunken sleep—how he was carried to bed and placed in her care, and how she beheaded him with his own sword while he slept. She and Abra, carrying the concealed head of Holofernes, have passed without question from the Assyrian camp and back to Bethulia. She displays the head, orders that it be hung from the city wall, and commands the soldiers of Bethulia to prepare to slaughter the Assyrians when they are shaken with fear after discovering the death of their general. The Israelites praise Judith and begin to organize festivities for her, but she halts their preparations and urges them to praise God rather than her, for it was God who saved them. The final number is a chorus of

36. The parts of Ozias and Holofernes are at times designated in the sources as for tenor (in tenor clef) and for soprano (in violin G clef, labeled as sung by the castrato Tenducci). The sources suggest that Tenducci sang the airs of two different roles in at least some of the performances.

praise. (See Table V-2, nos. 27, 27a, and 28, for the final chorus in the different versions.)

As can be seen in the structural outline, Table V-2, the main tonal area of the work is D, but G also receives some emphasis: acts I and III close in D, and act II closes in G, which is also the overture's key. The only numbers in minor are those of lamentation at the beginning of act I and the reflection on blasphemy, number 23. Most of the numbers in flat major keys relate to the Judith-Holofernes relationship: in act I, numbers 6 and 8, Judith sings of her plan; in act II, numbers 11, 12 and 13, Judith's plan is working, as Holofernes becomes infatuated with her and the Assyrians anticipate their victory. The tonality shifts to the sharp side in numbers 14–17 (A, D, G, and D, excluding no. 15a) as the Assyrian feast approaches and is held, and then returns to the flat key of F as Judith sings Holofernes to sleep. (No. 15a, Judith's pastoral hymn, is also in F.) At the beginning of act III, numbers 20–22 (in F, B-flat, and B-flat) relate to Judith's deed in the enemy camp and to the pending slaughter of the Assyrians.

The orchestra consists of strings, continuo (both organ and harpsichord are mentioned in the sources), pairs of horns, oboes, bassoons, flutes, trumpets, and timpani, and a harp. The trumpets and timpani are used in the final choruses of acts I and III and in the first chorus of act II; the harp is designated only in number 5, "Wake my harp to melting measures," where it doubles the notated harpsichord part in an obbligato accompaniment to the voice. Another obbligato part is in number 25: the oboe accompanies the soprano and plays solos in the ritornellos. In "No more the heathen shall blaspheme," two obbligato violoncellos and continuo accompany the voice; the ritornellos are elaborate, particularly the final one, which includes an unmeasured, notated cadenza for the violoncellos alone.

The only extended instrumental number is the three-movement "overture," which is an Italian sinfonia with movements in G major, E minor, and G major and with fast, slow, fast tempos.[37] The first and last movements have tonal structures roughly like those of sonata forms but with scarcely any development section, and the second movement is a rounded binary form. The overture is motivically independent of the oratorio proper. In act II, a six-measure instrumental interlude by strings and flutes accompanies Judith's entrance to Holofernes's banquet, following his recitative, "Silence each ruder sound, let nothing breathe but softest harmony"; these instrumental colors establish the mood for Holofernes's following speech about Judith as "another Venus."

Judith is typical of the mid-century in its mixture of traditional and newer styles. The most traditional are the da capo airs (nos. 15 and 25).

37. In the sources, no tempo mark is given for the third movement, but its minuet style would seem to require a relatively quick tempo.

TABLE V-2
Arne, *Judith*: Structural Outline

Numbers	Keys
1. Overture	G
ACT I	
2. Chorus of Israelites, "Father of mercies, lend thine ear"	a
3. Air. An Israelite Woman, "O torment, great, too great to bear"	g
4. Air. Ozias, "Be humble, suff'ring, trust in God"	D
5. Air. Abra, "Wake my harp! to melting measures"	G
6. Air. Judith, "Advent'rous lo! I spread the sail"	E♭
7. Chorus of Israelites, "When Israel wept, no comfort nigh"	G
8. Air. Judith, "Remember what Jehovah swore"	B♭
9. Air. Charmis, "Conquest is not to bestow, In the spear or in the bow"	C
10. Chorus of Israelites. "Hear! angels, hear! Celestial choirs"	D
ACT II	
11. Air. Judith, "Oh strive not with ill suited praise"	B♭
12. Air. Holofernes, "Adorn'd with every matchless grace"	E♭
13. Chorus of Assyrians, "Rejoice! rejoice! Judea falls"	E♭
14. Air. Abra, "Vain is beauty, gaudy flow'r"	A
15. Air. An Assyrian Woman, "Haste to the gardens of delight"	D

Note: The sequence of numbers in this table combines the information from the two manuscripts and the four librettos consulted (see above). The following comments on individual numbers describe the main differences among these versions; numbers for which there are no comments are substantially the same in all versions.

9. In the libretto of 1764 only, the text reads, "'Tis not in the spear, or bow, / Fame and conquest to bestow."

15–15a. In the libretto of 1764, for Lock Hospital, a hymn, no. 15a, is substituted for the sensual no. 15. (The music for the hymn is in GB-Lbl, 11517, ff. 4v–7v, but is missing in GB-T.) In 15a, the word "mead" replaces the word "plain" in the GB-Lbl manuscript.

16. The text of the B section is marked "not sung" in the libretto of 1761 and is missing from the other librettos.

20. The word "With" in both manuscripts is "Mongst" in all librettos.

Representing newer structures are the transformed da capo airs (A1-B-A2: nos. 3, 4, and 5; A1-A2: nos. 17 and 21). Airs with AA' forms (and tonal schemes differing from the transposed da capo) are numbers 9, 11, 14, and 18; and AB or AAB forms are numbers 6, 7, 8, 12, 20, and 23.

Characteristic in the airs in *Judith* are balanced phrases of early Classical style, together with linear continuo and orchestral accompaniments, Baroque dance styles, and quick harmonic rhythm. Examples V-6 through V-8 illustrate the simplest styles of airs. Example V-6 (from no. 9 in Table V-2) is sung by Charmis in act I following his recitative pro-

TABLE V-2
continued

Numbers	Keys
15a. Hymn. Judith, "How chearful along the gay mead [plain]"	F
16. Duet. Judith, Abra, "Oh thou, on whom the weak depend"	G
17. Air with chorus. Holofernes, Assyrians, "Hail, immortal Bacchus!"	D
18. Air. Judith, "Sleep, gentle cherub!—Sleep descend!"	F
19. Chorus of Assyrians, "Prepare the genial bow'r"	G
ACT III	
20. Air. Ozias, "With [mongst] heroes and sages recorded"	F
21. Air. Judith, "O Lord, our God! tremendous rise"	B♭
22. Chorus of Israelites, "Who can Jehovah's wrath abide"	B♭
23. Air. An Israelite Man, "No more the heathen shall blaspheme"	a
24. Chorus of Israelites, "Breath the pipe, the timbrel sound"	C
24a. Air. An Israelite Man, "The victor on his lofty seat"	?
25. Air. Judith, "Not unto us, but to his name"	F
26. Duet. Ozias, Abra, "On thy borders, o Jordan"	?
27. Chorus of Israelites, "Hear, angels, hear! Celestial choirs"	D
27a. Chorus of Israelites, "Here sons of Jacob let us rest"	D
28. Chorus of Israelites, "Hear! angels, hear! Celestial choirs"	D

21. The text of the B section is marked in the 1761 and 1773 librettos as not sung and is missing in the other librettos; the B section is not set to music in the manuscripts.

23. In the manuscript GB-Lbl, 11515, ff. 64r–67v, this number is misbound as an interruption of no. 8 (ff. 63v, 68r–70r).

24a and 26. These texts are printed in the 1761 libretto only; they are not set to music in either manuscript.

27a, 28. In all printed librettos but that of 1773, no. 28 (the same as no. 10) is the final chorus. In GB-Lbl, 11517, f. 57v, the words "Turn back immediately to the last chorus of the first Act where the . . . [?oratorio ?finishes]" are crossed out; another chorus, labeled "A new last chorus for the Oratorio of Judith" follows, on ff. 58r–73v (no. 27a, above). The libretto of 1773 and the music manuscript GB-T include only the new last chorus.

claiming that "upon this woman's strength we rest our hopes." The text of the air expresses the belief that conquest and victory go not to the valiant and strong but to those who trust in Jehovah; thus the air implies hope that Judith, because of her faith, will prevail against the enemy warriors. The musical setting blends the style of an optimistic, Baroque gavotte with that of a martial air. Triadic figures in the voice and orchestra suggest the military fanfare; to add power to the vocal line, the orchestra doubles it at the unison and octave. To the heavily doubled melody, the oboes play a countermelody (mm. 8–16), mostly in parallel

EXAMPLE V-6. continued

thirds and sixths. Other airs similar to this one in phrasing, dancelike quality, and texture are numbers 15 and 17 (in which the Chorus of Assyrians joins Holofernes in a drinking song).

The air from which Example V-7 is taken comes from act I (no. 5) and immediately follows Judith's accompanied recitative in which she tells Abra, "I feel my spirit stir'd with strange emotions. Raise some solemn strain whilst I retire and in meek meditation seek the Lord." While Judith meditates, Abra sings her "solemn strain" to the accompaniment of a harp and harpsichord in unison, together with pizzicato violins. Example V-7 shows the beginnings of the long ritornello and the first vocal section. This example illustrates the same degree of symmetry as the previous one but reveals an even simpler texture and a more lyrical melodic line, which stands out in particularly attractive relief against the rhythmically activated chordal accompaniment.

Judith sings Holofernes to sleep (act II, no. 18) in the air illustrated in Example V-8. Here again the phrases of the vocal line are symmetrical. The voice appropriately paints the words "sleep descend" (mm. 7–8) and "spread" (mm. 10–11). Perhaps the contrast between the active continuo and the slower moving upper parts is intended to symbolize the descent of sleep over Holofernes's drunken mind. Unlike the previous examples, this one is contrapuntal: the continuo line moves in eighth notes throughout most of the number and the violin parts (with their chains of suspensions) and the active viola part are contrapuntally conceived.

Excerpts from two heroic airs by Judith are shown in Examples V-9 and V-10. In act I, after Judith's prayer and heroic resolve to save the city of Bethulia, she sings an air (no. 6) in which the event she is about to undertake is compared to an adventurous voyage. Example V-9 begins near the end of the air's opening ritornello and shows the vigorous rhythmic style of the number's orchestral passages. Judith's first phrase is striking for its angular style. A whimsical touch is the pun on the word "lo!" (placed at the bottom of the phrase). The word "spread" (m. 20) is set by an appropriately spreading motive, which is repeated in the violins (mm. 20–21). The angular melodic style is characteristic of the air as a whole, as are coloratura passages—a short one is used to paint the word "guides" in this example. As usual with Arne, the phrases are symmetrical. The orchestral accompaniment is mostly supportive, rather than contrapuntal.

The air from which Example V-10 is taken (no. 21) follows Judith's recitative in act III in which she orders the Israelites to prepare to attack the Assyrians after they discover their decapitated general: "Then shall they fear and fly before you, while you thunder down, and overthrow them with a mighty slaughter." In the air, the words "battle dreadful," "storm," and "vengeance" are reflected in the vigorous orchestral and vocal activity. The sixteenth-note tremolo passages in the violins (mm. 27–28, 37–38), fanfare-styled vocal and instrumental lines, symmetrical

EXAMPLE V-7. *Judith*—Arne (Arne, *Judith**, pp. 20–21; Arne, "Judith"*, 1:191).

EXAMPLE V-7. continued

EXAMPLE V-7. continued

EXAMPLE V-7. continued

soft-   est,   sweet-   est   trea-   sures,

EXAMPLE V-8. *Judith*—Arne (Arne, *Judith**, p. 65; Arne, "Judith"*, 2:124).

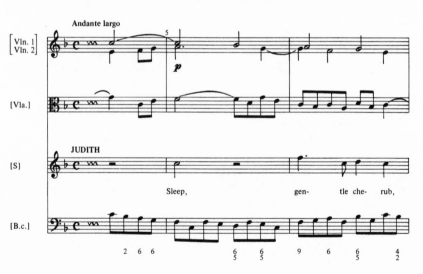

EXAMPLE V-8. continued

sleep, de-scend,   sleep,   de-scend,   thy heal-ing wings____

pro-tec-tive spread,_____ thy heal- ing wings pro- tec-   tive spread,

EXAMPLE V-9. *Judith*—Arne (Arne, *Judith**, pp. 28–29; Arne, "Judith"*, I:III).

EXAMPLE V-9. continued

EXAMPLE V-9. continued

vir- tue guides, guides,

EXAMPLE V-10. *Judith*—Arne (Arne, *Judith**, pp. 74–75; Arne, "Judith"*, 3:29).

EXAMPLE V-10. continued

rise,   rise,   tre- men- dous rise.

In bat- tle dread- ful

EXAMPLE V-10. continued

mount   the storm,   be-

EXAMPLE V-10. continued

EXAMPLE V-10. continued

phrases, and relatively slow harmonic rhythm are all characteristic of the number as a whole. Judith's call for God to rise elicits appropriate ascending lines in both the vocal and orchestral parts.

Prior to the duet of Judith and Abra (no. 16) in act II, Judith has received Holofernes's invitation to the banquet, and in recitative she has told Abra, "Hie we hence to this same banquet. God shall save me to whose almighty guidance I resign myself this night full prostrate on the earth. Let our warm vows in concord sweet aspire." The duet that follows is Judith and Abra's prayer for strength. Example V-11 shows the beginning of the duet's first vocal section, in which the "warm vows in concord sweet" of the singers consist in close imitation, a style prominent throughout the duet. As with the other examples, so also here the phrases are symmetrical, but this time they are three measures in length rather than Arne's usual four in *Judith*. Of contrapuntal interest between the voices and orchestra is the viola line of measures 13–15, which forms a countermelody to the vocal parts.

Of the fifteen recitative sections in the work, six have passages in which a personage begins in simple style but concludes with orchestral accompaniment, and four have speeches that are orchestrally accompanied throughout. All the latter occur in act II, the most dramatic act of the oratorio; Judith and Holofernes sing two such accompanied recitatives each. Those by Judith precede her first air in act II and the duet; Holofernes's occur in the banquet scene: the first before the drinking song, "Hail immortal Bacchus" (no. 17), and the second at Judith's entrance to the banquet. After the instrumental interlude for strings and flutes, Holofernes proclaims his admiration of Judith's beauty in an accompanied recitative beginning, "Fair Judith comes, another Venus by graces led."

The choruses of the oratorio are distributed evenly among the three acts. Choruses are located at the beginning of act I and at the end of each act; the others are internal. All the choruses are essentially in chordal style except the first and last in act III, (no. 22 and no. 27a, the "new" last chorus), which include fugal sections. The most imposing chorus of the oratorio is number 22, from which Examples V-12a and V-12b are drawn. Although the chorus is in B-flat, it begins outside the key, moving from G minor through F minor, A-flat, and E-flat, before settling in B-flat (Example V-12a, mm. 1–9). This rich harmonic language suggests late Baroque rather than early Classical practice. After the chordal opening (Example V-12a), comes a contrapuntal section (Example V-12b), which suggests the style of Handel, with three subjects for three phrases of the text. Chordal style returns but another contrapuntal section is introduced near the end of the chorus. This chorus and the oratorio's "new" final chorus (no. 27a) represent the closest approximations to Handel's style in the oratorio.

EXAMPLE V-12. *Judith*—Arne (Arne, "Judith"*, 3:60–63, 66–67).

Example a:

EXAMPLE V-12. continued

EXAMPLE V-12. continued

EXAMPLE V-12. continued

EXAMPLE V-12. continued

Example b:

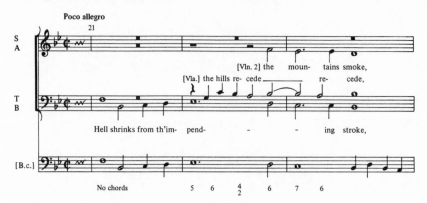

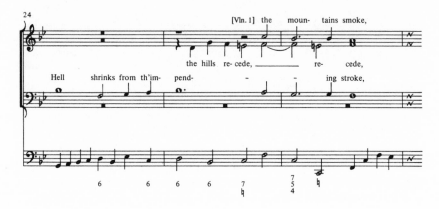

John Worgan: Hannah

Born in London, John Worgan (1724–90) was the brother of the organist and composer James Worgan (1715–53), and the father and grandfather of the composers Thomas Danvers Worgan (1774–1832) and George Worgan (1802–88).[38] A student of his brother and of Thomas Rosingrave, John Worgan took the Bachelor of Music at Cambridge in 1748 and the Doctor of Music there in 1775. An organist in several London churches and at Vauxhall Gardens (1753–61 and 1770–74), he was said to be an outstanding performer, comparable to Handel. For Vauxhall Gardens he composed numerous songs that were published singly and in collections. He also wrote keyboard works, cantatas, and

38. On John Worgan and the Worgan family, see Charles Cudworth, "Worgan," *New Grove*, 20:530–31.

anthems; his oratorios are *Manasseh* (1766; lost), *The Chief of Maon* (lost), *Gioas* (incomplete), and *Hannah*, published in 1764.[39] *Hannah* was performed (perhaps for the only time) at a Lenten concert on Tuesday, 3 April 1764, at the Kings Theatre in the Haymarket.[40]

The librettist of *Hannah*, Christopher Smart (1722–71), was a poet who wrote for the London stage in the 1740s and 1750s.[41] His translation of the Psalms was published with a collection of psalm tunes in 1765,[42] and some of his psalms were used in the libretto of the pasticcio oratorio *Omnipotence* (1774), adapted by Samuel Arnold to music of Handel. The libretto of *Hannah* is based on the story in the First Book of Samuel, chapters 1–2, about Elkanah and his two wives.[43] The oratorio is in three acts and includes the personages Elkanah (T); Hannah (S) and Peninnah (S), his two wives; a Handmaid to Peninnah (S); a Virgin attendant on Hannah (S); a Levite of Elkanah's Household (B); Eli (B), a priest; and a Chorus of Priests, Damsels, and Other Attendants (SATB). The dramatic action of the libretto (which takes some liberties with the biblical story) revolves around the two wives. In act I, scene 1, Peninnah and her Handmaid declare their pride in the many children Peninnah has given Elkanah and their resentment of the favored treatment that Hannah—who has had no children—receives from Ellkanah. In scene 2 Hannah expresses her gratefulness to Elkanah but feels deep guilt for having dishonored him by not bearing children. Elkanah reasures Hannah of his love and urges her not to "murmur against Providence and me"; and the Levite advises Hannah that "the remedy is not in man or musick for woes like thine" and admonishes her to trust in God and pray. In act II (a single scene), Peninnah upbraids Elkanah for his generosity to Hannah, whom she believes does not deserve it, but Elkanah replies, "I reward, but not presume to punish" Hannah. The Levite reproves both Peninnah and her Handmaid for their behavior toward Hannah, who prays for resignation to the will of God. In act III, scene 1, Elkanah and his household are in Shiloh for their annual prayers and sacrifices. Hannah vows that if she is given a son, she will dedicate him to the service of God, and she receives the blessing of Eli, who tells her, "I forsee thy sure success in all thy heart's desire." Hannah's response is the "Song of Hannah" (in the biblical account sung after the birth of Samuel, not

39. Worgan, *Hannah**. This publication includes the airs, ensembles, one chorus, and two accompanied recitatives; it omits the overture, five choruses (for which texts were printed in the libretto), and all simple recitatives.

40. This performance is the only one listed in *London Stage*.

41. See the list of performances of his works in *London Stage Index*.

42. *A Collection of melodies to the Psalms*, listed as no. 191 in Temperley, *Parish Church*, p. 376.

43. This paragraph is based on the printed libretto, *Hannah. An Oratorio. Written by Mr. Smart. The Musick composed by Mr. Worgan. As perform'd at the King's Theatre in the Hay-market.* (London, [1764]), copies in GB-Lbl: T. 657 (20) and R. M. 5. e. 6 (3).

before). This long number consists of six stanzas, sung in turn by Hannah (stanzas 1–2), a virgin (3), a trio and chorus (4), a levite (5), and Hannah (6). At the beginning of scene 2, Elkanah and Hannah express their joy at the birth of Samuel, and Hannah declares that "the first-fruits of our love I have devoted to serve his Maker only, and attend from early youth upon this holy place." The remainder of the oratorio consists of joyful expressions by the Virgin attendant on Hannah, and by Elkanah, Hannah, Eli, and the chorus; the final number is a "Grand Chorus" of praise to God.

The structural outline in Table V-3, although based on the incomplete musical source,[44] allows some observations about the use of keys. Worgan's minor keys reflect sombre thoughts: Hannah's lamentation (no. 3); the Levi's comments about widespread corruption (no. 9), made during his prayer at a "family sacrifice" before an altar; the frightening images ("moonless night," "death," "hurricane") during the first half of Elkanah's air in act II (no. 11), an air that turns to major in the second half with thoughts on the sweetness of home, love, and peace; and the comments in the trio (no. 19, stanza 4) on "the poor, the lowly and obscure" whom the Lord exalts. The keys of A and E major are used only by or in relation to Hannah and only for optimistic and joyful expressions. The key of A major is used three times: for the love duet between Hannah and Elkanah (no. 7); for Hannah's last air in act II (no. 15), a prayer for peaceful resignation; and for the air by a Virgin attendant on Hannah (no. 19, stanza 3), as she reflects on Hannah's triumph over the rival wife. The key of E major is reserved for one important occasion: the first two stanzas of the Song of Hannah (no. 19).

The orchestra consists of strings and pairs of flutes, oboes, bassoons, and horns. Among the airs the heaviest orchestration is found in Elkanah's first air (no. 4), a heroic piece in which he sings of greatness, praises Hannah, and closes with the words: "Is not Hannah then a name / glorious to the latest age?" The only air with an obbligato instrumental part is number 15, Hannah's prayer for resignation; there a violoncello plays not only solo obbligato figures to accompany the voice, but also an elaborate solo in the final ritornello.

The formal structures of the airs are relatively simple. Most have binary form. The several transformed da capo airs are numbers 1, 3, 5, and 17 (all A1-B-A2), and 2 and 4 (A1-A2). Ternary ABA' forms are numbers 6 and 12. The da capo form is absent, and only one air (no. 18) has a dal segno form; the sign is used to delete the opening ritornello.

Virtually all the airs reflect the early Classical style more strongly than the late Baroque: melodic lines are simple and clear, most successive phrases are of equal length, the harmonic rhythm tends to be slow, and texture is homophonic and uncomplicated. Example V-13 (no. 1 in Table V-3) is representative. As befits the procreative theme of this libretto, the

44. See above, n. 39.

TABLE V-3
Worgan, *Hannah*: Structural Outline

Numbers	Keys
ACT I	
Scene 1	
1. Air. Peninnah, "Say, ye turtles, as ye pair"	G
2. Air. Handmaid to Peninnah, "How joyful the triumph"	F
Scene 2	
3. Air. Hannah, "Since grief her misfortune shou'd suit"	c
4. Air. Elkanah, "Is not genius heav'nly fire"	C
5. Air. Hannah, "All our evils past and present"	B♭
6. Air. Levite, "There is no part of heav'n so high"	E♭
7. Duet. Hannah, Elkannah, "To thy lover flee for cover"	A
8. Air (Levite) and chorus, "Glory is thy due"	G
ACT II	
9. Air. Levite, "Far and wide corruption reigns"	d
10. Air. Peninnah, "Every bird that pipes a note"	D
11. Air. Elkanah, "When storms affright"	f/F
12. Air. Hannah, "When I send my thoughts to rove"	C
13. Air. Handmaid to Peninnah, "Female tempers ebb and flow"	B♭
14. Air. Levite, "Sweeter sleeps the village hind"	D
15. Air. Hannah, "O thou whom fancy sees"	A
16. Chorus. "Where choristers angelic throng" [not in musical source]	?
ACT III	
Scene 1	
17. Air. Hannah, "With what I scorn upbraid me not"	E♭
18. Air. Eli the Priest, "May he who can awake the dead"	F
19. Song of Hannah	
Stanzas 1–2, Hannah, "My heart with transport springs"	E
Stanza 3, a Virgin, "She that on dainties fed"	A
Stanza 4, Trio (Hannah, Virgin, Levite) and chorus,	
"The Lord exalts the poor"	f♯
Stanza 5, Levite, "The Lords audacious foe"	G
Stanza 6, Hannah, "The prince of peace shall tow'r"	D
Scene 2	
20. Air. Elkanah, "No more the dupe of vague mischance"	G
21. Air. Virgin attendant on Hannah, "The cherubs of the highest sphere"	B♭
22. Air (Elkanah) with chorus. "The Lord in highest bliss above"	F
23. Grand Chorus. "To Thee stupendous in thy ways" [not in musical source]	?

Note: The act and scene numbers are those of the printed libretto. All other numbers are those of the present author. The information in numbers 16 and 23 is based on the printed libretto; those numbers were not printed in the musical source. In no. 19, stanza 4, the word "poor" is taken from the musical source; the printed libretto reads "foe."

EXAMPLE V-13. *Hannah*—Worgan (Worgan, *Hannah**, p. 4).

EXAMPLE V-13. continued

text of the first air, one of the countless "bird" airs in oratorios and operas of the period, treats the bliss of turtle doves as they "pair, quickened by the vernal air"; although this is a comparison text, the relationship between the image and the personage is implied rather than explicit. Like most of the phrases in this minuetlike air, those in Example V-13 are four measures long. The basso continuo frequently repeats notes and most of the measures have only one or two chords. The orchestral parts provide simple support to the voice, sometimes doubling it (violins, mm. 1–4), at other times using repeated notes for background (violins, mm. 9–12). The ornaments in the vocal line and violin parts in the first two measures imitate the cooing of doves, and the role of the flutes is birdlike as well. The words "quickened by the vernal air" are not unexpectedly quickened by sixteenth notes.

Example V-14 (no. 9), which illustrates another type of air in *Hannah*, forms part of the Levi's prayer, which began as an accompanied recitative, on behalf of the House of Elkanah. To express the text's dark thoughts about reigning corruption, Worgan has set it in D minor with jagged melodic lines contrasting with conjunct ones; and to add power to the vocal line, he has doubled it, approximately, by various orchestral parts (continuo and viola in mm. 1–5, first violins and continuo in mm. 6–8, second violins in mm. 8–10). Perhaps because of the seriousness of the text, Worgan here uses a somewhat more complex accompaniment: the first violin, for instance, begins with an idea that is melodically and rhythmically independent of the vocal line.

An excerpt from the highpoint of the oratorio, the "Song of Hannah" (no. 19, stanza 1), is shown in Example V-15. Again the usual traits of Worgan's style in *Hannah* are evident, especially the prevailing four-measure phrases and slow harmonic rhythm. The text "My heart with transport springs" motivates an upward-springing melodic line at the beginning of both the first violin and vocal parts; the violin makes a special point of wide skips in measures 5–10. At the entrance of the voice, Worgan approximately repeats the opening ritornello, which at times doubles the voice, but in measures 19–22 ("to thee it springs") the voice adds its own leaps to the wider ones in the first violin. The second violin's harmonic filler springs through smaller intervals in measures 1–24, and the continuo and viola do their share of springing from one octave to another and through various intervals within the octave.

In Example V-16 (no. 19, stanza 3), a Virgin attendant on Hannah comments on the way the tables have turned with respect to Hannah and Peninnah. "She that on dainties fed" refers to Peninnah, and "the hungry," to Hannah. The air's text finishes with lines about Hannah's triumph: "The fruitful womb must fail, / the barren shall prevail, / and reckon to the seventh son." From the standpoints of harmony and texture, this is among the simplest airs of the oratorio and perhaps reflects the Handmaid's rustic character. The vocal phrases are predominantly symmetrical, as usual, but here they tend to be three measures long,

EXAMPLE V-14. *Hannah*—Worgan (Worgan, *Hannah**, p. 64).

EXAMPLE V-14. continued

where-fore what re- source re- mains, what re- source re- mains

EXAMPLE V-15. *Hannah*—Worgan (Worgan, *Hannah**, pp. 113–14).

EXAMPLE V-15. continued

EXAMPLE V-15. continued

EXAMPLE V-16. *Hannah*—Worgan (Worgan, *Hannah**, p. 120).

EXAMPLE V-16. continued

feast _____ be- gun, __ has __ the __ feast _____ be- gun

rather than the usual four. The A-major harmony remains static for the first seven measures, and the same bass note is retained with little exception for the first ten measures, until the approach to the cadence in measure 13.

John Stanley: The Fall of Egypt

Born in London, Stanley (1712–86) was blinded in a domestic accident at the age of two.[45] He began to study music when he was seven and made rapid progress under Maurice Greene at St. Paul's Cathedral. He was performing as an organist in London churches before he was twelve; by the time was twenty he had achieved considerable acclaim for his playing of voluntaries, and in 1729 he became the youngest person ever to be granted the Bachelor of Music degree at Oxford. Endowed with an extraordinary memory, Stanley was active not only as an organist, but also as a teacher, composer, and director of oratorios. From 1760 until his death he collaborated, at first with J. C. Smith the younger and later with Thomas Linley, Sr., in the continuation of Handel's oratorio series in London's theaters during Lent. Best known for his instrumental music, particularly his organ voluntaries, he also composed cantatas, sacred vocal music, a few stage works, and three oratorios. His *Jephtha* (librettist, John Free, b. 1712) dates from ca. 1751–57;[46] *Zimiri* (Hawkes-

45. For details of Stanley's life and works (including a thematic catalogue), see Williams, "Stanley."

46. No record of a performance has been found. See ibid., 1:180, 2:29–42.

FIGURE V-2. John Stanley (1712–86). (Anonymous engraving; from *The European Magazine and London Review* 6 [Sept., 1784]: 170.)

worth), was performed at Covent Garden in 1760 and 1761;[47] and *The Fall of Egypt* (Hawkesworth), at Drury Lane in 1774 and 1775. The last-named work exists in a manuscript music source; its libretto is extant in both manuscript and printed versions.[48]

The librettist of *The Fall of Egypt*, John Hawkesworth (1715?–73), wrote occasionally for the London stage from the 1750s until the time of his death.[49] His libretto for *The Fall of Egypt* is based on the Israelites' exodus from their Egyptian captivity, including the plagues visited on Egypt, as set forth in the Book of Exodus, chapters 7–15. The members of the large cast represent Egyptions and Israelites. The Egyptians are Pharaoh (T), his son Sephres (S), his sister Menytis (S), First and Second Eunuch Officers (S, S), and a Chorus of Egyptians (SATB); the Israelites are Moses (B), an Israelite Man (T), an Israelite Woman (S), the First Elder (T), the Second Elder (T), the First Israelite (T), the Second Israelite (S), an Israelite Messenger (T), and a Chorus of Israelites (SATB).

In part I, in the land of Goshen (a district of Egypt), an Israelite Man and Woman review the plagues and lament the ninth plague, darkness, which is now upon them. The Israelites want Moses to lead them in an escape from their captors during the darkness, but he refuses, telling them, "this land of bondage shall ye quit with glory, / and pass in triumph by the gate of Memphis." The scene changes to the palace of Pharaoh in Memphis; Pharaoh and the other Egyptians describe the frightful gloom. Gradually the light returns, and Moses enters to claim the freedom of his nation. Menytis urges her brother to let the Israelites go, but Pharaoh rejects her plea and the chorus of Egyptians closes part I by proclaiming that the arts of Moses will be in vain. At the beginning of part II the scene has changed to Goshen. Evening approaches, and Moses tells his people that tomorrow they will be free, which they scarcely dare to believe. Two hours after midnight in the outer court of the palace at Memphis, Pharaoh's officers, at first incredulous, discover that the plague of the death of the firstborn is upon them; Pharaoh's son, Sephres, has died on the very day that he was to be married; and Pharaoh has granted the Israelites their request. They rejoice in their sudden free-

47. The airs, duets, and one recitative were published in 1760. See ibid., 2:42–43.

48. The musical source for the following comments on this work is the manuscript in GB-Lcm: MS 596, in three volumes. (The published microfilm of it [Brighton: Harvester Press Microform Publications, n.d.] includes only volume 1.) The libretto sources used are the manuscript in the Larpent Collection, no. 369, published on microcard (San Marino: Henry E. Huntington Library and Art Gallery, 1953); and the printed libretto, *The Fall of Egypt. An Oratorio* (London, 1774), copies in GB-Lbl: 1344. N. 21 and GB-Lcm: Libretto XX. G. 20 (11). For a discussion of this oratorio and its sources, see Williams, "Stanley," 1:190–94, and 2:45–48.

49. See the entries under his name in *London Stage Index*.

dom and are on the march, when a Messenger arrives with the news that the Egyptians are pursuing them. Moses urges his people to have faith; he raises his rod and the Red Sea is suddenly divided. The final chorus of Israelites expresses astonishment at the miracle. As part III begins, the Israelites are passing through the Red Sea ahead of the Egyptians. The Israelites are joyful, yet still fearful of the enemy in pursuit. When they reach the other side, at Moses' command the waters meet and destroy the enemy. The Israelites rejoice for their safety and the miracle of God, yet they pity their enemy. Moses predicts the coming of a Prince of Peace, and the final chorus praises "the Lord who reigns supreme abroad."

The structural outline in Table V-4 reveals a basic tonal center of D major-minor: the first number of part I is in D minor, part II begins on the dominant and closes on the tonic (minor then major), and part III also closes in D. The key of the overture, G minor, does not neatly fit the basic tonal scheme; it was not composed for the occasion but was borrowed from one of Stanley's earlier works.[50] The minor keys are reserved for sorrowful affects, and those which are most remote from D major (nos. 6 in F minor and C minor; 13, in F minor) have texts in which Egyptians reflect on the plagues of darkness and the death of the first-born, respectively.

The instrumentation consists of strings, pairs of flutes, oboes, horns, trumpets, and timpani, and at least one bassoon.[51] This is the largest orchestra that Stanley employed.[52] The opening instrumental number is a traditional French overture; the fugue in the second part is based on an imposing subject made mostly of running sixteenth notes, and the last two measures of the work return to the style (and surely the slow tempo, though not marked) of the opening section. The French overture is followed by a minuet in binary form with both parts repeated. These are the only purely instrumental numbers of the oratorio. Near the end of part II, after Moses lifts his rod and the sea divides, the printed libretto refers to "a symphony expressing the commotion of the waters"; but the "symphony" is actually the opening ritornello of number 19, which paints the rushing water with running sixteenth notes.

Of the thirteen airs without chorus, eight have binary structure and two (nos. 2 and 22) are transformed da capo airs (A1-B-A2). One air is strophic (no. 1), one ternary (ABA', no. 20), and one through-composed (no. 23). Two of the airs are for two singers who do not sing simultaneously: number 1 is called in the source "Air by the Man & Woman

50. The French overture is found in Stanley's cantata, *The Power of Music* (1729), and also in one of his organ voluntaries from ca. 1750. Cf. Williams, "Stanley," 2:48.

51. In the source, the only indication of a bassoon part is in no. 13, where a note in a hand different from that which copied the music reads (vol. 2, p. 6) "bassoon con voce."

52. Williams, "Stanley," 1:190.

Numbers	Keys
Overture	g
PART I	
1. Air. Man, Woman, "The gliding stream whose silver wave"	d
2. Air. Man, "Freedom's charms alike engage"	G
3. Chorus. Israelites, "Hail! belov'd of man, of God"	D
4. Air. Woman, "In blooming youth the gentle maid"	e
5. Chorus. Israelites, "We hear thee and with transport trust"	E♭
6. Air. Pharaoh, Sephres, "O darkness! dreaded not in vain"	f/c
7. Air and chorus. Pharaoh, Egyptians, "Hence ye powers of death and night"	F
8. Air. Menytis, "Friendship is the joy of reason"	A
9. Duet. Pharaoh, Moses, "Fly, and see my face no more"	e
10. Chorus of Egyptians, "Hence! and try thy arts again"	C
PART II	
11. Air. First Israelite, "At early dawn the lab'ring hind"	A
12. Air. Moses, "By doubts and tears no more depres'd"	B♭
13. Air. Second Eunuch Officer, "Death, where 'er we turn we meet"	f
14. Air with chorus. Menytis, Chorus of Egyptians Virgins, "Alas! in blooming youth he died"	a
15. Air. Menytis, "How vain is grandeur's purpose pride"	F
16. Duet. Menytis, Pharaoh, "O! let my voice attention gain"	d
17. Air and chorus. Second Israelite, Chorus of Israelites, "Less are youthful charms to love"	F
18. Chorus. Israelites, "O words of horror!"	g
19. Chorus. Israelites, "It parts! the liquid walls behold"	d/D
PART III	
20. Air. Second Israelite, "How blest is he whose tranquil mind"	C
21. Chorus. "Tis done! the wond'rous journey's o'er"	A
22. Air. Moses, "Again the voice of God is heard"	E♭
23. Air. Moses, "O God of hosts! to thee we raise"	F
24. Air. First Israelite, "With gen'rous tears the dead deplore"	B♭
25. Chorus. Israelites, "Praise to the Lord who reigns supreme"	D

Note: No. 23 was originally composed in the bass clef for Moses and sung in F major; in the musical source it was subsequently changed to soprano clef for An Israelite and transposed to G major.

Alternately"; and in number 6, Pharaoh's air in F minor is continued by Sephres's in C minor. Of the two duets, number 16 is an A1-A2 form and number 9 is brief and through-composed.

The airs show a mixture of late-Baroque and early Classical styles. The relationship between the continuo and the vocal lines tends to be contrapuntal, while the melodic lines often proceed in balanced phrases. Example V-17 (from no. 1), in which an Israelite Woman sings of the plague that turned the waters into blood, illustrates the mixed style. The example consists of four four-measure phrases, each clearly marked by rhythmic and harmonic means; yet the continuo is essentially linear, and the harmonic rhythm is quick. The trio setting is also characteristically Baroque. Showing a slightly different mixture of styles is Example V-18 (from no. 4). Here the phrases are balanced, the harmonic rhythm slow, and the texture simple at the beginning; yet the rhythmic movement suggests the Baroque sarabande, and when the flute enters (mm. 9–12 and beyond) the texture is that of a trio.

A particularly moving number is the air begun by Pharaoh and continued by Sephres, with a text about the plague of darkness (no. 6); the beginning is shown in Example V-19. This air is akin in text and music to "Torments, Alas!" and "Total eclipse!" in Handel's *Samson*.[53] Like them, it is in minor and the voice begins without accompaniment; unlike them, however, this one is accompanied by continuo only—more characteristic of airs in Baroque than early Classical oratorios. This air is a typical Baroque expression: the main impluse is rhetorical, which results in a rather free grouping of measures; the continuo at times moves by step (mm. 7–13) and gives the impression of a contrapuntal line; the harmonies change from two to four times in most measures; and sequence plays an important role in melodic organization. Especially telling are the successive suspensions in measures 12–14.

Accompanied recitative is heard five times in the oratorio, and in all but one the orchestra plays sustained chords. The exception is the emotionally charged commentary by the First and Second Eunuch Officers about the plague that kills the firstborn, preceding number 13. When the First Officer tells the other that a "sudden blast, impetuous from the south, shook the proud palace to its base, and from the gen'ral groan on all sides echo'd round me loud shrieks of horror and languid moans of grief succeeded . . ." the orchestra punctuates with tone painting, mostly runs in thirty-second notes. Unusual is the arioso passage (just before no. 19), with chordal accompaniment, in which Moses says to his people, "Let me, while thus I lift my hand to heaven, teach ye, once more, to trust eternal truth." According to the printed libretto, "He lifts up his Rod, the sea is supposed to be suddenly divided." Later, before number 22, in a recitative accompanied by sustained strings Moses commands the waters to meet.

53. For examples see Smither, *Oratorio*, 2:274–75.

EXAMPLE V-17. *The Fall of Egypt*—Stanley (GB-Lcm: MS 596, vol. 1, p. 14).

EXAMPLE V-17. continued

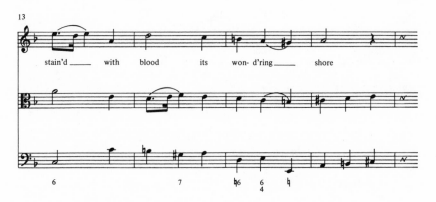

EXAMPLE V-18. *The Fall of Egypt*—Stanley (GB-Lcm: MS 596, vol. 1, p. 37).

EXAMPLE V-18. continued

ten- der joys and___ cares de- sign'd

EXAMPLE V-19. *The Fall of Egypt*—Stanley (GB-Lcm: MS 596, vol. 1, p. 63).

Of the ten choruses in the oratorio, three (nos. 7, 14, 17) are connected to preceding airs. In two of the choruses the orchestra includes trumpets and timpani (the only uses of these instruments in the oratorio): number 3, in which the Israelites hail the approach of Moses; and number 25, the final chorus, with a text praising the Lord. Six of the choruses (nos. 3, 7, 10, 14, 17, 25), have chordal texture throughout and four (nos. 5, 18, 19, 21) include passages of fugal or imitative texture. Several of the choruses are reminiscent of those in Handel's oratorios, especially number 21, in which chordal and fugal textures alternate and themes are ingeniously combined near the end.

Of particular interest in two of the choruses is Stanley's characterization of the Egyptians by 12/8 meter, quick tempo, and jig style. The first of these is the air and chorus sung by Pharaoh and the Egyptians (no. 7). At this point the light has begun to return after the plague of darkness, and Pharaoh's courage also returns; in a recitative he asks for music that will "conjure the pow'rs of darkness from the sky." At the beginning of the air (Example V-20), the first violins play a jig; Pharaoh enters without accompaniment to sing a "motto," and after the orchestra enters again, the voice continues, as does the jig in the first violins. The Baroque "motto" air was archaic by the 1770s, and Stanley's use of it here is probably a reflection of his Handelian oratorio model. When the chorus enters, they continue in the same rhythmic style. The other chorus (Example V-21) is the finale of part I; its text also begins "Hence," and this time the Egyptians mock Moses and send him on his way to try—in vain, they believe—more of his arts against them. Again the first violins play a jig, joined at times by the first oboe, and the jig continues while the chorus enters in simple, chordal style.

Samuel Felsted: Jonah

Little is known of the life of Felsted, the composer of probably the first oratorio written in the New World and the first one given a complete performance there. (See the end of chapter 4 for the performance history of *Jonah*.) The composer was "the son of William Felsted and Joyce Felsted (née Weaver), whose marriage may be the one recorded in the archives of Old Christ Church, Philadelphia, on May 1, 1741."[54] He may have been born on the island of Jamaica about 1743; his death is recorded in Kingston on 29 March 1802. He was organist at Saint Andrew's Parish for at least eight years, until his resignation in 1783. His three children, John, William, and Christina, were all organists in the Kingston area. Nothing is known of his musical training, but he may

---

54. All biographical information is drawn from Dox, "Felsted," which includes further details.

EXAMPLE V-20. continued

EXAMPLE V-21. continued

-gain, hence! and try thy arts a- gain

-gain, hence! and try thy arts a- gain

have spent some time in England, where he published his *Jonah* (for title page, see Figure V-3).[55] That publication, in keyboard reduction, is the only known source of the oratorio. The work was published by subscription,[56] and was dedicated to a Mrs. Dalling, presumably the wife of the Lieutenant Governor of Jamaica, whom Felsted thanks for patronage (see the dedication in Figure V-4). Felsted was also the composer of *Six Voluntarys, for the Organ or Harpsichord* (London: Thompson, [n.d.]). No other music by Felsted is known.

The libretto of *Jonah* is anonymous. Felsted would probably have been capable of writing it, for in 1771 he was called "an ingenious young Gentleman" of "merit in the three Sister Sciences, Poetry, Painting and Music."[57] The libretto is a condensation and poetic paraphrase of the Book of Jonah, often used for librettos since the seventeenth century. The story begins with the Lord telling Jonah to go to Nineveh and preach against the wickedness there; instead, Jonah flees and boards a ship for Tarshish. A great storm arises, which Jonah interprets as God's punishment, and to save the others on the ship he asks them to throw him overboard. God provides a whale to save him, by swallowing him, carry-

55. Felsted, *Jonah**. Copies in GB-Ge and Lbl; and US-Pu.

56. Nearly 250 subscribers, from both England and the New World, are listed in pp. 1–4 of the publication.

57. Letter of recommendation from Dr. James Smith of Jamaica to the American Philosophical Society in Philadelphia, 28 September 1771, quoted in Dox, "Felsted."

FIGURE V-3. Title page of Samuel Felsted's *Jonah,* published in keyboard reduction in 1775. (Reproduced by permission of GB-Lbl.)

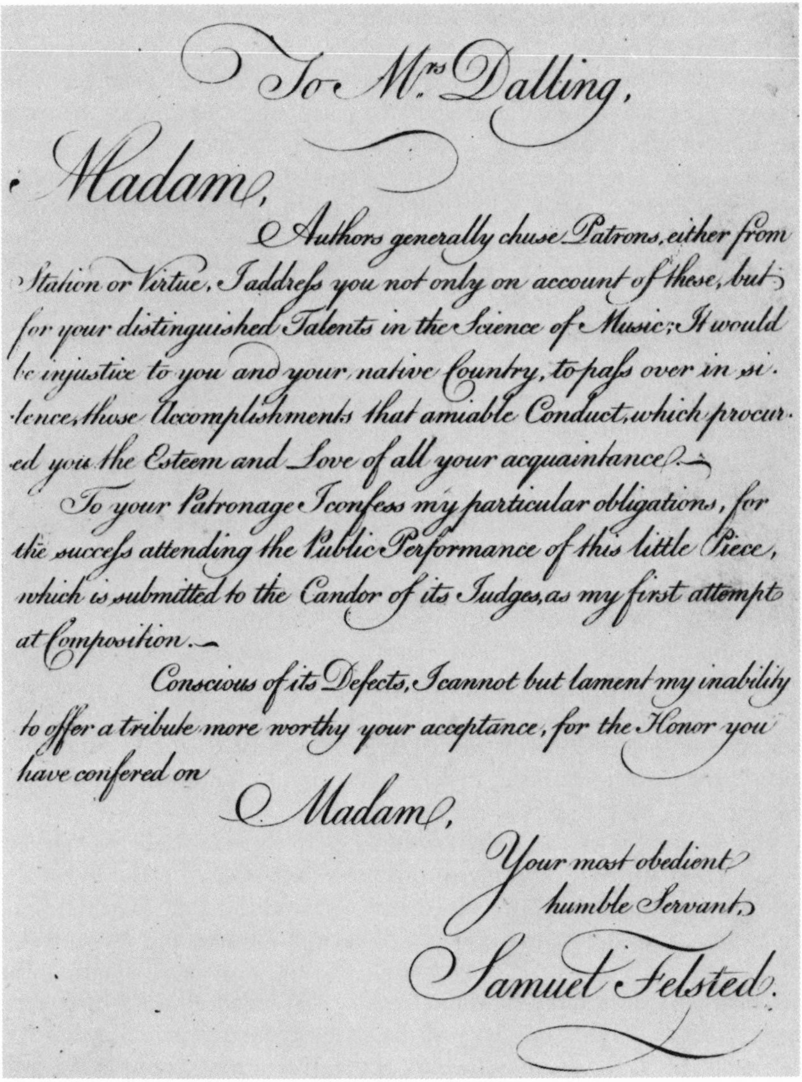

To Mrs Dalling.

Madam,

    Authors generally chuse Patrons, either from Station or Virtue. I address you not only on account of these, but for your distinguished Talents in the Science of Music; It would be injustice to you and your native Country, to pass over in silence, those Accomplishments that amiable Conduct, which procured you the Esteem and Love of all your acquaintance.

    To your Patronage I confess my particular obligations, for the success attending the Public Performance of this little Piece, which is submitted to the Candor of its Judges, as my first attempt at Composition.

    Conscious of its Defects, I cannot but lament my inability to offer a tribute more worthy your acceptance, for the Honor you have confered on

    Madam,

           Your most obedient
             humble Servant,

    Samuel Felsted.

FIGURE V-4. Dedication of Felsted's *Jonah*.
(Reproduced by permission of GB-Lbl.)

ing him to shore, and depositing him there. Again the Lord tells Jonah to go to Nineveh and preach against the evils of the city, which Jonah does successfully. The city repents and is saved from the Lord's anger. The one-part libretto includes no designated personages but implies the roles of Jonah (T) and a Narrator (T) who also sings the lines spoken to Jonah by the Lord. The chorus (SATB?)[58] sings twice: once as a Chorus of Ninevites and again as a nondramatic, final "Grand Chorus" of praise. The long opening recitative of the libretto condenses chapter 1 in the Book of Jonah, up to the point at which Jonah is swallowed by the whale; the two airs that follow, numbers 3 and 4 in Table V-5, correspond to chapter 2, Jonah's song from within the whale; and numbers 5–11 tell the story of chapter 3, through the repentance of the Ninevites. (Chapter 4, the final chapter in the Book of Jonah, is virtually always ignored in oratorio librettos, as it is here.)

As Table V-5 shows, the oratorio begins in F and later returns to F (no. 8) and moves to its relative minor (no. 10); the other airs and the first chorus are also in flat keys. Only the final chorus of praise is in a sharp key.

As the only source of the oratorio is a keyboard reduction, virtually nothing may be said of its original instrumentation and orchestration. The source includes a few instrumental cues, and according to the announcement of the work's Boston performance in 1789 (see the reference in chapter 4, n. 131), instrumental parts were to be performed by "a Society of Gentlemen with the band of his Most Christian Majesty's Fleet" (the French fleet); but the size and composition of the band is not known.

The overture is like an Italian sinfonia, with three movements marked Allegro, Andantino, and Allegro—all three in the key of F and in binary forms (with repeated sections in the second and third movements). Examples V-22a-c show the beginning of each movement and reveal traits of the early Classical style: homophonic texture, slow harmonic rhythm, *Trommelbass* (in Examples V-22a and c), and balanced phrases (sometimes extended). The simplicity of the style is characteristic of the work as a whole, as is the graceful melody of the Andantino (Example V-22b).

The four airs represent conservative structures for their time. None uses a transformed da capo scheme. Number 6 uses the dal segno to create a half da capo form; the B section is in the traditional relative minor. As represented in the source, number 4 has an AB structure, but it may have been intended as a da capo form: the A section has a text of fear, which is set in C minor, quick tempo, and duple meter; the B section's text is a prayer, set in the relative major, slower tempo, and triple meter. To interpret the number as a da capo structure does no violence to the text and allows the air to close in the tonic, as do all the

58. The choral voices are not specified in the source (a keyboard reduction), but the standard SATB seems appropriate.

TABLE V-5
Felsted, *Jonah*: Structural Outline

Numbers	Keys
1. Overture	F
2. Recit. Narrator, "Jonah, arise! to Nineveh repair"	
3. Air. Jonah, "Out of the deep, oh God I cry"	E♭
4. Air. Jonah, "Billows foam around my head"	c-E♭
5. Recit. Narrator, "The Lord commands, with haste the fish obeys"	
6. Air. Jonah, "My God and King, to Thee I sing"	B♭
7. Recit. Narrator, "Jonah, arise, again thy steps prepare"	
8. Air. Jonah, "Lord I obey, taught by thy pow'rful hand"	F
9. Recit. Jonah, "Repent, ye men of Nineveh, repent"	
10. Chorus of Ninevites, "Have mercy Lord and hear our plaintive cries"	d
11. Recit. Narrator, "God saw their works, he listen'd to their prayer"	
12. Chorus. "Tune your harps your voices raise"	D

other airs of the work.[59] Number 8 has a ternary ABA' structure with the B section in the relative minor; and number 3 is a binary form.

Examples V-23 and 24a-b are excerpted from Jonah's song from within the whale. Particularly effective in the simple prayer of Example V-23 (from no. 3) are the moments of dialogue between the voice and the instruments and the appoggiatura "sigh" figures on the words "deep," "cry," "sorrows," and "eye." Example 24a (from no. 4) first illustrates the beginning of the opening ritornello (mm. 1–5), and then the setting of the first two lines of the text. The key of C minor and the melodic contours of the ritornello and the text setting (both its vocal and continuo lines) represent the menacing, stormy billows with which Jonah is surrounded. Example 24b shows the beginning of the B section—a lyrical prayer with a graciously arching melodic line and simple accompaniment.

Example 25 (from no. 6) shows the setting of Jonah's spirited song of praise, rendered after he has been deposited on the shore by the whale. As may be seen at the beginning (mm. 1–4) the phrases are balanced and the harmonic rhythm slow, but the continuo is active, moving either in stepwise or arpeggiated motion. When the voice first enters (mm. 18–25), the balance of phrases continues, but the continuo momentarily becomes simpler. The coloratura passage of this example (mm. 44–48) is one of several in this air. Extended coloratura passages occur in number

59. The recording, Dox, "Felsted," successfully treats the air as a shortened da capo form.

EXAMPLE V-22. *Jonah*—Felsted (Felsted, *Jonah**, pp. 2, 4, 6).

Example a:

Example b:

EXAMPLE V-22. continued

Example c:

EXAMPLE V-23. *Jonah*—Felsted (Felsted, *Jonah**, p. 10).

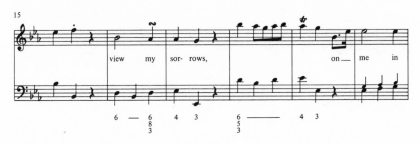

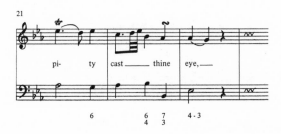

EXAMPLE V-24. *Jonah*—Felsted (Felsted, *Jonah**, pp. 12, 14).

Example a:

Example b:

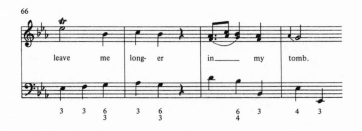

EXAMPLE V-25. *Jonah*—Felsted (Felsted, *Jonah**, p. 15).

EXAMPLE V-25. continued

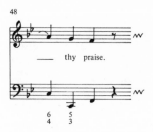

8 (not shown), Jonah's air of assent to God's command that he preach to the Ninevites.

Of the five recitatives in the oratorio, three (nos. 5, 7, and 11) are quite brief and in simple style. The opening recitative (no. 2) is the longest of the oratorio, for it tells the story of chapter 1 in the Book of Jonah; it begins as a simple recitative but ends with orchestral accompaniment.[60] Jonah's sermon to the Ninevites (no. 9) is labeled as an accompanied recitative. At the beginning of Example V-26 (no. 2) the Narrator quotes the Lord's command for Jonah to arise and go to Nineveh. Felsted is specific in his notation of declamation, with frequent use of dotted patterns. In measures 14–23, as the Narrator describes the storm, the orchestra enters with ascending runs in upper and lower register after the word "rise," in the bass only after "roar," higher runs ending with a fermata after the word "skies," and repeated notes approaching the cadence after the word "dismay."

The two choruses are simple but effective. They are essentially homophonic; counterpoint is minimal, and there are no fugal sections. As may be seen in the Grand Chorus, illustrated in Example V-27, the voice leading is not shown in the keyboard reduction of the source, but chordal style is evident.

*   *   *

60. Because it is known that instruments other than continuo were used in the work's performance, I interpret as orchestral the accompaniment motives, written in both bass and treble staves (see Example V-26, mm. 15–23).

EXAMPLE V-26. *Jonah*—Felsted (Felsted, *Jonah**, pp. 8–9).

EXAMPLE V-27. *Jonah*—Felsted (Felsted, *Jonah**, p. 24).

We have seen the enormous influence of Handel on English oratorio, both during and after his lifetime, in the continuing performance of his oratorios—in London, at the provincial festivals, and elsewhere, including the New World. Handelian influence is also evident in the English oratorios by other eighteenth-century composers, but traits of early Classical style also appear in their works. A characteristic that the English oratorio had in common with the North German, Protestant oratorio was an emphasis on the chorus, and that emphasis would seem to bode well for the acceptance of the Handelian oratorio in German-speaking lands. Yet the German oratorio, originally derived from that in Italian, proceeded along its independent path until late in the century. The English veneration of Handel through monumental performances was contagious, as is seen from Hiller's successes with *Messiah* in Germany. Yet the greatest impact of the Handelian oratorio on the genre in German was found in Vienna, where the patron Gottfried van Swieten fostered the performance of Handel's oratorios. Van Swieten encouraged Haydn, already inspired by the monumental performances of Handel that he heard in London, to compose *The Creation* and *The Seasons* to texts of English derivation and in his personal version of the English manner.

PART III

The German Oratorio

CHAPTER VI
Social Contexts of
the German Oratorio

Introduction: Terminology and Genre Definition

In German-speaking lands from the mid-eighteenth century to at least
the early nineteenth two concepts of oratorio existed side by side: the
traditional Baroque, Italianate, dramatic oratorio paralleled the development of the new, lyric, *empfindsam* oratorio. Some works share aspects
of both types, as we shall see, but for the sake of terminological discussion the two types are treated separately below and are designated simply
as the "lyric" and the "dramatic" oratorio. Both are long pieces in comparison with the usual German church cantata, but the lyric oratorio
tends to be shorter than the dramatic. Although the German term *Oratorium* (or the Italian, *oratorio*) was common for both types, a variety of
other terms were also applied to them, including *Abendmusik* (in Lübeck), *Cantate* (or *Kantate*), *geistliches Singgedicht*, *geistliches* (*lyrisches*,
religiöses, or *musikalisches*) *Drama*, and *musikalisches Gedicht*. As with
the Italian oratorio so also with the German, most of the terms by which
works are designated relate to the poetic composition, for the usual view
of a vocal piece was that of a literary work set to music, rather than a
musical work with words. Of the terms just mentioned, *Abendmusik* is
the only exception, for it refers to a performance context rather than a
literary work.

The Dramatic Oratorio

In Roman Catholic areas the German oratorio, which appeared in the
early eighteenth century but became increasingly prominent in mid-century, was essentially the same as the Italian oratorio in terminology and
genre definition—indeed, in virtually every respect but language. In fact,
some German oratorios are settings of Italian librettos in translation.
Furthermore, the occasions and manner of performance of the German
oratorio paralleled those of the Italian in the same regions.

In Protestant Germany the Italian word *oratorio* and its German form, *Oratorium* (borrowed from Latin), began to appear on the title pages of musical works with German texts and in German writings about literature and music in the first decade of the eighteenth century.[1] The dependence of Protestant German terminology and concept of oratorio upon Italian models is clear not only from the organization and style of the earliest German librettos and music but also from the earliest known comment on the genre in Protestant Germany, written in 1706 by Christian Friedrich Hunold (pseud., Menantes).[2] Other writings that show the Italian influence by stressing the dramatic nature and considerable length of an oratorio are those from the 1720s to the 1740s by Johann Adolph Scheibe and Johann Mattheson.[3] In the mid-century, Christian Gottfried Krause (1719–1770), in his *Von der musikalischen Poesie* (written in 1747, published in Berlin, 1752), continues to stress the dramatic quality of the genre. Krause describes "spiritual dramas or oratorios" ("geistliche Dramata oder Oratorien") as "a type of spiritual play" ("eine Art geistlicher Schauspiele") and notes that "many lack almost nothing [of the play] but the decoration of the stage and the costumes of the singers."[4] Late in the century, long after the ascendancy of the lyric oratorio in North Germany, some writers on music still considered the dramatic element to be of primary importance in oratorio. For instance, in 1783 Cramer's *Magazin der Musik*, published in Hamburg, carried a review of a recently printed text for a lyric oratorio and commented that the work should "rather be called a cantata than an oratorio, because dramatic action [Handlung] is the distinguishing feature of an oratorio."[5]

Despite the dependence upon the Italian model for terminology and genre definition, however, the German Protestant oratorio typically differs from that model in two important respects: the greater emphasis on chorus (which the German has in common with the English oratorio) and the inclusion of chorale tunes and texts. The combination of these traits suggests the German oratorio's close relationship to the church cantata; despite this relationship, however, in the first half of the century the church cantata and oratorio were usually seen as different genres. Krause, for instance, specifically excludes from the genre of oratorio those relatively short works for church that are purely reflective and made up of a few Bible verses and some arias and chorales—works that he terms *Kirchencantaten* or *Kirchenstücke*.[6] In the first half of the eigh-

1. For details, see Smither, *Oratorio*, 2:105.
2. Quoted in ibid., 2:105. The same quotation, in the original German and with a larger context, is found in Reimer, "Oratorium," p. 3.
3. Cited in Smither, *Oratorio*, 2:105–7.
4. Translated from Krause, *Poesie*, p. 470.
5. *Magazin der Musik* 1/1 (1783): 243–44. The anonymous author continues by criticizing Sulzer's treatment of oratorio (see below) as inadequate.
6. Krause, *Poesie*, p. 470. Highly exceptional is Erdmann Neumeister's use of the term *oratorio* for exactly the types of pieces that Krause excludes from the

teenth century the word *Oratorium* is rarely applied to a Protestant German church work that combines biblical narrative and poetic texts, such as oratorio Passions or *historiae* of any kind.[7] Krause is exceptional in including this type within the genre oratorio.[8]

An important type of dramatic oratorio in Protestant Germany—specifically in Lübeck—from the early eighteenth to the early nineteenth centuries was known by the terms *Oratorium, geistliches Singgedicht,* and *Abendmusik.*[9] The latter term was derived from the name of a concert series, the *Abendmusiken,* held in the late afternoon on five Sundays before Christmas in Lübeck's Marienkirche. As a composition, an *Abendmusik* was in five parts, one part to be performed on each of the five concerts. An *Abendmusik* was described by Caspar Ruetz (1708–55), the Kantor of St. Catherine's school in Lübeck, as "a complete *drama per musica* (as the Italians say), and it lacks only the action of the singers for it to be a spiritual *opera.* The poet bases [the text] on a biblical story and works it out according to the rules of theatrical poetry."[10] The title pages of the printed librettos usually refer to the composition as a *geistliches Singgedicht* and reserve the term *Abendmusik* for the name of the concert, as may be seen in the title page of A. C. Kunzen's *Absalon* (see Figure VI-1).[11] Yet such works were understood to be oratorios: for instance, Kunzen wrote the word *Oratorium* on the autograph manuscript of his *Absalon,* as shown in Figure VI-2.[12] Thus in the context of this Lübeck concert series, the terms *Oratorium, Abendmusik,* and *geistliches Singgedicht* were synonyms when applied to a musical composition.

The Lyric Oratorio and the Church Cantata

Although in Protestant Germany the dramatic, Italianate concept of oratorio continued throughout the eighteenth century and beyond, another one emerged in the mid-eighteenth century and became more prominent than the dramatic. The proponents of the new concept held that an oratorio is a work for divine service, and they supported the Enlighten-

---

category of oratorio: see Smither, *Oratorio,* 2:106–7, and Reimer, "Oratorium," p. 4.

7. See Smither, *Oratorio,* 2:106. Hereafter, the term *oratorio Passion* will refer to the type of Passion that J. S. Bach composed, with quoted biblical passages and inserted reflective numbers, which will be distinguished from *Passion oratorios,* with an entirely poetic text.

8. Krause, *Poesie,* p. 470.

9. The *Abendmusik* is treated more fully later in this chapter and in chap. 7.

10. Translated from Ruetz's *Widerlegte Vorurtheile von der Beschaffenheit der heutigen Kirchenmusik und von der Lebens-Art einiger Musicorum* (Lübeck, 1752), p. 44, as quoted in Stahl, "Ruetz," pp. 336–37.

11. Copy of libretto in B-Br: Fétis 4549.

12. Manuscript in D-LÜh: Mus. A160.

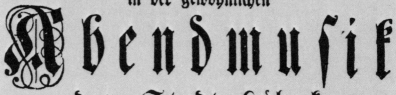

Abſalon.

Ein geiſtliches

Singgedichte.

Aus dem

XV. bis XVIII. Capitel des I Buchs Samuelis

genommen,

und

in der gewöhnlichen

Abendmuſik

der Stadt Lübeck

in der

Hauptkirche zu St. Marien

im Jahr 1761

zur Erbauung aufgeführet

von

Adolph Carl Kunzen.

Lübeck, gedruckt bey Johann Daniel Auguſt Fuchs.
Zu bekommen auf dem Werkhauſe zu St. Marien.

FIGURE VI-I. Title page of libretto to A. C. Kunzen's *Absalon* (1761), called a *Singgedichte* to be performed in the *Abendmusik*. (Courtesy of B-Br.)

FIGURE VI-2. Folio 1 of A. C. Kunzen's autograph manuscript of *Absalon*, called an *Oratorio*, the same work as represented in Figure VI-1. (Courtesy of D-LÜh.)

ment notion that only "useful" forms of music should be retained in church. "The Enlightenment held that the chief function of all church music was 'edification.' Everything that seemed to be edifying was to be kept; everything else was either to be abolished or to be revised. To 'edify' meant to induce feelings of reverence, whether they were only sentimental or more elevating in nature."[13] In accord with this view, the term *Oratorium* began to designate works with texts emphasizing the religious feelings aroused by familiar biblical stories, primarily those relating to the major feasts of the church year and thus to Jesus as the Messiah: mainly Christmas, the Passion, Easter, and Ascension. Rather than presenting the external events of the story in a connected, dramatic or narrative-dramatic text, as the traditional Baroque librettist had done, the poet assumed the listener's knowledge of the story and wrote a contemplative, lyric drama with personages who are usually unnamed and "idealized," and who express their sentiments about the story's events.[14] The absence of personages' names in the libretto involves the reader-listener in an active role. Rather than being an observer of a drama, he more readily identifies with the poet or the unnamed personage who experiences the feelings expressed in the text.

Drawing on the language and attitudes of Pietism and English nature poetry (popular in German translations of the time), the new lyric texts constitute a facet of *Empfindsamkeit* ("sensibility," or the "sentimental") in literature. The influence of Friedrich Gottlieb Klopstock's poetry on the lyric oratorio seems particularly strong—especially his odes, his *Messias* (the first three cantos of which were published in 1748), and his *empfindsam*, religious tragedy, *Der Tod Adams* (1757).[15] Arnold Schering, who treats the lyric libretto under the general heading, "The Messiah- and Idyl-Oratorio," aptly summarizes the changes from which the new viewpoint emerged: "An unusually heightened life of feeling, a changed relationship to religion, to nature, to society, brought forth two generations of which the most striking characteristic is usually grasped in the expression '*Empfindsamkeit*.' After a time of reason there followed a time of sentiment."[16] The most famous oratorio libretto of the new type was Carl Wilhelm Ramler's *Der Tod Jesu* (1754), set by numerous composers but best known in the setting (1755) by Carl Heinrich Graun.[17]

13. Feder, "Decline and Restoration," p. 323; Feder, "Verfall und Restauration," p. 221.

14. On the concept of the lyric drama in the eighteenth century, and for bibliography, see Wodtke, "Lyrisches Drama," 2:252–54.

15. For a summary of the characteristics and history of literary *Empfindsamkeit*, and for bibliography, see Liepe, "Empfindsame Dichtung." On relationships among *Empfindsamkeit*, Klopstock, and Pietism, see Sauder, *Empfindsamkeit*, pp. 58–64, and König, *Tod Jesu*, pp. 68–76.

16. Schering, *Oratorium*, p. 361; see his pp. 360–81 for the chapter on the oratorio with this type of text.

17. For details of the libretto and music, see chap. 8.

In the influential encyclopedia of the arts, *Allgemeine Theorie der schönen Künste* (Leipzig, 1771–74) edited and partly written by Johann Georg Sulzer (1720–79), the article "Oratorium" defines the genre entirely with reference to the newer, lyric type. Probably a collaborative writing by Johann Abraham Peter Schulz (1747–1800) and Johann Philipp Kirnberger (1721–83),[18] the article begins:

> *Oratorium.* (Poetry; music.) A spiritual, but completely lyric and short drama, which is performed with music, for use in divine service on high feast days. The designation of lyric drama indicates that here no gradually developing action, with striking events, intrigues, and interwoven ventures [*durch einanderlaufenden Unternehmungen*] takes place, as in the drama made for a play. The oratorio assumes various personages who are strongly moved by the noble religious subject of the feast that is being celebrated and who express their sentiments [*Empfindungen*] about it, now singly, now together, in a very emphatic manner. The purpose of this drama is to penetrate the hearts of the listeners with similar sentiments [*Empfindungen*].
>
> The material of the oratorio is therefore always a well-known thing, to the commemoration of which the feast is dedicated. Consequently it can be treated entirely lyrically, because here neither dialogue, nor narration, nor reports of what precedes are necessary.
> . . .
> Therefore the poet in the oratorio must completely avoid the epic and the usual dramatic expression, and where he wishes to narrate something or describe an event he must do it in a lyric tone. . . .[19]

This article focuses throughout on Ramler and Graun's *Tod Jesu*, which is said by the writer(s) to be "the best oratorio that I know."[20]

The article's definition of oratorio as a "completely lyric and short drama" and one "for use in divine service" raises the question of the relationship between the new lyric oratorio and the church cantata. What is meant by "short" can be judged by the model oratorio, Graun's *Tod Jesu*: Ramler's text is about 285 lines long, includes eleven choruses (six are chorales), eight recitatives (some quite long, one orchestrally accompanied), five arias, and one duet, and Graun's setting requires

---

18. According to Peter Schnaus, "Sulzer," *MGG*, 12:col. 1735, the articles on music in Sulzer's encyclopedia up to "Modulation" were written by Sulzer in collaboration with Kirnberger; from "Modulation" to "Präludium," by Schulz and Kirnberger; and from "Präludium" on, mainly by Schulz, who signed his articles "S." According to Schering, *Oratorium*, p. 368, the article "Oratorium" is by Schulz.

19. Sulzer, *Allgemeine Theorie*, 2/2:360.

20. Ibid., p. 361.

nearly two hours to perform.[21] This work is short in comparison with an opera or a dramatic oratorio in the Baroque tradition (which might last three hours or more) but is long in comparison with the usual church cantata (often less than a half-hour, rarely as long as an hour). If the lyric oratorio as described in the article is for divine service, its function is that of a church cantata. In fact, in the article "Cantate" (probably by Sulzer with the advice of Kirnberger), the church cantata and oratorio are regarded as a single genre: "There are two types of cantatas: the smaller [cantatas], for chamber music, in which there appears neither many voiced singing nor many voiced accompaniment by various instruments; and the larger [cantatas], for festive church music [*größere zur feyerlichen Kirchenmusik*], in which there are choruses, chorales, and other many voiced vocal numbers and a strong setting with various instruments. The latter are generally called oratorios [*Oratoria*]."[22] This treatment of the terms *oratorio* and *church cantata* as synonyms for festive church pieces is accepted by certain other writers of the time.[23] As further indication of the synonymous use of the two terms, it is noteworthy that Graun's *Tod Jesu* was called a *Cantate* on the title page of the score printed in 1760, yet on title pages of printed librettos and in newspaper notices of the late eighteenth and early nineteenth centuries it was called an *Oratorium* nearly as often as it was a *Cantate*.[24]

Shortly before the appearance of Sulzer's *Allgemeine Theorie*, John Brown's *Dissertation* (London, 1763) had been translated into German (Leipzig, 1769) by Johann Joachim Eschenburg (1743–1820). Brown's theories of the oratorio libretto (discussed in chapter 5) are in some respects similar to those in the article printed by Sulzer, particularly Brown's rejection of the traditional dramatic libretto in favor of one that is essentially lyric, that is, neither an epic nor an ode, but a union of the two. Brown's treatise in translation may have influenced the development of the lyric libretto in German, but if so, the degree of such influence remains a matter of speculation.

21. The recording of Graun's *Tod Jesu*, made in 1972 by the Heinrich Schütz-Kantorei Freiburg, the Badische Kammerorchester (Konzertmeister, Wolfgang Hock), conducted by Martin Gotthard Schneider (Da Camera Magna, SM 94038/39) lasts one hour and fifty minutes.

22. Sulzer, *Allgemeine Theorie*, 1/1: 254.

23. See the sources quoted in Reimer, "Oratorium," p. 6.

24. According to the *RISM* libretto files in D-Mbs, it is called an *Oratorium* on the title pages of librettos printed for performances in: n.p., 1761; Frankfurt, 1776; Copenhagen, 1778; Mainz, 1779; Stade, 1781; Cologne, 1787; Neuburg, 1793; Regensburg, 1800; Neuburg, 1803; Darmstadt, 1808; Brunswick, 1813; among numerous others. The work was consistently called an oratorio by the *Hamburger Correspondenten* in notices of its performances: see Menke, *Telemann*, Anhang A, pp. 40, 41, 44, 45, 48, 51, among others. For more on the genre of this work, see König, *Tod Jesu*, pp. 95–96.

The new concept of German oratorio espoused in the article "Oratorium" printed by Sulzer originated and was especially popular in Protestant Germany and was also adopted by some composers in Catholic areas. The dramatic oratorio, however, is ignored in that article—probably for aesthetic-partisan reasons—but it is grudgingly acknowledged in the article "Kirchenmusik": "In some German Protestant churches, they have even come to the tasteless notion of sometimes making church music dramatic. They perform oratorios [*Oratorien*], which are like small operas, in which recitatives, arias, and duets continually alternate among one another in the operatic manner, so that a dramatic action [*eine Handlung*] is presented by various personages. An invention of a senseless head, which to the shame of good taste is still retained in many places."[25]

The *Musikalisches Lexikon* (Frankfurt, 1802) by Heinrich Christoph Koch (1749–1816) presents a more balanced view of oratorio than does Sulzer's encyclopedia, for Koch recognizes both the lyric, *empfindsam* oratorio and the dramatic or operatic type; yet he follows Sulzer's work in disapproving of the latter. At the beginning of his article "Oratorium," Koch's definition is similar to Sulzer's: an oratorio is "a completely lyric drama of religious content for use in divine service" and it consists of "recitatives, arias, and choruses, which often, however, as with our modern church music in general, depart too much from the noble simplicity that should distinguish our music for divine service and incline too much toward the stole of opera music."[26] Unlike the article in Sulzer, that in Koch acknowledges the Italian roots of "the form that oratorios now have" and provides historical background that regards Archangelo Spagna as an oratorio reformer.[27] Koch considers length a criterion for distinguishing between an oratorio and a church cantata—a criterion traditional in Protestant Germany. Johann Mattheson had written in 1740 that an oratorio is both more dramatic and longer than the usual church piece;[28] and Koch, in the article "Cantate," writes of "the usual church piece [*die gewöhnlichen Kirchenmusik*]" as distinct from "the oratorio, which is of greater length."[29]

25. Sulzer, *Allgemeine Theorie*, 2/2:19. The article "Kirchenmusik" is probably by Sulzer with the advice of Kirnberger.

26. Koch, *Lexikon*, 2:1098.

27. Ibid., pp. 1098–99.

28. See the quotation from Mattheson's *Grundlage einer Ehren-Pforte* (Hamburg, 1740), in Smither, *Oratorio*, 2:106.

29. Koch, *Lexikon*, 1:302. For an earlier article that makes a similar distinction between church cantata and oratorio and that also champions the lyric, *empfindsam* oratorio, see the anonymous "Ueber die Beschaffenheit der musikalischen Oratorien, nebst Vorschläge zur veränderten Einrichtung derselben," *Musikalischer Almanach für Deutschland für das Jahr 1783*, p. 179.

Sponsors and Social Contexts

In the following sections, sponsors and contexts that are primarily sacred are treated separately from those primarily secular, but the sacred sections include those borderline cases in which the location of the performance is a church but the sponsor is secular (e.g., the Lübeck *Abendmusiken* and the first performance of Graun's *Tod Jesu* in Berlin). On the other hand, concerts given in nonreligious buildings, such as theaters and concert halls, are grouped with secular sponsors and contexts (e.g., the Concerts spirituels of Berlin and Schwerin).

Roman Catholic Areas

Religious Sponsors and Contexts. Although in German-speaking, Roman Catholic areas the Italian oratorio was cultivated mainly at courts that were leaders in Italian opera (e.g., Vienna, Dresden, and Mannheim), the German oratorio was heard primarily at more modest courts and in monasteries. Yet the occasions for the performances of Italian and German oratorios were much the same: both usually served to solemnize the Lenten period in general and Holy Week in particular, and for the latter occasion, both were sometimes performed before a model of Jesus' sepulchre, erected in a court chapel or a church. Furthermore, the German and Italian oratorio in Catholic areas were much alike in literary and musical structure and style.

Salzburg, with its archbishop's court, cathedral, and Benedictine university, was an active center of oratorio performance. Although some Italian oratorios were given there early in the century,[30] most Salzburg oratorios were in German and date from the 1740s to the early 1770s. The principal patron of oratorios in Salzburg appears to have been Archbishop Siegmund Christoph, Count of Schrattenbach (r. 1753–71), who was unaffected by Enlightenment viewpoints toward religious ceremony and music. His successor, Archbishop Hieronymous, Count of Colloredo (r. 1772–1803), was a man of the Enlightenment, who reformed and simplified religious observances and showed little interest in oratorio.[31] The principal composers of German oratorios for Salzburg were Johann Ernst Eberlin (1702–62), who became the court and cathedral Kapellmeister in 1749 but had been a cathedral organist since 1725;[32] Leopold Mozart (1719–87), in the service of the Salzburg archbishops since

30. As indicated in chap. 1.

31. On Archbishops Schrattenbach and Colloredo, see Martin, *Salzburgs Fürsten*, pp. 214–56.

32. For a thorough study of Eberlin's oratorios, see Haas, "Eberlin." Haas lists Eberlin's oratorios and school dramas on pp. 12–14. A complete Eberlin oratorio

1743;[33] Anton Cajetan Adlgasser (1729–77), court and cathedral organist beginning in 1750;[34] Michael Haydn (1737–1806), in the service of the archbishop from 1763;[35] and Wolfgang Amadeus Mozart, whose only German oratorio was composed in his tenth year: his *Die Schuldigkeit des ersten Gebots* (K. 35) was part I of a three-part work (part II was by M. Haydn, and III by Adlgasser).[36]

Regarding the frequency and occasions of Salzburg's German oratorio performances, a letter of 1755 from Leopold Mozart to a friend in Augsburg is informative:

> Another thing! Do you not have a good text for a so-called *oratorio*? If I were to have time, I would perhaps compose another one for Lent. Do you not have one like that which I did a year ago, namely *Christus begraben*?
>
> What was the one that Herr Seifert did awhile back for the *Collegium*? Perhaps you can produce mine for the comming Lent. I find nothing in it that he could object to; it is on the burial of Christ.
>
> If sometime a good text for a larger vocal work [Sing-*Musique*] comes to hand, send it to me; for every Lent each week we must *produce 2 oratorios*, and where do we find enough texts? It does not even have to be *de passione Christi*. It can also be another penitential story. For example, last year we performed the repentant Peter; and this year the penitent *David* will be done. . . .[37]

If two oratorios were performed each week every year in Lent, as this letter indicates, then the surviving sources, both librettos and music manuscripts, represent an extremely small proportion of the original

---

and exerpts from several others are published in Eberlin, *Der blutschwitzende Jesus**.

33. His oratorios are listed in Plath, "Leopold Mozart," *New Grove*, 12:677, and details of their sources are given in Carlson, "Leopold Mozart," pp. 186–93.

34. On his oratorios see Schneider, "Adlgasser," in which the composer's oratorios, all in German, are listed on pp. 39–40. The Latin works listed as oratorios in Rainer, "Adlgasser," pp. 387–88, and Reinhard G. Pauly, "Adlgasser" *New Grove*, 1:110, are actually school dramas (mostly spoken, with some music) rather than oratorios.

35. For a list of his oratorios, see Reinhard G. Pauly and Charles H. Sherman, "Michael Haydn," *New Grove*, 8:410–11.

36. Part I is printed in Mozart, W. A., *Die Schuldigkeit**; parts II and III are lost.

37. L. Mozart to J. Jak. Lotter (the Augsburg publisher of Mozart's violin treatise) 29 December 1755. Translated from Mozart, L., *Ausgewählte Werke**, pp. xxxi–xxxii. The oratorio *Christus begraben* mentioned in the letter is a complete revision of the one that Mozart set in 1741, the text of which is reprinted in ibid., pp. XIII–XV. On the two versions, see Carlson, "Leopold Mozart," pp. 187–88, 193.

repertoire. The printed librettos that have come to light thus far provide few specifics on the performance contexts of works by the above-mentioned Salzburg composers, except that most were for Lent.[38] Some oratorios were probably sung before a model of the holy sepulchre erected in the cathedral,[39] perhaps in conjunction with prayers and a sermon, and some were given in the archbishop's residence. *Die Schuldigkeit des ersten Gebots*, the three-part work mentioned above, was performed in the *Rittersaal* of the residence: part I on 12 March 1767 (the first Thursday in Lent), part II a week later, part III perhaps the following week, and part I again on 2 April.[40] This work and others like it may have been given as operas, with costumes, acting, and modest scenery.[41] A German oratoriolike work seems occasionally to have functioned as an *interludium* between the acts of a Latin school drama presented at the Benedictine university.[42]

The German oratorio was cultivated in a religious context in various communities and courts throughout the Habsburg lands. At the musically active Benedictine abbey of Kremsmünster, where Holy Week music performed at a model of Jesus' sepulchre may be traced back to the seventeenth century, that tradition was evidently still alive in the 1770s. In Holy Week of 1771 the music director, Georg Pasterwiz, performed at the sepulchre a German oratorio, *Der Heiland in Gethsemane*, by Fruktuos Räder (a Benedictine from Fulda),[43] and in 1775 he performed in the same context Graun's *Tod Jesu*,[44] a work identified mainly with

38. Little research has been done on this subject, but the contexts of Eberlin's oratorios are briefly treated in Haas, "Eberlin," pp. 15–17. See also Schneider, *Salzburg*, pp. 103–4 for further comments on oratorio contexts in Salzburg.

39. Haas, "Eberlin," p. 17. According to Martin, *Salzburgs Fürsten*, p. 230, in 1782 Archbishop Colloredo abolished the construction of the ornate *Grabtheater* and permitted only a simple sepulchre, with four candles, to be erected in the cathedral.

40. Cf. the foreword, by Franz Giegling, to Mozart, W. A., *Die Schuldigkeit**, p. VII. No information has come to light on the performance date of part III.

41. Ibid.; see also Mozart, W. A., *Die Schuldigkeit*(KB), pp. a/6–a/7. The printed libretto of *Die Schuldigkeit* (see facsimile of title page in Mozart, W. A., *Die Schuldigkeit**, p. XVII) does not bear a genre designation, but a contemporary diarist, Georg Hübner, calls it an *Oratorium* (cf. Klein, "Mozartiana," p. 183); the libretto for a similar three-part work of the following year, *Der Kampf der Busse und Bekehrung* (part I by M. Haydn, II by Adlgasser, and III by David Westermayer) is called an "*Oratorio* in dreyen Theilen vorgestellet" on the title page of its printed libretto (copy in D-Mbs: Slg. Her o 222). Although Giegling's assumption of staged performances of such oratorios would seem reasonable, given the tendencies of the time and the Salzburg tradition he describes, I have seen no clear evidence as to whether they were or were not staged.

42. See the discussion of Eberlin's *Sedecias* in Haas, "Eberlin," pp. 14–15.

43. Kellner, *Kremsmünster*, p. 451.

44. Ibid., p. 463.

Protestant Germany. At the same abbey in 1778, Johann Heinrich Rolle's *Der Tod Abel* (1769) contributed to the festivities of the annual election day of the abbot;[45] and in the 1790s and early 1800s performances were given of German oratorios by both Michael and Joseph Haydn, including the latter's *The Creation* and *The Seasons* in the year following the first Viennese performance of each.[46]

A collection of printed librettos in Göttweig attests to at least occasional performances from the 1720s to the 1770s of German oratorios in court chapels and parish and monastic churches in Graz, Göttweig, Krems an der Donau, and Vienna.[47] At Krems in the mid-eighteenth century, Johann Georg Zechner (1716–78) composed at least twelve German oratorios for Advent, Christmas, and Good Friday.[48] The manuscripts and printed librettos of the Good Friday works state that they were performed before a holy sepulchre erected in the parish church of St. Vitus in Krems. According to one of the librettos, the performance began at seven o'clock in the evening; whether prayers and a sermon formed part of the context (as they did for Italian oratorios performed before a sepulchre at the Viennese court chapel before 1740) is not known.[49]

Gregor Joseph Werner (1693–1766)—Joseph Haydn's predecessor as Kapellmeister at the Esterházy court in Eisenstadt—composed at least nineteen German oratorios between 1729 and 1762.[50] According to their printed librettos and manuscript sources, most, if not all, were intended for performance on Good Friday before a sepulchre."[51] For instance, the printed libretto of Werner's last oratorio, *Antiochus der wütente Tyrann, und Vorbild des künftigen Antichrist*, states that the work was performed on Good Friday, 11 April 1762, "in the High-Princely Esterházy Palace, at the Holy Grave."[52] As Joseph Haydn had arrived in the previous year to assume the duties of Kapellmeister, he may have been involved with this performance. Although such annual

45. Ibid., p. 473.

46. Ibid., pp. 497, 511, 566–67.

47. The collection is discussed and title pages of librettos are quoted in Riedel, "Göttweig."

48. For details, see Riedel, "Krems," pp. 310–15, 324–25 (list of oratorios and sources).

49. On the Viennese practice in the late seventeenth and early eighteenth centuries, see Smither, *Oratorio*, 1:371 and n. 12.

50. See the list of oratorios in Hubert Unverricht, "Werner," *New Grove*, 20:349. For studies of eight oratorios by Werner dating from 1729 to 1760 see Warner, "Werner."

51. Manuscript title pages testifying to this occasion and context for eight of Warner's oratorios are quoted in Warner, "Werner," pp. 18, 43, 57, 69, 79, 94, 105, and 118.

52. The complete title page is quoted in Landon, *Haydn*, 1:369.

Good Friday oratorios in German were evidently traditional in Eisenstadt before Haydn's tenure, the tradition was discontinued shortly after his arrival.[53]

In Prague some of the same religious orders that sponsored performances of Italian and Latin oratorios (see chapter 1) also sponsored German ones, though less frequently. According to extant librettos, the Premonstratensiens and Franciscan Capuchins may have presented more German oratorios than the other orders. In Prague the pattern noted elsewhere of giving performances on Good Friday before a holy sepulchre was followed. As in Salzburg, the number of German oratorios appears to have increased beginning in the 1740s.[54]

Secular Sponsors and Concerts: Vienna. The importance of Vienna's Tonkünstler-Societät for the cultivation of Italian oratorio in the 1770s was mentioned in chapter 1. By the end of that decade, however, Viennese tastes were beginning to change, and oratorios in German became increasingly popular.[55] The year 1779 marks the beginning of German oratorio in the Society's concerts: in Lent the oratorio was *Die Israeliten in der Wüste*, by Maximilian Ulbrich (1741?–1814; the work was repeated in Lent, 1783) and in Advent, Handel's *Judas Maccabaeus* in a German translation.[56] Among the other German oratorios performed on the Society's concerts up to 1810 are: in 1780, *Die Zurückkunft des verlorenen Sohnes* by Friedrich Hartmann Graf (1727–95); 1781, *Die Pilgrime auf Golgatha* by Johann Georg Albrechtsberger (1736–1809); 1794, *Die Hirten bei der Krippe zu Bethlehem* by Joseph Leopold Eybler (1765–1846); in Lent, 1798, 1799, and 1801, Joseph Haydn's *Die sieben letzten Worte unseres Erlösers am Kreuze*; in Advent of 1799, Haydn's *Die Schöpfung* (*The Creation*), performed in both Lent and Advent of 1800 and once each in 1804, 1805, 1807, 1809, and 1810; for Lent of 1801, Haydn's *Die Jahreszeiten* (*The Seasons*), repeated for both Lent and Advent of 1802 and once each in 1804, 1808, and 1809; and for Lent, 1810, *Die vier letzten Dinge*, by Eybler. The works by Eybler have

53. Further research is necessary to determine whether the discontinuation resulted from the influence of Enlightenment views.

54. For the data on which this paragraph is based, see the lists of librettos in Poštolka, "Strahow," and Bužga, "Osteroratorien."

55. Except when otherwise indicated, this paragraph is based on the lists and commentary in Hanslick, *Concertwesen*, pp. 30–35, and Pohl, *Tonkünstler-Societät*, pp. 43–68 (Pohl provides the fullest information), with further verifications of titles mostly in the composer articles of *New Grove*.

56. Handel's work was performed in an arrangement once thought to be by W. A. Mozart but probably by Joseph Starzer, and the translation was possibly by Baron Gottfried van Swieten. Cf. Holschneider, "Die *Judas-Macchabäus* Bearbeitung"; Gerhard Croll, "Starzer," *New Grove*, 13:81; and Edward Olleson, "Swieten," *New Grove*, 13:415.

texts of the lyric type, as does Haydn's *Die sieben letzen Worte*; the others have dramatic texts except for Haydn's *The Creation* and *The Seasons*, which are special cases, with mainly narrative text, treated below.

Oratorios were occasionally presented in Vienna at concerts other than those of the Tonkünstler-Societät. Beethoven first performed his *Christus am Oelberge*, for instance, on Tuesday, 5 April, in Holy Week of 1803, at a concert in the Theater-an-der-Wien, together with his first and second symphonies and third piano concerto.[57] On 15 November 1807 at the Theater in der Leopoldstadt, Ferdinand Kauer (1751–1831) gave the premier performance of his *Die Sündflut oder Noahs Versöhnungsopfer*.[58] A performance of this oratorio in the same theater on 24 December 1809 would seem to have included some staging, for the report in the *Allgemeine musikalische Zeitung* quoted the advertisement, which had invited the public to "see and hear" this grand performance.[59] Indeed, the advertisement pasted to the front cover of the manuscript in the Gesellschaft der Musikfreunde in Vienna speaks of Noah's construction of an altar of thanksgiving in part III, of a bright flame burning his sacrificial offering on the altar, and of a rainbow that appears as a monument and reminder that the world will never again be punished so severely.[60]

Clearly the most important single patron of oratorio in Vienna during the last two decades of the century was Baron Gottfried van Swieten (1733–1803). While living in Berlin (1770–77) as the Habsburg ambassador to the court of Frederick the Great, Swieten had become interested in earlier music, particularly that of J. S. Bach and Handel, which he would have heard in the soirées of Princess Anna Amalia of Prussia and in the Liebhaberkonzerte.[61] Upon his return to Vienna as Prefect of the Imperial Library, he began to sponsor performances of music by Bach and Handel, including oratorios by the latter, in the Library's rooms. Probably about 1785 he organized a society of aristocratic patrons of music called the Gesellschaft der Associierten, who sponsored private performances mainly of Handel's oratorios in the houses of the noble members. W. A. Mozart was employed to make arrangements of some of Handel's works, including *Acis and Galatea* (1788), *Messiah* (1789), and the *Ode for St. Cecilia's Day* and *Alexander's Feast* (1790). It is of interest that these four works, plus *Judas Maccabaeus* (also performed in

57. For details, see chap. 8.

58. Geck, *Deutsche Oratorien*, p. 16.

59. *Allgemeine musikalische Zeitung*, 12 (1809): 267. (The reporter states that he was unable to attend the performance.)

60. The advertisement is pasted to the verso of the front cover of the manuscript A-Wgm: III 14234 / Q 868.

61. For a summary of Swieten's life and works and a full bibliography, see Edward Olleson, "Swieten," *New Grove*, 18:414–15.

Vienna, possibly in Swieten's translation) were also the most popular of Handel's pieces in contemporary England (see Table IV-1 and the accompanying discussion).

Much interested in contemporary music as well as Handel and J. S. Bach, Swieten, while serving in Berlin, traveled to Hamburg expressly to meet C. P. E. Bach and commissioned him to write the six symphonies of 1773.[62] In 1788, the year after the publication of C. P. E. Bach's oratorio *Auferstehung und Himmelfahrt Jesu* (see chapter 8), Swieten sponsored performances of the work, on 26 February and 4 March, the third and fourth Tuesdays of Lent.[63] A published report following the event provides some insights into the private performances with which Swieten was involved. According to the report, the work with a text by Ramler,

> admirably set to music by the incomparable Hamburg Bach, was performed at the home of Count Johann Esterházy. The performance, by an orchestra of 86 players in the presence of and under the auspices of the Freiherr van Swieten, found the greatest appreciation amongst the most honorable company. The Royal-Imperial Capellmeister [W. A.] Mozart beat time and had the score, and the Royal-Imperial Capellmeister [Ignaz] Umlauff played the piano. The performance was splendid, for two general rehearsals had preceded it.
>
> During the performance of 4 March, the count had the engraved portrait of the Capellmeister Bach sent around the hall. The princesses and countesses present and the whole splendid nobility admired the great composer. A loud "vivat" followed, and three rounds of applause. Among the singers were Madame Lange, the tenor [Valentin] Adamberger, the bass [Ignaz] Saale, and 30 choristers. On 7 [March] the piece was performed in the Royal-Imperial National Theater.[64]

Although that report mentions only Swieten as patron, the location of the performance in the home of Count Esterházy and Mozart's participation would suggest that this was an event of the Associierten, of which Swieten was the leader.[65] Other new works sponsored by the Associierten and first performed at the house of a member, Prince

62. For specifics see Eugene Helm, "Bach, III: (9)," *New Grove*, 1:849 and 860.

63. The publication of Ramler's *Auferstehung* at Vienna in 1788 (in small format; see copy in GB-Lbl: 11748.aa.73) might have been undertaken to provide librettos for this performance; yet nothing to that effect is stated in the publication, and the version differs slightly from the one that Bach set.

64. *Musikalischer Almanach für Deutschland* (1789), pp. 121–22. In the report, the titles given to Mozart and Umlauff are erroneous.

65. The relationship of Count Johann to the Associierten is not known, but according to Landon, *Haydn*, 4:28, "Prince [Nikolaus?] Esterházy" was a member.

Schwarzenberg, are Haydn's *Seven Last Words*, *The Creation*, and *The Seasons*, for which Swieten was the writer and adapter of the texts. (On *The Creation* and *The Seasons*, see chapter 8.)

Protestant Areas

Religious Sponsors and Contexts. Although in Roman Catholic churches neither Italian nor German oratorios are known to have been performed during Mass,[66] in German Protestant churches an oratorio might form part of the principal worship service on a major feast day (see the comments published by Sulzer and Koch quoted early in this chapter). Any important feast of the church year could be an occasion for an oratorio during the service, but Passion oratorios intended for Holy Week are more numerous and more typical than those for any other time of the year. In the first half of the century the oratorio Passion was of special significance in Protestant churches during Holy Week, but after the midcentury the Passion oratorio became increasingly important as modifications reflecting Enlightenment thought were incorporated into the service. In the modified service the dramatic responsorial Passion and the oratorio Passion were increasingly considered "unedifying" and were abandoned in favor of "a reading of the Passion text by the minister, interrupted by the congregation's singing of chorale verses. . . . The central position was now held by the lyrical Passion oratorio, especially its smaller variant, the Passion cantata."[67]

Particularly significant for the cultivation of German oratorio in the first half of the century is Hamburg, where oratorios began to be performed quite early both in concerts and church services.[68] Johann Mattheson states that he introduced oratorios into the Hamburg cathedral in Christmas of 1715, and he performed oratorios there until 1728, when he resigned his directorship of the cathedral's music.[69] Georg Philipp Telemann (1681–1767)—as Kantor and music director in Hamburg—composed oratorio Passions for the city's churches, but his oratorios were performed primarily in concerts. An important exception is his Passion oratorio *Seliges Erwägen des Leidens und Sterbens Jesu Christi* (1728), which was given annually, in some years more than once, both in concerts and in the smaller churches, until long after the composer's

66. In France, however, Latin oratorios were occasionally performed during Mass. See the section of chapter 9 on LeSueur's oratorios; see also Smither, *Oratorio*, 1:424 and 427, on oratorios by M.-A. Charpentier.

67. Feder, "Decline and Restoration," pp. 363–64.

68. Cf. Smither, *Oratorio*, 2:107–20.

69. Cannon, *Mattheson*, p. 60; Smither, *Oratorio*, 2:114, 117. From the title pages of the oratorios cited in Cannon, *Mattheson*, pp. 161–88, it seems probable that some if not all were performed during divine service; Georg Feder, in "Oratorium," *MGG*, 10: col. 136, states that the oratorios were intended for divine service.

death; between 1786 and 1799, for instance, it was given seventeen times.[70] A newspaper notice from 1758 about the *Seliges Erwägen* is typical: the "beloved work" was to be performed on the second Friday of Lent "before and after the sermon" in the church of Hamburg's workhouse, prison, and poorhouse.[71] Carl Philipp Emanuel Bach (1714–88), Telemann's successor in Hamburg, continued the tradition of composing oratorio Passions for church service and oratorios for concerts, but some of the latter were also performed in churches, e.g., the Passion oratorio *Die letzten Leiden des Erlösers* (1770);[72] in 1782 Bach performed a portion of his *Die Auferstehung und Himmelfahrt Jesu* (1777–80) in church as Easter music.[73] When Bach published his oratorio *Die Israeliten in der Wüste* (composed 1769; published Hamburg, 1775), he noted in a Hamburg newspaper: "This oratorio has been so arranged for use, that it can be performed not for just one kind of ceremony, but at all times, within and without the church, purely to praise God, and indeed without offence to anyone who is a member of the Christian religion."[74]

Performances of oratorios in Berlin prior to the mid-century are virtually unknown.[75] In 1749 Johann Philipp Sack (1722–63), a teacher at the Berlin Cathedral School and from 1756 the Cathedral organist, established a society of amateur musicians, the Musikübende Gesellschaft, which was to play a significant role in oratorio performance.[76] Although the society performed mainly instrumental music, usually in Sack's home, it presented Passion oratorios on Good Friday, 9 April 1751, and Maundy Thursday, 11 April 1754.[77] The latter performance (and possibly the former) was given in the Cathedral, as a concert rather than within a service—the Cathedral was a Reformed church and thus did not use elaborate service music.

A particularly important event in Berlin on Wednesday of Holy Week, 26 March 1755, was the public premiere, at a concert in the Cathedral, of Graun's *Tod Jesu*.[78] The performers were those of the Musikübende Gesellschaft, plus professionals from the royal chapel, including C. P. E.

70. Menke, *Telemann*, p. 81; Martin Ruhnke, "Telemann," *New Grove*, 18:653.

71. Menke, *Telemann*, p. 42; a similar notice, p. 43.

72. Miesner, *Bach*, p. 70. Hamburg would seem to have been exceptional for continuing to cultivate the oratorio Passion in C. P. E. Bach's time.

73. Ibid., p. 75.

74. Translated from ibid., p. 74, as quoted from *Hamburger Correspondent*, no. 147 (14 September 1774).

75. For an apparently isolated instance of 1708, possibly performed in a church, see Smither, *Oratorio*, 2:124–25.

76. For details of this society, which lost its vitality after the death of its founder, see Loewenthal, *Berlin*, pp. 6–17.

77. Ibid., p. 13.

78. Ibid., p. 14. A private hearing of the work took place in or before February

Bach at the harpsichord, Johann Gottlieb Graun leading the violins, Agricola singing tenor and beating time, and two female opera singers as soloists. According to a newspaper report that appeared the following day, "Yesterday afternoon in the Cathedral Church a Passion oratorio was performed by the local Musikübende Gesellschaft. The gathering was unusually large, and even the rehearsal, which took place the previous day in the same church, had attracted a large crowd of listeners. Even her majesty the queen honored [the performance] with her presence."[79] (The king, Frederick the Great, was not mentioned and thus was not present; in principle opposed to religious music, he may never have heard Graun's famous *Tod Jesu*, but he did occasionally hear a religious work; four performances of Hasse's *Sant'Agostino* are said to have been given at one of his palaces in Potsdam in July, 1768.)[80] Graun's *Tod Jesu* continued to be performed annually in Berlin for well over a century. Although its premiere and many of its subsequent performances were given in concerts, it also became a standard work for Holy Week in church services throughout Protestant Germany until the late nineteenth century. Known and admired by many generations of Germans, Graun's *Tod Jesu* became as important in Germany as Handel's *Messiah* in England and America. By 1793, the *Berliner musikalische Zeitung* could state, "almost everyone knows at least part of the music by heart; innumerable performances on solemn occasions, particularly in church, have now already sanctified it, so that people have sung it almost from childhood."[81] Some librettos printed for performances of this work show a two-part division, which is not indicated in the printed score of 1760, and the work was apparently performed in two parts on Palm Sunday and Good Friday of 1759 in Berlin's St. Peter's Church.[82] Presumably the division into two parts was made to allow for the usual sermon, during a service, at the mid-point of two-part oratorios and cantatas. (See chapter 8 for more details on Graun's *Tod Jesu*.)

In Leipzig churches after the period of J. S. Bach, as elsewhere in Germany, the lyric Passion oratorio became more important than the oratorio Passion of the type that he composed. Examples from among the numerous librettos printed for performances of lyric Passion oratorios in Leipzig churches between the mid-eighteenth century and the early nineteenth are: *Der Christ bey dem Kreuze Jesu*, by C. E. Weinlich,

---

1755, at the home of the court preacher August Friedrich Wilhelm Sack, according to Lott, "Tod Jesu," p. 126.

79. Translated from Loewenthal, *Berlin*, p. 14, as quoted from the *Berlinische privilegierte Zeitung*, later called the *Vossische Zeitung* (1755), no. 37.

80. Mennicke, *Hasse und die Brüder Graun*, p. 520, n. 3.

81. 13 April 1793, p. 37, as translated by Howard Serwer in the preface to Graun, *Tod Jesu**, p. viii.

82. Dubinski, "Berlin," pp. 139–40.

performed at the Nicolaikirche on Palm Sunday and at the Thomas-kirche on Good Friday;[83] *Empfindung am Grabe Jesu: Ein Oratorium*, by Handel (a modified text to his *Funeral Anthem for Queen Caroline*), performed in the Nikolaikirche on Palm Sunday morning, and *Jesus in Gethsemane: Ein Oratorium*, by Antonio Rosetti [Anton Rösler], per-formed in the same church on Good Friday morning;[84] and *Empfindun-gen bey dem Kreuze des Erlösers: Ein Oratorium*, by J. Haydn (a Ger-man text to his *Stabat Mater*, often called an oratorio in the time), performed on Palm Sunday in the Nicolaikirche and Good Friday in the Thomaskirche.[85] From 1789 to 1801, when Johann Adam Hiller (1728–1804) was Kantor of the Thomasschule in Leipzig, Graun's *Tod Jesu* was the standard oratorio for services on Palm Sunday and Good Friday.[86]

In Dresden, Gottfried August Homilius (1714–85)—a student of J. S. Bach and in 1755–85 Kantor at the Kreuzkirche and teacher at the Kreuzschule—composed eight lyric Passion oratorios. All are larger than his cantatas, are divided into two parts, and were intended for services in the Kreuzkirche during Lent, especially on Holy Thursday and Good Friday.[87] Homilius's student and from 1785 his successor at the Kreuz-kirche and Kreuzschule, Christian Ehregott Weinlig (1743–1813), com-posed at least eleven lyric Passion oratorios between 1786 and 1812 for performance at the Kreuzkirche.[88] Characteristic of the myriad perfor-mances of lyric oratorios in court and parish churches of smaller com-munities are those at Bückeburg, Eisenach, Erlangen, Havelberg, Gotha, Lübeck, Rostock, and Schwerin.[89]

83. Undated libretto in D-LEm: I.B.51.

84. The two are printed together in a libretto dated 1814, in D-LEm: PT 1318.

85. Undated libretto in D-LEm: PT 1221. The libretto is divided into two parts, the second of which begins with the heading: "Nach der Predigt."

86. Schering, *Leipzig*, 3:649.

87. For details of Homilius's Passion oratorios and their sources, see John, *Homilius*, pp. 207–17, 227–28.

88. See the list of his oratorios in Dieter Härtwig, "Weinlig," *MGG*, 14:col. 412.

89. The following are a few indications of interest in such works in these communities: the works by J. C. F. Bach set to texts by Herder for performance in Bückeburg, 1772–76 (on Herder's texts, see chap. 7), and the performance of J. Haydn's *Die sieben letzten Worte* in Bückeburg (1802) as reported by a contem-porary and translated in Landon, *Haydn*, 1:98; Johann Ernst Bach's "O Seele, deren Sehnen" (1764), composed in Eisenach: cf. Joseph Kromolicki's "Vor-wort" to Bach, J. E., *Passionsoratorium**, p. V; Johann Balthasar Kehl's *Die Pilgrime auf Golgatha*, performed at Erlangen in 1762 (libretto in D-B: Mus. T 99/5); Johann Heinrich Rolle's *Das Leiden und Sterben des Welt-Erlösers*, per-formed in Havelberg, 1786 (libretto in D-B: Mus. Tr 815/20); on oratorio Pas-sions and Passion oratorios in Gotha, see Blankenburg, "Gotha"; on Lübeck, see Stahl, *Lübeck*, pp. 103, 105; on Schwerin and Rostock, see Meyer, *Mecklenburg-Schwerin*, pp. 55–57.

Of special importance for the history of the oratorio in Protestant Germany is the annual church concert series known as the *Abendmusiken* held in the Lübeck Marienkirche.⁹⁰ The *Abendmusiken* were begun by the Marienkirche organist Dietrich Buxtehude (ca. 1637–1707) in the early 1670s (following antecedents established by his predecessor, Franz Tunder); they were given annually for more than a century on the last two Sundays before Advent and the second, third, and fourth Sundays of Advent. Buxtehude's successors as directors of the *Abendmusiken* were the Marienkirche organists Christian Schieferdecker (1679–1732), Johann Paul Kunzen (1696–1756), his son Adolf Carl Kunzen (1720–81), and Johann Wilhelm Cornelius von Königslöw (1745–1833).

Only quasi-religious events, the *Abendmusiken* began at four o'clock in the afternoon, immediately following the church service's last chorale "Nun gottlob, es ist vollbracht" and the closing "Benedicamus Domino."⁹¹ Although the music was religious and performed in church, the financial support came mainly from the business community, and the *Abendmusiken* were viewed not as performances within a worship service but as spiritual concerts.⁹² The concerts were free of charge, but donations were welcome and a donor was given a printed libretto and assured of a good seat. Also free of charge until the mid-century were the dress rehearsals on Friday afternoons in the church organist's rehearsal hall. In 1752 admission began to be charged to these rehearsals, and in 1755 were moved to the large hall of the Lübeck stock exchange. The dress rehearsals increasingly attracted large crowds from Lübeck and its environs, and by the end of the century they had become a more important concert series than that in the church.⁹³ In 1800 the church authorities prohibited further *Abendmusiken* in the Marienkirche, because of the intolerable disturbance created by the members of the large concert audience who began to assemble during the afternoon service.⁹⁴ During the Napoleonic period, social confusion and troubles in Lübeck led to the abandonment of the *Abendmusiken* after the concerts of 1810.⁹⁵

90. For aspects of *Abendmusik* terminology, see above, in this chapter; on the librettos, see below, chap. 7. The principal writing on the Lübeck Abendmusiken is Stahl, "Abendmusiken"; see also Kerala Johnson Snyder, "Abendmusik," *New Grove*, 1:16. For a summary of the history and music of the *Abendmusiken* to the mid-century, and for more bibliography, see Smither, *Oratorio*, 2:81–102 and 120–21.

91. Cf. the comment of 1752 by Kaspar Ruetz, quoted in Stahl, "Ruetz," p. 337, n. 4.

92. See quotations to this effect from comments by Johann Adolph Scheibe and other contemporary sources in Stahl, "Abendmusiken," p. 29.

93. For details see ibid., pp. 30–33.

94. For details, see ibid., pp. 36–39.

95. Ibid., p. 38.

Secular Sponsors and Concerts. Oratorios in German formed an integral part of the burgeoning concert life, both private and public, in eighteenth-century Germany.[96] Concerts typically included oratorios during Lent, and sometimes during Advent, but occasionally outside these seasons as well. In Frankfurt, for instance, Telemann's oratorios were performed in concerts of his Collegium musicum as early as 1718.[97] Long after his departure from that city, in 1721, his oratorios continued to be heard there—until at least the 1750s—and the German oratorios of other composers (including Graun, Homilius, and Georg Anton Kreusser, 1746–1810) were also performed in Frankfurt's Lenten concerts.[98] In Schwerin, during the reign of the pietist duke Friedrich of Mecklenburg-Schwerin (r. 1756–85), secular music was prohibited at court, and *Concerts spirituels* were held twice each week. The concerts included numerous oratorios, mostly of the lyric type, composed by A. C. Kunzen, Johann Wilhelm Hertel (1727–89), Carl August Friedrich Westenholz (1736–89), Ernst Wilhelm Wolf (1735–92), Johann Friedrich Reichardt (1752–1814), J. G. Naumann, Friedrich Ludwig Benda (1752–92), and A. Rosetti.[99] In Magdeburg Johann Heinrich Rolle (1716–1785), the city's music director since 1751, founded a public concert series in 1764; the sixteen concerts per year took place in the Seidenkramer-Innung, where Rolle presented his nearly twenty dramatic oratorios between 1766 and 1785.[100] Many other German cities could be cited for concert performances of German oratorios, especially in the last quarter of the century, but the following account will treat three major ones: Hamburg, Leipzig, and Berlin.

Hamburg was an important center for the performance of oratorios in public concerts.[101] During Telemann's Hamburg period (1721–67), oratorios were frequently heard under his direction, at first in the Drillhaus, which served as a concert hall until 1761, and then in the new Concertsaal auf dem Kamp.[102] Passion oratorios were usually given several per-

96. For background on the development of concert life in Germany, see Preußner, *Bürgerliche Musikkultur.*

97. See Smither, *Oratorio,* 2:122–24.

98. See the concert chronology from 1713 to 1780 in Israël, *Frankfurt,* pp. 23–74: on the performance of Telemann's oratorios, pp. 23–38; on Graun's, p. 58; on Homilius's, p. 65; Kreusser's, p. 71.

99. See the works by these composers listed in Kade, *Mecklenburg-Schwerin*; see also, Dieter Härtwig, "Schwerin," *New Grove,,* 17:48–49; and Hans Erdmann, "Schwerin," *MGG,* 12:cols. 405–14.

100. On Rolle's life and works, and especialy the oratorios, see Kaestner, *Rolle*; Thomas A. Bauman, "Rolle," *New Grove,* 18:113–15; and Erich Valentin, "Rolle," *MGG,* 11:cols. 653–656. For a picture of the Seidenkramer-Innung, see Valentin, "Magdeburg," *MGG,* 8:col. 1474.

101. On some private concert performances of oratorios in Hamburg in 1707 and 1712, see Smither, *Oratorio,* 2:111 and 114.

102. See ibid., 2:118–20.

formances each year during Lent: most frequent among them were settings of the Brockes Passion by Telemann and Handel,[103] settings of Ramler's *Tod Jesu* by both Telemann and Graun, and Telemann's *Seliges Erwägen*.[104] Oratorios on other subjects by Telemann and his contemporaries were also performed occasionally throughout the year. Telemann usually repeated in public concerts his numerous oratorios composed for the *Kapitänsmusiken*,[105] and those for other special occasions, such as funerals, memorial services, weddings, special civic events, dedications of buildings, and ceremonies at the Gymnasium, many of which are listed in newspaper notices.[106] Hamburg's first subscription concert series that was open to the public, under the direction of the composer Friedrich Hartmann Graf, began in 1761 with the opening of the new concert hall. Graf's advance anouncement of the concerts states that they take place every Monday afternoon at five o'clock and calls special attention to "the spiritual pieces, which are set for Advent and Lent."[107] In the season 1761–62, Graf included Italian, Latin, and German oratorios, among them Graun's *Tod Jesu* and the premier performance of Telemann's last oratorio, *Der Tag des Gerichts* (1762).[108]

In 1768 C. P. E. Bach succeeded Telemann in Hamburg and continued many of the same traditions of composition and performance. Bach's public concerts, in the Drillhaus and the Concertsaal auf dem Kamp, included his own oratorios and others, including *Seliges Erwägen* by Telemann; *Die Hirten bei der Krippe zu Bethlehem* and *Die Auferstehung Christi* by Johann David Holland (1746–1827); *Die Jünger zu Emaus* by Jacob Schuback (1726–84); and Handel's *Messiah*, sung in a German translation written by Christoph Daniel Ebeling (1741–1817) and Klopstock, in 1775.[109] Bach's performance of *Messiah* was not, however, the first in Hamburg, for in 1772 Michael Arne (the son of Thomas Augustine) had performed at least part of it there, but it is not clear which language was used for that performance.[110] Arne's is the first known performance in Germany of an English oratorio by Handel. Ora-

103. On the Brockes text and settings by Keiser, Mattheson, Telemann, and Handel, see ibid., 2:111–14 and 130–38.

104. See the concert notices from the *Hamburger Correspondenten* listed in Menke, *Telemann*, Anhang A.

105. For details of the *Kapitänsmusiken*, see Maertens, "Kapitänsmusiken" (1966) and Maertens, "Kapitänsmusiken" (1975); for brief comments see Smither, *Oratorio*, 2:117–18.

106. See Menke, *Telemann*, Anhang A.

107. Translated from Sittard, *Hamburg*, p. 100.

108. Ibid.

109. Siegmund-Schultze, "*Messias*-Aufführungen," pp. 54–55; Siegmund-Schultze prints the Ebeling-Klopstock translation on pp. 73–94. On this performance, see also Miesner, *Bach*, p. 20; and Sittard, *Hamburg*, pp. 102–13.

110. Siegmund-Schultze, "*Messias*-Aufführungen," p. 52; see also Sittard, *Hamburg*, p. 110–11.

torios were also performed in concerts for the benefit of the poor, sponsored by the Freemasons and held in their lodge.[111] Private concert societies that sponsored oratorio performances, among other works, were Das Westphal'sche Concert, founded about 1770–71, and Die Gesellschaft Harmonie, founded in 1789.[112]

The Leipzig Concerts spirituels were mentioned in chapter 1 for the cultivation of Italian oratorio in Lenten concerts between 1750 and 1756, and again after 1763. An exception to the strong Italian preference in Leipzig was the performance in 1756 of Telemann's *Betrachtung über das Leiden und Sterben Jesu Christi*, which, however, was probably not a part of the Concerts spirituels.[113] In the 1763–78 series of the Großes Konzert, organized by Hiller, the only exceptions to Italian oratorios during Lent were two performances of Graun's *Tod Jesu*.[114] With the construction of the new Gewandhaus in 1781 and the establishment of a Gewandhaus series, in which Concerts spirituels were given in Advent and Lent (see chapter 1), the repertoire began to change, and German oratorios were preferred. Under Hiller's direction the German oratorios in the series included a balance of dramatic and lyric types (the former by Rolle, the latter by Graun and Johann Gottfried Schicht [1753–1823]), but beginning in 1785, when Schicht succeeded Hiller as musical director of the Gewandhaus concerts, the lyric type predominated (lyric works by Graun, Rolle, Rosetti, Johann Abraham Peter Schulz [1747–1800], Schicht, C. E. Weinlig, and E. W. Wolf; only two dramatic works, by C. P. E. Bach and Rolle).[115] Some particularly important events for the Gewandhaus were the performances of Handel's *Messiah* (1803), in German and in Mozart's arrangement; and Haydn's *Die sieben letzten Worte* (1788), *The Creation* (Gewandhaus, 1803; St. Paul's Church, 1800), and *The Seasons* (Gewandhaus, 1802; Schauspielhaus, 1801).[116]

In mid-centrury Berlin the Musikübende Gesellschaft was important for its role in concerts in the Cathedral. More significant for the cultivation of oratorio, however, was the concert series in Berlin known as the Liebhaberkonzerte, founded in 1766 by Friedrich Ernst Benda (1749–85) and Carl Ludwig Bachmann (1743–1809), and led by the latter from Benda's death till near the end of the century.[117] The members of the concert society met weekly for rehearsals and performed in concert each month an oratorio, an opera, or a cantata; their repertoire included works by Graun, Hasse, C. P. E. Bach, Rolle, and Handel. In the years 1783 and 1784 Johann Friedrich Reichardt (1752–1814) directed a series of Concerts spirituels during Lent in which both German and Italian

111. Sittard, *Hamburg*, pp. 112–13.
112. Ibid., pp. 113–20.
113. Schering, *Leipzig*, 3:269–70.
114. Ibid., p. 403.
115. See the lists of works in ibid., 3:492, and Dörffel, *Festschrift*, 1:184.
116. Dörffel, *Festschrift*, 2:23 and 26.
117. Blumner, *Sing-Akademie*, pp. 2–3.

oratorios were performed.[118] In 1786 came the first Berlin performance (described in chapter 4) of Handel's *Messiah*, in Italian, organized by Hiller and modeled on the 1784 Handel Commemoration in Westminster Abbey.

Of special importance for oratorio performance was the Berlin Sing-Akademie, of which the tentative beginnings date from about 1789. In that year, Carl Friedrich Christian Fasch (1736–1800), who was in the service of the Berlin court but also taught privately, began to present his students in private concerts of choral music. During the next several years the group grew ever larger and continued to meet regularly for rehearsals and to give private concerts. To gain more space, Fasch's society twice moved to new quarters in private homes; finally in 1793 they transferred to the building that housed the academies of arts and sciences. By association with their new location they became known as the Sing-Akademie. After the death of Fasch, Carl Friedrich Zelter (1758–1832) assumed the organization's directorship. This institution became important for the J. S. Bach and Handel revivals, but the members also sang contemporary oratorios and other choral works. Nearly every year on Good Friday from 1796 to 1884 they performed in concert Graun's *Tod Jesu*—a favorite of the court and the Berlin populace. In the 1790s and early 1800s the Good Friday concert was often given in the opera house. Other oratorios were rarely performed in the early period, for the Sing-Akademie concentrated mostly on shorter works; but Zelter's oratorio, *Die Auferstehung und Himmelfahrt Jesu*, with a lyric text by Ramler, was performed by the Sing-Akademie in 1807.[119]

118. Ibid., p. 4. On Reichardt's performance of Leo's *La morte d'Abel*, see above, chap. 3.

119. For the history of the Sing-Akademie to the early 1800s, see Blumner, *Sing-Akademie*, pp. 8–37 and the lists of works performed in *Anhang* V and VI.

CHAPTER VII

The Libretto and Music
of the German Oratorio

The Libretto

Roman Catholic Areas

The similarity between the German dramatic libretto in Roman Catholic areas and the Metastasian libretto probably reflects the cultural leadership of Vienna, for the Italian type was central to the Viennese oratorio tradition. Most librettists of dramatic German oratorios were local poets; no leading figure, no "German Metastasio," emerged whose works served as models. Some composers, however, set German translations of Metastasio's librettos and of other Italian texts. Eberlin, for instance, set Metastasio's *La Passione* in German as *Das Leiden unseres Heilandes Iesu Christi* and *S. Elena al Calvario* as *Die heilige Helena auf dem Schedelberg*; and the text of Eberlin's *Des heiligen Augustinus Bekehrung* is a translation of Maria Antonia Walpurgis's *La conversione di Sant'Agostino*, first set by Hasse.[1] (See the discussion of Hasse's version in chapter 8.) As most characteristics of the Metastasian oratorio described in chapter 2 apply equally to the German dramatic libretto in Catholic areas, only departures from that model are treated below.

Although the majority of German dramatic oratorios from Catholic areas follow the two-part division of the Italian libretto, works of one and three parts seem to have been more common among German oratorios than Italian. Of Eberlin's extant oratorios, five are in two parts, four in one part, and one in three parts.[2] Special cases are four other oratorios by Eberlin (three in German, one in Latin), which were intended as

1. Haas, "Eberlin," pp. 13–14.
2. Cf. the outlines of Eberlin's extant oratorios in ibid., p. 20 ff. According to Haas (pp. 15–16), the main librettist of Eberlin's oratorios was the Benedictine Jakob Anton [Marianus] Wimmer (1725–93), who signed his initials J. A. W.; more recent research suggests that those initials stand for Ignaz Anton Weiser (1701–85): cf. Klein, "Mozartiana," pp. 171–74, and Mozart, W. A., *Die Schuldigkeit*(KB), pp. a/12 and a/13.

interludes in Benedictine school dramas and are in two, three, and five parts. Among the one-part works is a Passion oratorio, *Der blutschwitzende Jesus*, which uses the Evangelist as a narrator.[3] The libretto is a metrical version of the Passion story, beginning with the Last Supper; the Evangelist sings only narrative in recitative, whereas the other personages have recitatives and arias: the Daughter of Sion (two arias), Peter (one), the Believing Soul (two), and Jesus (one). After the libretto reforms of Zeno and Metastasio, the role of Jesus rarely appeared in Italian oratorios, particularly to sing arias, but it did appear occasionally in German oratorios, as in this work. (See below for arias sung by Jesus in a Lübeck *Abendmusik*.) The chorus in this work is reserved for the final number. Another one-part oratorio for Salzburg is L. Mozart's *Christus begraben* (1741), of which only the libretto, written by Ignaz Anton Weiser (1701–85), is extant.[4] The oratorio includes three personages— Magdalene, Nicodemus, and Joseph of Arimathea—who reflect in dialogue (recitatives, six arias, one duet, and a final chorus) as they witness and participate in the burial of Jesus. Weiser was also the librettist of L. Mozart's one-part *Der Mensch ein Gottes Mörder*,[5] and the three-part *Die Schuldigkeit des Ersten Gebots*, by the ten-year-old W. A. Mozart, M. Haydn, and Adlgasser. Unlike the Metastasian libretto, the latter is neither biblical nor hagiographical, but an allegorical drama of the competition between the Spirit of the World and the Spirit of Christ—the latter assisted by Divine Righteousness and Divine Compassion—for the soul of "a lukewarm and later zealous Christian" ("ein lauer und hinnach eifriger Christ").[6] Part I by Mozart (the only surviving musical source) includes recitatives, seven arias, and a concluding trio. Werner's oratorios, written for the Esterházy court at Eisenstadt, are similar to the Metastasian oratorio, except for an emphasis on one-part works.[7] Unusual for its brevity is Zechner's one-part *Oratorio per il natale del nostro signore Giesù Christo*, with only three arias and a final chorus.[8]

Some of the German oratorios performed in the concerts of the Tonkünstler-Societät have dramatic librettos, as pointed out above. The one-

3. For a modern edition, see Eberlin, *Der blutschwitzende Jesus**.

4. On the identification of the poet and for related bibliography, see Carlson, "Leopold Mozart," p. 187. Called a cantata on its title page, the libretto is as long as the one-part works called oratorios by Eberlin, and in a letter of 1755 (quoted above, in chap. 6) L. Mozart refers to it, in its revised form, as an oratorio.

5. Described in Tagliavini, "Un oratorio sconosciuto."

6. Cf. the cast as listed in the facsimile of the printed libretto, in Mozart, W. A., *Die Schuldigkeit**, p. XVII; and the librettist's summary of the central ideas, quoted in Mozart, W. A., *Die Schuldigkeit* (KB), pp. a/11 and a/12.

7. Of the eight oratorios studied in Warner, "Werner," four are in one part, three in two parts, and one in three parts.

8. I am grateful to Dr. Goeffrey Chew for having given me a copy of his score, made from the manuscript parts in A-GÖ: Zechner 32.

part libretto for Beethoven's *Christus am Oelberge* (1803), written by Franz Xaver Huber (1755–1814), is a dramatic work, with language influenced by *Empfindsamkeit*.

Although the lyric oratorio was far more important in Protestant than Catholic areas, in the latter Graun's *Tod Jesu* was occasionally performed, and some concerts of the Tonkünstler-Societät included lyric works. The text of J. Haydn's *Die sieben letzten Worte unsers Erlösers am Kreuze* (ca. 1796) was arranged by Gottfried van Swieten from words that Joseph Friebert (Kapellmeister of Passau Cathedral) had in part borrowed from Ramler's *Tod Jesu* and adapted to Haydn's originally instrumental work.[9] Of the two works by Eybler performed at the concerts of the Tonkünstler-Societät, *Die Hirten* uses an anonymous text in two parts, and *Die vier letzten Dinge* is a three-part text by Josef Sonnleithner (1766–1835) on the end of the world and the Last Judgment. Although the latter text includes personages—three archangels and Adam and Eve—they all have essentially lyric lines that are narrative or descriptive, rather than dramatic.[10]

The librettos adapted by Swieten for Haydn's *The Creation* and *The Seasons* are special cases of English Handelian influence, which do not fit into the contexts of the dramatic and lyric types of the German libretto. Both librettos are treated in chapter 8.

Protestant Areas

The Dramatic Libretto. A stronghold of the dramatic oratorio in Protestant Germany was Lübeck, famous for the *Abendmusiken*, discussed in chapter 6. The text for all five parts of an oratorio, which would be performed in the course of five evenings, was printed in one booklet (see Figures VI-1 and VII-1 for characteristic title pages), and many such printed librettos survive.[11] Their librettists, mostly from Lübeck or nearby,[12] usually selected biblical subjects, among them: for Schieferdecker's works, Adam and Eve (1708), Gideon (1716), and Job (1720); for J. P. Kunzen, Haman (1749), Rebekah (1750), and Saul and David (1754); for A. C. Kunzen, the Israelites in the wilderness (1758),

---

9. Although not originally conceived as an oratorio, this work was widely regarded in its time as an oratorio of the lyric type.

10. For incipits of both works, comments on their sources, and bibliography, see Herrmann, *Eybler*, pp. 165–73. Eybler's *Hirten* does not use Ramler's text, despite the similarity of title.

11. For a general discussion of librettos for the *Abendmusiken* see Stahl, "Abendmusiken," pp. 50–54. Among the collections of printed librettos are those in B-Br (Fétis collection), D-B, and D-LÜh.

12. For biographical and bibliographical details on the poets, see Stahl, "Abendmusiken," pp. 44–49.

Bethulia saved by Judith (1759), Absalon (1761), David and Goliath (1762), and the youth of Nain (1776); and for Königslöw, three five-part librettos on different episodes of the Tobias story (1781–83), one on Esther (1787, see Figure VII-1), and one on the saving of the child Moses (1788). The text on the youth of Nain (*Der Jüngling zu Nain*), is exceptional as one of the few *Abendmusiken* based on the New Testament; it is also of interest for its treatment of the personage of Jesus, who sings two arias in part I, one in III, and one in IV—in contrast to the usual post-Zeno practice in Italian librettos of avoiding the Divinity as a personage. In some respects, however, the *Abendmusiken* are similar to the Metastasian libretto: they are virtually always dramatic and typically include four to six personages per part (performed on one concert), and the recitatives in free verse alternate with closed numbers (arias, ensembles, or choruses) in regular meter. Each part usually includes ten to fifteen numbers. Near the end of the century, in some years two or more works of one, two, or three parts—not always new works nor written for the occasion by local composers—were performed during the five concerts, and some of these were exceptional for their lyric librettos.[13]

The typical *Abendmusiken* differ remarkably from the Metastasian type and the German Catholic oratorio in the greater number of choruses and the types of texts and music used for them. In the *Abendmusiken* nearly one-half of all numbers are choruses, a proportion that considerably exceeds that of choruses in English oratorios, and their texts are of three types: chorale stanzas, biblical verses, and newly composed metrical stanzas. During the course of the century, there was evidently a considerable decrease in the use of chorale stanzas and biblical verses and a corresponding increase in newly composed texts for choruses.[14] Chorale and newly composed stanzas might be used at any point, but biblical verses were favored at the beginning and ending of a part. In the printed librettos, chorale texts are usually accompanied by identifications of the chorale tunes (often with the number in the chorale book used at the Marienkirche), suggesting audience participation in the singing.[15] Each part of an *Abendmusik* usually begins and ends with a chorus, although some begin with arias and recitatives. The text (and no doubt the music) of an opening chorus was sometimes repeated for symmetry at the end of a part. After the final chorus of part V, another chorus, designated *Schlußchor*, closes the entire *Abendmusik*. The *Schlußchor*, an epilogue of prayers and good wishes for Lübeck, its gov-

13. For a list of works by composers who were not Marienkirche organists, see Stahl, "Abendmusiken," pp. 42–43.

14. This conclusion and the following ones are based on my informal survey of a sample of printed librettos; firm conclusions must await further investigation.

15. This would be possible, of course, only if the chorale were set in simple style, as is true of the chorale in part V of J. P. Kunzen's *Absalon*, in D-LÜh: Mus. A, 160, [f. 23].

Esther,
ein geiftliches Singgedicht
von
Johann Benedikt Jacob von Königslöw
Prediger zu Holtorf und Capern
Hochgräfl. Gerichts Sattow.

In der gewöhnlichen

Abendmusik
der Stadt Lübeck

in der
Hauptkirche zu St. Marien
im Jahre 1787
zur Erbauung aufgeführt

von
Johann Wilhelm Cornelius von Königslöw

Lübeck
gedruckt von Georg Christian Green,
E. Hochedl. Hochw. Raths Buchdrucker.

Zu bekommen auf dem Werkhaufe zu St. Marien.

FIGURE VII-1. Title page of the libretto to *Esther*, a five-part *Abendmusik* of 1787 by Königslöw. (Courtesy of B-Br.)

ernment, the emperor, or the realm, is not necessarily related to the *Abendmusik*, but some librettists were able to relate it either to the oratorio's general theme or to the final chorus of part V.

In Magdeburg, one of Germany's most active composers and performers of dramatic oratorios from the 1760s to the 1780s was Johann Heinrich Rolle. His principal librettists, the Magdeburg minister Johann Samuel Patzke (1727–87) and the Halle University professor August Hermann Niemeyer (1754–1828), drew mainly on Old Testament subjects, among them the Exodus, Cain and Abel, the sacrifice of Isaac, and the daughter of Jephthah. Two of Niemeyer's dramatic librettos are exceptional: one for its New Testament story, the raising of Lazarus; and the other for its basis in a legend of martyrdom, Thirza and her sons. Rolle called his dramatic oratorios musical dramas (usually *ein musikalisches Drama* on the title page of a libretto or score), and most are divided into two or three parts—sometimes called acts or *Handlungen*. The printed librettos include vivid descriptions of scenes and actions, apparently to help the listener visualize the dramatic context; there is no evidence that any of Rolle's oratorios were performed as operas.[16] Reflecting the *Sturm und Drang* theater of the time, the librettos include strikingly dramatic dialogue and events—at times even gory. The dramatic impact is increased in the later librettos (most written by Niemeyer) at times by disregarding the traditional alternation of recitatives and closed numbers in favor of long complexes that mix choral-solo-ensemble participation and allow for a more flexible musical setting. Most of the librettos include five to seven personages, but some have many more. *Abraham auf Moria* (libretto by Niemeyer, 1776), for instance, includes fourteen personages plus two choruses. The chorus is important in these librettos (yet less so than in the *Abendmusiken*), but chorales are rare, for these works are more closely related to the theater and concert hall than to the church.[17]

The Lyric Libretto. That Friedrich Gottlieb Klopstock (1724–1803) strongly influenced the libretto of the lyric oratorio is assumed by Arnold Schering, who also states that at the time of his writing (1911) the details of such influence had yet to be investigated.[18] Even today the same situation prevails.[19] Yet the importance of Klopstock's poetic language for the poetry of *Empfindsamkeit* has been studied,[20] and Schering's hypothesis seems sound. Many librettos of the time are infused by Klopstock's language of intense, enraptured religious feeling, sharp contrasts, enthralled description of nature, and awesome mystical experience. Although he wrote no oratorio librettos, parts of his monumental *Mes-*

16. He composed his oratorios for his concert series in Magdeburg; they were also heard in Berlin's Liebhaberkonzerte, Leipzig's Concerts spirituels, Lübeck's *Abendmusiken* late in the century, and elsewhere.

17. For more on the librettos of Rolle's oratorios, and especially on *Lazarus*, see chap. 8.

18. Schering, *Oratorium*, p. 362; Schering treats Klopstock's influence on pp. 361–63.

19. For more recent comments on Klopstock's influence on oratorio librettos, see König, *Tod Jesu*, the section "Exkurs: Einfluß Klopstocks?" pp. 73–76.

20. See chap. 6, n. 15.

sias—in twenty cantos published between 1748 and 1773—were set by Telemann, Rolle, and others as lyric oratorios or cantatas. Telemann's setting, called on its libretto title page *Zween Auszüge aus dem Gedichte: der Messias* (Hamburg, [1759?]),[21] is a two-part work: part I is from the first canto, "Sing, unsterbliche Seele," of *Messias*, and part II, from the tenth, "Mirjams, und deine Wehmut."[22] Rolle set Klopstock's poetry in his *Messias* (1764), *David und Jonathan* (1766; not an oratorio but a brief dialogue), and *Der leidende Jesu* (1777).[23] Klopstock's tragedy, *Der Tod Adams* (1757) formed the point of departure for Patzke's dramatic libretto, *Adams Tod*, set by M. Haydn (ca. 1778).

In contrast to German dramatic librettos, which were usually written by local poets and set only once, the lyric librettos by Ramler and Zachariä were set by numerous composers and served as models for other librettists. In fact, a reviewer of 1761 spoke of Ramler as a "German Metastasio."[24]

A student at Halle, Carl Wilhelm Ramler (1725–98) moved to Berlin in 1745, taught philosophy at the Prussian cadet school from 1748 to 1790, and directed the Royal National Theater from 1787–96.[25] For more than thirty years he was the recognized spokesman for poetic taste in Berlin.[26] His three librettos for lyric oratorios (or cantatas, see the treatment of terminology early in chapter 6), written in the mid-century, were immensely popular. *Der Tod Jesu* was set by Telemann and Graun in 1755, and later by J. C. F. Bach, Christian Ernst Graf (1723–1804), Silvester Julius Krauß, and G. A. Kreusser;[27] borrowings from it are used in J. Haydn's *Die sieben letzten Worte*. Ramler's Christmas oratorio, *Die Hirten bei der Krippe zu Bethlehem*, was set by Johann Friedrich Agricola (1720–74), J. C. F. Bach, Georg Wilhelm Gruber (1729–96), Holland, Johann Balthasar Kehl (1725–78), Johann Friedrich Reichardt (1752–1814), Telemann, Daniel Gottlieb Türk (1750–1813), Stanislaus Spindler (1763–1819), and C. A. F. Westenholz; and his libretto for Easter and Ascension, *Die Auferstehung und Himmelfahrt*, by Agricola, J. C. F. Bach, C. P. E. Bach, Johann Gottfried Krebs (1741–1814), Reichardt, Johann Adolph Scheibe (1708–76), Telemann, Georg Joseph Vogler (1749–1814), and Zelter.

All three of Ramler's librettos were printed in collections of his poetry

21. See libretto in D-B: Mus. Tt 140.

22. For a detailed study of Telemann's setting, see Godehart, "Telemanns *Messias*."

23. Bauman, "Rolle," *New Grove*, 16:114.

24. *Bibliothek der schönen Wissenschaften* 7/1 (1761): 194, as quoted in König, *Tod Jesu*, p. 31.

25. Peter Branscombe, "Ramler," *New Grove*, 15:575; Richard Daunicht, "Ramler," *MGG*, 10:cols. 1908–9.

26. König, *Tod Jesu*, p. 78.

27. For brief comments on these composers and their settings, see König, *Tod Jesu*, pp. 34–39.

FIGURE VII-2. Title page of Ramler's collection of lyric oratorios or cantatas in an early edition. (Reproduced by permission of GB-Lbl.)

as one-part works,[28] but in their musical settings and performances some of them were divided into two or three parts.[29] In *Tod Jesu* Ramler indicates the type of setting (recitative, aria, duet, chorus, chorale) to be used for each of the numbers, and he specifies the traditional chorale tunes to which the chorale texts should be sung. He does not provide such indications for setting the texts of his other two librettos, and in neither of them does he include chorales. His intentions as to the type of setting are clear, for he follows the traditional metrical conventions of the musical libretto: regular meters for arias, ensembles, and choruses and freer ones for recitatives. The longest librettos are *Tod Jesu* (with twenty-five numbers, including recitatives) and *Auferstehung und Himmelfahrt* (twenty numbers). *Hirten bey der Krippe* (eight numbers), is quite brief—more like a cantata than an oratorio—but Westenholtz extends it by adding a chorale at the beginning, another at the end, and three within the work.

Ramler's librettos do not include named personages. To replace drama with lyricism and to intensify the role of the reader-listener as an active participant, the poet assumes the viewpoints of unnamed, "idealized," personages who witness, describe, and reflect upon the events of the story; in the process they reveal their feelings about the subject and its religious meaning. Characteristic of Ramler's texts is the beginning of the opening recitative in *Hirten bey der Krippe*:

Hier schläft es,—o wie süß!—	Here he sleeps,—o how sweet!—
Und lächelt in dem Schlafe,	and smiles in his sleep,
das holde Kind.	the noble Child.
Hier schläft das Kind vom Stamm	Here sleeps the Child from the
des Hirten David;	root of the shepherd David;
Hier schläft auf weichem Klee,	here sleeps on soft clover,
Auf frisch gemähten Blumen	on freshly cut flowers,
der Hirten Gott.	the shepherd God.
Ja! ja! der Hirten Gott![30]	Yes! Yes! The shepherd God!

28. For example, see Ramler, *Kantaten*.

29. Two-part performances of Graun's one-part setting of *Tod Jesu* are mentioned above (see the reference in chap. 6, n. 82). Agricola's *Auferstehung und Himmelfahrt* (1750s?; D-Bds, Mus. Ms. autogr. Agricola 4) is in one part, as is Krebs's (1774; D-B, Mus. Ms. 11,989); C. P. E. Bach's setting (1777–80; Bach, C. P. E., *Auferstehung**) is in two parts, and Zelter's (1807; printed librettos in D-B, Mus. Tz 103 [Berlin, 1810] and D-LEm, PT 2149 [Berlin, 1813]) is in three. Zelter's preface printed in both librettos explains his rationale for the three-part division. For one-part settings of *Hirten bey der Krippe* see Agricola (1750s?; D-Bds, Mus. Ms. autogr. Agricola 5), Westenholtz (1765; printed libretto in B-Br, Fétis 4545 [Schwerin, n.d.]), and Türk (1782; D-B, Mus. Tt 502 [Berlin, n.d.]).

30. Quoted from libretto (Leipzig: Breitkopfischen Buchdruckerey, 1784), possibly printed for Türk's setting, in D-LEm: 18 IB; and verified with a libretto

The use of present tense and of simple, direct language contribute a sense of intimacy; lyric description and emotional reaction are emphasized. The delicacy and idyllic quality of the images—the sweet, smiling child, the bed of clover and freshly cut flowers, the child as the shepherd God—and the exclamations and repetitions for emotional impact are characteristic of this libretto in general. The recitative continues for fourteen more lines of irregular meter, with pastoral images reflecting the ways in which the world is transformed by the birth of Jesus. Then the first aria speaks of the new period as a golden age and exhorts the shepherds to rejoice:

Hirten aus den goldnen Zeiten,	Shepherds from the golden age,
Blast die Flöten, rührt die Saiten!	blow your flutes, touch your strings!
Euer Tagewerk sey Freude,	Let your daily work be joy,
Euer Leben sey Gesang!	let your lives be song!
Gott der Hirten, dessen Macht	God of shepherds, whose might
Aus der Wüste Sin und Kades	made God's garden out of the
Einen Garten Gottes macht,	wilderness of Zin and Kadesh,
Ach! mit welchen Zungen	ah! with what tongues
Wird dein Lob gesungen?	will thy praise be sung?
Nimm zum Lobe meine Freude!	Take my joy for praise!
Meine Freude sey dein Dank!	Let my joy be thy thanks!
[Da capo]³¹	[Da capo]

Using the regular meter and da capo structure characteristic of the arias, the poet or anonymous personage addresses the shepherds of the Christmas story (A section) and then the mighty God of shepherds, whom he thanks with his joy (B section).

Quite different in content but equally emotive and representative of literary *Empfindsamkeit*—with the use of present tense, simple and direct language, idealized personages, and images drawn from nature—are Ramler's other two librettos, *Tod Jesu* and *Auferstehung*. Quotations from both, in the musical settings by Graun and C. P. E. Bach respectively, are treated in chapter 8.

Friedrich Wilhelm Zachariä (1726–77) attended the universities of Leipzig and Göttingen before moving to Brunswick in 1748 to become a teacher at the Collegium Carolinum, where he was appointed a professor in 1761.³² Active primarily as an editor and a poet, many of his lyric

definitely for Türk, printed for a *Konzert der Musikliebhaber zu Berlin* (n.d.) in D-B: Mus. Tt 502.

31. Quoted from sources as above—D-LEm: 18 IB; and D-B: Mus. Tt 502.

32. On his life and works, see the articles on him by Peter Branscombe in *New Grove*, 20:614; and by Urte Härtwig in *MGG*, 14: cols. 964–66.

poems appeared in published collections of songs. He was also a musician and published a few vocal and instrumental works. He wrote one dramatic oratorio text, *Die Pilgrime auf Golgatha* (1756), set by Albrechtsberger (see chapter 6), Kehl, Georg Simon Löhlein (1725–81), and Georg Abraham Schneider (1770–1839).[33] This one-part libretto with four personages and twenty-four numbers (including recitatives) uses language typical of *Empfindsamkeit* and the lyric oratorio, but is not based on a familiar story and thus includes more narrative and dramatic writing than does the lyric oratorio. The idea for the work would seem to have been derived from S. B. Pallavicino's *I pellegrini al sepolcro* (1742), set by Hasse. Zachariä's three lyric texts that are comparable in length to oratorios are *Die Tageszeiten* (1756), *Die Auferstehung* (1761), and *Das befreyte Israel* (1761), all of which were set by Telemann. In 1764 Rolle set the last-named libretto, but in a version that Christoph Christian Sturm (1740–86) had transformed into a dramatic work by the addition of new text and personages.[34]

Like Ramler, Zachariä does not include personages in his lyric librettos. *Tageszeiten* was possibly modeled on the long poem by James Thomson (1700–48), *The Seasons* (1726–30),[35] which was to form the basis of Swieten's libretto for J. Haydn's work of the same name. Consisting of four parts that reflect on times of the day—morning, noon, evening, and night—*Tageszeiten* is essentially a nature poem with relatively little religious content of the type characteristic of oratorio librettos in the time.[36] Thus it is a borderline work, between oratorio and secular cantata, as is Haydn's *The Seasons*. *Auferstehung* and *Israel*, however, are both within the main stream of the lyric oratorio.

Die Auferstehung as set by Telemann is in one part with twelve sections, numbered in the printed libretto, plus a final chorus.[37] Some of the sections begin with soloists and close with choruses, and others are entirely for soloists; although the type of solo setting is not indicated, the meters leave little doubt as to the poet's intentions. The libretto fluctuates between reflections on and descriptions of the Resurrection story in the present tense and narrations of it in the past tense. Thus the work begins with the anonymous personage approaching the grave of Jesus:

33. The setting by Schneider, not listed in the articles on him in *New Grove* or *MGG*, is listed in Geck, *Deutsche Oratorien*, p. 33, and dated 1807.

34. Kaestner, *Rolle*, pp. 29 and 51–52.

35. Schering, *Oratorium*, p. 381; Härtwig, "Zachariä," *MGG*, 14:col. 965.

36. The modern edition, Telemann, *Tageszeiten**(pv), is essentially a reproduction of the edition by Alfred Guttmann (Berlin: Deutscher Arbeiter-Sängerbund, 1928), in which the libretto includes even less religious content than does the original—Guttmann wished to eliminate the "pietistische Wendungen" (see the introduction by Guttmann, p. 2).

37. A copy of the libretto, *Die Auferstehung. Ein musikalisches Gedicht* (Hamburg: J. C. Piscator, [1761?]) is in D-B: Mus. Tt 123.

Du tiefe, todte, grauenvolle Stille

Ums heilige Grab; um des
  Geopferten,
Des gottversöhners Grab!
Verhülle mich! Verhülle
Mein Herz in Traurigkeit, mein
  Aug in Nacht!

You deep, deathly, dreadful
  stillness
around the holy grave; around the
  grave of the sacrificed one,
the grave of the God-Atoner.
Cover me! Cover
my heart in sorrow, my eyes in
  night

As the recitative continues, the personage sees that the sepulchre is open:

Doch wie? Das Grab is offen?—
  Leer!
Wie schauderts mich! Auch nicht
  den Todten mehr—

Yet what is that? The grave is
  open?—Empty!
How I shudder! No longer dead—

The chorus bursts forth, jubilantly proclaiming the Resurrection, and a narrative section follows, again in recitative:

Der Engel Gottes fuhr herab!
Schnell, wie der wetterleuchtende
  Blitz;
Sein Kleid war weiß, wie der
  schimmernde Schnee.

The angel of God came down!
Fast, as the summer lightening;

his clothing was white, as the
  shimmering snow.

Such lines as these are free elaborations of the Resurrection story in the Bible.

Zachariä's *Das befreyte Israel*, unlike most lyric oratorios, is based on an Old Testament passage: the canticle of Moses after the crossing of the Red Sea, from Exodus, chapter 15.[38] The same source is used by Handel for his *Israel in Egypt*. In one part divided into nine sections (numbered in the libretto printed for Telemann), the work consists largely of a free poetic paraphrase of its biblical source; like its source, it fluctuates between present and past tense. Probably because the libretto is a close paraphrase of the biblical passage, its language is less that of *Empfindsamkeit* than is the freer language of *Auferstehung*.

Especially important from the literary standpoint are the lyric oratorio

---

38. The full title of the libretto printed for Telemann is: *Das befreyte Israel. Ein musikalisches Gedicht. Nach Anleitung des Mosaischen Lobgesanges im 15 Capitel des 2 B. Mose* (Hamburg: Jeremias Conrad Piscator, [1761?]); a copy is in D-B: Tt 135. A modern edition of the oratorio is in Telemann, *Donerode; Befreite Israel**.

librettos of Johann Gottfried Herder (1744–1803), written between 1772 and 1776 at the Bückeburg court of Count Wilhelm of Schaumburg-Lippe, and set to music by J. C. F. Bach: *Die Kindheit Jesu: Ein Oratorium* (1772), *Die Auferweckung Lazarus: Eine biblische Geschichte zur Musik* (1773), and *Der Fremdling auf Golgatha: Eine biblische Geschichte mit Gesang* (1764, rev. 1776).[39] Among the significant literary figures of his time, Herder was an admirer of Klopstock and adopted in his librettos the vocabulary of *Empfindsamkeit* and lyric verse. Yet he used named personages and rejected the approach of those who did not; highly critical of Ramler's oratorios, he wrote: "Who sings, who narrates in the recitatives? Suddenly a useful teaching [is] drawn from the biblical story; through the whole no standpoint, no continuing thread of feeling [*Empfindung*], of plan, of purpose."[40] Herder includes five personages and a chorus of shepherds in *Kindheit Jesu*, and six personages and an undesignated chorus in *Auferweckung Lazarus*; in the latter work the personage of Jesus sings recitatives and joins Mary and Martha in a trio. Herder was the translator of Handel's *Messiah* for the first performances of that work in Weimar, 1780–81, under the direction of E. W. Wolf;[41] as late as 1824 Goethe vividly remembered the strong impact that the work made on him at those performances.[42]

Of the numerous other poets who wrote lyric oratorios, Heinrich Julius Tode (1733–97) may have been the most prolific. A Lutheran minister at Pritzier and later an alderman of the Schwerin Church Council, Tode wrote at least nineteen librettos for lyric oratorios and cantatas, mostly for composers who wrote for the Schwerin court.[43] Among these composers are J. W. Hertel, who set Tode's seven-part lyric Passion, one part of which is *Jesus in Gethsemane* (1780), set separately as a lyric oratorio by both E. W. Wolf (1788–89) and A. Rosetti (1790). The text by Christian Wilhelm Alers (1737–1806) for Telemann's *Der Tag des Gerichts* is in four parts, in which personages (most of whom are allegorical, but who provide a dramatic element) describe and reflect on the Last Judgement.[44] Karl Zinkernagel, of the Oettingen-Wallerstein court, wrote two lyric librettos, both with designated personages: *Der sterbende Jesus*, first performed in 1785 at Wallerstein in a setting by Ro-

39. The dates are those of the librettos, according to Walter Wiora, "Herder," *MGG*, 6:col. 206. For modern editions of the last two settings, see Bach, J. C. F., *Kindheit Jesu**, and idem, *Auferweckung Lazarus**.

40. Translated from Schering, *Oratorium*, p. 368, n. 2, as quoted from Herder's *Naschrift* to *Von deutscher Art und Kunst* (1773), p. 117.

41. For Herder's translation, see Siegmund-Schultze, "*Messias*-Aufführungen," pp. 73–94.

42. In Goethe's review of Reichardt's *Für Freunde der Tonkunst.* Cf. Friedrich Blume, "Goethe," *MGG*, 5:col. 440.

43. For a list of some of these, and for brief biographical information, see Meyer, *Mecklenburg-Schwerin*, pp. 81 (and n. 1), 121, 152, 161, and 268.

44. A modern edition is Telemann, *Tag des Gerichts**.

setti,[45] and *Die Auferstehung Jesu* (1794), set in 1794 by Ignaz von Beecke (1733–1803) and later by Friedrich Witt (1770–1836).[46]

Of special interest is the libretto of the remarkable poet and composer Joseph Martin Kraus (1756–92), who wrote both the text and music of his *Der Tod Jesu* (1776). Originally the second of a pair of oratorios (the first, *Die Geburt Jesu*, is lost), his *Tod Jesu* was strongly influenced by Klopstock's treatment of the Passion in his *Messias* and by Ramler's *Tod Jesu*. Kraus's one-part work, without personages, has been called "an oratorio of the *Sturm und Drang* movement" in both its literary and musical aspects.[47]

The Music: General Characteristics

Early Classical traits appear later in German oratorios than in Italian. Although such traits become increasingly common in the Italian oratorio beginning in the 1720s, they do so in the German oratorio only in the 1740s. North German oratorios written before that time—by Reinhard Keiser, J. S. Bach, and Telemann, among others—represent late Baroque style.[48] Before the 1740s the relatively few German oratorios in Roman Catholic areas—early works by G. J. Werner at Eisenstadt, for instance—exhibit more late Baroque than early Classical characteristics. Because of the relative conservatism of the German oratorio, the present section covers a shorter period—from the mid-eighteenth century to the beginning of the nineteenth—than does the comparable section on the Italian oratorio in chapter 2. In chapter 8 a more detailed treatment of seven oratorios will help illustrate the general comments of this section.

Among the aspects of the German oratorio that are relatively constant from the mid-eighteenth century to the early nineteenth are those of general structure that depend upon the text and have been mentioned above in the section on the libretto: considerable variety in the number of parts (from one to five, occasionally even more); the alternation between recitative on the one hand and aria, ensemble, or chorus on the other (characteristic of both dramatic and lyric oratorios in German); the frequent use of chorus; and the inclusion of chorales in Protestant works. Other constants, which the German oratorio has in common with the eighteenth-century oratorio in general, are the musical interpretation of the affects and imagery of the texts and the tendency toward

45. Libretto in D-Au (formerly D-HR: III, 8, 8 o, 1480).

46. Librettos in D-Au (formerly D-HR: III, 8, 8 o, 1480) and D-B: Mus. T 89/18, respectively.

47. It is so treated in the article, Van Boer, "Kraus"; for a discussion of the libretto and its relationship to Klopstock and Ramler, see ibid., pp. 70–72. For a modern edition of the work, see Kraus, *Tod Jesu**.

48. On earlier eighteenth-century German oratorio, see Smither, *Oratorio* 2:105–69.

overall tonal planning. Essentially the same patterns and phases of change—described in chapter 2 as early Classical, Classical, and late Classical—are found in the German oratorio. These changes are treated below in two overlapping periods: from the 1740s to the 1770s and from the 1770s to 1803 (the date of Beethoven's *Christus am Oelberge*).

From the 1740s to the 1770s

This period includes composers from both the Protestant North and the Catholic South who combined late Baroque and early Classical traits in their oratorios, and also contemporaneous composers who more fully represent the new style. Among the first group are Telemann in Hamburg and G. J. Werner, J. Haydn's predecessor, in Eisenstadt. For instance, in Telemann's later oratorios (1755–62)—such as *Der Tag des Gerichts* (1762—and in Johann Balthasar Kehl's *Die Pilgrimme auf Golgatha* (1762?–74)[49] some arias are found that mix the old and new textures and phrasing, and others are more clearly within the new style. In Werner's later oratorios hints of early Classical style appear in some arias, but fugal treatment is found not only in most of the oratorios' instrumental introductions—which often suggest the French overture with their slow beginnings followed by fugues—and also at times within the arias.[50]

More numerous in this period, however, are the oratorios that clearly reflect the new stylistic developments. Among the works that are available in musical sources and represent the early Classical style in Protestant Germany are: composed for Berlin, C. H. Graun's *Tod Jesu* (1755), treated below, and Agricola's *Die Hirten bey der Krippe* and *Auferstehung und Himmelfahrt*;[51] for the *Abendmusiken* in Lübeck, A. C. Kunzen's *Israels Abgötterei in der Wüsten* (1758) and *Absalon* (1761);[52] for Eisenach, Johann Ernst Bach's *Passionsoratorium* (1764);[53] for Bückeburg, J. C. F. Bach's *Die Kindheit Jesu* (1773) and *Auferweckung*

49. Manuscript source: D-LÜh: Mus. A 10a.

50. Eight of Werner's oratorios are described in Warner, "Werner," in which the conclusion, pp. 180–92, briefly treats Werner's mixture of new and old styles. As a tribute to Werner, in 1804 Joseph Haydn published as string quartets six of Werner's oratorio introductions (most with a slow first section followed by a fugue): see Werner, *Sechs Fugen**; for information on Haydn's publication, see Somfai, "Haydns Tribut." For six other oratorio introductions, see Werner, *Sechs Oratorienvorspiele**.

51. Manuscript sources for the Agricola works: D-Bds: Mus. Ms. autogr. Agricola 4 and 5, respectively.

52. These are the only two oratorios by A. C. Kunzen known to have been performed in *Abendmusiken* for which musical sources survive. *Israels Abgötterei*, D-Bds: Mus. ms. autog. A. K. Kunzen 2; *Absalon*, D-LÜh: Mus. A 160.

53. Modern edition: Bach, J. E., *Passionsoratorium**.

Lazarus (1773);[54] and for Altenburg, J. G. Krebs's *Auferstehung und Himmelfahrt Jesu* (1774).[55] In the Catholic South, Salzburg was of special importance, and the early Classical style is represented there by Eberlin's *Der blutschwitzende Jesus* and thirteen other extant oratorios, all from the mid-century;[56] Adlgasser's *Christus am Ölberg* (1754) and *Die wirkende Gnade Gottes* (1756);[57] L. Mozart's *Der Mensch ein Gottes Mörder*;[58] W. A. Mozart's *Die Schuldigkeit des ersten Gebots* (1767);[59] and Michael Haydn's six extant oratorios.[60] At Krems an der Donau, J. G. Zechner composed at least twelve German oratorios; his brief *Oratorio per il natale del nostro signore Giesù Christo* (1738) shows some early Classical tendencies.[61] Although all the composers and works in this list share, to a greater or lesser extent, the early Classical style, they differ not only in their individual musical languages but also according to the regions in which they were active. Compared with the composers in Catholic areas, for instance, those of the Protestant North characteristically place more emphasis on the chorus (including chorales) and tend to write in a slightly more complex harmonic and contrapuntal style. In oratorios of the South—those by Eberlin, for instance—the texture and harmonic language tend to be closer to the simple, Italian version of the early Classical style.

A number of the North German works just mentioned are settings of lyric librettos. In view of the close relationship between the lyric libretto and literary *Empfindsamkeit*, it is important to address the question of musical *Empfindsamkeit* in relation to oratorio. Although passages similar to what is generally called *empfindsamer Stil*, or *Empfindsamkeit*—the frequent use of sigh motives, sudden contrasts, and "sentimental" harmonies and melodic figures—may be found in many oratorios of this period (and in operas and church music as well), these traits alone would seem doubtful criteria for determining *empfindsamer Stil*.[62] Oratorio by

54. Modern edition: Bach, J. C. F., *Kindheit Jesu**.

55. Manuscript source: D-B: Mus. ms. 11989.

56. Modern edition: Eberlin, *Der blutschwitzende Jesus**. The other oratorios (four of which functioned as interludes in Benedictine school dramas) are described in Haas, "Eberlin."

57. Described in Schneider, "Adlgasser."

58. Described in Tagliavini, "Un oratorio sconisciuto."

59. Modern edition: Mozart, W. A., *Die Schuldigkeit**.

60. Listed in Charles H. Sherman's worklist in "Michael Haydn," *New Grove*, 8:410–11.

61. For the source see above, n. 8. Zechner's oratorios are listed in Riedel, "Krems," pp. 324–25.

62. On the characteristics of *empfindsamer Stil* and *Empfindsamkeit* in music, see Daniel Heartz, "Empfindsamkeit," *New Grove*, 6:157–59, and especially the analysis of *empfindsam* elements in the first recitative of Graun's *Tod Jesu*, which are essentially operatic elements; Helm, "Bach, III: (9)," *New Grove*, 1:851; and Newman, *Sonata in the Classic Era*, pp. 122–24.

its very nature—as a work for concert hall or church, often using relatively large forces—lacks the intimate quality associated in the eighteenth century with the musical evocation of the *Empfindungen*. That quality is the property of solo and small ensemble music, and especially of the clavichord, which requires an intimate environment—without which it can scarcely be heard—and allows for extreme delicacy of nuance. In fact, the clavichord is the most characteristic instrument of *empfindsamer Stil* and was the favorite of C. P. E. Bach, who is most closely associated with this style. Thus the terms *empfindsamer Stil* and *Empfindsamkeit* are questionable for the musical aspect of oratorios, operas, church cantatas, and other genres intended for large audiences, even though their texts might represent literary *Empfindsamkeit*.[63]

The arias of German oratorios from this period, in both the North and the South, are stylistically and structurally like those of Italian oratorios and serious opera. Arias typically use the full da capo form or the shortened, dal segno version that omits the opening ritornello (cf. Table II-1). The other abbreviated da capo forms (half, condensed, and quarter da capo—cf. Table II-2) are virtually absent, as are transformed da capo arias (cf. Table II-3).[64] German oratorios, like Italian, rarely include more than two ensembles—usually duets, or an occasional trio. Exceptional are the oratorios of Eberlin, in which trios, quartets, and quintets are heard.[65] Ensembles tend to be similar in structure to arias, except that non-da capo forms, including transformed da capo schemes, are sometimes found.

Most recitatives are in simple style, accompanied by basso continuo only. At particularly expressive points in the text or for the words of an important personage—Jesus, for instance—the simple recitatives tend to become arioso and to exhibit a contrapuntal relationship between the voice and continuo. Accompanied recitative appears from two to about five times within an oratorio; although some recitatives alternate between simple and accompanied style, particularly important ones are accompanied throughout. A curious exception in recitative practice is found in Eberlin's *Der blutschwitzende Jesus*. Except for one brief introductory recitative sung by Jesus and two by the Evangelist, both in simple style, the recitatives sung by Jesus, the Evangelist, and the Disciples (with texts based on the biblical Passion) are set as accompanied recitative and are modeled closely on chant recitation formulas.[66] Thus the work has a decidedly liturgical sound, and the orchestra is heard almost throughout.

Most choruses in German oratorios of this period mix chordal and

---

63. See also chap. 8, on Graun's *Tod Jesu* and C. P. E. Bach's *Auferstehung*.

64. According to Schneider, "Adlgasser," p. 55, arias in some of these forms, including arias in "Sonatensatzform," are found in Adlgasser's music for school dramas.

65. See the outlines of Eberlin's oratorios in Haas, "Eberlin," pp. 17–20.

66. For an analysis of the recitative and a comparison with chant formulas, see Haas, "Eberlin," pp. 26–28.

imitative styles, but the former predominates. Final choruses, however, tend to include more imitative writing and sometimes a fugue. Chorales are usually set in the simple, chordal style, but occasionally they are elaborated, with orchestral passages heard between the chorale phrases.

Protestant oratorios frequently begin with a vocal number, often a chorale, rather than an instrumental piece. Of the works listed above, for instance, those by Agricola, J. C. F. Bach, J. E. Bach, C. H. Graun, Krebs, and A. C. Kunzen all begin with a chorus (sometimes a chorale setting) or a recitative; Telemann's *Der Tag des Gerichts* begins with a French overture, as does Kehl's *Die Pilgrimme auf Golgatha*. In the South, introductory instrumental pieces are characteristic: mentioned above are Werner's introductions, usually called "Introductio," which recall the French overture, but he also used two- and three-movement introductions that suggest the style and structures of the Italian sinfonia;[67] Zechner's *Oratorio per il natale del nostro signore Giesù Christo* begins with a one-movement binary "Introitus"; all but one of Eberlin's oratorios begin with a one-movement *sinfonia* in binary form of a type that has been called a "primitive two-part sonata form";[68] and of the two oratorios by Adlgasser mentioned above, the first has a binary "Introduzione" comparable to the *sinfonie* of Eberlin's oratorios and the second approximates a French overture.[69]

From the 1770s to Beethoven's Christus (1803)

In this period are grouped composers who participated in the development of the Classical and late Classical styles. Included here for reasons of the styles of their later oratorios—despite the early dates and different styles of their first ones—are C. P. E. Bach and Rolle. Active as an oratorio composer in Hamburg, Bach wrote three major oratorios, *Die Israeliten in der Wüste* (1769; pub. Hamburg, 1775), *Die letzten Leiden des Erlösers* (1770); and *Auferstehung und Himmelfahrt Jesu* (1777–78; pub. Leipzig, 1787); the last-named work is discussed in chapter 8. From the 1750s to the 1780s, Rolle composed for Magdeburg six oratorios with lyric texts and nearly twenty with dramatic texts. Among the dramatic oratorios, for which he became well known, is *Lazarus, oder die Feyer der Auferstehung* (1778; pub. Leipzig, 1779; see chapter 8). Other oratorios that represent the styles of this period include: in Buchen, Kraus's *Der Tod Jesu* (1776);[70] in Dresden, Homilius's *Die Freude der*

67. In Werner, *Sechs Oratorienvorspiele**, the forms similar to the French overture are those for the oratorios *Daniel*, 1:22–33; *Der gute Hirt*, 1:34–50; *Die allgemeine Auferstehung*, 2:23–36; and *David*, 2:37–50. In two movements (Vivace and Molto allegro) is the introduction to *Debora*, 1:11–21; and in three movements (fast-slow-fast) is the introduction to *Judas Machabaeus*, 2:11–22.

68. Haas, "Eberlin," p. 24.

69. Schneider, "Adlgasser," p. 56.

70. Modern edition: Kraus, *Tod Jesu**.

Hirten über die Geburt Jesu (1777);[71] in Halle, Türk's *Die Hirten bei der Krippe zu Bethlehem* (pub. Leipzig, 1782);[72] in Berlin, J. C. Kühnau's *Das Weltgericht* (1783);[73] in Mainz, Kreusser's *Der Tod Jesu* (1783);[74] and in Leipzig, J. G. Schicht's *Die Feier der Christen auf Golgatha* (1784).[75] Two brief Danish works that, in translation, became popular oratorios in the German repertoire are F. L. A. Kunzen's *Die Auferstehung* (1796) and *Das Halleluja der Schöpfung* (pub. Zurich, 1797?).[76]

In Vienna, with its strong Italian oratorio tradition, the German oratorio was a rarity before this period. Beginning in 1779, however, German oratorios began to appear on the concerts of the Tonkünstler-Societät, as we have seen. The crowning Viennese achievements in oratorio were Haydn's *The Creation* (1798; pub. Vienna, 1800) and *The Seasons* (1801; pub. Leipzig, 1802)—the former published with German and English texts, the latter in two versions, German-French and German-English. Although Haydn's oratorios—strongly influenced by the English oratorio of Handel—represent a departure for the German oratorio, Beethoven's *Christus am Oelberge* (1803; pub. Leipzig, 1811) continues the German Passion-oratorio tradition, despite its unusually dramatic approach to the subject matter.

The styles and structures of arias in most oratorios of the period continue to parallel those in Italian oratorio and serious opera. The trend away from the da capo and dal segno aria and ensemble, noted in the discussion of the Italian oratorio, is clear also in the German oratorio. An indication of the trend may be seen even within the oratorios of one composer, C. P. E. Bach: in the first two of his oratorios listed above, nearly all the arias have either the da capo or dal segno form; in *Auferstehung*, however, there is only one.da capo aria and no dal segno. Also in the oratorios by other composers mentioned above, the da capo and dal segno forms become rare in the 1770s and 1780s and are virtually nonexistent by the 1790s. The most common substitute for the da capo and dal segno aria is the transformed da capo (cf. Table II-3). In Bach's *Auferstehung*, for instance, all arias but the one in da capo form have the A1-B-A2 form, as does the duet. The transformed da capo structures continue to be common to the end of the period under consid-

---

71. Described in John, *Homilius*, pp. 218–19.

72. Described in Serauky, *Halle*, 2:227–28; long musical examples in ibid., "Musikbeilagen," pp. 28–48.

73. For a long and enthusiastic review of this work (signed by "M***") as performed on 6 May 1783 in Berlin's Dreifaltigkeitskirche, with an orchestra of about 70 and a *Schülerchor* of 36, see Cramer's *Magazin der Musik* 1/2 (1783): 848–52.

74. See the long, favorable review in ibid., 1350–58.

75. For an unfavorable review, see ibid., 2/2 (1786): 879–82.

76. Manuscript sources: *Auferstehung*, D-LÜh: Mus. A 48a; *Halleluja*, D-LÜh: Mus. A 49a.

eration here—both Haydn and Beethoven use them. In the arias of *The Creation*, however, Haydn often retains the tonal but not the melodic relationships of the A1 and A2 sections. Ensembles, which become more frequent in this period, are also more varied, in part because the texts show greater variety. Particularly in dramatic ensembles, such as the trio in the finale-complex of Beethoven's *Christus*, the composer creates flexible structures that correspond to the exigencies of the text.

Accompanied recitative increasingly replaces simple recitative. Again, a comparison of the first two of C. P. E. Bach's oratorios listed above with the third is revealing: in the first two, about one-third of the recitatives are accompanied; in *Auferstehung*, however, all but one are accompanied. Around the turn of the century, some oratorios—those by F. L. A. Kunzen and Beethoven, for instance—include only accompanied recitatives; although Haydn uses both types, some of his most creative text setting in *The Creation* and *The Seasons* is found in the accompanied recitatives.

The influence of Gluck's close association of drama and music is suggested, to some extent, in Rolle's setting of the *Sturm und Drang* texts of his dramatic oratorios (and partially in the introductory instrumental pieces, mentioned below). Quite unusual for the 1770s and 1780s is Rolle's flexible intermingling of simple and accompanied recitative with ariosos, arias, ensembles, and choruses in the service of dramatic and musical continuity. (See the discussion of his *Lazarus* in chapter 8.)

The emphasis on the chorus that had long been characteristic of the German oratorio continues in this period, as does the use of the chorale in Protestant works. As in the period ca. 1740–70, the most common texture for choruses is chordal, with occasional imitative passages and sometimes a closing fugue. The strong Handelian influence that prompted the composition of Haydn's *The Creation* and *The Seasons* is clearly visible in the large number and variety of the choruses in those works—particularly those choruses containing fugues. Although the combination of soloists with chorus is relatively rare in German oratorio until the end of the century, one finds that combination in the oratorios of Rolle, no doubt stemming from his interest in intermingling various styles and textures mentioned above. In both *The Creation* and *The Seasons*, Haydn includes soloists with the choruses more often than not.

As in the previous period, some Protestant oratorios begin without an instrumental introduction. The first two of C. P. E. Bach's oratorios and the Kunzen works, for instance, have only orchestral introductions to their opening vocal numbers. Although Rolle uses the French overture as an introductory piece to to his *Lazarus* and Bach uses that form prior to the first appearance of Moses in *Die Israeliten* (probably to lend majesty to this important figure), the French overture disappears from oratorios during the course of the period under consideration. The instrumental pieces that begin oratorios or parts of oratorios are used increasingly to paint the mood of the first number or of the work as a whole—possibly another influence of Gluck's opera reform. Examples are the introductions to both parts of Bach's *Auferstehung*, the introductions to all three acts of Rolle's *Lazarus*, and the introduction to Türk's *Hirten*.[77] The introduction of *The Creation* is famous for its "representation of chaos"; and Beethoven's *Christus* begins with an evocation of the dark mood on the Mount of Olives.

77. Printed in Serauky, *Halle*, 2:31 (in "Musikbeilagen").

CHAPTER VIII

Selected German Oratorios

The seven works examined in this chapter represent the main tendencies in the German oratorio from the mid-eighteenth century to the beginning of the nineteenth. The oratorios are presented in chronological order except for the first two: C. H. Graun's *Der Tod Jesu* preceded Telemann's *Der Tag des Gerichts* by seven years, yet the latter is placed first, as it illustrates the style of an earlier generation. Included are works that represent both Protestant and Catholic areas and settings of both lyric and dramatic texts, plus the strong English influence seen in Haydn's oratorios.

Georg Philipp Telemann: Der Tag des Gerichts

Born in Magdeburg, Telemann received his early general and musical education there, in Zellerfeld, and in Hildesheim.[1] In 1701 he went to the University of Leipzig to study law, but musical activity soon dominated his life: within a year he became the musical director of the Leipzig opera and founded a student Collegium musicum, which gave regular public concerts, and in 1704 he was appointed organist at the Neue Kirche, the University church. Leaving Leipzig in 1705, he went first to Sorau as court Kapellmeister and then to Eisenach (1708) in the same position. In 1712 he moved to Frankfurt am Main to become director of the city's music, Kapellmeister of the Barfüsserkirche, and director of the Collegium musicum of the aristocratic and bourgeois Frauenstein Society, for which he composed instrumental works and oratorios.

Telemann began his long residence in Hamburg in 1721, where he was appointed Kantor of the Johanneum (the Latin school) and musical director of the five main churches. A year later he was offered but refused the position of Kantor at the Thomaskirche in Leipzig, a position that

---

1. On Telemann's life and works, see: Martin Ruhnke, "Telemann," *New Grove*, 18:647–59; idem, "Telemann," *MGG*, 13:cols. 175–211; Petzoldt, *Telemann*; and Kleßmann, *Telemann*.

was next refused by Christoph Graupner, and finally accepted by J. S. Bach. Except for an eight-month sojourn in Paris (1737), Telemann remained in Hamburg for the rest of his life. His schedule in Hamburg was an extremely demanding one: he was to compose two cantatas for each Sunday, a Passion each year, and special cantatas and oratorios for ceremonial occasions. In addition he established a Collegium musicum, which gave frequent public concerts, and he directed the Hamburg opera from 1722 until it closed in 1738.

Telemann was widely known and highly regarded. Writing in the journal *Critischer Musikus* in the late 1730s, Johann Adolph Scheibe ranks him together with Hasse, C. H. Graun, and Handel as among the best and most advanced of the German composers.[2] (Scheibe omits from his list of luminaries the name of J. S. Bach, who was less well known than the others and whose music he disliked for its outmoded complexity.)[3] Telemann's musical style, like that of many in his generation, reveals a mixture of old and new traits. His instrumental and secular vocal pieces represent the early Classic tendencies better than his sacred works, which are more learned in style, while his last oratorio reveals some of the newer characteristics, as will be shown.

An astonishingly prolific composer, Telemann wrote in virtually all the genres of his time. His output of oratorios and related works,[4] many of which are lost, includes forty-six oratorio Passions (one each year, 1722–67), six Passion oratorios,[5] thirty-six *Kapitänsmusiken* for the annual celebrations of the Hamburg city militia (an oratorio and a serenata for each celebration),[6] and about twelve other oratorios (the number depending on genre classification).[7] He composed the oratorio Passions and *Kapitänsmusiken* throughout his Hamburg career, but his other oratorios represent two periods: 1716–31 and 1755–62. From the earlier period come his first ten oratorios: seven for Frankfurt and three for

2. See the quotation from Scheibe's *Critischer Musikus* (2d edition, Hamburg, 1745), in Ruhnke, "Telemann im Schatten von Bach?" pp. 146–47.

3. For quotations from Scheibe that provide background and reasons for his dislike of Bach's style and preference for the composers named, see ibid., pp. 146–48; and for a quotation in English translation of Scheibe's criticism of J. S. Bach (without naming him) see David and Mendel, *Bach Reader*, p. 238.

4. See the lists of Telemann's oratorios, including modern editions, in Ruhnke, "Telemann," *New Grove*, 18:656, and idem, "Telemann, *MGG*, 13:cols. 193–94.

5. On Telemann's oratorio Passions and Passion oratorios, see Hörner, *Telemann*; and Menke, *Telemann*, pp. 78–84.

6. The number of Telemann's *Kapitänsmusiken*, not all extant, is established in Maertens, "Kapitänsmusiken" (1975), 1:5; see that work for an authoritative study of these works.

7. For a general survey of styles and structures in seven of the oratorios (including three from *Kapitänsmusiken*), see Rhea, "Telemann," 1:82–105 and 134–54; in 2:10–225 are transcriptions of excerpts from the oratorios. For further bibliography on Telemann's oratorios, see Wettstein, *Telemann*, pp. 45–47.

Hamburg. The Frankfurt oratorios include one of his most famous works, the Brockes Passion (1716, revised 1722), and his five oratorios on the subject of King David.[8] The early Hamburg works include a Passion oratorio of remarkable longevity, *Seliges Erwägen* (1728, text by Telemann), which continued to be performed to the end of the century. From the later period, 1755–62, most of the oratorios are settings of lyric librettos, among them texts by Joachim Johann Daniel Zimmermann: *Betrachtung der Neunten Stunde an dem Todes-Tage Jesu* (1755); Ramler: *Tod Jesu* (1755),[9] *Hirten bei der Krippe* (1759), and *Auferstehung und Himmelfahrt* (1760); Zachariä: *Befreite Israel* (1759) and *Auferstehung* (1761); Klopstock: sections of *Messias* (1759);[10] and Alers: *Tag des Gerichts* (1762), Telemann's last oratorio, which combines lyric and dramatic qualities.[11]

Telemann's *Tag des Gerichts* was first performed on 17 March 1762, the fourth Wednesday in Lent, in Hamburg's Concertsaal auf dem Kamp at a subscription concert directed by Friedrich Hartmann Graf.[12] In an advance announcement, the work was called "an oratorio [Sing-Gedicht] full of strong emotions"; the final number on the program was part I of Telemann's *Donnerode* (1756),[13] a poetic translation by Johann Andreas Cramer (1723–88) of the eighth and twenty-ninth psalms. *Tag des Gerichts* was also performed, together with Telemann's *Betrachtung der Neunten Stunde*, in the same concert hall on 21 March 1774, the fourth Thursday in Lent, at a concert directed by Hardenack Otto Conrad Zinck (1746–1832);[14] he was a student of C. P. E. Bach and later, in Schwerin, the composer of an oratorio on the same subject, *Das Weltgericht* (1780).[15]

8. See Smither, *Oratorio*, 2:121–24. In Ruhnke, "Telemann," *New Grove*, 18:656 and idem, "Telemann," *MGG*, 13:col. 192, this is considered a single oratorio in five parts; the title page of the printed libretto, however, speaks of "Fünff verschienenen Oratorien."

9. For details on the first performance of this work, see Lott, "Tod Jesu," p. 127.

10. For a detailed study, see Godehart, "Telemanns *Messias*."

11. For general comments on the work, see Annibaldi, "Telemann."

12. For a modern edition, see Telemann, *Tag des Gerichts**; for background information on the work, see the introduction to that edition, by Max Schneider, especially pp. LVII–LXIV. See also the historical and analytical essay by Ludwig Finscher, "Der Tag des Gerichts," in both German and English, which accompanies the 1967 recording of the work conducted by Nikolaus Harnoncourt on Telefunken, "Das alte Werk," SAWT 9484–9485.

13. The announcement is quoted in part in Sittard, *Hamburg*, p. 100. The announcement does not specify "part I" of the *Donnerode*, but according to Wolf Hobohm, in the foreword of Telemann, *Donnerode; Befreite Israel**, p. IX, the first known concert performance of part II dates from 26 April 1762.

14. Sittard, *Hamburg*, pp. 124–25.

15. Its sources (parts only) are listed in the Schwerin catalogue: Kade, *Mecklenburg-Schwerin*, 2:325.

The librettist of *Tag des Gerichts*, Christian Wilhelm Alers (1737–1806), was born in Hamburg and educated at the Johanneum where Telemann was Kantor; thus he would have known and probably studied with the composer. Alers studied theology at Helmstedt (1749–62) and then became the pastor at Rellingen and later at Ütersen.[16] In 1786–88 he published a three-volume collection of his poetry. Telemann set at least one other libretto by Alers, and C. P. E. Bach also set some of his poetry.[17]

Alers's libretto for *Tag des Gerichts* is subdivided into four parts, each of which is called a Contemplation (*Betrachtung*).[18] That word had been used previously by Telemann for each of the nine parts of his *Seliges Erwägen*, an early example of the lyric libretto.[19] As the word *Contemplation* suggests, the libretto is essentially lyric in conception, but it also includes the dramatic element of dialogue among its twelve named personages and the contrast between those who believe in Jesus and those who do not. Telemann did not adopt a strictly dramatic approach to the assignment of the twelve roles, most of which are allegorical, for the same role is sometimes sung by different voices. Four soloists could sing the work if each soloist sang more than one solo part and sang in the choruses, all of which are for SATB. The distribution of the solo roles among the voices in the four Contemplations is shown in Table VIII-1.

Part I (i.e., the First Contemplation) opens and closes with a Chorus of Believers (*Chor der Gläubigen*) who are convinced that the Lord will come and pass judgement. (See the structural outline in Table VIII-2.) Like allegorical prologues to some Baroque operas, part I consists of a dispute between opposing forces that figure in the work to follow: Disbelief and the Mocker ridicule the idea that the world will end and all will be judged; Reason, Religion, and the Chorus of Believers support that idea and predict the events of the oratorios's next three parts. Part II begins with an unidentified chorus that describes the thundering approach of Jesus coming to judge the world. Devotion continues the description with the recitative "There they are, the signs of devastation!," which is filled with impassioned, Klopstockian descriptions of horrendous natural and unnatural events and of awesome feelings. The fury of Devotion's descriptive recitative and aria (no. 7) gives way to Faith's recitative of reflection on the scene of devastation and also an arioso (no. 8) of blissful soaring "upwards from these desolate ruins" to see the choir of angels rejoicing and "the wounds of Jesus shimmering"; the

16. On Alers's life and works, see Max Schneider's introduction to Telemann, *Tag des Gerichts*, pp. LVII–LVIII.

17. Ibid., p. LVIII, n. 4.

18. That the work is in four parts is not unusual, for Protestant German oratorios ranged from one to as many as nine parts, as pointed out in chapter 7.

19. For two different prints of the libretto of *Seliges Erwägen*, undated but probably from Telemann's time, see D-B: Mus. Tt 153 and B-Br: Fétis 4548.

TABLE VIII-1
Telemann, *Der Tag des Gerichts*: Distribution of Solo Roles

Voices	Solo Roles in the Four Contemplations			
	I	II	III	IV
S	Religion	Faith	Archangel	The 3d Blessed
A	Reason		Devotion	The 2d Blessed, Faith
T	Mocker	Faith	Disbelief	The 1st Blessed
B	Disbelief	Devotion	Jesus	John

arioso closes with transports of joy: "He approaches, radiance is his apparel. O majesty! O bliss!"

Part III depicts the scene of the Last Judgement. In the opening recitative Devotion narrates and describes the coming of the angel of vengeance, who blows his trumpet for the resurrection of the dead; in an arioso (no. 9) the Archangel then commands the dead to arise and be judged, and separates the believers from the disbelievers. Devotion describes the approach of Jesus who then in an arioso (no. 10) beatifies the believers. They respond with a chorale-chorus, "Thou King of Glory, Jesus Christ" (no. 11). Disbelief and the Chorus of Vices agonize over the coming verdict and, in a paraphrase of Revelation 6:16, they yearn to die. Part III closes with Jesus's aria to the godless (no. 13), "Hence from my sight! You enemies of God, be damned!"

Part IV, sung in Heaven, is an exultant expression of joy, praise, and thanksgiving, in which the symmetries of the libretto are reinforced by the music. (See the brackets in the left-hand margin of part IV in Table VIII-2.) Part IV is framed by jubilant choruses in D major, nos. 14 and 21–22, the last two separated by a recitative sung by Faith, the only recitative in part IV. The internal numbers are organized by two interlocking textual-musical units in keys closely related to D major: nos. 15, 17, and 19 interlocking with 16, 18, and 20. In one of these units John quotes twice from Revelation (no. 15, "Now has come the salvation and the power and the kingdom," Rev. 12:10; and no. 19, "Worthy is the Lamb who was slain," Rev. 5:12), and the Chorus of the Blessed join in with "Holy is our God," set to a slight modification of the Gregorian *Te Deum* incipit written in chordal-chorale style; the same chorale is repeated as no. 17 and thus functions as a three-fold refrain (in nos. 15, 17, and 19). In the other interlocking unit, nos. 16, 18, and 20 have texts sung by the three Blessed (in order of ascending ranges: T, A, S), whose praises of God are accompanied by obbligato instruments (described below).

As Table VIII-2 shows, D major is the oratorio's key: most of part I,

TABLE VIII-2
Telemann, *Der Tag des Gerichts*: Structural Outline

Numbers	Keys
The First Contemplation	
Einleitung	D
1. Chorus of Believers, "Der Herr kommt"	D
2. Aria. Disbelief, "Fürchtet nur"	G
3. Aria. The Mocker, "Jetzt weiß ich's"	F
4. Aria. Reason, "Des Sturmes Donnerstimmen"	B♭
5. Chorus of Believers, "Dann jauchzet"	D
The Second Contemplation	
6. Chorus. "Es rauscht—so rasseln stark"	D
7. Aria. Devotion, "Da kreuzen verzehrende"	B♭
8. Arioso. Faith, "Ich aber schwinge mich"	F
The Third Contemplation	
9. [Arioso]. Archangel, "So spricht der Herr"	G
10. [Arioso]. Jesus, "Seid mir gesegnet"	a
11. Chorale-Chorus, the Faithful, "Du Ehren König"	a-E
12. Chorus of Vices, "Ach Hilfe! Weh uns!"	f
13. Aria. Jesus, "Hinweg von meinem Angesichte!"	B♭
The Fourth Contemplation	
14. Chorus of Angels and the Chosen, "Schallt"	D
15. Solo, Chorus. John, "Nun ist das Heil," & Chorale, Angels and the Chosen, "Heilig"	b
16. [Arioso]. 1st Blessed, "Ein Ew'ger Palm"	b
17. Chorale, Angels and the Chosen, "Heilig"	b
18. [Arioso]. 2d Blessed, "Heil! Wenn um des"	G
19. Solo, Chorus. John, "Das Lamm" & Chorale, the Blessed, "Heilig"	D-A
20. Aria. 3d Blessed, "Ich bin erwacht"	A
21. Chorus of the Blessed, "Lobt ihn"	D
22. Chorus of Heavenly Hosts, "Die Rechte"	D

the beginning of II, and all of IV emphasize that key and closely related ones. Throughout the work flat keys usually are used with texts of disbelief in God, transiency of physical existence, devastation, and the Last Judgement, whereas sharp keys relate to the heavenly sphere; but the symbolic use of keys is not consistent, probably for reasons of musical structure and variety. In part I, the aria of Disbelief moves only as far away from the main key as G major, for it is only the oratorio's second vocal number; but in number 3, sung by the Mocker, a text equally disbelieving is set in F major. In number 4 Reason describes in B-flat major the rolling of thunder, the tottering and falling of mountains, the raging within the womb of the earth, and the pride of ages that sinks into a mournful grave. Part II begins by reasserting the work's main key, but number 7 shifts to B-flat major for descriptions of lightning, roaring winds, and avenging fire at the approach of Jesus. Yet in number 8, the aria of Faith remains in the flat area. The Archangel, as a representative of Heaven, sings an arioso in G major in Part III. Jesus sings in the "neutral" key of A minor (no. 10), not previously heard; and the Faithful (no. 11) begin in the same key with their modal chorale of praise for the King of Glory, but they close on E major. Far removed from E major, and from the oratorio's main key of D major, is the F minor of the Chorus of Vices (no. 12), the key with largest number of flats used in the oratorio; the Vices curse their misdeeds and plead for death in words close to those of Revelation 6:16; in B-flat major (no. 13) Jesus then passes judgement on the godless, who are damned, to be tormented for ever in Hell. The spirit of jubilation and praise, which dominates the texts of part IV, evokes the key of D major and closely related keys to the end of the work.

The largest orchestral force of the oratorio—two trumpets, timpani, two oboes, strings, and continuo—is heard in the overture and in the choruses of parts I and IV, which have texts affirming faith and praising the Lord (nos. 1, 5, 14, 21, and 22). Most other numbers are given the normal accompaniment of oboes, strings, and continuo, but a few are of special interest for their unusual accompaniments. At the beginning of part III, in response to the text's reference to the angel's trumpet, which raises the dead, solo horn-calls (plus strings) accompany the recitative preceding the Archangel's aria (no. 9); solo horn-calls are also heard in the aria itself, and calls by three horns in block triads—for the same extramusical purpose—accompany the recitative that follows number 9. When Jesus beatifies the believers in part III (no. 10) an oboe obbligato accompanies his arioso line with agile counterpoint, while the strings provide minimal support with pizzicato chords. In part IV the three solo numbers sung by the Blessed are distinguished by solo obbligato instruments and continuo (without the usual string section): solo viola da gamba (no. 16), two solo violins (no. 18), and solo oboe and bassoon (no. 20).

In the instrumental Introduction (*Einleitung*), the oratorio's only instrumental number, Telemann reveals his strong Baroque roots by writing a French overture with the traditional tempo sequence (slow, fast, and brief slow ending) and binary structure with chordal style in the first part and fugal style in the second. The overture has no thematic relation to the oratorio proper, but trumpet-calls and tympani heard prominently in both sections make clear reference to the trumpets of the Last Judgement. The overture proper ends with a full cadence in the tonic, but that is followed by two long-held chords that return to the dominant in preparation for the opening chorus in the tonic.

Of the eleven numbers marked *aria* or *arioso* in Table VIII-2, five are conventional da capo arias (nos. 2, 3, 4, 7, and 13). (In this work Telemann does not use the dal segno mark, so common in the 1760s, to abbreviate the da capo form.) The B section of every da capo aria retains the tempo of the A section, uses new melodic material, and is tonally unstable, beginning and ending on different tonal centers. The aria of the Third Blessed (no. 20) is a setting of four stanzas of poetry to the musical scheme: A A' B C. Six of the solo numbers are ariosos—i.e., arialike numbers that are shorter than the usual aria (nos. 8, 9, 10, 16, and 18).[20] These tend to have less text repetition than arias and exhibit a binary structure similar to the A section of a da capo aria. The arioso of Jesus (no. 10) has a clear AAB form, with repeat signs for the first, brief section.

The arias reflect Telemann's position as a composer of an older generation who mixes the Baroque and early Classical styles. Balanced phrases are prominent, yet Baroque irregularities and spinning-out procedures are found at times, as in Example VIII-1. Taken from the beginning of the first vocal entrance in the aria of the Mocker (no. 3), that example consists of two eight-measure musical units, which correspond to the two sentences of the text (mm. 17–24, 25–32). Yet the internal divisions of these units are irregular (both could be treated as 3 + 5 measures), and in the second unit the vocal line is organized by a spinning-out procedure, perhaps to stress the text's meaning ("es täuscht mich," "it deceives me," mm. 27–30). Here and throughout the oratorio Telemann pays careful attention to word painting and textual expression; for instance, in the same example he provides a sixteenth-note "laugh" on "Lachen" (m. 21). Although the basso continuo of this example is initially noncontrapuntal, it soon becomes active and functions more as a Baroque than as an early Classical bass line. The other instrumental parts, too, suggest Baroque style, particularly the first violin, with its imitations of the voice (mm. 25–26) and its subsequent rhythmic and melodic figures (mm. 27–30).

Devotion's aria from part II (no. 7), shown in Example VIII-2, illustrates Telemann's mixture of melodic-rhythmic simplicity and complexity. The text, describing the crossing of the streaks of lightning that emanate from the flaming throne of Jesus as he approaches to judge the world, are set to two phrases of five and seven measures. The vocal line in the first phrase is simple (regular quarter-note motion, syllabic text setting, ascending sequence) as is the continuo (mostly repeated notes).

20. Only one of these, no. 8, is called *arioso* in a source of the time, the libretto for the 1762 performance: cf. Telemann, *Tag des Gerichts**, "Revisions-Bericht," p. LXXVII. I have followed that edition in adding *arioso* for the other numbers so designated in Table VIII-2.

EXAMPLE VIII-I. *Der Tag des Gerichts*—Telemann (Telemann, *Tag des Gerichts**, pp. 21–23).

EXAMPLE VIII-I. continued

-sicht, es täuscht mich eu'r Ge- sicht, es tauscht

mich, es täuscht mich eu'r Ge- sicht.

Now I know, you over-wise heads, why no mocking, no bitter laughter could make you better. Your appearance deceives me.

EXAMPLE VIII-2. *Der Tag des Gerichts*—Telemann (Telemann, *Tag des Gerichts**, pp. 58–60).

EXAMPLE VIII-2. continued

EXAMPLE VIII-2. continued

Consuming streaks of lightning cross each other and shoot down from the flaming seat of the Judge.

Word painting is important in the vocal line, which consists of descending motives and terminates with a descent of a seventh (on "Richters herab," mm. 9–10). More complex and functioning more as Baroque than early Classical accompaniments are the violin parts, in which descending "lightning" motives constantly cross to paint the text, "Da kreuzen verzehrende Blitze." In the second vocal phrase (mm. 11–17) the text and melody are modified: the melodic material is extended to paint the word "flaming" (sixteenth notes, mm. 13–14), while the violins continue to cross but also imitate the voice with sixteenth-note "flames" of their own.

The arias illustrated by Examples VIII-1 and VIII-2 represent the stylistic mixture found in both arias and ariosos of the oratorio as a whole; but in part IV the numbers sung by the Second Blessed (no. 18) and the Third Blessed (no. 20) are closer to the simplicity of early Classical style than any others of the work, and appropriately so, for they must reflect the pure, simple, joyful innocence of the Blessed. The aria of the Third Blessed is illustrated in Example VIII-3. The symmetrical four-measure phrases and simple continuo are characteristic of the entire aria; yet the number is not without a modicum of contrapuntal interest, provided by the obbligato oboe and bassoon parts, which occasionally imitate the vocal line, as does the oboe in measures 14–15.

In parts I–III most of the numbers listed in Table VIII-2 are preceded by recitatives that have texts that are either argumentative (in part I) or narrative and descriptive (in parts II and III). The only numbers in parts I–III that are not preceded by recitatives are the opening choruses of parts I and II (both are narrative choruses) and the chorale-chorus of the Faithful in part III (no. 11, a direct response to Jesus' preceding arioso). As a finale of praise and joy, part IV has little need of the style of dialogue, narrative, and description found in the other parts; recitative appears only once, between nos. 21 and 22. The accompaniments of recitatives with continuo only are usually simple and traditional, but on occasion they are active and expressive, as is the recitative of Disbelief that precedes his aria in part I.

Accompanied recitative is heard four times in the oratorio, but twice it grows out of simple recitative. The two passages that are entirely accompanied are those preceding number 7 in part II and number 9 in part III. The first of these (see Example VIII-4 for its first half) is the most impressive—indeed, among the most memorable moments in the oratorio—for its powerful description of the devastation at the end of the world. First comes the roaring thunder (mm. 2–3), then the scattering flames (mm. 4–7), then a striking harmonic shift from major to minor (m. 7) and a series of sustained, chromatically altered chords of the sixth and seventh for "Shudders never felt before." Next, the lines "The sweet harmony of the spheres dissolves in rude discord" (mm. 11–13) are represented at first by "sweet" thirds and sixths in the violins, followed by a "rude" dissolution in discordant sounds—clearly "wrong" notes; with

EXAMPLE VIII-3. *Der Tag des Gerichts*—Telemann (Telemann, *Tag des Gerichts**, p. 105).

I have awakened in God's image in wisdom and righteousness.

EXAMPLE VIII-4. *Der Tag des Gerichts*—Telemann (Telemann, *Tag des Gerichts**, pp. 54–55).

EXAMPLE VIII-4. continued

EXAMPLE VIII-4. continued

EXAMPLE VIII-4. continued

gelinde ... der Ster- nen Hee- re wei- chen aus ih- rem al- ten Gleis ... *gelinde*

There they are, the signs of devastation! Hear how the loud thunderclaps roar!
Far around they scatter flames and threaten the earth, threaten the stars,
threaten to destroy their powers. Shudders never felt before fill with unbearably
sharp pain the oppressed hearts of mortals. The sweet harmony of the spheres is
dissolved in rude discord—the storm whips the clouds into swift flight—the
hordes of stars depart from their ancient course— . . .

thirty-second notes in the violins "the storm whips the clouds into swift
flight," and with offbeat rhythms in the violins and violas "the hordes of
stars depart from their ancient course." The remainder of the recitative
(not in the example) is equally pictorial and closes with rushing scale
passages in the violins to represent the raging waves.

Characteristic of a German oratorio in its time, this work places special emphasis on the chorus. As Table VIII-2 shows, half of the numbers
(not counting recitatives) are choruses. Parts I and III include two choruses, part II only one, and part IV, six. The chorus at the beginning of
part II is anonymous and has a narrative text, but the other choruses are
all designated as groups of personages. An emphasis on vertical sonority,
on chordal rather than contrapuntal style, reflects the early Classical
tendencies of the work, yet some of the choruses include contrapuntal
sections. The "amen" section at the end of number 21 is outstanding and
exceptional for its counterpoint. The opening and closing choruses of the
oratorio (Examples VIII-5 and VIII-6) illustrate the prevailing choral
style; *colla parte* orchestration, contributing to the chordal emphasis, is
used in both. As these are festive choruses, they use trumpets and timpani, and Example VIII-6 uses horns as well. The opening chorus, Example VIII-5, with its text about the coming of the Lord and many thousand saints, is appropriately like a march, whereas the final chorus is a

Selected German Oratorios 395

EXAMPLE VIII-5. *Der Tag des Gerichts*—Telemann (Telemann, *Tag des Gerichts**, p. 5).

The Lord is coming with many thousand saints. . . .

EXAMPLE VIII-6. *Der Tag des Gerichts*—Telemann (Telemann, *Tag des Gerichts**, p. 115).

The right hand of the Lord is raised! The right hand of the Lord is victorious!

quick, joyful, victorious dance in triple meter with hemiola cadences. The chorale of the Faithful, number 11 (see Example VIII-7), together with the chorale-refrain in part IV (numbers 15, 17, and 18) constitute the simplest choruses of the work. Of greatest interest for its textures and word painting is the opening chorus of part II, which describes the coming of Jesus (Example VIII-8). The thunder, like the rumbling of chariots, is represented by tremolo in all the strings at the beginning, and the continuo and viola continue the tremolo almost throughout, while the violins play other pictorial figures. The choral parts enter separately—breathlessly, as it were, and with astonishment, commenting on the thunder—at dramatic silences (mm. 6–7 and 10–11). The chorus asks "Who is it?" and answers "It is Jesus!" with his name at the peak of the phrase in long notes and at a sudden halt in the rushing, rumbling orchestral sounds. In measure 15 another text segment begins that speaks of Jesus' being borne on a bolt of lightning, at which point the violins paint the lightning in arpeggiated figures of sixteenth notes. This dramatic and descriptive chorus is then followed by the powerful accompanied recitative (illustrated in Example VIII-4) discussed above.

EXAMPLE VIII-7. *Der Tag des Gerichts*—Telemann (Telemann, *Tag des Gerichts**, p. 75).

Thou king of glory, Jesus Christ, God the Father's eternal Son art thou.

EXAMPLE VIII-8. *Der Tag des Gerichts*—Telemann (Telemann, *Tag des Gerichts**, pp. 44–45).

EXAMPLE VIII-8. continued

EXAMPLE VIII-8. continued

It is thundering—thus rumble powerfully rolling chariots. Who is it? It is Jesus! Borne on lightning . . .

Carl Heinrich Graun: Der Tod Jesu

Graun was born in 1703 or 1704 in Wahrenbrück, about forty miles north of Dresden, where he attended the Kreuzschule from 1714 to 1721.[21] At the Kreuzschule he received thorough training in singing, keyboard instruments, and composition; together with other students, he sang in the chorus of the Dresden opera. He became a tenor in the Brunswick court opera in 1725 and two years later was appointed vice-Kapellmeister. In 1735 he moved to Rupin as tenor and then Kapellmeister at the court of Crown Prince Frederick. When Frederick acceded to the Prussian throne in 1740, he appointed Graun the Royal Kapellmeister, a position that the composer retained until his death in 1759.

In his lifetime Graun was considered along with the somewhat older Hasse as an outstanding representative of modern Italian *opera seria* in Germany. Between 1727 and 1735 Graun composed six operas for Brunswick, and after 1741, twenty-six major operas for Berlin. The composer of numerous secular cantatas and some instrumental and sacred works, Graun gained posthumous fame largely for his only oratorio, a setting of Ramler's *Tod Jesu*, first performed in 1755 at a concert in the Berlin Cathedral (see chapter 6). As we have seen, this tremendously popular work was singled out in Sulzer's encyclopedia as an outstanding example of oratorio, and it "occupied until the late 19th century a position in Germany analogous to that of Handel's *Messiah* in England and America."[22]

The librettist of *Tod Jesu*, Carl Wilhelm Ramler, has been treated above (in chapter 7) for his special importance in the history of the oratorio; his three lyric, *empfindsam* librettos were widely admired and set by numerous composers. Ramler wrote *Tod Jesu* at the request of Princess Anna Amalia of Prussia, Frederick the Great's sister.[23] An important patroness of music, she, unlike her brother, was fond of sacred works. A composition student of her Kapellmeister, Johann Philipp Kirnberger (1721–83), the princess had originally intended to set Ramler's text to music, but she subsequently asked Graun to do it. She did, however, set the opening chorale and first chorus, which Kirnberger later published.[24]

Both the libretto and score of *Tod Jesu* were originally printed in one

21. For Graun's biography see Eugene Helm, "Graun," *New Grove*, 7:644–46; Werner Freytag, "Graun," *MGG*, 5:cols. 710–20; and Mennicke, *Hasse und die Brüder Graun*, pp. 447–90.

22. Helm, "Graun," *New Grove*, 7:646.

23. For background on *Tod Jesu*, see Howard Serwer's preface to Graun, *Tod Jesu**, pp. vii–x.

24. Kirnberger's *Die Kunst des reinen Satzes in der Musik*, vol. 1 (Berlin and Königsberg, 1774), pp. 226–28 (for the opening chorale); vol. 2 (Berlin and Königsberg, 1776–79), part 2, pp. 75–88 (first chorus).

FIGURE VIII-1. Carl Heinrich Graun (1703–4—1759). (Mezzotint of 1752 by V. D. Preisler after a portrait by Andreas Möller. Reproduced by permission of the Bild-Archiv of A-Wn.)

part;[25] the work was probably intended to be sung without a pause or a sermon at the mid-point. A performance in two parts took place in Berlin in 1759, however, and three librettos printed in Lübeck show a division between numbers 14 and 15.[26] (See the separation between those numbers in Table VIII-3.) Number 14 is an imposing fugal chorus, entirely suitable as a final number for part I of an oratorio, and it occurs just past the mid-point of the oratorio's duration—a pause following that number would seem more appropriate than at any other point if one wished to present the oratorio in two parts. Although the extent to which it was performed in two parts has yet to be investigated, such a performance would follow the tradition of framing a sermon with music in Protestant services and would allow a concert audience to rest during the nearly two hours required for a performance.

Like most lyric librettos, this one has only unnamed, "idealized" personages. Also unnamed are the choruses (including the chorales), which clearly represent an idealized congregation of Christians. In the first performance (and probably in others) the congregation was expected to join in the singing of all the chorales except the rather complex number 24.[27] Throughout the libretto Ramler indicated which of the text's stanzas were to be set as recitatives, arias, duet, choruses, and chorales, and he provided the names of the chorale tunes to be used with the chorale texts. Following traditional libretto procedures, Ramler assigned most of the narration and description to recitatives and the reflection to the other numbers; yet his recitatives are lyric in tone and include reflections and reactions to the situation, and the other numbers include some description. Ramler's version of the Passion draws freely from all the Gospels, and he frequently quotes from or paraphrases the New and Old Testaments; most of the chorale stanzas in the work originated in the seven-

25. The earliest print of the libretto is that made for the first performance in 1755: *Der Tod Jesu: Eine Cantate, nach der Composition des Königl. Capellmeisters Herrn Grauns, zum erstenmahl in der Ober- Pfarr- und Domkirche zu Berlin, auf Veranstaltung der Musicübenden Gesellschaft daselbst aufgeführet den 26sten Märtz 1755* (Berlin: Fried. Wilh. Birnstiel, [1755]), cited from König, *Tod Jesu*, p. 138, n. 2. The earliest print of Graun's musical score is *Der Tod Jesu: Eine Cantate in die Musik gesetzt* (Leipzig: Johann Gottlob Immanuel Breitkopf, 1760); a copy is in US-Wc, among other libraries. That print is the main source for Graun, *Tod Jesu**, on which the present study is based.

26. On the performance in Berlin, 1759, see chapter 6. The three Lübeck librettos, which are undated, are in D-LÜh: G37, G8g, G8i. On the title page of the last-named libretto, a manuscript note reads "Charfreitag März 24 1837 in der Börse, dir: G. Hermann." Thus that libretto was for a concert performance held in the city's stock exchange.

27. For that number, the instruction "Will not be sung along with by the congregation" is given in the printed libretto of 1775. Cf. Serwer's preface to Graun, *Tod Jesu**, p. x.

TABLE VIII-3
Graun, *Der Tod Jesu*: Structural Outline

Numbers	Keys
1. Chorale (chorus). "Du, dessen Augen Flossen"	E♭/c
2. Chorus. "Sein Odem ist schwach"	c
4. Aria (S). "Du Held, auf den die Köcher"	B♭
5. Chorale (chorus). "Wen hab' ich sonst"	B♭
7. Aria (S). "Ein Gebeth um neue Stärke"	G
9. Aria (T). "Ihr weichgeschaffnen Seelen"	E♭
10. Chorus. "Unsre Seele ist gebeuget"	f
11. Chorale (chorus). "Ich will von meiner Missethat"	A♭
13. Aria (B). "So stehet ein Berg Gottes"	D
14. Chorus. "Christus hat uns ein Vorbild gelassen"	A
15. Chorale (chorus). "Ich werde Dir zu Ehren"	a
17. Duet (SS). "Feinde, die ihr mich betrübt"	C
19. Aria (S). "Singt dem göttlichen Propheten"	B♭
20. Chorus. "Freuet euch alle ihr Frommen"	F
21. Chorale (chorus). "Wie herrlich ist"	F
24. Chorale (chorus & solo B). "Ihr Augen weint"	g/G
25. Chorus. "Hier liegen wir"	E♭

Note: The numbering in this table is that of the modern edition: Graun, *Tod Jesu**; recitatives, numbered in that edition, are omitted from the table.

teenth century.[28] Of the six chorale texts, Ramler wrote original texts for only the first and last, numbers 1 and 24 (in Table VIII-3).

The first two numbers of the libretto, a chorale and a chorus, express strong reactions to a drama in progress assumed to be understood by the listener. The chorale addresses Jesus, asking, "where is the valley, the retreat that shelters Thee, Jesus?" and the chorus observes, "His breath is weak, his days are made short." Not until the first recitative (no. 3), however, does the listener become aware of the starting point for Ramler's account of the Passion:

Gethsemane! Gethsemane!	Gethsemane! Gethsemane!
Wen hören deine Mauren	Whom do thy walls hear,
so bange, so verlassen trauren?	lamenting so anxiously, so desolately?
Wer ist der peinlich langsam sterbende?	Who is it that dies in slow torment?

28. For full details on the biblical and chorale sources of the libretto, see König, *Tod Jesu*, pp. 150–52.

Ist das mein Jesus? Bester aller Menschenkinder,	Is that my Jesus? Thou best of all mankind,
du zagst, du zitterst, gleich dem Sünder,	art thou shivering and shaking like a sinner,
dem man sein Todesurtheil fält?	upon whom a death sentence has fallen?
Ach seht! er sinkt, belastet mit den Missethaten	Ah, look, he sinks, burdened with the sins
von einer ganzen Welt.	of an entire world.
Sein Herz, in Arbeit, fliegt aus seiner Hölle,	His heart, laboring, flies from his bosom;
sein Schweiß rollt purpurroth	his sweat drips purple-red
die Schläf' herab; er ruft: Betrübt ist meine Seele!	from his temples. He cries out: "My soul is sorrowful
bis in den Tod!	even unto death."

Thus the oratorio betrays its Enlightenment origin by beginning not with the Last Supper and the institution of the Sacrament of the Eucharist, as do most Orthodox Lutheran oratorio Passions and Passion oratorios,[29] but instead, with Jesus' suffering in the Garden of Gethsemane.[30] This recitative illustrates the lyric tone of Ramler's combined narration, description, and reaction. His intimate, *empfindsam* style is revealed in his use of the present tense and the first person ("my Jesus") and the close, first-hand witnessing of Jesus' physical and emotional state, beginning with "Ah look, he sinks" and ending with the quotation of Jesus' words as he cries out in agony.

In the next three recitatives (nos. 6, 8, and 12), similar in literary style to the one quoted above, the story is told—in intensely emotional yet highly economical verse—of Jesus' waking his followers ("And look! Sleep has overcome the disciples. . . ."), being taken by the soldiers ("Now arms clash, spears gleam in the light of torches, and murderers invade. I see assassins: Oh! it is happening to him!"), being judged, and carrying his cross (". . . and with shocking wrath [Judah] lays on the bloody one the beams on which he will slowly, slowly die . . ."). The arias, choruses, and chorales that follow the recitatives reflect on the heroism of Jesus, His power of consolation, the conversion of sinners, and, in number 14, his example, which we should follow.

After a chorale of courage, number 15, the narrative recitatives (nos. 16, 18, and 22) continue the story: Jesus is nailed to the cross, and virtually all the episodes of the Gospel stories, including His seven last

29. On the distinction between the oratorio Passion and the Passion oratorio, see chapter 6, n. 7.

30. König, *Tod Jesu*, p. 48. On the relationship between Ramler's *Tod Jesu* and the Enlightenment, as opposed to Orthodox, religious viewpoints, see König's chapter "Der religiöse Inhalt: Eine Passionsdichtung im Geiste der Aufklärung," pp. 42–67.

words, are worked into the relatively brief recitatives. The death of Jesus closes number 22, and the last recitative, number 23, describes the lamentation of the seraphim and the catastrophic events after Jesus' death. Following each of these recitatives the other numbers—arias, duet, choruses, and chorales—reflect feelingly upon and draw Christian lessons from the narrative. The final chorus prays to Jesus to "accept our offering" and to "let worship be thy thanks, offered by everyone."

Graun's musical setting of Ramler's text offers a unique combination of modern operatic style in the arias and recitatives, learned style in the choruses, and the quite simple, church style of the Enlightenment in the chorales—a combination that surely contributed to its extraordinary longevity. Certain characteristics associated with musical *Empfindsamkeit* are heard occasionally in the work, especially in the accompanied recitatives. Nevertheless, to classify the oratorio in general as an example of musical *empfindsamer Stil* would exaggerate the role of its *empfindsam* elements, for drawing-room intimacy and *empfindsam* subtlety are absent from the oratorio as a whole.

The main tonal center of the oratorio, as shown in Table VIII-3, is E-flat major. The opening chorale is essentially in that key (see the discussion of Example VIII-13), and the final chorus (no. 25) is in E-flat major. Flat keys predominate throughout the work. The numbers with sharp keys (nos. 7, 13, 14, and part of 24) may have been written in those keys for affective reasons, for all have optimistic texts: that of number 7, in G major, begins with a reflection on Jesus' "Prayer for new strength to carry out noble works"; the text of number 13, in D major, comments on Jesus as "a mountain of God, with feet in the storm and head in the sunshine"; number 14, in A major (the farthest away from the work's main key), observes that "Christ has left us a model," and number 24 alternates between texts with contrasting affects: "Weep, thou eyes!" set in G minor and "Do not cry!" in G major.

The orchestra for *Tod Jesu* requires strings and pairs of flutes and bassoons, and probably oboes.[31] The winds play obbligato parts only in the duet (number 17), in which the two flutes at times provide soli accompaniments to the voices. There are no orchestral movements in the work—a chorale substitutes for the usual overture. And like some oratorio overtures of the time, the opening chorale ends (as illustrated in Example VIII-13) with a transition to the next number.

The five arias and one duet of the oratorio are all in dal segno form, common in the mid-century, in which the sign eliminates the opening ritornello at the repetition of the A section.[32] In all the arias and the duet

31. According to Serwer's preface to Graun, *Tod Jesu*, p. x, the score calls for two oboes, yet oboes are not indicated in the edition; presumably they would have doubled the violins, as is characteristic of the time. For comments on the orchestral forces probably used at the first performance, see ibid., pp. ix–x.

32. On the interpretation of the dal segno indication in these numbers, see Serwer's preface to Graun, *Tod Jesu**, pp. x–xi.

the melodic material in the B section differs from that in A, and in three of the five arias (nos. 4, 7, and 9) the tempo and meter of the B section contrast with that of A. The arias in Graun's work reveal a closer affinity with the early Classical style than do those in Telemann's oratorio treated above. Less inclined to complicated accompaniment figures, Graun writes textures that allow the voice to stand out in greater relief; his phrases are usually written in multiples of two measures but are sometimes varied in length by extensions and elisions. Representative is Example VIII-9, from number 9—the aria that follows the recitative narration of Peter's denial of Jesus. The melodic line of the aria proceeds in clear, two-measure groupings, with an extension (mm. 16–17) on a melisma for the word "Schmerz" to express pain, yet the balance is quickly restored in measures 18–19, despite the chromatic quick-note passages expressive of weeping and pain. The string parts and continuo play unobtrusive accompaniment figures, at times doubling the vocal line. A particularly telling effect is the flatted leading tone when the voice first enters, to express the word *weak* ("*weich*geschaffnen"). Representing the simplest early Classical style is the optimistic minuet, number 7 (Example VIII-10), which comments on Jesus' prayer for new strength in the Garden of Gethsemane. When the vocal line enters it is doubled at the upper and lower octaves by the first violin and first bassoon, respectively; the harmony is simple, the harmonic rhythm slow, and counterpoint virtually absent, and Lombardic rhythms decorate the third measure of first two phrases. Ever conscious of opportunities for word painting, Graun shows that the prayer "parts the clouds" by ascending violin runs that "part" the vocal line (mm. 32–35) and that it "presses on to the Lord" by syncopations on *dringt* (mm. 36–39). Each aria of the oratorio includes at least a brief coloratura passage of six to eight measures; number 19, an aria of praise, includes the longest one, seventeen measures, on the word *Dank* in the phrase, "singt ihm Dank" ("sing thanks to him").

A recitative precedes every aria, and, following the convention of setting dramatic librettos, Graun writes the recitative and aria for the same voice; a recitative (S) also precedes the duet (SS), and near the end two recitatives (first simple, then accompanied) for bass are grouped together before the final chorus. The six simple recitatives in the oratorio are set in a highly affective manner by declamatory, harmonic, and contrapuntal means. Every simple recitative includes quotations of Jesus' words, and these are set off by arioso style, usually with imitation between the continuo and vocal lines. Examples VIII-11a-c illustrate the contrast between the narrative-descriptive passages, with their characteristic, long-note accompaniment, and the quotations from Jesus, in arioso style. Example VIII-11a (from no. 6) is the end of the scene in which Jesus finds his disciples sleeping in the Garden of Gethsemane. The narrative portions (mm. 21–23 and from the end of 26 to the middle of 28) have simple declamation and accompaniment, but the quotations from Jesus

EXAMPLE VIII-9. *Der Tod Jesu*—Graun (Graun, *Tod Jesu**, pp. 56–58).

EXAMPLE VIII-9. continued

EXAMPLE VIII-9. continued

You weak souls, you cannot err for long; soon you will hear reproachful conscience, soon pain will burst forth from you in weeping.

EXAMPLE VIII-10. *Der Tod Jesu*—Graun (Graun, *Tod Jesu**, pp. 40–41).

EXAMPLE VIII-10. continued

A prayer for new strength to carry out noble works parts the clouds, presses on to the Lord, . . .

EXAMPLE VIII-11. *Der Tod Jesu*—Graun (Graun, *Tod Jesu**, pp. 38, 52–53, 164–65).

Example a:

EXAMPLE VIII-11. continued

The friend of mankind stands contemplating them and speaks with a gentle countenance looking down upon them: "The spirit is willing, only the flesh is weak"; and he bows down, softly touching Peter's hand: "Even you are no longer awake? O watch and pray, my brothers!"

Example b:

EXAMPLE VIII-II. continued

He, however, without fear, approaches the enemy; magnanimously he speaks: "Are you seeking me? If I am the one you seek, then let my friends go."

Example c:

EXAMPLE VIII-II. continued

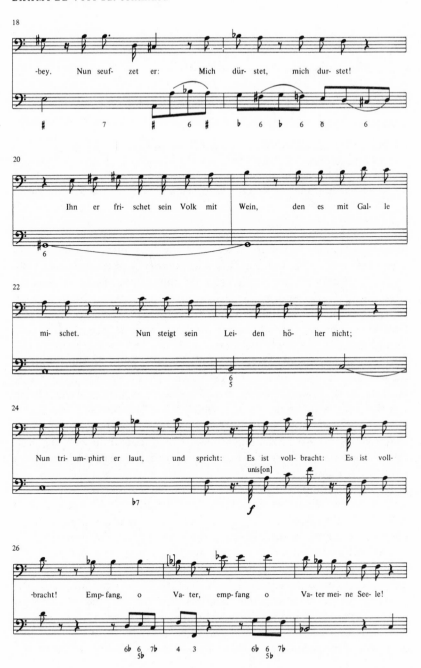

EXAMPLE VIII-II. continued

29

Und neigt sein Haupt auf sei- ne Brust und stirbt.

6   4+   6   ♯

He calls: "My God, my God, why hast thou forsaken me." And see, the dark moment passes. Now he sighs: "I am thirsty." His people refresh him with wine mixed with gall. Now his suffering increases no more; now he speaks loud and triumphant: "It is fulfilled! Receive, O Father, my soul!" and he bows his head on his breast and dies.

(mm. 24–26 and 28–30) are based on a few repetitions of a basso ostinato freely imitated in the vocal line; the number ends, however, with the end of the quotation set by the usual closing formula for recitatives. In Example VIII-11b (from no. 8) Jesus, still in Gethsemane, "without fear, approaches the enemy; magnanimously he speaks"; the voice freely imitates the continuo, and both paint the scene with martial rhythms and triadic fanfares. Example VIII-11c (from no. 22) includes the fourth through the seventh of the Seven Last Words of Jesus. In the setting of the fourth and fifth Words (mm. 14–15 and 18–19) the vocal line freely imitates the continuo—these Words have similar melodic motives. Graun sets the sixth Word (mm. 25–26), which Jesus "speaks loud and triumphant," with an ascending triadic motive; and, for the first time in a recitative in this work, the composer doubles Jesus' line with the continuo in order to add power. The seventh Word, the death of Jesus, is set with simple dignity.

The two accompanied recitatives use orchestral motives to paint the text and unify sections;[33] but the second and longer one (no. 23) is of special interest because of a phrase that is repeated to unify the entire number—a rhetorical device also in Ramler's text for the recitative. Example VIII-12 includes the first two-thirds of number 23. Following the death of Jesus (and immediately following Example VIII-11c), this recitative describes with appropriate orchestral figures the lament of the seraphim, the earthquake, the darkness, and the opening of tombs at Jesus' death. The refrain, "Er ist nicht mehr!" first appears in measures 7–8 and returns in 10–11 and three more times, including the final measures of the recitative; always followed or preceded by the orchestral

33. See chapter 7, n. 62, for reference to a discussion of and quotations from the first accompanied recitative, no. 3.

EXAMPLE VIII-12. *Der Tod Jesu*—Graun (Graun, *Tod Jesu**, pp. 166–68).

EXAMPLE VIII-I2. continued

laut: Er ist nicht mehr!

Der Er- de Tie- fen schal- len wie- der: Er ist nicht

EXAMPLE VIII-12. continued

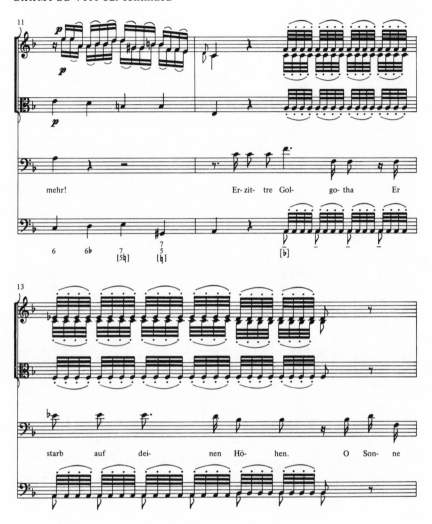

EXAMPLE VIII-12. continued

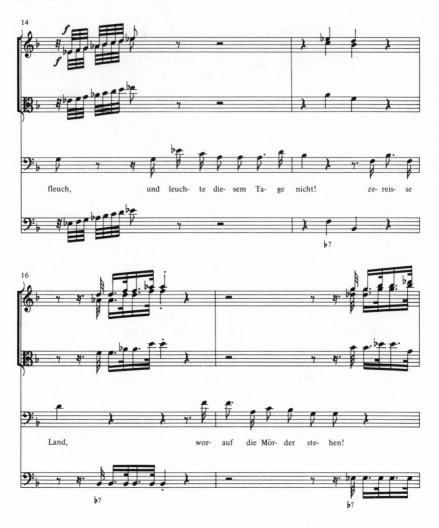

EXAMPLE VIII-12. continued

Ihr Grä- ber thut euch auf!

The seraphim come down from all the stars and loudly lament: "He is no more!" The depths of the earth echo: "He is no more!" Shudder, Golgatha, he died on your heights! Flee, O sun, and do not light this day! Break open this ground on which the murderers stand! You graves, open! . . .

passage seen in measure 8, the refrain not only helps unify the section but also intensifies the quality of lamentation.

This oratorio includes more choruses than any other type of number, and more than any of the other numbers, they are responsible for the work's solemn quality. Of the eleven choruses, six are chorales, all but one of which are given simple, chordal settings. The first number—Ramler's text set to the tune of "O Haupt voll Blut und Wunden," illustrated in Example VIII-13—shows the style of harmony and texture characteristic of most of the chorale settings. This opening chorale fluctuates between E-flat major (mm. 1–5) and C minor (mm. 6–9); after moving through closely related keys, it cadences in E-flat (m. 35) before going to the dominant of C minor in preparation for number 2, a chorus in that key. In the exceptional, more complex chorale movement (no. 24), the chorale tune and text, "Weep, thou eyes," is stated three times (by SA soli, then SAT soli, and finally SATB tutti) in simple, chordal style and in G minor; following each statement a bass solo contradicts the affect of the chorale with the text, "Do not cry! The lion from the stem of Judah has overcome," set to a lively melodic line in G major. The number closes with the third solo passage, in G major.

Of the five choruses that are not chorales, four include imitative or fugal texture: number 2 begins with a chordal section that introduces two fugatos on different subjects; 10 alternates between chordal and

EXAMPLE VIII-13. *Der Tod Jesu*—Graun (Graun, *Tod Jesu**, pp. 1–2).

Thou whose eyes were flowing the moment you saw Zion, . . . Persecutors of his soul, have you already murdered him?

imitative styles; 14 is a double fugue; 20 begins in chordal style and continues as a fugue; and 25, the final number, is chordal throughout, and it is the only chorus in dal segno form. Thus in the choruses Graun places greater emphasis on learned style than does Telemann in the work treated above. Like Telemann, however, Graun fully exploits the word-painting and expressive possibilities of the chorus's texts. An illustration of the combination of chordal and contrapuntal textures is the beginning of number 2, shown in Example VIII-14: the instruments anticipate—with the off-beat, *suspiratio* figure—the text's reference to Jesus' weakness of breath, which the chorus, in chordal texture, emphasizes by a

EXAMPLE VIII-14. *Der Tod Jesu*—Graun (Graun, *Tod Jesu**, pp. 2–5).

EXAMPLE VIII-14. continued

EXAMPLE VIII-14. continued

EXAMPLE VIII-14. continued

EXAMPLE VIII-14. continued

His breath is weak; his days are made short . . .

diminished seventh chord on the word *weak* ("schwach", mm. 3 and 5) and by "sigh" motives (mm. 6–7). At the next phrase of text, "His days are made short," note values become shorter (sixteenth notes are heard for the first time) and fugal texture begins; and with measures 17–19 the word *abgekurzet* is repeatedly "made short," as it were, by rests separating the syllables.

By far the most ingenious chorus of the oratorio is number 14, illustrated in Example VIII-15a-c. To reflect the notion of imitation in the text ("Christ has given us a model, so that we should follow in his footsteps"), Graun composed a double fugue. Written with the *alla breve* time signature associated with *stile antico* and with *colla parte* orchestration, the chorus opens with a four-voice exposition based on the first subject and the first phrase of text (Example VIII-15a), then moves to another four-voice exposition based on the second subject and the second phrase of text (Example VIII-15b), and finally combines both musical subjects and textual phrases (Example VIII-15c); near the end are passages of stretto (mm. 53–57, among others not shown in the example) and augmentation (mm. 58–61, not shown).

Christian Friedrich Daniel Schubart (1739–91), writing in 1785, offers the following critical comments on Graun's *Tod Jesu* in general and on the double fugue in particular: this work, he says, "caused the entire

EXAMPLE VIII-15. *Der Tod Jesu*—Graun (Graun, *Tod Jesu**, pp. 96–97, 98–99, 99–100).

Example a:

EXAMPLE VIII-15. continued

EXAMPLE VIII-15. continued

Christ has left us a model, . . .

Example b:

EXAMPLE VIII-15. continued

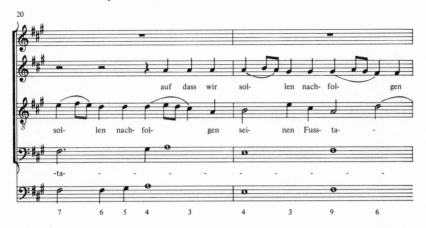

. . . so that we should follow in his footsteps.

EXAMPLE VIII-15. continued

Example c:

EXAMPLE VIII-15. continued

Christ has left us a model, so that we should follow in his footsteps.

world to gaze in wonder, even though one can say, justifiably, that it has too worldly an aspect. But Graun did this with serious intention; the Angel takes on a pilgrim's manner, in order to speak with those who live in a lowly state—God! who has ever composed a fugue such as "Christ has given us a model. . . ."[34]

Carl Philipp Emanuel Bach: Auferstehung und Himmelfahrt Jesu

The second surviving son of Johann Sebastian Bach and his first wife Maria Barbara, Emanuel Bach was born in Weimar in 1714.[35] He studied music with his father and attended the Lutheran seminary in Cöthen and the Thomasschule in Leipzig. In 1731 he entered the University of Leipzig as a law student, while he lived with his parents, assisted his father, and began his composing career with works for keyboard and other instruments. He continued his law studies from 1734 to 1738 at the University of Frankfurt an der Oder; in Frankfurt he composed, performed, and gave keyboard lessons.

In 1738 Emanuel joined the musical establishment of Crown Prince Frederick in Rupin (where Johann Joachim Quantz and the Graun brothers, among others, had already been appointed), and two years later when Frederick became king, Emanuel moved to Berlin to serve as court harpsichordist for royal chamber music. In Berlin Emanuel was active as a composer—primarily of solo keyboard music, which was to be central to his career—and also as the author of the important treatise, *Versuch über die wahre Art das Clavier zu spielen* (*Essay on the True Art of Playing Keyboard Instruments*) published in Berlin in 1753. By the 1750s he became dissatisfied with conditions in Berlin for a variety of reasons and began to seek positions elsewhere. When Telemann, his godfather, died in Hamburg in 1768, Emanuel applied for his position, was hired, and began his tenure there as Kantor of the Johanneum and director of music in the five principal churches; he retained that position till his death in 1788.

Bach's schedule in Hamburg was fully as demanding as Telemann's, and like his predecessor, he established a concert series. During his Hamburg years he wrote keyboard works, chamber music, symphonies, and songs, all genres in which he had previously composed; but an important change of direction in Hamburg resulted from his obligation to write religious choral music. Most of his choral works and all his oratorios

---

34. As translated from Schubart's *Ideen zu einer Ästhetik der Tonkunst* (written in 1774–75, published in Vienna, 1806), p. 81, in Ratner, *Classic Music*, p. 367.

35. On C. P. E. Bach's life and works, see Eugene Helm, "Bach III: (9)," *New Grove* 1:63; and Miesner, *Bach*.

FIGURE VIII-2. Carl Philipp Emanuel Bach (1714–88). (Lithograph by Heinrich E. von Wintter. Courtesy of D-Mbs.)

date from his Hamburg period. Like Telemann, Bach composed one Passion per year (twenty-one Passions) and a large number of other choral works—some of which were called oratorios—for special occasions.[36] The most significant of his oratorios are *Die Israeliten in der Wüste* (H 775, W 238), composed in 1769 (published in Hamburg, 1775), with a

36. On style in Bach's oratorios and cantatas, see Chamblee, "Bach"; on his Hamburg works in general, see Miesner, *Bach*.

text by the Hamburg poet Daniel Schiebeler;[37] *Die letzten Leiden des Erlösers* (H 776, W 233), composed in 1770, text mainly by Luise Karsch, a student of Ramler; and *Auferstehung und Himmelfahrt Jesu* (H 777, W 240), composed 1777–78 (published in Leipzig, 1787), text by Ramler.[38] *Israeliten* is his only dramatic oratorio; the other two are settings of lyric texts, with unnamed personages.

Bach's *Auferstehung* is among the most original oratorios of its time, and this quality may well have been responsible for the relatively few sales of the Breitkopf edition of 1787.[39] To console his publisher, Bach wrote in that year: "Although this Ramler cantata is by me, I can still assert, without foolish egotism, that it will last many years, because it is one of my important masterworks, from which young composers can learn something. In time it will sell as well as Graun's *Tod Jesu*. At first there is difficulty with all such things that are written for instruction and not for women and musical cream puffs [musikalische Windbeutel]. My *Heilig* and my *Israeliten* are also faltering just now, but I am not worried; finally they will be sought out again."[40]

Auferstehung was first performed on the third Wednesday in Lent, 18 March 1778, under the composer's direction, in Hamburg's Concertsaal auf dem Kamp.[41] According to a Hamburg newspaper, the work was a great success: "Our composer and singers honored themselves in the rivalry of showing their talents in the composition of this strong and expressive music and received the admiration of their worthy leader and all connoisseurs present."[42] The work appears to have been admired by the Viennese patron Gottfried van Swieten, who sponsored a performance of it in 1788 (see chapter 6).

Bach's libretto closely corresponds to Ramler's text but includes some small deviations.[43] Ramler's *Auferstehung* is a sequel to his *Tod Jesu* in

---

37. For a modern edition of this work, see: Bach, C. P. E., *Israeliten**. The "H" numbers in the references to C. P. E. Bach's works are those of Eugene Helm, in *New Grove*, 1:861, and in Helm's forthcoming thematic catalogue of Bach's music; the "W" numbers are those of Alfred Wotquenne's *Thematisches Verzeichnis der Werke von Carl Philipp Emanuel Bach (1714–1788)* (Leipzig, 1905).

38. For a modern edition, which is the source for the following comments on this work, see Bach, C. P. E., *Auferstehung**.

39. On the problems of the publication and its sales, see Hase, "Bach," pp. 102–4.

40. Bach to Johann Gottlob Immanuel Breitkopf, 1787?, translated from Hase, "Bach," p. 104.

41. Sittard, *Hamburg*, p. 107.

42. Translated from the *Hamburger Correspondent*, no. 45, as quoted in Sittard, *Hamburg*, p. 107.

43. One deviation is the substitution of the aria "Wie Bang hat dich mein Lied" (no. 7) for the original aria "Sey gegrüßet." According to the announce-

that it begins with the Resurrection and continues to the Ascension; and the same *empfindsam* literary style is common to both. In the recitatives of *Auferstehung*, Ramler's unnamed personages narrate and describe the events of the story by paraphrase, elaboration, and at times quotation from the Bible (especially of the words of the biblical characters) and the recitatives include some lyric reflection as well. The choruses (all set for SATB), arias (S, T, B), and duet (ST) reflect upon the content and implications of the recitatives and at times add further description. The opening chorus of part I (no. 2 in Table VIII-4) assumes the listener's understanding of the story and expresses the faith that God will not "leave his soul in Hell, nor allow Thy Holy One to be consumed." The first recitative (no. 3; recitatives are omitted from Table VIII-4) describes the trembling of Judea and the natural and unnatural phenomena that accompany the Resurrection (see Example VIII-20), then the descent of the Archangel Michael, who "comes down and rolls away the heavy stone from the grave of his King." The aria that follows (no. 4; see Example VIII-17) contributes further description and conveys the ecstatic reaction of the unnamed personage who witnesses the Resurrection. The remaining three recitatives of part I relate the entrance of the three Marys into Jesus' tomb (no. 6), the meeting of Mary Magdalene with Jesus (no. 8, see Example VIII-21), and the meeting of the other women with Jesus (no. 10). The final chorus of part I, "Death, where is your sting?" is a close paraphrase of 1 Corinthians 15:55–56.

Part II begins with the longest recitative text of the oratorio (no. 14, forty-two lines; the others range from thirteen to twenty), freely based on the story of the two men and Jesus on the way to Emmaus (Luke 24:13–31). The recitative includes a long quotation in which Jesus teaches the men (as an elaboration of verse 27) and in the process tells a condensed version of the Passion story. The other two recitatives of part II treat (in no. 17) the appearance of Jesus to his eleven disciples together with the story of doubting Thomas, and (in no. 20) the Ascension of Jesus, who is surrounded by "the blessed companions of his pilgrimage. Astonished, they see the radiance of his face. In a bright cloud they see the chariot of fire waiting. . . ." The concluding text is a long chorus of jubilation.

Bach's setting of this *empfindsam* libretto uses a much richer harmonic vocabulary than is characteristic of oratorios of the time, and it is filled with striking contrasts and surprises in virtually every element of the music. The work is replete with poignant sigh motives and other figures calculated to render the text in the most touching manner. One might, in fact, consider this an oratorio in *empfindsamer Stil* but for the magnitude of the work and its forces and the monumentality of some of its

---

ment, in Cramer's *Magazin der Musik* 2/1 (1784–85): 258, of the publication of the work, the new aria text was written by Ramler at the request of Bach, so that the work could include an *adagio* aria.

TABLE VIII-4
C. P. E. Bach, *Auferstehung*: Structural Outline

Numbers	Keys
PART I	
1. Einleitung	d
2. Chorus. "Gott, du wirst seine Seele"	D
4. Aria (B). "Mein Geist, voll Furcht"	c
5. Chorus. "Triumph! Triumph!"	E♭
7. Aria (S). "Wie bang hat dich mein Lied"	B♭
9. Duet (S, T). "Vater deiner schwachen Kinder"	d
11. Aria (T). "Ich folge dir, verklärter Held"	D
12. Chorus. "Tod! Wo ist dein Stachel?"	G
PART II	
13. Einleitung	e
15. Aria (B). "Willkommen, Heiland!"	A♭
16. Chorus. "Triumph! Triumph!"	E♭
18. Aria (T). "Mein Herr, mein Gott"	g
19. Chorus. "Triumph! Triumph!"	E♭
21. Aria (B). "Ihr Tore Gottes"	B♭
22. Chorus. "Gott fähret auf mit Jauchzen"	E♭

Note: The numbering in this table is that of the modern edition: Bach, C. P. E., *Auferstehung**; recitatives, numbered in that edition, are omitted.

numbers. Nor is the label *Sturm und Drang* more satisfactory, for the libretto so clearly represents literary *Empfindsamkeit*. Bach's oratorio is simply a product of his personal and unconventional musical style and his evident desire to offer an intense setting of the Ramler text.

In Bach's *Auferstehung* the key of E-flat is one of joy and triumph, an unusual use for this key in oratorios of the time. As shown in Table VIII-4 the oratorio ends in E-flat with a jubilant chorus for the Ascension. The texts of the three other choruses in E-flat (beginning "Triumph! Triumph!") express the triumph of the Resurrection (nos. 5 and 16) and of the Ascension (no. 19); all three have essentially the same music and thus form a unifying refrain for the oratorio as a whole. Eleven of the fifteen numbers (excluding tonally unstable recitatives) are also in flat keys. The gloom of death in the oratorio's D-minor orchestral introduction—with its dark instrumental sounds (no. 1; see Example VIII-16a)—precedes a chorus of hope in D major (no. 2) and a recitative narrating the Resurrection (no. 3, partially quoted above). Tonal symmetries in part I are the repeated pairing of D minor and D major (nos. 1–2 and 9–11); and those pairs frame three numbers in flat keys (nos. 4, 5, and 7).

The close relationship between G major (no. 12) and its relative minor (no. 13) forms a smooth tonal connection between the two parts.

The orchestra consists of pairs of flutes and oboes (but flutes and oboes are never used in the same number), one bassoon, two horns, three trumpets, and timpani, plus strings and continuo. The largest instrumental forces are used in the four joyful choruses in E-flat: the three refrain choruses and the final chorus. Flutes are heard in the first chorus, which has a text of hope, and in the duet, which also includes muted strings and has a text of consolation. Of special interest are the obbligato passages for trumpet in one of the tenor arias (no. 11) and for bassoon in one of the bass arias (no. 15). The most powerfully orchestrated aria is number 21 for bass, which follows the narrative of the Ascension and includes trumpet and horn fanfares alternating with vocal phrases.

The surprises in this work begin with the instrumental introductions to both parts, for they are brief and unconventional. Shown in their entirety in Examples VIII-16a-b, both are marked *adagio molto*, both close with a diminuendo, and both lead harmonically to the following number. The introduction to part I is remarkably simple and poetic; surely intended to convey the melancholy associated with Jesus' death and with the time between the Crucifixion and Resurrection, this introduction consists of a single melodic line played in three octaves by the violas, violoncellos, and double basses. The motive of a "contracting" diminished third (a descending diminished third resolving upward chromatically) is characteristic (see mm. 5, 9, 13, 17–19); the number closes on the dominant in preparation for the D-major chorus of hope that follows. The equally simple introduction to part II is composed of a few harmonic progressions activated by syncopated figures first in the violins, then in the lower strings. This number closes with some fascinating tonal ambiguity: an augmented sixth (m. 6, between the two lowest voices) that resolves (mm. 6–7) to suggestions of both A minor and E minor and in which the bass voice forms the leading tone to the opening E-minor chord of the following recitative.

Only one of the six arias is in da capo form (no. 11 in Table VIII-4), and none uses the dal segno. In four of the arias (nos. 4, 15, 18, and 21) Bach used the transformed da capo (A1-B-A2). With one exception (no. 21) the B sections of the arias contrast in tempo with the A1 and A2 sections, and the melodic material of B is always a contrast. One aria (no. 7) has an AB form with the sections marked *adagio* and *allegro*, respectively; in this case a repetition of the A text would have been illogical. Coloratura writing is not an important part of the vocal style. Although most of the arias do have one or more coloratura passages, they tend to be brief, no more than three or four measures in length; no such passage is more than eight measures long, and one aria (no. 21) has no coloratura passages. As shown below, Bach's orchestral accompaniments to the vocal lines in the arias and duet tend to be more active and

Example a:

Example b:

at times more contrapuntal than is typical in his time, yet the vocal lines are not obscured by this activity.

The extreme detail with which Bach characteristically treats each thought of his aria texts is illustrated in Examples VIII-17a-b, taken from number 4, which follows the recitative describing the Resurrection. In Example VIII-17a the trembling for fear and joy, basic to the first thought in the text, is represented by an opening ritornello and accompaniment of dotted sixteenths and thirty-seconds in the violins; "the rock bursts," by a descending skip of a sixth; "the night," by low pitches in the voice and orchestra, *pianissimo* and without horns; "becomes light," by an upward leap of a seventh and a sudden *fortissimo* in the orchestra, with added horns; "see how he hovers in the air," by *piano* syncopated

EXAMPLE VIII-17. *Auferstehung*—C. P. E. Bach (Bach, C. P. E. *Auferstehung**, pp. 16–18, 20–21).

Example a:

EXAMPLE VIII-17. continued

EXAMPLE VIII-17. continued

EXAMPLE VIII-17. continued

schwe- bet, seht wie von sei - - nem An- ge- sich- te die

Glo- - - - - - - - - - - - -

EXAMPLE VIII-17. continued

My soul, filled with fear and joy, trembles! The rock bursts, the night becomes bright! See how he hovers in the air, see how from his countenance the halo of divinity shines forth, . . .

Example b:

EXAMPLE VIII-17. continued

Did Jesus not struggle with a thousand pains? Did not his God receive his soul?
Did his blood not flow from his heart?

figures in the violins; and the "halo [or glory] of divinity" by a melisma of nearly three measures. The B section of the aria (Example VIII-17b), with its text recalling Jesus' struggle, pain, and flowing blood, is set in *adagio* tempo and begins in the uncommon key of B-flat minor; chromatic progressions pass through the even less common A-flat minor (m. 33) before a momentary arrival on C minor (m. 39). Meanwhile the voice declaims the text with sigh motives (on "nicht," "tausend," "Schmerzen," and "Blut"), and with descending chromatic lines at the phrase "Floß nicht sein Blut."

The duet (no. 9, illustrated in Example VIII-18) begins with a delicate and simple accompaniment (with continuo silent, to lighten the sonority) and includes many of the sigh motives (with *forte-piano* marks for the orchestra in mm. 13–15) so characteristic of the work as a whole. In measure 11 Bach interprets the text by placing a rest on the strong beat and the word "schwachen" on a "weak" beat. When the voices join together, either in parallel thirds and sixths or in counterpoint, the vocal-orchestral texture becomes more active—a texture less characteristic of the time than of Bach. Especially interesting is the orchestral effect of divided violas (rare in oratorios of this period) and flutes doubling the voices at the unison and octave, while the violins play decorated versions of the vocal lines and the continuo is silent (mm. 39–44).

The bass aria (no. 21) shown in Example VIII-19 follows the narration of the Ascension and is the most majestic of all the solo numbers in the oratorio. The voice commands that the gates of Heaven be opened and does so in fanfares of mounting tension, the top notes of which rise from b-flat through d' and e'-flat to f' (mm. 8–11). That command is introduced and accompanied by other fanfares for strings, horns, and trumpets, written in unison and octaves. After an effective pause (m. 12) following the initial flurry of activity, the same rhythmic style continues as the voice describes Christ the King's entrance into his realm.

Of the seven recitatives all but one (no. 17, the story of doubting Thomas) are orchestrally accompanied; but only number 3 (Example VIII-20), which describes the Resurrection, is in that style throughout. With an opening crescendo in the timpani and strings, dotted patterns, and dissonances, the orchestra prepares for and accompanies the text describing the awesome trembling of Judea, the earthquakes, and the backward flowing of the Jordan. At the Andante the voice rises an octave and a half to paint the central text of the oratorio's first part: "The Lord of the earth arises from its womb."

In all recitatives that mix simple and accompanied style, the former is used mostly for narrative texts and the latter for quotations or paraphrases from biblical persons, usually from Jesus. Example VIII-21 illustrates the procedure. Simple style is used for the first section of recitative, which narrates the entrance of Mary Magdalene by asking who it is who enters the garden and weeps, and then describes Jesus' appearance in the garden. In a style reminiscent of the accompaniment to Jesus' words in J.

EXAMPLE VIII-18. *Auferstehung*—C. P. E. Bach (Bach, C. P. E. *Auferstehung**, pp. 59–61).

EXAMPLE VIII-18. continued

EXAMPLE VIII-18. continued

EXAMPLE VIII-18. continued

EXAMPLE VIII-18. continued

Father of Thy weak children, he who has fallen, he who is sorrowful, hears from
Thee his first consolation. . . . Consoler, Father, Friend of Mankind, oh how
with every tear Your merciful heart is softened. . . .

EXAMPLE VIII-19. continued

EXAMPLE VIII-19. continued

EXAMPLE VIII-19. continued

Der Kö- nig zie- het in sein Reich,

You gates of God, open! The King enters his realm, . . .

EXAMPLE VIII-20. *Auferstehung*—C. P. E. Bach (Bach, C. P. E. *Auferstehung**, pp. 10–12).

EXAMPLE VIII-20. continued

Ju- dä- a zit- tert! Sei- ne Ber- ge be- ben! Der

Jor- dan flieht den Strand! Was zit terst du, Ju- dä- ens Land? Ihr

EXAMPLE VIII-20. continued

EXAMPLE VIII-20. continued

11

Schoß, tritt auf den Fels, und zeigt der stau-nen- den Na-tur sein Le- ben.

Judea trembles! Its mountains shake! The Jordan flees its banks! Why do you tremble, land of Judea? You mountains, why do you shake so? What was the matter, Jordan, that your current flowed backward? The Lord of the earth arises from its womb, steps on the rock, and shows his life to astonished nature.

EXAMPLE VIII-21. *Auferstehung*—C. P. E. Bach (Bach, C. P. E. *Auferstehung**, pp. 55–57).

B solo

Wer ist die Si- o- nit- tin, die vom Gra- be so schüch-tern in den Gar-ten flieht und

B.c.

4

wei- net? Nicht lan- ge. Je- sus selbst er- schei- net, doch un- er-

EXAMPLE VIII-21. continued

EXAMPLE VIII-21. continued

EXAMPLE VIII-21. continued

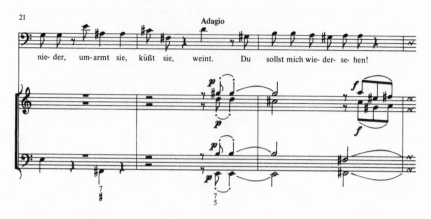

Who is the daughter of Sion, who from the grave so timidly into the garden flees and weeps? Not for long. Jesus himself appears, but unrecognized, and speaks to her: O daughter, why do you weep? Sir, tell me, did you take my Lord from this grave? Where does he lie? Ah, allow me to bring him back, that I might sprinkle him with my tears, that I might anoint him with these ointments in death, as I anointed him in life—Mary! Thus calls her Friend with a gentle voice, revealing his own form—Mary. My Master, ah! She falls at his feet, embraces him, kisses him, and weeps. You shall see me again! . . .

S. Bach's *St. Matthew Passion* and in other Passions before it,[44] sustained strings accompany Jesus' first words after the Resurrection, "O daughter, why do you weep?" The same string accompaniment continues for the dialogue between Mary and Jesus, but the words of Jesus, when he reveals himself to her ("Maria," in mm. 16 and 19), are emphasized by motivic accompaniment. Simple style returns for more narrative passages (mm. 17–18 and 20–22), but they are followed by string accompaniment for the dialogue between Mary and Jesus. Of further interest in this recitative is the rhetorical manner of Bach's text setting: in measure 4 the pause after the question mark that precedes the comment, "Not for long," and the longer notes on "lange"; the changes of tempo (mm. 12, 20, and 22) for convincing rhetorical declamation; and the telling rhythmic and melodic differentiation of the text segments within the scene (mm. 19–22) where Mary recognizes Jesus, falls at his feet, embraces him, kisses him, and weeps.

Unlike most German oratorios (including Bach's other two major ones listed above), *Auferstehung* does not include chorales. It is of interest that the setting of the same text by Bach's Berlin colleague, Agricola—a setting that Bach would probably have known—uses chordal-chorale style for the three refrain chorus texts, "Triumph! Triumph!" Although

44. On early examples in this tradition, see Smither, *Oratorio*, 2:41.

Bach follows Agricola in repeating virtually the same music for the text repetitions, he prefers to set the text in a jubilant allegro, with full winds and fanfare-style melodic lines in the orchestra and mainly chordal style in the vocal parts. With two exceptions all six of the choruses in the oratorio are essentially in chordal style. The exceptions are those ending each of the two parts and including fugues. Bach set the long final text of the oratorio, a text of rejoicing for the Ascension, as a monumental choral rondo in six sections (beginning at mm. 1, 79, 172, 215, 255, and 287, respectively), the last of which is the fugue. The first five sections include: brilliant fanfares for trumpets and timpani; mainly chordal writing for the chorus but some imitative sections and occasional long roulades (especially on "Jauchzen"); some powerful choral unison passages ("Der Herr ist König," mm. 113–17 and 129–33), without orchestra, and based on the same melodic figure heard with the words "Ihr Tore Gottes" at the beginning of the preceding aria (see the figure of Example VIII-19, mm. 6–7); and pictorial effects on "The sea roars, the rivers rejoice" ("Das Meer brause, die Wasserströme frohlocken," mm. 153–61). The closing four-part fugue (see Example VIII-22 for part of the first exposition) has a giguelike subject with *colla parte* orchestration for the strings and woodwinds and with occasional reinforcements by the brass and timpani; stretto passages appear near the end (mm. 323ff., 349ff., and 372ff.); and the oratorio closes with a brief chordal "halleluja."

Johann Heinrich Rolle: Lazarus, oder die Feyer der Auferstehung

Rolle was born in 1716 in Quedlinburg (about thirty miles south-west of Magdeburg).[45] His father, the composer and organist Christian Friedrich (1681–1751), was the Quedlinburg Kantor from 1709 until 1721 when he accepted a Kantorate in Magdeburg and subsequently became the city's music director. Together with Kuhnau and J. S. Bach, he judged a new organ in Halle (1716), and he competed with J. S. Bach for the Kantorate in Leipzig. Johann Heinrich studied music with his father and served as an organist in Magdeburg from 1732 until 1736 when he moved to Leipzig. According to early biographers, he studied law at the University of Leipzig, but no documentation to that effect has been found.[46] In Berlin he served as a violinist and violist in Frederick the

45. On Rolle's life and works, and especialy the oratorios, see Kaestner, *Rolle*; Thomas A. Bauman, "Rolle," *New Grove*, 16:113–15; and Erich Valentin, "Rolle," *MGG*, 11:cols. 653–656.

46. On the presumed law studies in Leipzig, see Kaestner, *Rolle*, p. 7; the law studies are questioned by Valentin, "Rolle," *MGG*, 11:col. 653; and Bauman, "Rolle," *New Grove*, 16:114.

All that has breath, praise the Lord, hallelujah!

Great's court orchestra from 1741 until 1747, and he is said to have been in close contact with the Graun brothers, the Bendas, and C. P. E. Bach. He returned to Magdeburg in 1747 to become the organist of the Johanniskirche. Upon the death of his father, he succeeded him as Kantor and city music director and retained these positions until his death in 1785.

Of special importance to Rolle's development as an oratorio composer in Magdeburg was his participation in an association of intellectuals, including at various times: Johann Wilhelm Ludwig Gleim, Klopstock, Sulzer, Samuel Patzke, and August Hermann Niemeyer. The association was established in 1760 as the *Gelehrten Clubb*, in 1763 became the *Literarische Gesellschaft*, and continued to function at least until the late 1780s. From discussions in this group arose the idea of a public concert series to be directed by Rolle; founded in 1764 and called the *öffentliche Concerte*, this was among the earliest concert series in Germany. Prior to that date Rolle's Magdeburg compositions—Passions, brief oratorios,

FIGURE VIII-3. Johann Heinrich Rolle (1716–85). (Engraving by Christian Gottlieb Geyser after a painting by Jacob Adolph Fischer. Reproduced by permission of the Bild-Archiv of A-Wn.)

and motets—had been heard only in the Johanniskirche. The sixteen *öffentliche Concerte* per year, mainly of Rolle's works, were given in a guildhall, the Seidenkramer-Innungshaus.[47] Between 1766 and 1785 Rolle composed nearly twenty large-scale dramatic oratorios for this series, most of them based on Old Testament subjects. About half of these works were published in keyboard reductions in Leipzig between 1771 and 1787, usually subtitled *ein musikalisches Drama*; they were widely performed and made Rolle famous throughout Germany.

Many of the librettos for Rolle's oratorios, both lyric and dramatic, were written by his associates in the *Gelehrten Clubb*, Klopstock, Patzke, and Niemeyer. Although his six lyric works (mostly on the Passion) are characteristic of the mainstream of oratorio in North Germany, the dramatic ones differ in their modern theatrical orientation from virtually all other German dramatic oratorios. The texts by Niemeyer—especially his *Abraham auf Moria* (1776), *Lazarus* (1778), and *Thirza und ihre Söhne* (1779)—are the most theatrical and reflect the *Sturm und Drang* movement current in the theater of the time.[48]

August Hermann Niemeyer (1754–1828) was a theologian and a prolific writer, both of theological works and of poetry; in 1779 he became a professor at the University of Halle and from 1808 to 1816 was also that university's chancelor and rector. Characteristic of his librettos is the emphasis on the gloom and anguish of the situations, which usually deal with death, and the awesomeness of supernatural events. His works show strong contrasts of affect, a flair for extravagant language (as opposed to the simple, direct intimacy of *empfindsam* librettos), and remarkable dramatic continuity, all of which Rolle skillfully emphasizes in his musical settings. Essential to the effect of *Sturm und Drang* theater in Rolle's late oratorios are the detailed descriptions of scenes, scene changes, and actions given in both the printed librettos and keyboard reductions of the music; these descriptions give the listener-reader an imaginary scenic context for the music and thus intensify the dramatic impact. No evidence is known of staged performances of Rolle's oratorios, but the scenic descriptions provide sufficient information for effective staging. Given the anticipation of German romantic theater in Niemeyer's texts, it is no surprise that in 1820 Franz Schubert began a setting of *Lazarus* (D689) and as late as 1832 the libretto of *Thirza* was highly praised in the journal *Caecilia*.[49]

Rolle's setting of Neimeyer's *Lazarus, oder die Feyer der Auferstehung* (Lazarus, or the Celebration of the Resurrection) dates from 1778 and

47. For a picture of the Seidenkramer-Innungshaus, see Valentin, "Magdeburg," *MGG*, 8:col. 1474.

48. For a summary of this movement, and for comments on Rolle's *Sturm und Drang* works, see Daniel Heartz, "Sturm und Drang," *New Grove*, 18:311–12.

49. For Schubert's setting of act I and act II as far as no. 23, see Schubert, *Lazarus**; for the *Caecilia* comment, see Nauenburg, "Aphorismen," p. 244.

was published in a keyboard reduction in 1779.[50] Based on the story in John 11:1–44 of Jesus' raising of Lazarus, the libretto is divided into three acts (*Handlungen*). Its themes are death and resurrection, with much emphasis on death—the stress and anxiety of death as well as the peace of dying as a believer in Christ. In most of act I Lazarus approaches his death, which occurs just before the solo-choral complex that ends the act; in act II he is buried; and in act III he is awakened from death by Jesus, whose supernatural act is attended by an unearthly quiet followed by an earthquake and a thunderstorm.

The vivid theatrical character of the libretto is no doubt responsible for the absence of a role for Jesus, who is central to the story but does not appear; He does, however, appear in some other German librettos of the time. In this work as in Metastasio's librettos, the words of Jesus are always narrated in past tense by other personages, and only the effects of His miracle—not the miracle itself—are "seen" by the audience.

As described at the beginning of the printed libretto and keyboard reduction, the scene of the first act is "a garden before a rural house. Mary and Martha, the sisters of Lazarus, lead their sick brother out of the house, under the shadows of a palm tree, and lay him gently down on a flowered lawn. His face is pale but not distorted."[51] In recitatives, Lazarus (T) says he knows he is about to die and wishes in his final hour to enjoy God's creation. He urges his sisters not to weep. Martha (S) laments in recitative, and Mary prays, in a simple aria, for his eternal rest (no. 4, in Table VIII-5; see below, Example VIII-24). Nathan (T) arrives, says he has just come from Jesus, and in a recitative closely paraphrases Jesus' words about Lazarus: "This sickness is not unto death, but for the glory of God, that through it the Son of God may be glorified" (John 11:4; see Example VIII-27). Nathan prays (no. 9) that he, too, may go as gently to his grave as Lazarus. Martha and Mary speak of Lazarus's courage, and Mary sings a comparison aria (no. 11) in which God's love is likened to a solid rock in the midst of the waves in the sea. Jemina (S) enters, and Lazarus, who feels blessed to see her, refers to her as "daughter of the resurrection," for Jesus had raised her from the dead (Mark 5:21–43). Lazarus requests from her a song of death and resurrection. She sings (no. 13) of the sleep of the guiltless, which was her sleep, and in the following accompanied recitative (no. 14, "Nun entflog auf schnellen Schwingen") she describes her supernatural experience: her spirit's entrance into Heaven, her welcome there by the angels, and the blinding shimmer of God in the distance, and the way she was suddenly called

50. The sources for the present comments are the keyboard reduction, Rolle, *Lazarus**; the manuscript copy in US-Wc: M1500/.R64L3; and printed librettos in B-Br: Fétis, 4548 (a bound volume including two different librettos lacking names of place and publisher, one dated 1783 and the other undated) and in D-B: Mus. Tr. 814.

51. Rolle, *Lazarus**, p. 6.

TABLE VIII-5
Rolle, *Lazarus*: Structural Outline

Numbers	Keys
1. Overture	E♭
ACT I	
4. Aria. Maria, "Steh im letzten Kampf"	F
9. Aria. Nathanael, "Wenn ich nachgerungen"	B♭
11. Aria. Maria, "Gottes Liebe! Fels im Meer"	D
13. Aria. Jemina, "So schlummert auf Rosen"	A
15. Nathanael, Jemina, Maria, Martha, Chorus, "Heiliger, verlaß ihn nicht"	c
ACT II	
17. Aria. Simon, "Wehe! Wehe!"	d
19. Double Chorus, Maria, Martha, Jemina, Nathanael, "Sanft und still Schläft"	E
20. Chorus. "Du nimmst ihn auf"	E
23. Aria. Martha, "Hebt mich, der Stürme"	D
25. Duet. A Youth, Jemina, "Mein stiller Abend"	g
26. Chorus. "Wiedersehn! sey uns gesegnet"	C
ACT III	
28. Aria. Maria, "Auferwecker!"	C
30. [Arioso]. Maria, "So fließt der Thau"	E♭
32. [Arioso]. Simon, "Und nun? Die Gräber"	a
33. Chorus and solo (B). "Preis dem Erwecker!"	D
34. Chorus and soloists (S, A). "Er kam, mit Trost des Himmels"	D
35. Chorus and solo (B). "Er ist erwacht!"	D
37. Aria. Lazarus, "O daß mit Himmelharmonien"	F
38. Chorus and Lazarus, "Mehr! viel mehr!"	F
40. Aria. Simon, "In Wetterwolken eingehült"	c
42. Duet. Lazarus, Jemina, "Ich will dich"	B♭
43. Double Chorus. "Heilige Städte"	E♭

Note: The numbers and designations *aria*, *duet*, and *chorus* in this table are those printed in a libretto of the period (in B-Bn: Fétis, 4548), undated but corresponding to the text of Rolle, *Lazarus**. Numbers 30 and 32 were called "aria" in the libretto but are so brief that they are labeled "arioso" in the table. All omitted numbers are recitatives.

back to life by the words of Jesus, "Awake, awake my daughter!" As Lazarus grows weaker, Martha, Mary, Nathan, and Jemina see that his end is near, and they pray. At the close of a long accompanied recitative, Lazarus dies (see Example VIII-28). All present pray for him (no. 15) and the chorus of Friends of Lazarus, who have gradually assembled, join in a final prayer.

In act II "the scene is a verdant meadow filled with gravestones and with palms and cedars planted all around. In the background a small grove, and in the distance a path to Lazarus's dwelling."[52] The act opens with an anguished "lost" scene by Simon (B)—a Sadducee, the only unbeliever in the drama, and a characteristic *Sturm und Drang* figure— who is tormented by fear of death and annihilation. According to the "stage" directions he "enters with wild agitation" and sings an accompanied recitative (no. 16), beginning with a line familiar in both opera and oratorio (cf. the lines of Peter, "Dove son: Dove corro," after his denial of Jesus, in Metastasio's *La passione*, quoted in chapter 2, "Recitatives"):

Wo bin ich? Wo bin ich?	Where am I? Where am I?
Weh! Gräber um mich—bemooßte Steine,	Alas! Graves around me— moss-covered stones,
Blumen aus Staube gesproßt, und modernden Menschengebeine,	flowers sprouting from dust, and recent human bones,
Tod und Vernichtung um mich her!	death and annihilation around me!

His fear increases as he sees an open grave and wonders whether it is for him, and with his aria of fear (no. 17; see Example VIII-26) the scene reaches its climax. Nathan enters and in recitative tries to console him; he tells Simon to stay awhile, for they are now bringing Lazarus to his grave. In the distance, two choruses of the Friends of Lazarus, plus soloists (no. 19) follow the procession and sing of the gentleness of their friend's sleep. Martha sings an aria, reflecting her suffering, in which she wishes to follow her brother in death (see Example VIII-25). Lazarus is laid to rest during the duet of a Youth (T) and Jemina (no. 25), and in the final chorus with soloists (no. 26, "Wiedersehn!") Lazarus's friends bid him farewell.

The scene of act III is "as in the first act, before the house of the deceased."[53] In an opening recitative Martha paraphrases and quotes from the biblical scene in which she says to Jesus, "Lord, if thou hadst been here my brother would not have died," and Jesus replies, "Thy brother shall rise" (John 11:21–27). Both sisters of Lazarus take hope, and Mary expresses hers in an aria (no. 28) and a brief arioso (no. 30). Then the orchestra continues and "the scene changes into the meadow before the grove, as in the beginning of the second act."[54] In the background of the new scene, two choruses of the Friends of Lazarus, plus Mary, Martha, and Nathan, stand around the grave of Lazarus, and in

52. Ibid., p. 29.
53. Ibid., p. 57.
54. Found in all copies of the printed libretto cited above, following "So fließt der Thau" (no. 30) but not found in Rolle, *Lazarus**, pp. 62–63.

the foreground stands Simon, who expresses, in an accompanied recitative (no. 31, "Wie ich wanke! Wie ich irre!"), even more torment than when last seen. He falls to the ground in agony—but suddenly he feels an awesome stillness:

RECITATIVE

Wie wird mir? Welche heil'ge Stille?	What is happening to me? What holy stillness?
Der Klage Lied im Hayn verstummt!—	The song of lament in the grove has become silent!
Es schweigt das Thal, die Ebne— neues Leben	The valley is quiet, the plain— new life
Durchathmet die Naturen!— Immer stiller!	Breathes through nature!— Ever stiller!
[Arioso, no. 32]	
Und nun? Die Gräber——	And now? The graves——
Sie sinken unter mir! Die Donner—Schlag auf Schlag!	They sink under me! The thunder—bolt upon bolt!
Zertrümmert Gott den Erdkreis? Rettet,	Is God shattering the world? Save,
O rettet—rettet ich versinke!	oh save me—save me, I am being swallowed up!
(Er eilt wild von der Scene.)	(He rushes wildly from the scene.)

It now becomes clear that Simon has experienced the phenonena accompanying the supernatural moment of Lazarus' awakening from the dead: the chorus sings, triumphantly, "Praise to the awakener!" (no. 33), which initiates a series of choruses (nos. 33–35) of rejoicing and praise. Nathan then explains to Simon, who has returned, that Lazarus lives again; Lazarus enters from the grove, arms outstretched, "Welcome my brothers," and sings a recitative and aria (no. 37) of praise. After a chorus and further recitatives, Simon understands what has happened and confesses that he is born again: first in a recitative, "O day of jubilation! I am born anew, the name death rings sweetly in my ears . . .," and then in an aria (no. 40) of confidence in the face of the Last Judgement. Thus the theme of resurrection extends beyond Lazarus' awakening to Simon's rebirth. After a duet of praise (no. 42) sung by Lazarus and Jemina, the two who had been awakened by Jesus, the final chorus praises the resurrection of Lazarus and comments on the resurrection of the dead on the day of the Last Judgement and on the eternal morning, which follows the night of the grave.

As shown in Table VIII-5, the overture to the oratorio and the last chorus of act III are in E-flat, the main tonal center of the work; E-flat (and its relative minor) are the keys with the greatest number of flats in this oratorio. Although the key of E-flat appears again in recitatives and in the arioso no. 30, the relative minor of E-flat and its parallel major (C minor and major) are heard more often and at important points. In C minor Lazarus begins his first speech about his impending death (no. 2), and he dies after singing in the dominant minor of C minor (see the turn to G minor near the end of Example VIII-28), which leads to C minor for the final number of of act I; act II begins (with an accompanied recitative) and ends in C major; the first aria of act III (no. 28) is in C major; and Simon's aria (no. 40) is in C minor. The central portion of each act moves to sharp keys: act I, as far away from the tonic as A major; act II farther away, to E major; and act III to D major. In general, sharp keys are used to set texts expressing hope and peace.

Of special interest in the general structure of *Lazarus* (and of Rolle's other late dramatic oratorios) is the emphasis on musical continuity and flexibility—perhaps a reflection of Gluck's close association of music and drama in his reform operas. In Rolle's dramatic oratorios, simple and accompanied recitative, aria, arioso, and choral styles are intermingled to match the continuous dramatic development in the libretto. In *Lazarus*, for instance, from the beginning of the overture to the end of number 9 the music flows continuously, with smooth harmonic and rhythmic connections between numbers: a transition leads from the overture to the next number, an accompanied recitative (no. 2), which is followed without pause by Mary's simple recitative (no. 3) and her aria (no. 4), which has no ritornello; numbers 5–7 are recitatives (simple-accompanied-simple) that follow without pause; and Nathan's aria (no. 9) has no opening ritornello but closes with five orchestral measures followed by a double bar (the first one since the beginning of the act). Another long section of continuous music occurs between numbers 29 and 35, beginning before and concluding after the awakening of Lazarus. Especially in this section, with its two ariosos, Rolle moves flexibly and skillfully from one style to another, depending on the requirements of his text. The three choruses (nos. 33–35) form a single unit of choral-solo writing, and the intermingling of choral and solo passages is heard in most of the other choruses as well.

Rolle requires a large orchestra for *Lazarus*, including strings, pairs of flutes, oboes, bassoons, and horns, three trumpets, and timpani. The only extended instrumental piece is number 1, which follows the traditional structure and style of the French overture (and Rolle uses the French term, *ouverture*). Acts II and III both begin with brief orchestral introductions to recitatives. The introduction to act III (Example VIII-23) is of special interest. According to the "stage" directions, Mary, whose brother had died at the end of act I, is "strolling about, in deep thought" ("tiefsinnig umhergehend"), and the instrumental passage expresses her mood. Surprising for its time is the chromaticism, especially in measures 3–4, which consists of a chromatically descending stream of parallel diminished seventh chords, marked *tenuto* to heighten their effect. As we shall see, Rolle introduces similar chromatic passages elsewhere for expressive purposes.

Four of the arias (nos. 4, 11, 23, and 40) have transformed da capo structures (A1-B-A2); number 28 is the only da capo aria and the only aria with a contrasting tempo in the B section (Larghetto-Allegro-Larghetto); the remaining arias are either in binary or rondolike forms. Number 9 is unusual for its arrangement of text and tempos: a text with eight lines is set to music as A (Vivace, lines 1–4), B (Larghetto, lines 5–8), and B' (Larghetto continuing, lines 1–4 repeated). Number 37, a binary structure ending on the dominant, is harmonically continued by the following chorus. Probably for reasons of Rolle's emphasis on dramatic and musical continuity, mentioned above, four of the arias (nos. 4, 8, 11, and 23) begin without a ritornello.

The styles of the arias and duets range from simple, sentimental, songlike pieces often with dancelike rhythms (nos. 4, 13, 25, 28, and 42) to more powerful numbers bordering on bravura style (nos. 9, 11, 17, 23, 37, and 40). Representing the simpler style is the first aria of the oratorio (no. 4), the beginning of which is shown in Example VIII-24. Mary has just urged Martha not to disturb Lazarus with her lamenta-

EXAMPLE VIII-24. *Lazarus*—Rolle (Rolle, *Lazarus**, p. 8; US-Wc: MI500.R64L3, vol. 1, pp. 24–25).

EXAMPLE VIII-24. continued

Frie- den ihm die See- le — sey.

Help the tired one, in the final struggle, Lord of death, that his soul be filled
with sublime, sweet peace.

tion, and in the aria Mary prays that her brother may die in peace.
Accompanied by muted strings, often in thirds and sixths and with considerable doubling of the vocal line, the simple, triadic, symmetrical
melody of Mary's aria reflects her desire that Lazarus's "soul be filled
with sublime, sweet peace."

The aria that is closest to bravura style is Martha's (no. 23), sung
shortly before the burial of Lazarus. Her preceding accompanied recitative, a lament for her brother, closes with her fervent wish that she might
die and sink into the grave with him. In the extravagant text of her aria,
of which the beginning is shown in Example VIII-25, she asks to be lifted
up by the "wing of the storm, from the hill of death," and wishes to
follow Lazarus "through towering waves, through all the stars' orbits."
With ascending vocal lines and upward-rushing thirty-second notes in
the strings, Rolle depicts the images of the text in this example, and
slightly later in the aria he sets the image of "the stars' orbits" by an
eight-measure coloratura passage, mostly of sixteenth notes, which
reaches the high a'' four times.

Rolle's chromaticism in the service of an anguished text is illustrated in
Simon's aria (no. 17, see Example VIII-26), which follows his equally
tortured accompanied recitative in his first appearance, at the beginning
of act II. Tormented by thoughts of death and trembling at the open
grave, which he thinks might be his own, he begins with two chromatic
sighs ("Wehe! Wehe!"), while the basses play a trembling, repeated-note
chromatic descent of a perfect fourth (mm. 8–13). In a subsequent
phrase Simon's line ascends chromatically and is doubled by the basses in
repeated eighth notes (mm. 17–21) as he sings of his shaking limbs. The
words "open grave" are each time depicted by a half-measure rest and a

EXAMPLE VIII-25. *Lazarus*—Rolle (Rolle, *Lazarus**, p. 44; US-Wc: MI500.R64L3, vol. 1, pp. 124–26).

EXAMPLE VIII-25. continued

Lift me up, wing of the storm, from the hill of death; through towering waves, through all the stars' orbits do I wish to follow him.

EXAMPLE VIII-26. *Lazarus*—Rolle (Rolle, *Lazarus**, p. 32; US-Wc: M1500.R64L3, vol. 1, pp. 90–92).

EXAMPLE VIII-26. continued

EXAMPLE VIII-26. continued

EXAMPLE VIII-26. continued

Woe! Woe! Woe, from the horrid thoughts of death, all my limbs shake, before my feet the open grave.

descending leap of an octave, first returning upward (mm. 24–25), then proceeding stepwise downward to the low *A* (mm. 28–29 and 30–31).

We have seen that an important feature of the oratorio is its dramatic and musical continuity and the intermingling of styles that helps to achieve it. Example VIII-27 from act I illustrates some of that flexibility. At the beginning of the example Nathan tells Lazarus that he has come to bring him the words of Jesus (mm. 3–8). When Nathan begins to quote Jesus, his words are set in triple meter and arioso style (mm. 9–20)—in fact, Jesus' words are consistently set in arioso throughout the oratorio. After the quotation (m. 21) Nathan continues in accompanied recitative, and the final cadence of the recitative falls on the first note of Nathan's aria (no. 9, not shown in the example), which begins without a ritornello.

The accompanied recitative shown in Example VIII-28, the death scene of Lazarus, is of special interest for the sensitivity that Rolle shows toward the text. After a simple beginning, a chromatic bass underlines Lazarus's words "the footstep of death" (mm. 28–30), and diminished seventh chords express the word "death" ("Tod"); more chromaticism, diminished sevenths, and dissonances are heard at "I am ready to walk the dark path" (mm. 31–34); a shift to G minor and its dominant, with simpler harmony (fewer dissonances and less chromaticism), accompanies the prayer, "Lord, my Shepherd, lead Me!" (mm. 37–39); chromaticism returns at "Ah, if my heart breaks" (mm. 40–41); and the final prayer, "Thou full of grace, do not abandon me!" (mm. 42–45), is again in G minor, with simpler harmony and "sweet" parallel thirds in the flutes and violins.

Essentially *Lazarus* includes only six choruses, all of which are choral-solo complexes, for numbers 19–20 of act II constitute one unit, as do numbers 33–35; none of the choruses is a chorale. Each act ends with a chorus; internal choruses are in act II (no. 20) and act III (nos. 33–35 and 38). Most of the choruses are in chordal style and are thus more like operatic choruses than those for church works. In act III, numbers 33 and 35 (which have similar melodic material) both close with fugato sections, and the final chorus of act III also has some fugal texture, but none of the choruses includes an extended fugue.

Ich, als der Bo- te kam, stand dicht an sei- ner Sei- te horch-te da der ho-hen

Weis- heit sei- ner Re- de; Geh, sprach- er, und sa- ge mei- nen Freun- den:

Nicht zum To- de, nicht zum To- de leigt La- za-rus,

hoch wer- det ihr den Sohn des Va- ters

prei- sen, den Sohn des Va- ters— prei- sen.

EXAMPLE VIII-27. continued

I came as a messenger; I stood close to His side, hearkened to the noble wisdom of His words; go, He said, and tell my friends: Lazarus does not lie unto death; greatly will you glorify the Son of the Father! I hurried to you—no, no, that is not death!

EXAMPLE VIII-28. *Lazarus*—Rolle (Rolle, *Lazarus**, pp. 24–25 US-Wc: M1500.R64L3, vol. 1, pp. 71–74).

EXAMPLE VIII-28. continued

EXAMPLE VIII-28. continued

EXAMPLE VIII-28. continued

Herz nun bricht, dann, Gna-den-vol- ler, dann, Gna-den-vol- ler,

dann ver-wirf mich nicht, dann ver-wirf mich nicht!

I am dying! Ah, now comes the footstep of death! I am ready to walk the dark path! It is so dark! Lord, my Shepherd, lead me! Ah if my heart now breaks, then, Thou full of grace, do not abandon me! . . .

Joseph Haydn: The Creation *and* The Seasons

Reflecting English and Handelian influence, Haydn's *The Creation* (1798) and *The Seasons* (1801) are among the greatest masterworks of the composer's later years and of the late Classical style. Both were enthusiastically received at their first performances, yet by neither their composer nor later generations have they been judged of equal importance.[55] In the nineteenth and twentieth centuries, *The Creation* found its way into the "standard" repertoire of choral societies in German- and English-speaking countries, whereas *The Seasons* has been relatively seldom performed. It is of terminological interest that Haydn called *The Creation*, but not *The Seasons*, an oratorio on the title page of the first edition, probably because of the lesser religious emphasis in the later work. Yet in Haydn's time *The Seasons* was widely considered an oratorio, as it usually is today. For reasons of space and because of the greater importance of *The Creation* in the history of the oratorio, that work will form the focus of attention in the present section. After the treatment of *The Creation*, a few general comments on *The Seasons* will follow.

The Creation

The biographical sketch of Haydn provided in chapter 3, in relation to his Italian oratorio *Il ritorno di Tobia*, mentions his two visits to London of 1791–92 and 1794–95, as the featured composer and musical director of the Salomon concerts. Haydn could not have lived in London during those years without being affected by the overwhelming veneration accorded to Handel; the English Handelian tradition was to exert a powerful influence on his subsequent oratorio composition—especially on *The Creation*, but also on *The Seasons*. Haydn's first sojourn in London began in January 1791, and just five months later he attended the gigantic Handel Festival in Westminster Abbey, from 23 May to 1 June (see chapter 4). Seated in a box near the royal family, he heard monumental performances of *Israel in Egypt* and *Messiah* complete, and excerpts from *Esther, Saul, Judas Maccabaeus,* and *Deborah*. He had heard Handel oratorios before, at the Viennese performances sponsored by Baron Gottfried van Swieten, but the English performances, particularly at this festival, were of an entirely different order. If the report by Giuseppe Carpani, who knew Haydn, is accurate, Haydn "confessed . . . that when he heard the music of Hendl [*sic*] in London, he was struck as if he had been put back to the beginning of his studies and had known nothing up to that moment. He meditated on every note and drew from

---

55. On the reception of *The Creation* in Haydn's time, see Landon, *Haydn*, 4:318–23, 572–601; and of *The Seasons*, see ibid., 5:37, 41–49, 182–99.

FIGURE VIII-4. Joseph Haydn (1732–1809). (Stipple engraving by Thomas Hardy. Reproduced by permission of the Bild-Archiv of A-Wn.)

those most learned scores the essence of true musical grandeur."[56] Other reports, too, confirm Haydn's admiration for Handel's oratorios.

Near the end of Haydn's second visit to England came the initial impetus for his composition of *The Creation*. His biographer Albert Christoph Dies, whose book was based on conversations with Haydn, summarizes the initial stage of the oratorio's history: "The first suggestion for

56. Giuseppe Carpani, *Le Haydine* (Milan: C. Buccinelli, 1812), pp. 162–63, as translated in Landon, *Haydn*, 3:84.

this work came from Salomon in London. Since he had been fortunate in so many musical undertakings up to then, and Haydn had contributed no little to his fortune, his courage for new undertakings was always greater. Salomon resolved to have a great oratorio written by Haydn, and delivered to him for that purpose an already old text, in the English language. Haydn had doubts about his knowledge of the English language, did not undertake it, and finally left London on August 15, 1795."[57]

When he returned to Vienna, Haydn showed the libretto to Swieten, one of the city's most important patrons of music, an admirer of both Handelian oratorio and Haydn's music, and the arranger of the text to Haydn's *Seven Last Words*. In a letter to the periodical *Allgemeine musicalische Zeitung* some months after the first performances of *The Creation*, Swieten provided some important information about the work's early history and its libretto. According to his letter, the libretto was written

> by an unnamed author who had compiled it largely from *Milton's* Paradise Lost, and had intended it for *Handel*. What prevented the great man from making use of it is unknown; but when *Haydn* was in London it was looked out, and handed over to the latter with the request that he should set it to music. At first sight the material seemed to him indeed well chosen, and well suited to musical effects, but he nevertheless did not accept the proposal immediately; he was just on the point of leaving Vienna, and he reserved the right to announce his decision from there, where he wanted to take a closer look at the poem. [On his return] he then showed it to me, and I found myself in agreement with the verdict he had given. But I recognized at once that such an exalted subject would give *Haydn* the opportunity I had long desired, to show the whole compass of his profound accomplishments and to express the full power of his inexhaustible genius; I therefore encouraged him to take the work in hand, and in order that our Fatherland might be the first to enjoy it, I resolved to clothe the English poem in German garb. In this way my translation came about. It is true that I followed the plan of the original faithfully as a whole, but I diverged from it in details as often as musical progress and expression, of which I already had an ideal conception in my mind, seemed to demand. Guided by these sentiments, I often judged it necessary that much should be shortened or even omitted, on the one hand, and on the other that much should be made more prominent or brought into greater relief, and much placed more in the shade. . . .[58]

57. Gotwals, *Haydn*, pp. 37–38, as translated by Gotwals from Dies, *Biographische Nachrichten von Joseph Haydn* (Vienna, 1810).

58. Letter dated Vienna, end of December 1798, printed in *Allgemeine Musi-*

Neither Dies nor Swieten mentions the name of the original English librettist. Haydn's friend and first biographer Georg August Griesinger says the author was "Lidley";[59] yet, according to recent scholarship, "no likely librettist by that name can be found."[60] It has been conjectured that "Lidley" was actually Thomas Linley senior (1733–95) and that, as an improbable author of the libretto, he may simply have made a copy of it available to Salomon and thus to Haydn.[61]

Some form of the libretto must have been available to Haydn by 1796, for he appears to have begun the sketches of *The Creation* in that year.[62] The degree of musical collaboration between Swieten and Haydn is unclear, but Swieten offered numerous suggestions (treated below) on the musical setting of the libretto. A story recounted by the well-known poet and playwright, Franz Grillparzer, would make Swieten's musical role important, for the latter "had each piece, as soon as it was ready, copied and pre-rehearsed with a small orchestra. Much he discarded as too trivial [*kleinlich*] for the grand subject. Haydn gladly submitted [*fügte sich*], and thus that astonishing work came into being which would be admired by coming generations. I have all this from the lips of a well-informed contemporary who himself took part in these pre-rehearsals."[63]

By late in 1797 Haydn had finished the first draft of all, or most, of *The Creation*;[64] and by April the parts had been copied for the first performance, which was sponsored by Swieten's Gesellschaft der Associirten and given in the Schwarzenberg Palais, the residence of one of the members.[65] The public rehearsal took place on 29 April and the first performance proper on 30 April 1798. Given under Haydn's direction with a probable performing force of about 180,[66] the work was greeted with enormous enthusiasm by the audience and press alike, and repeat

kalische Zeitung, 1 (1798–99):254–55; translation from Olleson, "Haydn's Creation," p. 150.

59. Griesinger, *Biographische Notizen über Joseph Haydn* (Leipzig, 1810), translated in Gotwals, *Haydn*, pp. 37–38.

60. Olleson, "Haydn's Creation," p. 152.

61. For details, see ibid., pp. 152–53, 162–63.

62. Landon, *Haydn*, 4:116.

63. Translated from Grillparzer's *Sämtliche Werke* (Stuttgart, 1893), 15/4:124, as quoted in Walter, "Swietens handschriftliche Textbücher," p. 242, by Landon, *Haydn*, 4:353.

64. Landon, *Haydn*, 4:265.

65. The Schwarzenberg Palais, which no longer exists, was in the Mehlmarkt (now the Neuer Markt). See endpapers, no. 1.

66. It is not clear whether the number of ca. 180 (see Landon, *Haydn*, 4:449–50) is that of the orchestra or the total performing force, but the latter seems more in keeping with Viennese tradition of large forces for such works at this time.

performances were given in the same place on 7 and 10 May.[67] In 1799 *The Creation* was performed again at the Schwarzenberg Palais on 2 and 4 March, in the Burgtheater (see endpapers no. 4 and Figure I-3) on 19 March (all Lenten performances), and on 22 and 23 December in the Burgtheater for the annual Advent concerts of the Tonkünstler-Societät. From the first performance until 1810 *The Creation* was performed at least forty-five times in Vienna and frequently in other European centers as well.[68]

The earliest surviving manuscript scores of *The Creation* include Haydn's conducting score and three others made under the supervision of his personal copyist, Johann Essler.[69] In February 1800 the first edition of *The Creation* in full score was published by the composer; later issues were made by Breitkopf & Härtel in Leipzig.

The first edition of *The Creation* bore a title page in both German and English and included bilingual text underlay (the earliest known example of bilingual underlay for a major work) so that the oratorio might be sung in either language.[70] Until recently, scholars and performers alike have assumed that Swieten had changed his original English model so drastically that the German text should be considered original and the English a translation—according to Donald Francis Tovey and others, "a re-translation by a German from the German."[71] This assumption has resulted in the assignment of a higher priority to the German than to the English; the latter, widely considered too weak for performance, is rarely heard in its original version.[72] Nevertheless, conclusions contrary to the general assumptions about the English text are strongly suggested by recent research into the manuscript and printed sources of *The Creation* and into the details of Haydn's text setting. The following summary of the results of the new research cites the main bases for the reassessment of the English text's priority: "The English text to the *Creation* as we

67. See the quotations from diaries and press notices in ibid., 4:318–21.

68. See the list of Viennese performances (together with dates, places, sponsors, performers, and literature) in Brown, *Haydn's "The Creation,"* Table 1, pp. 7–10. I am grateful to Professor A. Peter Brown for sending me page proofs of his forthcoming book.

69. The most recent study of the manuscript and printed sources of *The Creation* is Brown, *Haydn's "The Creation,"* which is a study in performance practice. For other comments on the early and modern sources, see Landon, *Haydn*, pp. 390–93. The sources used for the present study are Haydn, *Creation**-E; Haydn, *Creation**-M; and Haydn, *Creation**-P.

70. This paragraph summarizes the conclusions primarily of Temperley, "Libretto of *The Creation*" and partially of Olleson, "Haydn's *Creation.*" See those articles for the details of their arguments and for documentation.

71. Tovey, *Essays*, 5:120.

72. According to Temperley, "Libretto of *The Creation,*" p. 189, the Peters vocal score "still prints it essentially unaltered." On a forthcoming revision of the Peters vocal score, see below, n. 78.

know it from the printed score, was to a considerable extent simply compiled by van Swieten from his model,"[73] and thus much of it may be considered "original"; Swieten intended the music to fit the text in both languages;[74] although Haydn worked mainly from the German text, he probably had the English in mind, either as he composed or revised, for the music, on occasion, fits the English better than the German;[75] before the work's first publication, Swieten went through the score to fit all the English words to music and probably was the writer of the alternative musical notes as required;[76] the English texts printed for the first performances in London (1800) used the original "Lidley" version to make corrections and modifications, which shows a close relationship between Swieten's English version and the "Lidley" version;[77] and finally, "Whatever the shortcomings of the English text of *The Creation*, we can see now that there are compelling reasons for preferring it to any other, German or English, for performances in the English-speaking world. The composer made clear by his actions that he wanted this text to have equal authority with the German; and in many ways it must be closer to his own thoughts than any 'improved' English version can be."[78]

The libretto of *The Creation* is in three parts, as it no doubt was in the "Lidley" version, for Swieten stated in the letter quoted above that he "followed the plan of the original faithfully as a whole." Relatively few German oratorios are three-part works, but most of Handel's oratorios are, and the three-part oratorio was traditional in England; thus *The Creation* comes by its three-part structure quite naturally. The original English librettist relied on three sources for the compilation of his text: the stories of the Creation found in the first two books of Genesis, from which the oratorio's narrative derives; John Milton's *Paradise Lost*, especially book 7, on which the descriptive and lyrical passages are based; and the Psalms, which are paraphrased in some texts of praise at the ends of the Days of Creation.[79] The narrative-reflective libretto treats the first four Days in part I and the fifth and sixth in part II; part III focuses on Adam and Eve in Paradise and consists mostly of lyric and idyllic texts. (See Table VIII-6 for a structural outline.) In the "Lidley" version, each Day may have consisted of four phases: (1) a narrative from Genesis, (2) Genesis paraphrase and commentary, (3) words introducing the

73. Olleson, "Haydn's *Creation*," p. 160.

74. Ibid., p. 160, and Temperley, "Libretto of *The Creation*," p. 199.

75. Temperley, "Libretto of *The Creation*," pp. 199, 204.

76. Ibid., pp. 199–200, 204.

77. Ibid., p. 194.

78. Ibid., p. 211. Nicolas Temperley "has prepared a version faithful to the original English text, which is to be incorporated into the vocal score of the C. F. Peters edition," according to Brown, *Haydn's Creation*, p. xv.

79. For details, see Olleson, "Haydn's *Creation*," pp. 156–59; and Landon, *Haydn*, 4:346–49.

TABLE VIII-6
Haydn, *The Creation*: Structural Outline

Numbers	Keys
PART I	
1. Einleitung: Die Vorstellung des Chaos—Introduction: The Representation of Chaos	c-C
[*First Day*]	
RA. Raphael, "Im Anfange schuf Gott"—"In the beginning God created"	i-III
Chorus. "Und der Geist Gottes"—"And the spirit of God"	III-I
RA. Uriel, "Und Gott sah das Licht"—"And God saw the light"	I
2. Aria with chorus	
Aria. Uriel, "Nun schwanden vor dem Heiligen Strahle"—"Now vanish before the holy beams"	A:I
Chorus	
"Verzweiflung, Wut und Schrecken"—"Despairing, cursing rage"	iii
"Und eine neue Welt"—"A new created world"	I
[*Second Day*]	
3. RA. Raphael, "Und Gott machte das Firmament"—"And God made the firmament"	—
4. Chorus with solo. Gabriel, "Mit Staunen sieht das Wunderwerk"—"The marv'lous work beholds amaz'd"	C
[*Third Day*]	
5. RS. Raphael, "Und Gott Sprach"—"And God said"	—
6. Aria. Raphael, "Rollend in schäumenden Wellen"—"Rolling in foaming billows"	d-D
7. RS. Gabriel, "Und Gott sprach: Es bringe die Erde"—"And God said: Let the earth"	—
8. Aria. Gabriel, "Nun beut die Flur"—"With verdure clad"	B♭
9. RS. Uriel, "Und die himmlischen Heerscharen"—"And the heavenly host"	—
10. Chorus. "Stimmt an die Saiten"—"Awake the harp"	D
[*Fourth Day*]	
11. RS. Uriel, "Und Gott sprach: Es seyn Lichter"—"And God said: Let there be light"	—
12. RA. Uriel, "In vollem Glanze"—"In splendour bright"	D-C
13. Chorus, Gabriel, Uriel, Raphael, "Die Himmel erzählen"—"The heavens are telling"	C

Note: The numbers are those of the Eulenburg miniature score (No. 955), 1925, and of Landon, *Haydn*, 4:388–90. The abbreviations RA and RS stand for accompanied recitative and simple recitative, respectively.

TABLE VIII-6
continued

Numbers	Keys
PART II	
[Fifth Day]	
14. RA. Gabriel, "Und Gott sprach: Es bringe das Wasser"—"And God said: Let the waters bring forth"	—
15. Aria. Gabriel, "Auf starkem Fittige"—"On mighty pens"	F
16. RS, RA. Raphael, "Und Gott schuf große Wallfische"—"And God created great whales"	d
17. RS. Raphael, "Und die Engel"—"And the angels"	—
18. Trio. Gabriel, Uriel, Raphael, "In holder Anmuth"—"Most beautyfull appear"	A
19. Trio (Gabriel, Uriel, Raphael) with chorus, "Der Herr ist groß"—"The Lord is great"	A
[Sixth Day]	
20. RS. Raphael, "Und Gott sprach: Es bringe die Erde"—"And God said: Let the earth"	—
21. RA. Raphael, "Gleich öffnet sich der Erd Schoß"—"Strait opening her fertile womb"	—
22. Aria. Raphael, "Nun scheint in vollem Glanze der Himmel"—"Now heav'n in fullest glory shone"	D
23. RS. Uriel, "Und Gott schuf den Menschen"—"And God created man"	—
24. Aria. Uriel, "Mit Würd' und Hoheit angetan"—"In native worth and honour clad"	C
25. RS. Raphael, "Und Gott sah jedes Ding"—"And God saw ev'ry thing"	—
26. Chorus. "Vollendet ist das große Werk"—"Achieved is the glorious work"	B♭
27. Trio. Gabriel, Uriel, Raphael, "Zu dir, o Herr"—"To thee each living soul"	E♭
28. Chorus. "Vollendet is das große Werk"—"Achieved is the glorious work"	B♭
PART III	
29. RA. Uriel, "Aus Rosenwolken bricht"—"In rosy mantle"	E-C
30. Duet (Adam and Eve), with chorus, "Von deiner Güt"—"By thee with bliss"	C
31. RS. Adam, "Nun ist die erste Pflicht erfüllt"—"Our duty we performed now"	—
32. Duet. Eve, Adam, "Holde Gattin"—"Graceful consort"	E♭
33. RS. Uriel, "O glücklich Paar"—"O happy pair"	—
34. Chorus with soloists (SATB). "Singt dem Herren alle Stimmen!"—"Sing the Lord, ye voices all!"	B♭

Heavenly Host, and (4) words of praise by the Heavenly Host.[80] If that was the original scheme, Swieten omitted, shortened, and/or combined these phases for some of the Days. The solo personages in parts I and II of Swieten's libretto are the archangels Gabriel (S), Uriel (T), and Raphael (B), who sing the narrative and most of the commentary and participate with the chorus in songs of praise;[81] the chorus (always SATB) usually represents the Heavenly Host. In part III the main personages are Adam (B) and Eve (S); Uriel sings brief introductory recitatives, and the chorus participates in one of Adam and Eve's duets and sings with four unnamed soloists in the last number.

The libretto's treatment of the elements created on each of the six Days is shown in the following outline. (The outline includes references to Genesis 1 but not to Genesis 2, for the narrative depends less frequently and specifically on Genesis 2. Phases 3 and 4, the words introducing the Heavenly Host and the words of praise, are combined in the outline under the heading *Praise*.)

PART I

First Day
    1. *Genesis 1:1–4*—heaven, earth, light.
    2. *Commentary*—light, the fallen angels.
Second Day
    3. *Genesis 1:6–7*—division of the waters.
       Commentary—storms, winds, lightning, thunder, floods, hail, snow.
    4. *Praise*—the Heavenly Host.
Third Day
    5. *Genesis 1:9–10*—seas, earth.
    6. *Commentary*—sea, mountains, rocks, plains, rivers, brooks.
    7. *Genesis 1:11*—grass, trees.
    8. *Commentary*—grass, flowers, plants.
  9–10. *Praise*—the Heavenly Host.
Fourth Day
    11. *Genesis 1:14–16*—lights in the firmament: [sun, moon], stars.
    12. *Commentary*—sun, moon, stars.
    13. *Praise*—the Heavenly Host.

PART II

Fifth Day
    14. *Genesis 1:20*—fish, birds.
    15. *Commentary*—birds: eagle, lark, dove, nightingale.
    16. *Genesis 1:21–22*—whales, command to multiply.

80. Temperley, "The Libretto of *The Creation*," pp. 196–98; see Temperley's Table 2, summarizing the possible structure of the original, on his p. 197; that table has influenced my outline of the libretto.
81. In Swieten's earliest version, the angels were nameless; the names were

17–18. *Praise and commentary*—by the archangels (hills, water, birds, fish).

19. *Praise*—archangels and Heavenly Host.

Sixth Day

20. *Genesis 1:24*—beasts.

21. *Commentary*—beasts: lion, tiger, stag, horse, cattle, sheep, insects, worm.

22. *Commentary*—birds, fish, heavy beasts; but creation incomplete.

23. *Genesis 1:26*—man.

24. *Commentary*—man, woman.

25. *Genesis 1:31*—survey of creation.

26–28. *Praise*—the Heavenly Host.

PART III

29. Narrative introduction to duet and chorus.

30. Duet (Adam and Eve) and chorus of praise for the Creation.

31. Adam and Eve's introduction to their duet.

32. Love duet of Adam and Eve.

33. Uriel's suggestion of the fall from Grace by Adam and Eve.

34. Chorus of thanksgiving and praise.

As an aspect of Swieten's collaboration with Haydn on the music of *The Creation*, it is of interest that the manuscript libretto with which Swieten supplied the composer is filled with suggestions for musical setting, many of which Haydn followed.[82] A text with so many images of natural phenomena lends itself amply to the kind of word painting that Handel practiced, and some of these word-painting techniques were still current in Haydn's time. Swieten was specific in many of his pictorial suggestions, and *The Creation* abounds in *Thonmahlerey* ("tone painting," as it was commonly called in Haydn's time) and in various kinds of symbolism. Some nineteenth- and early twentieth-century critics raised strenuous objections to Haydn's word painting, but recent critics are more charmed than offended by the good-humored naiveté of this element in *The Creation*.[83]

An interesting aspect of symbolism is found in the tonal organization of *The Creation*.[84] The main tonal center of the work is C, a key that is

added before the first performance. For details, see Landon, *Haydn*, 4:350; and Walter, "Swietens handschriftliche Textbücher," p. 250.

82. For Swieten's comments in his manuscript of the libretto, see Walter, "Swietens handschriftliche Textbücher," pp. 250–59; the comments are translated into English in Landon, *Haydn*, 4:350–52.

83. On the tone painting in *The Creation* and criticism of it, see Landon, *Haydn*, 4:342–45 and 403–8. For a detailed study of text-music relationships in Haydn's oratorios, see Riedel-Martiny, "Haydns Oratorien."

84. The treatment of tonal symbolism in this paragraph is based on much

introduced at several significant points: number 1 begins in C minor and closes in C major (see Table VIII-6); C major returns at the end of the second Day (no. 4) and at the end of the fourth Day (no. 13, which closes part I); in part II, C major is heard after God creates man (no. 24); and in part III, when Adam and Eve first sing, in paradise (no. 30). Yet part III ends in B-flat, rather than C, for symbolic reasons: Adam and Eve, central to part III, are lower beings than the angels, and as Uriel suggests in a recitative (no. 33), they will fall from Grace. Their position and their fall are symbolized by the B-flat ending of part III. Long before, however, Haydn had prepared for the final deflection to B-flat: the first stable key in part II is F, and part II closes in B-flat. Furthermore, early in part III the flat tonal areas of Adam and Eve are suggested. Their first duet (with chorus, no. 30) begins and ends in C major (for they are still associated with the Heavenly Host), but in the center section of that number the tonality moves remarkably far afield on the flat side, passing through F, B-flat, A-flat, G-flat, E-flat minor, F minor, G minor, G major, and again to C major (for the last time in the oratorio); and their love duet (no. 32) is in the key of E-flat. The tonal symbolism with respect to Adam and Eve is matched by stylistic symbolism, for in comparison with the magnificent C-major duet with chorus (no. 30), the love duet (discussed below) and the final chorus of the oratorio are notably simple and of a "lower" style.[85]

Haydn's orchestra for *The Creation* is unusual in the size and constitution of the wind section: pairs of flutes, oboes, clarinets, and bassoons; one contrabassoon, two horns, two trumpets, timpani, and three trombones (alto, tenor, and bass). The composer had rarely written for clarinets before; the contrabassoon was virtually unknown in Viennese music (but Haydn had heard it in the Handel festival in Westminster Abbey); and three trombones, though associated with Viennese church music, were unusual in oratorios. The score is filled with highly inventive orchestral effects.[86]

The title "Introduction: The Representation of Chaos," which appears at the beginning of part I, describes the number's intended extramusical content.[87] This highly original piece of program music represents chaos

more extensive treatments of that subject in two writings, to be consulted for details: Levarie, "Closing Numbers of *Die Schöpfung*," especially pp. 319–20; and Landon, *Haydn*, 4:397 and 399–403.

85. Details in Levarie, "Closing Numbers of *Die Schöpfung*," pp. 316–19. Levarie's study successfully counters Tovey's recommendation (in Tovey, *Essays*, 5:145–46) that performers delete the last four numbers of *The Creation* and end the work with no. 30.

86. On the orchestration of this work, see Landon, *Haydn*, pp. 408–13.

87. For Heinrich Schenker's reductive analysis of the tonal structure of "Chaos," see Schenker, "Chaos." For analytic comments on most of the numbers in *The Creation*, see Landon, *Haydn*, 4:413–26; and Tovey, *Essays*, 5:114–46.

at first by its stark beginning, shown in the first measure of Example VIII-29a: a long C, with fermata, played by full orchestra in unison and octaves—the C is initially without order, without tonal function, neither major nor minor. In the next few measures the mode and tonal functions become slightly clearer; the extremely effective, lonely first violin melody in measures 3–5, which begins over a leading-tone diminished-seventh chord, would help to confirm the C-minor key but for the deceptive cadence on the VI chord in the first inversion (m. 5). Contributing to the vagueness, dissonance, and pathos of the piece's first section is the recurring sigh motive of a descending half-step and its inversion, treated in imitation; its pitches function in various harmonic contexts as chord tones, suspensions, and long appoggiaturas. (See Example VIII-29a, in the violoncello, viola, violin 1–2, oboe 1–2, flute 1–2, and in mm. 8–9, double bass and violoncello). Throughout the introduction, Haydn evokes the notion of chaos by groping, shifting, tenuous effects, especially through orchestration, texture, and unexpected harmonies, with dissonances and chromatic inflections. His seven sketches for "Chaos" show the pains he took, in revisions, to "dematerialize" the texture.[88]

The evocation of chaos, however, is accomplished by an orderly process. According to a recent interpretation, "Stylistically, the movement combines Fuxian counterpoint with the fantasia bass line and unmeasured rhythms of C. P. E. Bach, as elucidated in the Versuch. Essentially, 'Chaos' is an instrumental movement in a bizarre motet style, a ricercar functioning as an exordium."[89] Structurally, the number moves from C minor to E-flat major and back to C minor. Rhythmically active motives are introduced and manipulated. The triplet motive that first appears in the bassoon part (m. 6 in Example VIII-29a) continues to be prominent for several measures in other parts and returns briefly in the nebulous C-minor recapitulation. The D-flat section (beginning at m. 21, not in the example) is a surprising parenthesis in the long-range progression from C minor to E-flat major, the latter reached on a six-four chord (see Example VIII-29b, m. 26). During this parenthesis a particularly significant rising and falling motive appears in the flute and oboe parts (Example VIII-29b, mm. 22–24), supported by a series of diminished seventh chords, which form dissonances with the D-flat pedal point in the lower strings. The instrumental "Representation of Chaos" proceeds directly into the first recitative, where Haydn clarifies the meaning of the flute and oboe motive just mentioned: as shown in Example VIII-29c, he repeats essentially the same motive with the words "and the world was without form and void."

The first recitative continues directly into the first chorus, which is a

88. For a reproduction of the sketches and a discussion of the process of "dematerialization," see Landon, Haydn, 4:356–74.
89. Brown, Haydn's "The Creation," p. 31.

Example a:

EXAMPLE VIII-29. continued

EXAMPLE VIII-29. continued

Example b:

EXAMPLE VIII-29. continued

Example c:

EXAMPLE VIII-29. continued

Example d:

EXAMPLE VIII-29. continued

justly famous passage: Haydn's setting of the text, "And the spirit of God moved upon the face of the waters; and God said: Let there be Light, and there was Light." The chorus sings the first part of the text *sotto voce* and the orchestra plays *pianissimo*; but the word *light* at the end of the passage (Example VIII-29d, m. 86) is illuminated by the first C-major cadence in the oratorio and by overwhelming orchestral fireworks: a sudden *tutti*, played *fortissimo*, for three and one-half measures, which includes the previously unheard bass trombone, contrabassoon, and strings without mutes. The ascending fourths in the soprano (mm. 83–86) may have been inspired by Handel's setting of "Let there be light" in *Samson*,[90] but purely Haydn's is the arrival at C major after so long a preparation and the sudden burst of sound at the word *light*. A typically Haydnesque touch in this passage is the priceless pizzicato in measure 8; that pizzicato, on the dominant, must surely be the very moment in which God caused light to appear—the C major *tutti*, *fortissimo*, is simply the effect of that cause. A member of the audience at the first full rehearsal observed that Haydn had kept secret, even from Swieten, his representation of light in *The Creation* until that moment, and that when it was finally heard, "the enchantment of the electrified Viennese was so general that the orchestra could not proceed for some minutes."[91]

Only five of the numbers in *The Creation* are set as arias without chorus (nos. 6, 8, 15, 22, and 24). A glance at the outline of the libretto given above will show that the text of each aria is a commentary on a feature of the Creation, and that most of the commentaries provide ample opportunities for conventional word painting. In the arias, and even more in the accompanied recitatives (see below), Haydn displays a delightfully playful approach to musical imagery. He virtually never misses an opportunity for word painting, either by the voice or by the orchestra; although his general approach to word painting is conventional, he treats the conventions with uncommon attention to detail—a characteristic also noted in relation to his earlier oratorio, *Tobia*. For instance, in his representation of water (no. 6) he distinguishes between the sea "rolling in foaming billows" (mm. 1–27), the river "thro' th'open plains outstretching wide in serpent error" (mm. 50–72), and the brook, which "softly purling glides on" (mm. 73–121); in the famous bird aria (no. 15) Haydn distinguishes among the various activities and songs of the several types of birds; and with more than a touch of humor, in number 22 he introduces a grunt in the bassoon and contrabassoon in octaves—on their lowest notes (B'-flat and the octave below) and *fortissimo* in the midst of a *piano* passage—to represent the "heavy beasts" (m. 40), and he soon repeats the effect but at a higher pitch (m. 44). Although coloratura passages are less important in *The Creation* than in

90. Cited in Smither, *Oratorio* 2:279, Example VII-20, m. 7.
91. Report by Fredrik Samuel Silverstolpe, as quoted in Mörner, "Haydniana," p. 28 and translated in Landon, *Haydn*, 4:318.

Tobia, they are found on occasion, as in Gabriel's two arias (nos. 8 and 15).

Perhaps because the commentaries on the Creation in the aria texts do not suggest traditional aria structures, the common ternary and transformed da capo structures are absent (at least melodically speaking) from all but one of the arias: for number 8—Gabriel's aria about the grass, flowers, and plants—Haydn wrote a transformed da capo. He set the first six lines of text to A1 and repeated them in A2, and he set lines seven through nine to a tonally unstable B section (mm. 38–51, passing through D-flat, A-flat, and B-flat minor). The other arias behave tonally but neither textually nor melodically like transformed da capo structures.

Four numbers of *The Creation* are written for ensembles combined with chorus (no. 13, trio; 19, trio; 30, duet; and 34, quartet), and three are for ensembles alone (no. 18, trio; 27, trio; and 32, duet). With the exception of the love duet of Adam and Eve (no. 32) all the ensembles, with or without chorus, have texts of praise and are written in an exalted and sometimes contrapuntal style. Differing strikingly from the other ensembles and from virtually all other numbers in *The Creation*, however, is the love duet of Adam and Eve, for it includes music in popular style. Organized as a two-tempo AB structure in E-flat, the duet begins in adagio and triple meter with expressions of devotion set to cantabile lines, sung first by Adam and then by Eve; the duet continues with the two voices in a combination of contrapuntal texture and parallel thirds and sixths. But a surprise comes at the beginning of the B section with the change to allegro and duple meter (see Example VIII-30) suggested by the text, "The dew-dropping morn, o how she quickens all!" Here the lovers spring into a dance, an *écossaise*—a type of contredanse enjoyed in Viennese ballrooms around 1800.[92] This dance is stylistically the "lowest" music in *The Creation*, evokes an attitude of social entertainment in a popular environment contrasting with the previous duet (no. 30) of praise and prayer in the company of angels, and forms a part of the "deliberate fall from the elevated level of [Adam and Eve's] first duet,"[93] a fall represented also by the tonal centers, as we have seen.

In the accompanied recitatives of *The Creation* are found some of the oratorio's most imaginative, charming, and at times humorous moments (the latter especially important, humor being so rare in oratorio). The first passage of accompanied recitative occurs within the "Introduction" and is mentioned above in connection with Example VIII-29c. Number 3, the second accompanied recitative, includes both a Genesis text and a commentary on it; 14 and 16 have only texts from Genesis; 12 and 21 are commentaries; and 29 is a narrative introduction to part III. A glance at the contents of those numbers in the outline of the libretto

92. Levarie, "Closing Numbers of *Die Schöpfung*," p. 318.
93. Ibid., p. 319.

EXAMPLE VIII-30. *The Creation*—Haydn (Haydn, *Creation**-E, pp. 335–36).

given above will suggest the aspects of Creation that Haydn paints in
these recitatives; the tone painting usually occurs in the orchestra before
the words are sung. As in the arias, so also in the recitatives Haydn
distinguishes carefully among the elements that he paints. In number 3,
for instance, he provides a specific, clearly identifiable motive in the
orchestra to represent each of the seven natural phenemona mentioned
in the text: the storms, winds, lightning, thunder, rain, hail, and snow.
Among the most celebrated of his orchestral images are those in number
12: the sunrise (whole notes in violin 1 and flute 1, rising by step through
an interval of a tenth and accompanied by countermelodies) and moon-
rise (half notes in violoncello and double bass, rising through an eleventh
and accompanying the vocal line). In number 16 the command to multi-

ply is accompanied by divided lower strings. Haydn's zest for amusing musical pictures is particularly evident in number 21 where he represents in turn: the lion, tiger, stag, horse, cattle, sheep, insects, and worm. The simple recitatives of the oratorio are of minimal musical interest, except for number 31, a dialogue between Adam and Eve, which prepares for their love duet and is the oratorio's only recitative that is dramatic in the sense of operatic exchange between personages.

Like the Handelian oratorio and that of North Germany, *The Creation* makes frequent use of chorus. Yet Haydn rarely uses his chorus without soloists. Of the ten numbers in which chorus participates (see Table VIII-6: nos. 1, 2, 4, 10, 13, 19, 26, 28, 30, 34), only three are for chorus alone (nos. 10, 26, 28), and two of those (nos. 26 and 28) function as the first and last units of a tripartite choral-trio complex. Except for number 1, in which choral participation is brief and narrative, and number 2, a commentary, the choruses have texts of praise. The element most striking in the choruses of Handel's oratorios is also characteristic of those in *The Creation*: the immense variety, both from number to number and within numbers. Haydn skillfully varies the choral-solo relationships, the textures, and the styles, and as in the other numbers of the oratorio he shows in the choruses a constant sensitivity to the meaning of the text. These traits are heard in number 2, for instance, which begins with an andante aria sung by Uriel (in A moving to E) about the newly created light that banishes darkness—the play of light and dark are clearly and effectively contrasted by register, orchestration, and harmony. At Uriel's text about the fallen angels, "Affrighted fled hell's spirits black in throngs, down they sink in the deep of abyss to endless night," the tempo changes to allegro moderato, the tonality shifts to the darker C minor, and orchestral lines descend chromatically. The chorus enters ("despairing, cursing rage attends their rapid fall"), with a fugato on a disjunct, descending figure moving to A minor; but at "a new created world springs up at God's command" the bright A major returns, with smooth melodic lines (mostly repeated notes and conjunct motion) and chordal texture. Again the text about the fallen angels is heard, as is the music of Uriel and the chorus, and the piece concludes in A major with a repeat of the choral section on the "new created world."

A particularly festive, neo-Handelian song of praise is number 10, for chorus without soloists. The opening and closing sections, predominantly declamatory and chordal, frame a fugue that includes stretto and quasi-augmentation. Number 13, "The heavens are telling of the glory of God," a favorite number of *The Creation* in the nineteenth century, is probably still the best-known chorus in *The Creation*. Its text of praise closes the fourth Day and part I of the oratorio. Written for chorus and the three archangels as soloists, the large two-part structure begins (allegro) immediately with the first choral section (without introductory ritornello); after alternation between choral and solo sections, begins the second part (più allegro), which includes an extended fugue, continuing

EXAMPLE VIII-31. *The Creation*—Haydn (Haydn, *Creation**-E, pp. 108–9, 116, 122–23).

Example a:

Example b:

Example c:

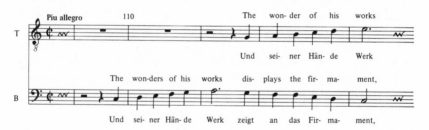

until the chordal close. The number is a model of economy. It is almost entirely in C major (the last time that key will be heard until no. 30), and most of the melodic material is derived from the first few measures, as is shown in Example VIII-31a-c: the bracketed portion of Example VIII-31a is reused in modified form by the soloists (Example VIII-31b), and the fugue subject (see the first two entrances in Example VIII-31c) is modeled on the second vocal phrase of the piece (Example VIII-31a, mm. 8–12).

The magnificent three-part complex that closes part II of the oratorio begins with a brief chorus (no. 26) in B-flat that has the same initial text and some of the same musical material as the next chorus (no. 28). The two choruses, both in B-flat, frame a trio (no. 27) in E-flat, sung by the three archangels. Particularly noteworthy is the double fugue, which begins after the opening chordal section, with the text "Glory to his name for ever, he sole on high exalted reigns, alleluja."

The oratorio's last number in C major, Number 30, which consists of the duet and chorus of praise, would seem to function as the work's finale but for the important matter of balance and the fall of Adam and Eve, which must follow.[94] Organized as a two-tempo structure, number 30 begins with an adagio section in *alla breve* time and in C major; focusing on Adam and Eve's duet, "By thee with bliss, o bounteous Lord," the section includes simple, supporting choral passages, mostly in chordal style. Especially effective near the end of the first section are the solo timpani rolls (thirteen of them), to emphasize the repeated words, "his name be ever magnified" (but perhaps more appropriate for the word "resound" in German: "Sein Lob erschall in Ewigkeit"—"Let his praise resound in eternity"). The second section, allegretto, in 2/4 time and beginning in F major, continues the exchanges of solo and choral parts, but the role of the chorus becomes more prominent, and includes fugato passages as well as chordal ones. The second section moves far afield tonally (as mentioned above), finally returning to a C-major choral conclusion. The oratorio's final chorus with four soloists, number 34, is again a two-tempo structure with an andante chordal beginning followed by an allegro double fugue and a chordal ending; but the whole is in simpler style than number 30. The role of the soloists in number 34 is to interject melismatic "amen" passages.

The Seasons

Within a year after the first performance of *The Creation*, Haydn was already at work on *The Seasons*;[95] it was first performed on 24 April 1801 in the Schwarzenberg Palais under the sponsorship of the Gesellschaft der Associierten. The work was enthusiastically received by the audience; the reviews of the early performances were generally positive but objections were raised to some of the tone painting.[96] In 1802 *The Seasons* was published in Leipzig by Breitkopf & Härtel in two editions: German-French and German-English.

Like the libretto of *The Creation*, that of *The Seasons* was adapted by Swieten from an English source. In this instance, however, the source was not originally an oratorio libretto but a poem by James Thomson (1700–

94. Tovey recommends (Tovey, *Essays*, 5:145–46) performing nos. 29 and 30 immediately after 28, as the finale of part II, and deleting the rest of the oratorio; this procedure, however, would defeat Haydn's probable purpose of representing the fall from grace, as mentioned above, and would destroy the work's balance.

95. Landon, *Haydn*, 4:454.

96. On the circumstances of the early performances and on the early reviews, see ibid., 5:37, 41–47.

48), *The Seasons*—a nature poem with a strong element of deism—originally published in parts between 1726 and 1730, as a whole in 1730 and revised in 1745, and in a German translation by Barthold Heinrich Brockes at Hamburg in 1745.[97] For this work Swieten had to condense and rewrite far more than for *The Creation*. Although the German libretto for *The Seasons* borrows occasionally from Brockes's translation, the English version owes little to Thomson and reveals Swieten's inadequacy in the English language. (The poor English text may be one reason for the infrequent performances of the work in English-speaking countries.) The structure, content, and expression in Swieten's text falls far short of the quality of *The Creation*, and Haydn was not entirely happy with it. The libretto is in four parts, "Spring," "Summer," "Autumn," and "Winter," and includes three personages: Simon (B), a farmer; · Hanne (S), his daughter; and Lucas (T), a young country boy; these personages function as narrators, as did the archangels in *The Creation*. The chorus enters twelve times, and half of the choruses include solo or soli sections by the personages named above. Although some of the choruses bear personage designations—"Chorus of Peasant-People," "Chorus of Girls and Lads," "Chorus of Peasants and Hunters"—most are undesignated. As a representative of the oratorio genre, *The Seasons* is a borderline case because of the unusually few religious references of a traditional kind in its text. The work's early sources do not bear a genre designation, but it was widely considered an oratorio in Haydn's time (and still is, in our own); yet on occasion it was called a "Cantate," as in Hummel's catalogue (1806) of the Esterházy collection.[98]

As with *The Creation*, Swieten offered Haydn numerous musical suggestions—frequently about tone painting—and again Haydn followed many of them.[99] *The Seasons* is filled with musical pictures of natural phenomena, one of which includes the croaking of frogs (in no. 18), which Haydn himself later regretted. He is quoted as having written, "This whole passage with its imitation of the frogs, was not my idea. I was forced to write this Frenchified trash,"[100] presumably by Swieten, who, however, rejected the notion that Haydn had been "forced."[101]

Despite Haydn's attitude toward the libretto, *The Seasons* includes some of the best music of the composer's late period. Especially worthy of careful study are: the introductory number to each season (no. 1, 9,

97. Ibid., 5:93–95; for a detailed discussion of the libretto, see ibid., pp. 93–118. Brockes was the author of a famous Passion oratorio text, set by Handel among other composers (see Smither, *Oratorio*, 2:111, 113–14, 130–34).

98. Harich, "Inventare," p. 96.

99. For Swieten's suggestions quoted in German, see Walter, "Swietens handschriftliche Textbücher," pp. 259–77; for English translations, see Landon, *Haydn*, 5:115–18.

100. Letter, Haydn to A. E. Müller, 31 December 1801, as translated in Landon, *Haydn*, 5:187.

101. Landon, *Haydn*, 5:187.

19, 29); the joyful, folklike, and sometimes boisterous quality in certain numbers (2, 4, 10, 22, 26, 28, 34, 36); the more serious arias (nos. 13, 15, 24, 30, 32, 38); and the serious choruses, with and without soloists (choruses with fugues: nos. 6, 8, 20, 39; without fugues: nos. 11, 17, and 18).[102]

Ludwig van Beethoven: Christus am Oelberge

Born at Bonn in 1770, Beethoven moved to Vienna in 1792, where he remained until his death in 1827. Among the most widely admired and influential composers in Western music, Beethoven is of special importance for his individual approach to the expansion and modification of the Classical style, by which he ushered in the musical language of the Romantic era. Since the nineteenth century his life and works have usually been divided into three periods: the first, formative period ending about 1802, the middle period lasting to about 1812, and the final period extending from 1813 to his death. Recent Beethoven research has tended to retain the three-period division for both musical and biographical reasons but to refine and qualify it.[103] Beethoven's only oratorio, *Christus am Oelberge* (Christ on the Mount of Olives), dates from 1803; thus a general consideration of the first two periods will assist in providing a context for understanding that work.

When Haydn passed through Bonn in 1792, en route to Vienna after his first sojourn in London, arrangements were made for the young Beethoven to study with the celebrated master in Vienna.[104] A well-known local musician, Beethoven had been the music student of his father and various other local teachers, especially the court organist Christian Gottlob Neefe (1748–98). Regarded as an accomplished pianist—by some as a promising composer—Beethoven had acquired several highly placed admirers, among them Count Ferdinand Waldstein, who would long remain a friend and patron. Elector Maximilian Franz, in whose orchestra Beethoven played viola, agreed to support the young musician's study in Vienna and assumed he would return to Bonn—which, however, he did not do.

Moving to Vienna in 1792, Beethoven studied counterpoint with Haydn for only a year, but was dissappointed with Haydn's teaching and simultaneously sought help from the composer Johann Schenk. After

102. The numbers are those in Haydn, *Seasons*-E; Haydn, *Seasons*-M; and Landon, *Haydn*, 5:121–23. For full discussions of the sources and the music of *The Seasons*, see Landon, *Haydn*, 5:121–82; and Tovey, *Essays*, 5:146–61.

103. On the three style periods and the need to refine and qualify them, see Joseph Kerman and Allan Tyson, "Beethoven," *New Grove*, 2:376–78.

104. For Beethoven biography, see: Kerman and Tyson, "Beethoven," *New Grove*, 2:354–76; Solomon, *Beethoven*; and Thayer, *Beethoven*.

FIGURE VIII-5. Ludwig van Beethoven (1770–1827). (Bronz bust, 1812, by Franz Klem. Courtesy of the Beethovenhaus, Bonn.)

Haydn left for his second visit to England, Beethoven continued counterpoint studies with the Kapellmeister of St. Stephen's Cathedral, Johann Georg Albrechtsberger (1736–1809). On an informal and irregular basis Beethoven studied Italian text setting with the imperial Kapellmeister Antonio Salieri (1750–1825), probably between 1798 and 1801.[105] During the 1790s Beethoven successfully established himself as a virtuoso pianist and composer, made valuable contacts among the Viennese aristocracy, and played frequently in their homes.

By the early 1800s his professional and financial successes were considerable, yet in letters of June and July 1801, he confessed to friends in Bonn that for nearly two years he had experienced increasing deafness.[106] He wrote of his anxiety, his anticipation of drastic difficulties in his professional and social life, his avoidance of social functions for fear his loss of hearing would be detected, and the necessity of resignation to his deafness. In the spring of 1802 Beethoven went to the small town of Heiligenstadt, outside Vienna, where he spent the summer composing. In October, before returning to Vienna, he wrote the famous and moving document known as the "Heiligenstadt Testament," addressed to his two brothers—yet also addressed, in some passages, to mankind in general—a document that reveals the frame of mind in which he approached the composition of his oratorio and other works of the next few years.[107] In this will, found among his papers after his death, Beethoven presents himself as having descended to the depths of despair because of his loss of hearing and as having contemplated suicide—and still he has determined to go on living and composing. He speaks of his art as having held him back from suicide and of virtue as having upheld him in his time of misery, and he bids farewell to his brothers. According to Maynard Solomon's perceptive interpretation of this document:

> The Heiligenstadt Testament is a leave-taking—which is to say, a fresh start. Beethoven here enacted his own death in order that he might live again. He recreated himself in a new guise, self-sufficient and heroic. The testament is a funeral work, like the *Joseph* Cantata and *Christ on the Mount of Olives*. In a sense it is the literary prototype of the *Eroica* Symphony, a portrait of the artist as hero, stricken by deafness, withdrawn from mankind, conquering his impulses to suicide, struggling against fate, hoping to find "but one day of pure joy." It is a daydream compounded of heroism, death,

---

105. On the dates of Beethoven's studies with Salieri, see Kramer, "Beethoven," p. 22.

106. For details of and quotations from these letters (to Franz Wegeler and Karl Amenda) and for perceptive interpretations of them, see Solomon, *Beethoven*, pp. 112–14; and Tyson, "Heroic Phase," pp. 140–41.

107. The Heiligenstadt Testament is quoted and interpreted in Solomon, *Beethoven*, pp. 116–21.

and rebirth, a reaffirmation of Beethoven's adherence to virtue and to the categorical imperative.[108]

Thus Beethoven would return to the theme of the hero, reflected in the Heiligenstadt Testament, in his *Christus am Oelberge* (1803) and the *Eroica* Symphony (1803), but also in the opera *Leonore* (in its first version, 1804–5; later called *Fidelio*).

Early in 1803 Emanuel Schikaneder (1751–1812) commissioned Beethoven to write an opera for his large and lavish Theater-an-der-Wien, which had opened in 1801, and Beethoven moved his lodgings to the theater. Beethoven's engagement at the theater included an opportunity to give a concert there, for which he hastily composed his first dramatic vocal work, the oratorio *Christus*—in one letter he said he had composed it in two weeks and in another in several weeks (see below). Appropriately and traditionally for the performance of a Passion oratorio, the concert took place on Tuesday in Holy Week, 5 April 1803. Beethoven's student, secretary, and copyist, Ferdinand Ries (1784–1838), offers

108. Ibid., p. 121.

FIGURE VIII-6. The Theater-an-der-Wien, Vienna, where Beethoven's *Christus am Oelberge* was first performed. (Anonymous aquarelle; from Eisler, *Das bürgerliche Wien*, p. 184.)

some fascinating insight into the haste with which the performance was prepared. The final rehearsal was scheduled for eight o'clock in the morning on the day of the performance. Ries was summoned to Beethoven early, at about five o'clock:

> I found him in bed, writing on *separate* sheets of paper. To my question what it was he answered "*Trombones.*" The trombones also played from *these* sheets at the performance.

> Had someone forgotten to copy these parts? Were they an afterthought? I was too young at the time to note the artistic interest of the incident; but probably the trombones were an afterthought, as Beethoven might as easily have had the *uncopied parts* as the copied ones. The rehearsal began at eight o'clock in the morning. . . . It was a terrible rehearsal, and at half past two everybody was exhausted and more or less dissatisfied.

> Prince Karl Lichnowsky, who attended the rehearsal from the beginning, had sent for bread and butter, cold meat and wine, in large baskets. He pleasantly asked all to help themselves, and this was done with both hands, the result being that good nature was

restored again. Then the Prince requested that the oratorio be rehearsed once more from the beginning, so that it might go well in the evening and Beethoven's first work in this genre be worthily presented. And so the rehearsal began again. The concert began at six o'clock, but was so long that a few pieces were not performed.[109]

Included in the concert were the first and second symphonies, the third piano concerto, and the oratorio—the last three were premier performances. It is not known what works intended to be performed were omitted.

Beethoven's concert was a financial success, but the reviews of the oratorio were mixed. The *Allgemeine Musikalische Zeitung* was alone in stating that *Christus* had been received with "extraordinary approval";[110] three months later that report was countered by another correspondent in the same journal who wrote, "In the interest of truth, I am obliged to contradict a report in the *Musikalische Zeitung*; Beethoven's cantata did not please." The *Zeitung für die Elegante Welt* found the oratorio generally good, and spoke of the "excellent effect" of the trombones in the aria of the Seraph (actually a recitative of the Seraph—probably the parts Beethoven had written the morning of the performance—see below); the *Freymüthige* liked single passages in the oratorio but said it was "too long, too artificial in structure and lacking in expressiveness, especially in the vocal parts. The text, by F. X. Huber, seemed to have been as superficially written as the music."

Beethoven's correspondence shows that he was not entirely pleased with the oratorio and that he revised it before publication. On 26 August 1804 he wrote to Breitkopf & Härtel that the work had not been published "because I have added an entirely new chorus and have also made a few alterations, the reason being that I wrote the whole work in a few weeks and that naturally some passages did not altogether satisfy me later on."[111] Despite Beethoven's efforts to get the oratorio published, however, only in 1811 did it appear, as opus 85. On 23 August 1811 Beethoven wrote apologetically about the work to the publisher, Breitkopf & Härtel: "I have just begun to revise the oratorio. . . . Here and there the text must remain in its original form. I know that the text is extremely bad. But once one has thought out a whole work which is based even on a bad text, it is difficult to prevent this whole from being destroyed if individual alterations are made here and there."[112] And

109. Thayer, *Beethoven*, 1:328–29.
110. This and all other periodical quotations in this paragraph are taken from ibid., 1:330.
111. As quoted in Tyson, "Beethoven's *Christus*," p. 552.
112. As quoted in ibid., p. 552. As this and the previous letter indicate, the 1803 version differed from the published version; for a study which reconstructs the 1803 version on the basis of sketches and other primary sources, see ibid.

again he apologized for the work on 9 October 1811: "Arrange for the oratorio, and in general everything else, to be reviewed by whomever you like. . . . The only point to consider in connection with my oratorio is that it was my first work in that style and, moreover, an early work, and that it was written in a fortnight and during all kinds of disturbances and other unpleasant and distressing events in my life (my brother happened to be suffering from a mortal disease). . . . What is quite certain is that now I should compose an absolutely different oratorio from what I composed then."[113] According to Anton Schindler, "in later years [Beethoven] unhesitatingly declared that it had been a mistake to treat the part of Christ in the modern vocal style."[114] Despite the mixed reviews and Beethoven's misgivings, however, *Christus* was frequently performed during the composer's lifetime, continued to receive at least occasional performances in Germany after his death, and became a favorite in England.[115]

The librettist of *Christus*, Franz Xaver Huber (1755–1814), was a Viennese satirist, diarist, and librettist. Prior to writing *Christus* he had produced librettos for a comic opera and a *Singspiel*, both set by Franz Xaver Süssmayer (1766–1803), and an opera libretto for Peter Winter (1754–1825). *Christus*, his only oratorio libretto, is in one part, divided into six numbers (see Table VIII-7).[116] Each number consists of a recitative followed by an aria, ensemble, chorus, or combination of chorus and soloists. Conceived as a short dramatic work (about fifty minutes long in Beethoven's setting), the libretto includes three solo personages—Jesus (T), a Seraph (S), and Peter (B)—plus choruses of Soldiers (TTB), Disciples (TT), and Angels (SATB). As we have seen, a role for Jesus was more common in the German oratorio of the later eighteenth century than in the Italian. Yet the best-known Passion oratorio in the time, Graun's *Tod Jesu*, has no named personages—Jesus' words are quoted by unnamed narrators. It may be that Huber and Beethoven included a role for Jesus on the basis of comments on Graun's work found in the article on recitative in Sulzer's *Allgemeine Theorie der schönen Künste*, which Beethoven had consulted shortly before writing *Christus*.[117]

The entire oratorio takes place on the Mount of Olives. In number 1, Jesus prays to his Father for strength and expresses his sorrow and ter-

113. As quoted in ibid., p. 553.

114. As quoted in Thayer, *Beethoven*, 1:330.

115. In the *Allgemeine musikalische Zeitung* (vols. 5–32) thirty-three performances of the oratorio are noted between 1803 and 1830 in German-speaking lands, Holland, Scandinavia, and Russia. In 1814 Sir George Smart introduced *Christus* in London; later (because of the "offensive," operatic role for Jesus) it was supplied with new words for England and often performed as *Engedi, or David in the Wilderness*.

116. Unless otherwise indicated, the comments on the libretto and music of *Christus* are based on the 1811 version, as printed in Beethoven, *Christus**.

117. Kramer, "Beethoven," p. 38.

TABLE VIII-7
Beethoven, *Christus*: Structural Outline

Numbers	Keys
1. Introduzione	
Orchestral introduction	e♭
Accomp. recit. Jesus, "Jehovah, du mein Vater!"	
Aria. Jesus, "Meine Seele ist erschüttert"	c
2. Accomp. recit. Seraph, "Erzittre, Erde! Jehovah's Sohn liegt"	
Aria with Chorus of Angels. Seraph, "Preist, preist des	
Erlösers Güte"	G
3. Accomp. recit. Seraph, Jesus, "Verkündet, Seraph, mir dein Mund"	
Duet. Seraph, Jesus, "So ruhe denn mit ganzer Schwere"	A♭
4. Accomp. recit. Jesus, "Willkommen, Tod! den ich am Kreuze"	
Chorus of Soldiers, "Wir haben ihn gesehen"	C
5. Accomp. recit. Jesus, "Die mich zu fangen ausgezogen sind"	
Chorus of Soldiers, Chorus of Disciples, "Hier ist er"	D
6. Accomp. recit. Peter, Jesus, "Nicht ungestraft soll"	
Trio. Seraph, Jesus, Peter, "In meinen Adern wühlen"	B♭
Chorus of Soldiers, Chorus of Disciples, Jesus,	
"Auf! auf! ergreifet den Verräter"	B♭-C
Chorus of Angels, "Welten singen Dank und Ehre"	C

Note: The numbers are those of Beethoven, *Christus**.

ror; a Seraph arrives (no. 2) and, addressing mankind, speaks of the
suffering of Jehovah's Son, urges praise for the Redeemer, hails the re-
deemed, and prophesies the woe of the unredeemed. A chorus of Angels
repeats part of the Seraph's text. In the opening recitative of number 3
Jesus asks if his Father has taken pity, but the Seraph replies that the
sacred mystery of reconciliation must be fulfilled; the two sing a duet in
which Jesus resigns himself to the will of his Father and the Seraph
trembles at Jesus' sorrows. In the recitative of number 4 Jesus welcomes
his death, which is for the good of mankind; the Soldiers enter, convinced that Jesus cannot escape. In number 5 Jesus sees that those sent to
take him draw near; the Soldiers see him and are about to seize and bind
him, while the confused Disciples, suddenly surrounded by soldiers, beg
for mercy. In the recitative of the final number, Peter wishes revenge, but
Jesus tells him to put up his sword. During the trio Peter expresses his
anger, Jesus preaches of love and forgiveness, and the Seraph warns
mankind to listen to the holy teaching. The Soldiers are about to seize
Jesus, and the Disciples fear persecution, torture, and death. In the final
chorus the Angels praise the Son of God and rejoice.

Especially in the first part of the libretto, the language is close to that of the *empfindsam* oratorio, which originated several decades earlier but was still popular. The last few lines of the recitative and the entire aria of number 1 illustrate this language of feeling:

RECITATIVE

. . .

Ach sieh! wie Bangigkeit, wie Todesangst	Ah see how anxiety, how mortal terror
mein Herz mit Macht ergreift!	with power seize my heart!
Ich leide sehr, mein Vater!	I suffer greatly, my Father!
O sieh! ich leide sehr: erbarm' dich mein!	Oh see! I suffer greatly: have mercy upon me!

. . .

ARIA

Meine Seele ist erschüttert von den Qualen, die mir dräun.	My soul is deeply shaken by the torments which threaten me.
Schrecken fasst mich, und es zittert	Terror grips me, and my body
grässlich schaudernd mein Gebein.	horribly trembles and shudders.
Wie ein Fieberfrost ergreifet mich, die Angst, beim nahen Grab,	Like a feverish chill, fear of the approaching grave seizes me,
und von meinem Anlitz träufet statt des Schweisses Blut herab.	and from my brow drips blood instead of sweat.
Vater! tief gebeugt und kläglich	Father! Bowed down deep and wretched,
fleht dein Sohn hinauf zu dir:	thy son beseeches thee:
deiner Macht ist Alles möglich,	to thy power all is possible,
nimm den Leidenskelch von mir!	take the cup of sorrow from me!

If the language is in part modeled on that of *Empfindsamkeit*, however, the structure is not; this essentially dramatic work is diametrically opposed to the lyric texts of Ramler and the type of oratorio espoused in the article "Oratorium" in Sulzer's *Allgemeine Theorie der schönen Künste*.

The drama in the libretto is that of Jesus' innocent suffering and heroic self-sacrifice. Considering Beethoven's own feelings while in Heiligenstadt six months before he set this text, such a theme and such stanzas as those quoted must surely have had a deep personal meaning to him. He was soon to explore further the subject of heroism: "both in its subject matter and in its size [*Christus*] opens—however haltingly and imperfectly—the path to the *Eroica* and to *Fidelio*. The 'heroic' style seemed to be struggling for emergence, and *Christus* is a step toward that emergence. . . ."[118] Certain literary and musical relationships between *Christus* and *Leonore/Fidelio* are clear. The themes of "undeserved suffering, isolation, deprivation, hopes and fears concerning deliverance . . . link both oratorio and opera with Beethoven's own life."[119] Beethoven set both Christ and Florestan as tenors, and "the figure of Christ in the oratorio foreshadows that of the operatic hero: he might be called an *Ur-Florestan*. Both Christ and Florestan are under the threat of a painful death but are resigned to the will of God: Florestan is lying in the dark, Christ (according to Beethoven's stage direction, which never found its way into the published score) is on his knees. In each case a long and sombre prelude in the minor [beginning of act II in the opera, of no. 1 in the oratorio] depicts the lone figure's plight."[120] In *Christus* the Seraph and Jesus join in a duet, as do Florestan and Leonore ("O namenlose Freude!") in the opera.

The principal tonal area of *Christus* is C (see Table VIII-7): C minor is used in the first aria, C major in number 4, the dominant in number 2, and its dominant in number 6, and C major in the final chorus. (Beethoven again used the movement from C minor to C major in the Fifth Symphony, another work from his "heroic phase.") An architectonic logic may be seen in the use of the flat keys below and above the opening key: number 1 is in E-flat minor; 3, a fifth below, in A-flat; and the first two sections of 6, a fifth above, in B-flat. In the introduction Beethoven uses the extremely unusual key of E-flat minor to represent the gloom of the scene and situation. (In *Fidelio*, the beginning of act II, much like the beginning of the oratorio in concept and orchestration, is in the key of F minor.)

The orchestra of *Christus* includes pairs of flutes, oboes, clarinets, bassoons, horns, trumpets, and timpani; three trombones (ATB); and strings. The only extended instrumental writing is the dark, adagio orchestral introduction with its muted strings, melodic material mainly in the lower strings, mostly low dynamic level, ominous horn-calls, and soft timpani solos. Tonally the number moves essentially from E-flat minor to B-flat minor and back again, but with surprises, such as the shifts from E-flat minor to E major to B-flat minor (mm. 13–18). At the end a turn to the dominant of C minor prepares for the beginning of Jesus' recitative, "Jehovah, du mein Vater!"

The recitatives in *Christus*, all orchestrally accompanied, are of interest in relation to the models and traditions on which they depend. The relationship between the first recitative and the oratorio's orchestral introduction, for instance, is similar to that in Haydn's *Creation*: in both works the introduction is connected to the recitative and the mood and certain melodic-rhythmic materials from the introduction reappear in

---

118. Solomon, *Beethoven*, p. 192.
119. Tyson, "Beethoven's *Christus*," p. 582.
120. Tyson, "Heroic Phase," p. 140.

the recitative. Also suggestive of Haydn's work is Beethoven's approach to tone painting in the first recitative. As in Haydn's music, the tone painting anticipates the words: in measures 68–72, tutti chords with double-dotted rhythmic figures (a traditional symbol for a king or for God), marked *maestoso* and *fortissimo*, anticipate the lines that begin, "Ich höre deines Seraphs Donnerstimme" ("I hear the thundering voice of thy Seraph"), and the same tone painting is repeated (mm. 77–81) before the words "O Vater! ich erschein' auf diesen Ruf" ("O Father, I appear at this call"). Near the end of the recitative, at the words about Jesus' anxiety and terror (the text quoted above), Beethoven's expressive technique is conventional for this affect (see Example VIII-32): off-beat rhythms in the strings (mm. 94–98) suggest the *suspiratio* figure that Graun used in *Tod Jesu*, as noted above (Example VIII-14), just after the introductory chorale, when he wished to paint Jesus' weakness of breath. Also conventional are the sigh motives on "sieh'" (Example VIII-32, mm. 95, 102) and "sehr" (mm. 100, 103)—a motive common in the Graun work. The extent of Beethoven's familiarity with Graun's *Tod Jesu* is not clear, but it was among the few oratorios published in score and widely available, and quotations from it were among those Beethoven studied in the article on recitative in Sulzer's *Allgemeine Theorie der schönen Künste*.[121] The unusual and highly expressive final cadence of the recitative (mm. 103–4) is like a cadence in a C. H. Graun cantata that Beethoven knew from his study of the same article.[122]

The entrance of the Seraph in *Christus* is similar in some respects to that of the Queen of the Night in Mozart's *Die Zauberflöte*.[123] Both enter to a roll on the timpani, and the Seraph's words, "Erzittre Erde!" (Example VIII-33), recall those of the Queen of the Night, "O zittre nicht!" (Like the Queen of the Night's aria, the Seraph's, which follows this recitative, is in coloratura style but less florid than "O zittre nicht!") Also of interest at the entrance of the Seraph is the inescapable suggestion (given the angelic tradition in oratorio) of tone painting—the Seraph flutters down from heaven in a sequence of eighth- and sixteenth-note figures (mm. 5–7 in Example VIII-33). The next recitative of the Seraph, in number 3, is also preceded by a quick, descending line in the strings, but the motive is different (Example VIII-34). In this recitative Jesus asks the Seraph if the eternal Father has taken pity on Him. Following the words "Thus speaks Jehovah," the Seraph delivers the message from the

121. On the possibility that Beethoven turned to Graun's *Tod Jesu* for reference while composing *Christus*, see Kramer, "Beethoven," pp. 37–38; according to Kramer (p. 38), "it is not clear from Carl Czerny's account of Beethoven's first contact with Graun's *Tod Jesu* whether this took place before or after the completion of *Christus*."

122. For a study of Beethoven's copies of Graun's recitatives from the article in Sulzer's *Allgemeine Theorie*, see Kramer, "Beethoven," especially pp. 26–27, where this cadence is discussed.

123. The similarities are mentioned in Tyson, "Beethoven's *Christus*," p. 583.

EXAMPLE VIII-32. *Christus*—Beethoven (Beethoven, *Christus**, p. 9).

EXAMPLE VIII-32. continued

Ah, see how anxiety, how mortal terror with power seize my heart! I suffer greatly, my Father! Oh see! I suffer greatly: have mercy upon me!

EXAMPLE VIII-33. *Christus*—Beethoven (Beethoven, *Christus**, p. 19).

EXAMPLE VIII-33. continued

EXAMPLE VIII-33. continued

Tremble, earth, for Jehovah's son lies here . . .

EXAMPLE VIII-34. *Christus*—Beethoven (Beethoven, *Christus**, pp. 49–50).

EXAMPLE VIII-34. continued

Thus speaks Jehovah: Until fulfilled is the sacred mystery of reconciliation, so long shall the human race remain cast down, robbed of eternal life.

Father that the Son must die to fulfill the "sacred mystery of reconciliation." The Father's words (mm. 7–13) are set in a highly effective repeated-note "chant" style, in slow tempo, with an organ-like accompaniment (winds, violoncello, double bass) in which the alternating minor and major triads move downward in alternating major and minor thirds (A minor, F major, D minor, B-flat major, G minor, E-flat major, C minor, A-flat major, F minor), and the Father's message ends with a suspension cadence suggesting *stile antico*. Beethoven marked this passage "stark deklamiert und accentuiert" ("strongly declaimed and accented");[124] that marking, however, did not find its way into the published version. This is the passage that the reviewer in the *Zeitung für die Elegante Welt* much admired at the first performance. Manuscript evidence strongly suggests that the three trombone parts in this accompaniment were last-minute additions; they are probably the parts that Ries saw Beethoven writing early in the morning on the day of the last rehearsal for the first performance.[125]

Both of the arias have transformed da capo structures. In Jesus' aria (in no. 1), an A1-A2 structure, all three stanzas of text are set in the A1 section, which moves from C minor to E-flat major. The A2 section recapitulates most of the material and all text of A1, but begins in C major, moves through an unstable area and closes in C minor. The text of this aria (quoted in full above) offers opportunities to paint Jesus' shaking, trembling, and shuddering, of which Beethoven takes full and conventional advantage. The Seraph's aria (no. 3) begins with a larghetto setting of the first stanza as an introduction and continues with an allegro using the next two stanzas, which are set in an approximation of the A1-A2 structure. The A2 section, however, includes an important new element: after the 1803 performance, Beethoven added a chorus to the Seraph's recapitulation (mm. 123–205), then added a new chorus (with the Seraph), beginning at the allegro molto.[126] The Seraph's part is extremely demanding in both the 1803 sections and the later additions: it ascends to d''' at one point (m. 85), c''' with an alternate e''' at another (m. 164), and includes a written cadenza near the end (m. 288), which begins on c'''.

The two ensembles present quite different types of texts. In the duet (no. 3), the texts of the two personages are similar: Jesus resigns himself to the Father's will and the Seraph empathizes with his terror. Thus the musical styles of the personages are essentially the same. The duet is cast roughly in the form: A (Jesus), A' (Seraph), B (both). As in Jesus' aria, so in this duet Beethoven carefully expresses individual words, particularly

124. Ibid., p. 559, n. 11, describes the marking as found over the words of the Seraph in the autograph score in Berlin.

125. Ibid., p. 559, n. 11.

126. For details of the structure in the 1803 version and of the added material, see ibid., pp. 560–66.

the shuddering and trembling of the Seraph. The duet closes with a four-measure transition that modulates to the next number and was added after 1803.[127] The trio forming part of the finale complex has a text of contrasts: Peter shouts that his "blood boils in righteous fury," Jesus sings of his teaching "to love all men," and the Seraph urges mankind to heed the words from "the mouth of a God." Peter begins the trio with his impetuous words and melody; Jesus continues in a gentle, lyric vein; and the Seraph's style is similar to that of Jesus. When the three combine, Peter's lines stand rhythmically and melodically apart from those of the other two. An interesting touch near the end is Jesus' approach to his cadenza (mm. 119–25): the words "ich lehrt' euch bloss allein, die Menschen alle lieben" ("I taught you only to love all men") are set entirely "alone," without accompaniment ("bloss allein"—"only" or "alone")—the only chord comes at a rest in the vocal line. This type of word painting is surprising in Beethoven because of its rarity in music after the Baroque era.

Of the three choruses, the first (in no. 2) is largely chordal in the section added to the Seraph's recapitulation (mentioned above); but the new (post-1803) section, beginning at the allegro molto, becomes imitative and includes jagged melodic lines to express the reference to those who reject Jesus, and descending lines to express "Verdammung" ("damnation"). The essentially dramatic chorus in number 5 depicts the soldiers seeking Jesus, in a marchlike rhythm and tempo, and the Disciples' fear of the soldiers. This mainly declamatory chorus is of less musical interest than the others. The most imposing chorus is that of the Angels at the end of the oratorio. After a powerful, chordal maestoso with majestic, orchestral dotted patterns that suggest the beginning of a French overture, the tempo changes to allegro for the final C-major fugue, the first few measures of which are shown in Example VIII-35a. Written with an *alla breve* time signature and mostly *colla parte* orchestration, the fugue's subject appears in the voices and a countersubject at first in the orchestra. After working out this material at some length, and including stretto passages, Beethoven introduces a fugal section on a new subject (see Example VIII-35b), this time in the voices alone and with an active accompaniment in the strings, and he manipulates this subject until the final, massive, chordal ending.

*   *   *

The discussion of the German oratorio brings to a close the treatment of oratorios with texts in the three major languages in which they were written. In the eighteenth century, oratorio was more assiduously cultivated in Italy, England, and German-speaking lands than in other geographical areas. Other than oratorio in the three languages discussed

127. Ibid., p. 566.

EXAMPLE VIII-35. *Christus*—Beethoven (Beethoven, *Christus**, pp. 107, 112–13).

Example a:

Praise Him, you choirs of angels, loudly in holy sounds of rejoicing.

EXAMPLE VIII-35. continued

Example b:

EXAMPLE VIII-35. continued

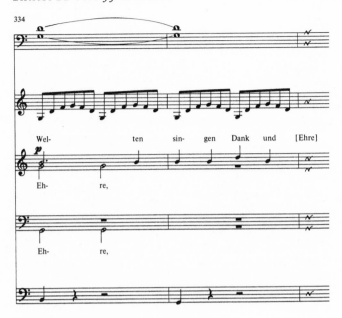

Let the universe sing thanks and glory . . .

thus far, that in French—partially derived from the Italian oratorio, but also with purely French qualities—has received the most scholarly attention, and the following chapter is devoted to it. Research on oratorio in other areas and languages is in its infancy. The Spanish and Portuguese oratorio appears to derive from the Italian, the Scandinavian from the German, and the Russian from a combination of Italian, German, and English influences (English by way of Haydn) together with native Russian traditions.

PART IV

*The Oratorio in French
and Other Languages*

§● CHAPTER IX

The French Oratorio

Introduction: Terminology and Genre Definition

In Paris of the late seventeenth and early eighteenth centuries, Marc-Antoine Charpentier (ca. 1645–50 to 1704) was virtually alone as a composer of oratorios; his were in Latin and modeled on those of his Roman teacher, Giacomo Carissimi.[1] Between Charpentier's death and the mid-century, few oratorios are known to have been performed in Paris.[2] Only in the late 1750s, when oratorios in French began to be heard in the Concert spirituel, did the genre become widely known among Parisians. The extent to which oratorios may have been performed in French cities other than Paris is unknown. Thus the present chapter focuses primarily on the oratorios of the Parisian Concert spirituel but also examines the highly unusual terminology, genre conception, and oratorios of Jean-François Le Sueur (1760–1837).

In respect to works performed in the Concert spirituel, the term *oratorio* or *oratoire* (both spellings were used) typically designated a musical setting, for soloists, chorus, and instruments, of a sacred dramatic text, usually in French but occasionally in Latin; the manner of performance was that of a "concert," without scenery, costumes, or acting.[3] Thus the French used the term in approximately the same way as the Italians and the English, and as the Germans did for their dramatic oratorio. Yet the brevity of the French oratorio distinguishes it from most oratorios in other languages. Usually forming only part of a program at the Concert spirituel, the French oratorio lasted only twenty to thirty minutes and was thus even shorter than the typical German lyric oratorio. The importance of the chorus distinguishes the French oratorio from the Italian, but not from the English or German. Exceptions to the typical French

1. On Charpentier's oratorios and the few by other composers, and for bibliography, see Smither, *Oratorio*, 1:419–34.

2. These few are treated in Foster, "Oratorio in Paris," pp. 72–80 and 129; Foster's is the most important writing on the Parisian oratorio, and the present chapter depends heavily upon it.

3. For more details on French oratorio terminology, see ibid., pp. 69–72.

terminology and genre description include a few secular works that were called oratorios by the French press (but not on title pages of music or librettos). Other terms were also exceptionally applied to the genre, among them *idylle, motet, cantate sacrée, cantate religieuse, hiérodrame* (or *hyérodrame*), and *drame sacré*. The oratorio with an operatic presentation did not become a part of French practice until the early nineteenth century, and even then it was rare; operas based on biblical subjects, like the five-act *Jephté, tragédie lyrique* (1732) by Michel Pignolet Montéclair (1667–1737), were not considered oratorios by either their composers or the press. The use of the term *oratorio* in the writings of Le Sueur and on the title pages of his music is exceptional and is treated below, together with his music.

Social Context

The Concert spirituel, among the earliest concert series in Europe, was established in 1725 for the purpose of presenting concerts on religious holidays when the Académie royale de musique (the royal opera) was required to be closed. The series continued without interruption until 1790 and distinguished itself as the principal institution for concerts not only in Paris but in all of Europe. Celebrated traveling virtuosi, both vocal and instrumental, were heard there, as was the music of Europe's leading composers.

According to the royal privilege granted to the founder of the series, the oboist and composer Anne Danican Philidor (1681–1728) was permitted to "establish and present public concerts of spiritual music" during the three weeks from Passion Sunday (the fifth Sunday of Lent) through Low Sunday (Quasimodo or the octave of Easter) inclusive, and on Pentecost, All Saints (1 November), Christmas, all the feasts of the Virgin, and on the eve of every feast.[4] In principle these holidays permitted a larger number of concerts per year than were actually given. Throughout the series' history the number appears to have varied from about ten to over fifty per year but averaged about twenty-five. For most of the sixty-six years of the series' existence, the concerts were given in the Salle des Cent suisses, located in the Tuileries Palace, which stood across from the Tuileries Garden (along the present Avenue Général Lemonnier).

Originally the repertoire of the Concert spirituel excluded works with

4. The quotation and content of this sentence are taken from a notarized document of the time, quoted in Pierre, *Concert spirituel*, p. 15, which specifies the conditions to which Philidor agreed. In his book, the most important work on the Concert spirituel, Pierre lists all programs of the series in an appendix. For a treatment of the Concert spirituel published in 1900 but still useful, see Brenet, *Concerts*, pp. 115–346. Brief summaries of the series are found in Anthony, *French Baroque Music*, pp. 21–23; and Daval, *Musique en France*, pp. 123–52.

French texts and fragments from operas; this exclusion, specified in Philidor's privilege, was to protect the interests of the royal opera.[5] During his directorship of the series (1725–27) and that of succeeding directors until the 1750s, the programs consisted primarily of instrumental music and large motets in Latin. The motets represented prominent French composers of the past and present—Michel-Richard de Lalande (1657–1726) was a favorite—and the instrumental works were by both French and foreign composers.

Only in 1755, when Jean-Joseph Cassanéa de Mondonville (1711–72) assumed the musical direction of the series, did the concerts begin to include sporadic performances of works with French texts, usually oratorios. The first oratorio performed in the Concert spirituel was Mondonville's *Les Israélites à la montagne d'Horeb* (text by Claude-Henri de Fuzée, Abbé de Voisenon), given on 14 March 1758 (Tuesday after Passion Sunday).[6] The program of the concert was typical of the Concert spirituel in this period: a symphony (unidentified), the motet "Deus misereatur" by Pierre Just Davesne (ca. 1745–66 to 1783), a violin concerto composed and performed by Pierre Vachon (1731–1803), two Italian arias sung by Madame Violante Vestris de Giardini (ca. 1732–91), the overture to *Daphnis et Alcimadure* by Mondonville performed on the organ by Claude-Bénigne Balbastre (1727–99), a solo motet sung by Mademoiselle Marie Fel, and Mondonville's oratorio as the final number.[7] That oratorio received thirteen performances in the Concert spirituel between 1758 and 1762,[8] the last year in which Mondonville directed the concerts. The innovation of a French oratorio in the Concert spirituel pleased most of the reviewers but also confused them, for they were uncertain what to call the piece; they labeled it variously as " 'motet françois,' 'poëme françois,' 'motet françois en forme d'oratorio,' and 'oratorio françois.' "[9] Mondonville's next oratorio, *Les fureurs de Saül* (1758), was performed ten times during his directorship. His *Les Titans* (1761), performed four times, had a secular text and was not called an oratorio but is much like his two works which were designated oratorios. Other oratorios performed in the Concert spirituel during the same period are Jean-Nicolas Loiseau de Persuis's *Le passage de la mer Rouge* (1759) and Davesne's *La conquête de Jérico* (1760).

Between 1762 and 1773 the directors of the Concert spirituel evidently had little interest in oratorios because none were performed. However, a change of directorship in 1773 brought changes in the series; oratorios returned, and they continued to be heard in the Concert spirituel until its

5. Pierre, *Concert spirituel*, p. 15.
6. Mondonville's oratorios are treated in Foster, "Oratorio in Paris," pp. 80–82.
7. Pierre, *Concert spirituel*, p. 275.
8. In this and the next two paragraphs, all performance statistics are taken from Foster, "Oratorio in Paris," appendix, pp. 127–33.
9. Ibid., p. 80.

demise in 1790. From 1773 to 1777 the directors of the series were Pierre Gavinès (1728–1800), Simon Leduc (?before 1748–1777), and François-Joseph Gossec (1734–1829); the next and final director was Joseph Legros (1739–93), who ran the series from 1777 to 1790. In the period 1774–90, the most active one for oratorios in the Concert spirituel, at least thirty-six new oratorios by twenty-seven composers were heard, and the total number of oratorio performances was at least 138. Paris may have been the most active European city outside of Italy for the performance of new oratorios—brief as they were—during this seventeen-year period.

A representative list of oratorios heard in the Concert spirituel between 1774 and 1790 is found in Table IX-1.[10] The mixture of well-known and obscure composers listed (in alphabetical order) is typical of the series. The texts of most oratorios were in French but a few were in Latin. In Table IX-1 the only works with Latin texts are Giroust's *Passage de la mer Rouge*, adapted from Exodus 14 in the Vulgate Bible, and Philidor's popular *Carmen seculare*, with a text adapted from Horace. Although Philidor's work is not typical of the oratorios in the series, it was considered an oratorio (at least by the press) in its time. Most composers of oratorios for the Concert spirituel also composed operas, as did the majority of those listed in Table IX-1. Among the exceptions are Lepreux, a choirmaster at the Sainte-Chapelle;[11] and Beaumesnil, a singer who had retired from the Opéra and the royal chapel at the time she wrote her oratorio.[12] She is the only woman known to have composed an oratorio for the series.

The performing forces for the oratorios at the Concert spirituel varied according to the changing views—and probably the economics—of the series' directors.[13] In the earliest period of oratorios, that of Mondonville (1758–62), the total number of available performers ranged from about ninety-four to ninety-nine: twenty-seven to thirty strings, about twelve winds, forty-four to forty-seven chorus singers, and ten vocal soloists. The chorus was divided about equally among the voice parts: *premier dessus* and *second dessus* (first and second treble), *haute-contre* (male alto), *taille* (tenor), *basse-taille* (low tenor or baritone), and *basse-contre* (bass). Before the mid-century in the Concert spirituel the *premier dessus* was sung by males and the *second dessus* by females; at the end of 1751, however, four men were placed on the *second dessus* and two women replaced them on the *premier dessus*. In 1765 women completely replaced men on the two *dessus* parts, but in 1769–70 those parts again included men. In the next oratorio period—that of Gavinès, Leduc, and

10. The table is adapted from ibid., appendix, pp. 129–33, which provides a complete chronological list of eighteenth-century Parisian oratorios, with performance data and comments on librettists and sources.

11. Pierre, *Concert spirituel*, p. 183.

12. Ibid., p. 189.

13. This paragraph is based on ibid., pp. 76–78.

FIGURE IX-1. Handbill advertising a Concert spirituel (Paris, 1779), which included the oratorio *Samson*, with a text by Voltaire and music by Giuseppe Maria Cambini. (Reproduced by permission of F-Po.)

Gossec, beginning in 1774—the strings were increased to forty-two, the winds to sixteen, and the total number of performers to 133; both men and women were still used on the *dessus* parts. Under the directorship of Legros (1777–90), however, the size of the chorus was reduced to between nineteen and twenty-seven, which shrank the total number to between eighty-six and ninety-five. The soloists in oratorios at the Concert spirituel usually were the singers of the Opéra, and the members of the orchestra and chorus were drawn from the Opéra, the royal chapel, and church choirs.

Of the other concert institutions in Paris, the only one known to have performed oratorios—but rarely—was the Concert des amateurs, founded and directed by Gossec in 1769 at the Hôtel de Soubise.[14] In 1780 the institution changed its name to the Concert de la Loge olympique (a name that bore Masonic implications). Two of Rigel's oratorios heard in the Concert spirituel were also given in this series: *La sortie d'Egypte*, performed twice in 1775–76 at the Concert des amateurs, and *Jephté*, once in 1783 at the Concert de la Loge olympique.[15]

14. Brenet, *Concerts*, pp. 357–66.
15. Foster, "Oratorio in Paris," pp. 130, 132.

TABLE IX-1
A Selective List of Oratorios Performed in the Concert spirituel, 1774–90

Composer	Title	Years and No. of Performances
Cambini, Giuseppe Maria (1746–1825)	Le sacrifice d'Isaac	1774–88, ca. 8
Idem	Joad	1775, 3
Idem	Samson	1779, 3
Giroust, François (1737–99)	Passage de la mer Rouge	1784, ?
Idem	Les fureurs de Saül	1781, 1
Gossec, François-Joseph (1734–1829)	La nativité	1774–83, ca. 9
Idem	L'arche d'alliance devant Jérusalem	1781–82, 4
Lenoble, Joseph (1753–1829)	La mort d'Absalon	1782, 1
Lepreux, André-Etienne (?–?)	Les fureurs de Saül	1786–87, 3
Méreaux, Nicolas-Jean Le Froid de (1745–1797)	Samson	1774–77, 4
Idem	Oratoire tiré des choeurs d'Esther de Racine	1775–76, 5
Idem	La résurrection	1780, 2
Philidor, François-André Danican (1726–95)	Carmen seculare	1780–88, ca. 15 complete or partial
Rigel, Henri-Joseph (1741–99)	La sortie d'Egypte	1774–88, 33
Idem	La destruction de Jéricho	1778–85, 10
Idem	Jephté	1784, 2; 1788, 1
Sacchini, Antonio (1730–86)	Esther	1786–90, 10
Salieri, Antonio (1750–1825)	Le jugement dernier	1788, 2
Villard de Beaumesnil, Henriette-Adélaïde (?–?)	Les Israëlites poursuivis par Pharaon	1784–85, 3
Vogel, Johann Christoph (1756–88)	Jephté	1781–82, 3

Oratorios appear not to have been performed in Parisian churches, except for four curious oratoriolike works by Le Sueur given in 1786–87 at Notre-Dame Cathedral. In the Napoleonic period Le Sueur composed works that he called oratorios for the Tuileries Chapel (see below).

In 1803 an innovation for Paris was the performance of a staged pasticcio oratorio, arranged by Christian Kalkbrenner (1755–1806) and Ludwig Wenzel Lachnith (1746–1820). The title page of the printed libretto bears the work's genre and its manner and place of performance (see Figure IX-2).[16] The following quotation from the libretto's *Avertissement* explains the point of view of the pasticcio's arrangers:

> Italy long ago adopted the Oratorio in action. Following its example, we offer to the public this endeavor, indeed less through the ambition of attempting something new, than through the desire of varying the pleasures of a Nation sensible to the charms of harmony, but even more to dramatic impressions, for the most alluring sounds cannot long distract it from the need of occupying its heart, its spirit, or its eyes. The Concerts spirituels, which formerly gave concerts [l'Academie de Musique], despite the concurrence of the most celebreted talents, never appeared to produce on the public all that one would have had the right to hope from them. Without renouncing the advantages of a genre, we have believed ourselves able to add to its effect, in giving a framework to the different pieces of music, in supporting them by scenic movement and variety of costumes and decorations.
>
> The title ORATORIO prescribed to us the law of choosing only a religious subject; and the gathering together of the airs that we would present demanded an action clear enough, [and] simple enough to permit only that recitative which is necessary for understanding the scenes, so that the airs themselves would be the principal development of the action. These airs we have chosen from the works of the great composers, foreign and national: PAESIELLO, CIMAROSA, MOZART, HAYDN, HANDEL, NAUMANN, GOSSEC, AND PHILIDOR.[17]

The authors of this *Avertissement* are correct in their assessment of Italian practice, as we have seen, and they are probably correct in their suggestion that the work represented a new approach to oratorio for Paris. French operas based on biblical subjects had long been known in Paris, but they were essentially dramatic works and were not considered oratorios. In *Saül*, however, the emphasis appears to have been on the airs, rather than on drama; the pasticcio seems to have been conceived as a scenic concert work—indeed, as a scenic oratorio.

Although the scenic oratorio appears to have been a short-lived genre in Paris, the success of *Saül* must have been sufficient to encourage the same composers to undertake a similar pasticcio in 1805: *La prise de Jéricho, oratorio en trois parties, représenté sur le Théatre de l'Académie Impériale de Musique, le 21 germinal an XIII*.[18] Again the composers

16. Copies of the libretto in F-Pn: Th^B 256 (4) and Th^B 1871. The musical sources of *Saül* are F-Pc: Ms. 8339, 8340 (1–6), 8341, 8342, and 8344. In 1805 *Saül* was performed in Vienna at the Redoutensaal, for the benefit of the poor, according to the *Allgemeine musikalische Zeitung* 7 (1804–5): 320–21.

17. Translated from the libretto F-Pn: Th^B 256 (4), p. [iii].

18. Copy of printed libretto: F-Pn: Th^B 1933. The musical sources are in F-Pc: Ms. 8126.

SAÜL,

ORATORIO MIS EN ACTION;

REPRÉSENTÉ

SUR LE THÉATRE DES ARTS,

LE 16 GERMINAL AN XI.

A PARIS,

Chez { BALLARD, Imprimeur du Théâtre des Arts, rue J.-J. Rousseau, n°. 14; DEFRELLE, Libraire, cloître St.-Honoré, n°. 11.

AN XI (1803).

FIGURE IX-2. Title page of the staged pasticcio oratorio *Saül*, assembled by Kalkbrenner and Lachnith. (Reproduced by permission of F-Pn.)

whose music is adapted are named, and they include Mozart, Haydn, Paër, Sacchini, Nicolini, Cimarosa, Piccini, and [?A.] Scarlatti.

The Libretto

Most librettists of the oratorios for the Concert spirituel are little-known figures.[19] Among the few exceptions is Michel-Paul-Guy de Chabanon (1729 or 1730 to 1792), the librettist of Gossec's *La nativité*, who was also the author of two *tragédies lyriques* and various widely read treatises on music theory and aesthetics.[20] Another exception is Pierre Louis Moline (1740–1821), who wrote four librettos set to music for the Concert spirituel: *La résurrection* (set by Méreaux), *L'arche d'alliance devant Jérusalem* (Gossec), *Jephté* (Vogel), *Les fureurs de Saül* (Giroust), and *La mort d'Absalon* (Lenoble). Moline was extremely active as a librettist for the French stage and is best known for his French adaptation of Raniero de Calzabigi's libretto for Gluck's *Orphée* (1774). One of the well-known authors whose works were adapted as oratorio texts is Voltaire, whose *Samson* was originally written for Rameau in 1731–32, was arranged for Méreaux's oratorio *Samson*, and was again set by Cambini. Méreaux also set part of Racine's *Esther* as an oratorio, and Cambini, in his *Joad*, set selected texts from Racine's *Athalie*.

As we have seen, most oratorios for the Concert spirituel were sung in French—Latin was rare. As a glance at the titles in Table IX-1 will show, Old Testament subjects were overwhelmingly favored—even more so than for dramatic oratorios in other languages and geographical areas. The few New Testament oratorios are based only on the Nativity and Resurrection stories. The Passion oratorio, so prominent in other languages and regions, did not form part of the Concert spirituel. (But see below on the Passion oratorios of Le Sueur for the Tuileries Chapel.) Although the Moline-Méreaux *La résurrection* begins with a lamentation for the Passion and Crucifixion of Jesus—sung by Mary, Martha, Mary Magdalene, and Joseph of Arimathea—the work emphasizes the Resurrection. The treatment of the biblical stories is, of course, limited by the necessary brevity of the French oratorio; little time is allowed for characterization or development of plot. Like the librettists for the German lyric oratorio of the same period, the French librettists characteristically selected biblical episodes that were already familiar to the audience and could thus be presented in a few numbers, usually between five and ten per oratorio. The long tradition of the grand motet in the Concert

19. All librettists whose names are known are listed in Foster, "Oratorio in Paris," pp. 129–33.

20. All oratorios mentioned in this paragraph are represented in Table IX-1, which may be consulted for composers' full names and dates and for performances at the Concert spirituel.

spirituel, which the oratorio tended to replace, must have influenced the poet's and composer's conception of the genre. About one-third to one-half of the numbers in a French oratorio are choruses; a chorus usually ends an oratorio and frequently begins one as well. Of common occurrence are choral-solo and choral-ensemble numbers, in which the chorus and soloist(s) alternate and overlap. The distinction—characteristic of librettos in other languages—of a freer verse for recitative than for the air, ensemble, or chorus is found in the French libretto.

The Music: General Characteristics

The earliest musical sources for oratorios performed in the Concert spirituel date from the second period of that series' cultivation of the genre, 1774–90. The music in the sources represents a combination of early Classical and Classical styles, with little remaining trace of Baroque style.[21]

The instrumentation most commonly includes strings and pairs of flutes, oboes, horns, and bassoons; less frequently included are clarinets, trumpets, and trombones. Overtures and other instrumental numbers are rare; given the context of French-oratorio performances within the Concert spirituel, an overture may have been viewed as unnecessary. Often, however, the opening vocal number will begin with an extended orchestral introduction in lieu of an overture.

The airs, recitatives, and ensembles tend to be relatively simple, with emphasis on clear declamation of the text and appropriate word painting and expression. Little of the virtuosic, coloratura style common in the Italian oratorio is found in the French. The airs and ensembles are usually brief and cast in binary, ternary, or transformed da capo structures; occasionally the dal segno sign is used for an abbreviated da capo form, but the full da capo form is extremely rare. The recitatives are always orchestrally accompanied, and they constitute some of the most affective sections of the oratorios.

Like the airs and ensembles, the choruses pay special attention to text declamation, painting, and expression. The choral texture is almost exclusively chordal. Unlike oratorios in most other languages and regions, choral fugues are not a part of the style, and the few points of imitation are brief. (Philidor's *Carmen seculare* does include a fugue, but that work is highly exceptional.)[22] Following the French tradition, the choral parts are usually designated as *dessus* (many choruses have both *premier* and *second dessus*), *haute-contre*, *taille* (sometimes the designations *haute-taille* and *basse-taille* are used), and *basse* (sometimes, *contra-basse*).

21. For more details about musical style and structure in French oratorios than are given in this brief survey, see Foster, "Oratorio in Paris," pp. 84–114.
22. For a quotation from the fugue, see ibid., pp. 98–99.

The Music: Selected Oratorios

Henri-Joseph Rigel: La sortie d'Egypte

Born in Wertheim, Germany, Rigel (originally Riegel; 1741–99) is said to have studied with Jommelli in Stuttgart, and he may have studied with Franz Xaver Richter in Mannheim.[23] By early 1767 he was in Paris, where he remained for the rest of his life and became one of the city's most respected composers of instrumental and vocal music, including operas, oratorios, motets, and revolutionary hymns. In 1783 he was appointed *maître de solfège* at the Ecole royale de chant and, after the Revolution, a professor *première classe* of piano at the Conservatoire. In 1783 and 1787–88 he was the *chef d'orchestre* at the Concert spirituel. The first of Rigel's three oratorios (see Table IX-1), *La sortie d'Egypte*, was by far the most popular, receiving thirty-three performances at the Concert spirituel and two at the Concert des amateurs between 1774 and 1788; the work was given again in Paris as late as 1822.[24]

The librettist of *La sortie* was Chabanon de Maugris (1735–80), the brother of the more famous librettist and writer on music, Michel-Paul-Guy de Chabanon. The personages are Moses (B), an Israelite (T), an unidentified soloist (S) added in 1786 to scene 1, a quartet of Israelites (SSTB), a Chorus of Egyptians (SATB), a Chorus of Israelites (SATB) and a Coryphaeus (A, soloist from the chorus), and a double chorus of Israelites (SA) and Egyptians (TB). Based on the story of the Israelites' departure from their Egyptian captivity, the libretto derives from Exodus 11–15. The work is divided into six scenes (see Table IX-2), and begins in the midst of the exodus with a quartet of Israelites (and a recitative and ariette added in 1786) commenting on a sudden change in their favor: God has seen their miseries and heard their innocent cries and has marched ahead of Moses, their leader. In scene 2 Moses assures the Israelites that they are free and that the power of Pharoah has been subdued by the greater power of God; in an ariette, he asks God to strike down his enemies. Scene 3 is one of lamentation: the Egyptians petition the God of the Jews to cease his blows, for they are suffering from the tenth plague, the death of the firstborn throughout Egypt. At the beginning of scene 4 Moses orders the Israelites to recognize the power of their God and to march forth, for the moment of their deliverance is at hand. A Coryphaeus and the chorus sing a march, which eventually is interrupted: according to a note in the manuscript at the beginning of scene 5, "The march is interrupted by an orchestral passage [une trait de Symphonie], which expresses the distant tumult of an army, the gallop of

23. On Rigel's biography, see Barry S. Brook and Richard Viano, "Rigel," *New Grove*, pp. 16:16–18.

24. Ibid., 16:17; on Rigel's oratorios, see Foster, "Oratorio in Paris," pp. 88–92. The source for the following comments on Rigel's *La sortie d'Egypte* is the autograph manuscript in F-Pc: Ms. 7369.

TABLE IX-2
Rigel, *La sortie d'Egypte*: Structural Outline

Numbers	Keys
[Scene 1]	
Quartet [des Israelites], "Quel changement soudain!"	B♭
*[Recit. (accomp.). "Du Dieu d'Israël la colère"	E♭]
*[Ariette. "Si de nos tirans odieux"	E♭]
Scene 2	
Recit. Moïse, "Oui peuple! tu verra la fin de tes allarmes"	
Ariette. Moïse, "Frappe, frappe grand Dieu!"	f
Scene 3	
Choeur Lamentable des Egyptiens, "Arrête, arrête"	c
Scene 4	
Recit. Moïse, "Israël! de ton Dieu"	
Marche. Coryphé, Choeur [des Israelites], "Nous marchons"	E♭
Scene 5	
Recit. (accomp.). Un Israelite, Moïse, "Un bruit confus s'eleve"	(C)
Scene 6	
[Double Chorus]. Israelites, Egyptiens, "Ô prodige inouï"	C
Choeur. Chant de Victoire, "Je reconnais ton bras"	C

*Added in 1786.

Note: The term *scene* and the numbers are those of the source, F-Pn: Ms. 7369.

horses, etc."[25] After the brief orchestral passage, an Israelite comments on the noises and the pursuit of the enemy, and Moses commands the waters of the Red Sea to part. At the beginning of Scene 6 "the symphony expresses the profound calm of the sea."[26] For the double chorus of Israelites and Egyptians that follows, according to the score, "the Israelites must be on one side and the Egyptians on the opposite side."[27] As the Israelites proceed they sing of the miracle of the water opening before them, and the Egyptians voice their thirst for vengeance. Suddenly, after a general pause, the Egyptians cry out, for the water is closing in on them. In the final number the Israelites praise God for their salvation.

The tonal structure of the work shows a movement from flat keys to C major. Minor keys are used for Moses' ariette of anger (F minor), in which he asks God to strike down the enemy, and for the lamentation of the Egyptians (C minor).

25. F-Pc: Ms. 7369, p. 51.
26. Ibid., p. 54.
27. Ibid.

The orchestra consists of strings plus pairs of oboes, bassoons, clarinets, horns, trumpets, and timpani. Although the work has no overture, the thirty-measure orchestral introduction to the opening quartet serves as an introduction to the oratorio. Important orchestral sections include: a march signaling the start of the exodus at the beginning of scene 4, which is introduced by the clarinets, oboes, bassoons, horns, violas, and contrabasses (violins and violoncellos join only at the vocal entrance); the interruption of the march, at the beginning of scene 5, by the strings, trumpets, and timpani; and, at the beginning of scene 6, the expression of the calmness of the sea by a "symphony" of strings, horns, oboes, and bassoons.

Both of the ariettes—the one sung by Moses (the only one in the original version) and the one added in 1786—have transformed da capo structures. In scene 2 in Moses' ariette of anger he calls down the wrath of God on the Egyptians. As shown in Example IX-1, the number includes the triadic figures characteristic of traditional martial music. The text of the ariette added to scene 1—a text of hope, anticipating freedom and victory—is set in a relatively virtuosic manner, with numerous recurrences of high b″-flat, but without coloratura. In both of these airs syllabic text setting is more typical than melismatic.

The opening quartet has a dal segno form in which the sign supresses repetition of the long opening instrumental section that begins the oratorio. The A section is predominantly in chordal style. The B section begins with solo passages—while the orchestra paints the waves of the Nile, mentioned in the text—and continues with paired voices (SS and TB) singing mostly in parallel thirds before the return to A. Declamatory text setting predominates.

All four of the recitatives are orchestrally accompanied: three use strings only, but the strings are joined by the trumpets and timpani in the recitative of scene 5, where the noises of the distant Egyptian army are heard. The simplest recitative accompaniment of the oratorio, however, is the solemn chordal setting of Moses' command that the waters part.

Like the other numbers of the oratorio, the choruses emphasize textual declamation by largely chordal, homorhythmic writing. The first chorus, in which the Egyptians lament the plague that has killed their firstborn children, is in ABA′ structure. The beginning of the A and A′ sections, for SATB, is shown in Example IX-2; there, in *mezza voce* and essentially declamatory style, the Egyptians plead with the God of the Jews to stop the plague. The B section begins with a solo passage sung by one woman about her dead child, and then three sopranos lament the deaths of their children before the return to the music of Example IX-2. The chorus in scene 4, preceded by the instrumental march that serves as an introduction, as mentioned above, has a simple march tune sung by the Coryphaeus and the full chorus in alternation; of special interest is the careful attention to dynamics in this chorus, which was praised in the

EXAMPLE IX-1. *La sortie d'Egypte*—Rigel (F-Pc: Ms. 7369, pp. 22–23).

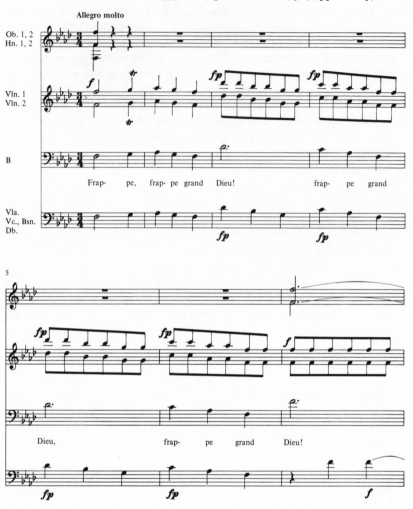

EXAMPLE IX-I. continued

EXAMPLE IX-I. continued

Strike, strike, great God, that thy proud enemies fall, buried in the dust of the dead.

EXAMPLE IX-2. *La sortie d'Egypte*—Rigel (F-Pc: Ms. 7369, pp. 32–34).

EXAMPLE IX-2. continued

EXAMPLE IX-2. continued

EXAMPLE IX-2. continued

EXAMPLE IX-2. continued

Stop, God of the Jews! Stop, calm thy wrath, o death, suspend thy blows.

Journal de Paris on 26 March 1777 as a chorus "avec toutes les grada-
tions du *crescendo*."[28] The victory chorus, which closes the oratorio, has
a martial style and is essentially chordal but with two brief points of
imitation.

The most dramatic choral number of the oratorio is the double chorus
in scene 6. After the opening symphony mentioned above, which expresses the calm of the sea, the chorus of the Israelites passing through
the Red Sea (SA, on one side of the stage) alternates with that of the
Egyptians pursuing them (TB, on the opposite side). The difference of
style between the Israelites and the Egyptians—both declamatory, but the
Israelites in *alla breve* and the Egyptians in 12/8—was praised by the
reviewer in the *Journal de Paris*, 26 March 1777, who described it as a
contrast of "chant simple et pur des Israélites avec les cris de fureur des

28. Quoted in Brenet, *Concerts*, p. 309.

Egyptiens."[29] After three alternations of the two choirs the Egyptians musically "overtake" the Israelites, and the two groups sing simultaneously in their respective meters (see Example IX-3, mm. 68–73). Following another pair of alternations, a fermata on a dominant chord (m. 85) signals the safety of the Israelites, after which the Egyptians cry out—with wavelike accompaniment in the orchestra—that the waves tremble and subside (mm. 86–92). The section closes with a seven-measure return to the calmness of the introduction to this scene.

François-Joseph Gossec: La nativité

Gossec (1734–1829) was born in Vergnies, Hainaut (south-west Belgium) and received his early musical training in Walcourt, Maubeuge, and Antwerp where he sang in the choir of the Cathedral of Notre Dame. Probably in 1751 he went to Paris with a letter of introduction to Rameau, who secured a position for him as violinist and bass player in the private orchestra of the famous patron Alexandre-Jean-Joseph Le Riche de La Pouplinière (1693–1762). From 1762 to 1770 Gossec served as director of the private theater of Louis-Joseph de Bourbon, Prince of Condé, at Chantilly, and about 1766 he also served Louis-François de Bourbon, Prince of Conti, as *ordinaire de la musique*. In 1769 Gossec founded the Concert des amateurs, which he directed until he, Leduc, and Gaviniès assumed leadership of the Concert spirituel, 1773–77 (see above). From 1782 to 1784 Gossec led the supervisory committee of the Opéra, and in 1784 he became the director of the Ecole royale de chant; in 1795 he became an inspector of the Conservatoire and professor of composition there. Among the most prolific composers in France of his time, Gossec wrote much instrumental music of which his symphonies are particularly important. His vocal music includes operas, sacred music, revolutionary pieces, and two oratorios.

The most popular of Gossec's oratorios (listed in Table IX-1), *La nativité* received about nine performances at the Concert spirituel.[30] Although the work is said to have been composed in 1759, it probably dates from the year of its first performance on Christmas Eve of 1774.[31] The oratorio was the final number in a concert typical of the series,

29. Quoted in ibid., p. 309.

30. The *Saül* (F-Pc: Ms. 8340), thought to be a third oratorio by Gossec (see Foster, "Oratorio in Paris," pp. 93–94), is music by him used in the scenic pasticcio oratorio *Saül* (1803), arranged by Kalkbrenner and Lachnith (see above).

31. On the title page and in the introduction of the modern edition, Gossec, *Nativité* (a vocal score), the editor assumes the number "1759" on the title page of the manuscript (F-Pc: Rés. F. 1132) to be a date; Foster, "Oratorio in Paris," pp. 92 and 130, apparently follows that editor in the same assumption. But "1759" is found on the manuscript title page twice, once preceded by "N°," and seems to be an old catalogue number, comparable to (and probably in the same

EXAMPLE IX-3. *La sortie d'Egypte*—Rigel (F-Pc: Ms. 7369, pp. 65–66, 68–69).

EXAMPLE IX-3. continued

EXAMPLE IX-3. continued

EXAMPLE IX-3. continued

EXAMPLE IX-3. continued

EXAMPLE IX-3. continued

EXAMPLE IX-3. continued

Israelites: Preserve from danger the innocent dove, before [our steps] . . .
Egyptians: . . . implacable vengeance, for a culpable people will feel their blows;
soon they will yield, this odious people, [who] cross the abyss open before our
eyes; . . . but the sea trembles, the wave subsides . . .

which included in the following order: a symphony and the motet "Christe redemptor" by Gossec, an oboe concerto by Julien-Amable Mathieu (1734–1811), the motet "Cantate Domino" by Honoré Langlé (1741–1807), a new symphonie concertante for two violins by Simon Leduc, a solo motet by Méreaux, a concerto for violin composed and performed by Louis-Henri Paisible (1748–82), and finally Gossec's *La nativité*. The review of the concert in the *Mercure de France* praised the work and termed it both an *oratoire* and a *motet*:

> This concert finished with the *Nativité*, a new oratorio with two choirs, composed by M. Gossec. This motet had a very great success. The first duo is fresh and delicious music; the air sung by M. Legros is charming. The Sleep of the Shepherds, interrupted by extraordinary signs, is a symphonic piece with a very grand effect, even dramatic, as was the chorus, *Quel sort funeste nous menace?* The Chorus of Angels was placed above the vault of the hall, and that illusion added to the very good effect of the piece; but perhaps [the oratorio is] a little too long, as was the last chorus, [which is] susceptible to being abridged.[32]

The *Mercure de France* reported that even outside of the Christmas season, that is, in March 1775, another presentation of the Concert spirituel had "finished with the *Nativité*, oratorio [oratoire] with two choirs, by M. Gossec, which was requested again; music of a brillant and imposing effect."[33] By 1779 the work was well known and highly valued. An enthusiastic reviewer of the Christmas Eve and Christmas Day performances in that year wrote:

> What a difference between the frivolous sensations of the concertos and the impetuous and varied movements that the oratorio of M. Gossec produced! A subject analogous to the feast of the day; a style full of grace and majesty; of astonishing effects of harmony; the happiest combinations of instruments, their mixture with the voice, which from time to time imitates the song of the nightingale or the rolling of thunder; the chorus of shepherds that appeared in the orchestra and of the angels, which one could not see at all but could hear from an immense distance; that species of dialogue between the inhabitants of the earth on the one hand and the inhabitants of heaven, which one would believe assembled on a cloud; the air of a noël, which the composer had placed in the midst of this grand and rich tableau, carried the illusion and the interest to the

---

hand as) those found on the title pages of the Francesco Feo manuscripts in the same collection (F-Pc: Ms. 1955–59).

32. *Mercure de France*, January 1775, pp. 180–82.

33. Ibid., March, 1775, p. 149. This performance is not listed in Pierre, *Concert spirituel*.

FIGURE IX-3. François-Joseph Gossec (1734–1829). (Lithograph, 1820, by Julien Boilly. Reproduced by permission of GB-Lcm.)

most captivating degree for the public and the most flattering for M. Gossec.[34]

La nativité, the only oratorio libretto by M.-P.-G. de Chabanon, is divided into eight numbers, as shown in Table IX-3.[35] The personages are a Shepherdess (S), a Shepherd (A, in the alto clef but probably sung by a male alto), a Narrator (T), a Voice (S) from heaven, one of the Magi (B), a Chorus of Shepherds (SATB), a Chorus of Angels (SSAT), and an unspecified Chorus (SATB) on earth, which joins with the Angels at the end. The first two numbers and part of the third express the tranquility of the Shepherds' evening: in number 1 they begin to rest from their labors, and the birds gather to sing; in number 2 a Shepherd draws an analogy between their protection of their flocks and God's protection of them; in number 3, while the shepherds sleep, a Narrator describes the peace of the fields, which is suddenly disturbed, for the heavens open and a bright light is seen. The fear and trembling of the Shepherds is depicted in number 4; the Shepherds believe they will be punished for their sins and they ask for mercy. In the brief recitative of number 5 a Voice from heaven announces the birth of a Savior and tells the Shepherds to go to Bethlehem. The duet and chorus of number 6 depict their journey, and on their arrival one of the Magi, in number 7, shows them the God whom they seek, and the Chorus of Angels sings "Glory to God." The final number is a dialogue between the Chorus of Angels in heaven and the Chorus [of Shepherds?] on earth, singing praises to God.

The oratorio closes in D major and begins in the dominant of that key. The key farthest away from that center is C minor, used in number 4 to depict the fear of the Shepherds; after that number closes in C minor, reassurance comes immediately in C major in the recitative of the Voice from heaven. The only other minor key is in number 2, where A minor, in contrast to the preceding A major, paints the evening scene.

The instrumentation includes strings plus pairs of flutes, oboes, clarinets, bassoons, and timpani; two horns are used until the last number, which requires four. The longest passages for the orchestra alone are the introductions to numbers 1 and 3, both written to establish delicate moods. Number 1, as befits a pastorale, is in 6/8 time and begins with a drone in the horns, bassoons, and lower strings, while the upper strings play a simple, lilting melody; all strings are muted throughout the number. The orchestra again introduces a peaceful scene in number 3, for this

---

34. Translated from Brenet, *Concerts*, p. 308, as quoted from *Mercure de France*, January 1779, p. 48.

35. The source used for the following comments on the libretto and music is in F-Pc: Rés. F. 1132.

TABLE IX-3

Gossec, *La nativité*: Structural Outline

Numbers	Keys
1. Pastorale. Bergère, Berger, "Bergers cesons nos travaux"	A
2. [Air]. Berger, "Chères brebis dans cette enciente"	a
3. Sommeil des Bergers. [Recit.] Chant [Narrator], "De ces paisibles champs"	D-C
4. Choeur [des Bergers], Berger, "Quel sort funeste nous menace?"	c
5. [Recit.] Une Voix, "Bergers rassurez-vous, un Dieu Sauveur"	C
6. Marche des Bergers. [Duet] Bergère, Berger, & Choeur, "Nous que pour ses enfants Dieu"	C
7. Récit. Un Mage, Choeur d'Anges, "Habitans des hameaux"	C-D
8. Choeur d'Anges, "Gloire au Dieu toutpuissant"	D

Note: Numbers are those in or implied by the source, F-Pc: Ms. Rés. F. 1132.

is night music—adagio, pizzicato strings, and sustained tones in the clarinets and horns—played while the Shepherds sleep.

Both the structure and the melodic style of the oratorio tend to be simple, in keeping with the pastoral theme, yet there are ornamental passages. Number 2, an air in binary form, has the kind of simplicity shown in the first part of Example IX-4 (mm. 12–23); in the second part of the same number, however, slightly more elaborate passages appear, one of which is shown later in the same example (mm. 33–38).

Like the air, the duet (no. 1) begins in a simple style but becomes elaborate in the middle section of its dal segno form, where bird calls are painted in both the voice and the orchestra. In Example IX-5 the nightingale is depicted, with its trills and runs, as mentioned by the reviewer of 1779.

All the choruses are predominantly in chordal style. They are harmonically simple, and even the chromatic passage in the chorus expressing the Shepherds' fear (no. 4) is effected mainly by passing tones and chords over a pedal point, as shown in Example IX-6. The next chorus, depicting the journey of the Shepherds to Bethlehem, is based on the noël "Où s'en vont ces gais Bergers?" according to the oratorio's manuscript source.[36] The final chorus is the simplest one of all, and simple style was prudent for the kind of performance practice Gossec had in mind. In the manuscript source (a copy) one reads a passage marked "Observation autographe de Gossec," as follows:

36. F-Pc: Rés. F. 1132, p. 59.

EXAMPLE IX-4. *La nativité*—Gossec (F-Pc: Rés. F. 1132, pp. 27–28, 30).

EXAMPLE IX-4. continued

Dear flock, within that enclosure, near your shepherds, you show, without fear.... We are his flock, he will ward off [the evils] ...

EXAMPLE IX-5. *La nativité*—Gossec (F-Pc: Rés. F. 1132, pp. 21–23).

EXAMPLE IX-5. continued

EXAMPLE IX-5. continued

The nightingale is heard, it charms the wood all around . . .

EXAMPLE IX-6. *La nativité*—Gossec (F-Pc: Rés. F. 1132, pp. 49–50).

EXAMPLE IX-6. continued

Before thy compassionate eyes may our iniquity be obliterated.

Chorus of Angels Separated from the Orchestra

This chorus was placed above the vault of the Salle du Concert spirituel in Paris, in the dome of the palace of the Tuileries; it was heard perfectly without being seen and created an illusion. The chorus master who conducted it based his beat on that of the conductor of the large orchestra whom he observed through a small opening the size of a cupped hand, made in the ceiling.[37]

Such a drastic spatial separation of performers is apparently unique for an oratorio in this period. The illusion created by the means described never failed to captivate the reviewers and, no doubt, the audience as well.

37. Translated from F-Pc: Rés. F. 1132, p. 71. The original French and a translation are printed in the introduction to Gossec, *La Nativité**.

All three recitatives (nos. 3, 5, and 7) are orchestrally accompanied. The most extensive and dramatic one is number 3, in which the Narrator describes the miraculous events that interrupt the sleep of the Shepherds. After the opening orchestral "night music," the narrator comments on the peacefulness of the scene; then a powerful orchestral crescendo representing the brilliant light is followed by the Narrator's description (punctuated with short runs by flutes and violins) of the striking scene that accompanies the angelic announcement of the birth of Christ.

The Oratorios of Jean-François Le Sueur

Le Sueur and His Concept of Oratorio. Born in 1760 at Abbeville, Picardy, Le Sueur was trained in the choir schools of Abbeville and Amiens.[38] In 1777 he was named choirmaster at the small Norman town of Sées; two years later he spent several months in Paris as assistant choirmaster at the church of the Holy Innocents and studied harmony and composition with the abbé Nicolas Roze (1745–1819). He served as choirmaster of the cathedrals in Dijon (1779–82) and Le Mans (1782–83) and of the collegiate church of St. Martin in Tours (1783). In 1784 Le Sueur returned to Paris as choirmaster of the church of the Holy Innocents, and in 1786–87 he was choirmaster at Notre-Dame cathedral for slightly more than a year. In the post-Revolutionary period, Le Sueur launched his operatic career with the succesful opera *La caverne* (1793), became well known for his hymns performed at the festivals of the Revolution, and was made an inspector of teaching at the Conservatoire (1795–1802). In 1804 Napoleon appointed him to succeed Giovanni Paisiello as director of the Tuileries Chapel. Le Sueur held that position alone until the Restoration (1814), after which he held it jointly at first (1814–16) with Johann Paul Aegidius Martini (1741–1816) and then (1816–30) with Luigi Cherubini (1760–1842); the Tuileries Chapel was closed in 1830. Le Sueur taught composition at the Conservatoire from 1818 until his death in 1837. His most famous student was Hector Berlioz (1803–69), who began studying with him in 1822 and in the following year composed a Latin oratorio, *Le passage de la mer rouge* (lost), perhaps suggested by Le Sueur's biblical oratorios in Latin. That Berlioz greatly admired Le Sueur is clear from his writings, including two obituaries of his teacher.[39]

Active primarily as a composer of church music and opera, Le Sueur was particularly well known for his music for the Tuileries Chapel. Seventeen volumes of his sacred works, including eleven that he labeled oratorios, were published between 1826 and 1841. Most of these works

38. The most important writings on Le Sueur and his music are the monumental studies, Mongrédien, *Le Sueur*, and Mongrédien, *Catalogue*.

39. On these writings, with bibliography, see Mongrédien, *Le Sueur*, 2:994–98.

FIGURE IX-4. Jean-François Le Sueur (1760–1837). (Lithograph, 1821, by Julian Boilly. Courtesy of the Stockholm Musikhistoriska museet.)

were composed for the Tuileries Chapel and exist in the chapel's manuscript repertoire, but some were altered for the purpose of publication.[40]

As a young composer Le Sueur was a modernist with a strong desire to reform church music. In his position at Tours he had difficulties with his superiors for attempting to introduce new practices into the service.[41] At Notre-Dame he was dismissed from his position because of a scandal resulting from his innovative, oratoriolike music composed for Mass on four major feasts—Christmas, Easter, Pentecost, and the Assumption— and performed in the cathedral by large forces, including singers from

40. On the manuscript and printed sources of Le Sueur's music, see Mongrédien, *Catalogue*.

41. Mongrédien, *Le Sueur*, 1:36.

the Opéra.[42] To explain, defend, and justify his "reform" works for these four feasts, Le Sueur wrote small treatises about them, which set forth his aesthetic point of view and presented the "plans"—analytic guides, or sets of program notes—for the music and text.[43] According to his treatises music must imitate nature, particularly the sentiments; as the imitation of the sentiments results in drama, music is essentially dramatic. Church music, Le Sueur argues, must be musically and dramatically unified and composed for a specific feast day.

The text of his music for the four major feasts at Notre-Dame include the Ordinary of the Mass, with additional biblical and liturgical passages that relate to the "drama" of the feast but not all of which form a part of the liturgy of the day. In his program notes Le Sueur gives dramatic interpretations of both the Ordinary and the additional texts. The Gloria of the Mass, for instance, is interpreted differently for each of the four feasts. At the beginning of the Gloria in his Christmas Mass Le Sueur says that an angel sings the announcement to the shepherds: "Gloria in excelsis Deo, et in terra pax hominibus bonae voluntatis";[44] then the shepherds sing a march as they proceed toward Bethlehem: "Laudamus te, benedicimus te";[45] when the shepherds arrive at the crib of Jesus, they adore him, singing: "Adoramus te, glorificamus te."[46] For the Easter Mass, however, Le Sueur says that the patriarchs, the prophets, and the just ones of the Old Testament who are leaving limbo at the precise moment of the Resurrection are those who sing the first part of the Gloria;[47] later on Mary Magdalene asks Jesus for forgiveness as she sings an air to another part of the Gloria: "Domine, Fili unigenite, Jesu Christe," etc.[48] In the music for Pentecost the disciples of Jesus sing the first part of the Gloria;[49] later the apostles make a vow for the formation of the church with these words from the Gloria: "Domine Deus, Agnus Dei, Filius Patris," etc.[50] And for the feast of the Assumption, the beginning of the Gloria is sung by the heavenly escort of the triumphant Virgin Mary;[51] and later the first Christians and apostles, "motionless and

42. On Le Sueur's Notre-Dame episode, see ibid., 1:51–70.

43. The treatises are: Le Sueur, *Essai* (Noël, 1786); *Exposé* (Noël, 1787); *Suite de l'essai* (Pâque); *Exposé* (Pentecôte); and *Exposé* (Assomption). For a full discussion of the treatises, see Mongrédien, *Le Sueur*, 1:100–204. The following treatment of Le Sueur's treatises and concept of oratorio is condensed, paraphrased, and partially quoted from Smither, "Le Sueur."

44. Le Sueur, *Exposé* (Noël, 1787), pp. 11–13 of separate pagination at end of volume.

45. Ibid., p. 15.

46. Ibid., p. 16.

47. Le Sueur, *Suite de l'essai* (Pâque), p. 75.

48. Ibid., p. 77.

49. Le Sueur, *Exposé* (Pentecôte), 55–56.

50. Ibid., pp. 57–58.

51. Le Sueur, *Exposé* (Assomption), pp. 89–90.

siezed with emotion, bow down while singing: Adoramus te, glorifica-mus te," etc.[52]

Thus, by providing a programmatic interpretation of every section within these church works, Le Sueur establishes dramatic contexts for the words and the music. He recognizes and clearly states that the pro-grams are essential to an understanding of the works: "It is necessary . . . to know the dramatic intentions of the musician. It is for this reason that he is forced to publish them—for the understanding of the rational plan of this music, which conveys only the pantomime of a species of drama of which the situations are not at all indicated by gesture, nor by other means that the dramatic art employs, but only by the musical accent and arrangement of the words."[53] Indeed, the sung texts and the musical settings, without the program notes, could not convey the composer's dramatic intentions.

Each of the reform works described in the treatises is divided into three parts: part I includes the Kyrie and Gloria; part II, the Credo; and part III, the remainder of the Mass, including a motet for the Elevation and the "Domine salvum" (a prayer for the king). The works differ in their motet texts for the Elevation and the texts Le Sueur added to the Ordinary to make the works more narrative, dramatic, and proper to the feast. Each work begins with a programmatic overture, either with or without voices—the extra-musical meanings of the overtures are fully interpreted in the commentary—and programmatic orchestral preludes and interludes occur between and within the vocal numbers.

The relationship of these four works to oratorio is clarified in Le Sueur's treatise on his music for the Assumption. Responding to the criticism that his reform works would lead to opera in church, he states: "It is not pretended at all, as ill-intentioned people have wanted to have it understood, that my efforts would lead to a wish to display to the eye, so to speak, each situation that I have indicated. My purpose is only to force myself to produce the effect that results from an oratorio. Now an *oratorio* is a species of dramatic poem. When one hears it sung at the Concert spirituel, one understands the situations only through the music and the arrangement of the words. These situations, then, are repre-sented only to the imagination."[54] Le Sueur is, of course, entirely famil-iar with the oratorio tradition in Paris, and he does not call his reform works oratorios—rather, he calls them "music in quite a new genre."[55] Nevertheless, he wants them to create the effect of oratorios, and Donald Foster has coined the useful term "mass-oratorio" for these pieces.[56]

52. Ibid., p. 90.
53. Le Sueur, *Exposé (Pentecôte)*, pp. 3–4.
54. Le Sueur, *Exposé (Assomption)*, p. 108.
55. Le Sueur, *Essai (Noël, 1786)*, p. 4.
56. For Foster's treatment of Le Sueur's "mass-oratorios," with special atten-tion to the one for Christmas, see Foster, "Oratorio in Paris," pp. 114–27.

Nearly twenty years after writing these innovative works for Notre-Dame, Le Sueur turned again to dramatic composition for the Mass. In the music that he composed between 1804 and 1815 for the Tuileries Chapel, he provided two designations: *mass* and *oratorio*. On their manuscript title pages he called them Masses, presumably to indicate their intended function; yet on their title pages in published form, he called them oratorios, presumably to indicate their genre—the following discussion will refer to them as oratorios.[57] They all have Latin texts, set in music as recitatives, airs, ensembles, and choruses. Four are based on Old Testament stories (*Ruth et Noëmi, Ruth et Booz, Debbora*, and *Rachel*), four on the New Testament (*Oratorio de Noël* and three Passion oratorios), and three are coronation oratorios. Although Le Sueur drew the words for his biblical oratorios from well-known stories in the Vulgate, most of his librettos are not, in themselves, either narrative or dramatic. The *Oratorio de Noël* is evidently based on part of the 1786 Christmas "mass-oratorio" for Notre-Dame, and the coronation oratorios use a variety of liturgical and biblical texts appropriate for a coronation.

For all the works that Le Sueur calls oratorios, he includes theatrical, scenic descriptions, in French, printed usually at the tops or bottoms of the pages in the printed scores. His dramatic concept of the works—even those without dramatic texts—is evidently his rationale for calling them oratorios. They are oratorios in the same unusual sense as his four "mass-oratorios" for Notre-Dame. Exceptional among Le Sueur's works for the Tuileries Chapel are the two oratorios on the subject of Ruth, treated below; they are his only extant works that could be called oratorios according to the generally accepted meaning of that word in France of his time: both have narrative-dramatic texts and personages who speak in first person.

During Napoleon's time the performance context for Le Sueur's oratorios composed for Mass in the Tuileries Chapel reflected the taste of the emperor, who was not noted for his piety.[58] Napoleon and his entourage were said to have been impatient at Mass, and he would not tolerate a long service. The works in the Tuileries Chapel repertoire range from fifteen to twenty minutes in length; thus each of Le Sueur's oratorios would last approximately as long as, and be performed concurrently with, the celebration of Mass. The performing forces at the Tuileries Chapel during the decade 1804–14 increased from about forty singers and instruments in 1804 to fifty-three in 1810, and to about a hundred in 1814; the singers included those active at the Opéra.[59]

57. For a survey of Le Sueur's oratorios for the Tuileries Chapel, see Mongrédien, *Le Sueur*, 2:873–907.

58. On the service and the music in the Tuileries Chapel under Napoleon, see ibid., 2:803–19, 867–71.

59. Ibid., 2:810.

The "Ruth" Oratorios: Ruth et Noëmi *and* Ruth et Booz. Le Sueur's oratorios that are closest to the French oratorio tradition, *Ruth et Noëmi* and *Ruth et Booz*, were composed for the Tuileries Chapel.[60] The manuscript sources are undated, but according to a letter from Le Sueur to his copyist the works existed in 1811 and represent the Napoleonic period.[61] Both oratorios were included in one volume of Le Sueur's published sacred works, and the printed scores are essentially the same as the extant manuscripts of the Tuileries Chapel repertoire.[62] The two were conceived as complementary oratorios, according to the title page of the publication: "Ruth and Naomi, Historical Oratorio with Large Choruses, Followed by Ruth and Boaz, Another Historical and Prophetical Oratorio with Large Choruses, Drawn from the Book of Ruth, Which [Ruth and Boaz] Is the Complement of the First." A note printed at the end of the first oratorio explains not only the relationship between the works but also their functions: "End of the historical oratorio of RUTH and NAOMI, forming, at the chapel of the palace, a first Sunday Mass. It is followed by RUTH and BOAZ, another historical and prophetical oratorio, which is the complement of the first and is performed the following Sunday."[63] Because the oratorios are complementary, they are treated together in the following comments.

Le Sueur compiled and adapted the texts of both oratorios from the Book of Ruth in the Vulgate Bible. According to the biblical story, because of famine Elimelech emigrated from Bethlehem to Moab with his wife Naomi (Noemi in the Vulgate and the Douay translation) and their two sons, who then married Moabite women, Ruth and Orpha. Elimelech and the two sons died, and when the famine had ended at Bethlehem, Naomi wished to return home. She urged her daughters-in-law to remain in their homeland, but Ruth insisted on staying with her. During the barley harvest in Bethlehem Ruth followed the tradition of the poor by gleaning in the fields behind the harvesters. The field belonged to Boaz (Booz in the Vulgate and Douay spelling), a wealthy relative of Elimelech. Boaz treated Ruth kindly, and Naomi suggested that a marriage be arranged between them. Ruth requested the marriage, and Boaz married her after a closer relative had ceded his rights and Boaz had purchased Elimelech's property. The son of Boaz and Ruth was Obed, the grandfather of David.[64]

Ruth et Noëmi is based on the first chapter of Ruth, in which Naomi

60. For a brief discussion of both works, see ibid., 2:879–81.

61. Ibid., 2:865.

62. For descriptions of the manuscript and printed sources, see Mongrédien, *Catalogue*, pp. 49–50 and 267–72. The source used for the following comments on these oratorios is the printed volume in which both are found, Le Sueur, *Ruth**.

63. Le Sueur, *Ruth**, p. 58.

64. For details and background, see P. J. Calderone, "Ruth," *New Catholic Encyclopedia* (New York: McGraw-Hill, 1967), 12:761–62.

decides to return to Bethlehem, urges Ruth and Orpha to remain in Moab, and is finally met at the gates of Bethlehem by the Israelites. The solo personages are Naomi (S), Ruth (S), and the chorus (SATB, SSTT), which first plays the role of the Companions and Relatives of Ruth and Orpha, and then that of the Hebrews, Shepherds, and Harvesters. Orpha does not have a solo role, but is designated as a soprano of the chorus in scene 1; thus a listener must know of and imagine her presence without hearing her. Le Sueur divides *Ruth et Noëmi* into five sections, each of which he calls a "scène religieuse" (see Table IX-4). As in his other oratorios, Le Sueur provides copious descriptive notes in French, which in the published scores are printed (in extremely small type) at the top or bottom of a page or are embedded within the score. These notes fulfill three functions: to give a French translation or paraphrase and at times a religious interpretation of the Latin text; to describe the personages' actions, which could not be inferred from the words being sung; and to provide background and continuity by explaining a part of the drama that could not otherwise be understood. The notes reveal the considerable extent to which Le Sueur imagined his oratorios as staged dramas, even though they were intended for unstaged performance during Mass.

In scene 1, Ruth and Orpha with their companions and relatives accompany Naomi to the road that leads to Bethlehem. According to the descriptive notes, when Naomi urges Ruth and Orpha to return to their people, she embraces them, and they weep. Both Ruth and Orpha wish to go on with her, but finally "Orpha, her companions, and the chorus let themselves be persuaded by Naomi. Orpha, in tears, embraces her and starts to return with her companions and relatives to her Moabite country. But Ruth remains with Naomi without wishing to leave her."[65] Le Sueur calls scene 2 a "chorus and hypocritical symphony [symphonie hypocritique] for the farewells and the departure of Orpha and her companions." Scene 3 begins with Naomi urging Ruth to follow Orpha and her companions back to Moab, but Ruth, in a *chant agité*, insists on going with her to Bethlehem and declares, in the words of Ruth 1:16, "Entreat me not to leave you or to return from following you; for where you go I will go, and where you lodge I will lodge; your people shall be my people, and your God my God." This *chant agité* continues, without pause, into scene 4 and fills all of that scene—except for Naomi's six-measure recitative at the end—and part of scene 5. According to the notes, in scene 4 Naomi and Ruth are proceeding to Bethlehem, and as they approach the city the Israelites come out to meet them; the Israelites "express themselves only through their mute gestures and their pantomime of admiration for Naomi; they greet her and render homage to this woman so beloved, so respected in their country. Naomi, by a courteous gesture, full of goodness, acknowledges their recognition."[66] At the end

65. Le Sueur, *Ruth**, p. 18.
66. Ibid., p. 32.

TABLE IX-4
Le Sueur, *Ruth et Noëmi*: Structural Outline

Numbers	Keys
Scene 1	
Chorus (SATB), Noëmi, "Noëmi egressa es"	c
Air. Noëmi, "Ne vocetis me Noëmi"	E♭
Scene 2	
Chorus (SSTT). "Ah! Noëmi!"	c
Scene 3	
Rec. Noëmi, Ruth, "Orpha osculata es socrum"	E♭
Chant agité. Ruth, "Ne adverseris mihi"	E♭
Scene 4	
Chant agité (cont.). Ruth, "[et ubi morata] fueris et ego pariter morabor"	E♭-B♭
Scene 5	
Chant agité (cont.). Ruth, Chorus (SATB), "Quocumque perrexeris tecum"	B♭-E♭

Note: The scene numbers are those of the source.

of scene 4 Naomi still urges Ruth to return, but at the beginning of scene 5 (which continues from scene 4 without pause) Ruth becomes even more emphatic about staying with Naomi, and the chorus of Israelites join and alternate with Ruth in her assertions that she will remain. According to a note, at length Naomi "breaks her silence" as she joins with Ruth and the chorus and sings that it is God's will ("hoc Deus voluit!") for Ruth to stay. Near the end of the work, according to another note, "Ruth and Naomi prepare to leave for Bethlehem, raising their eyes and hands toward heaven" as they sing of placing their hope in heaven; the Israelites "also accompany the music with the same pantomime."[67]

For *Ruth et Booz*, Le Sueur draws his text from the end of the first chapter in the Book of Ruth, from passages in the remaining three chapters, and, for the final "prophetic chorus," from Genesis, Isaiah, Revelation, and other books of the Bible.[68] This oratorio has two solo personages, Ruth (S) and Boaz (T). Naomi does not sing but the listener must assume her presence because Ruth sings to her in scene 3, according to the notes, after which Naomi has an exit. The chorus (SSTB, SSTTB, and SSTTTBB) plays the role of the Israelites and Harvesters until scene 6, in which it represents the Elders, Prophets, and Levites. The first "scène religieuse," called "Première pastorale" (see Table IX-5), is a chorus of

67. Ibid., p. 56.
68. Ibid., p. 120.

the Israelites and Harvesters (SSTB), who narrate the story of Naomi's return and Ruth's gleaning in the fields behind the harvesters. In her air of scene 2, Ruth asks Naomi for permission to continue gleaning and says that God will come to their aid. A note at the end of scene 3 paraphrases and elaborates Ruth 2:3: "It happened that the owner of the field where Ruth just left Naomi, her beautiful mother, to continue to glean the grain abandoned by the harvesters, belonged to Boaz."[69] This note prepares for the beginning of scene 4, in which Boaz comes to the field and asks the Harvesters who this girl is. In the "2me pastorale," the chorus replies, and Boaz orders them to let her continue to glean grain. In Boaz's air of scene 4 he tells Ruth she may continue and also may drink and eat with his harvesters as if she were one of his own; the chorus joins him in expressing kindness toward her. In her air with chorus, Ruth thanks Boaz for his graciousness. Scene 5, the "Marche pastorale," is entirely instrumental. A long descriptive note, which provides continuity between scenes 4 and 6, begins: "Following this chorus, which ends the fourth scene, and during the resumption of the panto-mime and pastorale music that leads to the sixth scene, Naomi informs her beautiful daughter that Boaz is a descendent of Abraham by Phares, and that he is a close relative of Elimelech, husband of Naomi and father

69. Ibid., p. 69.

of Mahalon, the spouse of Ruth.—Boaz, in the presence of Naomi, swears by the God of Israel that he will take Ruth for his wife, for all the people of the city know that she is a young woman filled with virtue. . . ."[70] The note continues the story up to the preparations for the wedding. Another note at the beginning of scene 5 describes the procession of the Israelites to the city gate, where the wedding will take place. Scene 6 begins with a note describing the large crowd gathered for the marriage; both the note and the Latin text of this "choeur prophétique" make clear that from this marriage an illustrious child will be born.

Despite the complementary relationship between the two Ruth oratorios, they have different tonal centers, as Tables IX-4 and IX-5 show. In *Ruth et Noëmi* the main tonal center is E-flat and only flat keys are used, whereas the the main center of *Ruth et Booz* is C. Yet the oratorios have some tonal areas in common, for both begin in C (minor in the first oratorio, major in the second), and the second oratorio moves to flat keys for two of its numbers. Perhaps the emphasis on flat keys in the first oratorio results from the elements of sorrow and conflict in that work— the sorrow of Naomi's parting from the Moabites and from Orpha, and the conflict between Ruth's faithfulness to Naomi and the latter's insistence that she return to Moab. It is not surprising that variety in tonal centers is minimal, for Le Sueur's approach to his sacred works is one of extreme economy of means and simplicity, at times to the point of austerity.[71]

The instrumentation of the two oratorios is the same: strings and pairs of flutes, clarinets, oboes, bassoons, and horns. Neither oratorio begins with an overture. The only number for orchestra alone is the "Marche pastorale," scene 5 of *Ruth et Booz*; that number has in common with the traditional pastorale a simple, cantabile melody and a repeated pedal point in the bass throughout, but its time signature is C rather than the 6/8 or 12/8 more common in the pastorale.

In these oratorios neither the airs nor the long *chant agité* in *Ruth et Noëmi* have the conventional formal structures found in most oratorios of the time. Le Sueur uses repetition of phrases and brief sections but not recapitulation in the usual sense. Instead, the airs are essentially through-composed, and their structures and procedures correspond to the meanings and attitudes of the prose texts. In their melodic, harmonic, and orchestral aspects, the airs tend to be simple; neither coloratura nor any type of virtuosity forms a part of the style. Phrase structures are usually balanced, often in units of three measures.

Example IX-7, from Naomi's air in scene 1 of *Ruth et Noëmi*, shows Le Sueur's typical responsiveness to his text. This is the first vocal entrance, which follows a five-measure orchestral introduction—in both

70. Ibid., p. 115. By the phrase "spouse of Ruth" (epoux de Ruth) Le Sueur probably meant "intended spouse of Ruth."
71. Cf. Mongrédien, *Le Sueur*, 2:877–79.

EXAMPLE IX-7. *Ruth et Noëmi*—Le Sueur (Le Sueur, *Ruth**, pp. 14–16).

EXAMPLE IX-7. continued

EXAMPLE IX-7. continued

Call me not Naomi, that is, beautiful; but call me Mara, that is, bitter . . .

oratorios the introductions tend to be brief, if they exist at all. Here Naomi, whose husband and two sons have died, tells her daughters-in-law and their companions not to call her Naomi, which means beautiful, but Mara, which means bitter ("amaram"). The air begins with Le Sueur's customary simplicity in both the vocal and orchestral parts and shows balanced phrases in three-measure units. At the word "amaram" (m. 21), the mode shifts to the minor form of the dominant, the strings play agitated scale passages, and a diminished-seventh chord is heard (m. 23) at the approach to the emphatic cadence on F major, for the repetition of "id est amaram."

The beginning of Ruth's long *chant agité* (Example IX-8), which extends from scene 3 into scene 5 of *Ruth et Noëmi*, does not have an orchestral introduction and offers an immediate response to Naomi's urging that Ruth return to Moab. Le Sueur describes the tempo and mood as "Allegro agitato e risoluto" and provides dotted rhythms and staccato arpeggios to express Ruth's agitated emotional state. Again three-measure phrases are characteristic here.

Although the simple, diatonic harmony of Examples IX-7 and IX-8 is typical of both oratorios, chromaticism is sometimes found in the service of word painting or expression, as illustrated in Example IX-9. In this

EXAMPLE IX-8. *Ruth et Noëmi*—Le Sueur (Le Sueur, *Ruth**, p. 28).

Be not against me, that I should leave thee and depart . . .

EXAMPLE IX-9. *Ruth et Booz*—Le Sueur (Le Sueur, *Ruth**, pp. 64–65).

EXAMPLE IX-9. continued

EXAMPLE IX-9. continued

se- quens,_ se- quens_mes- so- rum_ ves- - ti- gi-

-a; et_ col- li- gam_ spi- cas_ post_ ter- ga me-

EXAMPLE IX-9. continued

If thou wilt, I will go into the field and glean the ears of grain that escape the hands of the harvesters, following in the footsteps of the harvesters; and I will glean the ears of grain behind the harvesters.

example, from the air in scene 2 of *Ruth et Booz*, Ruth speaks of gleaning the ears of grain that escape the hands of the harvesters. On the words "fugerint manus mentitium" ("escape the hands of the harvesters"), Le Sueur paints the scene by "escaping" from his usual diatonic simplicity: in measures 26–30 he writes a melodic-harmonic sequence involving a chromatic bass line with a falling motive (which continues for nearly an octave) and places diminished-seventh chords at the beginnings of measures. To carry his text painting even further, at the words "sequens messorum vestigia" ("following in the footsteps of the harvesters," mm. 32–36) he represents "footsteps" and "following" by the sequential repetition and imitation of an ascending motive of two eighth notes.

The recitatives are all orchestrally accompanied but include highly effective moments that are totally unaccompanied, which appear between phrases by the chorus or orchestra. The opening scene of *Ruth et Noëmi* is an especially effective alternation between the chorus and orchestra on the one hand, and Naomi's unaccompanied recitative phrases on the other. The recitatives are carefully calculated for clear declamation.

The chorus is particularly important in both oratorios, and the choral texture is typically chordal. Le Sueur seems to have desired a kind of solemn, monumental archaism in the choruses, a style that he describes in a note as "patriarchal."[72] The two pastorales in *Ruth et Booz*, scenes 1 and 3, illustrate this patriarchal style. Example IX-10 shows the choral narrative at the opening of scene 1, with the pedal point in the low strings, the recitations on the notes c and g in the bass and tenor voices, and the simple, almost folklike melody in the soprano and first violin parts.

On occasion Le Sueur departs from his usual chordal texture in the choruses and introduces momentary and minimal counterpoint, as may be seen in Example IX-11 from scene 5 of *Ruth et Noëmi* and Example IX-12 from Ruth's air with chorus in scene 4 of *Ruth et Booz*. Those examples also show the two styles of orchestration found in these works: the orchestral accompaniment with rhythmic figures different from those of the chorus (Example IX-11), and the *colla parte* style (Example IX-12), used to create a massive effect. The pedal point so common in the choruses of the oratorio is seen in Example IX-12.

*   *   *

Although French oratorio performance was confined almost exclusively to the Concert spirituel between the late 1750s and 1790 (Le Sueur's works were important exceptions), French composers were relatively active in oratorio composition—much more so, for instance, than English composers. The basic elements of the French oratorio—a narrative-dramatic libretto based on a biblical story—were common to oratorio in other languages and regions. Yet in its brevity and choral emphasis the French oratorio was molded to the specific needs and taste of the Parisian context in which it was heard. As we shall see, France's southern neighbors across the Pyrenees also molded their oratorios to suit local taste and context, while depending heavily upon the Italian oratorio as a model.

72. His long note at the bottom of Le Sueur, *Ruth**, p. 70, mentions this simple, "patriarchal" style and its desired manner of performance.

EXAMPLE IX-10. *Ruth et Booz*—Le Sueur (Le Sueur, *Ruth**, p. 59).

EXAMPLE IX-10. continued

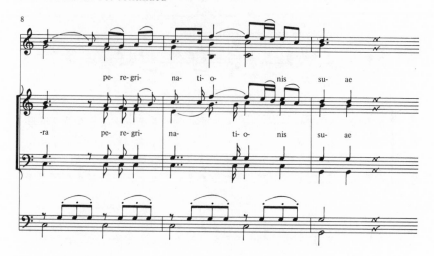

Naomi came with Ruth, the Moabitess, her daughter-in-law, she came from the land of her sojournment . . .

EXAMPLE IX-11. *Ruth et Noëmi*—Le Sueur (Le Sueur, *Ruth**, pp. 42–43).

EXAMPLE IX-II. continued

EXAMPLE IX-II. continued

EXAMPLE IX-II. continued

Ruth: Be not against me that I should leave thee, for
   wherever thou shalt go I will go . . .
Chorus: Be not against her that she should leave thee, for
   wherever thou shalt go she will go . . .

EXAMPLE IX-12. *Ruth et Booz*—Le Sueur (Le Sueur, *Ruth**, pp. 115–16).

EXAMPLE IX-12. continued

... and she said: the heart of [thy] handmaid has found grace in thy eyes ...

CHAPTER X

The Oratorio in Other Languages

Oratorios with texts in Italian, English, German, and French have claimed the major attention of music historians who have an interest in this genre. Although oratorios in those languages appear to represent the main stream of eighteenth-century development, so little is known about oratorios in other languages that the task of determining their relative historical and musical importance has yet to be undertaken. The present chapter considers oratorios in three language groups, for which preliminary investigations make possible a brief survey: Spanish and Portuguese (in Europe only—oratorio in the New World remains to be investigated), Scandinavian, and Slavic.

The Spanish Oratorio

From what is known of the social context, libretto, and music of the Spanish oratorio, it resembles the Italian oratorio in most respects. Yet some unmistakable Spanish aspects appear in the libretto, and when more music has been studied, that too may reveal some Spanish elements. The following account, however, depends mostly on the work by Carreras y Bulbena[1] and on printed librettos, from which a few conclusions are drawn not only about the libretto but about the social context and music as well.

Social Context

The earliest known oratorio performances in Spain date from the eighteenth century. According to Carreras y Bulbena, the first oratorio to be performed there was an Italian work given at the Barcelona court of the Habsburg archduke Charles, the brother of Emperor Joseph I and from 1711 the emperor Charles VI. Charles was in Barcelona from 1705 to 1711, and late in that period an Italian oratorio by Nicolo Porsile,

1. Carreras, *Oratorio*.

probably *L'esaltazione di Salomone*, is said to have been given at his court.[2] Because of the Habsburg presence in Barcelona and strong Italian influence in the city, it is not surprising that the earliest cultivation of oratorio—a genre of Italian origin—took place there.

The earliest Spanish oratorio known to the present writer, an *Oratorio mystico, y alegórico* (Barcelona, 1717),[3] was composed by Francisco Valls (1665–1747), the maestro de capilla of the Barcelona Cathedral from 1709 to 1740.[4] The title page of its printed libretto (see Figure X-1) provides information about the social context of its performance: the performers were members of the cathedral chapel under Valls's direction, and the work was given in the monastery of St. Cajetan (which would probably have been that of the Theatines) for the veneration of "the Most Holy Mary of the Pilar," who is the subject of the oratorio and is depicted in an illustration on the libretto's title page.[5] From this work of 1717 to the early nineteenth century, Barcelona appears to have been the chief center of the Spanish oratorio; yet so little research has been done on the genre in Spain that one cannot be certain at present whether the available sources accurately reflect the activity of the time.[6]

Probably the most active location in Barcelona for the performance of oratorios—from at least 1729 to the early nineteenth century—was the church of San Felipe Neri, home of the Barcelona Congregation of the Oratory, founded in 1673.[7] Whether the Oratorians in Barcelona ran an oratorio season comparable to those of the Oratorians in Italian cities (see chapter 1) remains to be investigated.[8] The printed librettos for the oratorios performed at San Felipe Neri frequently include a note, between the two parts, which reflects a typical Oratorian practice: "There follows a discourse of a half hour." José Picañol (d. 1769?), an organist,

2. Ibid., p. 135. Carreras y Bulbena gives no documentation for the performance.

3. Libretto copy in E-Mn: T/24123. I wish to thank William J. Smither, without whose personal intervention in expediting receipt of materials from E-Mn the conclusions based on those materials would very likely have been impossible.

4. On Valls see Robert Stevenson, "Francisco Valls," *New Grove*, 19:507. Stevenson does not list this oratorio, nor, to my knowledge, is it mentioned in any previous literature.

5. Our Lady of the Pillar, the name of a splendid church (1681) in Zaragoza, contains a shrine with a statue of the Virgin Mary and Child on a pillar; the statue is said to have been brought there by the Virgin Mary. The feast day of Our Lady of the Pillar is celebrated in Spain on 12 October. Cf. Metford, *Dictionary*, p. 200.

6. Thus far, I have found more sources in Barcelona than elsewhere. In the chapter on Spain in Carreras, *Oratorio*, pp. 135–55, Barcelona is emphasized, possibly because he was Catalan and worked mostly in Barcelona.

7. Gasbarri, *Spirito*, p. 186.

8. The church of San Felipe Neri owns a small collection of librettos, mostly of oratorios performed there. Other sources of works performed there are in E-Bc; see the catalogue, Pedrell, *Càtalech*.

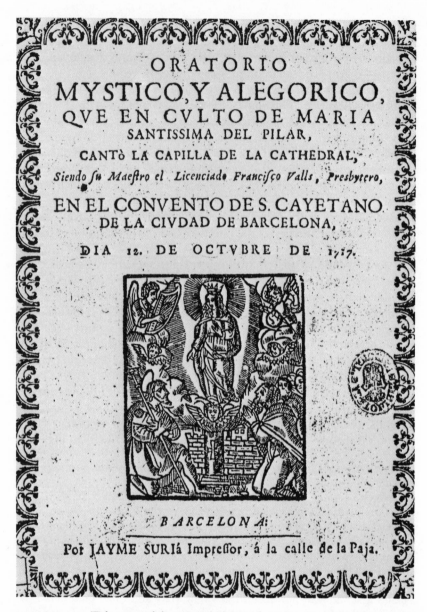

FIGURE X-1. Title page of the printed libretto for the earliest Spanish oratorio known to date. (Courtesy of E-Mn.)

composer, and assistant maestro de capilla to Valls at Barcelona Cathedral, is known to have composed eight oratorios that were performed by the cathedral chapel in the church of San Felipe Neri, four of which are dated: *Traslación del Testamento desde la casa de Aminadab á la nueva fábrica de Sión* (1729), *El triunfo del pecado* (1730), *El Machabeo de la ley de gracia, San Serapio mártyr* (1731), and *Amore consurgens*

(1732).[9] From this early period on, it is common for libretto title pages to state that oratorios were performed in this church by the cathedral chapel—the cathedral is located only a few steps away from San Felipe Neri. Three oratorios by Pujol—*El juicio particular* (1770), *Santo Tomas*, and *San Felipe Neri*—were performed in the Oratorians' church;[10] and Francisco Queralt (1740–1825)—maestro de capilla at Barcelona Cathedral for many years until his death—composed at least seventeen oratorios for performance at San Felipe Neri between 1771 and the early nineteenth century.[11] Carlos Baguer (1768–1808), organist at the cathedral, composed seven oratorios, most for San Felipe Neri.[12] Other composers for the Oratorians were Emanuel Thomas y Maymí, Domingo Arquimbau, Juan Bros, Ramón Aleix, and Mateo Ferrer.[13]

Oratorios were performed in several other churches and monasteries of the same city. Three oratorios by Jaime Casella (1690–1764) given at the church of Santa María del Mar were *Betulia libertada* (1726), *La igual justicia de Dios* (1729), and *Vencer matando y muriendo* (1731);[14] and late in the century oratorios heard at the same church include *La presentación de Nuestra Señora* (n.d.) by Ramón Aleix and *Las dos sillas de San Eloy* (1799) by José Cau, who also composed at least three other oratorios in the 1790s.[15] The oratorio by Valls of 1717, mentioned above, was given in a monastery, and at least occasional monastic sponsorship of oratorios continued. In 1736 an anonymous work was performed in the monastery of the Minor Clerks Regular (the Caracciolines), according to a printed libretto: *Oratorio, en culto de San Adauto mártir. En nuestra casa de San Sebastian, de padres clérigos reglares menores de la ciudad de Barcelona. Año de 1736* (Barcelona: Juan Piferrer, [1736]);[16] and in 1739 an *Oratorio armónico* (Barcelona: Los Herederos de Joan Pablo y María Martí, [1739]) by Salvador Figuera (maestro de capilla of Santa María del Mar) was sponsored by a confraternity and performed in the monastery of San Francisco for the veneration of St. Anthony of Padua (see Figure X-2).[17] The libretto's title page includes a list of six leaders (*mayorales*) of the confraternity (*cofadria*), with their full titles. The extent to which confraternities sponsored oratorios in Spain remains to be investigated.

The Jesuits at the Barcelona church of Belén began to sponsor oratorio

9. See the list in Carreras, *Oratorio*, p. 137.

10. Ibid., p. 139.

11. For lists see ibid, p. 143; and Eleanor Russell, "Francisco Queralt," *New Grove*, 15:504.

12. For lists, see Carreras, *Oratorio*, pp. 143–44; Almonte Howell, "Carlos Baguer," *New Grove*, 2:32. Sources in E-Bc.

13. Carreras, *Oratorio*, p. 144.

14. Ibid., p. 137.

15. Ibid., pp. 144–45.

16. Libretto copy in E-Mn: T/26546.

17. Libretto copy in E-Mn: T/24150.

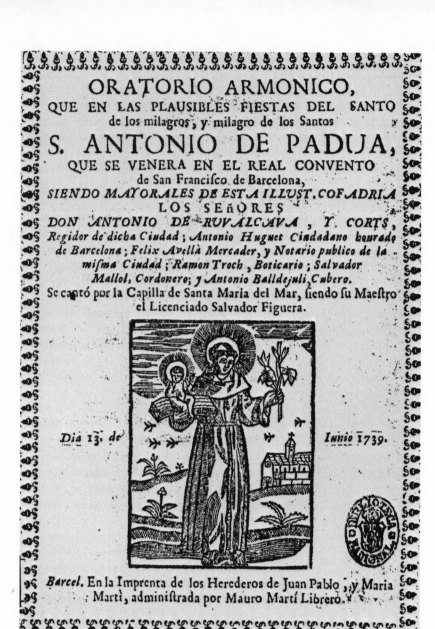

ORATORIO ARMONICO,
QUE EN LAS PLAUSIBLES FIESTAS DEL SANTO
de los milagros, y milagro de los Santos
S. ANTONIO DE PADUA,
QUE SE VENERA EN EL REAL CONVENTO
de San Francisco de Barcelona,
SIENDO MAYORALES DE ESTA ILLUST. COFADRIA
LOS SEñORES
DON ANTONIO DE RUVALCAVA, Y CORTS,
Regidor de dicha Ciudad; Antonio Huguet Ciudadano beurado
de Barcelona; Felix Avellà Mercader, y Notario publico de la
misma Ciudad; Ramon Troch, Boticario; Salvador
Mallol, Cordonero; y Antonio Balldejuli, Cubero.
Se cantó por la Capilla de Santa Maria del Mar, siendo su Maestro
el Licenciado Salvador Figuera.

Dia 13. de   Iunio 1739.

Barcel. En la Imprenta de los Herederos de Juan Pablo, y Maria
Martì, administrada por Mauro Martì Librero.

FIGURE X-2. Title page of the printed libretto for an oratorio sponsored by a
confraternity and performed in the Barcelona monastery of San Francisco for
the veneration of St. Anthony of Padua in 1739. (Courtesy of E-Mn.)

performances immediately upon the completion of that church in 1729;[18] three oratorios performed there—composed by José Pujol (fl. 1734–98), the successor of Valls as maestro de capilla of Barcelona Cathedral—are *La nave del mercader* (1734), *Hermosa nube del día* (1745), and *El triunfo de Fael* (1755).[19] At the royal chapel of the Palau (palace), José Durán (d. 1802)—the chapel's maestro de capilla from 1755 to 1780, who had been a student of Durante in Naples—composed at least sixteen Spanish oratorios.[20] He may have written them for the Palau, but he performed at least one for the female students and teachers in a convent, according to the libretto's title page.[21]

Valencia and Palma de Mallorca are the earliest known locations of Spanish oratorio performances after those in Barcelona. As early as 1720 an oratorio was written by the maestro de capilla at Valencia Cathedral, Pedro Rabassa (or Rabasa, 1683–1767), to celebrate the feast of St. John the Baptist's Nativity (24 June) in the Congregation of the Oratory in his city: *Oratorio sacro a San Juan Bautista. Que se cantó en su día, en la real Congregación de San Felipe Neri, de la Ciudad de Valencia, est año 1720* (Valencia: Antonio Bordazar, [1720]).[22] According to a libretto of 1721, Miguel Suav,[23] the maestro de capilla of the cathedral of Palma on the island of Mallorca, composed an oratorio with the following title: *Oratorio histórico, y alegórico con que a expensas de la devoción, se celebrò la festividad de María Santíssima del Pilar, en la real iglesia de Santa Anna de esta ciudad de Palma . . . cantado el día 12 octubre de 1721* ([Palma]: Pedro Ant. Capó, [1721]). Performed in the church of Santa Anna, this oratorio is yet another celebration of the feast day of "Most Holy Mary of the Pilar" (see above, Figure X-1, and n. 5); also the title page of this libretto bears an illustration of the Virgin Mary standing on a pillar and holding the Christ Child. According to another printed libretto, Pedro Martínez, a composer working in Valencia in 1729, wrote a work for the Oratorians at Palma: *Oratorio sacro al*

18. Carreras, *Oratorio*, p. 139.

19. Barton Hudson, "Pujol, José," *New Grove*, 15:450.

20. They are listed in Carreras, *Oratorio*, pp. 141–42, without indication of the places of performance.

21. *La victoriosa Esther. Oratorio sacro alegorico, que en los solemnes cultos, que consagran a la Sma. Virgen María en su presentacion al templo, las señoras de las clases de la escuela, y compañia de María en el religiosisimo convento de las Reverendas Madres de la Enseñanza, y Compañia de María de la ciudad de Barcelona, cantó la real capilla de Nra. Sra. del Palao, siendo su maestro el señor Josef Durán, día 21. de noviembre de 1776* (Barcelona: Los Herederos de María Angela Martí, [1776]). Copy in E-Bf (unnumbered).

22. Libretto copy in E-Mn: T/24517. This saint has two feast days, 24 June for the nativity and 29 August for the beheading, but the text of the oratorio suggests that the work celebrated the former.

23. On the title page of the libretto (copy in E-Mn: T/24151) the printing of the second letter in the composer's name is not clear; furthermore, "v" could be "u." Thus the name could be Svav, Svau, Suau, or even Siav or Siau.

nacimiento de Christo señor nuestro. Que se cantara en la iglesia de la Congregación del Oratorio de San Phelipe [sic] *Neri de la ciudad de Palma á 23. Enero del año 1729* ([?Palma], en casa de Gerónimo Frau, [1729]).[24] In the printed libretto, a note between the two parts indicates the delivery of a half-hour sermon. Three more printed librettos attest to oratorio performances at other churches in Palma: an *Oratorio allegórico al santíssimo sacramento* (1735), by Carlos Julian, was performed (possibly for a Forty Hours Devotion) in Palma Cathedral;[25] a *Sacro oratorio que consagra a la Reyna de los Angeles* (1737), by Juan Rossel, in the convent of the Capuchin Mothers ("Madres Capuchinas");[26] and an *Oratorio al feliz tránsito del glorioso esposo de María santíssima San Joseph* (1756), by Carlos Julian, in the convent of Nuestra Señora del Carmen.[27]

Printed librettos attest to sporadic oratorio performances in other towns and cities of Spain. In the vicinity of Barcelona is the smaller town of Gerona, where Manuel Gónima (ca. 1712–ca. 1793) composed an oratorio for the Jesuit church in 1745;[28] and in the same town, in the 1770s and 1780s, numerous performances were given of several oratorios by Manuel Juncá, Jaime Balius, and Domingo Arquimbau.[29] In Manresa, also near Barcelona, José Maseví composed at least one oratorio for the Jesuit church;[30] there is other evidence showing that oratorios were performed in Vich, Torroella de Montgrí, and other smaller towns.[31] Little evidence has been found thus far of oratorio performances in other regions of Spain, but unusual librettos from Seville (1726) and Valladolid (1747) are treated below.

Two librettos printed for oratorio performances in Madrid in 1742 and 1760 are of special interest, for they suggest the possibility of a tradition that would bear further investigation.[32] Both oratorios were performed at the royal choir school (the Colegio de Niños Cantores) on 4 December, the feast of St. Barbara, the school's patron saint. The earlier work was composed by Antonio Corvi y Moroty, maestro de capilla of the school, and the later one was by Francesco Corselli, the school's maestro de capilla and rector. Both librettos bear the royal coat of arms at the top and have similar title pages. The earlier one reads *Oratorio que se ha de cantar en el Real Colegio de su magestad, al iris de*

24. Copy in E-Mn: T/24583.
25. Libretto copy in E-Mn: T/24563.
26. Libretto copy in E-Mn: T/24141.
27. Libretto copy in E-Mn: T/22403.
28. Carreras, *Oratorio*, pp. 139–40.
29. Ibid., p. 145.
30. Ibid., p. 140.
31. Ibid., p. 145.
32. Libretto copies in E-Mn: T/24118 (for the libretto of 1742) and T/23791 (for that of 1760).

paz la gloriosa virgen, y mártyr Santa Bárbara, a quien se dedica, como patrona, y titular del oratorio, en el día 4. de diciembre de este año de 1742 (n. p., [1742]), and the later one is represented in Figure X-3. Both are two-part Italianate librettos, which would accord with the court's interest in Italian music. These librettos pose the question of what sort of music was used for the school's annual celebrations of the feast of St. Barbara, and whether that feast was regularly celebrated by an oratorio. Another printed libretto from Madrid, dated 1742 and set by Giovanni Battista Mele (1701–after 1752), was performed in an essentialy Italian context, as the title page shows: *Oratorio sacro al glorioso mártyr San Genaro, que se ha de cantar en la sagrada iglesia pontifical, y real de S. Pedro, y S. Pablo, de la casa-hospital de los italianos de esta corte, en este año de 1742* (Madrid: n. p.).[33] The subject of the oratorio is the patron saint of Naples (San Gennaro, St. Januarius), and the church in which it was performed (Saints Peter and Paul) was that of the Italian hospital. According to the dedication (to the governors of the hospital), this was an annual celebration of that saint's feast; again the question arises of the possibility of other oratorios performed for the same occasion in other years.

The Libretto and Music

Most librettos of Spanish oratorios closely follow the Italian model in both subject matter and structure. The majority are in two parts, but occasionally a work is in one or three parts. The librettos consist mainly of alternations between recitatives on the one hand and arias, ensembles, or choruses on the other. The arias are often marked as da capo structures, with the incipit of the first line of the A section printed after the B section. The choruses are few and usually appear at the end of a part, although sometimes also at the beginning or within a part. Some oratorios have no choruses but close with an ensemble or an aria.

Occasionally in Spanish librettos, however, one finds an unmistakable Spanish feature: the word *coplas* (couplets or stanzas) appears as a heading for a number. To understand the full implication of that word in an oratorio libretto requires further research, but from the librettos known to date two possible interpretations arise, relative to two different contexts. The word *coplas* may refer to stanzas in a popular, native style, which are sung in a strophic setting, as opposed to those labeled *aria*, which follow Italian conventions and are normally given a da capo setting. When a number labeled *coplas* consists of a series of stanzas and each is followed by a refrain (occasionally labeled *estribillo*), the resulting structure is analogous to that of the Spanish *villancico*—a brief genre (often lasting no longer than five or six minutes), which in its religious

33. Copy in E-Mn: T/24071.

FIGURE X-3. Title page of the printed libretto for an oratorio by Francesco Corselli performed at the royal choir school in Madrid on 4 December 1760, the feast day of St. Barbara, the school's patron saint. (Courtesy of E-Mn.)

form substituted for the responsories in matins on important feast days.[34] Sections of alternating *coplas* and *estribillo* are sometimes found within an otherwise typical, Italianate libretto. Oratorios known thus far that include such reflections of the *villancico* date from the first half of the eighteenth century; from the mid-century on, the known librettos are based purely on the Italian oratorio model.

The libretto for Valles's *Oratorio místico e alegórico* (Barcelona, 1717), mentioned above, is essentially a one-part, Italianate work: recitatives and arias alternate, and the arias are marked as da capo forms. About half-way through, however, a brief section appears that suggests the *villancico* but does not bear the designations *coplas* and *estribillo*. In that section, after a short trio sung by Faith, Hope, and Charity, Jacob sings a series of three four-line stanzas, and following each stanza a *coro* (possibly performed by those who had sung the trio) repeats the trio's last line as a refrain. A more explicit reflection of the *villancico* is found in the anonymous *Oratorio, en culto de San Adauto* (Barcelona, 1736), mentioned above, for it includes the term *coplas*. The oratorio begins with a structure that is much like a *villancico*: an opening chorus (called *coro* but functioning as an *estribillo*) is marked as an alternation between settings for eight voices and those for fewer voices; next begin the *coplas* (so marked), consisting of six stanzas set as solos, which alternate with an eight-voice choral refrain of two lines from the introductory chorus. After this opening number the libretto proceeds with recitatives, arias, ensembles, and choruses, more or less in the Italian manner. The *Sacro oratorio* (Palma, 1737), composed by Juan Rossell, mentioned above, is a one-part, essentially Italianate libretto, but at about the middle the word *coplas* appears above two four-line stanzas sung by the personage Grace, and each stanza is followed by a one-line choral refrain. At the end of the libretto the words "*Conclusion. Coplas*" appear as a heading, and the remainder of the oratorio proceedes as if it were a short *villancico*—six-line solo stanzas alternate with a two-line choral refrain, and the refrain is expanded to four lines at the end of the oratorio. A similar pattern is followed in the oratorio by Picañol, *Pastor, y mercenario a un mismo tiempo. Oratorio sacro* (Barcelona: María Martí, viuda, n. d.),[35] in which a section of *coplas* (so marked) appears at about the mid-point, and the oratorio closes with another section of *coplas*. The *coplas* sections in this work differ from those in the one previously discussed, however, for here they do not include a choral refrain, but the oratorio does end with a chorus.

An interesting libretto from Seville, dated 1726, was set to music by Joseph Magallanes, maestro de capilla of the collegiate church of San Salvador. It was sung in the chapel of San António, the national chapel of

34. On the villancico in Spain, and for bibliography, see Isabel Pope, "Villancico," *New Grove* 19:767–69.

35. Libretto copy in I-Mn: V/e-67-13.

the Portuguese, to celebrate the inauguration of a gilded altarpiece for which most of the funds had been donated by the king of Portugal, John V, according to the title page.[36] This libretto includes a dedication to the king, followed by the texts of four pieces, each divided into *estrivillo* [sic] and *coplas* (i. e., four *villancicos*). After these four pieces comes a work called an *oratorio*, organized as an *Introducción* followed by seven sections. Each of the first six sections consist of a recitative, an aria, and some *coplas*; and the seventh section includes a recitative, an *estrivillo* [sic], and some *coplas*. Thus the oratorio absorbed elements of the preceding *villancicos*.

A curious exception among the Spanish librettos for its quotations from secular literature is an *Oratorio armónico* (Valladolid: Los Figueroas, 1747) with a text in praise of San Pedro Regalado, set by Joseph Mir y Llusà, maestro de capilla in Valladolid (see title page in Figure X-4).[37] As the title page suggests, the four personages are the great Latin poets Horace, Virgil, Claudian, and Ovid. These classic poets sing the virtues of San Pedro Regalado in recitatives, arias, and ensembles throughout the two-part oratorio; the texts are based on specific passages from their writings and are documented in marginal notes. The oratorio closes with a quartet of the four personages. An appendage to the libretto, with the heading *Villancicos*, comes after the final number, and this is followed by three *villancicos* in praise of San Pedro Regalado. These *villancicos* form a popular counterpart to the more literary oratorio on the same subject, but the performance relationship between the oratorio and the *villancicos* is not clear; the latter may have been performed after the oratorio, as part of a service.

The Portuguese Oratorio

Virtually no research has been done on the Portuguese oratorio; no work exists for Portugal like that by Carreras y Bulbena for Spain. The following comments are based largely on information supplied by the Gulbenkian Foundation in Lisbon.[38]

36. *Letras, que se cantaron el día diez y seis de junio en la capilla nacional de S. Antonio de los Portugueses, en la festiva solemnidad, quanto solemne fiesta, que consagra dicha nacion en nombre del muy alto y muy poderoso Señor Don Juan V. Rey de Portugal, su venerado patrono en el estreno de su dorado retablo, la mayor parte con limosnas de dicho augusto monarca, à quien se dedican, con un oratorio poetico, que se cantò por la tarde, en continuacion de tan referentes cultos, &c. Puestos en musica por Don Joseph Magallanes, maestro de capilla de la insigne Iglesia Colegial de Señor San Salvador de esta ciudad de Sevilla* ([Seville]: Diego Lopez de Haro, 1726). Quoted from the RISM libretto file in P-Lcg.

37. Libretto copy in E-Mn: T/24106.

38. I am grateful for the assistance of Maria Fernanda Cidrais, at P-Lcg, who sent me photocopies of the RISM libretto files which I requested.

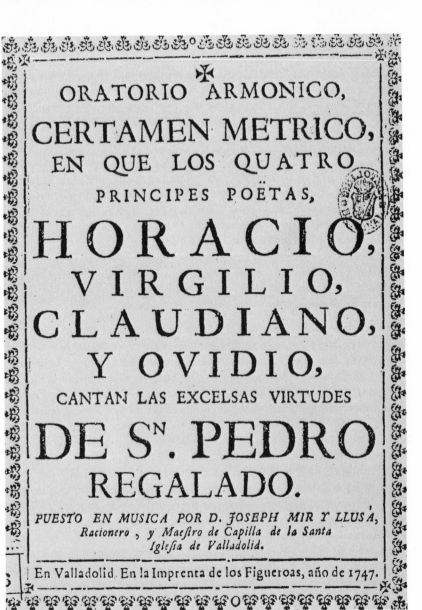

ORATORIO ARMONICO,

CERTAMEN METRICO,

EN QUE LOS QUATRO

PRINCIPES POËTAS,

HORACIO,

VIRGILIO,

CLAUDIANO,

Y OVIDIO,

CANTAN LAS EXCELSAS VIRTUDES

DE Sᴺ. PEDRO

REGALADO.

PUESTO EN MUSICA POR D. JOSEPH MIR Y LLUSÁ,
Racionero, y Maeſtro de Capilla de la Santa
Igleſia de Valladolid.

En Valladolid. En la Imprenta de los Figueroas, año de 1747.

FIGURE X-4. Title page of the printed libretto for an oratorio set by Joseph Mir y Llusà, in which classical poets sing the praises of San Pedro Regalado. (Courtesy of E-Mn.)

The earliest known Portuguese oratorio dates from 1719 and was performed in Lisbon Cathedral. Its composer, Jayme de la Té y Sagau (ca. 1680–1736), of Catalan birth, was brought to Lisbon in 1708 by the Jesuit diplomat Alvaro Cienfuegos, who helped arrange the marriage between John V and Marianna, the sister of Leopold I of Austria.[39] The composer wrote Italian-style cantatas in honor of the new queen, as well as various works for palace festivities, and he was active as a music publisher. The title page of the libretto for his oratorio reads,

> Oratorio que se cantó, con varios instrumentos, in 22. de enero: fiesta del glorioso, invicto, mártir, S. Vicente, patrón de ambas Lisboas: en la Metropolitana Cathedral del Oriente. Siendo mayor-domos los señores, arcediano de Santarén Hierónimo Leyte, Malleyros, y Joseph Feyo de Castelbranco, canónigo de dicha Ca-thedral, y su maestro de capilla el racionero Francisco de Costa, y Sylva. Compusó los metros el señor canónigo Julian Maciel, y la música, D. Jayme de la Te, y Sagau. Lisboa Occidental, en la Im-prẽta de Musica. Año 1719 . . .[40]

Thus the work's occasion was the feast day of St. Vincent (22 January), Lisbon's patron saint, and its libretto was written by Julian Maciel. The cathedral's maestro de capilla was Francisco de Costa y Silva (also known as da Costa e Silva, d. 1727). The libretto, which does not include personages, is in one part of twenty-two vocal numbers, excluding recita-tives, of which there are three accompanied and seven in simple style. The libretto is well annotated in regard to the musical setting. The work apparently opened with a sonata for all the instruments; those men-tioned are strings, bassoons, trumpets, and timpani. The first and last vocal numbers are for four voices (possibly choruses); and there are seven solo arias, two duo arias, seven solo or unspecified *coplas*, and four duo *coplas*. In these instances the word *coplas* appears to mean stanzas for strophic setting as opposed to da capo arias. Extant librettos for the same work were printed for its performances in 1721, 1722, and 1723, and also for the celebration of St. Vincent's day in the cathedral.[41]

In the year 1720 a different oratorio was performed in Lisbon Cathe-dral for the feast of St. Vincent. This one was written by the Spanish composer, Antonio Literes (1673–1747), of the royal chapel in Madrid, who was comissioned to compose not only the oratorio but a *villancico* to be performed on the vigil of the feast.[42] The work includes four

39. Robert Stevenson, "Jayme de la Té y Sagau," *New Grove*, 18:711.
40. Libretto copies in P-C: R-17–18 (32); and P-Ln: Res. 198 P (10) and Res. 208 P (10).
41. Libretto copies in P-Ln. For 1721, Res. 198 P (14) and Res. 208 P (13); for 1722, Res. 198 P (16); and for 1723, Res. 198 P (18).
42. Robert Stevenson, "Antonio Literes," *New Grove*, 11:79. The title page reads, *Oratorio que se cantó, con varies instrumentos, en 22 de enero: fiesta del*

personages—Amor, Culto, Lusitania, and Inveja Infernal—and a chorus (set as a double chorus of eight voices). According to the printed indications in the libretto, the work included an opening chorus for eight voices, five arias, one aria with chorus, eight recitatives, one duo, and one trio. Numbers designated by Spanish or Portuguese terms are those called *tonada* (one example), *estribilo* (two), *seguidilla* (two), and *endecha* (one).

Whether the above-mentioned oratorios performed at Lisbon Cathedral established a tradition has yet to be investigated. One would assume that more Portuguese oratorios were composed in the first half of the century, and more may come to light as research continues. In the second half of the century the trend in Lisbon was to perform Italian oratorios (see chapter 1). Occasionally Metastasio's oratorios were translated into Portuguese, including *Izac figura de Jesu Christo* (Lisbon, 1766), *A Paixão de Jesus Christo* (Lisbon, 1781), and *Joseph reconhecido* (n. d.).[43]

The Oratorio in Denmark and Sweden

In the eighteenth century few oratorios were composed to texts in Scandinavian languages. Court and public performances of oratorios were relatively rare, and when they did occur, they were usually in Italian or German. In the main centers of oratorio cultivation, Copenhagen and Stockholm, the former led the way in native-language oratorio.

During the reign of the Pietist Christian VI (1730–46), opera was forbidden in Copenhagen, and concert life—usually performances that combined amateurs and professionals—began to take its place. In 1740 Johann Adolph Scheibe was named Kapellmeister to the Danish court; he retired from that position after Christian VI died, but thereafter he remained in Denmark. Scheibe was an important figure in the burgeoning concert life of the 1740s, and two decades later, with his Passion *Den døende Jesus* (1762), he became a pioneer in the use of Danish for a large sacred work.[44] Yet throughout the second half of the century more ora-

---

glorioso, invicto, mártir, S. Vicente, patron de ambas Lisboas: en la Metropolitana Cathedral del Oriente siende mayordomos los señores Dean Juan Cesar de Meneses; y Sylvestre de Sousa Sorres, canonigo de dicha Cathedral; y su maestro de capilla el quartanario Francisco de Costa y Silva. Compuse la musica Don Antonio Literes, musico de la Real Capilla de Madrid. Lisboa Ocidental, en la Imprenta de Musica Año 1720. Libretto copies in P-Ln: Res. 198 P (12) and Res. 208 P (11).

43. Libretto copies of librettos of the first two in P-Pm: P. B. P. M., N-7–9 (10); and of the third in P-C: Misc., vol. 587 (5).

44. Schousboe, "Protestant," pp. 633–34.

torios were performed in foreign languages than in Danish, among them Jommelli's *La passione* (performed in 1775), Hasse's *Giuseppe riconosciuto* (1778), Paisiello's *La passione* (1786), Salieri's *La passione* (1786), and Friedrich Heinrich Himmel's (1765–1814) *Isacco figura del Redentore* (1795 and 1796).[45] The Italian oratorios were given in various contexts, but mainly by the musical society, Det Harmoniske Selskab (The Harmonic Society). Handel's *Messiah* was performed in Copenhagen in 1786 in the wake of London's Commemoration of Handel of 1784.[46] Only late in the century did the Danish court and concert audiences become interested in Danish oratorios. Johann Abraham Peter Schulz (1747–1800), who became royal Kapellmeister and director of the Royal Danish Theater in 1787, directed the Court Passion Concerts in Passion Week beginning in 1788.[47] In 1787–88 he composed for one of these concerts a Passion oratorio in Danish, *Maria og Johannes* (Mary and John; text by Johannes Ewald, 1743–81), performed in the court chapel at Christiansborg in 1789.[48] His next two Passion oratorios in Danish are *Christi død* (The Death of Christ; text by Jens Baggesen, 1764–1826), performed at Christiansborg, Lent, 1792;[49] and *Frelserens sidste Stund* (The Redeemer's Last Hour; text by Viktor Kristian Hjort, 1765–1818), performed for a charitable purpose in March 1794 at Copenhagen's Trinity Church.[50] Friedrich Ludwig Aemilius Kunzen (1761–1817) succeeded Schulz, who was pensioned from his position in 1795 for reasons of health. In addition to Kunzen's activities as court Kapellmeister and director of the Royal Theater, he became the conductor of Det Harmoniske Selskab. In 1796 he composed the Danish oratorio *Opstandelsen* (Resurrection; text by Thomas Thaarup, 1749–1821), which is a two-part work with personages; and in 1797 the German oratorio, *Das Halleluja der Schöpfung* (1797; by Baggesen), a one-part work without personages.[51] The latter work, the text of which was probably suggested by a Klopstock ode, *Das grosse Halleluja* (1766), became extremely popular in Germany; *Opstandelsen*, in a translation

---

45. Printed librettos for Copenhagen performances of all these works are cited in Sartori, "Catalogo."

46. According to the report of the performance in Cramer's *Magazin der Musik* 2/2 (1786): 960–67, the performance, which was poor, resulted directly from the newspaper reports of the Handel Commemoration.

47. Rieß, "Schulz' Leben," p. 234.

48. Ibid. The work was published in tablature with Danish text in 1790; a keyboard-vocal version was edited by C. F. Cramer and published in Copenhagen in 1790; and a full score in German was published in Copenhagen in 1791. For a modern edition with German text, see Schulz, *Maria**.

49. Rieß, "Schulz' Leben," p. 251. Manuscript source in D-Bds. Modern piano-vocal score: Schulz, *Christi**.

50. Ibid. Manuscript in German translation, D-Bds.

51. Printed librettos in D-LÜh: K6c (*Auferstehung*) and K6f (*Hallelujah*).

as *Die Auferstehung,* was also widely performed there. In 1801 Kunzen directed 200 performers in two performances of Haydn's *The Creation.*

All the composers of Danish oratorios named above—Scheibe, Schulz, and F. L. A. Kunzen—were North Germans, and their oratorios represent the dominant trend in the region of their origin and training. The Danish librettos that they set—as well as Baggesen's *Das Halleluja der Schöpfung*—were lyric oratorios, a type prominent in Germany, and the musical styles of the extant works (by Schulz and Kunzen) are Classical.

Stockholm's public concert life began as early as 1731, when Johann Helmich Roman (1694–1758) organized public concerts in which amateurs joined with members of the royal chapel; the sacred repertoire they performed was either Italian or German.[52] The same pattern continued in the second half of the century. Examples of the works performed are Graun's *Tod Jesu,* given frequently; *La passione* (Metastasio's text) by Francesco Uttini (1723–95), performed in 1776; and *Isacco figura del redentore* (Metastasio) by Naumann, in 1788. In April 1786 Handel's *Messiah* was performed in Stockholm about a month after its performance in Copenhagen;[53] and on 3 April 1801 Stockholm heard Haydn's *The Creation,* thanks to efforts of the Haydn student Paul Struck (1776–1820).[54] According to Torben Schousboe, the "first Swedish oratorio" was *Försonaren på Golgatha* (text by S. Ödmann), composed by Johann Christian Friedrich Haeffner (1759–1833);[55] it was first given in the university town of Uppsala on 19 March 1809 and appears to belong more to the succeeding period than the previous one, for it inaugurated a tradition of choral music in nineteenth-century Uppsala.[56]

The Russian Oratorio

During the course of the eighteenth century oratorios in Italian and occasionally German were heard in Slavic lands, and some of these have been mentioned above. The extent to which Slavic-language oratorio texts were set to music and performed, however, is unknown. The following discussion focuses exclusively on the Russion oratorio because that has been the subject of research.[57]

52. Martin Tegen, "Stockholm," *MGG,* 12:cols. 1370–71; Ingmar Bengtsson, "Johan Helmich Roman," *New Grove,* 16:119.

53. Myers, *Handel's "Messiah,"* p. 271, n. 11.

54. Tegen, "Stockholm," *MGG,* 12:col. 1371. For details, see Hennerberg, "Haydns Oratorium."

55. Schousboe, "Protestant," p. 633.

56. Folke Bohlin, "Johann Christian Friedrich Haeffner," *New Grove,* 8:20.

57. The most recent and extensive study of oratorio in Russia of the eighteenth and early nineteenth centuries is Hughes, "Degtiarev," which reports on much

Introduction: Terminology, Genre Definition, Social Context

The word *oratorio*, when used by composers active in eighteenth- and early nineteenth-century Russia and by the Russian intelligentsia, must surely have referred primarily to oratorios of the types treated in the preceding chapters, for numerous oratorios by foreign composers were performed in Lenten concerts in both Saint Petersburg and Moscow.[58] With the great influx of Italian opera composers and performers to Russia during the century, an Italian concept of the genre would have been widely known. Among the Italian oratorios heard in Russia were *La passione* by Jommelli, given in Petersburg, 1779; *Giuseppe riconosciuto* by Alessio Prati (1750–88), Petersburg, 1783; *La passione* by Paisiello, Petersburg, 1783, in the Catholic Church; *Betulia liberata* by Mathias Stabingher (ca. 1750–ca. 1815), Moscow, 1783; *La morte d'Abele* by Piccini, Moscow, 1793, Petrovsky Theater; and *Betulia liberata* by G. B. Anselmi (?–?), Moscow, 1796. These all have texts by Metastasio and represent the Italian dramatic oratorio. Among the non-Italian oratorios performed in Russia that would have had a bearing on the Russian concept of oratorio are *Les Israëlites au Mont-Oreb* (possibly the same text by Abbé de Voisenon that Mondonville set; see chapter 9) by Louis-Henri Paisible (1748–82), performed in Petersburg, 1779; *Abraham auf Moria* by Rolle, Petersburg, 1783, German Theater; *Samson* by Handel, Moscow, 1783; and *Die sieben Worte* by Haydn, Moscow, 1789. The works by Paisible, Rolle, and Handel are all dramatic oratorios; that by Haydn was loosely called an oratorio in its time and relates to the German lyric oratorio. In the early nineteenth century Haydn's *The Creation* and *The Seasons* were first heard and highly praised almost immediately upon the publication of their scores: *The Creation*, in both Petersburg and Moscow, 1801;[59] and *The Seasons*, in both cities in 1803.[60]

The only eighteenth-century works with Russian texts that are known to have been designated oratorios were written by Giuseppe Sarti (1729–1802), who was active in Petersburg from 1784 to 1801. Sarti's works that are labeled oratorios in their manuscript sources are *Gospodi vozzvakh k tebe* (1785; reworked in 1790 as *Pomili mia, Bozhe*), *Tebe Boga khvalim* (1786), *Tebe Boga khvalim* (1789), and *Slava v vyshnykh Bogu* (1792).[61] These differ considerably from the foreign oratorios listed in the preceding paragraph, all of which represent categories of the Western oratorio. Sarti's oratorios are based on texts from the Russian

---

Soviet research. The following discussion of the subject depends heavily on Hughes's work.

58. See the list in Mooser, *Opéras.*

59. See the reports in the *Allgemeine musikalische Zeitung* 4 (1802): 344–46, 385–96.

60. For full information on these and other performances of Haydn's oratorios in Russia, see Steinpress, "Haydns Oratorien in Russland."

61. Sarti's oratorios are discussed in Hughes, "Degtiarev," pp. 91–97.

Orthodox liturgy, are narrative but not dramatic, include little or no connective recitative between the long numbers, place primary emphasis on choral numbers (with double chorus) and less on ensembles and solos, and derive stylistically from Russian Orthodox choral music. As monumental festive pieces, Sarti's oratorios were performed in concert (never in the Orthodox church, which did not allow instruments) by large forces, and they emphasized sensational effects of sound and sight, including numerous percussion instruments, the *rogovoi orkestr* (a horn band unique to Russia, described below), cannon fire, and fireworks. Sarti's *Gospodi vozzvakh k tebe* was performed during Lent of 1785 in Petersburg at the palace of his patron, Gregorii Potemkin (ca. 1743–91).[62] One of his oratorios was performed in Petersburg during a public Lenten concert season in 1800, which included an Italian oratorio by Guglielmi (perhaps his *Debora e Sisara*) as well as "a Russian oratorio, composed by Mr. Sarti, with a *rogovoi orkestr*, chorus, and solo singing by the best Russian singers."[63]

The only known discussion of oratorio terminology in Russia of the period is an essay by the poet Gavril Romanovich Derzhavin (1743–1816) in a manuscript of 1808 with the heading, "Discussion of Lyrical Poetry."[64] In 1777 Derzhavin entered the civil service in Petersburg and for a while he was the private secretary to Catherine the Great (r. 1762–96). He must surely have been well informed of the literary and musical genres of his time. Derzhavin defines oratorio as "a musical composition, to a certain extent dramatic, but more lyrical, revived from the ancient Greek, mixed with choruses, and dependent upon tragedy."[65] He presents his view of the history of oratorio, then contrasts oratorio with opera:

> Oratorio differs from opera in the fact that oratorio has a religious content and characters from the holy writings of the Old and New Testaments; but opera—at least opera cast in a higher tone—is taken from pagan, Greek mythology, or ancient and modern history. In an oratorio, the singing characters do not deck themselves up in theatrical dress, but in opera, they wear whatever is appropriate to the character and the situations.
>
> In oratorio, the singers do not act and there is very little dramatic dialogue among the characters (they hardly speak to each other);

62. Mooser, *Opéras*, p. 65.

63. As translated from the *Sankt-Peterburgskie Vedemosti*, no. 18, (2 March 1800), reprinted in the *Russkaia muzykal'naia gazeta*, no. 40 (1902): 943, in Hughes, "Degtiarev," p. 99.

64. "Rassuzhdenie o liricheskoi poezii," in a manuscript with the title "Raznye bumagi, otnociashchiesia k besede" ("Various Papers Related to a Conversation"), in USSR-Lsc. The manuscript is discussed and partially quoted in Hughes, "Degtiarev," pp. 76–91.

65. Hughes, "Degtiarev," pp. 76–77.

but in opera the dialogues are connected dramatically. The goal of oratorio is none other than to inspire in the listeners exactly those sincere feelings which are being sung about; but in opera, actions are presented, and characters must explain the plot and similar dramatic appurtenances.[66]

This treatment of oratorio reflects the author's familiarity with the foreign works listed above, performed in eighteenth-century Russia—nearly all were of the dramatic type, yet in comparison with opera, as Derzhavin points out, the drama is minimal.

It is clear from his later statements in the essay that Derzhavin considers the chorus of primary importance to oratorio:

If recitatives, arias, duets, and such songs are to be included in an oratorio for the setting of the music, or if they are essential for the flow and ebb of the music, then those should as much as possible be infrequent and abbreviated, used only for inspiration or, so to speak, for the rousing of the choral singing. For the chorus is the main component of an oratorio. It is the voice of the church or, better, of the whole universe, glorifying its creator with lips united. By the same token, dramatic characters are permitted in an oratorio only to give the composer the opportunity to excel in his art by presenting the nuances of feeling and passions.[67]

The emphasis on the chorus in this passage may reflect the influence of Haydn's *The Creation* and *The Seasons*, which were greatly admired in Russia. The emphasis may also reflect the influence of Russian Orthodox church music, which is indeed "the voice of the church."

A curious aspect of Derzhavin's essay, however, is the absence of Sarti's name and any mention of his oratorios. Derzhavin says, in fact, "I do not know of a single oratorio in our language composed for any special occasion whatsoever, except the translation by Mr. Karamzin of Haydn's *The Creation*."[68] That Derzhavin ignores Sarti's oratorios is understandable in view of his essentially Western definition of the genre; yet despite that view and his omission of Sarti, Derzhavin presents a model oratorio text, set in the previous year (1807) by Sigismund Neukomm (1718– 1858), "Gospodi! vozsylaiut k Tebe svoi mol'by" ("O Lord, they send up their prayers to You"),[69] which is a prayer to the health of the emperor and is much like the texts of Sarti's oratorios.

The oratorio by Degtiarev, discussed below, borrows from both the

66. As translated in ibid., p. 77.

67. As translated in ibid., p. 80.

68. As translated in ibid., p. 73. On the translation by Karamizin, an important writer and historian of the time, see Steinpress, "Haydns Oratorien in Russland, pp. 88–90.

69. Quoted in Hughes, "Degtiarev," pp. 83–84.

Western oratorio tradition as revealed in Derzhavin's essay and the Russian tradition of Sarti and Orthodox church music. As we shall see, the reviewers of the Degtiarev work considered it the first Russian oratorio, an assessment that agrees with Derzhavin's claim that none had been written up to his time.

Stepan Anikievich Degtiarev: Minin i Pozharskii, ili Osvobozhdenie Moskvy (Minin and Pozharskii, or The Liberation of Moscow)

Born in Borisovka in the Ukrainian province of Kursk, Degtiarev (1766–1813) was a serf of the Sheremetev family and was sent to the family's choir school at seven years of age.[70] After his voice changed, he was among the few who were retained in the school to study music and theater and was later permitted to attend Moscow University as an auditor of lectures in philology and foreign languages—Italian and possibly French. It has long been said that he was sent to Italy in the 1790s in the company of Giuseppe Sarti to study composition, but the story of his Italian sojourn has been questioned in recent literature, for lack of evidence.[71] It is uncertain with whom he studied composition, but probably with visiting Italian composers and most likely with Sarti; if he did not also study with Dmitrii Stepanovich Bortnianskii (1751–1825), Degtiarev was clearly influenced by his music. In 1789 Degtiarev became the teacher of choral concertos for the Sheremetev chapel, and in 1790 he assumed the duties of musical director for Sheremetev's court in Moscow. After Catherine the Great's death in 1796 and the ascendancy of her son, Paul I (1754–1801), the center of cultural life shifted from Moscow to Petersburg; Count Nikolai Petrovich Sheremetev moved to Petersburg when he entered diplomatic service in 1797, and Degtiarev was required to move with him. Virtually nothing is known of the composer's professional life in Petersburg, but he is known to have worked on gaining his freedom. In 1805 he published his Russian translation of the *Regole armoniche* (Venice, 1775; 2d ed., Venice, 1797) by Vincenzo Manfredini (1737–1799); that translation, made from the second edition, represents an important step in the rendering of Western musical terminology in the Russian language. After Count Nikolai Petrovich's death in 1809 Degtiarev joined with other serfs in petitioning for his freedom; it was never granted (contrary to assertions of earlier biographers),[72] but he was

70. On Degtiarev's biography, see ibid., pp. 104–72. The present treatment of Degtiarev relies heavily on Hughes and adopts her transliteration, rather than that of Geoffrey Norris, "Stepan Anikiyevich Degtyaryov," *New Grove*, 5:325.

71. The probability of an Italian sojourn is repeated in Norris, "Degtyaryov," *New Grove*, 5:325; but see the review of literature and evidence in Hughes, "Degtiarev," pp. 128–30.

72. Including Norris, "Degtyaryov," *New Grove*, 5:325; but see Hughes, "Degtiarev," pp. 163–64, 170–71.

given a pass to go where he wished. He then returned to Moscow (1809), where he remained until the French occupation, during which he was probably in Kursk; he was in Moscow again, probably late in 1812, and he died in the spring of the next year.

According to Degtiarev's obituary, he was the composer of *khorovye konserty* (choral concertos—*a cappella*, polyphonic works for the Orthodox church service), which were "masterpieces" and which foreign composers arranged for instruments, and the oratorio *Minin i Pozharskii*.[73] The obituary also speaks of another oratorio, "without doubt the most important," in progress at the time of his death, called *Torzhestva Rossii, ili istreblenie vragov iaia, i begstvo Napoleona* (The Triumphs of Russia, or the Destruction of Her Enemies and the Flight of Napoleon).

The first two performances of *Minin i Pozharskii* were given in Moscow during Lent, on 9 March and 6 April 1811.[74] Both took place in the large and elegant building, across from the Kremlin Wall, then known as the Assembly of the Russian Nobility and today called the Dom Soiuza (the House of the Soviets), and renowned as the hall in which deceased Soviet leaders lie in state.[75] Performed in a period of increasing nationalism and growing fear of Napoleonic power, this patriotic oratorio struck a strongly sympathetic chord in the audience and reviewers. The reviewer for the Muscovite *Vestnik Evropy* in April 1811 well represents the enthusiasm with which the work was generally received:

On March the ninth, the Moscow public had the pleasure of hearing the first Russian oratorio, *Osvobozhdenie Muskvy* [The Freeing of Moscow], composed by Mr. Degtiarev, who is known for his many excellent choral music compositions. Those aware of Degtiarev's talent long ago expected from him some kind of major composition for full chorus. The expectation has been fulfilled: with his oratorio, Mr. Degtiarev proved that he can place his own name on a level with those of the first-rank composers in Europe. Few musical compositions by even the most famous foreign composers have been received with such praise from the general public as was the musical oratorio of Mr. Degtiarev. Applause accompanied almost every couplet of the oratorio. The orchestra consisted of almost 200 solely Russian musicians and singers under the direction of Mr. Degtiarev himself. The majestic choruses with the music of the *rogovoi orkestr*, the most lovely arias, the harmonic modulations of the tonalities, and the masterful fugues—which all together comprise the oratorio—affirm forever the praise of Deg-

73. The obituary is translated in Hughes, "Degtiarev," pp. 168–69.
74. For accounts of these performances, as reflected in reviews, see ibid., pp. 410–23.
75. For interior and exterior photographs of the building, see ibid., p. 266.

tiarev among his compatriots and even within other countries, for the oratorio has already been translated into Italian by one scholarly man and will be sent along with the text to Naples.[76]

In common with other reviewers, this one sees *Minin i Pozharskii* as "the first Russian oratorio," calls attention to the large performing force, and makes special mention—in this patriotic and nationalistic time—that all the performers were Russians. If a score was indeed sent to Naples, it has been lost.

Degtiarev receives high praise in the review just quoted, but still higher praise in a later one, in the *Zhurnal dramaticheskii*: "After the *Oratorios* by Haydn, it was amazing to hear of the arrival on the *Musical Scene* of a new oratorio, almost equally magnificent, almost equally perfect as the first ones! . . . At this point, [Mr. Degtiarev] is still the first of all Russians to dare such a significant undertaking in musical art and his venture, judging by the consensus of our connoisseurs and music lovers, was crowned with success." The reviewer closes his piece with a return to his opening comparison: "We conclude our remarks with sincere gratitude to the Russian Degtiarev. And we say that now without a doubt we will have our own Haydn, our own Mozart, and Cherubini, and so forth."[77]

Minin i Pozharskii received a posthumous performance on 20 February 1818 in connection with the unveiling of a monument to the heroes Minin and Pozharskii; the monument had been sculpted by Ivan Martos (1752–1835) and stands in what is known today as Red Square.[78] As part of the lavish unveiling ceremonies, the oratorio was performed for the benefit of invalids in the same hall as the performance of 1811; the persons involved in the performance are said to have numbered around 300.[79]

The librettist of *Minin i Pozharskii*, Nikolai Dmitrievich Gorchakov (ca. 1780–1847), a well-educated member of the gentry, wrote poetry as well as articles and monographs on many subjects, including Orthodox religious history and the city of Moscow, where he lived.[80] Gorchakov drew the material for his libretto from an episode in Russian history— the so-called Time of Troubles (1596 or 1598 to 1613)—in which a crisis of leadership, caused by the extinction of the Riurik dynasty and the absence of a successor to the throne, resulted in Polish control of the

---

76. As translated in ibid., pp. 412–13, from *Vestnik Evropy*, 55 (1811): 228–30.

77. Excerpted from the translation of the entire review in Hughes, "Degtiarev," pp. 417–18, of the original in *Zhurnal dramaticheskii*, 4 (18 April 1811): 559–61.

78. For the history of this monument within the context of Minin and Pozharskii in Russian literature and art, see Hughes, "Degtiarev," pp. 240–67.

79. For quotations from reviews of this performance, see ibid., pp. 423–25.

80. For Gorchakov's biography, see ibid., pp. 173–99.

FIGURE X-5. The monument to Minin and Pozharskii (left and right, respectively) whose heroic deeds are commemorated in Degtiarev's oratorio *Minin i Pozharskii* (Moscow, 1811). The oratorio was given a second performance (Moscow, 1818) to celebrate the unveiling of the monument. (Courtesy of Carol Bailey Hughes.)

throne and of Moscow.[81] (This is the same period from which Modest Musorgsky derived the events portrayed in his opera *Boris Godunov*, begun in 1868.) The protagonists of the oratorio are the historical figures Kuz'ma Minin (d. 1616), a middle-class merchant in Nizhni-Novgorod (present-day Gorki), and Dmitrii Mikhailovich Pozharskii (1578–1642), a minor prince. The historical Minin, an eloquent orator and effective organizer, stirred the officials of his town to initiate action that would free Moscow from Polish control, and he was able to negotiate sound financial backing for the campaign. The military leadership was entrusted to Pozharskii, who had established a reputation for his military skill. The Minin and Pozharskii movement to free Moscow grew rapidly and was joined by one Volga town after another. The battle for Moscow, which took place in 1612, succeeded against the Poles. A new tsar was needed, and Pozharskii was proposed, but he refused to accept the nomination. The final choice was Mikhail Romanov (r. 1613–45), who was distantly related to the Riurik line. His coronation established the Romanov dynasty, which ruled until the Bolshevik Revolution of November 1917.

The personages in Gorchakov's libretto are Minin (T), Pozharskii (T), Avramii Palitsyn (B, an early seventeenth-century priest and chronicler of the Time of Troubles), Ol'ga (S, Pozharskii's wife), and Trubetskoi (T, historically a seventeenth-century prince).[82] The chorus, extremely important in the oratorio, represents the Russian people. The libretto is divided into three acts and begins with Palitsyn's announcement of the grave news that Russia and Moscow have been given over to the enemy. Minin asserts that Russia must be saved. The chorus agrees and asks who the leader will be; Minin proposes, "Pozharskii! He is worthy above all men: a distinguished hero of the Fatherland." Again the chorus supports Minin with full agreement. After choral and solo numbers devoted to the greatness of the cause and the need to fight and sacrifice for Russia, and after a prayer to the Omnipotent Creator for help, Minin urges the people to go to Pozharskii and ask his assistance. The first act closes with a chorus of hope that Pozarskii will be the leader. In act II Minin and Palitsyn visit Pozharskii (who, historically, was recovering from battle wounds) to ask for his assistance, and he immediately announces his eagerness to help. Ol'ga says she wishes to go with him and "to give women an example of how they should love their country, the law, their husbands, and hold sacred all that serves to glorify Russia."[83] Her husband is overwhelmed with her noble and exemplary spirit, but he objects, for he wishes to protect her from the horror of war. They sing

81. For a summary of the historical events and the folk and literary traditions based on them, see ibid., pp. 201–39.

82. The entire libretto is reproduced in Russian (both in Cyrillic alphabet and transliterated) and in English in ibid., pp. 460–88; the libretto is discussed in ibid., pp. 285–312.

83. In no. 13 of Table X-1.

a duet of their love and the pain of separation, which, however, must be put aside for the Fatherland; Ol'ga says she will pray that her husband may return safely, and she sings a recitative and aria on the power of love, which can bring the sweetest peace even among the cries of the wounded. The act closes with prayers for help from the Most High, expressed in a trio (Minin, Pozharskii, and Palitsyn) and a chorus. Between acts II and III the battle has taken place, and act III begins with reflections on the victory and the triumph of the Fatherland. Ol'ga expresses her joy that God has saved her husband's life, and the chorus sings of their happiness. Trubetskoi enters, however, to remind the people that not all is concluded, for there is still no tsar. Pozaharskii is acclaimed as the right one to mount the throne, but he refuses and instead names Mikhail Romanov as Russia's next ruler. The chorus proclaims Mikhail as tsar and closes the oratorio with a prayer to God for happiness in Russia.

This libretto represents a striking change from the traditional libretto of the eighteenth and early nineteenth centuries, for it is, essentially, a patriotic, nationalistic expression. Yet here the genre has not lost its religious roots—there are numerous prayers, usually for Russia, as well as musical suggestions of Orthodox church music.

As may be seen in Table X-1 the first number of the oratorio begins in D minor but soon turns to D major, and the final number of act III is in D major.[84] The other keys of the work may have been selected for reasons of suitability to the instruments or voices and for variety, but the attitudes of the texts may also have influenced the choices. In act I the tonality moves to F minor for the prayer in number 7. In act II more flat keys are used, perhaps because of the texts about impending war, the tears of the Russian people, and the unhappiness of separation from loved ones that war causes, all of which are important themes in that act. The prayer in act II (no. 18)begins in the minor mode, as did that in act I, but closes (no. 19) in G major. Act III, one of victory, praise, and joy, returns to D major and its dominant and subdominant; number 34, a prayer, begins in G minor but ends (no. 35) in D major.

The oratorio shows Degtiarev's interest in musical and dramatic continuity, for numbers are at times linked by transitions to recitatives, and the recitatives—all of which are orchestrally accompanied—usually function tonally as transitions to the numbers that follow. The musical continuity begins at the end of the first-act introduction, which closes on the dominant after a transition preparatory to the first recitative. Other linkings are numbers 3 to 4, 5 to 6, 11 to 12, and 34 to 35. (As indicated by the bracket in Table X-1, nos. 3–4 form a unit: the chorus in 4 has the

84. The musical source used for the following comments is Degtiarev, *Minin**; for a discussion of the work's manuscript sources in libraries of the Soviet Union, see Hughes, "Degtiarev," pp. 269–84; on the work's musical structures and styles, see ibid., pp. 313–409.

TABLE X-I
Degtiarev, *Minin i Pozharskii*: Structural Outline

Numbers	Keys
ACT I	
1. Introduction (orchestra)	d/D
2. Rec. Palitsyn, Minin, "Gotov'tes'"	—
⌐3. Chorus. "Beda, beda postignet nas"	D
⌐4. Rec. Minin, "Pozharskago! Dostoinee on vsekh"	—
Chorus. "Emu vruchim my zhrebyi svoi"	D
⌐ Rec. Minin, "Kogda soglasie soediniaet"	—
5. Aria. Minin, "Poidem dushami s'edinimsia"	C
6. Chorus. "Dadim sebia, kak rossam srochno"	C
7. Duet. Minin, Palitsyn, "Velik i vsemogushch Tvorets"	f
Chorus. "Ego desnitsei ukreplenny"	f
8. Rec. Minin, "Poidem k Pozharskomu i vozvestim emu"	C
Chorus. "Emu, emu prilichna slava"	C
ACT II	
9. Introduction (orchestra)	F
10. Rec. Pozharskii, Minin, "Chto vizhu ia? Tam voiny vokrug stoiat"	—
11. Duet (arioso). Minin, Palitsyn, "Iavi: iavi v sebe zashchitnikaty"	b♭
12. Aria. Palitsyn, "Idi spasat' svobodu"	E♭
13. Rec. Pozharskii, Ol'ga, "Syny otechestva, idu ia s vami"	—
14. Duet. Pozharskii, Ol'ga, "Kogda rastanus' ia s toboi"	B♭
15. Rec. Ol'ga, Pozharskii, "Prosti, prosti suprug liubeznyi"	—
16. Aria. Ol'ga, "Vezde liubov' proizvodila"	E♭
17. Rec. Pozharskii, Minin, "Gotov'tes' voiny"	—
18. Trio. Minin, Pozharskii, Palitsyn, "Iavi, Vsevyshnii pomoshch'"	g
Chorus with trio. "Iavi, Vsevyshnii pomoshch'"	g
19. Chorus. "K Tebe, k Tebe vzyvaem vse!"	G
ACT III	
20. Introduction (orchestra)	C
21. Rec. Minin, Palitsyn, "Velikii podvig sovershilsia"	—
22. Chorus. "Slava Mininu sPozharskim"	D
23. Chorus. "Chti prestol', zakony pravdu"	A
24. Rec. Pozharskii, "Spodvizhnikov moikh potomstvo ne zabudet"	—
25. Trio. Minin, Pozharskii, Palitsyn, "Posle strakha, bur' voennykh"	E♭
26. Rec. Ol'ga, Pozharskii, "Supruga moego Vsevyshnii sokhranil"	—
27. Aria. Ol'ga, "Est'li v svete chto milee"	G
28. Chorus. "Schastlivaia cheta, vy slava nashikh dnei"	D
29. Rec. Trubetskoi, Palitsyn, "Ne vse, ne vse eshche svershilos'"	—
30. Chorus. "Pozharskii svobodil Rossiiu"	f/F
Rec. Palitsyn, Minin, Pozharskii, "Primi pochtennyi vozhd' pravlen'e"	—

Note: The numbers in this table are those of the printed edition, Degtiarev, *Minin**.

TABLE X-I
continued

Numbers	Keys
31. Aria. Pozharskii, "He l'shchus' ia vlastiiu verkhovnoi"	B♭
32. Rec. Minin, Pozharskii, "Velikii chelovek, primer dlia"	D
33. Chorus. "Voskliknem slava Bogu"	D
34. Chorus. "Tebe, Vladyko tvari vsei"	g
35. Chorus. "Uslyshi v vysoty nebes"	D

same music, but not the same text, as that in 3.) Several of the numbers (7, 8, 18, 30) are themselves complexes of solo or ensemble and choral units.

The instrumentation of *Minin i Pozharskii* is one of its most fascinating aspects in that it reflects a mixture of Western and specifically Russian elements. In addition to the usual strings, the orchestra includes a woodwind section of piccolos, flutes, bassoons, English horns, clarinets, and basset horns; a brass section of trumpets, horns, and *rogovoi orkestr*; and a percussion section of snare drum, triangle, timpani, marching cymbals, bass drum, and cannon battalion. The instrumental numbers are the long introductions to the acts: act I begins with a sonata-form in allegro tempo but with a largo sostenuto introduction; act II, with a larghetto in binary form for three basset horns and two horns, an instrumentation perhaps chosen to suggest a pastoral atmosphere for the presumably rural location of the act; and act III, with a two-movement battle symphony, treated below. While the introductions to acts II and III are special cases, most other numbers of the oratorio use the kind of orchestration one expects from oratorios in the late Classical period in the West (Vienna or Naples), as exemplified in the works of Joseph Haydn or Pietro A. Guglielmi. Certain aspects of the instrumentation and orchestration, however, reflect Russian traditions.

The *rogovoi orkestr* originated in the mid-eighteenth century, flourished until around 1800, and became obsolete in the course of the early nineteenth century.[85] In such an ensemble each player would play a single tone on a simple, straight, conical horn (some so long as to require an assistant to support the bell), and the tones would be rhythmically combined and synchronized to create melodic lines, harmonies, and simple polyphonic textures. Listeners, including Louis Spohr, reported their enchantment with the sound and visual effect of these horn bands, which performed as independent ensembles as well as with larger instrumental

85. The *rogovoi orkestr* and the literature about it are treated in ibid., pp. 328–41.

and choral groups. Referred to in scores as *tube, toube,* or *taube,* the *rogovoi orkestr* was characteristic of festive, celebratory works, as composed by Giuseppe Sarti and others, and is used to create an atmosphere of celebration in *Minin i Pozharskii.* When Haydn's *The Creation* was first performed in 1801 the *rogovoi orkestr* substituted for trombones, which were not yet available in Petersburg; a German reviewer commented on the "extraordinary effect" and said "the sounding of these horns frequently brought forth amazement and delight."[86]

The *rogovoi orkestr* is not used alone in Degtiarev's oratorio but is combined with instruments and voices in six numbers, three of which are prayers: 1) the duet and chorus in number 7, a prayer to the "Great and Omnipotent Creator," to help "return peace to Russia"; 2) the final chorus of act II, another prayer, "To You, to You we all cry! You are great with Your power. We extol You forever and ever"; 3) the instrumental introduction to act III; 4) the chorus in act III (no. 28), which comments on the happiness of Pozarskii and Ol'ga who are reunited; 5) the chorus (no. 30) that proposes Pozarskii as the tsar; and 6) the penultimate chorus (no. 34), another prayer, "To You, most holy Lord of all creatures, we sing a song of praise." Example X-1 shows the manner in which the *rogovoi orkestr* is used in the trio from act II (no. 18). In these measures the horn ensemble joins the orchestra in providing a simple harmonic support to the voices, yet the visual and sonorous quality of the performance would have added a specifically Russian color to an otherwise rudimentary passage.

In addition to the *rogovoi orkestr,* unusual features of the oratorio are the use of the wind instruments as a military band and the introduction of a cannon battalion. As pointed out in the libretto summary, the battle of Moscow takes place between acts II and III. Degtiarev depicts the battle in his instrumental introduction to act III, which consists of two movements: Alla marcia, in binary form and in C major; and Allegro vivace, an exposition-recapitulation form that begins in C minor and ends in C major. The military band plays throughout the first movement and enters near the end of the second. The band is notated separately in the manuscript score and may have constituted a separate unit, possibly a military organization. The battle scene proper is the first half of the second movement, the C-minor section; after the battle the mode changes to major to prepare for the victorious expressions at the beginning of act III. The second movement is composed within the tradition of battle symphonies, with syncopations, contrasting dynamics, percussion, and tremolo strings, but its scoring includes cannon, which are to fire on the beat, as shown in Example X-2. In the example, the cannon alternates between firing in quarter notes on the first and third beats of the measure and in half notes on the first half. (One wonders whether the half-notes for cannon would constitute two firings in rapid succession or

86. See the report in *Allgemeine musikalische Zeitung* 4 (1802): 344–46.

Behold the Most High, our help.

perhaps a simultaneous double firing as an accent.) It is not known how the battalion of cannoneers might have been conducted, nor where they would have been located. The effect of this battle for Moscow must have been startling, yet within the same tradition as Sarti's festive oratorios with cannon and fireworks.

The musical structure and style as reflected in the oratorio's five arias is characteristic of that of the late eighteenth century in Italy, but with perhaps fewer florid vocal lines. All arias have the transformed da capo structure (A1-B-A2); the B sections provide contrast but are not development sections. Example X-3 is taken from the longest and most elaborate aria of the oratorio, that of Palitsyn in act II (no. 12), in which he urges Pozharskii to lead the campaign to free Russia from the enemy. This aria proceeds without pause after the duet arioso (no. 11), and the first note of the example is the last note of the duet. The fanfare melodic style at the beginning of the vocal line is entirely within the eighteenth-century tradition of setting martial texts, and both the vocal and orchestral writing represent the Classical style as found in oratorio and opera. The last part of the example shows the extreme of florid vocal writing in the oratorio, and it appears near the end of the aria on the words, "Vanish unhappy tears. Return peace to Russia."

In the trio near the end of act II (no. 18), a through-composed number, the oratorio's three central personages ask for divine help before they go into battle, and they are joined at the mid-point by the chorus and the *rogovoi orkestr*. Both the trio and the trio-choral sections have chordal texture at first and then brief points of imitation. The second trio, for the same three personages in act III (no. 25), has a transformed da capo structure (A1-B-A2) and frequent pairing of voices, with the third voice imitating or sometimes opposing the other two. The longest and most intricate duet is the one in act II sung by Pozharskii and Ol'ga (no. 14), which begins in larghetto tempo as the two speak of the torment of parting, but turns to allegro as Pozharskii says, "Away with sad thoughts, yearn to save the Fatherland!" while Ol'ga says she will pray for his safety. The textures are varied, including imitation, parallel thirds and sixths (sometimes in melismatic passages), and the alternation of solo sections. In the duet and chorus of act I (no. 7), the duet is frequently in paired thirds and sixths; the chorus enters at about the midpoint.

As mentioned above, the recitatives are orchestrally accompanied and tend to have the tonal functions of transitions to the following numbers. The orchestra punctuates the vocal phrases by either chords or motivic passages or accompanies them in sustained-chord style. Word painting is not a significant feature of the oratorio, in the recitatives or elsewhere, but in the recitatives the orchestral passages respond to and express the emotional qualities of the text. A good example is number 17, Pozharskii's call to battle ("Prepare yourselves, warriors. Put on your swords and helmets. Sons of the Fatherland, follow behind us."), which is accompanied by orchestral tremolo, winds, brass, and percussion.

With the chorus entering fourteen times, *Minin i Pozharskii* is comparable in its choral emphasis to the most chorally oriented of the eighteenth-century German and English oratorios. Most of the choruses mix chordal passages with contrapuntal ones, but a few are purely chordal (nos. 6, 8, and 34), and two are fugues, which appear, conventionally, as the finales to acts II and III. Of greater interest, however, are the choruses with mixed textures. Some of these are close in style to the choral

EXAMPLE X-3. continued

EXAMPLE X-3. continued

Go forth to save freedom, all hearts are devoted to you. . . . Return peace to Russia.

music of the Orthodox church, a style for which Degtiarev was well known and admired. The choral excerpt in Example X-4 is strongly suggestive of Russian church music—except for the orchestral parts, absent in music of the Orthodox church—and is characteristic of several of the choruses in this oratorio. The example is taken from the victory chorus near the beginning of act III (no. 22). Particularly close to church music are measures 13–15 with their repetitions of "slava" ("glory"), alternating in antiphonal style between the highest and lowest voices, while the alto voice sings chantlike repeated notes. Suggesting the choral concerto of Russian church music, Example X-5 (from no. 23) illustrates the alternation between three-part soli and tutti passages so often found in that genre and this oratorio.

Although *Minin i Pozharskii* represents the late eighteenth century for its melodic, harmonic, and textural styles—in both their Western and Russian manifestations—it also heralds a new beginning. Nationalism in the arts had been a growing tendency in Russia, as in other nations and areas of the late eighteenth century, but during the nineteenth and twentieth centuries that tendency matures and bears fruit in a variety of musical genres. Furthermore, in oratorio, traditionally a sacred genre, secular and nationalistic content become increasingly prominent. In its nationalistic libretto and musical content as well as its secular text (but with a strong sacred element) Degtiarev's *Minin i Pozharskii* foreshadows some future developments in oratorio.

EXAMPLE X-4. *Minin i Pozharskii*—Degtiarev (Degtiarev, *Minin**, pp. 109–10).

EXAMPLE X-4. continued

EXAMPLE X-4. continued

Glory to Minin and Pozharskii, liberators of Moscow.

EXAMPLE X-5. continued

EXAMPLE X-5. continued

Honor the throne, the law, the truth. Preserve the pure faith. Vanquish on the seas and on land, and rule half of the earth.

❧   Summary and Prospect

We have seen that various meanings were attached to the term *oratorio* in different geographical areas—and sometimes within one and the same area—during the eighteenth and early nineteenth centuries; nevertheless, a common thread unites most of these meanings. In the Classical era, regardless of language and geography, the term *oratorio* usually referred to a musical setting of a libretto based on a religious subject, the source of which was characteristically the Bible, more often the Old Testament than the New; the lives of saints were also prominent subjects, especially in librettos from Roman Catholic areas. Highly exceptional was the application of the term *oratorio* to a secular work, but that application became increasingly prominent in the nineteenth and twentieth centuries. Librettos of oratorios in the Classical era were usually divided into two or three parts, sometimes called acts, but some librettos were in only one part and others in four or five. Like an opera libretto, each part or act was further divided into recitatives, arias, ensembles, and choruses. Librettos usually included narrative, dramatic, and lyric passages, but they sometimes emphasized one of these qualities, especially the dramatic or lyric, more than the others.

The musical setting of the libretto in the solo and ensemble numbers of Italian and German oratorios tended to follow the styles and structures of serious opera, and the changes in the course of the century were approximately the same as in opera. A close relationship between changes in opera and oratorio continued in the nineteenth and twentieth centuries, yet eighteenth-century tendencies were revived. The choruses in oratorios of the Classical era were usually more contrapuntal than operatic choruses and were more numerous in English and German than in Italian oratorios. The musical aspects of the English oratorio were strongly influenced by Handel, but more recent styles appeared as well. Handel continued to influence the English oratorio of the nineteenth century, and to some extent that of the twentieth century. In France, oratorios performed at the Concert spirituel also emphasized the chorus and showed the influence of both the grand motet and opera. Our limited current knowledge of oratorio in Spain and Portugal suggests the Italian oratorio as a model and the influence of the *villancico*. The single Russian oratorio treated in this volume points to the influence of the

Italian and English oratorio and of the choral styles used in Orthodox church music.

In the Classical era, oratorios were widely performed throughout Europe and were beginning to be heard in the New World. Italy, where oratorio had originated in the seventeenth century, continued to offer a greater variety of social contexts for oratorios and thus a larger number of performances than any other geographical area. With the possible exception of the Iberian Peninsula, oratorios outside of Italy tended to be performed only during the Lenten season or on special or relatively rare occasions such as the English festivals. As eighteenth-century public concert life grew, oratorios became a part of that life; and in the nineteenth and twentieth centuries the public concert hall has been the primary place for the performance of oratorios.

From the mid-eighteenth century on, especially in Italy but to a lesser extent north of the Alps, Italian oratorios were increasingly performed with operatic staging, costumes, and acting; yet throughout Europe the characteristic manner of performing an oratorio, in any language, continued to be that of a concert, with music in the hands of the singers. Although much more research needs to be done on performing practices, available evidence suggests that in London, at the English provincial festivals, in Vienna, and occasionally elsewhere, the performing forces for oratorios increased from relatively modest choral and orchestral groups in the mid-century to larger ones—at times monumental in size— by the beginning of the nineteenth century. Monumentality continues to be characteristic of oratorio performances in the nineteenth and twentieth centuries.

At the end of the Classical era the Italian oratorio began to decline in social demand and frequency of performance. However, a brief revival of Italian oratorio appeared in the late nineteenth and early twentieth centuries. Around 1800 the oratorio was still Handelian in England, and oratorios were still performed during Lent and in festivals, but few new English oratorios—even fewer noteworthy ones—were composed. In the course of the nineteenth century, however, Mendelssohn and others shared the Handelian hegemony. The German oratorio at the turn of the nineteenth century was dominated by works of the lyric type, also reflected in the few Danish works of the time. Haydn's late oratorios, however, showed a strong Handelian influence, which became increasingly important in nineteenth-century Germany as Handel's oratorios became better known there. In France, with the demise of the Concert spirituel in 1790, the principal context of oratorio performance disappeared; yet in the early nineteenth century sporadic oratorio performances were given, and by mid-century oratorios began to appear with increasing frequency in French concert programs. In 1811 an important Russian oratorio by Degtiarev foreshadowed an interest of the nineteenth and twentieth centuries in nationalistic oratorios.

Some Title Pages of Italian and
Latin Printed Librettos Mentioned
in the Text

The following title pages are offered as documentation of statements made in
the text, for the most part in chapter 1, in regard to the social contexts of Italian
oratorios. The title pages have been copied from a variety of sources, including
the librettos themselves, but especially from Sartori, "Catalogo." Following the
imprint (in parentheses), the author of the libretto (L) is given, then the composer of the music (M), if known and not given on the title page; then follow
the sigla of one or more libraries who own copies of the libretto. Library shelf
numbers are supplied for those librettos seen by the present author. Other library sigla are taken from various sources, the most important of which is Sartori, "Catalogo."

*L'Abele. Componimento sacro per musica da cantarsi nell'oratorio della
veneranda Arciconfraternita di S. Maria della Morta la sera del venerdì santo.
Poesia del sig. abate Pietro Metastasio poeta di sua maestà cesarea e catolica.
Musica del signor Leonardo Leo maestro della real cappella di Napoli* (Bolo-
gna: S. Tommaso d'Acquino, 1739). I-Bc, Bca.
*Abramo. Oratorio cantato nella cappella di S.A.S.E. di Baviera l'anno
M.DCC.XXXI. La poesia è del sig. Domenico Lalli, poeta di S.A.S.E. di
Baviera* (Munich: Appresso Maria Maddalena Riedlin, Vedova, n.d.). M:
[Pietro Torri]. D-Mbs: 4e 198 B4. ital. p. 225.
*L'Abramo. Sacra azione a lode del Santissimo Sacramento esposto nell'insigne
tempio della Beatissima Vergine de' Miracoli presso S. Celso, da recitarsi in
occasione degli essercizj spirituali ne' giorni 8. 9. 10 febbrajo 1755. Poesia del
sig. dottore Francesco Tosi, fra gli Arcadi Merilgo. Musica del signor Antonio
Negri, maestro di capella di detto insigne tempio ec.* (Milan: Giambatista
Bianchi, n.d. [Imprimatur: 24 December 1754]). I-Ma, Mb.
*Adamo ed Eva. Componimento sagro da cantarsi nell'oratorio della nobilissima
Arciconfraternita e Spedale di S. M. della Morte la sera del venerdì santo
dell'anno 1775. Musica del celebre sig. Giuseppe Misliweck detto il Boemo*
(Bologna: Gaspare de' Franceschi, n.d.). I-Bca, Rn.
*L'adorazione delli tre re magi al bambino Gesù nella capanna di Betlemme.
Oratorio da cantarsi nella Congregazione dell'Immacolata Concezione eretta*

nella Casa Professa di S. Fedele de' RR. PP. della Compagnia di Gesù il dì 9 gennaio 1722. Musica del sig. D. Antonio Vivaldi maestro di capella di camera di S. A. S. il sig. prencipe Filippo langravio d'Assia d'Armestath (Milan: Eredi di Domenico Bellagatta, 1722). I-Mb.

Aemulatio inter divinum amorem et fidem in morte S.Joannis Francisci Regis S. I. (Palermo: Ang. Felicella, 1740). M: Giovanni Statella. I-PLcom.

L'angelica costanza dell'umanità ne'suoi dolori. Oratorio a quattro voci da cantarsi nell'oratorio dell'illustrissima Arciconfraternita di S. Maria della Morte di Bologna la sera del venerdì santo dell'anno 1720 (Bologna: Rossi e compagni, n.d.). I-Bas, MOe, Rn, Vgc.

L'appostolo dell'Etiopia: S. Matteo. Oratorio a quattro voci cantato la sera del giovedì li 11 aprile 1726 nella illustrissima prima arciconfraternita di Bologna Santa Maria della Vita (Bologna: Gio. Battista Bianchi, n.d.). I-Bc, Bca, Rn.

Aqua e rupe Horeb. Carmina praecindenda psalmo miserere. Modos fecit Balth. Galuppi chori moder. filiae Xenodochii S. Lazari Mendicantium cecinerunt. Ann. Repar. Sa. 1750 (Venice: n.p., 1750). I-Bu, Rc, Vcg.

L'armeria e la galleria dell'augustissima casa d'Austria aperte ed esposte per illustrare la sollenità di S. Rosalia V. P. celebrata nell'anno 1721. Dall'illustrissimo senato palermitano. Li signori . . . (Palermo: Antonio Epiro, 1721). I-PLcom: CXXXVI.C.213(16).

Il beato Riniero. Oratorio a quattro voci da cantarsi la sera delli XV marzo 1742 nell'oratorio dell'illustrissima prima arciconfraternità di Bologna Santa Maria della Vita posto novamente in musica da diversi autori (Bologna: S. Tommaso D'Acquino, n.d.). I-Bc, Bca.

La Betulia liberata. Dramma sacro del sig. abate Pietro Metastasio, romano, da rappresentarsi nel Teatro della Rua dos Condos nella quaresima dell'anno 1773 (Lisbon: Stamperia Reale, 1773). I-Rsc, P-Ln.

La caduta di Gerusalemme. Componimento poetico da cantars nell'oratorio dell'illustrissima prima arciconfraternità di Bologna S. Maria della Vita il primo giovedì del la quaresima 1727. Musica del signor Luca Antonio Predieri accademico filarmonico e maestro di capella di detta arciconfraternità (Bologna: Gio. Battista Bianchi, n.d.). I-Bc, Rn.

Cantata per la Natività della Beatissima Vergine in occasione dell'accademia pubblica del Collegio Nazareno. Musica del sig. abbate Gio. Niccolò Checconi. (Rome: Giovanni Zempel, 1739.) I-Rc, Rli, Vgc.

Cantata per la Natività della Beatissima Vergine in occasione della publica accademia nel Collegio Nazareno. (Rome: Giovanni Zempel, 1753). M: Rinaldo da Capua. Librettos with virtually identical title pages and same composer date from 1754–57, 1760, and 1780. All librettos in I-Vgc and various other locations.

Cantata per la Natività della Beata Vergine in occasione della pubblica accademia nel Collegio de' Nobili delle Scuole Pie d'Urbino consecrata a sua eccellenza monsignore Branciforte Colonna arcivescovo di Tessalonica e presidente della legazione d'Urbino. (Urbino: Stamperia Camerale, 1760). M: Rinaldo di Capua. I-Vgc.

Cantata per l'Assunzione della Beatissima Vergine in occasione della publica accademia nel collegio episcopale di S. Lorenzo Giustiniani in Murano diretto da i CC. RR. delle Scuole Pie. (Venice: Simone Occhi, 1752). I-Li.

Cantate a gloria del santissimo Sacramento esposto nell'insigne tempio della

Beatissima Vergine de' Miracoli presso S. Celso, in occasione degli esercizj spirituali alli 26. 27. e 28 febbrajo 1729. Poste in musica dal M. rev. sig. Dionigi Erba, maestro di cappella del detto insigne tempio, e date alle stampe da un divoto della Beata Vergine (Milan: Carlo Giuseppe Quinto, n.d.). I-Bc.

La cena del Signore. Componimento per musica applicato al suo santiss. sepolcro e cantato nell'augustissima cappella della sac. cesarea e catt. real maestà di Carlo VI imperador de' Romani sempre augusto l'anno 1720 (Vienna: Gio. Van Ghelen, n.d.). L: Pietro Pariati; M: Johann Joseph Fux. I-Ms.

La colpa originale piangente alle culle del Redentore. Oratorio sacro da recitarsi il giorno 8 di gennaro 1723 nella Congregazione dell'Immacolata Concezione eretta nella Casa Professa di S. Fedele de' RR. PP. della Compagnia di Gesù. Musica del sig. Gio. Maria Marchi organista della metropolitana (Milan: Giuseppe Agnelli, 1723). I-Mb.

Componimento per musica per la primiera Messa celebrata dal reverendo signor D. Giuseppe Cerlone, sacerdote napolitano (Naples: Catello Longobardo, 1771). I-Nn: Sala 6. Misc. A. 32 (9).

Componimento sagro per musica da cantarsi nel Palazzo Apostolico nella notte del Ss.mo Natale dell'anno 1740. Musica del signor Felice Doria (Rome: Stamperia della reverenda Camera Apostolica, 1740). I-Bu, Fm, MAC, Rc, Vgc.

Componimento sagro per musica sopra la nascita del Redentore da cantarsi il dì 4 gennajo 1735 nella insigne chiesa collegiata e parrochiale di S. Marco in occasione della solenne disputa sopra la dottrina cristiana da farsi dalle zitelle parrocchiane di essa chiesa, di Giovanni Gambogj romano (Rome: Gio. Zempel, 1735). I-Mb.

I conforti di Maria Vergine addolorata per la morte del suo Divin Figliuolo. Da cantarsi nell'oratorio della nobilissima Arciconfraternità di S. Maria della Morte la sera del venerdì santo. Poesia del molto reverendo padre D. Carlo Innocenzio Frugoni cher. reg. somasco. Musica del sig. Giacomo Antonio Perti mastro di capella della perinsigne collegiata di S. Petronio e di detto oratorio (Bologna: Lelio dalla Volpe, 1723). I-Bas, Bc, Bca. Similar title pages for same work performed for same occasion in 1734 (I-Bas, Bca) and 1745 (I-Bas, Vgc).

La conversione di S. Ignazio. Oratorio da cantarsi alla corta elettorale Palatina l'anno MDCCXL. Poesia del s. Lorenzo Santorini, poeta e segretario di S.A.S.E. Musica del s. Carlo Pietro Grua, maestro di capella di S.A.S.E. (Mannheim: Dalla Stamperia Majeriana, 817409. D-HEu: G 2811 VII, 3.

Il convito di Baldassarre. Oratorio da rappresentarsi nel Teatro Nuovo sopra Toledo nella quadragesima del corrente anno 1786 (Naples: Vincenzo Flauto, n.d.). M: di diversi autori. I-Vgc.

Coronatio Salomonis. Drama sacrum cecinendum a piis virginis choristis Noscomii Incurabilium recurrente solemnitate Transfigurationes Domini. Modos fecit D. Antonius Calegari (Venice: n.p., 1780). I-Vcg.

David e Bersabea. Oratorio di Paolo Rolli F.R.S. Composto da Nicolò Porpora per la nobiltà britannica (London: Sam. Avis, 1734.). BG-Lbl: 11714.aa. 22(9).

David poenitens. Actio sacra pro virginibus choristis in Nosocomio Divi Lazari Mendicantium recurrente solemni triduo hebdomadae majoris. . . . (Venice: Apud Aloysium Milocco, 1775). M: Ferdinando Bertoni. I-Bc: Lib. 7418.

David poenitens. Oratorio da cantarsi nel teatro privilegiato presso alla porta d'Italia in Vienna nell'Advento dell'anno 1775 . . . (Vienna: Giuseppe Kurzböck, 1775). M: Ferdinando Bertoni. D-DT: Mus. t-8.

Debora e Sisara. Azione sacra per musica di Carlo Sernicola P. A. da rappresentarsi nel real Teatro di S. Carlo nella quaresima dell'anno 1788. Dedicata alla S. R. M. di Ferdinando IV. Nostro amabilissimo sovrano. (Naples: Vincenzo Flauto, 1788). M: Pietro [Alessandro] Guglielmi. US-Wc: ML48/.S4241.

Debora e Sisara. Azione sacra per musica da rappresentarsi nel regio Teatro di Via della Pergola la quaresima del 1791 sotto la protezione dell'A. R. di Ferdinando III arciduca d'Austria . . . gran-duca di Toscana ec. ec. ec. (Florence: Albizziana, 1791). L: Carlo Sernicola P. A.; M: Pietro [Alessandro] Guglielmi, maestro di capp. napoletano. I-Bc, Fc, Nc.

Debora e Sisara. Azione sacra eseguita alla presenza di S. M. il re di Polonia nell'oratorio di corte la settimana santa dell'anno 1791 (Warsaw: P. Dufour, Cons: Aulico di S. M. e Dirett: della Stamperia del R. Corpo de Cadeti, 1791). L: Carlo Sernicola; M: Pietro Guglielmi. PL-Wu: XVIII.1.4477.

Debora e Sisara. Componimento sacro destinato cantarsi nell'oratorio dell'illustrissima Arciconfraternita di S. Maria della Morte la sera del Venerdì Santo dell'anno 1795 da' signori sagristani del primo quadrimestre. Musica del signor Pietro Guglielmi maestro di cappella napolitano (Bologna: S. Tommaso d'Aquino, n.d.). I-Bc, Bca (Malvezzi), Bam (Fondo moderno), Fm.

La decollazione di S. Gio. Battista. Componimento poetico cantato nell'oratorio dell'illustrissima prima arciconfraternità di Bologna di S. Maria della Vita la sera delli 3 aprile dell'anno 1721. Musica del sig. Giacomo Cesare Predieri, maestro di cappella della metropolitana e di detta arciconfraternità ed accademico filarmonico (Bologna: li Bianchi, n.d.). I-Bc, Bca.

La deposizione dalla croce di Gesu Cristo salvador nostro. Azione sacra, da cantarsi nella regia elettoral capela di Dresda il Sabato Santo. Dell'anno MDCCXLVIII. Poesia del Abbate Gio: Claudio Pasquini . . . Fu posta in musica dal sig.r Gio: Adolfo Hasse . . . (n.p. n.d.). Italian and German on facing pages. D-B: Mus. Th. 251.

La deposizione dalla croce e sepoltura del Redentore. Componimento sacro da cantarsi nell'oratorio dell'illustrissima Arciconfraternita di S. Maria della Morte la sera del venerdì santo dell'anno 1787. Posto in musica dal signor Gaspare Gabellone maestro di cappella napolitano (Bologna: S. Tommaso d'Aquino, n.d.). I-Bam, Bc.

Dialogo pastorale a gloria del nato Redentore da recitarsi il dì 7 gennaio 1720 nella ven. Congregazione dell'immaculata Vergine posta nella Casa Professa di S. Fedele de' RR. PP. della Compania di Gesù. Musica del signor Gioanni Perroni maestro di capela in S. Maria delle Grazie etc. (Milan: Domenico Bellagatta, 1720). I-Mb.

La divina providenza. Dramma armonico per la festività del glorioso patriarca S. Gaetano Thiene fondatore de' Cherici Regolari. Da rappresentarsi da' figliuoli del regal Conservatorio di Santa Maria di Loreto in quest'anno 1720. Posto in musica da Vito-Domenico Gagliarda figluolo dello stesso conservatorio (Naples: Gio. Francesco Paci, 1720). I-Msartori.

Elia al Carmelo. Cantata per la Natività della Beatissima Vergine in occasione della pubblica accademia nel Collegio Nazareno (Rome: Giovanni Zempel,

1761). M: Rinaldo di Capua. B-Bc, GB-Lbl, I-MAC, Rc, Vgc.

L'esiglio di S. Silverio papa e martire. Componimento poetico cantato nell'oratorio dell'illustrissima prima arciconfraternità di Bologna S. Maria della Vita la quaresima dell'anno 1720 (Bologna: Rossi e compagni, n.d.). I-Bc.

L'Ester palermitana S. Rosalia applaudita con giubilo univsale della Sicilia nel magnifico trionfo di Conca d'Oro in quest'anno 1728. Dalla fervorosa divozione dell'eccellentissimo senato palermitano grande di Spagna, li signori . . . (Palermo: Antonio Epiro, 1728). I-PLcom: CXXXVI.C.213(36).

Il figliuol prodigo. Azione sacra per musica applicata al santissimo sepolcro, da cantarsi nell'imperial capella di Dresda il venerdì santo dell'anno 1747. La poesia è del signor . . . Gio. Claudio Pasquini . . . *La compositione della musica è del signor Gio. Giorgio Schürer.* ([Dresden] V.va Stössel, n.d.). B-Bc, F-Pn, US-Wc.

Gesù bambino adorato dalli pastori. Oratorio da cantarsi nella Congregazione dell'Immacolata Concezione eretta nella Casa Professa di S. Fedele de' RR. PP. della Compagnia di Gesù il giorno 11 gennajo 1726. Musica del sig. Gio. Battista S. Martini (Milan: Eredi di Domenico Bellagatta, 1726). I-Mb.

Gesù Cristo deposto dalla croce e sepolto. Componimento sacro da cantarsi nell'oratorio della nobilissima Arciconfraternità di S. Maria della Morte la sera del venerdì santo dell'anno 1794. Musica del signor G. G. (Bologna: Lelio dalla Volpe, n.d.). I-Bc, Bca.

Giacob. Oratorio rappresentato sul teatro (Valenciennes: Gabriello Francesco Henry, stampagore regio, 1709). M: [Pietro Torri]. B-Bc: UU 20501.

Giacobbe. Azione sacro-pastorale per musica a cinque voci da cantarsi in Bruna nella quaresima dell'anno 1731 per commando di sua altezza . . . *il cardinale Wolffgango Annibale di Schrattenbach* . . . *La poesia è del sig. dott. Giov. Batista Catena, segretario attuale di s. altezza eminent. Musica di Wenceslao Gurezki dell'attuale servizio di s. altezza eminent.* (Brno: Giacomo Massimiliano Swoboda, 1731). I-Bc, Mb.

Giacobbe. Componimento da cantarsi nella ven. real capella di Nostra Signora della Soledad . . . *ricorrendi il sesto sabato della settimana di Passione dell'an. 1799 che si celebra da congregati detta R. R. cappella per pia divozione di sua real maestà Ferdinando III re delle due Sicilie, essendo maggiordomi li signori D. Giuseppe Gravina principe di Montevago, D. Pietro Napoli de' principi di Bonfornello, ten. col. degli eserciti di S. M. e com. del R. cast. del Molo, D. Giuseppe del Castell-*(Palermo: Solli, 1799). L: Gio. Francesco Fattiboni, patrizio cesenate; M: Pietro Guglielmi. I-Rc.

Gioas. Componimento sagro da cantarsi nella sera della festività di Santa Fermina protettrice della città di Civita Vecchia l'anno 1774, dedicato alla medesima santa dal magistrato di essa città li signori Stefano Bianchi, Vincenzo Fiori, Pietro Dumas, Sigismondo Vidau, visconti camarlinghi (Rome: Lorenzo Capponi, n.d.). L: Pietro Metastasio; M: Giovanni Valentini accad. filarmonico. I-Rn.

Gioas re di Giuda. Oratorio del sig. abate Pietro Metastasio romano, posto in musica dall'eccellentissimo signore D. Marc'Antonio Carafa de' duchi di Traetto, da cantarsi nella cappella privata dell'eccellentissima . . . *duchessa di Giovenazzo la sera delli 26 decembre 1757* (Rome: Generoso Salomoni, 1757). I-Rn, Vc.

Gioas re di Giuda. Oratorio da cantarsi per clementissimo ordine di sua altezza eminentissima elettorale emerico Giuseppe, della S. Sede di Magonza arcivescovo . . . la poesia è del celebre . . . Metastasio . . . La musica è del signore Giuseppe Michl (Mainz: Nella Stamperia privilegiata dell'Ospedale di S. Rocco, 1772?–74). D-MZp: 172.

Il Gioas re di Giuda. Sacro componimento drammatico per musica da cantarsi in camera alla presenza della real fedelissima maestà l'augustissima signore D. Maria I, regina di Portogallo degli Algarvi etc. il 31 marzo 1778, felicissimo giorno natalizio di sua real fedelissima maestà l'augustissima signora D. Maria Vittoria regina madre (Lisbon: Stamperia Reale, 1778). M: Antonio da Silva. B-Bc, BR-Rn, I-Rc, P-Lt.

Giuditta figura di Cristo, di Maria, e della Chiesa. Componimento sacro da cantarsi nel venerabil' Oratorio del Buon Giesù di Foligno, in occasione, che negl'ultimi tre giorni del carnovale dell'anno 1745., s'espone ivi, solennemente, alla pubblica adorazione de fedeli il Santissimo Sacramento, in una macchina, rappresentante il trionfo della stessa Guiditta. Dedicatto all'illustr. e reverend. monsignore Mario Maffae ottomio pastore di detta città, e sua (Foligno: Feliciano e Filippo Campitelli Stamp. Vescovili, n.d.). M: Giuseppe Carcani. I-Bc, FOLc, PESo, Rvat (Casimiri).

Giuseppe riconosciuto. Melodrama da rappresentarsi nell'essercizi vespertini de' RR. PP. dell'Oratorio (Naples: Felice Carlo Mosca, 1736). M: Giuseppe Terradellas, alunno del Collegio de' Poveri di Gesucristo. I-Nc: 5.5.4.a-b.

L'innocenza vendicata. Componimento da cantarsi nella solenne accademia degli scolari della rettorica delle Scuole Pie in occasione dell'apertura d'un nuovo oratorio nelle medesime scuole. Dedicato al Beato Giuseppe Calasanzio. (Florence: Stamperia Arcivescovile, 1759). I-Rc.

Invito alle spirituali nozze con Gesù Cristo. Dramma sacro composto dal molto illustre e reverendo signore D. Giambattista Paderni Accademico Industrioso ed Infiammato ed umilmente offerto in attestato di parentela da Antonio Maria Minelli alla molto reverenda madre suor Nicola Guzmana Maria Antonia al secolo . . . Catterina Lucia Rossi cittadina bolognese professante i voti solenni di religione nel nobilissimo . . . monistero di S. Pietro Martire (Bologna: Stamperia del Sassi, 1779). I-Bam.

Isacco figura del Redentore. Azione sacra per musica applicata al santissimo sepolcro e cantata nell'augustissima cappella della sacra cesarea e cattolica maestà di Carlo VI imperadore de' Romani sempre augusto l'anno 1740 (Vienna: Gio. Pietro Van Ghelen, n.d.). L: Pietro Metastasio; M: Luca Antonio Predieri. A-Wgm, D-W.

Isacco figura del Redentore. Azione sacra per musica applicata al santissimo sepolcro da cantarsi nell'imperial capela di Dresda il Venerdì Santo dell'anno 1753. La poesia è del sig. abbate Pietro Metastasio. La musica è del sig. Gio. Georgio Schürer. (Dresden: C. H. Hagenmüller, n.d.). CS-Pu.

Isacco figura del redentore. Da recitarsi nel real Conservatorio di S. Onofrio. Dedicato a S. E. Il signor D. Francesc'Antonio Perrelli . . . ed all'illustrissimi signori governatori di detto real conservatorio (Naples: Amato Cons., 1765). M: Vincenzo Bellini, primo alunno del detto real conservatorio. I-Rc.

Jefte in Masfa. Oratorio a quattro voci da rappresentarsi in Firenze nel Teatro di Via del Cocomero nell'autunno dell'anno 1776 (Florence: Anton Giuseppe Pagani, 1776). L: N. N. [Abate Semplici]; M: Francesco Ipolito Barthélémon, maestro di capp. francese, direttore e primo violino degli Oratorj nel Real Teatro di Haymarchet a Londra. I-Bc.

Jonathas. Actio sacra musicalibus numeris expressa a D. Ferdinando Bertoni pro virginibus choristis in Noscomio D. Lazari Mendicantium dum recolitur solemne triduum hebdomadae majoris anni 1771 (Venice: Angelum Pasinelli, 1771). I-PAc, Rc, Vcg, Vgc.

Maria Vergine confortata in casa di Zaccaria ed Elisabetta nella contemplazione della passione e morte del suo figlio Gesù. Dialogo a quattro voci e più strumenti da cantarsi nella ven. real cappella di Nostra Signora della Soledad delli nobili spagnoli e signori officiali militari, esistente nella ven. chiesa dei RR. PP. canonici regolari dell'Ordine della SS. Trinità della Redenzione dei Cattivi, nel piano del regio palazzo di questa città di Palermo, nel secondo sabbato di quaresima di quest'anno 1753. Non essendo esposto il Divinissimo Sacramento. Celebra questa festa per sua pia divozione monsignor Fr. D. Giuseppe Melendez . . . arcivescofo della città di Palermo (Palermo: A. Epiro, 1753). M: Salvatore Bertini. PLcom.

Il martirio di S. Eugenia. Tragedia sacra da rappresentarsi nel regal conservatorio de figliuoli di S. Onofrio di questa città di Napoli nel carnevale del corrente anno 1722. Di Leone Costantino Fularco. Dedicata all'illustriss. . . . signora D. Marcella Mauleon De Amato . . . (Naples: n.p., 1722). M: Nicola Porpora. I-Fm.

Il martirio di S. Ferma vergine e martire romana. Oratorio a quattro voci di G. B. F. poste in musica dal sig. Gio. Battista Costanzi romano, maestro di cappella dell'eminentissimo signor cardinale Ottoboni. Da cantarsi nella sala del Collegio Germanico e Ungarico di Roma (Rome: Stamperia Komarek, 1733). I-Li, MAC, Nc.

El materno amor de Maria SS. de la Soledad, resignado la divina justizia. Dramma sacro a 4. vozes, y muchos instrumentos, que se deve cantar en la venerable real capilla del N. S. de la Soledad existente en la venerable yglesa de la Ss. Trinidad en el llano del regio palazio, el sexto sabado de quaresma de este año 1739. Puesta en nota del sig. David Perez maestro de capilla. No siendo expuesto el Divinissimo Sacramento (Palermo: Antonio Epiro, 1739). GB-Lbl: 639.f.28(28).

La morte d'Abel. Componimento sacro-drammatico del signor abbate Metastasio da cantarsi nelle quarantore del carnevale nella chiesa del Giesù di Palermo (Palermo: Pietro Bentivegna, 1754). M: Girolamo Abbos. I-PLcom.

La morte d'Abelle. Oratorio a cinque voci da cantarsi nella venerabile Compagnia di S. Niccolo del Ceppo di Firenze la sera del dì 6 dicembre 1738. In occasione di solennizarsi la festa di detto santo. (Florence: P. G. Viviani, 1738). L: Metastasio; M: Leonardo Leo. I-Tu.

Moyses in Nilo. Modi sacri recinendi a piis virginibus choristis in Noscomio de Pietate nuncupato recurrente festo Nativitatis B. Mariae Virginis. Modos fecit D. Bonaventura Furlanetto chori magister et moderator. (Venice: Typis Dominici Battifoco, 1771). I-Rc, Vmc.

Oratorio per la Santissima Vergine addolorata da cantarsi nel venerdì santo nella Congregazione de' Fratelli della Natività di Maria Vergine eretta nella casa de' PP. Cherici Regolari Minori in S. Lorenzo in Lucina (Rome: A. de Rossi, 1738). L: Paolo Felici; M: Antonio Berti. C-Tu.

Oratorio per la Santissima Vergine addolorata da cantarsi nel venerdì santo nella Congregazione de Fratelli della Natività di Maria Vergine eretta nella casa de PP. Cherici Regolari Minori di S. Lorenzo in Lucina. Dedicata all'illustrissimo . . . D. Ottavio Maria Lancellotti principe di Mazzano etc.

(Rome: Ansillioni, 1739). L: Domenico Crisolini, tra gli Arcadi Crisomelio Bocalide; M: Marco Comestabile. I-Bc, Vgc.

Oratorio per l'Assunzione della B.ma Vergine da cantarsi nel Collegio Clementino. Musica del sig. Giuseppe Valentini (Rome: Stamperia della Rev. Cam. Apost., 1730). I-Bc, PLcom, PESo.

Il paradiso perduto. Componimento sacro per musica da cantarsi nell'Oratorio de' RR.PP. della Congregazione dell'Oratorio di Roma (Rome: Fulgoni, 1802). Lib. by Giovanni Battista Rasi; mus. by Pietro [Alessandro] Guglielmi. I-Rsc: Libretto vol. 165.1

Il paradiso terrestre. Oratorio in onore di S. Luigi Gonzaga cantato in Bologna nella solenne coronazione dell'imperatore della dottrina cristiana l'anno 1763 (Bologna: Lelio dalla Volpe, n.d.). M: Bartolommeo Del Bello veneziano, accad. filarmonico di Bologna e maestro di capp. della città di Cento. I-Bc, Bca, Bu, et al.

La passione di Gesù Cristo e i dolori della Vergine Madre in cinque cantate del sig. dott. Guido Riviera. I-Ma (for the following three titles).

Cantata 1: *Cristo coi discepoli nell'orto agonizzante, confortato dal angiolo. Cantata prima da recitarsi alla sera del primo venerdì di quaresima nella reale Congregazione dell SS.mo Entierro in S. Fedele. Musica del sig. Gio. Battista San Martino maestro di cappella della suddetta reale Congregazione* (Milan: Pietro Francesco Malatesta, 1743).

Cantata 2: *Cristo nell'orto tradito da Giuda. Cantata seconda da recitarsi alla sera del secondo venerdì di quaresima . . .* (n.p., n.d.).

Cantata 3: *Cristo giudicato del pretorio di Pilato. Cantata terza da recitarsi alla sera del terzo venerdì di quaresima . . .* (n.p., n.d.).

La passione di Giesù Cristo, nostro signore. Oratorio sacro cantato nella chiesa dei PP. della Compagnia di Giesù, giovedi & venerdi santo alle sette di sera (Bamberg: Johann Georg Klietsch, 1754). D-WÜu: Rp XV, 50.

La passione di Gesù Cristo nostro signore. Componimento sagro del canonico Carlantonio Morichini posto in musica dal signor Giovanni Cordicelli da cantarsi in memoria de' dolori della SS.ma Vergine nel venerdì santo a sera nell'oratorio delli Fratelli della ven. Congregazione della SS.ma Natività di M. V. entro la casa de' PP. Chierici Regolari Minori in S. Lorenzo in Lucina di Roma l'anno 1755 (Rome: Generoso Salomoni, 1755). I-Vgc.

La passione di Gesù Cristo nostro signore. Componimento sacro per musica da cantarsi la sera del 15 marzo in Campidoglio nell'appartamento del principe Rezzonico senator di Roma (Rome: Dalle stampe di Filippo Neri, 1790). L: Pietro Metastasio; M: Giovanni Paisiello. I-Mcom, Vgc.

La passione di Gesù Cristo signor nostro. Componimento sacro per musica applicato al suo santissimo sepolcro e cantato nell'augustissima cappella della sacra cesarea e cattolica real maestà di Carlo VI imperatore de' Romani sempre augusto l'anno 1730 (Vienna e Roma: Pietro Ferri, n.d.). L: Pietro Metastasio; M: Antonio Caldara. A-Wn, I-Fm, Rl, Rvat, Vgc.

La passione di Gesù Cristo signor nostro. Componimento sacro del signor abate Pietro Metastasio . . . M: Nicolò Jommelli. I-Rsc, Vgc.

La passione di Gesu Cristo signor nostro. Oratorio da cantarsi nella cappella elettorale Palatina la sera del venerdi santo dell'anno M.DCC.LIV. Per comando del ser. elett. (Mannheim: Stamp. elett., Nicola Perron, n.d.). L: [Metastasio]; M: Ignaz Holzbauer. D-HEu: G2811, II, 2.

La passione di Gesù Cristo signor nostro. Oratorio sacro da cantarsi nel real palazzo dell'Ajuda per festeggiare l'augusto nome del serenissimo signore D. Giuseppe principe del Brasile li 19 marzo 1783 (Lisbon: Stamperia Reale, 1783). L: Pietro Metastasio; M: Luciano Xavier dos Santos. BR-Rn, I-Rc, P-EVp.

La passione di nostro signore Gesù Cristo. Azione sacra eseguita alla presenza di S. M. il re di Polonia nell'oratorio di corte li 2 aprile 1784 (Warsaw: Pietro Dufour, 1784). L: Pietro Metastasio; M: Giuseppe Paisiello. PL-GD, Wu, WRol.

I pellegrini al sepolcro. Oratorio da cantarsi nella capella elettorale Palatina la sera del venerdì santo dell'anno M.DCC.LXVIII. Per comando del ser. elett. (Mannheim: Nella Stamperia del'Accademia, [1768]). L: [Stefano Benedetto Pallavicino]; M: Johann Adolf Hasse. D-HEu: G 2811.3 (14/1). Same work also performed on Good Friday, 1769.

I pellegrini al sepolcro di nostro salvatore. Oratorio. Die Pilgrime bey dem heil. Grabe, ein musikalisches Gespräch. Wird aufgeführt in der Kirche der Gesellschaft Jesu zu Innsbruck an dem heiligen Charfreitag und Charsamstag Abends um acht Uhr (Innsbruch: gedr. m. Wagnerischen Schriften, 1769.) L:[Stefano Benedetto Pallavicino]; M: [Johann Adolf Hasse]. D-As: 4°. Tonk. 197.

Pel le nozze di Salomone colla figlia del re di Egitto, simbolo dell'unione di Gesù Cristo con la chiesa, e con la B. Vergine, che principalmente la rappresenta. Epitalamio tratto dal Salmo XLIV. Da cantarsi nel Conservatorio della Pietà celebrandosi la festa di S. Maria del Carmine (n.p.: 1780). I-Nn: Sala 6, Miscell. A.32(14).

Peregrini ad sepulcrum servatoris nostri. Oratorium musicum decantatum feria V hebdomadae sanctae hora 7 vespertina Fuldae in templo PP. S.J. 1768 (Fulda: Joh. Christoph Dempter, 1768). L: [Stefano Benedetto Pallavicino]; M: Johann Adolf Hasse. D-FUl: Fuld 45/60.

Per la morte del Redentore. Oratorio a quattro voci di Domenico Lalli per servizio di . . . monsign. prencipe del S.R.I. e vescovo d'Erbipoli . . . La musica è del sign. Fortunato Chelleri maestro di capella di detta sua altezza (Würzburg: Arrigo Engmanno, [1730?]). D-WÜu.

Per la promozione al cardinalato del sereniss. real infante di Spagna Don Luigi. Cantata fatta recitare nel regio palazzo di sua maestà cattolica dall'eminentiss. e reverendiss. signor cardinale De Acquaviva di Aragona ministro della medesima presso la Santa Sede. Componimento del sig abate Bernardo Bucci posto in musica dal signor Benedetto Micheli (Rome: Gio. Maria Salvioni, 1735). I-MAC, PLcom.

Per la solenne esposizione del SS. Sagramento in una machina rappresentante Daniele nel Lago de' Leoni nel venerabile Oratorio del Buon Gesù di Foligno ne' tre giorni antecedenti alla quaresima dell'anno 1749. Drama sagro dedicato all. . . . (Foligno: Pompeo Campana, 1749). Invenzione e pittura della macchina di Nicola Epifani di Foligno. L: Neralco, Pastore Arcade; M: Giuseppe Dol di Monaco di Baviera. I-FOLc.

Per la solenne esposizione del SS. Sagramento in una machina rappresentante il sagrificio d'Abramo nel ven. Oratorio del Buon Gesù di Foligno ne' tre giorni antecedenti alla quaresima dell'anno 1751. Drama sagro dedicato all' ill.mo . . . monsign. Mario Maffei vescovo vigilantissimo di detta città (Foligno:

Francesco Fofi, 1751). [Invenzione e pittura della macchina di Niccola Epifani di Foligno.] L: Neralco Pastore Arcade; M: Niccola Vettori agostiniano di Firenze. I-FOLc.

Pharisaei conversio ad sepulchrum. Modi sacri tribus prioribus diebus majoris hebdomadae a piis Noscomii Pauperus Derelictorum virginibus recinendi. A Dom. Francisco Piticchio magistro panormitano musice espressi (Venice: n.p., 1782). I-Vcg.

Il popolo di Giuda liberato dalla morte per intercessione della regina Ester. Componimento sacro per musica da cantarsi nell'oratorio de' RR. PP. della Congregazione dell'Oratorio di Roma (Rome: Pallade, 1768). L: G. N. C.; M: Antonio Sacchini. GB-Lbl, I-Fm, Rv, Vc. (Another libretto, same title-page wording, librettist, and composer [Rome: Salvioni, 1777]). I-Bc, Vc.

Il popolo di Giuda liberato dalla morte per intercessione della regina Ester. Componimento sagro per musica da cantarsi nel Collegio Germanico-Ungerico l'anno 1769 (Rome: Angelo Maria Ansillioni, n.d.). L: G. N. C.; M: Antonio Sacchini. I-Vgc.

I portenti del Divino Amore. Componimento sacro drammatico di Francesco Cerlone da cantarsi in casa del signor D. Angelo Perrotti in occasione della prima S. Messa che celebra il novel sacerdote D. Pietro Perrotti suo degnissimo figlio (Naples: Flauto, 1775). M: del signor D. . . . maestro di cappella napoletano. I-Nn: Sala 6. Miscell. A. 32 (12).

La religione trionfante in S. Tomaso d'Acquino. Componimento sacro musicale da cantarsi nella chiesa de PP. Serviti il dì 7 marzo, festa di detto santo e dall'autore religioso servita dedicato al merito grande di sua exccellenza D. Gio. Antonio de Boxadors, conte di Cavallà ec., cavaliere dell'ordine insigne del Tonson d'Oro, intimo attuale consigliere di stato di S.M.C. e catt. e del supremo Consiglio di Flandra ec (Vienna: Andreas Hevinger, 1726). I-Bc.

Il ritorno di Tobia, azione sacra per musica di Gio. Gastone Boccherini Lucchese, . . . da cantarsi ne' teatri privilegiati di Vienna l'anno 1775. (Vienna: Presso Giuseppe Kurzboeck, [1775]). M: Joseph Haydn. CS-Pu: GY 3500.

Il ritorno di Tobia. Oratorio sacro da cantarsi nel real palazzo dell'Ajuda per celebrare l'augusto nome del serenissimo signore don Giuseppe principe del Brasile li 19 marzo 1784 (Lisbon: Stamperia Reale, [1784]). L: Giovanni Gastone Boccherini; M: Joseph Haydn. I-Fc, PAc, Rc, Vgc, P-Lt.

Rubri Maris trajectus sive promissae terrae a limine salutatio. Dramaticum carmen quod pro sollemni fidelium vita functorum recordatione in templo divae Mariae Angelorum ad echiam anniversaria, sollersque Pietas Regalis Montis Mortuorum, in eôdem instituti, statis diebus canendum curavit. Kalendis Nempe & quartô Nonas Novembres. (Naples: Ex typografia Manfrediana, 1773). M: Gennaro Manna. I-Nlp: Lib. A373(1)

Rut nel campo di Booz. Azione sacra da cantarsi nel regal monistero di Reginaceli in occasione della monacazione dell'eccellentissima signora D. Giulia Riario Ruspigliosi de' duchi Riario, marchesi di Corlato ec. (Naples: Muziana, 1759). L: Tegrillo Alfirense P.A.; M: Nicolò Conti maestro di capp. dello stesso regal monistero. I-Nn.

Sacrificium Abraham. Introductio ad psalmum Miserere concinenda a filiabus Xenodochii Incurabilium musicis modulis exornata a D. Baldassare Galuppi chori moderatore et magistro (Venice: Modesti Fentii, 1764). I-Vcg, Vnm.

Il sacrifizio d'Abramo. Rappresentato in occasione di essere accettata in

religione la nobil donna contessa Cecilia Mariscotti nel monistero de' SS.
Gervasio e Protasio (Bologna: Per Giuseppe Maria Fabri nella stamperia di S.
Tommaso d'Acquino, 1732). M: Giovanni Battista Martini? I-Bca, Bc.

Il sacrifizio di Gefte. Dramma sacro di Felice Martelli, poeta arcade e
accademico quirino, da recitarsi nella città dell'Aquila solennizandosi la
festività del glorioso protettore S. Emidio a 6 di ottobre dell'anno 1789.
Dedicato al merito incomparabile dell'ill.mo signore D. Domenico Falconi
patrizio Aquilano e barone di Torre di Toglia. Per cura e zelo de' procuratori
D. Eleuterio Basile e D. Francesco Santili (L'Aquila: Giuseppe Maria Grossi,
1789). I:Nlp: Lib. A664(2).

Li sacri sponsali dell'anima religiosa col verbo incarnato. Oratorio a 4. voci, da
cantarsi nella chiesa del venerabile monastero dell'Immacolata Concezione di
Maria Vergine, nel prender l'abito religioso col nome di S.or Maria Nazarena
la signora D.na Petronilla Ventimiglia e Spinola, De' Principi di Belmontino
. . . Sotto il governo della molto rev. madre suor Rosa Felice Ventimiglia
quarta volta abbadessa (Palermo: Antonio Epiro, 1739). M: da Don . . .
maesstro di cappella del medesima monastero. GB-Lbl: 639.f.28(24).

Sancta Maria Magdalena. Oratorium concinendum in Templo D. Lazari
Mendicantium ejusdem Sanctae Mariae Magdalenae recurrentibus annuis
solemniis die 22 julii anno Domini 1740. Expressit modulis Balthasar
Galuppi (Venice: Carolum Pecora, 817409). I-Rc, Vcg.

S[anctus] Petrus et S. Maria Magdalena. Sacra isagoge ad psalmum Miserere.
Cantabunt filiae chori pii Noscomii Incurabilium. Modos fecit Joannes
Adolphus Hasse, Frideici Augusti III Poloniae regis et electoris Saxonici,
musices moderator (Venice: Joseph Rosa, 1758). I-Rc, Vnm.

S[ant'] Elena al Calvario dell'ab. Metastasio poeta cesareo. Componimentio in
musica nuova da cantarsi a cinque voci nell'oratorio de' RR. PP. di S.
Girolamo della Carità. Dedicato all'eccellentissimo principe il sig. duca di
Rohan-Chabot principe di Leone . . . maresciallo di campo ed armate di S. M.
cristianissima ec. ec. ec. (Rome: Barbiellini alla Minerva, 1779). M: Fortunato
Luciani. I-Nc.

Sant'Elena al Calvario. Componimento sacro per musica fatto cantare in
quaresima nella sua residenza elettorale di Bonna da S.A.S.E. Clemente
Augusto arcivescovo et elettore di Colonia, gran maestro dell'Ordine
Teutonico . . . duca dell'una e l'altra Baviera etc. etc. etc. (Bonn: Vedova
Rommerskirchen suoi eredi nella stamperia di S.A.S.E. di Colonia, 1740). F-
Pn.

S[ant'] Elena al Calvario. Componimento sacro per musica a cinque voci del sig.
ab. Pietro Metastasio romano da cantarsi nel Collegio Germanico Ungarico
l'anno 1780 (Rome: Casaletti, n.d.). M: Nicola Luciani. I-Vgc.

La SS. Vergine addolorata. Oratorio a tre voci da cantarsi nel venerdì santo da'
confratelli della ven. Congregazione della SS. Nascita di Maria Vergine nel
loro oratorio dentro la casa de' padri Chierici Regolari Minori in S. Lorenzo
in Lucina (Rome: Raffaelle Peveroni, 1729). M: Alessandro de Rossi. I-Li.

La SS.ma Vergine addolorata. Oratorio a tre voci di D. M. pastore arcade da
recitarsi la sera del venerdì santo nella ven. Congregazione della Natività di
Maria Vergine eretta nella casa de' PP. Chierici Regolari Minori in S. Lorenzo
in Lucina. Dedicato all'e.mo . . . cardinale Giuseppe Renato Imperiali (Rome:
Gio. Battista de Caporali, 1733). M: Giuseppe Valentini. I-Li.

La SS.ma Vergine addolorata. Oratorio a tre voci da recitarsi la sera del venerdì santo nella ven. Congregazione della Natività di Maria Vergine eretta nella casa de' PP. Chierici Regolari Minori in S. Lorenzo in Lucina. Dedicato al r.mo padre Giovan Matteo preposito generale de' Chierici Regolari Minori di S. Lorenzo in Lucina ad istanza de' fratelli divoti (Rome: Gio. Battista de' Caporali, 1736). L: Paolo Felici; M: Antonio Berti. (Cf. Oratorio per la Santissima Vergine addolorata, 1738, listed above.) I-Vgc.

La SS.ma Vergine addolorata. Oratorio a tre voci da cantarsi la sera del venerdì santo nell'oratorio della Congreg. de' confratelli della S.ma Nascita di Maria Vergine eretta entro la casa de PP. Chierici Regolari Minori in S. Lorenzo in Lucina. Dedicato al merito impareggiabile dell'e.mo . . . cardinale Luigi Belluga Moncada del titolo di S. Prisca e protettore delle Spagne ecc. ad istanza de' confratelli divoti di essa congregazione (Rome: Gio. Zempel, 1737). L: Antonio Piacentini romano; M: Marco Comestabile romano. I-Li, Vgc.

La SS.ma Vergine addolorata. Componimento sacro per musica a tre voci da cantarsi nel venerdì santo dalli confratelli della vener. Congregazione della SS. Nascita di Maria Vergine nel loro oratorio entro la casa de' PP. Chierici Regolari Minori in S. Lorenzo in Lucina. Dedicato all'illustrissimo . . . monsignore Bernardino Giraud ad istanza di due fratelli divoti (Rome: Antonio de' Rossi, 1745). L: Gaetano Roccaforte romano; M: Francesco Maria Paci romano. I-Bc, Vgc.

Sermo discipulorum Christi in Vespere Diei Parasceve. Sacra isagoge ad psalmum Miserere cantabunt piae virgines choristae in Nosocomio Divi Lazari Mendicantium appellato. Recurrente solemni triduo hebdomadae majoris. Modos fecit Ferdinandus Bertoni chori magister et moderator (Venice: Angelus Pesinelli, 1760). I-Bc, Rc, Vcg.

La sposa de' sacri cantici. Componimento drammatico da cantarsi per lo solenne ingresso nel venerabil monastero della SS.ma Concezione detto il Monaster Nuovo in Via della Scala dell'illustrissima signora Margherita Ginori con nome di donna Caterina Teresa Maria Margherita (Florence: Bernardo Paperini, 1742). M: Lorenzo Fago di Napoli, detto Tarantino. D-Hs.

Lo sposalizio di Abigaille con Davide. Componimento sacro per musica da cantarsi in occasione che veste l'abito religioso nel real monastero di Reginaceli di Napoli la eccellentissima signora D. Argentina Mollo de' duchi di Lusciano (Naples: Manfrediana, 1767). M: Antonio Sacchini. I-Rc.

Tertia dies, sive Pium ascetarum colloquium in illa verbis Mulier ecce filius tuus . . . Carmen praecinendum psalmo Miserere a filiabus Nosocomii S. Lazari Mendicantium recurrente hebdomada majori anni 1767. Modos fecit Ferdinandus Bertoni chori ejusdem moderator ac magister (Venice: Angelum Pasinellum, [1767]). I-Rc, Vcg, Vgc.

Il trionfo della casta Susanna. Componimento sacro a quattro voci e più stromenti da cantarsi nel venerabile e real monistero del SS. Salvatore in occasione di prender l'abito monacale la sig. suor Maria Casimira detta nel secolo D. Catarina Drago e Naselli. Sotto il felice governo della reverenda madre suor Giuseppa Melchiora Lanza seconda volta abadessa. Musica del sig. Gio. Gualberto Brunetti (Palermo: Agnelo Felicella, 1742). I-PLn.

Il trionfo della castità di Santo Alessio. Dramma di Nicola Corvo dedicato all'illustriss. . . . la sig. contessa Camilla Barberini Borromei vice-regina nel regno di Napoli. Da rappresentarsi nel Real Conservatorio, detto delli

Turchini, con musica di Lionardo Leo figliuol dello stesso conservatorio (Naples: Felice Mosca, 1713). I-Bc, Bu.

Il trionfo della croce. Dialogissimo del conte Antonio Zaniboni P. A. in occasione di darsi solennemente la Croce a fanciulli della Dottrina Cristiana nella chiesa decanale e parrocchiale di S. Sigismondo. Dedicato al . . . senatore Sigismondo Malvezzi marchese di Castel Guelfo ecc. (Bologna: Ferdinando Pisarri, 1752). I-Bca (Malvezzi).

Il trionfo della religione. Componimento per musica da cantarsi per il solenne ingresso nel ven. monastero di S. Martino in Via della Scala dell'ill.ma sig.ra contessa Maria Elisabetta Barbolini. . . . Musica del sig. Bartolommeo Felici (Florence: Anton Maria Albizzini, 1747). I-Fm.

Il trionfo della religione e dell'amore. Da celebrarsi per musica nel giorno festivo di S. Benedetto alla presenza degli augustissimi regnanti nel monastero di Nostra Signora del Monferrato dell'ordine di S. Benedetto sotto la direzione del padre Antonio abbate di detto monastero l'anno 1725 li 22 aprile. La musica è di Antonio Caldara, vice maestro di S.M.C. La poesia è di Cristoforo Bonlini, patrizio veneto (Vienna: Gio. Pietro van Ghelen, 1725). A-Wgm, I-Vgc.

Il trionfo della vocazione religiosa contro le lusinghe del mondo. Componimento per musica da cantarsi nella chiesa delle nobili religiose di S. Pier Maggiore, in occasione dell'ingresso in monastero dell'illustriss. sig. contessa Maria Cammilla Pierucci (Florence: Andrea Bonducci, 1752). L: del dottor Damiano Marchi; M: Bartolomeo Felici. I-Bsf, Fc.

Il trionfo di David nella disfatta di Golia. Cantata a tre voci da festeggiarsi nel solenne triduo che rinnuova nella Terra di Figline del Valdarno di Sopra nel presente anno 1770. In onore di Santa Massimina vergine e martire . . . benefica protettrice di detta terra (Florence: G. B. Stecchi e A. G. Pagani, 1770). L: Niccolò Salvemini, canonico nel Collegio di S. Giuliano di Castiglione Fiorentino Acc. Apat. Etrusco; M: Abate Giuseppe Feroci, maestro di capp. di detta collegiata. I-Fm, Rc.

Il trionfo di Mardocheo. Componimento sacro per musica da cantarsi nell'oratorio de' reverendi padri della Congregazione dell' Oratorio di Roma (Rome: G. Salomoni, 1774). M: Giovanni Batista Borghi. GB-Lbl, I-Rc, Vgc.

Il trionfo di Mardocheo. Componimento sagro per musica da cantarsi nel Collegio Germanico Ungarico l'anno 1778 (Rome: Casaletti, n.d.). M: Giovanni Batista Borghi. I-Rc.

Il trionfo di Mardocheo. Componimento sagro per musica da cantarsi nell'oratorio de' RR. PP. della Congregazione dell'Oratorio di Roma (Rome: Stamperia di Filippo Neri e Luigi Vescovi, 1785). M: Giovanni Batista Borghi. I-Rc, Vc, Vgc.

Triumphus Judith. Cecinerunt piae virgines choristae in Noscomio nuncupato Pauperum Derelictorum recurrente festo Deiparae in coelum Assumptae. Accedunt cantica recinenda in aliis Vesperis quorum omnium modos fecit Antonius Cajetanus Pampani academicus filarmonicus chori magister ac moderator emeritus (Venice: Typographia Pinelliana, 1757). I-Rc, Vcg.

L'umiltà coronata alla santità di nostro signore Benedetto Terzodecimo sommo pontefice. Oratorio per musica da recitarsi nella chiesa di S. Domenico di Bologna li 6 febbrario 1725. Per l'annua solennità solita celebrarsi dallo Studio dell'Ordine de' Predicatori nella translazione del santo dottore angelico Tommaso d'Acquino. (Bologna: Stampe de' Peri, 1725). [Dedicated by the "studenti di sagra teologia dell'Ordine de Predicatori dal convento di S. Domenico di Bologna."] L: Giannalberto Bianchi di Verona, sacerdote dell'Ordine de Predicatori, Accademico Intrepido di Ferrara; M: Pietro Baldassari, maestro di capella della congregazione dell'oratorio di S. Filippo di Brescia. I-Bc, Fc.

L'umiltà coronata. Componimento da cantarsi per comando di sua eccellenza il signor Pietro Capello . . . ambasciatore ordinario al Sommo Pontefice per la . . . republica di Venezia. Nel giardino pensile del Pubblica Palazzo di S. Marco, ridotto ad uso d'anfiteatro (Rome: Chracas, 1727). I-Ms, Rli, Rv, Rvat, Vgc,

L'umiltà coronata. Oratorio per musica da recitarsi nella chiesa ducale di Santa Maria delle Grazie li 20 Marzo 1725 per l'annua solennità solita celebrarsi dallo Studio dell'Ordine de' Predicatori del santo dottore angelico Tommaso D'Acquino (n.p., n.d. Imprimatur: Milan, 10 March 1725). Dedicated by the "padri studenti delle Grazie di Milano." L: Giannalberto Bianchi; M: Pietro Baldassari. I-Mb.

Vexillum fidei. Cecinerunt piae virgines choristae in Noscomio appellato Incurabilium, recurrente solemni triduo majoris hebdomadae. Modos fecit Vincentius Ciampi, chori magister et moderator (Venice: n.p., 1761). I-Pu, Rc, Vcg.

Le virtù in gara per lodare S. Filippo Neri. Componimento sacro per musica da cantarsi nell'Oratorio de' RR. PP. della Congregazione dell'Oratorio di Roma (Rome: Fulgoni, 1802). L: Carlo Antonio Femi. M: Girolamo Mango. GB-Lbl: 11715.e49(20).

Il vota di Jefte. Dramma sacro per musica da cantarsi nella città dell'Aquila in occasione si celebra nella chiesa cattedrale il dì anniversario della prodigiosa liberazione dal tremuoto seguito nel dì 6 ottobre 1762, in ringraziamento al di lei amantissimo tutelare S. Emidio vescovo e martire . . . (L'Aquila: Emidio Mariani, [1801]). M: maestro di cappella di Lionessa. I-Nlp: Lib. A664(4).

§● APPENDIX B

Checklist of Composers of
Italian and Latin Oratorios,
ca. 1720–1820

Given the current state of research in the history of oratorio, this list must be regarded as tentative and by no means exhaustive. It is offered in the hope that it might serve as a preliminary checklist for further research. The oratorios by some of the composers listed are known from librettos only, others from music manuscripts. The present author has seen many of the extant sources of the oratorios by the composers in the list, but the vast majority have yet to be studied.

The list derives from searches of reference works (of which Sartori, "Catalogo," was particularly important) as well as searches in libraries of the United States and Europe. (I am grateful to Denis and Elsie Arnold for sending me a list of composers of oratorios for Venice from their forthcoming book, Arnold, *Oratorio in Venice*, which the reader should check for further information.) All composers have been checked in *New Grove* and *MGG*; composers found in neither of those works have been checked in *La musica: Dizionario*. The majority of the composers are found in one of those reference works. The list is divided into two parts: part 1 for composers whose birthdates are known or can be reasonably estimated (listed in chronological order by year of birth), and part 2 for those whose dates are unknown and cannot be estimated (listed in chronological order by date of earliest oratorio). The four columns in part 1 provide the following information, from left to right: the composer reference number; the composer's birth and death dates, as given in the most recent reference work (usually *New Grove*); the composer's name; the number of oratorios by the composer (pasticcio and partial works are omitted; when the number of oratorios differs from that in the above-mentioned reference works, the number given conforms to the best available sources—Sartori, "Catalogo" or printed librettos known to the present author); and the cities where the composer's oratorios were first performed, according to the best sources available. (The cities are given in chronological order of first performance, but names of cities are not repeated.) The list is followed by an alphabetical index of composers. For the purposes of this list, the word *oratorio* is interpreted as it is in the chapters on the Italian oratorio as a whole.

Ref. No.	Composers' Dates	Composers' Names	No. of Ors.	Cities Where First Performed
1	ca. 1660–1729	Monari, Clemente	8	Cremona, Modena, Forlì, Bologna
2	1660–1741	Fux, Johann Joseph	14	Vienna
3	ca. 1664– ca. 1730	Cesarini, Carlo Francesco	13	Rome, Florence
4	1668–1727	Gasparini, Francesco	12	Florence, Naples, Venice, Vienna, Rome, Ancona, Città di Castello, Ancona, Lucca
5	ca. 1670–1755	Bencini, Pietro Paolo	7	Rome
6	1670–1747	Bononcini, Giovanni	6	Bologna, Modena, Rome, Vienna
7	ca. 1670–1736	Caldara, Antonio	43	Venice, Mantua, Rome, Vienna, Salzburg
8	?–1740	Marchi, Giovanni Maria	9	Milan
9	1679–1744	Sarro, Domenico Natale	8	Naples, Rome, Genoa, Bologna
10	1679–1745	Zelenka, Jan Dismas	3	Dresden
11	ca. 1680?–? fl. 1730–42	Bencini, Antonio	4	Rome, Monte Giorgio, Bologna
12	ca. 1680– ca. 1740	Conti, Lorenzo	17	Florence
13	1680–1750	Porsile, Giuseppe	13	Vienna
14	ca. 1680– after 1759	Valentini, Giuseppe	8	Rome
15	1683–1729	Heinichen, Johann David	1	Dresden
16	1684–1755	Durante, Francesco	4	Naples, Rome, Venice
17	?–1736 (oratorios, 1724–28)	Monza, Carlo Antonio	6	Viterbo, Rome, Ancona, Bologna
18	1684–1762	Manfredini, Francesco Onofrio	6	Bologna, Pistoia
19	1685–1769	Redi, Giovanni Niccola Ranieri	5	Florence
20	1686–90–1757	Chelleri, Fortunato	8	Mannheim, Würzburg, Dresden
21	1686–1746	Fiocco, Jean-Joseph	5	Brussels
22	1686–1739	Marcello, Benedetto	5	Venice, Rome, Vienna

Ref. No.	Composers' Dates	Composers' Names	No. of Ors.	Cities Where First Performed
23	1686–1768	Porpora, Nicola (Antonio)	6	Naples, Venice, London, Vienna, Dresden
24	1688–1767	Predieri, Luca Antonio	7–10	Bologna, Vienna
25	ca. 1690–1757	Bellinzani, Paolo Benedetto	2	Ancona, Urbino
26	?–? (oratorios, 1730s)	Chiochetti, Pietro Vincenzo	11	Genoa
27	ca. 1690–1755	Porta, Giovanni	1	Venice
28	1690–1768	Veracini, Francesco Maria	8	Florence, Düsseldorf, London
29	ca. 1690–1730	Vinci, Leonardo	1	Naples
30	1691–1761	Feo, Francesco	12	Naples, Bologna, Genoa, Prague, Rome
31	1692–1753	Ristori, Giovanni Alberto	3	Dresden
32	ca. 1692–1740	Giacomelli, Geminiano	2	Genoa
33	1694–1744	Leo, Leonardo	6	Naples, Atrani, Bologna, Lecce
34	1695–1776	Felici, Bartolomeo	8	Florence, Bologna
35	1698–1765–67	Logroscino, Nicola Bonifacio	4	Brno, Catania, Palermo
36	1698–1754	Schiassi, Gaetano Maria	6	Bologna, Lisbon
37	1699–1759	Conti, Ignazio Maria	7	Vienna
38	1699–1778	Deichel, Josef Anton	1	Eichstätt
39	1699–1783	Hasse, Johann Adolf	11	Vienna, Venice, Dresden
40	?–after ca. 1765	Chiarini, Pietro	1	Venice
41	ca. 1700–1757	Cordans, Bartolomeo	1	Venice
42	ca. 1700–after 1768	Brusa, Francesco	5	Venice
43	ca. 1700–1773	Grua, Carlo Pietro	5	Mannheim
44	ca. 1700–1763	Platti, Giovanni Benedetto	3	Würzburg
45	1700–1701–75	Sammartini, Giovanni Battista	2	Milan
46	1702–3–71	Graun, Johann Gottlieb	1	Berlin
47	ca. 1702–78	Corselli, Francesco	2	Parma
48	1703–79	Carcani, Giuseppe	5	Foligno, Venice
49	1703–55	Harrer, Gottlob	1	Leipzig
50	1704–78	Costanzi, Giovanni Battista	23	Rome, Foligno, Todi, Florence, Genoa, Venice

Ref. No.	Composers' Dates	Composers' Names	No. of Ors.	Cities Where First Performed
51	1705–43	Gurecký, Václav Matyáš	3	Brno
52	ca. 1705–75	Pampani, Antonio Gaetano	11	Fermo, Venice
53	ca. 1705–ca. 80	Rinaldo di Capua	4	Rome
54	1706–85	Galuppi, Baldassare	27	Venice, Bologna, Rome, Florence,
55	1706–84	Martini, Giovanni Battista (Padre)	4	Bologna, Foligno, Camerino, Fermo
56	1706?–84?	Bernasconi, Andrea	5	Munich, Venice
57	1708–75	Duni, Egidio	2	Bitonto
58	1708–72	Reutter, Georg (Jr.)	8	Vienna
59	1708–96	Sabatino, Nicola	3	Genoa, Palermo
60	1709–89	Richter, Franz Xaver	2	Mannheim, Stams
61	ca. 1710–81	Aurisicchio, Antonio	2	Rome
62	1710–49	Bayer, Andreas	1	Würzburg
63	1710–36	Pergolesi, Giovanni Battista	1	?Naples (questionable authenticity)
64	1711–88	Bonno, Giuseppe	4	Vienna
65	1711–83	Holzbauer, Ignaz	4	Mannheim, Vienna
66	1711–88	Latilla, Gaetano	5	Venice
67	1711–78	Perez, David	4	Palermo, Rome, Padova
68	1713–1801	Sala, Nicola	1	Naples
69	1713–1803 or 1806	Scalabrini, Paolo	1	Bologna
70	1713–51	Terradellas, Domingo (Domenico) Miguel Bernabe	2	Naples
71	1714–82	Avondano, Pedro Antonio	5	Lisbon
72	1714–74	Jommelli, Nicolò	9	Naples, Venice, Rome, Palermo, Pistoia
73	1715–79	Manna, Gennaro	8	Naples
74	1715–77	Wagenseil, Georg Christoph	2	Vienna
75	1715–72	Zonca, Giuseppe	1	Bonn, Bologna, Munich
76	ca. 1715–92	Casali, Giovanni Battista	11	Rome, Foligno, Bologna
77	1717–85	Mazzoni, Antonio (Maria)	5	Bologna, Faenza, Pesaro, Gubbio, Genoa
78	1718?–1779	Ferradini, Antonio	1	Prague
79	1719?–62	Ciampi, Vincenzo	4	Venice

Ref. No.	Oratorio Dates	Composers' Names	No. of Ors.	Cities Where First Performed
80	1719–1812	Gibelli, Lorenzo	5	Bologna
81	1720–90	Corbisiero, Antonio	2	Naples, ?Venice
82	1720?– after 1774	Scolari, Giuseppe	1	Lisbon
83	ca. 1720–86	Schürer, Johann Georg	3	Dresden
84	ca. 1720– after 1788	Cocchi, Gioacchino	11	Venice
85	1723–95	Uttini, Francesco Antonio Baldassare	3	Bologna, Stockholm
86	1723–97	Rutini, Giovanni Marco	3	Florence
87	ca. 1724–1787	Cröner, Franz Carl Thomas	1	Munich
88	1725–1813	Bertoni, Ferdinando	48	Venice
89	?ca. 1725– after 1810	Fischietti, Domenico	4	Florence, Venice, Prague
90	1726 or 1727– 1787	Starzer, Joseph	1	Vienna
91	1727–97	Anfossi, Pasquale	22	Rome, Venice, ?Florence
92	1727–96	Gabellone, Gaspare	4	Bologna, Rome, Cava
93	1727–79	Traetta, Tommaso	1	Venice
94	1728–95	Insanguine, Giacomo	1	Naples
95	1728–1804	Guglielmi, Pietro Alessandro	7	Rome, Naples, Madrid
96	1728–1800	Piccini, Niccolò	4	Naples, ?Rome
97	1729–93	Feroci, Giuseppe	6–7	Castiglione Fiorentino, Arezzo, Valdarno, Florence
98	1729–74	Gassmann, Florian Leopold	1	Vienna
99	ca. 1729–97	Sales, Pietro Pompeo	8	Augsburg, Mannheim, Ehrenbreitstein, Koblenz
100	1729–1802	Sarti, Giuseppe	3	Venice, Florence
101	ca. 1730– after 1802	Corbisieri, Francesco	1	Venice
102	1730–86	Sacchini, Antonio	8	Bologna, Venice, Rome
103	1732–71	Brixi, František Xaver	9	Prague
104	1732–1809	Haydn, Franz Joseph	1	Vienna
105	1732–70	Majo, Gian Francesco (de)	6	Naples, Bologna
106	1734–1808	Santos, Luciano Xavier dos	1	Lisbon

Ref. No.	Composers' Dates	Composers' Names	No. of Ors.	Cities Where First Performed
107	ca. 1735–1808 or later	Silva, João Cordeiro da	1	Lisbon
108	1736–1800	Fasch, Carl Friedrich Christian	1	Berlin
109	ca. 1736–45 to 1812	Rispoli, Salvatore	1	Naples
110	ca. 1737–97	Crispi, Pietro Maria	12	Rome
111	1737–81	Mysliveček, Josef	6	Padua, Florence, Prague
112	1737–88	Zannetti, Francesco	4	Perugia, Castello, Florence, Arezzo
113	1738–96	Borghi, Giovanni Battista	7	Rome, Loreto, Camerino, Bologna, Bamberg
114	1738–1817	Furlanetto, Bonaventura	34	Venice
115	1739–99	Dittersdorf, Carl Ditters von	4	Grosswardein, Johannesberg, Vienna
116	1739–66	Ritschel, Johannes	1	Mannheim
117	1744–1829	Bellini, Vincenzo [Tobia] Nicola	8	Naples, Catania
118	1740–1817	Gatti, Luigi	4	Mantua, Brescia
119	1740–1816	Paisiello, Giovanni	6	St. Petersburg, Naples
120	1741–1808	Bartélémon, François-Hippolyte	1	Florence
121	1741–1801	Lucchesi, Andrea	2	Venice
122	1741–1801	Naumann, Johann Gottlieb	11	Dresden, Padua
123	1743–1805	Boccherini, Luigi	1	Lucca
124	1743–1818	Gazzaniga, Giuseppe	8	Verona, Venice, Crema, Parma, Modena, Bergamo
125	1744–1812	Martinez, Marianne von	2	Vienna
126	1745–1816	Michl, Joseph Willibald	1	Mainz
127	1747–98	Alessandri, Felice	2	Rome, Padua
128	1747–1818	Kozeluch, Leopold	3	Prague, Vienna
129	1748–1812	Schuster, Joseph	4	Dresden, Venice
130	1748–1806	Seydelmann, Franz	3	Dresden
131	1749–1801	Cimarosa, Domenico	7	Venice, Milan, Naples
132	ca. 1750–1812	Calegari, Giuseppe	2	Padua, Florence

Composers Whose Birthdates Are Unknown (continued)

Ref. No.	Oratorio Dates	Composers' Names	No. of Ors.	Cities Where First Performed
133	1750–88	Prati, Alessio	1	St. Petersburg
134	1750–1825	Salieri, Antonio	4	Vienna
135	ca. 1750–ca. 1815	Stabingher, Mathias	1	Moscow
136	ca. 1752–1810	Bianchi, Francesco	4	Venice
137	1752–1813	Lima, Braz Francisco de	1	Lisbon
138	1752–1814	Reichardt, Johann Friedrich	1	Berlin
139	1752–1837	Zingarelli, Niccolò Antonio	8	Milan, Naples, Florence, Birmingham
140	ca. 1753–98	Giordani, Giuseppe (Giordaniello)	5	Naples, Bologna, Macerata, Ascoli, Lisbon, Dresden
141	1753–1817	Kospoth, O. C. E. von	2	Venice
142	1754–after 1820	Marinelli, Gaetano	2	Naples
143	1754–1822	Caruso [Carusio], Luigi	4	Bologna, Nocera, Perugia
144	1755–1826	Andreozzi, Gaetano	5	Rome, Jesi, Naples, Palermo
145	1755–1829	Vallaperti, Giuseppe	3	Leonessa
146	1756–91	Mozart, Wolfgang Amadeus	2	(for Padua, not performed), Vienna
147	1757–1828	Calegari, Antonio	3	Padua, Venice
148	1758–1819	Moreira, Antonio Leal	1	Lisbon
149	1759–1833	Silva Leite, Antonio da	1	Lisbon
150	1760?–65–ca. 1810	Gardi, Francesco	9	Venice
151	ca. 1760–1814	Tarchi, Angelo	2	Mantua, Florence
152	1762–1842	Nicolini, Giuseppe	7	Naples, Cesena, Venice
153	ca. 1763–1817	Guglielmi, Pietro Carlo	1	Naples
154	1763–1845	Mayr, Simon	10	Venice, Forlì, Florence, Bergamo, Naples
155	1764–1826	Federici, Vincenzo	1	Naples, Palermo
156	1765–1814	Himmel, Friedrich Heinrich	1	Berlin, Copenhagen
157	1766–1846	Weigl, Joseph	2	Vienna
158	1767–1845	Ruggi, Francesco	1	Naples
159	1767?–after 1845	Brunetti, Antonio	4	Bologna, Ascoli, Chieti
160	1769–1840	Bonfichi, Paolo	21	Rome
161	1771–1839	Paer, Ferdinando	3	Parma, Dresden

Composers Whose Birthdates Are Unknown (continued)

Ref. No.	Oratorio Dates	Composers' Names	No. of Ors.	Cities Where First Performed
162	1772–1807	Cartellieri, Casimir Antonio	1	Vienna
163	1773–1832	Generali, Pietro	1	Florence
164	1782–1847	Catugno, Francesco	1	Naples
165	1784–1841	Morlacchi, Francesco	4	Perugia, Dresden
166	1792–1868	Rossini, Gioacchino	1	Naples

PART 2: *Composers Whose Birthdates Are Unknown*

Ref. No.	Oratorio Dates	Composers' Names	No. of Ors.	Cities Where First Performed
167	1697–1727	Vinchioni, Cintio	9	Viterbo, Rome
168	1706–55	Negri, Antonio	6	Milan
169	1718–36	Berti, Domenico Antonio	11	Rome
170	1720–25	Mellini, Francesco	5	Messina
171	1723	Giordani, Domenico Antonio	1	Rome
172	1732	Hendler, Wolfgang	1	Würzburg
173	1736–56	Bisso, Matteo	5	Bologna, Genoa, Venice
174	1737–59	Wassmuth, Georg	4	Würzburg, Bamberg
175	1738	Pera, Girolamo	1	Brno
176	1738	Trapani, Luca	1	Palermo
177	1739–41	Conti, Nicola	3	Naples
178	1739–40	Statella, Giovanni	2	Palermo
179	1740	Pulejo, Antonio	1	Palermo
180	1742–50	Sbacchi, Guglielmo	2	Palermo
181	1745–63	Seaglias, Angiolo	5	Macerata, Pergola, Iesi, Foligno
182	1750–64	Magherini, Giuseppe Maria	2	Fermo, Rome
183	1751–85	Bergamo, Antonio	2	Venice, Rome
184	1752–54	Garzia, Francesco	2	Rome
185	1753–59	Lustrini, Bartolomeo	2	Rome
186	1753–66	Maraucci, Giacomo	4	Naples, Florence
187	1766–79	Luciani, Fortunato	2	Rome
188	1770	Parise, Gaetano	1	Naples
189	1772	Naselli, Diego	1	London
190	1774	Cornet, Enrico	1	Viterbo
191	1774–90	Valentini, Giovanni	7	Rome, Venice
192	1775	Santucci, Michele	1	Naples

Composers Whose Birthdates Are Unknown (continued)

Ref. No.	Oratorio Dates	Composers' Names	No. of Ors.	Cities Where First Performed
193	1777	Moreschini, Paolo	1	Macerata
194	1778	Ferrari, Litterio	1	Naples
195	1778	Silva, António da	1	Lisbon
196	1778–82	Morosini, Giuseppe	6	Venice
197	1779–1804	Gargiulo, Angelo	3	Fabriano, Spello
198	1781–86	Piticchio, Francesco	3	Venice, Vienna
199	1784–93	Baini, Lorenzo	3	Venice, Rome
200	1787	Calvi, Giovanni Battista	1	Milan, Narni
201	1791	Issola, Gaetano	1	Lisbon
202	1792	Scolari, Giacomo	1	Pesaro
203	1793	Cavi, Giovanni	1	Lisbon
204	1793–97	Conventati, Domenico	3	Macerata, Camerino
205	?ca. 1795	Motta, João Pedro de Almeida	?1	Lisbon
206	1797–98	Crescini, Camillo	2	Rome
207	1798	Longarini, Giovanni Battista	1	Lisbon
208	1802	Mango, Girolamo	1	Rome
209	1812	Angeletti, Nicola	1	Naples
210	1813	Confidati, Luigi	1	Rome
211	1817	Agolini, Lucca	1	Rome
212	1818	Moro, Antonio del	1	Lucca
213	1819	Lepri, Giovanni Giacomo	1	Rome

Index of Composers Listed in Appendix B

The index provides last names only, except where two composers have the same last name. Each name is followed by a composer reference number.

℘ Bibliography

This bibliography includes all the sources referred to by short title in the main body of the book and also a few that are not referred to but may prove useful to the reader who wishes to pursue further oratorio studies. Materials fully identified in the main body, mostly encyclopedia articles and primary sources, are omitted. An asterisk following a short title indicates music.

Aaron, "Tuckey"
    Aaron, Amy. "William Tuckey, a Choirmaster in Colonial New York." *The Musical Quarterly* 64 (1978): 79–97.
Abert, *Jommelli*
    Abert, Hermann. *Niccolo Jommelli als Opernkomponist*. Halle: Erhardt Kallas, 1908.
Alaleona, *Oratorio*
    Alaleona, Domenico. *Storia dell'oratorio musicale in Italia*. Milan: Fratelli Bocca, 1945. Reprint, with different pagination, of *Studi su la storia dell'oratorio musicale in Italia*. 1908.
Allegemeine musikalische Zeitung (Leipzig), 7 (1804–5), 12 (1809).
Anfossi, *Betulia**
    Anfossi, Pasquale. *La Betulia liberata* [facsimile]. The Italian Oratorio 1650–1800, edited with introductions by Joyce L. Johnson and Howard E. Smither, vol. 30. New York: Garland Publishing, forthcoming.
Anfossi, *Giuseppe**
    ———. *Giuseppe riconosciuto* [facsimile]. The Italian Oratorio 1650–1800, edited with introductions by Joyce L. Johnson and Howard E. Smither, vol. 29. New York: Garland Publishing, forthcoming.
Annibaldi, "Telemann"
    Annibaldi, Claudio. "L'ultimo oratorio di Telemann." *Nuova rivista musicale italiana* 3 (1969): 221–35.
Anthony, *French Baroque Music*
    Anthony, James R. *French Baroque Music from Beaujoyeulx to Rameau*. New York: W. W. Norton, 1974.
Arcari, *Metastasio*
    Arcari, Paolo. *L'arte poetica di Pietro Metastasio: Saggio critico*. Milan: Libreria Editrice Nazionale, 1902.
Arne, *Judith**
    Arne, Thomas Augustine. *Judith. An Oratorio. As it is Perform'd at the Theatre-Royal in Drury Lane*. London: I. Walsh, [1764].
Arne, "Judith"* (GB-T: 985)

————. "Judith. An Oratorio in Three Acts." [Shelfmark of GB-T: Ms. Tenbury 985; now housed in GB-Ob]. Music Manuscripts from the Great English Collections. Series 2: The Music Collection of St. Michael's College, Tenbury. Brighton, England: John Spiers, Harvester Press Microform Publications, n.d.

Arnold, "Conservatories"

Arnold, Denis. "Orphans and Ladies: The Venetian Conservatories (1680–1790)." Proceedings of the Royal Musical Association 89 (1962–63): 31–47.

Arnold, Oratorio in Venice

Arnold, Denis and Elsie. The Oratorio in Venice. Royal Musical Association Monographs, 2. London: The Royal Musical Association, 1986.

Bach, C. P. E., Auferstehung*

Bach, Carl Philipp Emanuel. Auferstehung und Himmelfahrt Jesu. Oratorium für 3 Solisten, gemischten Chor und Orchester. Wtq 240. Edited by Gábor Darvas. Budapest: Editio Musica; Zurich and New York: Eulenburg, 1974.

Bach, C. P. E., Israeliten*

————. Die Israeliten in der Wüste: Oratorium. Edited by Gábor Darvas, English text by Hans-Hubert Schönzeler. London, Zurich, Mainz, and New York: Eulenburg, 1971.

Bach, J. C. F., Auferweckung Lazarus*

Bach, Johann Christoph Friedrich. Die Auferweckung Lazarus (1773). Edited by Georg Schünemann, revised by Hans Joachim Moser. Denkmäler deutscher Tonkunst, ser. 1, vol. 56. Wiesbaden: Breitkopf & Härtel; Graz: Akademische Druck-U. Verlagsanstalt, 1959.

Bach, J. C. F., Kindheit Jesu*

————. Die Kindheit Jesu (1773). Edited by Georg Schünemann, revised by Hans Joachim Moser. Denkmäler deutscher Tonkunst, ser. 1, vol. 56. Wiesbaden: Breitkopf & Härtel; Graz: Akademische Druck-U. Verlagsanstalt, 1959.

Bach, J. E., Passionsoratorium*

Bach, Johann Ernst. Passionsoratorium ["O Seele, deren Sehnen."] Edited by Joseph Kromolicki, revised by Hans Joachim Moser. Denkmäler deutscher Tonkunst, ser. 1, vol. 48. Wiesbaden: Breitkopf & Härtel; Graz: Akademische Druck-U. Verlagsanstalt, 1959.

Baker, "Marcello"

Baker, Helen E. "The Oratorios of Benedetto Marcello (1686–1739) as a Reflection of His Musical Thought and Milieu." Ph.D. dissertation, Rutgers, The State University of New Jersey, 1982.

Beechey, "Chilcot"

Beechey, Gwilym. "Thomas Chilcot and His Music." Music and Letters 54 (1973): 179–96.

Beethoven, Christus*

Beethoven, Ludwig van. Christus am Oelberge. Oratorium. Op. 85. Ludwig van Beethoven's Werke. Vollständige kritisch durchgesehene überall berechtigte Ausgabe, ser. 19, no. 205. Leipzig: Breitkopf & Härtel, n.d. [1862–65].

Bertoni, David*

Bertoni, Ferdinando. David poenitens [facsimile]. The Italian Oratorio 1650–

1800, edited with introductions by Joyce L. Johnson and Howard E. Smither, vol. 25. New York: Garland Publishing, forthcoming.

Blankenburg, "Gotha"

Blankenburg, Walter. "Die Aufführungen von Passionen und Passionskantaten in der Schloßkirche auf dem Friedenstein zu Gotha zwischen 1699 und 1770." In *Festschrift Friedrich Blume zum 70. Geburtstag*, edited by Anna Amalie Abert and Wilhelm Pfannkuch, pp. 50–59. Kassel: Bärenreiter, 1963.

Blume, *Classic and Romantic*

Blume, Friedrich. *Classic and Romantic Music: A Comprehensive Survey.* Translated by M. D. Herter Norton. New York: W. W. Norton, 1970.

Blume, *Evangelische Kirchenmusik*

———. *Geschichte der Evangelischen Kirchenmusik.* Kassel: Bärenreiter, 1965.

Blume, *Protestant Church Music*

———, et al. *Protestant Church Music: A History.* New York: W. W. Norton, 1974.

Blumner, *Sing-Akademie*

Blumner, Martin. *Geschichte der Sing-Akademie zu Berlin: Eine Festgabe zur Säcularfeier am 24. Mai 1891.* Berlin: Horn & Raasch, 1891.

Bonno, *Isacco**

Bonno, Giuseppe. *Isacco figura del redentore* [facsimile]. The Italian Oratorio 1650–1800, edited with introductions by Joyce L. Johnson and Howard E. Smither, vol. 21. New York: Garland Publishing, forthcoming.

Boyd, "Stanley"

Boyd, Malcolm. "John Stanley and the Foundling Hospital." *Soundings* 5 (1975): 73–81.

Brandenburg, "Bonn"

Brandenburg, Sieghard. "Die Kurfürstliche Musikbibliothek in Bonn und ihre Bestände im 18. Jahrhundert." *Beethoven-Jahrbuch,* neue Folge, zweite Reihe, 7 (1971–72, pub. 1975): 7–47.

Brenet, *Concerts*

Bobillier, Marie [Brenet, Michel]. *Les concerts en France sous l'ancien régime.* Paris, 1900. Reprint. New York: Da Capo Press, 1970.

Brook, *Breitkopf*

Brook, Barry S., ed. *The Breitkopf Thematic Catalogue, 1762–87.* New York: Dover Publications, 1966.

Brown, *Dissertation*

Brown, John. *A Dissertation on the Rise, Union, and Power, the Progressions, Separations, and Corruptions, of Poetry and Music. To which is prefixed, The Cure of Saul. A Sacred Ode.* London: L. Davis and C. Reymers, 1763.

Brown, *Haydn's "The Creation"*

Brown, A. Peter. *Performing Haydn's "The Creation": Reconstructing the Earliest Renditions.* Bloomington: Indiana University Press, in press.

Brumana, "Perugia"

Brumana, Biancamaria. "Per una storia dell'oratorio musicale a Perugia nei secoli XVII e XVIII." *Esercizi: Arte, Musica, Spettacolo* 3 (1980, Istituto di Storia dell'Arte Medioevale e Moderna, Università degli Studi, Perugia): 97–167.

Burney, *Account*
  Burney, Charles. *An Account of the Musical Performances in Westminster-Abbey, and the Pantheon, May 26th, 27th, 29th; and June the 3rd, and 5th, 1784. In Commemoration of Handel.* 1785. Reprint. Amsterdam: Frits A. M. Knuf, 1964.
Burney, "Commemoration"
  ———. "Commemoration of Handel." In Burney, *Account.*
Burney, *France and Italy*
  ———. *The Present State of Music in France and Italy: or, The Journal of a Tour through those Countries undertaken to collect Materials for A General History of Music.* London: T. Becket and Co., 1771.
Bužga, "Osteroratorien"
  Bužga, Jaroslav. "Einige Quellen zur Geschichte der Osteroratorien in Prag und Brno (Brünn) und der Ostermelodramen aus Olomouc (Olmüz) im 18. Jahrhundert." In *De musica disputationes pragenses,* edited by Academia Verlag der Tschechoslowakischen Akademie der Wissenschaften Prag, 1:151–71. Kassel: Bärenreiter, 1972.
Cahn-Speyer, *Seydelmann*
  Cahn-Speyer, Rudolf. *Franz Seydelmann als dramatischer Komponist.* Inaugural-Dissertation . . . Universität München. Leipzig: Breitkopf & Härtel, 1909.
Caldara, *Joaz**
  Caldara, Antonio. *Joaz* [facsimile]. The Italian Oratorio 1650–1800, edited with introductions by Joyce L. Johnson and Howard E. Smither, vol. 12. New York: Garland Publishing, forthcoming.
Cannon, *Mattheson*
  Cannon, Beekman C. *Johann Mattheson: Spectator in Music.* Yale Studies in the History of Music, vol. 1. New Haven: Yale University Press, 1947.
Carlson, "Leopold Mozart"
  Carlson, David Moris. "The Vocal Music of Leopold Mozart (1719–1787): Authenticity, Chronology and Thematic Catalog." Ph.D. dissertation, University of Michigan, 1976.
Carreras, *Oratorio*
  Carreras y Bulbena, José Rafael. *El oratorio musical desde su origen hasta nuestros días.* Barcelona: Tipografía "L'Avenç," Ronda de la Universidad, 20, 1906.
Cauthen, "Jommelli"
  Cauthen, Paul. "The Oratorios of Niccolò Jommelli." M.A. thesis, University of North Carolina at Chapel Hill, 1982.
Chamblee, "Bach"
  Chamblee, James Monroe. "The Cantatas and Oratorios of Carl Philipp Emanuel Bach." 2 vols. Ph.D. dissertation, University of North Carolina at Chapel Hill, 1973.
Cistellini, "Neri"
  Cistellini, Antonio. "San Filippo Neri e la sua patria." *Rivista di storia della chiesa in Italia* 23 (1969): 54–119.
Conati, "Rossini"
  Conati, Marcello. "Between Past and Future: The Dramatic World of Rossini in *Mosè in Egitto* and *Moïse et Pharaon*." *19th Century Music* 4 (1980): 32–47.

Cone, *Musical Form*
  Cone, Edward T. *Musical Form and Musical Performance*. New York: W. W. Norton, 1968.
Coyer, *Voyages*
  Coyer, [Gabriel François]. *Voyages d'Italie et de Hollande*. 2 vols. Paris: Chez la Veuve Duchesne, 1775.
Cvetko, *Musique slovène*
  Cvetko, Dragotin. *Histoire de la musique slovène*. Maribor: Založba Obzorja, 1967.
Daval, *Musique en France*
  Daval, Pierre. *La musique en France au XVIIIe siècle*. Paris: Payot, 1961.
David and Mendel, *Bach Reader*
  David, Hans T., and Mendel, Arthur. *The Bach Reader: A Life of Johann Sebastian Bach in Letters and Documents*. Revised, with a supplement. New York: W. W. Norton, 1966.
Dean, *Oratorios*
  Dean, Winton. *Handel's Dramatic Oratorios and Masques*. London: Oxford University Press, 1959.
Degtiarev, *Minin**
  Degtiarev, Stepan Anikievich. *Minin i Pozharskii, ili Osvobozhdenie Moskvy: Oratoriia*. [Minin and Pozharskii, or The Liberation of Moscow.] Piano-vocal score edited by K. Chernov. Moscow: Petr Iurgenson, n. d. [1907?–8].
Dittersdorf, *Ester**.
  Ditters von Dittersdorf, Carl. *La liberatrice del popolo giudaico, ossia l'Ester* [facsimile]. The Italian Oratorio 1650–1800, edited with introductions by Joyce L. Johnson and Howard E. Smither, vol. 24. New York: Garland Publishing, forthcoming.
Dizionario biografico
  Dizionario biografico degli italiani. 26 vols. to date. Rome: Istituto della Enciclopedia italiana, 1960–.
Dörffel, *Festschrift*
  Dörffel, Alfred. *Festschrift zur hundertjährigen Jubelfeier des Einweihung des Concertsaales im Gewandhause zu Leipzig*. Vol. 1: *Geschichte der Gewandhausconcerte zu Leipzig*. Leipzig: [Breitkopf & Härtel], 1884. Vol. 2: *Statistik der Concerte im Saale des Gewandhauses zu Leipzig*. Leipzig: [Breitkopf & Härtel], 1881.
Downes, "Johann Christian Bach"
  Downes, Edward O. D. "The Operas of Johann Christian Bach as a Reflection of the Dominant Trends in Opera Seria 1750–1780." Ph.D. dissertation, Harvard University, 1958.
Dox, "Felsted"
  Dox, Thurston J. [Record jacket notes to recording:] Samuel Fested. *Jonah: An Oratorio*. The Catskill Choral Society, Thurston Dox, Conductor. Ocean, N.J.: Musical Heritage Society, MHS Stereo 4870L, recorded and issued in 1983.
Dubinski, "Berlin"
  Dubinski, Max. "Beiträge zur Musikgeschichte Berlins während des siebenjährigen Krieges." *Die Musik*, yr. 11/4, vol. 44 (1911–12): 137–42.
Eberlin, *Der blutschwitzende Jesus**
  Eberlin, Johann Ernst. *Oratorium, Der blutschwitzende Jesus, nebst Anhang:*

Stücke aus anderen Oratorien. Edited by Robert Haas. Denkmäler der Tonkunst in Österreich, vol. 55. Vienna: Universal-Edition; Leipzig: Breitkopf & Härtel, 1921.

Edelmann, "Haydns *Il ritorno di Tobia*"
Edelmann, Bernd. "Haydns *Il ritorno di Tobia* und der Wandel des 'Geschmacks' in Wien nach 1780." In *Joseph Haydn Tradition und Rezeption: Bericht über die Jahrestagung der Gesellschaft für Musikforschung Köln 1982*, pp. 189–207. Kölner Beiträge zur Musikforschung, edited by Klaus Wolfgang Niemöller, vol. 144. Regensburg: Gustav Bosse Verlag, 1985.

Eisler, *Atlas des Wiener Stadtbildes*
Eisler, Max, ed. *Historischer Atlas des Wiener Stadtbildes*. Arbeiten des Kunsthistorischen Instituts der Universität Wien (Lehrkanzel Strzygowski), Bd. 16. Vienna: Verlag der Deutschösterreichischen Staatsdruckerei, 1919.

Eisler, *Das barocke Wien*
———, ed. *Historischer Atlas der Wiener Ansichten: Das barocke Wien*. Arbeiten des I. Kunsthistorischen Instituts der Universität Wien (Lehrkanzel Strygowski), Bd. 33. Vienna and Leipzig: Erlach & Wiedling, 1925.

Eisler, *Das bürgerliche Wien*
———, ed. *Historischer Atlas der Wiener Stadtansichten: Das bürgerliche Wien, 1770–1860*. Arbeiten des I. Kunsthistorischen Instituts der Universität Wien. (Lehrkanzel Strzygowski), Bd. 38. Vienna: Druck und Verlag der Österreichischen, 1929.

Elkin, *Concert Rooms*
Elkin, Robert. *The Old Concert Rooms of London*. London: Edward Arnold, 1955.

Enciclopedia cattolica
Enciclopedia cattolica. 12 vols. Vatican City: Ente per l'Enclicopedia cattolica e per il libro cattolico, 1950.

Encyclopedia of Music in Canada. Edited by Helmut Kallmann, Gilles Potvin, and Kenneth Winters. Toronto: University of Toronto Press, 1981.

Engel, "Quellen"
Engel, Hans. "Die Quellen des klassischen Stiles." In *Report of the Eighth Congress, New York, 1961*, International Musicological Society, edited by Jan LaRue, 1:285–304. Kassel: Bärenreiter, 1961.

Engländer, *Naumann*
Engländer, Richard. *Johann Gottlieb Naumann als Opernkomponist (1741–1801). Mit neuen Beiträgen zur Musikgeschichte Dresdens und Stockholms*. Leipzig: Breitkopf & Härtel, 1922.

European Magazine and London Review (London), 5(March, 1784):165.

Feder, "Bemerkungen"
Feder, Georg. "Bemerkungen über die Ausbildung der klassischen Tonsprache in der Instrumentalmusik Haydns." In *Report of the Eighth Congress, New York, 1961*, International Musicological Society, edited by Jan LaRue, 1:305–13. Kassel: Bärenreiter, 1961.

Feder, "Decline and Restoration"
———. "Decline and Restoration," translated by Reinhard G. Pauly. In *Protestant Church Music: A History*, by Friedrich Blume et al., pp. 317–404. New York: W. W. Norton, 1974.

Feder, "Verfall und Restauration"

_____. "Verfall und Restauration." In *Geschichte der Evangelischen Kirchenmusik*, by Friedrich Blume, with the collaboration of Ludwig Finscher, Georg Feder, Adam Adrio, and Walter Blankenburg, pp. 215–69. 2d ed. Kassel: Bärenreiter, 1965.

Felsted, *Jonah**
  Felsted, Samuel. *Jonah: An Oratorio, Disposed for a Voice and Harpsichord.* London: Longman, Luckey & Broderip, for the author, 1775.

Feo, *Oratorium pro defunctis**
  Feo, Francesco. *Oratorium pro defunctis* [facsimile]. The Italian Oratorio 1650–1800, edited with introductions by Joyce L. Johnson and Howard E. Smither, vol. 17. New York: Garland Publishing, forthcoming.

Florimo, *Napoli*
  Florimo, Francesco. *La scuola musicale di Napoli e i suoi conservatori, con uno sguardo sulla storia della musica in Italia.* 4 vols. Naples: Vin. Morano, 1880–82.

Fonseca Benevides, *Theatro de S. Carlos*
  Fonseca Benevides, Francisco da. *O Real Theatro de S. Carlos de Lisboa desde sua fundacão em 1793 até á actualidate: Estudo historico.* Lisbon: Typographia Castro Irmão, [1883].

Foster, "Oratorio in Paris"
  Foster, Donald H. "The Oratorio in Paris in the 18th Century." *Acta musicologica* 47 (1975): 67–133.

Fürstenau, *Dresden*
  Fürstenau, Moritz. *Zur Geschichte der Musik und des Theaters am Hofe zu Dresden, nach archivalischen Quellen.* 2 vols. Dresden: Rudolf Kuntze, 1861–62.

Galuppi, *Adamo**
  Galuppi, Baldassare. *Adamo caduto* [facsimile]. The Italian Oratorio 1650–1800, edited with introductions by Joyce L. Johnson and Howard E. Smither, vol. 19. New York: Garland Publishing, forthcoming.

Gasbarri, *Oratorio fil.*
  Gasbarri, Carlo. *L'oratorio filippino (1552–1952).* Rome: Istituto di Studi Romani, 1957.

Gasbarri, *Spirito*
  _____. *Lo spirito dell'Oratorio di S. Filippo Neri.* Brescia: Morcelliana, 1949.

Gassmann, *Betulia**
  Gassmann, Florian. *La Betulia liberata* [facsimile]. The Italian Oratorio 1650–1800, edited with introductions by Joyce L. Johnson and Howard E. Smither, vol. 26. New York: Garland Publishing, forthcoming.

Gazeteer and New Daily Advertiser (London), 25 February 1766.

Geck, *Deutsche Oratorien*
  Geck, Martin. *Deutsche Oratorien 1800 bis 1840: Verzeichnis der Quellen und Aufführungen.* Quellen-Kataloge zur Musikgeschichte, ed. Richard Schall, vol. 4. Wilhelmshaven: Heinrichshofen's Verlag, 1971.

Gehmacher, "Gatti"
  Gehmacher, Monika. "Luigi Gatti: Sein Leben und seine Oratorien mit thematischem Katalog des Gesamtschaffens." Ph.D. dissertation, University of Vienna, 1959.

Godehart, "Telemanns *Messias*"

Godehart, Günther. "Telemanns *Messias.*" *Die Musikforschung,* 14 (1961): 139–55.

Goethe, *Italian Journey*

Goethe, Johann Wolfgang. *Italian Journey (1786–88).* Translated by W. H. Auden and Elizabeth Mayer. London: William Collins, Sons and Co., 1962.

Goethe, *Die italienische Reise*

———. *Die italienische Reise: Die Annalen.* Gedenkausgabe der Werke, Briefe und Gespräche. Edited by Ernest Beutler, vol. 11. Zurich: Artemis-Verlag, 1950.

Gossec, *La Nativité**

Gossec, François-Joseph. *La Nativité (The Nativity): Oratorio.* Vocal Score. New York: Alexander Broude, Inc., 1966.

Gossett, "Operas of Rossini"

Gossett, Philip. "The Operas of Rossini: Problems of Textual Criticism in Nineteenth-Century Opera." Ph.D. dissertation, Princeton University, 1970.

Gottron, *Mainz*

Gottron, Adam. *Mainzer Musikgeschichte von 1500 bis 1800.* Beiträge der Stadt Mainz, vol. 18. Mainz: Stadtbibliothek, 1959.

Gotwals, *Haydn*

Gotwals, Vernon. *Haydn: Two Contemporary Portraits.* A translation with introduction and notes of the *Biographische Notizen über Joseph Haydn* by G. A. Griesinger and the *Biographische Nachrichten von Joseph Haydn* by A. C. Dies. Madison: University of Wisconsin Press, 1968.

Graun, *Tod Jesu**

Graun, Carl Heinrich. *Der Tod Jesu.* Edited by Howard Serwer. Collegium musicum, Yale University, ser. 2, vol. 5. Madison: A-R Editions, 1975.

[Grosley], *Italy*

[Grosley de Troyes, Pierre Jean]. *New Observations on Italy and Its Inhabitants. Written in French by two Swedish Gentlemen.* Translated by Thomas Nugent. 2 vols. London: Printed for L. Davis and C. Reymers, Printers to the Royal Society, 1769.

Haas, "Eberlin"

Haas, Robert. "Eberlins Schuldramen und Oratorien." *Studien zur Musikwissenschaft* 8 (1921): 9–44.

Hadamowsky, *Barocktheater*

Hadamowsky, Franz. *Barocktheater am Wiener Kaiserhof, mit einem Spielplan (1625–1740).* Vienna: A. Sexl, 1955. Offprint from the *Jahrbuch der Gesellschaft für Wiener Theaterforschung 1951–52.*

Hanbury, *Church-Langton*

Hanbury, William. *The History of the Rise and Progress of the Charitable Foundations at Church-Langton: Together with the Different Deeds of Trust of that Establishment.* London: Printed for the Benefit of the Charity, 1767.

Hanslick, *Concertwesen*

Hanslick, Eduard. *Geschichte des Concertwesens in Wien.* Vienna: Wilhelm Braumüller, 1869.

Hardie, "Leo"

Hardie, Graham H. "Leonardo Leo (1694–1744) and His Comic Operas *Amor vuol sofferenza* and *Alidoro.*" Ph.D. dissertation, Cornell University, 1973.

Harich, "Inventare"
    Harich, Janos. "Inventare der Esterházy-Hofmusikkapelle in Eisenstadt." *The Haydn Yearbook* 9 (1975): 5–125.
Hase, "Bach"
    Hase, Hermann von. "Carl Philipp Emanuel Bach und Joh. Gottl. Im. Breitkopf." *Bach Jahrbuch* 8 (1911): 86–104.
Hasse, *Sant'Agostino**
    Hasse, Johann Adolph. *La conversione di Sant'Agostino: Oratorio.* Edited by Arnold Schering; revised by Hans Joachim Moser. Denkmäler deutscher Tonkunst, ser. 1, vol. 20. 1905. Wiesbaden: Breitkopf & Härtel, 1958.
Hasse, *Sant'Elena**
    _____. *Sant'Elena al Calvario* [facsimile]. The Italian Oratorio 1650–1800, edited with introductions by Joyce L. Johnson and Howard E. Smither, vol. 28. New York: Garland Publishing, forthcoming.
Haydn, *Creation**-E
    Haydn, Franz Joseph. *Die Schöpfung. Text nach Milton's "Verlorenem Paradies" von Lidley. Deutsch G. von Swieten. Oratorium. / The Creation. Words after Milton's "Paradise Lost" by Lidley. German by G. von Swieten. Oratorio.* [Miniature score.] London, Zurich, New York: Ernst Eulenburg, Edition Eulenburg [no. 955], [1925].
Haydn, *Creation**-M
    _____. *Die Schöpfung.* [Edited by Eusebius Mandyczewski.] Joseph Haydns Werke: Erste kritische durchgesehene Ausgabe, ser. 16, vol. 5. Leipzig, Berlin: Breitkopf & Härtel, [1924].
Haydn, *Creation**-P
    _____. *Die Schöpfung. Oratorium.* Klavierauszug. Leipzig: C. F. Peters [Edition Peters. J. H. Schöpf], n.d.
Haydn, *Seasons**-E
    _____. *Die Jahreszeiten. The Seasons. Les Saisons. Oratorium.* London, Zurich, Mainz, New York: Ernst Eulenburg, Edition Eulenburg, [no. 987], n.d.
Haydn, *Seasons**-M
    _____. *Die Jahreszeiten.* [Edited by Eusebius Mandyczewski.] Joseph Haydns Werke: Erste kritische durchgesehene Ausgabe, ser. 16, vol. 6–7. Leipzig, Berlin: Breitkopf & Härtel, [1922].
Haydn, *Tobia**
    _____. *Il ritorno di Tobia: Oratorio (1775/1784).* Edited by Ernst Fritz Schmid. Joseph Haydn Werke, ser. 1, vol. 1, pts. 1–2. Munich-Duisburg: G. Henle, 1963.
Hayes, *Anecdotes*
    Hayes, William. *Anecdotes of the Five Music-Meetings, on Account of the Charitable Foundations at Church-Langton: In Which Many Misrepresentations, and Gross Falsehoods Contained in a Book, Intitled, The History of the Above Foundations, are fully Detailed, and Confuted, upon Indubitable Evidence. . . .* Oxford: W. Jackson, 1768.
Hell, *Opernsinfonie*
    Hell, Helmut. *Die neapolitanische Opernsinfonie in der ersten Hälfte des 18. Jahrhunderts: N. Porpora, L. Vinci, G. B. Pergolesi, L. Leo, N. Jommelli.* Münchner Veröffentlichungen zur Musikgeschichte, vol. 19. Tutzing: Hans Schneider, 1971.

Hennerberg, "Haydns Oratorium"
    Hennerberg, Carl F. "Det först Uppförandet i Stockholm av Haydns
    Oratorium Skapelsen." *Svensk Tidskrift för Musikforskning* 3 (1921): 37–
    51.
[Henslowe], "Barthélémon"
    [Henslowe, Cecilia Maria]. "Memoir of the Late F. H. Barthélémon." In *Selections from the Oratorio of Jephthe in Masfa . . . by the Late F. H. Barthélémon*, pp. 5–10. London: Clementi, Colherd & Collard, 1827.
Herrmann, *Eybler*
    Herrmann, Hildegard. *Thematisches Verzeichnis der Werke von Joseph Eybler*. Musikwissenschaftliche Schriften, vol. 10. Munich-Salzburg: Emil Katzbichler, 1976.
Hicks, "Smith"
    Hicks, Anthony. "The Late Additions to Handel's Oratorios and the Role of the Younger Smith." In *Music in Eighteenth-Century England: Essays in Memory of Charles Cudworth*, edited by Christopher Hogwood and Richard Luckett, pp. 147–69. Cambridge: Cambridge University Press, 1983.
Hill, "Florence I"
    Hill, John Walter. "Oratory Music in Florence, I: *Recitar Cantando*, 1585–1685." *Acta musicologica* 51 (1979): 108–36.
Hill, "Florence II"
    ———. "Oratory Music in Florence, II: At San Firenze in the Seventeenth and Eighteenth Centuries." *Acta musicologica* 51 (1979): 246–67.
Hill, "Florence III"
    ———. "Oratory Music in Florence, III: The Confraternities from 1655 to 1785." *Acta musicologica*, in press.
Hill, "Life and Works"
    ———. "The Life and Works of Francesco Maria Veracini." 2 vols. Ph.D. dissertation, Harvard University, 1972.
Hill, "Veracini"
    ———. "Veracini in Italy." *Music and Letters* 56 (1975): 257–76.
Hiller, "*Messias*"
    Hiller, Johann Adam. *Nachricht von der Aufführing des Händelschen "Messias" zu Berlin, den 19. May 1786*. Berlin: Christian Sigismund Spener, [1786].
Holschneider, "Die *Judas Macchabäus* Bearbeitung"
    Holschneider, Andreas. "Die *Judas-Maccabäus* Bearbeitung in der Österreichischen Nationalbibliothek." *Mozart-Jahrbuch* (1960–61): 173–81.
Hörner, *Telemann*
    Hörner, Hans. *Gg. Ph. Telemanns Passionsmusiken: Ein Beitrag zur Geschichte der Passionsmusik in Hamburg*. Inaugural-Dissertation, University of Kiel. Borna-Leipzig: Universitätsverlag von Robert Noske, 1933.
Hughes, "Degtiarev"
    Hughes, Carol Bailey. 'The Origin of 'The First Russian Patriotic Oratorio': Stepan Anikievich Degtiarev's *Minin i Pozharskii* (1811)." Ph.D. dissertation, University of North Carolina at Chapel Hill, 1984.
Hunter, "Haydn's Aria Forms"
    Hunter, Mary. "Haydn's Aria Forms: A Study of the Arias in the Italian Op-

eras Written at Eszterháza, 1766–1783." Ph.D. dissertation, Cornell University, 1982.

Husk, *Account*

Husk, William Henry. *An Account of the Musical Celebrations on St. Cecilia's Day in the Sixteenth, Seventeenth, and Eighteenth Centuries*. . . . London: Bell and Daldy, 1857.

Isotta, "*Mosè*"

Isotta, Paolo. "*Mosè*." In *Guida all'opera*, edited by Gioacchino Lanza Tomasi, vol. 2, pp. 567–77. 2 vols. Milan: Mondatori, 1971.

Isotta, *Rossini*.

———, ed. *Gioacchino Rossini: Mosè, in Egitto, Azione tragico-sacra / Moïse et Pharaon, Opera en quatre actes / Mosè, Melodramma sacro in quattro atti*. Opera: Collana di guide musicali, directed by Alberto Basso, ser. 1, no. 4. Turin: Unione Tipografico-Editrice Torinese, 1974.

Israël, *Frankfurt*

Israël, Carl, comp. *Frankfurter Concert-Chronik von 1713–1780*. Frankfort on the Main: Verein für Geschichte und Altertumskunde, 1876.

John, *Homilius*

John, Hans. *Der Dresdner Kreuzkantor und Bach-Schüler Gottfried August Homilius: Ein Beitrag zur Musikgeschichte Dresdens im 18. Jahrhundert*. Tutzing: Hans Schneider, 1980.

Johnson, "Oratorio"

Johnson, Joyce L. "The Oratorio at Santa Maria in Vallicella in Rome, 1770–1800." 2 vols. Ph.D. dissertation, University of Chicago, 1983.

Jommelli, *Betulia**

Jommelli, Nicolò. *La Betulia liberata; La passione di Gesù Cristo* [facsimile]. The Italian Oratorio 1650–1800, edited with introductions by Joyce L. Johnson and Howard E. Smither, vol. 18. New York: Garland Publishing, forthcoming.

Jommelli, *Passione**

———. *La passione di Nostro Signore Giesù Cristo: oratorio. Musica del signor Jomelli, poesia del signor Metastasio*. London: Printed and Sold by R. Bremner, opposite Somerset House in the Strand, [n.d. 1765?–1770]

Jommelli, *Passione**(pv)

———. *La passione di Gesù Cristo*. Transcribed, harmonised, and reduced to vocal score by G. Francesco Malipiero. I classici della musica italiana, no. 15 (quaderni 63–66). Milan: Istituto Editoriale Italiano, 1919.

Kade, *Mecklenburg-Schwerin*

Kade, Otto. *Die Musikalien-Sammlung des Grossherzogl. Mecklenburg-Schweriner Fürstenhauses aus den letzten zwei Jahrhunderten*. 2 vols. Schwerin: Sandmeyerschen Hofbuchdruckerei, 1893

Kaestner, *Rolle*

Kaestner, Rudolf. *Johann Heinrich Rolle: Untersuchungen zu Leben und Werk*. Königsberger Studien zur Musikwissenschaft, vol. 13. Kassel: Bärenreiter, 1932.

Kallmann, *Canada*

Kallmann, Helmut. *A History of Music in Canada 1534–1914*. Toronto: University of Toronto Press, 1960.

Kamieński, *Hasse*

Kamieński, Lucian. *Die Oratorien von Johann Adolf Hasse*. Leipzig: Breitkopf & Härtel, 1912.

Kamper, *Hudební Praha*

Kamper, Otkar. *Hudební Praha v XVIII. věku*. [Musical Prague in the 18th Century] Prague: Melantrich, [1938]

Kellner, *Kremsmünster*

Kellner, Altman. *Musikgeschichte des Stiftes Kremsmünster, nach den Quellen dargestellt*. Kassel: Bärenreiter, 1956.

Kirkendale, U. *Caldara*

Kirkendale, Ursula. *Antonio Caldara: Sein Leben und seine venezianisch-römischen Oratorien*. Wiener Musikwissenschaftliche Beiträge, vol. 6. Graz: Hermann Böhlaus Nachf., 1966.

Klein, "Mozartiana"

Klein, Herbert. "Unbekante Mozartiana von 1766/67." *Mozart-Jahrbuch* (1957): 168–85.

Kleßmann, *Telemann*

Kleßmann, Eckart. *Telemann in Hamburg: 1721–1767*. Hamburg: Hoffmann und Campe, 1980.

Koch, *Lexikon*

Koch, Heinrich Christoph Koch. *Musikalisches Lexikon*. 2 vols., continuous pagination. 1802. Facsimile reprint in 1 vol. Hildesheim: Georg Olms, 1964.

König, *Tod Jesu*

König, Ingeborg. *Studien zum Libretto des "Tod Jesu" von Karl Wilhelm Ramler und Karl Heinrich Graun*. Schriften zur Musik, vol. 21. Munich: Musikverlag Emil Katzbichler, 1972.

Kramer, "Beethoven"

Kramer, Richard A. "Beethoven and Carl Heinrich Graun." In *Beethoven Studies*, edited by Alan Tyson, 1:18–44. 1 vol. to date. New York: W. W. Norton, 1973–.

Kraus, *Tod Jesu**

Kraus, Joseph Martin. *Der Tod Jesu*. Edited by Bertil H. van Boer, Jr. Recent Researches in the Music of the Classic Era. Madison, Wisconsin: A-R Editions, [forthcoming].

Krause, *Poesie*

[Krause, Christian Gottfried]. *Von der musikalischen Poesie*. 2d ed. Berlin: Johann Friedrich Voß, 1753. Facsimile reprint. Leipzig: Zentralantiquariat der Deutschen Demokratischen Republik, 1973.

Laland, *Voyage*

Le Français De Lalande, Joseph Jérôme. *Voyage d'un françois en Italie, fait dans les années 1765 & 1766*. 8 vols. Paris: Desaint, 1769.

Landon, *Haydn*

Landon, H. C. Robbins. *Haydn: Chronicle and Works*. 5 vols. Bloomington: Indiana University Press, 1976–80.

LaRue, Review of Rosen, *Sonata Forms*

LaRue, Jan. Review of Rosen, *Sonata Forms*. In *Journal of the American Musicological Society* 34 (1981): 557–66.

Lauschmann, "Pražské oratorium"

Lauschman, Josef Jaromir. "Pražské oratorium 18. století." ["Das Prager

Oratorium im 18. Jahrhundert."] Ph.D. dissertation, University of Prague, 1939.

Leo, *Abel**-F

Leo, Leonardo. *La morte d'Abel* [facsimile]. The Italian Oratorio 1650–1800, edited with introductions by Joyce L. Johnson and Howard E. Smither, vol. 16. New York: Garland Publishing, forthcoming.

Leo, *Abel**-P1

_____. *La morte di Abel. Oratorio in due parti per soli, coro e orchestra.* Poesia di Pietro Metastasio. Elaborazione di Giuseppe Piccioli. Milan: Carisch S. p. A., 1959.

Leo, *Abel**-P2

_____. *La morte di Abel. Oratorio in due parti per soli, coro e orchestra.* Poesia di Pietro Metastasio. Elaborazione di Giuseppe Piccioli. Riduzione per Canto e Pianoforte. Milan: Carisch S. p. A., 1959.

Le Sueur, *Essai* (*Noël*, 1786)

Le Sueur, Jean-François. *Essai de musique sacrée ou musique motivée et méthodique pour la fête de Noël.* . . . Paris: Chez la veuve Hérissant, 1786.

Le Sueur, *Exposé* (*Assomption*)

_____. *Exposé d'une musique une, imitative et particulière à chaque solemnité . . . la fête de l'Assomption.* . . . Paris: Chez la veuve Hérissant, 1787.

Le Sueur, *Exposé* (*Noël*, 1787)

_____. *Exposé d'une musique une, imitative et particulière à chaque solemnité . . . la fête de Noël.* Paris: Chez la veuve Hérissant, 1787.

Le Sueur, *Exposé* (*Pentecôte*)

_____. *Exposé d'une musique une, imitative et propre à chaque solemnité . . . la Pentecôte.* . . . Paris: Chez la veuve Hérissant, 1787.

Le Sueur, *Suite de l'essai* (*Pâque*)

_____. *Suite de l'essai sur la musique sacrée et imitative . . . la fête de Pâque.* . . . Paris: Chez la veuve Hérissant, 1787.

Le Sueur, *Ruth**

_____. *Ruth et Noëmi, oratorio historique à grands choeurs, suivi de Ruth et Booz, autre oratorio historique et prophétique à grands choeurs, tiré du Livre de Ruth, il qui est le complément du premier.* 8ème livraison . . . des Oeuvres religieuses de M. Le Sueur. Paris: J. Frey, [1835].

Levarie, "Closing Numbers of *Die Schöpfung*"

Levarie, Siegmund. "The Closing Numbers of *Die Schöpfung*," in *Studies in Eighteenth-Century Music*, edited by H. C. Robbins Landon in collaboration with Roger E. Chapman, pp. 315–22. New York: Oxford University Press, 1970.

Lichtenthal, *Dizionario*

Lichtenthal, Pietro. *Dizionario e bibliografia della musica.* 4 vols. Milan: Antonio Fontana, 1826.

Liepe, "Empfindsame Dichtung"

Liepe, Wolfgang. "Empfindsame Dichtung." In *Reallexikon der deutschen Literaturgeschichte*, 2d ed., edited by Werner Kohlschmidt, et al., 1:343–45. Berlin: Walter de Gruyter, 1958.

Loewenthal, *Berlin*

Loewenthal, Siegbert. *Die Musikübende Gesellschaft zu Berlin und die*

Mitglieder Joh. Philipp Sack, Fr. Wilh. Riedt und Joh. Gabr. Seyffarth. Inaugural-Dissertation, Universität Basel. Bern: Polygraphischen Gesellschaft
Laupen, 1928.

London Stage

The London Stage 1660–1800: A Calendar of Plays, Entertainments &
Afterpieces Together with Casts, Box-Receipts and Contemporary Com-
ment. Edited with critical introductions by William Van Lenner (pt. 1:
1660–1700); Emmett L. Avery (pt. 2, vols. 1–2: 1700–1729); Arthur H.
Scouten (pt. 3, vols. 1–2: 1729–47); George Winchester Stone, Jr. (pt. 4,
vols. 1–3: 1747–76); Charles Beecher Hogan (pt. 5, vols. 1–3: 1776–
1800). 11 vols. Carbondale, Ill.: Southern Illinois University Press, 1960–
68.

London Stage Index

Index to: The London Stage 1660–1800. Compiled, with an introduction by
Ben Ross Schneider, Jr. Foreword by George Winchester Stone, Jr.
Carbondale and Edwardsville, Ill.: Southern Illinois University Press, 1979.

Lott, "Tod Jesu"

Lott, Walter. "Die beiden Uraffführungen des *Tod Jesu* im März 1755."
Monatsschrift für Gottesdienst und kirchliche Kunst 29 (1925): 123–27.

Lumbroso and Martini, *Confraternite romane*

Lumbroso, Matizia Maroni, and Martini, Antonio. *Le confraternite romane*
nelle loro chiese. Roma: Fondazione Marco Besso, 1963.

Lysons, *Three Choirs*

Lysons, Daniel, et al. *Origin and Progress of the Meeting of the Three Choirs*
of Gloucester, Worcester & Hereford, and of the Charity Connected with
It. Gloucester: Chance and Bland, 1895.

McClymonds, *Jommelli*

McClymonds, Marita. *Niccolò Jommelli: The Last Years, 1769–1774.* Studies
in Musicology, no. 23. Ann Arbor: UMI Research Press, 1980.

McCredie, "Smith"

McCredie, "John Christopher Smith as a Dramatic Composer." *Music and*
Letters 45 (1964): 22–38.

McGee, "Halifax"

McGee, Timothy J. "Music in Halifax, 1749–1799." *Dalhousie Review* 49
(1969): 377–87.

Mackerness, *Social History*

Mackerness, Eric David. *A Social History of English Music.* London:
Routledge and Kegan Paul, 1964.

McVeigh, "Violinist"

McVeigh, Simon W. "The Violinist in London's Concert Life, 1750–1784:
Felice Giardini and His Contemporaries." D. Phil. dissertation, Oxford
University, 1980.

[Maddison], *Examination*

[Maddison, Robert]. *An Examination of the Oratorios Which Have Been Per-*
formed This Season at Covent-Garden Theatre. London: G. Kearsly, R. Davis, J. Walter, 1763.

Maertens, "Kapitänsmusiken" (1966)

Maertens, Willi. "Georg Philipp Telemanns Hamburger 'Kapitänsmusiken.'"
In *Festschrift für Walter Wiora zum 30 Dezember 1966*, edited by Ludwig

Finscher and Christoph-Hellmut Mahling, pp. 335–41. Kassel: Bärenreiter, 1967.

Maertens, "Kapitänsmusiken" (1975)
_____. "Georg Philipp Telemans Hamburger Kapitänsmusiken." 2 vols. Ph.D. dissertation, University of Halle, 1975.

Magazin der Musik. Edited by Carl Friedrich Cramer. 2 vols. Hamburg: In der musikalischen Niederlage, 1783–86. Reprint, 2 vols. in 4 vols. Hildesheim: Georg Olms, 1971.

Mann, "Smith"
Mann, Alfred. "Handel's Successor: Notes On John Christopher Smith the Younger." In *Music in Eighteenth-Century England: Essays in Memory of Charles Cudworth,* edited by Christopher Hogwood and Richard Luckett, pp. 135–45. Cambridge: Cambridge University Press, 1983.

Marcello, *Joaz**
Marcello, Benedetto, *Joaz* [facsimile]. The Italian Oratorio 1650–1800, edited with introductions by Joyce L. Johnson and Howard E. Smither, vol. 13. New York: Garland Publishing, forthcoming.

Marciano, *Oratorio*
Marciano, Giovanni. *Memori historiche della Congregatione dell'Oratorio.* 5 vols. Naples: De Bonis, Stampatore Arcivescovale, 1693–1702.

Martin, *Salzburgs Fürsten*
Martin, Franz. *Salzburgs Fürsten in der Barockzeit, 1587 bis 1812.* Salzburg: Bergland-Buch, 1949.

Massachusetts Centinel (Boston), 14, 21, 27, 28 October; 25 November, 2 December 1789.

Mattei, "Filosofia-Riforma"
Mattei, Saverio. "La filosofia della musica o sia La riforma del teatro. Dissertazione." In *Opere del signor abate Pietro Metastasio, con dissertazioni, e osservazioni,* 3:iii–xlviii. 5 vols. Nice: Società Tipografica, 1883–85.

Mattei, "Filosofia-Salmi"
_____. "La filosofia della musica, o sia La musica de' Salmi." In *I Salmi tradotti dall'ebraico originale, ed adatti al gusto della poesia italiana,* 6:188–221. 9 vols. Padua: Stamperia del Seminario, 1780.

Menke, *Telemann*
Menke, Werner. *Das Vokalwerk Georg Philipp Telemann's: Überlieferung und Zeitfolge.* Erlanger Beiträge zur Musikwissenschaft, vol. 3. Kassel: Bärenreiter, 1942.

Mennicke, *Hasse und die Brüder Graun*
Mennicke, Carl. *Hasse und die Brüder Graun als Symphoniker: Nebst Biographien und thematischen Katalogen.* Leipzig: Breitkopf & Härtel, 1906.

Mercure de France (Paris), January, March, 1775.

Messiter, *Trinity Church*
Messiter, Arthur Henry. *A History of the Choir and Music of Trinity Church, New York, from its Organization, to the Year 1897.* New York: Edwin S. Gorham, 1906.

Metastasio, *Opere*
Metastasio, Pietro. *Tutte le opere.* Edited by Bruno Brunelli. 5 vols. Milan:

Arnoldo Mondatori, 1943–54.

Metford, *Dictionary*

Metford, J. C. J. *Dictionary of Christian Lore and Legend.* London: Thames and Hudson, 1983.

Meyer, *Mecklenburg-Schwerin*

Meyer, Clemens. *Geschichte der Mecklenburg-Schweriner Hofkapelle.* Schwerin: Verlag von Ludwig Davids, 1913.

Meyer-Baer, "Conservatories"

Meyer-Baer, Kathi. "Communications: [The Conservatories of Venice]." *Journal of the American Musicological Society* 24 (1971): 139–40.

MGG

Die Musik in Geschichte und Gegenwart. Edited by Friedrich Blume. 16 vols. Kassel: Bärenreiter, 1949–79.

Miesner, *Bach*

Miesner, Heinrich. *Philipp Emanuel Bach in Hamburg: Beiträge zu seiner Biographie und zur Musikgeschichte seiner Zeit.* Leipzig: Breitkopf & Härtel, [1929].

Millner, *Hasse*

Millner, Fredrick L. *The Operas of Johann Adolf Hasse.* Studies in Musicology, no. 2. Ann Arbor: UMI Research Press, 1976.

Mongrédien, *Catalogue*

Mongrédien, Jean. *Catalogue thématique de l'oeuvre complète du compositeur Jean-François Le Sueur (1760–1837).* Thematic Catalogue Series, no. 7. New York: Pendragon Press, 1980.

Mongrédien, *Le Sueur*

————. *Jean-François Le Sueur: Contribution à l'étude d'un demi-siècle de musique française (1780–1830).* 2 vols. Bern, Frankfurt, Las Vegas: Peter Lang, 1980.

Mooser, *Annales*

Mooser, R. Aloys. *Annales de la musique et des musiciens en Russie au XVIIIe siècle.* 3 vols. Geneva: Editions du Mont-Blanc, [1948–51].

Mooser, *Opéras*

————. *Opéras, intermezzos, ballets, cantates, oratorios joués en Russie durant le XVIIIe siècle, avec l'indication des oeuvres de compositeurs russes parue en Occident à la même époque: Essai d'un répertoire alphabétique e chronologique.* 3d ed. Basel: Bärenreiter, 1964.

Morini, *La Pergola*

Morini, Ugo. *La R. Accademia degli Immobili ed il suo teatro "La Pergola" (1649–1925): Cronistoria compilata per incarico del Conte Bali Alberto Della Gherardesca, Presidente dell'Accademia.* Pisa: Ferdinando Simoncini, 1926.

Morning Chronicle and London Advertiser (London), 7 March 1778.

Mörner, "Haydniana"

Mörner, C.-G. Stellan. "Haydniana aus Schweden um 1800." *Haydn-Studien* 2 (1969): 1–33.

Mozart Briefe

Mozart Briefe und Aufzeichnungen: Gesamtausgabe. Edited by Wilhelm A. Bauer, Otto Erich Deutsch, and Joseph Heinz Eibl. 7 vols. Kassel: Bärenreiter, 1962–75.

Mozart, L., *Ausgewählte Werke**

Mozart, Leopold. *Ausgewählte Werke*. Edited by Max Seiffert. In Denkmäler deutscher Tonkunst, ser. 2: Denkmäler der Tonkunst in Bayern, 9/2. Leipzig: Breitkopf & Härtel, 1908.

Mozart, W. A., *Betulia liberata**
Mozart, Wolfgang Amadeus. *Betulia liberata*. Edited by Luigi Ferdinando Tagliavini. In *Wolfgang Amadeus Mozart, neue Ausgabe sämtlicher Werke*. Serie 1, Werkgruppe 4, Band 2. Kassel: Bärenreiter, 1960.

Mozart, W. A., *Davidde penitente**
———. *Davidde penitente: Oratorium*. In *Wolfgang Amadeus Mozart's Werke: Kritisch durchgesehene Gesammtausgabe*. Serie 4: Cantaten und Oratorien; Zweite Abtheilung: Oratorien, no. 5. Leipzig: Breitkopf & Härtel, 1882.

Mozart, W. A., *Die Schuldigkeit**
———. *Die Schuldigkeit des ersten Gebots*. Edited by Franz Giegling. In *Wolfgang Amadeus Mozart, Neue Ausgabe sämtlicher Werke*. Serie 1, Werkgruppe 4, Band 2. Kassel: Bärenreiter, 1958.

Mozart, W. A., *Die Schuldigkeit*(KB)
———. *Die Schuldigkeit des ersten Gebots. Kritischer Bericht*. Edited by Franz Giegling. In *Wolfgang Amadeus Mozart, Neue Ausgabe sämtlicher Werke*. Serie 1, Werkgruppe 4, Band 2. Kassel: Bärenreiter, 1958.

Münster, "Max Emanuel"
Münster, Robert. "Die Musik am Hofe Max Emanuels." In *Kurfürst Max Emanuel: Bayern und Europa um 1700*, vol. 1, *Zur Geschichte und Kunstgeschichte der Max-Emanuel-Zeit*, edited by Hubert Glaser, pp. 295–316. Munich: Hirmer, 1976.

Münster, "München"
———. "Das kurfürstliche München." In *Musik in Bayern*, edited by Robert Münster and Hans Schmidt, pp. 91–206. 2 vols. Tutzing: Schneider, 1972.

Münster, "Torri"
———. "Neu aufgefundene Opern, Oratorien und szenische Kantaten von Pietro Torri." *Musik in Bayern* 13 (1976): 49–58.

Musikalischer Almanach
Musikalischer Almanach für Deutschland auf das Jahr 1789, edited by Johann Nikolaus Forkel. Leipzig: Im Schwickertschen Verlage, [1789].

Musikalisches Kunstmagazin. Edited by Johann Friedrich Reichardt. 2 vols. Berlin: Im Verlage des Verfassers, 1782, 1791. Reprint, 2 vols. in 1 vol. Hildesheim: Georg Olms, 1969.

Myers, *Anna Seward*
Myers, Robert Manson. *Anna Seward: An Eighteenth-Century Handelian*. Williamsburg, Va.: The Manson Park Press, 1947.

Myers, "Fifty Sermons"
———. "Fifty Sermons on Handel's *Messiah*." *The Harvard Theological Review* 39 (1946): 217–41.

Myers, *Handel's "Messiah"*
———. *Handel's "Messiah": A Touchstone of Taste*. New York: Macmillan, 1948.

Mysliveček, *Passione**
Mysliveček, Josef. *La passione* [facsimile]. The Italian Oratorio 1650–1800, edited with introductions by Joyce L. Johnson and Howard E. Smither, vol. 23. New York: Garland Publishing, forthcoming.

Nauenburg, "Aphorismen"
Nauenburg, Gustav. "Aphorismen über das religiöse Drama, insofern es für die Musik bestimmt ist." *Caecilia: Eine Zeitschrift für die musikalische Welt* 14 (1832): 231–46.

Naumann, *Passione**
Naumann, Johann Gottlieb. *La passione di Gesù Cristo* [facsimile]. The Italian Oratorio 1650–1800, edited with introductions by Joyce L. Johnson and Howard E. Smither, vol. 27. New York: Garland Publishing, forthcoming.

New Catholic Encyclopedia. 15 vols. New York: McGraw-Hill, 1967.

New Grove
The New Grove Dictionary of Music and Musicians. Edited by Stanley Sadie. 20 vols. London: Macmillan Publishers Ltd., 1980.

New York Journal (New York), 4 January 1770, 11 January 1770.

Newman, *Sonata in the Classic Era*
Newman, William S. *The Sonata in the Classic Era.* 3d ed. New York: W. W. Norton, 1983.

Olleson, "Haydn's *Creation*"
Olleson, Edward. "The Origin and Libretto of Haydn's *Creation*." *The Haydn Yearbook* 4 (1969): 148–67.

Oschmann, "Zelenka"
Oschmann, Susanne. "Die Oratorien von Jan Dismas Zelenka." Ph.D. dissertation, University of Cologne, 1984.

Ozolins, "Pasquini"
Ozolins, "The Oratorios of Bernardo Pasquini." Ph.D. dissertation, University of California at Los Angeles, 1983.

Paisiello, *Passione**
Paisiello, Giovanni. *La passione di Gesù Cristo* [facsimile]. The Italian Oratorio 1650–1800, edited with introductions by Joyce L. Johnson and Howard E. Smither, vol. 31. New York: Garland Publishing, forthcoming.

Pasquetti, *Oratorio*
Pasquetti, Guido. *L'oratorio musicale in Italia.* 2d ed. Florence: Successori Le Monnier, 1914.

Pastore, *Leo*
Pastore, Giuseppe A. *Leonardo Leo.* Galatina: Editore Pajano, 1957.

Pedrell, *Càtalech*
Pedrell, Felip. *Càtalech de la biblioteca musical de la Diputació de Barcelona.* 2 vols. Barcelona: Palau de la Diputació, 1908–9.

Peiser, *Hiller*
Peiser, Karl. *Johann Adam Hiller: Ein Beitrag zur Musikgeschichte des 18. Jahrhunderts.* Leipzig: Hug & Co., 1894.

Pennsylvania Packet, and Daily Advertiser (Philadelphia), 30 May 1786.

Petzoldt, *Telemann*
Petzoldt, Richard. *Georg Philipp Telemann.* Translated by Horace Fitzpatrick. New York: Oxford University Press, 1974.

Pierre, *Concert spirituel*
Pierre, Constant. *Histoire du Concert spirituel, 1725–1790.* Publications de la Société française de musicologie, ser. 3, vol. 3. Paris: Société français de musicologie, Heugel et Cie., 1975.

Pohl, *Tonkünstler-Societät*
  Pohl, Carl Ferdinand. *Denkschrift aus Anlass des hundertjährigen Bestehens der Tonkünstler-Societät im Jahr 1862 reorganisiert als "Haydn," Witwen- und Waisen- Versorgungs-Verein der Tonkünstler in Wien.* Auf Grundlage der Societäts-Acten bearbeitet. Vienna: Selbstverlag des "Haydn" (Stadt, Schottenhof), in commission bei Carl Gerold's Sohn, 1871.
Porpora, *Nascita di Gesù**
  Porpora, Nicola. *Oratorio per la nascita di Gesù Cristo* [facsimile]. The Italian Oratorio 1650–1800, edited with introductions by Joyce L. Johnson and Howard E. Smither, vol. 20. New York: Garland Publishing, forthcoming.
Poštolka, "Strahow"
  Poštolka, Milan. "Libretti der Musiksammlung Strahow." *Miscellanea musicologica* 25–26 (1973): 79–97.
Preußner, *Bürgerliche Musikkultur*
  Preußner, Eberhard. *Die bürgerliche Musikkultur: Ein Beitrag zur deutschen Musikgeschichte des 18. Jahrhunderts.* 2d ed. Kassel: Bärenreiter, 1950.
Pritchard, "Musical Festival"
  Pritchard, Brian W. "The Musical Festival and the Choral Society in England in the Eighteenth and Nineteenth Centuries: A Social History." Ph.D. dissertation, University of Birmingham, England, 1968.
Pritchard and Reid, "Festival Programmes"
  Pritchard, Brian; and Reid, Douglas. "Some Festival Programmes of the Eighteenth and Nineteenth Centuries." *R. M. A. Research Chronicle* 5 (1967): 51–79 ("1. Salisbury and Winchester"); 6 (1966): 3–23 ("2. Cambridge and Oxford" with addenda to "1. Salisbury and Winchester," communicated by Arthur D. Walker); 7 (1967): 1–27 ("3. Liverpool and Manchester" with addenda to "2. Cambridge and Oxford," communicated by Gwilym E. Beechey); 8 (1970): 1–33 ("4. Birmingham, Derby, Newcastle upon Tyne and York" with addenda to "1. Salisbury and Winchester," communicated by Betty Mathews).
Processo
  Il primo processo per San Filippo Neri nel codice vaticano latino 3798 e in altri esemplari dell'Archivio dell'Oratorio di Roma. Edited by Giovanni Incisa della Rocchetta, Vian Nello, and Carlo Gasbarri. 4 vols. Studi e testi, vols. 191, 196, 205, and 224. Vatican City: Biblioteca Apostolica Vaticana, 1957–63.
Prophet, *Hanbury*
  Prophet, John. *Church Langton and William Hanbury.* Wymondham: Sycamore Press, 1982.
Public Advertiser (London), 27 February 1773.
Quadrio, *Poesia*
  Quadrio, Francesco Saverio. *Della storia e della ragione d'ogni poesia.* 5 vols. Bologna and Milan: Pisarri, F. Agnelli, A. Agnelli, 1739–1752.
Radiciotti, *Rossini*
  Radiciotti, Giuseppe. *Gioacchino Rossini: Vita documentata, opere ed influenza su l'arte.* 3 vols. Tivoli: Arti Grafiche Majella di Aldo Chieca, 1927–29.
Raguenet, *Comparison*

Raguenet, François. *A Comparison between the French and Italian Musick and Operas.* [Translated by J. E. Galliard?] 1709. Reprint. London: Gregg, 1968.

Rainer, "Adlgasser"
Rainer, Werner. "Verzeichnis der Werke A. C. Adlgassers." *Mozart-Jahrbuch* (1962–63): 280–91.

Ramler, *Kantaten*
Ramler, Karl Wilhelm. *Geistliche Kantaten.* Berlin: Bey Ch. Fr. Post, 1760.

Ratner, *Classic Music*
Ratner, Leonard G. *Classic Music: Expression, Form, and Style.* New York: Schirmer Books, 1980.

Raugel, *Oratorio*
Raugel, Félix. *L'oratorio. Formes, écoles et oeuvres musicales.* Paris: Larousse, 1948.

Reimer, "Oratorium"
Reimer, Erich. "Oratorium" (1972). In *Handwörterbuch der musikalischen Terminologie,* edited by Hans Heinrich Eggebrecht. Wiesbaden: Franz Steiner Verlag, [1972–].

Reutter, *Betulia*
Reutter, Georg von. *La Betulia liberata* [facsimile]. The Italian Oratorio 1650–1800, edited with introductions by Joyce L. Johnson and Howard E. Smither, vol. 14. New York: Garland Publishing, forthcoming.

Rhea, "Telemann"
Rhea, Claude H., Jr. "The Sacred Oratorios of Georg Philipp Telemann." 2 vols. Ed.D. dissertation, Florida State University, 1958.

Ricci des Ferres-Cancani, *Morlacchi*
Ricci des Ferres-Cancani, Gabriella. *Francesco Morlacchi (1784–1841): Un maestro italiano alla corte di Sassonia.* "Historiae musicae cultores" biblioteca, no. 11. Florence: Leo S. Olschki, 1958.

Riedel, "Göttweig"
Riedel, Friedrich W. "Die Libretto-Sammlung in Benediktinerstift Göttweig." *Fontes artis musicae* 1 (1966): 105–11.

Riedel, "Krems"
———. "Beiträge zur Geschichte der Musikpflege an der Stadtpfarrkirche St. Veit zu Krems." In *950 Jahre Pfarre Krems,* edited by Farry Kühnel, pp. 300–323. Krems an der Donau: Pfarre Krems a. d. Donau, 1964.

Riedel-Martiny, "Haydns Oratorien"
Riedel-Martiny, Anke. "Das Verhältnis von Text und Musik in Haydns Oratorien." *Haydn-Studien* 1 (1967): 205–40.

Rieß, "Schulz' Leben"
Rieß, Otto. "Johann Abraham Peter Schulz' Leben." *Sammelbände der internationalen Musikgesellschaft* 15 (1913–14): 169–270.

Rolle, *Lazarus**
Rolle, Johann Heinrich. *Lazarus, oder die Feyer der Auferstehung, ein musikalisches Drama, in Musik gesetzt, und als ein Auszug zum Singen beym Klaviere herausgegeben von. . . .* Leipzig: Johann Gottlob Immanuel Breitkopf, 1779.

Rosen, *Classical Style*
Rosen, Charles. *The Classical Style: Haydn, Mozart, Beethoven.* New York: W. W. Norton, 1972.

Rosen, *Sonata Forms*
———. *Sonata Forms*. New York: W. W. Norton, 1980.
Rossini, *Mosè**
Rossini, Gioacchino. *Mosè in Egitto: Azione tragico-sacra*. Facsimile edition
of Rossini's original autograph manuscript, edited with an introduction by
Philip Gossett. Early Romantic Opera. 2 vols. New York: Garland Publish-
ing, Inc., 1979.
Ruhnke, "Telemann im Schatten von Bach?"
Runke, Martin. "Telemann im Schatten von Bach?" In *Hans Albrecht im
Memoriam*, edited by Wilfried Brennecke and Hans Haase, pp. 143–52.
Kassel: Bärenreiter, 1962.
Sacchini, *Esther**
Sacchini, Antonio. *Esther* [facsimile]. The Italian Oratorio 1650–1800, edited
with introductions by Joyce L. Johnson and Howard E. Smither, vol. 22.
New York: Garland Publishing, forthcoming.
Sadie, "Concert Life"
Sadie, Stanley. "Concert Life in Eighteenth Century England." *Proceedings of
the Royal Musical Association* 85 (1958–59): 17–30.
Sartori, "Catalogo"
[Sartori, Claudio]. *Primo tentativo di catalogo unico dei libretti italiani a
stampa fino a 1800.* [Photocopy of card catalogue.] Milan: Ufficio Ricerca
Fondi Musicali, n.d.
Sauder, *Empfindsamkeit*
Sauder, Gerhard. *Empfindsamkeit*. Vol. 1: *Voraussetzungen und Elemente.* 1
vol. to date. Stuttgart: J. B. Metzler, 1974.
Scarlatti, *Oratorii**
Scarlatti, Alessandro. *Gli oratorii.* 5 vols. to date. Rome: De Santis, 1964–.
Schenker, "Chaos"
Schenker, Heinrich. "Haydn: Die Schöpfung. Die Vorstellung des Chaos."
Das Meisterwerk in der Musik: Ein Jahrbuch 2 (1926): 161–70 and
Anhang XIII [analytic graph].
Schering, "Beiträge"
Schering, Arnold. "Neue Beiträge zur Geschichte des italienischen Oratoriums
im 17. Jahrhundert." *Sammelbände der internazionalen Musikgesellschaft* 8
(1906–7): 43–70.
Schering, *Leipzig*
———. *Musikgeschichte Leipzigs*, vol. 3: *Johann Sebastian Bach und das
Musikleben Leipzigs im 18. Jahrhundert.* Leipzig: Fr. Kistner & C. F. W.
Siegel, 1941.
Schering, *Oratorium*
———. *Geschichte des Oratoriums.* Kleine Handbücher der Musikgeschichte
nach Gattungen, vol. 3. 1911. Reprint. Hildesheim: Georg Olms, 1966.
Schmid, "Tobia"
Schmid, Ernst Fritz. "Haydns Oratorium *Il ritorno di Tobia*, seine Entstehung
und seine Schicksale." *Archiv für Musikwissenschaft* (1959): 292–313.
Schmid, "Zierpraxis"
———. "Joseph Haydn und die vocale Zierpraxis seiner Zeit." In *Bericht über
die internationale Konferenz zum Andenken Joseph Haydns*, edited by B.
Szabolcsi and D. Bartha, pp. 117–29. Budapest: Akadémiai kiadó, 1961.
Schneider, "Adlgasser"

Schneider, Constantin. "Die Oratorien und Schuldramen Anton Cajetan Adlgassers." *Studien zur Musikwissenschaft* 18 (1931): 36–65.

Schneider, *Salzburg*

———. *Geschichte der Musik in Salzburg von der ältesten Zeit bis zur Gegenwart*. Salzburg: R. Kiesel, 1935.

Schnitzler, "Draghi"

Schnitzler, Rudolf. "The Sacred Dramatic Music of Antonio Draghi." Ph.D. dissertation, University of North Carolina at Chapel Hill, 1971.

Scholes, *Burney*

Scholes, Percy A. *The Great Dr. Burney: His Life, His Travels, His Works, His Family and His Friends*. London: Oxford University Press, 1948.

Schousboe, "Protestant"

Schousboe, Torben. "Protestant Church Music in Scandinavia." In *Protestant Church Music: A History*, by Friedrich Blume et al., pp. 611–36. New York: W. W. Norton, 1974.

Schubert, *Lazarus**

Schubert, Franz. *Lazarus oder: Die Feier der Auferstehung*. In *Franz Schuberts Werke: Kritisch durchgesehene Gesammtausgabe*, [edited by Eusebius Mandyczewski, Johannes Brahms, et al.]. Ser. 17, no. 1. Leipzig: Breitkopf & Härtel, 1892.

Schulz, *Christi**

Schulz, Johann Abraham Peter. *Christi død*. Oratorium af J. Baggesen. Piano reduction by Christian Barnekow. Copenhagen: Samfundet til Udgivelse af Dansk Musik, 1879.

Schulz, *Maria**

———. *Maria und Johannes: Passions-Oratorium*. Edited by Jan Goens. Keyboard Reduction with Text by Ulrich Haverkampf. Wiesbaden: Breitkopf & Härtel, 1978.

Seibel, *Heinichen*

Seibel, Gustav Adolph. *Das Leben des Königl. Polnischen und Kurfürstl. Sächs. Hofkapellmeisters Johann David Heinichen nebst chronologischem Verzeichnis seiner Opern . . . und thematischem Katalog seiner Werke*. Leipzig: Breitkopf & Härtel, 1913.

Serauky, *Halle*

Serauky, Walter. *Musikgeschichte der Stadt Halle*. Vol. 2/2: *Von Wilhelm Friedemann Bach bis Robert Franz*. Beiträge zur Musikforschung, no. 8. Halle: Max Neimeyer, 1942.

Shaw, *Handel's "Messiah"*

Shaw, Watkins. *The Story of Handel's "Messiah": 1741–1784. A Short Popular History*. London: Novello & Company Ltd., 1963.

Shaw, *Three Choirs*

———. *The Three Choirs Festival: The Official History of the Meetings of the Three Choirs of Gloucester, Hereford and Worcester, c. 1713–1953*. Worcester and London: Published for The Three Choirs Festival by Ebenezer Baylis & Son Ltd., 1954.

Siegmund-Schultze, "*Messias*-Aufführungen"

Siegmund-Schultze, Walter. "Über die ersten *Messias*-Aufführungen in Deutschland." *Händel-Jahrbuch* 6 (1960): 51–109.

Sievers, "Rom"

Sievers, Georg Ludwig Peter. "Ueber den heutigen Zustand der Musik in

Italien, besonders zu Rom." *Caecilia: Eine Zeitschrift für die musikalische Welt* 1 (1824): 201–60.

Sittard, *Hamburg*
Sittard, Josef. *Geschichte des Musik- und Concertwesens in Hamburg vom 14. Jahrhundert bis auf die Gegenwart*. Altona and Leipzig: A. C. Reher, 1890.

Small, "Smith"
Small, Barbara M. "The Life and Works of John Christopher Smith the Younger." D.Phil. dissertation. Oxford University, in progress.

Smith, *Paradise**
Smith, John Christopher. *Paradise Lost. An Oratorio*. London: I. Walsh, [1760].

Smither, "Forty Hours"
Smither, Howard E. "The Function of Music in the Forty Hours Devotion of 17th- and 18th-Century Italy." In *Gloria, Laus, et Honor . . . Tribute to Gwynn S. McPeek*. . . . New York: Gordon and Breach, in press.

Smither, "Haydns *Il ritorno di Tobia*"
_____. "Haydns *Il ritorno di Tobia* und die Tradition des italienischen Oratoriums." In *Joseph Haydn Tradition und Rezeption: Bericht über die Jahrestagung der Gesellschaft für Musikforschung Köln 1982*, pp. 160–88. Kölner Beiträge zur Musikforschung, edited by Klaus Wolfgang Niemöller, vol. 144. Regensburg: Gustav Bosse Verlag, 1985.

Smither, "Le Sueur"
_____. "The Concept of Oratorio in the Music and Writings of Jean-François Le Sueur." Paper read at the 13th Congress of the International Musicological Society, Strasbourg, 2 September 1982. (Forthcoming, in the congress report.)

Smither, *Oratorio*
_____. *A History of the Oratorio*. Vol. 1: *The Oratorio in the Baroque Era: Italy, Vienna, Paris*. Vol. 2: *The Oratorio in the Baroque Era: Protestant Germany and England*. Chapel Hill: University of North Carolina Press, 1977.

Smither, "Sacred Opera"
_____. "Oratorio and Sacred Opera, 1700–1825: Terminology and Genre Distinction." *Proceedings of the Royal Musical Association* 106 (1979–80): 88–104.

Solomon, *Beethoven*
Solomon, Maynard. *Beethoven*. New York: Schirmer Books, a Division of Macmillan Publishing Co., Inc., 1977.

Somfai, "Haydns Tribut"
Somfai, László. "Haydns Tribut an seinen Vorgänger Werner." *The Haydn Yearbook* 2 (1963–64): 75–80.

Sonneck, *Concert-Life*
Sonneck, Oscar G. *Early Concert-Life in America (1731–1800)*. Leipzig: Breitkopf & Härtel, 1907. Reprint, Wiesbaden: Dr. Martin Sändig, 1969.

Stahl, "Abendmusiken"
Stahl, Wilhelm. "Die Lübecker Abendmusiken im 17. und 18. Jahrhundert." *Zeitschrift des Vereins für Lübeckische Geschichte und Altertumskunde* 29 (1938): 1–64.

Stahl, *Lübeck*

————. *Musikgeschichte Lübecks*. Vol 2: *Geistliche Musik*. Kassel: Bärenreiter, 1952.

Stahl, "Ruetz"

————. "Kaspar Ruetz. Ein lübeckischer Zeit- und Amtsgenosse J. S. Bachs." In *Gedenkboek aangeboden aan Dr. D. F. Scheurleer op zijn 70sten Verjaardag*, edited by Guido Adler et al., pp. 327–38. The Hague: Martinus Nijhoff, 1925.

Steblin, *Key Characteristics*

Steblin, Rita. *A History of Key Characteristics in the Eighteenth and Early Nineteenth Centuries*. Studies in Musicology, no. 67. Ann Arbor: UMI Research Press, 1983.

Steinpress, "Haydns Oratorien in Russland"

Steinpress, Boris. "Haydns Oratorien in Russland zu Lebzeiten des Komponisten." *Haydn-Studien* 2 (1969): 77–112.

Strohm, *Opernarien*

Strohm, Reinhard. *Italienische Opernarien des frühen Settecento (1720–1730)*. Annalecta musicologica, vol. 16/1–2. 2 vols. Cologne: Arno Volk Verlag Hans Gerig, 1976.

Sulzer, *Allgemeine Theorie*

Sulzer, Johann Georg. *Allgemeine Theorie der schönen Künste in einzeln, nach alphabetischer Ordnung der Kunstwörter auf einander folgenden Artikeln abgehandelt*. 2 pts. in 2 vols. each. Leipzig: M. G. Weidmanns Erben und Reich, 1773–75.

Tagliavini, "Un oratorio sconisciuto"

Tagliavini, Luigi Ferdinando. "Un oratorio sconosciuto di Leopold Mozart." In *Festschrift Otto Erich Deutsch*, edited by Walter Gerstenberg, Jan LaRue, and Wolfgang Rehm, pp. 187–95. Kassel: Bärenreiter, 1963.

Telemann, *Donnerode; Befreite Israel**

Telemann, Georg Philipp. *Die Donnerode; Das befreite Israel*. Edited by Wolf Hobohm. In *Georg Philipp Telemann, Musikalische Werke*, vol. 22. Kassel: Bärenreiter, 1971.

Telemann, *Tag des Gerichts**

————. *Der Tag des Gerichts: Ein Singgedicht in vier Betrachtungen von Christian Wilhelm Alers*. Edited by Max Schneider; revised by Hans Joachim Moser. Denkmäler deutscher Tonkunst, ser. 1, vol. 28. 1907. Wiesbaden: Breitkopf & Härtel, 1958.

Telemann, *Tageszeiten**(pv)

————. *Die Tageszeiten*. Piano reduction. Edited by Dietrich Höfert. Stuttgart: Carus-Verlag, 1981.

Temperley, "Libretto of *The Creation*"

Temperley, Nicholas. "New Light on the Libretto of *The Creation*." In *Music in Eighteenth-Century England*, edited by Christopher Hogwood and Richard Luckett, pp. 189–211. Cambridge: Cambridge University Press, 1982.

Temperley, *Parish Church*

————. *The Music of the English Parish Church*. 2 vols. Cambridge: Cambridge University Press, 1979.

Teuber, *Theater*

Teuber, Oscar. *Geschichte des Prager Theaters von den Anfängen des Schauspielwesens bis auf die neueste Zeit*. 2 pts. Prague: A. Haase, 1883–85.

Thayer, *Beethoven*
 Thayer, Alexander Wheelock. *Thayer's Life of Beethoven*. Revised and edited
 by Elliot Forbes. Princeton: Princeton University Press, 1967.
Tovey, *Essays*
 Tovey, Donald Francis. *Essays in Musical Analysis*, vol. 5, *Vocal Music*. Lon-
 don: Oxford University Press, 1937.
Trexler, "Ritual in Florence"
 Trexler, Richard C. "Ritual in Florence: Adolescence and Salvation in the Re-
 naissance." In *The Pursuit of Holiness in Late Medieval and Renaissance
 Religion: Papers from the University of Michigan Conference* [1972], edited
 by Charles Trinkaus and Heiko A. Oberman, pp. 200–271. Studies in Me-
 dieval and Reformation Thought, vol. 10. Leiden: E. J. Brill, 1974.
Troutman, "Naumann"
 Troutman, Leslie Anne. "Johann Gottlieb Naumann: *La passione di Gesù
 Cristo* 1767 and 1787." M.A. thesis, University of North Carolina at
 Chapel Hill, 1984.
Tyson, "Beethoven's *Christus*"
 Tyson, Alan. "The 1803 Version of Beethoven's *Christus am Oelberge*." *The
 Musical Quarterly* 56 (1970): 551–84.
Tyson, "Heroic Phase"
 ———. "Beethoven's Heroic Phase." *The Musical Times* 110 (1969): 139–41.
Van Boer, "Kraus"
 Van Boer, Bertil, Jr. "*Der Tod Jesu* von Joseph Martin Krauss—ein Oratorium
 der Sturm und Drang-Bewegung." In *Joseph Martin Kraus in seiner Zeit*,
 edited by Friedrich W. Ridel, pp. 65–82. Munich and Salzburg: Emil
 Katzbichler, 1982.
Vitali, "Colonna"
 Vitali, Carlo. "Giovanni Paolo Colonna maestro di cappella dell'oratorio
 filippino in Bologna: Contributi bio-bibliografici." *Rivista italiana di
 musicologia* 14 (1979): 128–54.
Walter, *Geschichte*
 Walter, Friedrich. *Geschichte des Theaters und der Musik am kurpfälzischen
 Hofe*. Forschungen zur Geschichte Mannheims und der Pfalz, edited by
 Mannheimer Altertumsverein, vol. 1. Leipzig: Breitkopf & Härtel, 1898.
Walter, "Swietens handschriftliche Textbücher"
 Walter, Horst. "Gottfried van Swietens handschriftliche Textbücher zu
 Schöpfung und *Jahreszeiten*." *Haydn-Studien* 1 (1967): 241–77.
Warner, "Werner"
 Warner, Charles J. "A Study of Selected Works of Gregor Joseph Werner
 (1695?–1766)." Ph.D. dissertation, Catholic University, 1965.
Weber, *Musical Classics*
 Weber, William. *The Rise of Musical Classics in Eighteenth-Century England*.
 Forthcoming.
Weil, "Forty Hours"
 Weil, Mark. "The Devotion of the Forty Hours and Roman Baroque Illu-
 sions." *Journal of the Warburg and Courtauld Institutes* 37 (1974): 218–
 78.
Weilen, *Theatergeschichte*
 Weilen, Alexander von. *Zur Wiener Theatergeschichte: Die vom Jahre 1629
 bis zum Jahre 1740 am Wiener Hofe zur Aufführung gelangten Werke*

theatralischen Characters und Oratorien. Schriften des Österreichische Vereins für Bibliotekwesen. Vienna: Alfred Hölder K. u. K. Hof- und Universitäts-Buchhändler, 1901.

Weissman, *Ritual Brotherhood*

Weissman, Ronald F. E. *Ritual Brotherhood in Renaissance Florence.* New York: Academic Press (Harcourt Brace Jovanovich), 1969.

Werner, *Sechs Fugen**

Werner, Gregor Joseph. *Sechs Fugen für Streichquartett, nach der Erstveröffentlichung von Joseph Haydn.* [Edited by] Walter Höckner. Locarno: Edizioni Pegasus, [1963].

Werner, *Sechs Oratorienvorspiele**

———. *Hat Oratórium-előjáték. Sechs Oratorienvorspiele.* Edited by Jenó Vécsey. Musica Rinata, nos. 12–13. 2 vols. Budapest: Zenemúkiadó, 1968.

Wesley, *Journal*

Wesley, John. *The Journal of the Rev. John Wesley . . .* Edited by Nehimah Curnock. 8 vols. 1909. Reprint. London: Epworth, 1938.

Wettstein, *Telemann*

Wettstein, Hermann. *Georg Philipp Telemann: Bibliographischer Versuch zu seinem Leben und Werk 1681–1767.* Hamburg: Verlag der Musikalienhandlung Karl Dieter Wagner, 1981.

Williams, "Stanley"

Williams, A. Glyn. "The Life and Works of John Stanley (1712–86)." 2 vols. Ph.D. dissertation, University of Reading, 1977.

Wodtke, "Lyrisches Drama"

Wodtke, Friedrich Wilhelm. "Lyrisches Drama." In *Reallexikon der deutschen Literaturegeschichte,* 2d ed., edited by Werner Kohlschmidt et al., 2:252–54. Berlin: Walter de Gruyter, 1958.

Wöchentliche Nachrichten und Anmerkungen die Musik betreffend. Edited by Johann Adam Hiller. No. 1 (1766).

Wolf, *Stamitz*

Wolf, Eugene K. *The Symphonies of Johann Stamitz: A Study in the Formation of the Classic Style, with a Thematic Catalogue of the Symphonies and Orchestral Trios.* Utrecht/Antwerp: Bohn, Scheltema & Holkema; The Hague/Boston: Martinus Nijhoff, 1981.

Wolff, "Leo"

Wolff, Hellmuth Christian. "Un oratorio sconosciuto di Leonardo Leo." *Rivista italiana di musicologia* 7 (1972): 196–213.

Worgan, *Hannah**

Worgan, John. *Hannah: An Oratorio as Perform'd at the Kings Theater in the Haymarket. . . Opera Prima.* London: Printed for the Author by Mrs. Johnson, 1764.

Yorke-Long, "Maria Antonia"

Yorke-Long, Alan. "Maria Antonia of Saxony." In *Music at Court: Four Eighteenth Century Studies,* by Alan Yorke-Long, pp. 71–93. London: Weidenfeld and Nicolson, 1954.

Zimmermann, *Tobit*

Zimmermann, Frank. *The Book of Tobit.* New York: Harper and Brothers, 1958.

❧ Index

The index includes persons, places, institutions, terms, concepts, and works. The names of composers and librettists are placed in parentheses after the titles of their works, as follows: (composer / librettist), (composer only).

—musical settings by: Leo, 67, 89–98 (analysis); Piccini, 209, 618; Reutter, 52; Seydelmann, 84

La morte di San Filippo Neri (Anfossi / Femi), 63, 84

Morzin, Count, 160

Mosè in Egitto: azione tragico-sacra (Rossini / Tottola), 34, 85–86, 182

motet: influence of, on French oratorio, 547–48

Mozart, Leopold, 340, 341, 357, 371

Mozart, Wolfgang Amadeus, xv, 76, 77, 341, 345, 346, 354, 357, 371, 523, 545, 547

Musorgsky, Modest, 625

Muzzillo, Canon, 114

Mysliveček, Josef, 77

Nabal (Handel pasticcio, arr. by Smith / Morell), 242

Napoleon, 577, 581

La nativité (Gossec / Chabanon), 547, 559; analysis of, 567–77

Naumann, Johann Gottlieb, 37, 78, 84, 352, 545

La nave del mercader (Pujol), 607

Neefe, Christian Gottlob, 513

Neri, Philip, 7, 11

Neukomm, Sigismund, 620

Neumayr, Franz: *Idea perfectae conversionis sive Augustinus*, 99

Nicolini, Giuseppe, 547

Niemeyer, August Hermann, 360, 464, 466

Norris, Thomas, 247n

North, Lord, 219

Ode for St. Cecilia's Day (Handel / Dryden), 345

Ödmann, S., 617

Omnipotence (Handel pasticcio, arr. by Arnold / Arnold and Toms), 242, 291

opera: *opera sacra* as term for staged oratorio, 34, 83. *See also* oratorio

Opstandelsen (Kunzen, F. L. A. / Thaarup), 616, 617

oratoire. See oratorio, term

oratorio: audiences at performances in Florence, 18–19; audiences at performances in Rome, 13–14; compared with opera, 53, 59, 64; decorations for concert performances, 5, 18, 27–29, 31, 35, 40–41; frequency of performances in Italy, 6, 8–11, 23n; operatic staging of, 5–6, 31, 32–34, 50, 64–65, 83, 85, 182, 342, 540, 544–47; periodization, 68,

370; secular work treated as, 199–200, 208–9; similarities to opera, 4–5; as unstaged genre, 4. *See also* churches, oratories, and other sites of oratorio performances; oratorio, term; pasticcio oratorio

oratorio, term: in America, 237; in England, 199–200, 201, 240; in France, 539–40, 541, 545; in Germany, 331–40; in Italy, 3–6; in Russia, 618, 619–21; semantic change of, in Italy, 6, 33–34; in works of Le Sueur, 580–81

Oratorio, en culto de San Adauto mártir (anonymous), 605, 611

Oratorio al feliz tránsito del glorioso esposo de María santíssima San Joseph (Julian), 608

Oratorio allegórico al santíssimo sacramento (Julian), 608

Oratorio armónico (Figuera), 605, 606

Oratorio armónico (Mir y Llusà), 612, 613

Oratorio histórico, y alegórico (Suav), 607

Oratorio mýstico e alegórico (Valls), 603, 604, 611

oratorio Passion, German, 347, 348, 349, 378

Oratorio per il natale del nostro signore Giesù Christo (Zechner), 357, 371, 373

Oratorio per la SS. Vergine del Rosario (Leo), 88

Oratorio que se ha de cantar en el Real Colegio (Corselli), 608, 610

Oratorio que se ha de cantar en el Real Colegio (Corvi y Moroty), 608–9

Oratorio sacro al glorioso mártyr San Genaro (Mele), 609

Oratorio sacro al nacimiento de Christo señor nuestro (Martínez), 607

Oratorio sacro a San Juan Bautista (Rabassa), 607

Oratorio Tedesco al Sepolcro Santo (Heinichen), 40

Orphée (Gluck / Calzabigi), 547

Osborne, Francis, the duke of Leeds, 213

Ottoboni, Pietro, 9, 30

overture, sinfonia, introduction: in Arne, T., *Judith*, 265; in Bach, C. P. E., *Auferstehung und Himmelfahrt Jesu*, 439; in Beethoven, *Christus am Oelberge*, 522–23; in Bertoni, *David poenitens*, 141, 142–44; in Classical oratorio, 83; in early Classical oratorio, 75, 370, 373; in English oratorio, 244–45; in Felsted, *Jonah*, 318; in French oratorio, 548; in German oratorio, 375–76; in Graun,

C. H., *Der Tod Jesu*, 406; in Guglielmi,
P. A., *Debora e Sisara*, 185; in Hasse, *La
conversione di Sant'Agostino*, 101; in
Haydn, J., *The Creation*, 498–99, 500–
502; in Haydn, J., *Il ritorno di Tobia*,
168, 169–70; in Jommelli, *La passione
di Gesù Cristo*, 118–19; in Leo, *La
morte d'Abel*, 90–91; in Rolle, *Lazarus,
oder die Feyer der Auferstehung*, 471; in
Smith, *Paradise Lost*, 250; in Stanley,
The Fall of Egypt, 305; in Telemann,
Der Tag des Gerichts, 383

La pace de Kamberga (Heinchen), 36
Paer, Ferdinando, 15, 37, 85, 547
Paisible, Louis-Henri, 567, 618
Paisiello, Giovanni, 15, 43, 85, 545, 577,
616, 618
A Paixão de Jesus Christo (libretto after
Metastasio), 615
Pallavicino, Stefano Benedetto, 44, 52, 366
Pamphili, Benedetto, 9
Paradise Lost (Smith / Stillingfleet), analy-
sis of, 245–57, 258–61
Pariati, Pietro, 52
Pasquini, Giovanni Claudio, 52
Le passage de la mer rouge (Berlioz), 577
Passage de la mer Rouge (Giroust), 542
Le passage de la mer Rouge (Persuis), 541
La passione di Gesù Cristo, libretto by
Metastasio, 56–60, 469
—musical settings by: Caldara, 52; Grua,
44; Jommelli, 47, 115–37 (analysis),
209, 616, 618; Morlachi, 85; Naumann,
78; Paisiello, 43–44, 85, 616, 618;
Reichardt, 217; Salieri, 77, 616; Santos,
42; Starzer, 77; Uttini, 617. See also *A
Paixão de Jesus Christo*
Passion oratorio, German, 347, 348, 349,
350, 378
Passionsoratorium (Bach, J. E.), 370
Pasterwiz, Georg, 44, 50, 342
pasticcio oratorio, 33, 241, 242; from
Handel's music, 208, 210; in Paris, 544–
47
*Pastor, y mercenario a un mismo tiempo.
Oratorio sacro* (Picañol), 611
Patzke, Johann Samuel, 360, 362, 464, 466
Paul I, Tsar of Russia, 621
I pellegrini al sepolcro di nostro Signore, li-
bretto by Pallavicino, 366; musical set-
ting by Hasse, 44, 47, 70
Pepusch, Johann Christoph, 245
Pera, Girolamo, 43
Peregrini ad sepulcrum servatoris nostri

(Hasse / Pallavicino), 44
performance practice: in Italy, 9, 13; manner of conducting at Commemoration of
Handel, 226–28. *See also* performing
forces
performing forces: at Commemoration of
Handel, 226; in English provincial festi-
vals, 220–22, 229; in Foundling Hospi-
tal Chapel, 212; in Haydn, J., *Il ritorno
di Tobia*, 161; in Hiller, J. A., Berlin per-
formance of *Messiah*, 231, 232; in Lon-
don theaters, 210–11; in the Parisian
Concert spirituel, 542–43
Perrotti, Angelo, 30
Perrotti, Pietro, 30
Persuis, Jean-Nicolas Loiseau de, 541
Petrovich, Count Nikolai, 621
Philidor, Anne Danican, 540, 541
Philidor, François-André Danican, 542,
544, 545, 548
Picañol, José, 603, 611
Piccini, Niccolò, 547, 618
Pierucci, Contessa Maria Cammilla, 30
Pietism, 336
Die Pilgrime auf Golgatha, libretto by
Zachariä, 366
—musical settings by: Albrechtsberger,
344, 366; Kehl, 366, 370, 373; Löhlein,
366; Schneider, 366
pitch notation, xvii
Poesie sacre drammatiche, librettos by
Zeno, 4
Polli, Francesco, 43
Pomili mia, Bozhe (Sarti), 618
Porpora, Nicola, 43, 47, 69
Porsile, Giuseppe, 52, 69
Porsile, Nicolo, 602
Potemkin, Gregorii, 619
Pouplinière. *See* La Pouplinière
Pozharskii, Dmitrii Mikhailovich, 625
Prati, Alessio, 618
Predieri, Luca Antonio, 52
La presentación de Nuestra Señora (Aleix),
605
Price, Robert, 246
*La prise de Jéricho, oratorio en trois par-
ties, représenté sur le Théatre de
l'Académie Impériale de Musique, le 21
germinal an XIII* (Kalkbrenner and
Lachnith), 545
The Prodigal Son (Arnold / Hall), 217, 219
Prota, Ignazio, 114
Providence (Fisher), 213, 219
Puccini, Giacomo, 181
Pujol, José, 605, 607

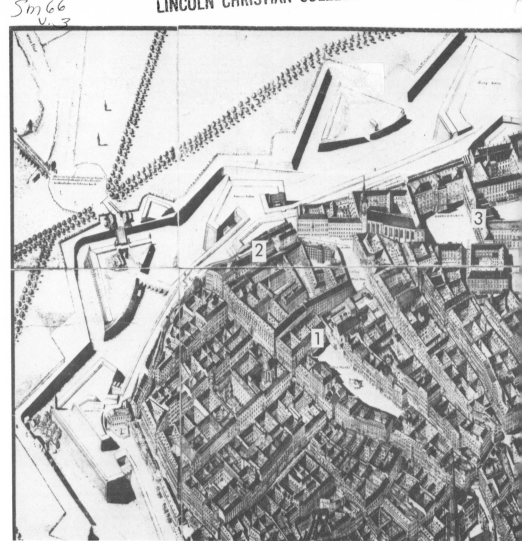

Endpapers A map of Vienna, 1769–74, showing some eighteenth-century locations of oratorio performances (after Eisler, *Atlas des Wiener Stadtbildes*, pl. XLII–XLIII.)